LA PERDIDA

La PERDIDA

Jessica Abel

PANTHEON BOOKS   NEW YORK

This book's epigraph is from *Under the Volcano* by Malcolm Lowry.

Library of Congress Cataloging-in-Publication Data

Abel, Jessica.
La perdida / Jessica Abel.
p. cm.
English and Spanish.
ISBN 0-375-42365-6
1. Graphic novels. I. Title.

PN6727.A25P47 2006 741.5'973—dc22 2005052123

www.pantheonbooks.com
Printed in the United States of America
First Edition
9 8 7 6 5 4 3 2

TO MATT
whose idea it was to go to Mexico in the first place

¿LE GUSTA ESTE JARDÍN
QUE ES SUYO?
¡EVITE QUE SUS HIJOS LO DESTRUYAN!

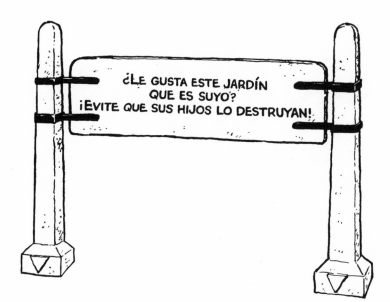

A Note on the Use of Spanish in This Book

I've written dialogue in chapter one as it's spoken; that is, in English when it's in English, and in Spanish when it's in Spanish (with "subtitles"). From chapter two on, however, the vast majority of dialogue is meant to be spoken in Spanish, so I dispensed with subtitles and simply "translated" the dialogue. From then on, when characters are speaking in English, that fact will be indicated by <arrow brackets>.

However, throughout the "Spanish" dialogue I've sprinkled words actually written in Spanish, particularly where the words have a particularly Mexican feel. All these words are translated in the glossary, at the back of the book. The glossary also contains explanations of some key locations and other cultural information.

All through the book, I've omitted the traditional use of italics for words in a foreign language, as I feel their constant use would be more distracting than helpful.

LA PERDIDA

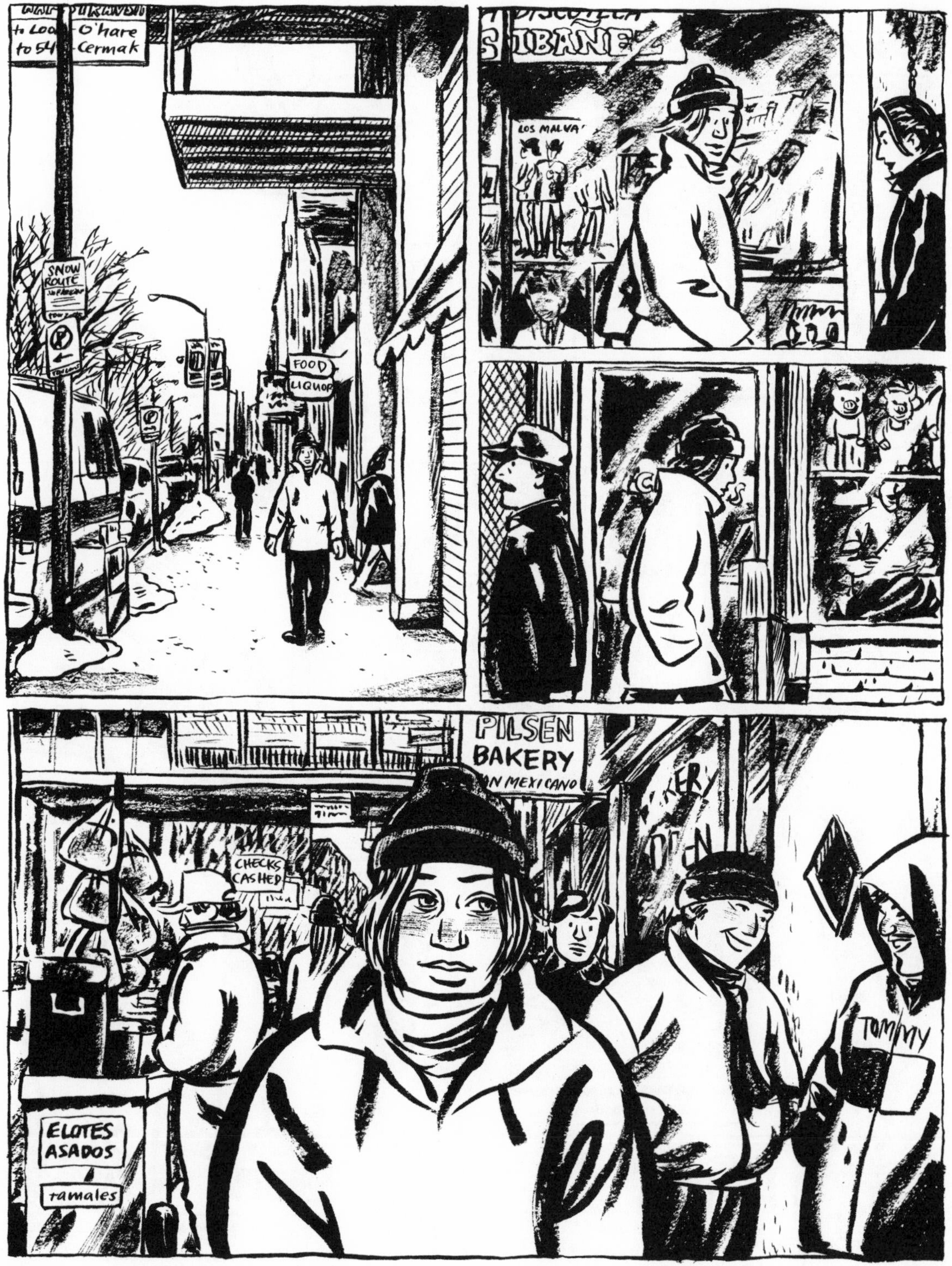
O'hare
Cermak
SNOW ROUTE
FOOD
LIQUOR
LOS MALVA'
PILSEN
BAKERY
CHECKS CASHED
ELOTES ASADOS
tamales
TOMMY

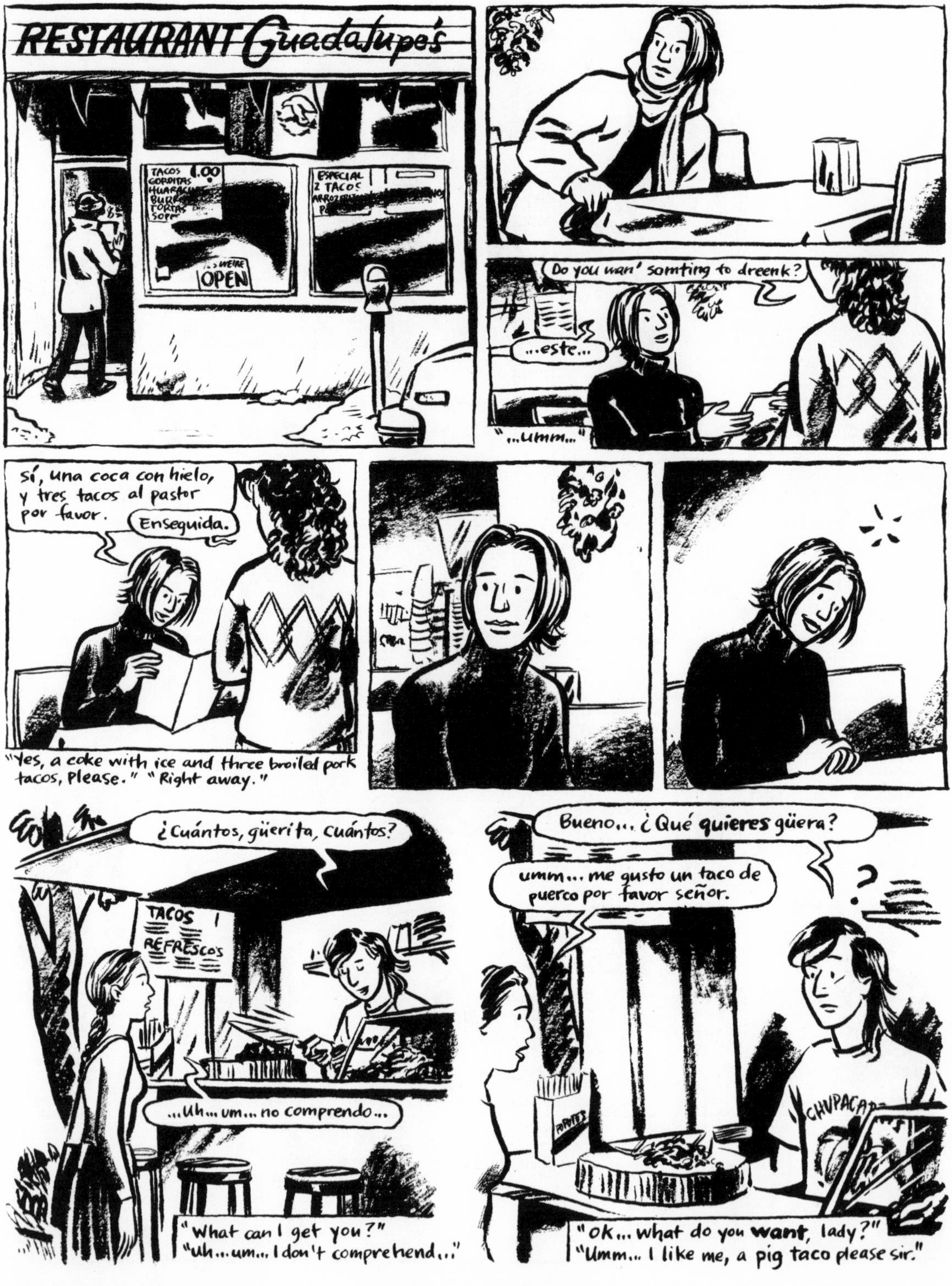
RESTAURANT Guadalupe's
TACOS 1.00
GORDITAS
ESPECIAL
2 TACOS
OPEN
Do you wan' somting to dreenk?
...este...
"...umm..."
sí, una coca con hielo, y tres tacos al pastor por favor.
Enseguida.
"Yes, a coke with ice and three broiled pork tacos, Please." "Right away."
¿Cuántos, güerita, cuántos?
TACOS
REFRESCO's
...uh...um...no comprendo...
"What can I get you?" "uh...um...I don't comprehend..."
Bueno... ¿Qué **quieres** güera?
umm... me gusto un taco de puerco por favor señor.
?
CHUPACA
"ok... what do you **want**, lady?" "Umm... I like me, a pig taco please sir."

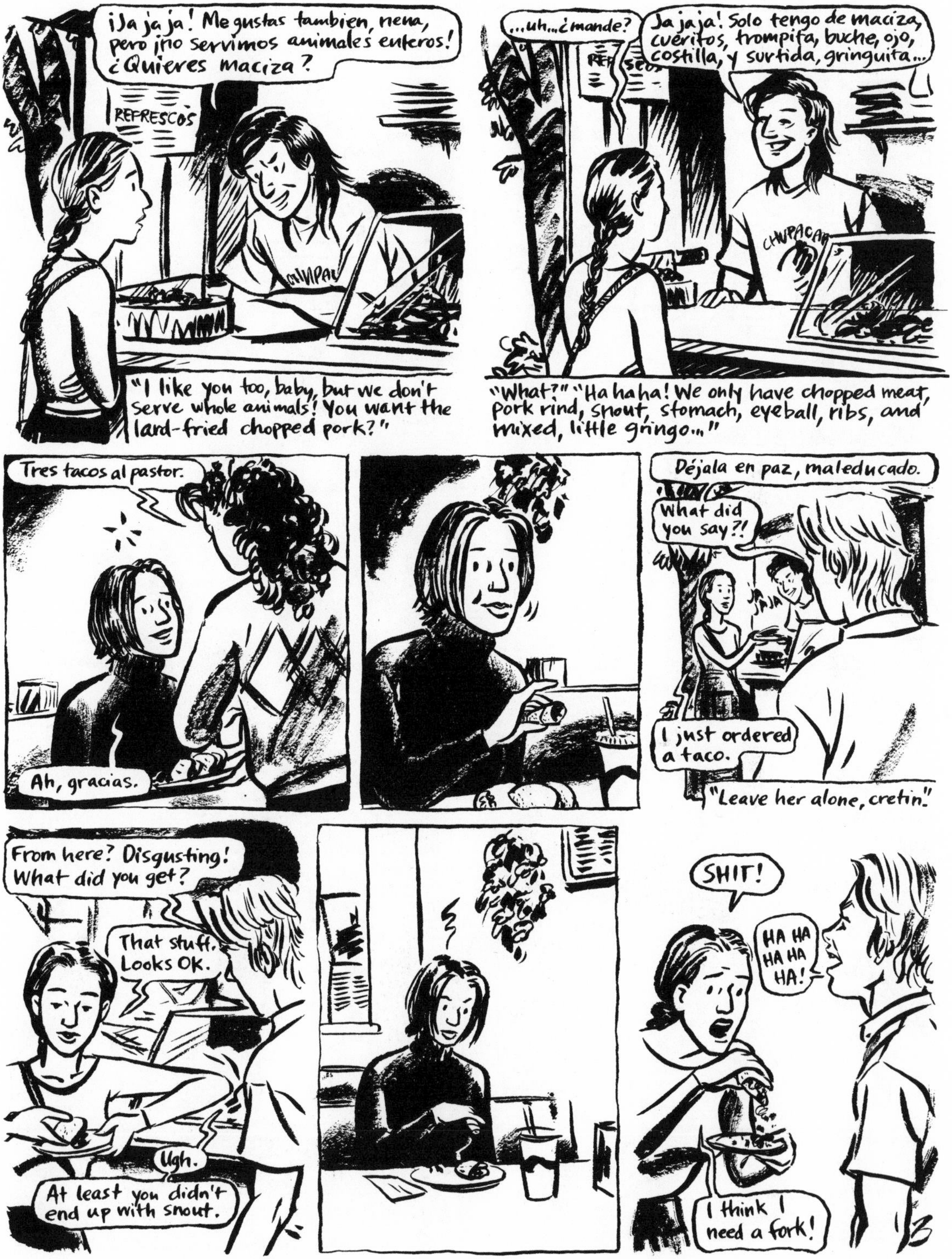
¡Ja ja ja! Me gustas tambien, nena, pero ¡no servimos animales enteros! ¿Quieres maciza?
REFRESCOS
"I like you too, baby, but we don't serve whole animals! You want the lard-fried chopped pork?"
...uh...¿mande?
Ja ja ja! Solo tengo de maciza, cueritos, trompita, buche, ojo, costilla, y surtida, gringuita...
CHUPACA
"What?" "Ha ha ha! We only have chopped meat, pork rind, snout, stomach, eyeball, ribs, and mixed, little gringo..."
Tres tacos al pastor.
Ah, gracias.
Déjala en paz, maleducado.
What did you say?!
JAJA
I just ordered a taco.
"Leave her alone, cretin."
From here? Disgusting! What did you get?
That stuff. Looks OK.
Ugh.
At least you didn't end up with snout.
SHIT!
HA HA HA HA HA!
I think I need a fork!

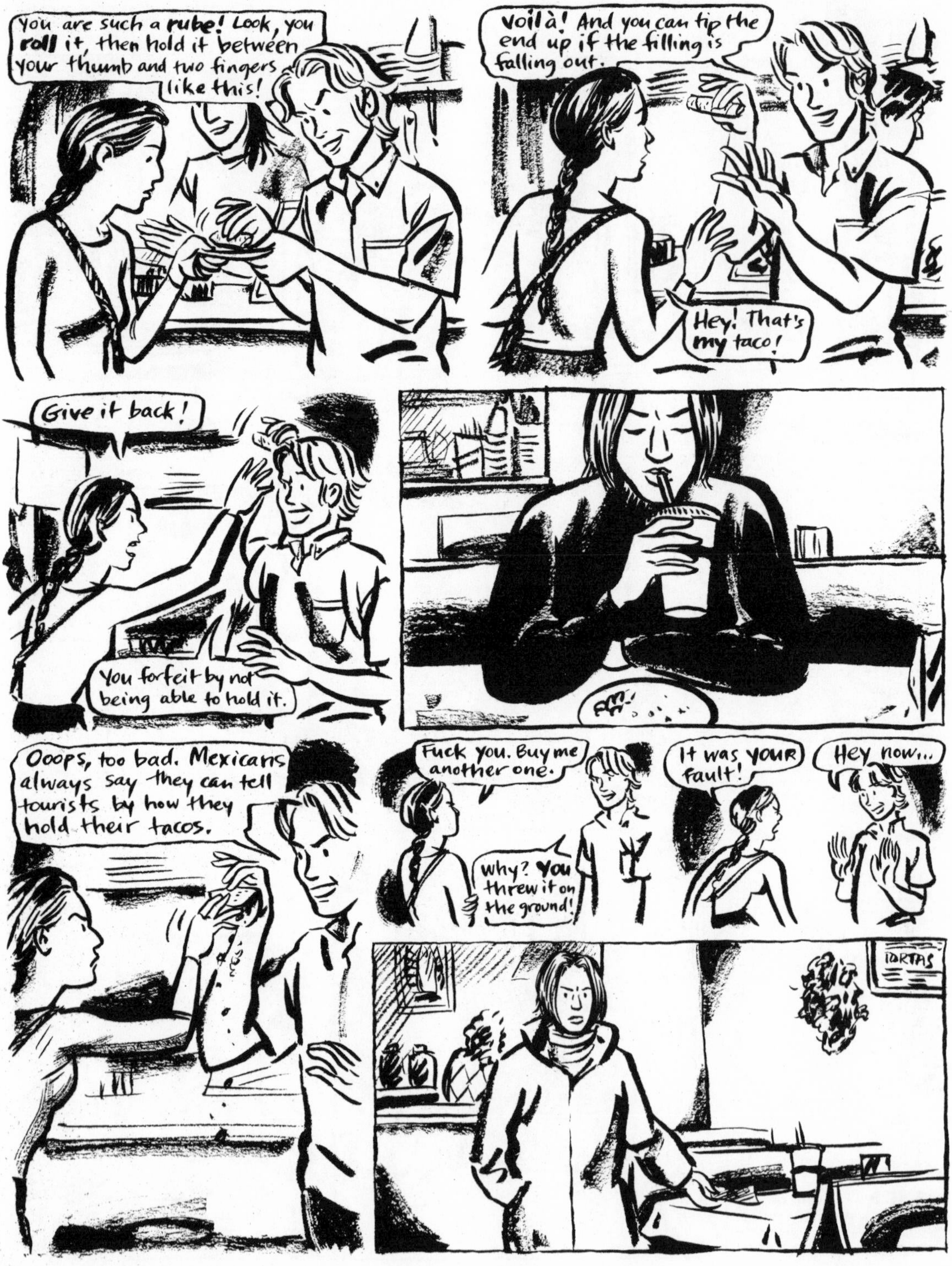

You are such a rube! Look, you roll it, then hold it between your thumb and two fingers like this!
voilà! And you can tip the end up if the filling is falling out.
Hey! That's my taco!
Give it back!
You forfeit by not being able to hold it.
Ooops, too bad. Mexicans always say they can tell tourists by how they hold their tacos.
Fuck you. Buy me another one.
Why? You threw it on the ground!
It was YOUR fault!
Hey now...
TORTAS

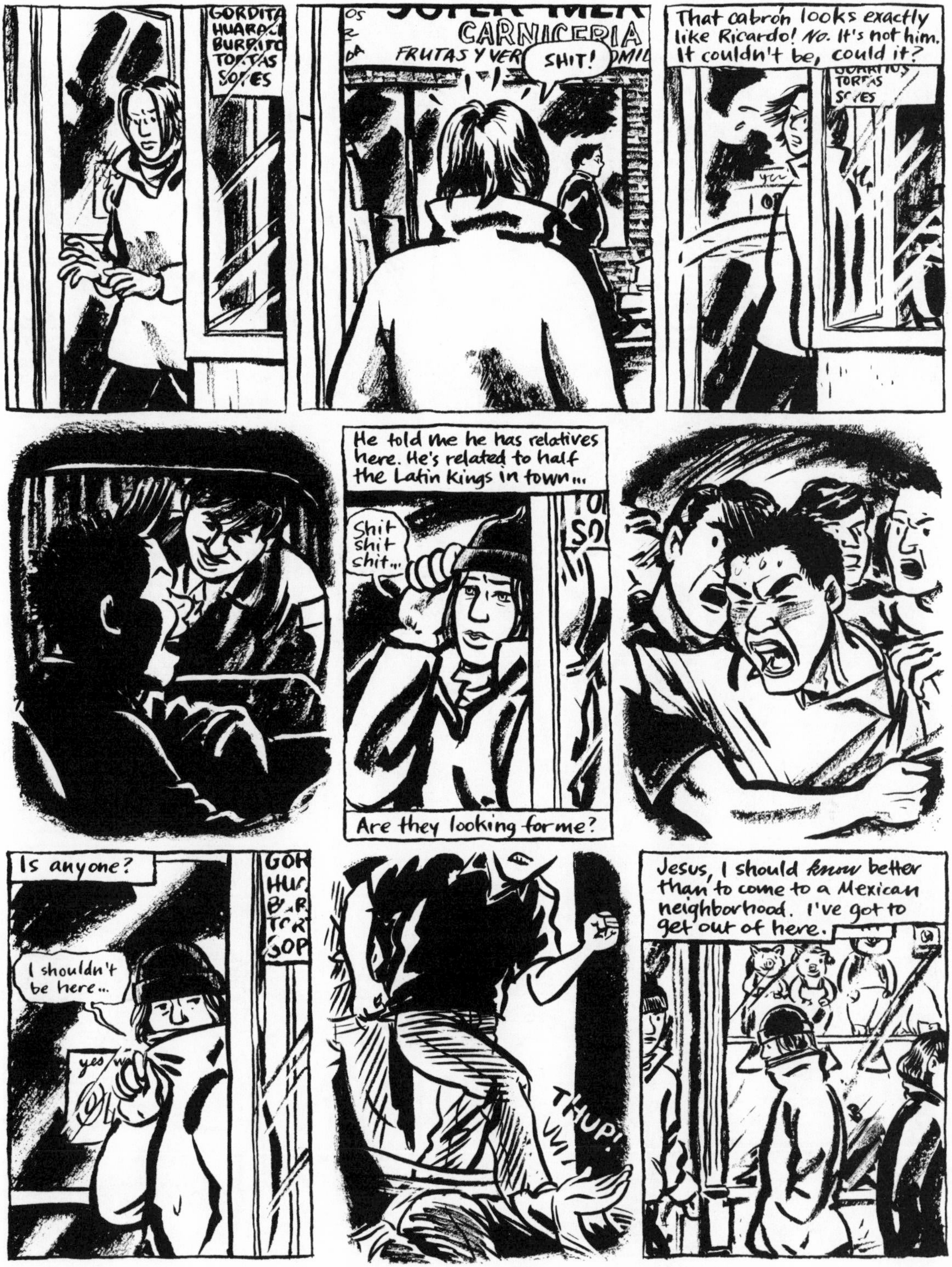

GORDITA
HUARAC
BURRITO
TORTAS
SOPES
CARNICERIA
FRUTAS Y VER
SHIT!
That cabrón looks exactly like Ricardo! No. It's not him. It couldn't be, could it?
TORTAS
SOPES
He told me he has relatives here. He's related to half the Latin Kings in town...
Shit shit shit...
Are they looking for me?
Is anyone?
I shouldn't be here...
THUP!
Jesus, I should *know* better than to come to a Mexican neighborhood. I've got to get out of here.

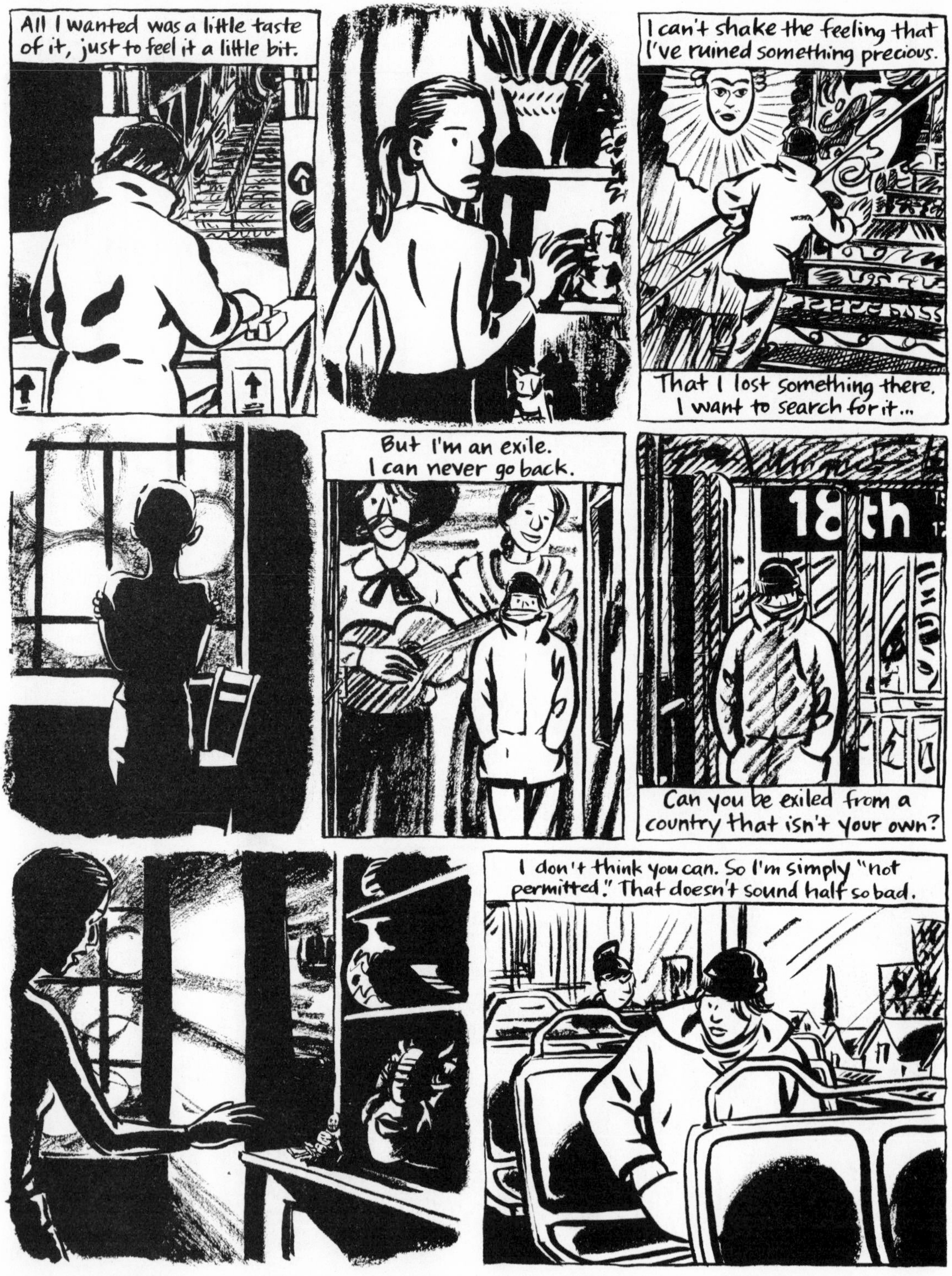
All I wanted was a little taste of it, just to feel it a little bit.
I can't shake the feeling that I've ruined something precious.
That I lost something there. I want to search for it...
But I'm an exile. I can never go back.
18th
Can you be exiled from a country that isn't your own?
I don't think you can. So I'm simply "not permitted." That doesn't sound half so bad.

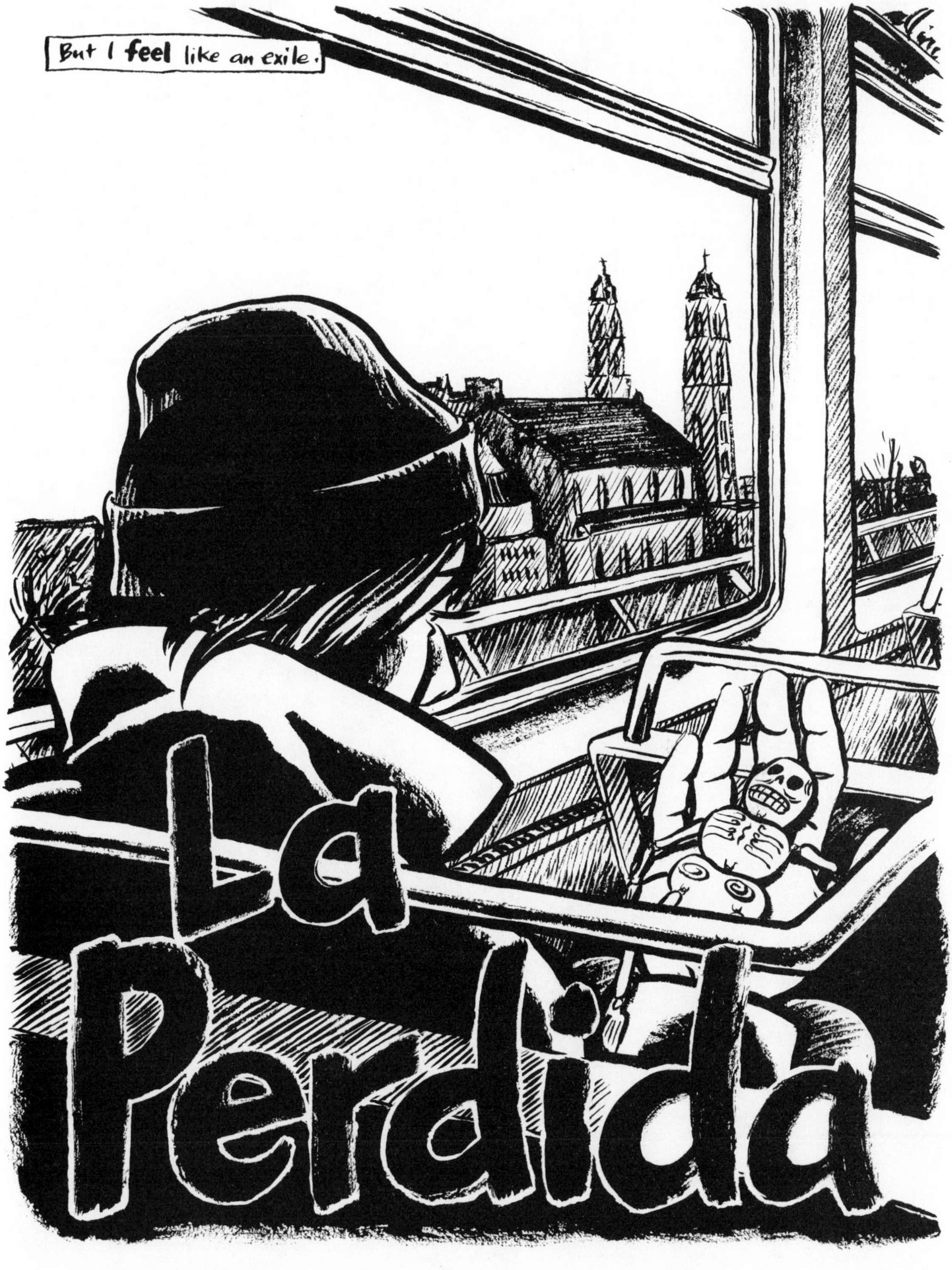
But I feel like an exile.
La Perdida

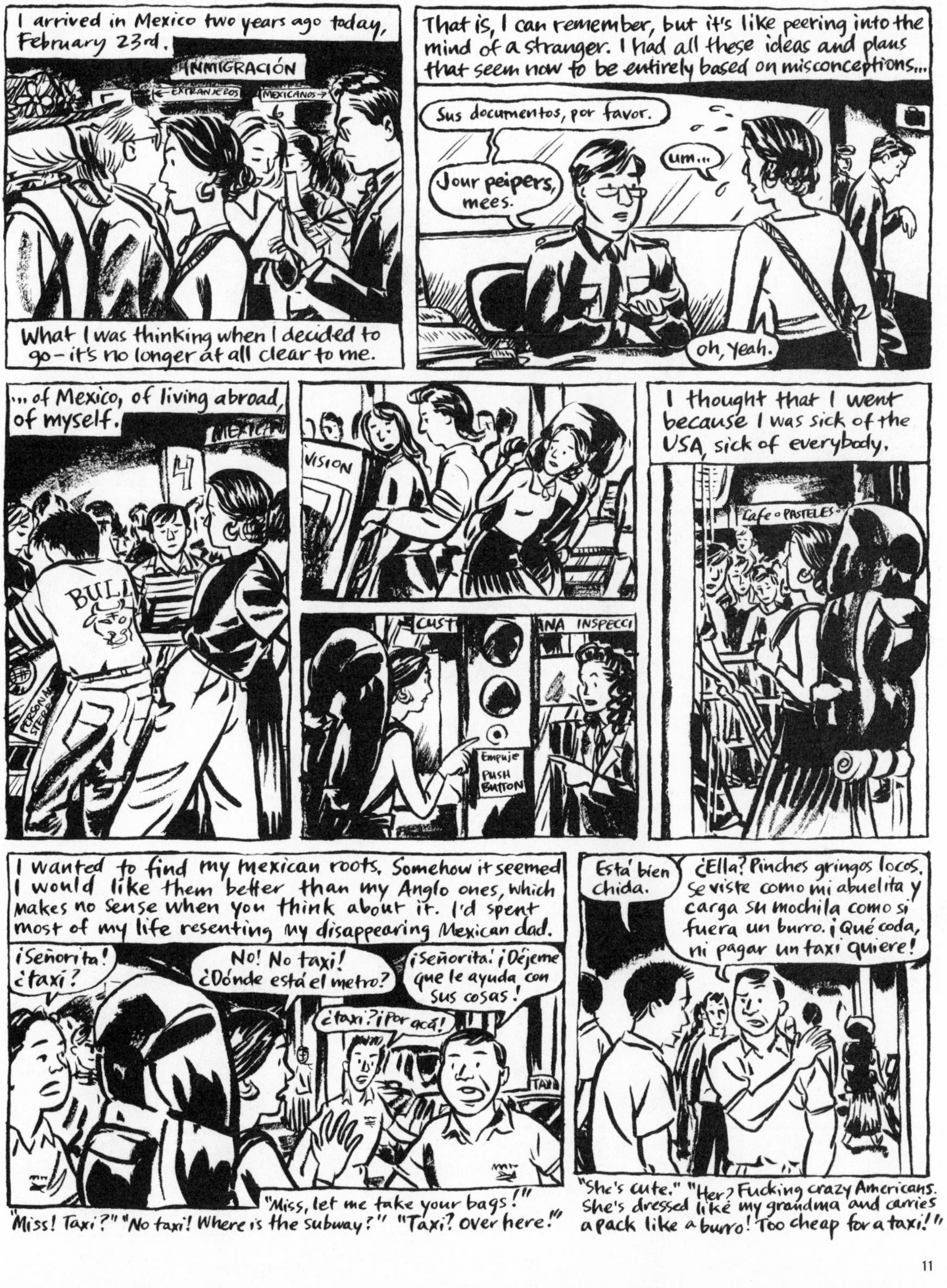

I arrived in Mexico two years ago today, February 23rd.
INMIGRACIÓN
EXTRANJEROS
MEXICANOS
What I was thinking when I decided to go - it's no longer at all clear to me.
That is, I can remember, but it's like peering into the mind of a stranger. I had all these ideas and plans that seem now to be entirely based on misconceptions...
Sus documentos, por favor.
Jour peipers, mees.
um...
oh, yeah.
... of Mexico, of living abroad, of myself.
BULL
VISION
CUST
NA INSPECCI
Empuje
PUSH BUTTON
I thought that I went because I was sick of the USA, sick of everybody.
Cafe • PASTELES
I wanted to find my Mexican roots. Somehow it seemed I would like them better than my Anglo ones, which makes no sense when you think about it. I'd spent most of my life resenting my disappearing Mexican dad.
¡Señorita! ¿taxi?
No! No taxi! ¿Dónde está el metro?
¡Señorita! ¡Déjeme que le ayuda con sus cosas!
¿taxi? ¡Por acá!
TAXI
"Miss, let me take your bags!"
"Miss! Taxi?" "No taxi! Where is the subway?" "Taxi? Over here!"
Está bien chida.
¿Ella? Pinches gringos locos. Se viste como mi abuelita y carga su mochila como si fuera un burro. ¡Qué coda, ni pagar un taxi quiere!
"She's cute." "Her? Fucking crazy Americans. She's dressed like my grandma and carries a pack like a burro! Too cheap for a taxi!"

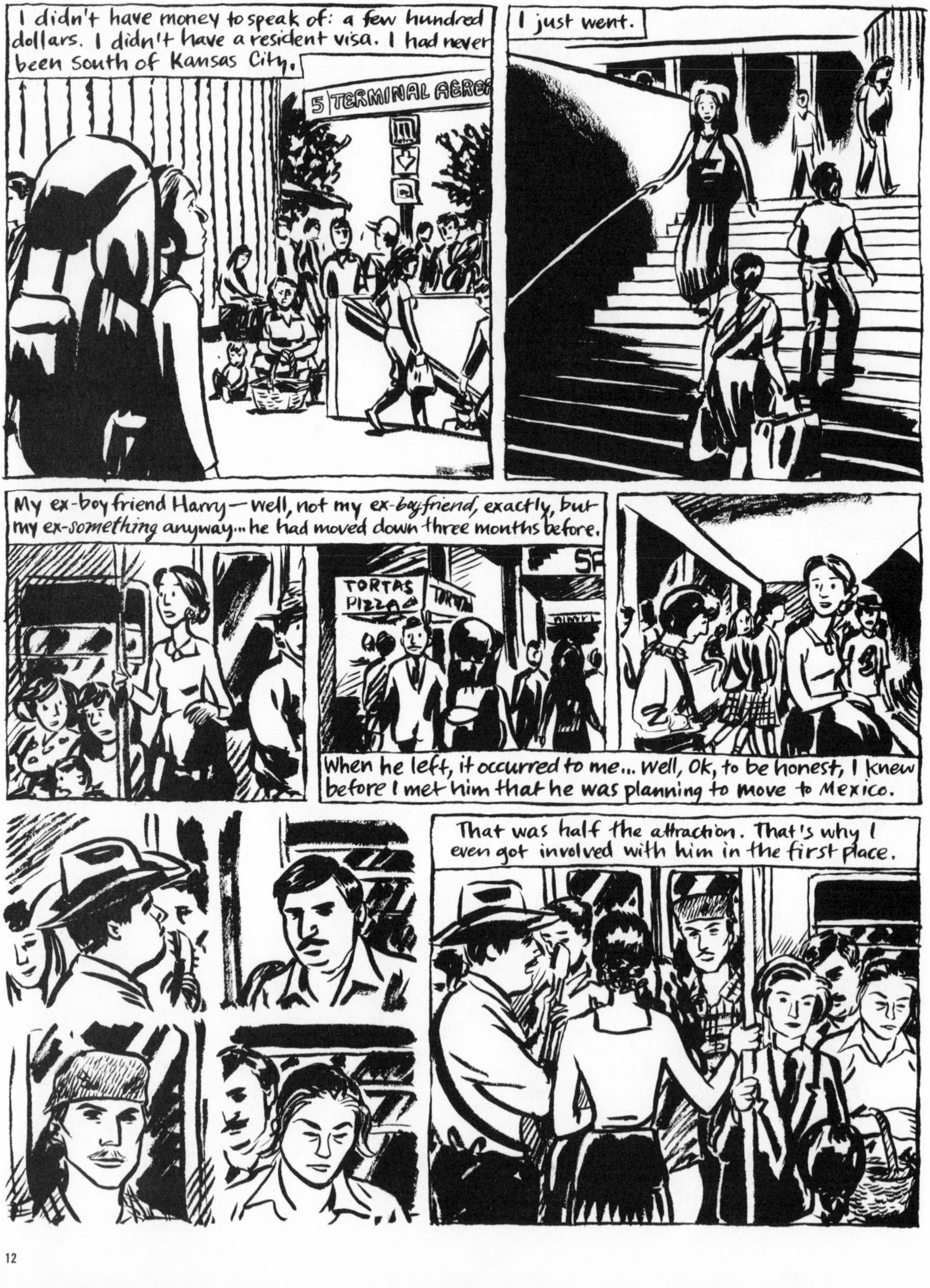

I didn't have money to speak of: a few hundred dollars. I didn't have a resident visa. I had never been south of Kansas City.
5 TERMINAL AEREA
I just went.
My ex-boyfriend Harry—well, not my ex-*boyfriend*, exactly, but my ex-*something* anyway... he had moved down three months before.
TORTAS
PIZZA
When he left, it occurred to me... Well, Ok, to be honest, I knew before I met him that he was planning to move to Mexico.
That was half the attraction. That's why I even got involved with him in the first place.

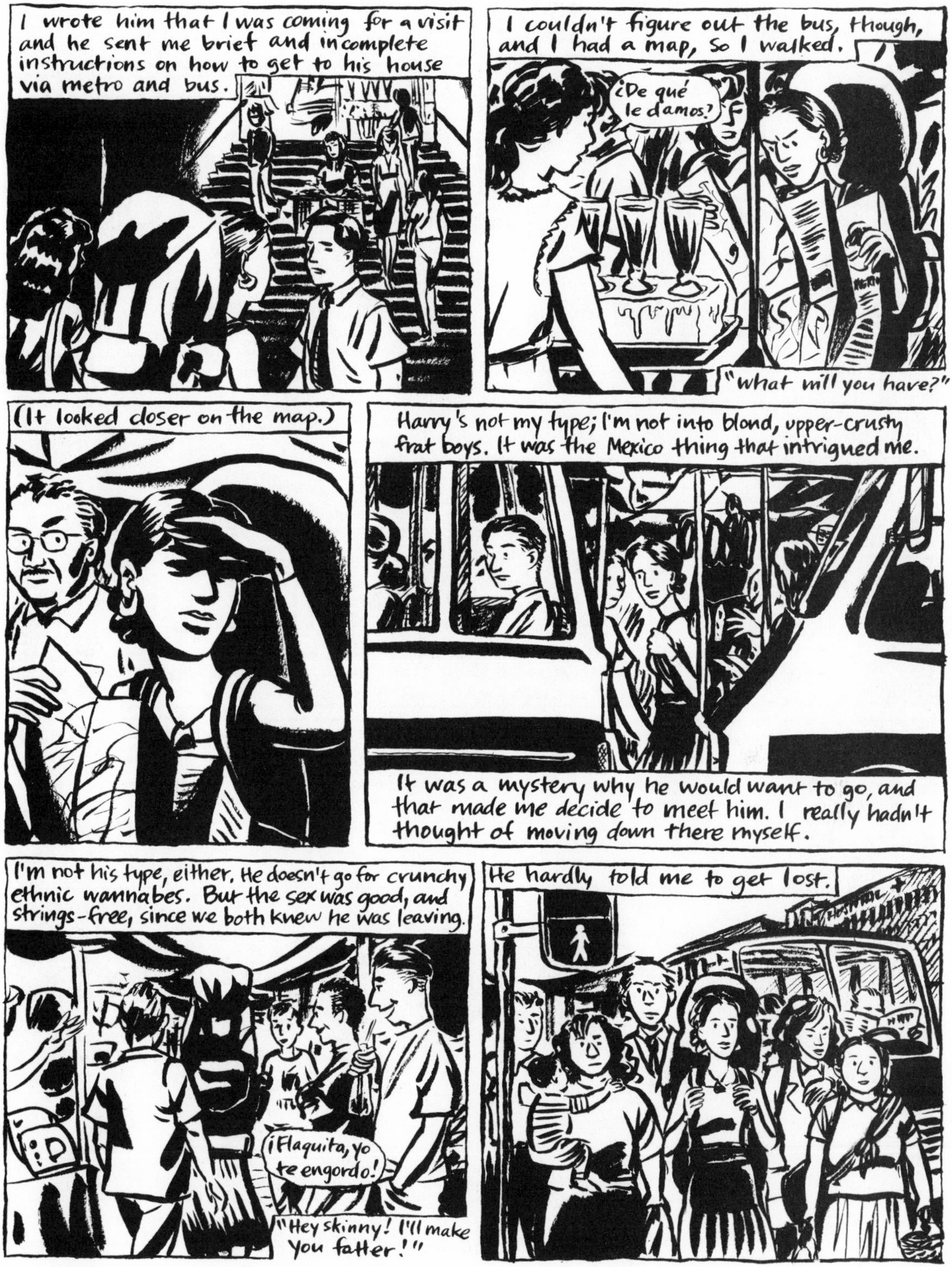
I wrote him that I was coming for a visit and he sent me brief and incomplete instructions on how to get to his house via metro and bus.
I couldn't figure out the bus, though, and I had a map, so I walked.
¿De qué le damos?
"What will you have?"
(It looked closer on the map.)
Harry's not my type; I'm not into blond, upper-crusty frat boys. It was the Mexico thing that intrigued me.
It was a mystery why he would want to go, and that made me decide to meet him. I really hadn't thought of moving down there myself.
I'm not his type, either. He doesn't go for crunchy ethnic wannabes. But the sex was good, and strings-free, since we both knew he was leaving.
¡Flaquita, yo te engordo!
"Hey skinny! I'll make you fatter!"
He hardly told me to get lost.

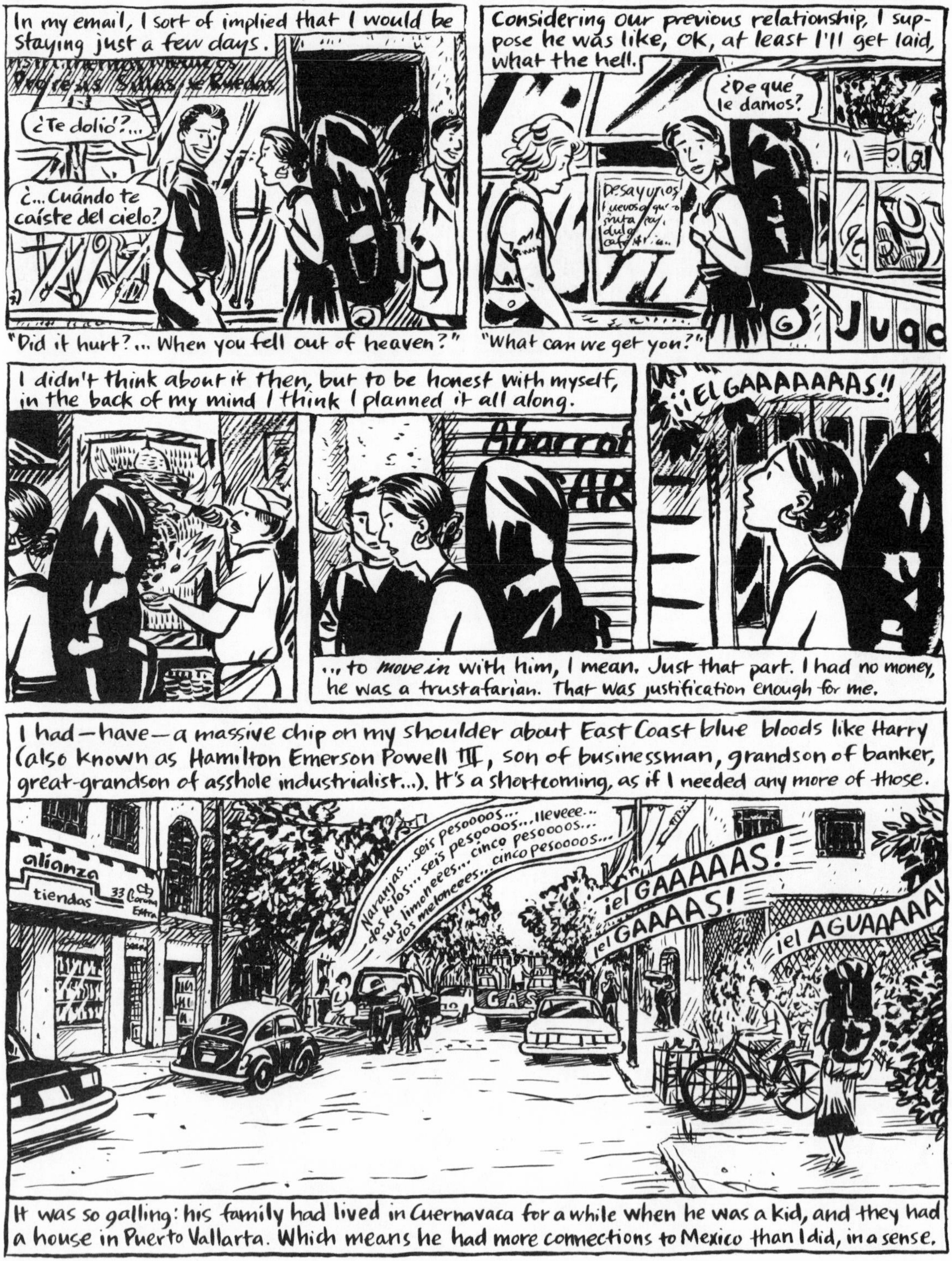

In my email, I sort of implied that I would be staying just a few days.
¿Te dolió?...
¿...Cuándo te caíste del cielo?
"Did it hurt?... When you fell out of heaven?"
Considering our previous relationship, I suppose he was like, OK, at least I'll get laid, what the hell.
¿De qué le damos?
"What can we get you?"
Jugo
I didn't think about it then, but to be honest with myself, in the back of my mind I think I planned it all along.
...to move in with him, I mean. Just that part. I had no money, he was a trustafarian. That was justification enough for me.
¡¡El GAAAAAAS!!
I had—have—a massive chip on my shoulder about East Coast blue bloods like Harry (also known as Hamilton Emerson Powell III, son of businessman, grandson of banker, great-grandson of asshole industrialist...). It's a shortcoming, as if I needed any more of those.
alianza
tiendas
Naranjas... seis pesooos... lleveee... dos kilos... seis pesooos... lleveee...
sus limoneees... cinco pesooos...
dos meloneees... cinco pesooos...
¡el GAAAAAS!
¡el GAAAAS!
¡el AGUAAAAA!
GAS
It was so galling: his family had lived in Cuernavaca for a while when he was a kid, and they had a house in Puerto Vallarta. Which means he had more connections to Mexico than I did, in a sense.

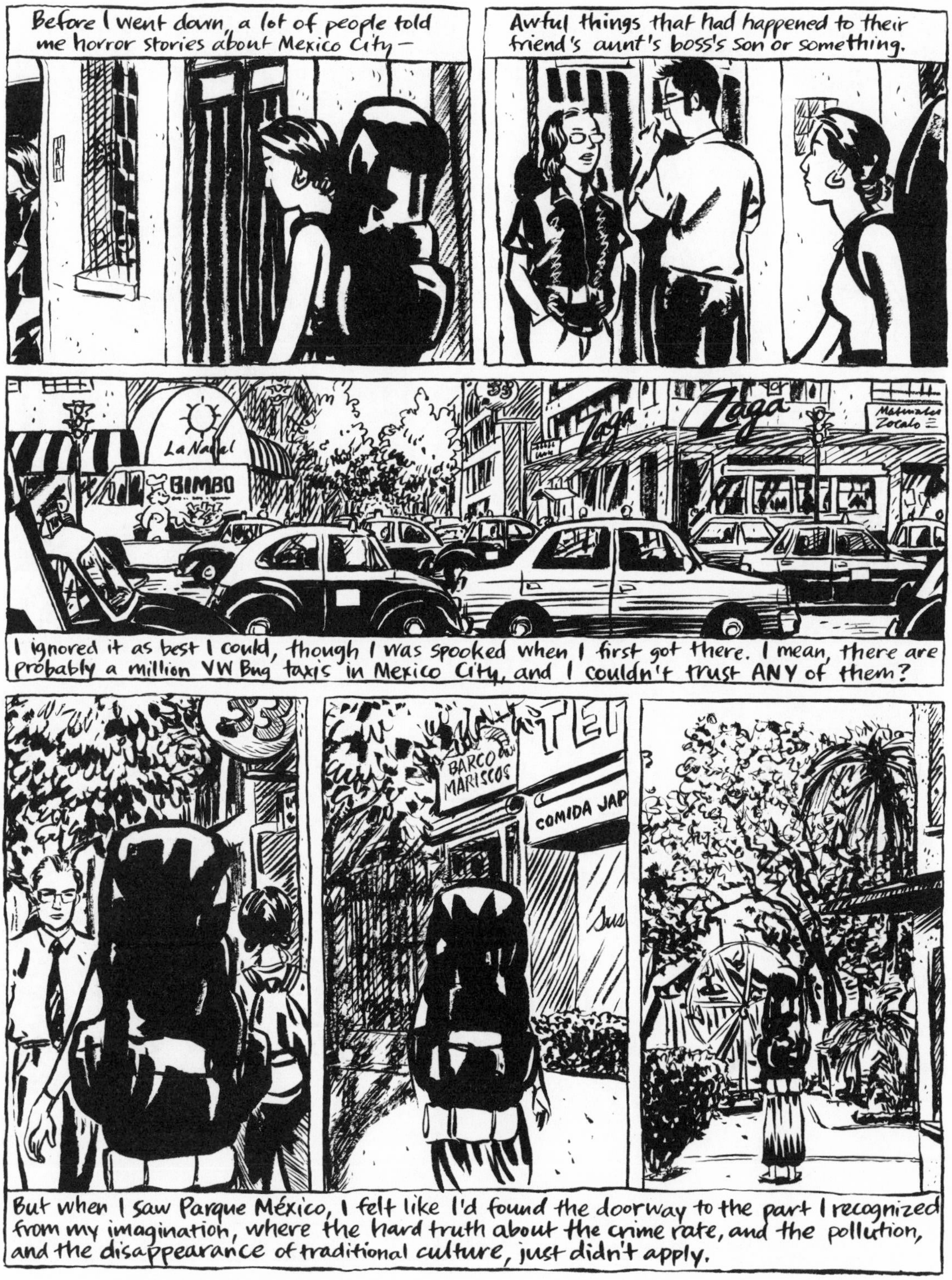
Before I went down, a lot of people told me horror stories about Mexico City—
Awful things that had happened to their friend's aunt's boss's son or something.
La Naval
BIMBO
Zaga
Zaga
I ignored it as best I could, though I was spooked when I first got there. I mean, there are probably a million VW Bug taxis in Mexico City, and I couldn't trust ANY of them?
33
BARCO MARISCOS
COMIDA JAP
But when I saw Parque México, I felt like I'd found the doorway to the part I recognized from my imagination, where the hard truth about the crime rate, and the pollution, and the disappearance of traditional culture, just didn't apply.

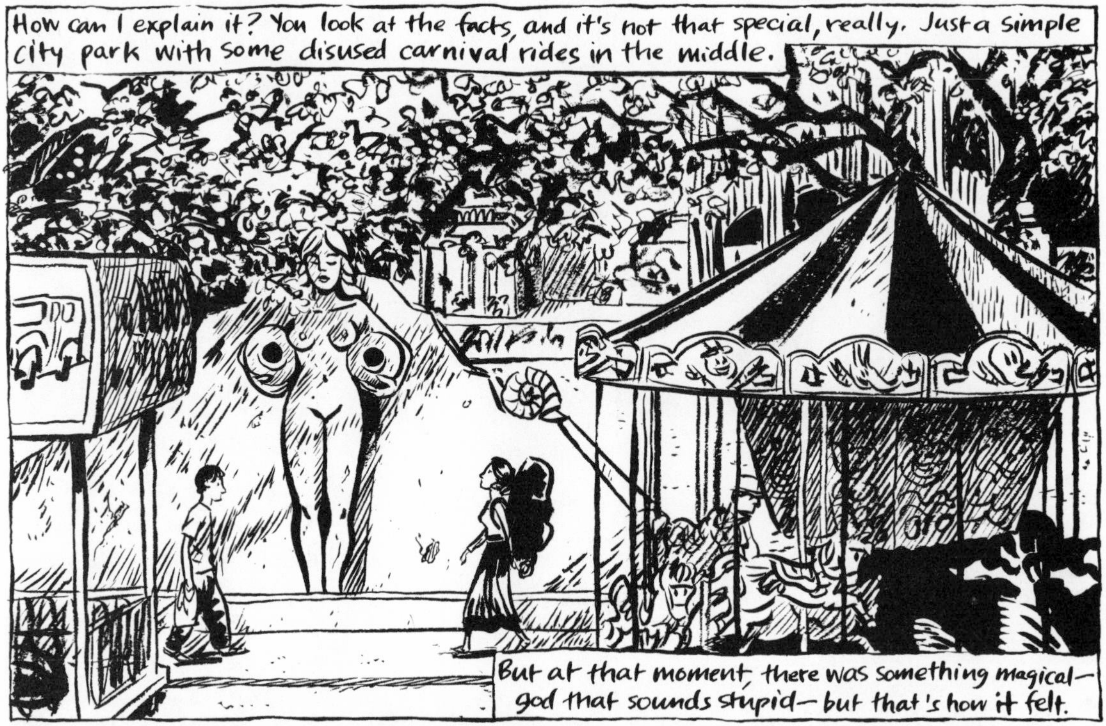
How can I explain it? You look at the facts, and it's not that special, really. Just a simple city park with some disused carnival rides in the middle.
But at that moment, there was something magical—god that sounds stupid—but that's how it felt.

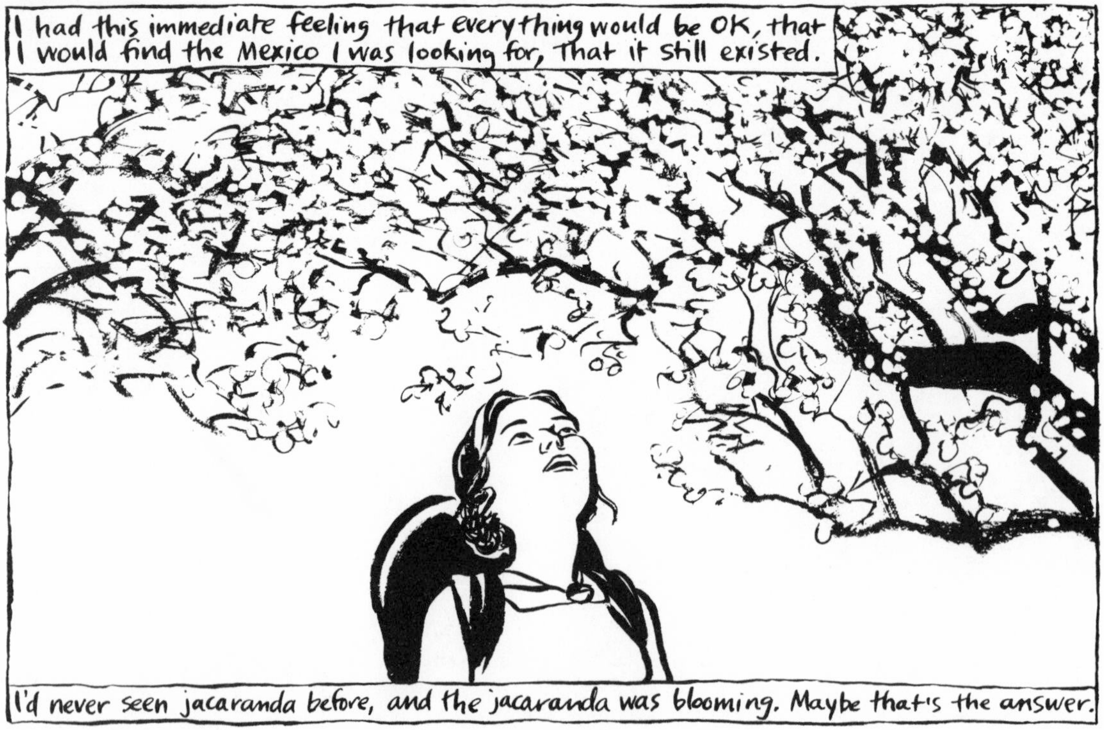
I had this immediate feeling that everything would be OK, that I would find the Mexico I was looking for, that it still existed.
I'd never seen jacaranda before, and the jacaranda was blooming. Maybe that's the answer.

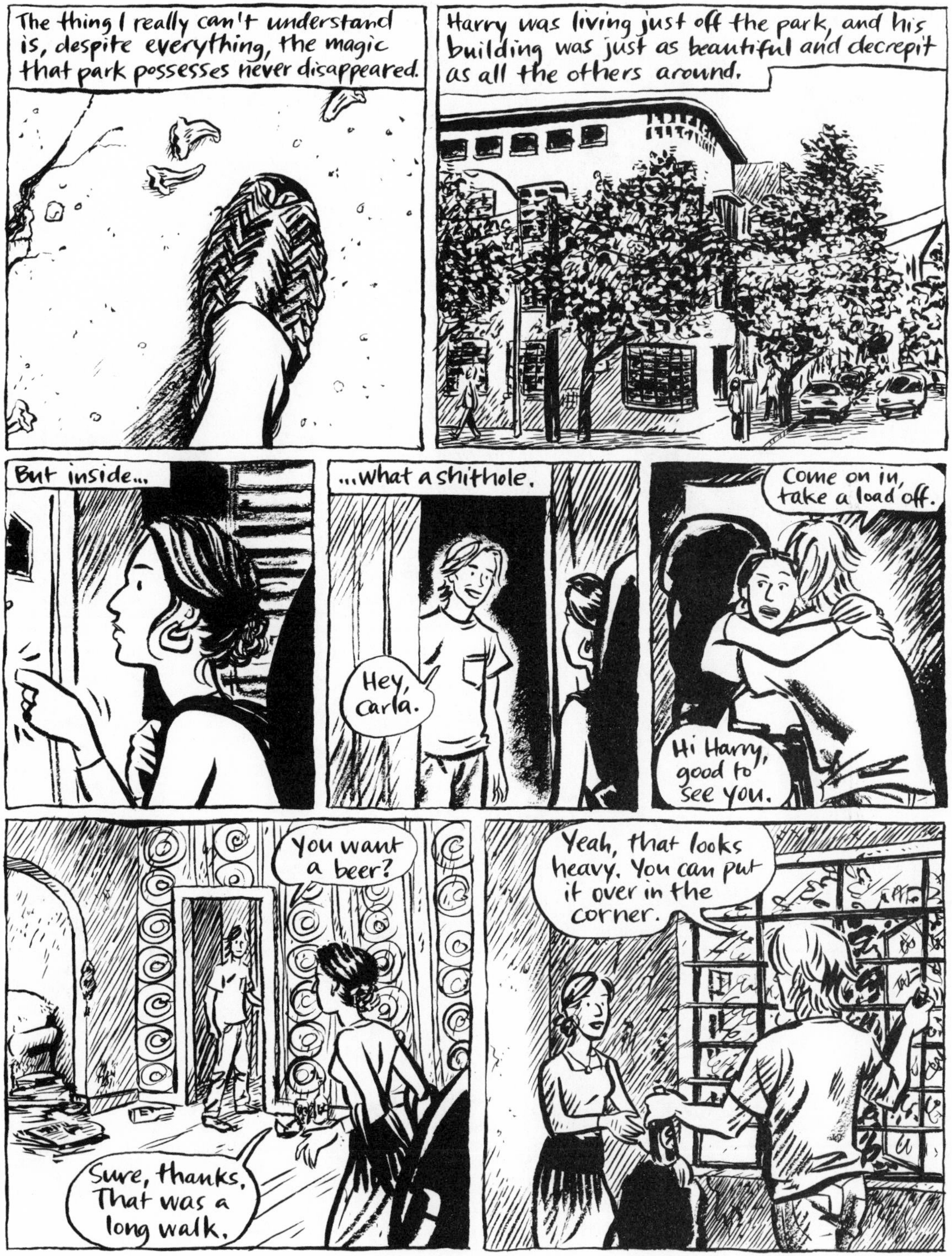
The thing I really can't understand is, despite everything, the magic that park possesses never disappeared.
Harry was living just off the park, and his building was just as beautiful and decrepit as all the others around.
But inside...
...what a shithole.
Hey, Carla.
Come on in, take a load off.
Hi Harry, good to see you.
You want a beer?
Sure, thanks. That was a long walk.
Yeah, that looks heavy. You can put it over in the corner.

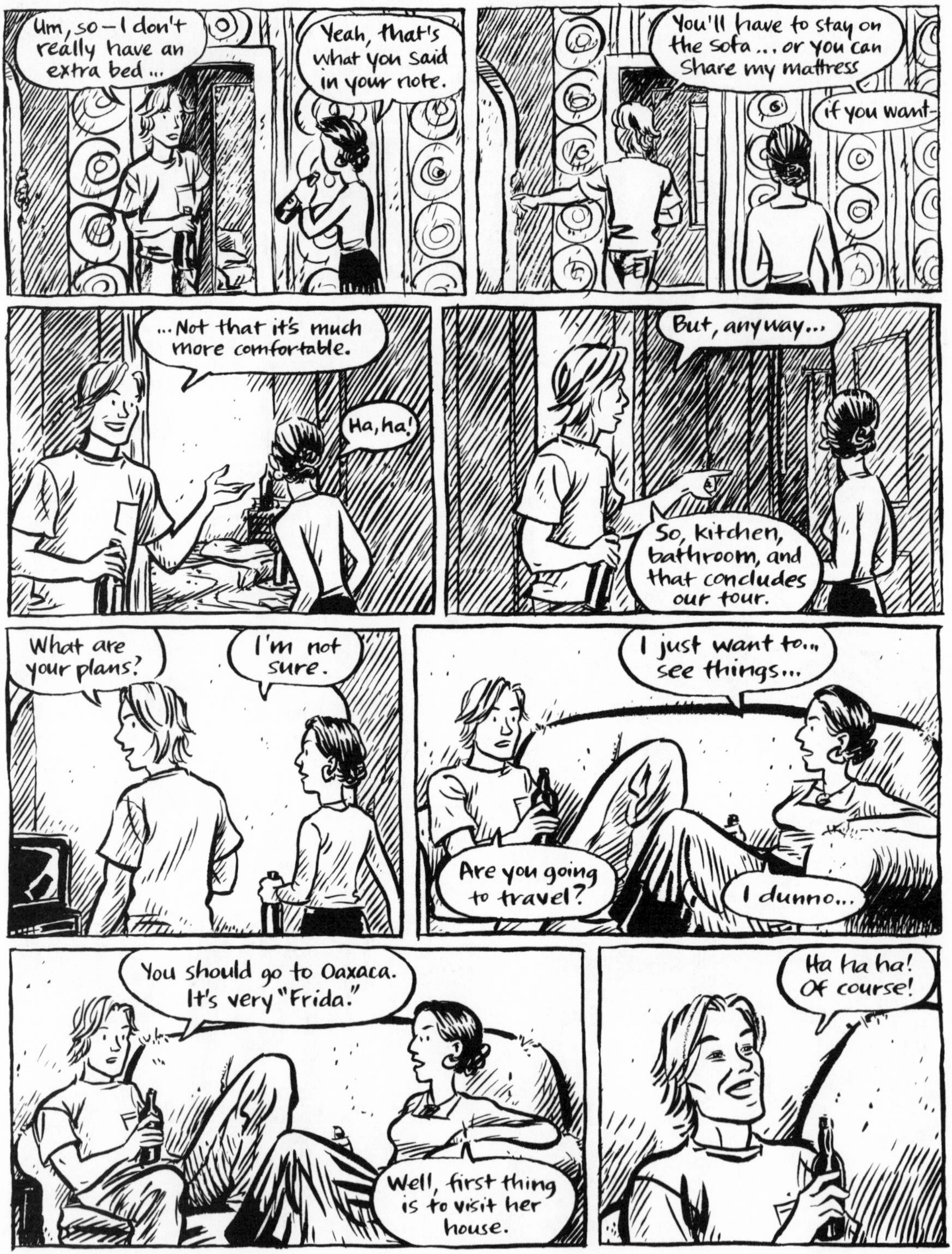
Um, so—I don't really have an extra bed...
Yeah, that's what you said in your note.
You'll have to stay on the sofa... or you can share my mattress
if you want-
...Not that it's much more comfortable.
Ha, ha!
But, anyway...
So, kitchen, bathroom, and that concludes our tour.
What are your plans?
I'm not sure.
I just want to... see things...
Are you going to travel?
I dunno...
You should go to Oaxaca. It's very "Frida."
Well, first thing is to visit her house.
Ha ha ha! Of course!

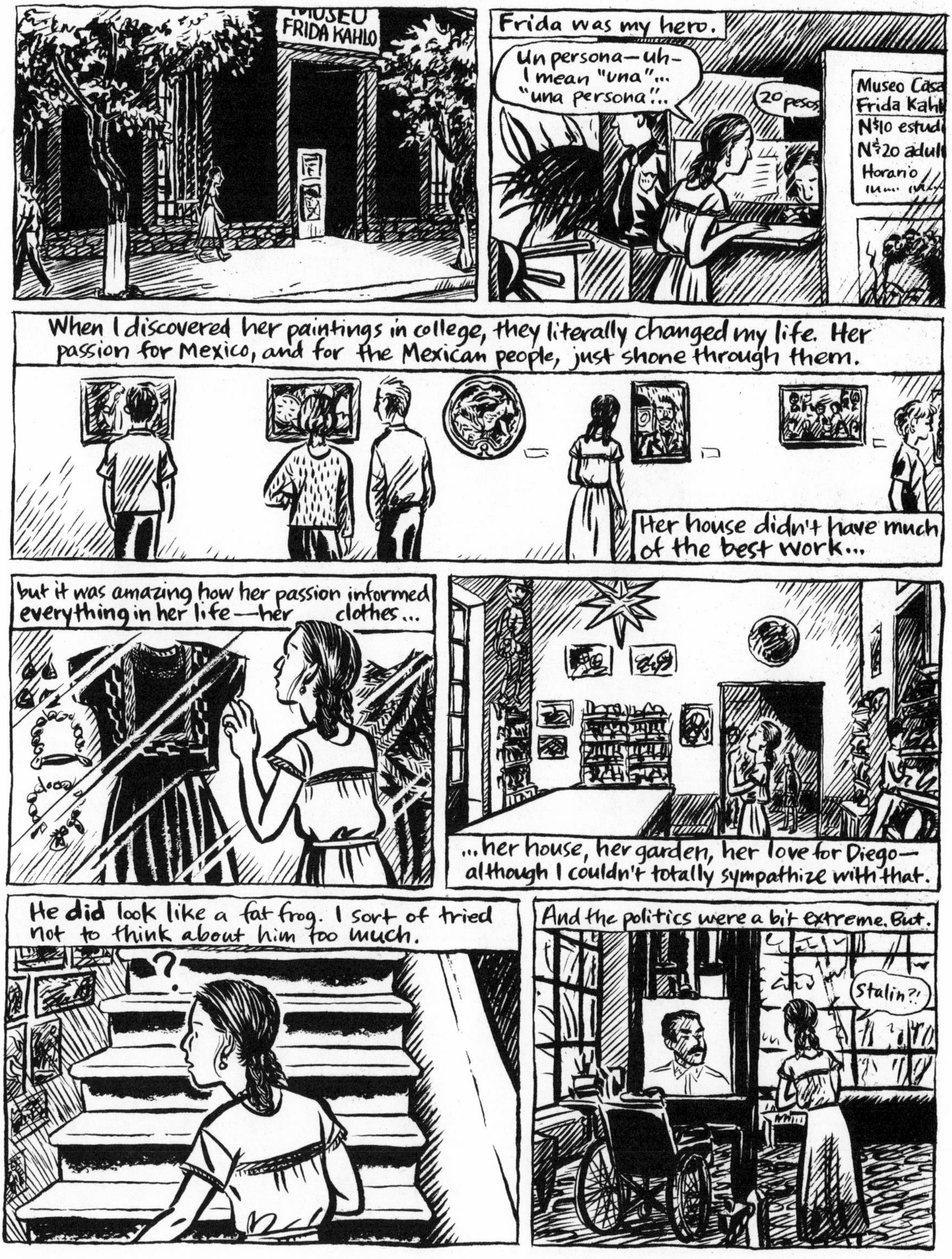
MUSEO FRIDA KAHLO
Frida was my hero.
Un persona—uh—I mean "una"... "una persona"...
20 pesos
Museo Casa Frida Kahl
N$10 estud
N$20 adul
Horario
When I discovered her paintings in college, they literally changed my life. Her passion for Mexico, and for the Mexican people, just shone through them.
Her house didn't have much of the best work...
but it was amazing how her passion informed everything in her life—her clothes...
...her house, her garden, her love for Diego—although I couldn't totally sympathize with that.
He did look like a fat frog. I sort of tried not to think about him too much.
?
And the politics were a bit extreme. But.
Stalin?!

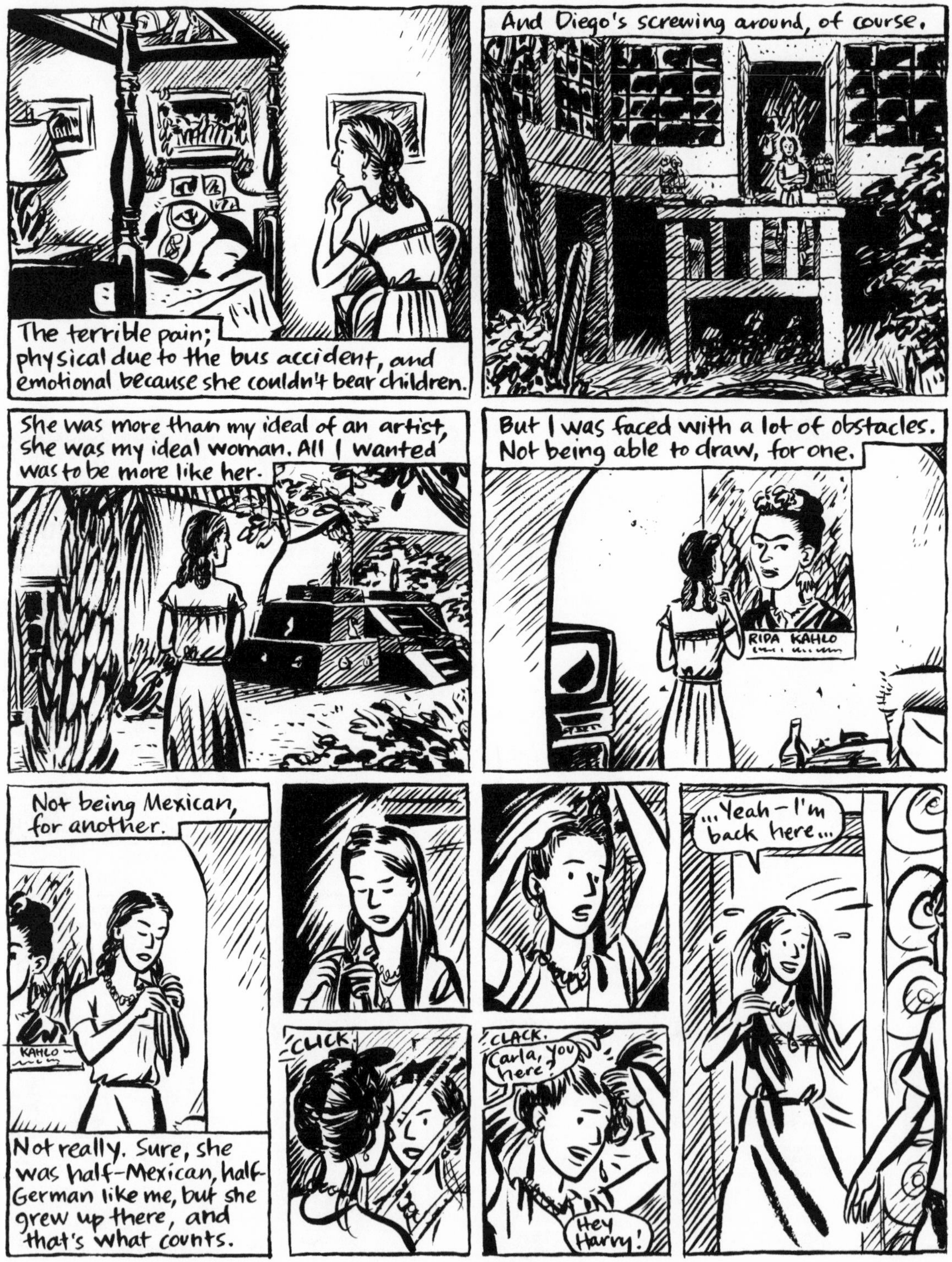

The terrible pain; physical due to the bus accident, and emotional because she couldn't bear children.
And Diego's screwing around, of course.
She was more than my ideal of an artist, she was my ideal woman. All I wanted was to be more like her.
But I was faced with a lot of obstacles. Not being able to draw, for one.
RIDA KAHLO
Not being Mexican, for another.
KAHLO
Not really. Sure, she was half-Mexican, half-German like me, but she grew up there, and that's what counts.
CLICK
CLACK.
Carla, you here?
Hey Harry!
...Yeah-I'm back here...

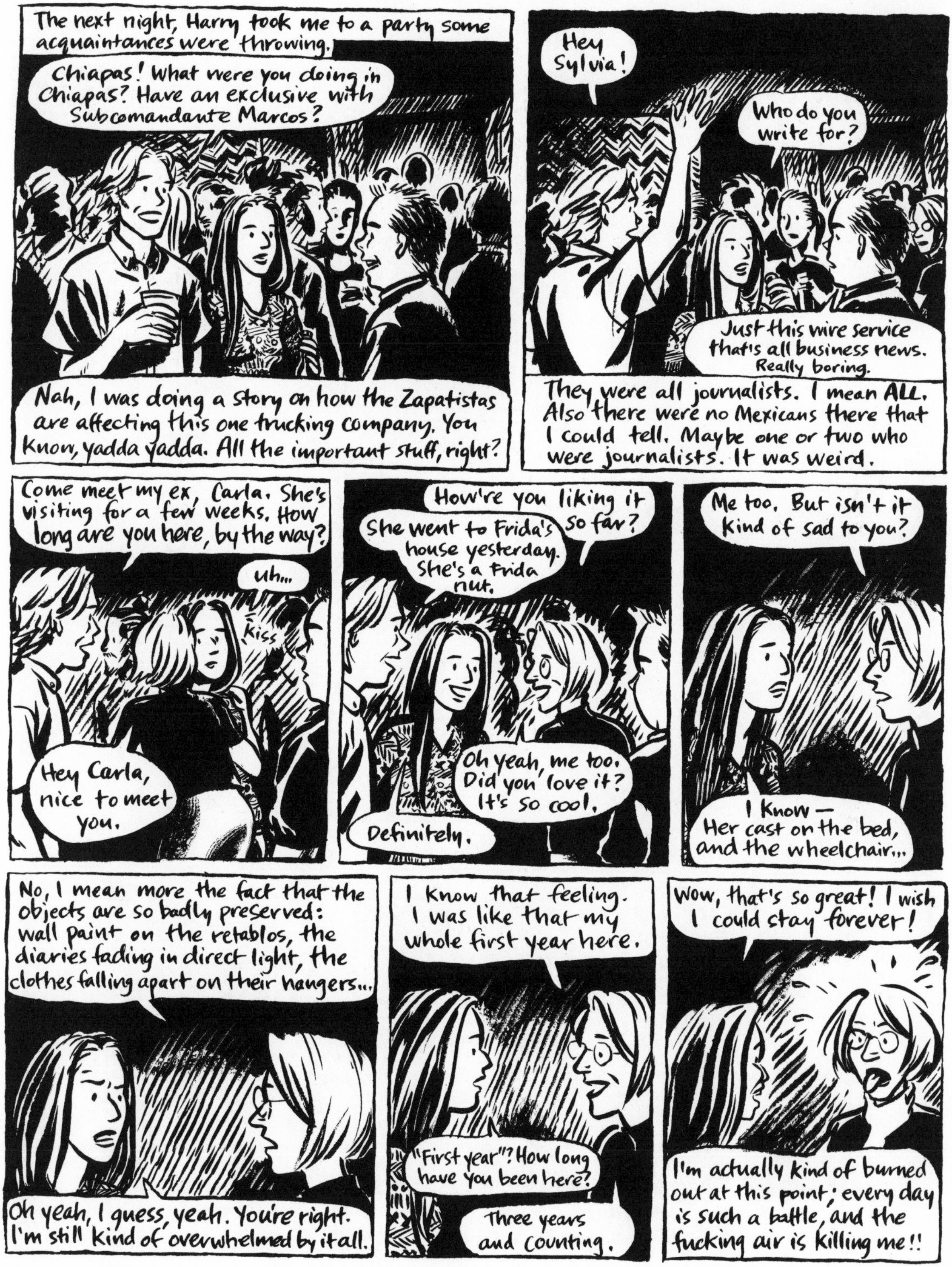

The next night, Harry took me to a party some acquaintances were throwing.
Chiapas! What were you doing in Chiapas? Have an exclusive with Subcomandante Marcos?
Nah, I was doing a story on how the Zapatistas are affecting this one trucking company. You know, yadda yadda. All the important stuff, right?
Hey Sylvia!
Who do you write for?
Just this wire service that's all business news. Really boring.
They were all journalists. I mean ALL. Also there were no Mexicans there that I could tell. Maybe one or two who were journalists. It was weird.
Come meet my ex, Carla. She's visiting for a few weeks. How long are you here, by the way?
uh...
kiss
Hey Carla, nice to meet you.
How're you liking it so far?
She went to Frida's house yesterday. She's a Frida nut.
Oh yeah, me too. Did you love it? It's so cool.
Definitely.
Me too. But isn't it kind of sad to you?
I know — Her cast on the bed, and the wheelchair...
No, I mean more the fact that the objects are so badly preserved: wall paint on the retablos, the diaries fading in direct light, the clothes falling apart on their hangers...
Oh yeah, I guess, yeah. You're right. I'm still kind of overwhelmed by it all.
I know that feeling. I was like that my whole first year here.
"First year"? How long have you been here?
Three years and counting.
Wow, that's so great! I wish I could stay forever!
I'm actually kind of burned out at this point; every day is such a battle, and the fucking air is killing me!!

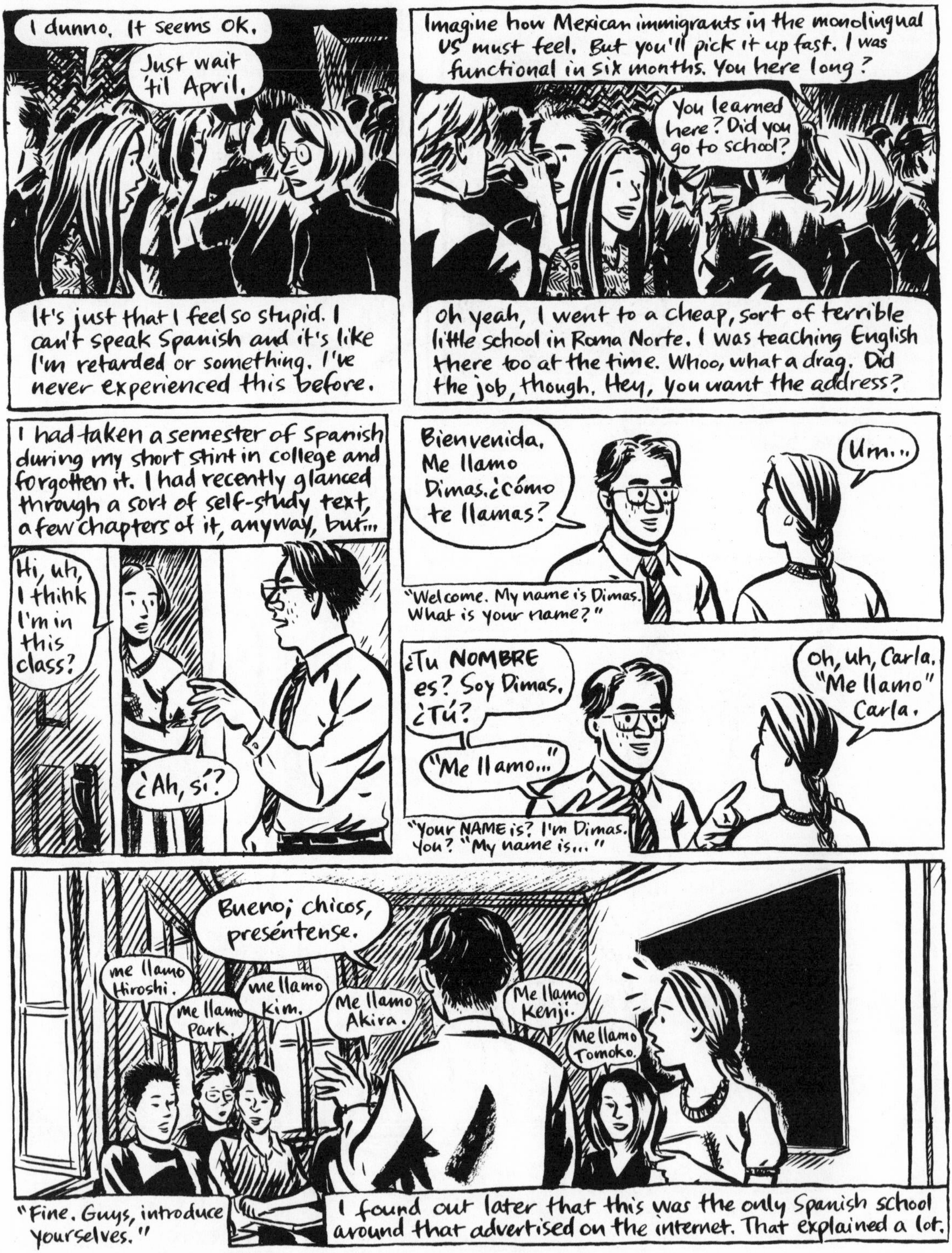

I dunno, It seems OK.
Just wait 'til April.
It's just that I feel so stupid. I can't speak Spanish and it's like I'm retarded or something. I've never experienced this before.
Imagine how Mexican immigrants in the monolingual US must feel. But you'll pick it up fast. I was functional in six months. You here long?
You learned here? Did you go to school?
Oh yeah, I went to a cheap, sort of terrible little school in Roma Norte. I was teaching English there too at the time. Whoo, what a drag. Did the job, though. Hey, you want the address?
I had taken a semester of Spanish during my short stint in college and forgotten it. I had recently glanced through a sort of self-study text, a few chapters of it, anyway, but...
Hi, uh, I think I'm in this class?
¿Ah, sí?
Bienvenida. Me llamo Dimas. ¿Cómo te llamas?
Um...
"Welcome. My name is Dimas. What is your name?"
¿Tu NOMBRE es? Soy Dimas. ¿Tú?
"Me llamo..."
Oh, uh, Carla. "Me llamo" Carla.
"Your NAME is? I'm Dimas. You?" "My name is..."
Bueno; chicos, preséntense.
me llamo Hiroshi.
Me llamo Park.
me llamo Kim.
Me llamo Akira.
Me llamo Kenji.
Me llamo Tomoko.
"Fine. Guys, introduce yourselves."
I found out later that this was the only Spanish school around that advertised on the internet. That explained a lot.

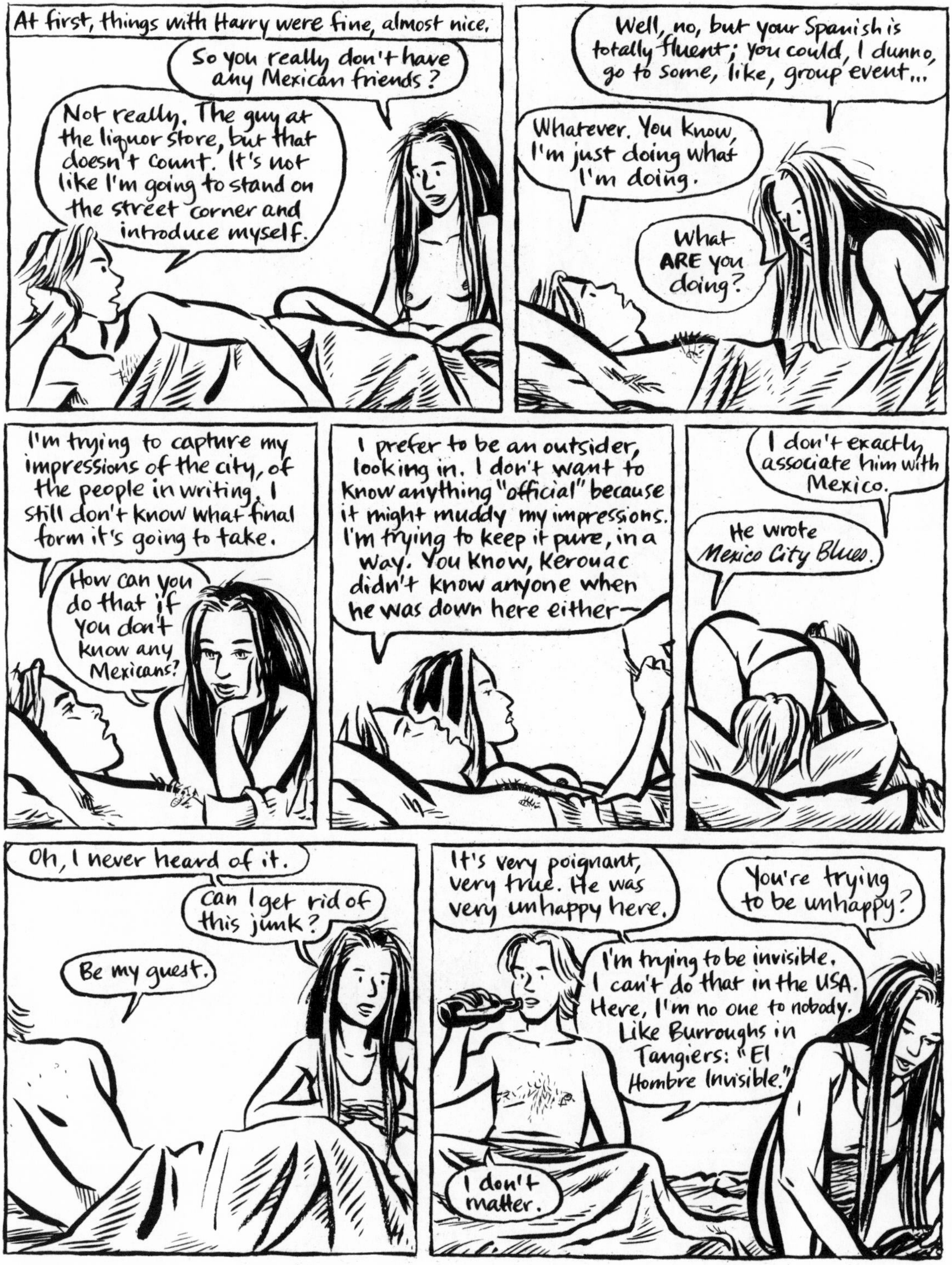

At first, things with Harry were fine, almost nice.
So you really don't have any Mexican friends?
Not really. The guy at the liquor store, but that doesn't count. It's not like I'm going to stand on the street corner and introduce myself.
Well, no, but your Spanish is totally fluent; you could, I dunno, go to some, like, group event...
Whatever. You know, I'm just doing what I'm doing.
What ARE you doing?
I'm trying to capture my impressions of the city, of the people in writing. I still don't know what final form it's going to take.
How can you do that if you don't know any Mexicans?
I prefer to be an outsider, looking in. I don't want to know anything "official" because it might muddy my impressions. I'm trying to keep it pure, in a way. You know, Kerouac didn't know anyone when he was down here either—
I don't exactly associate him with Mexico.
He wrote Mexico City Blues.
Oh, I never heard of it.
Can I get rid of this junk?
Be my guest.
It's very poignant, very true. He was very unhappy here.
You're trying to be unhappy?
I'm trying to be invisible. I can't do that in the USA. Here, I'm no one to nobody. Like Burroughs in Tangiers: "El Hombre Invisible."
I don't matter.

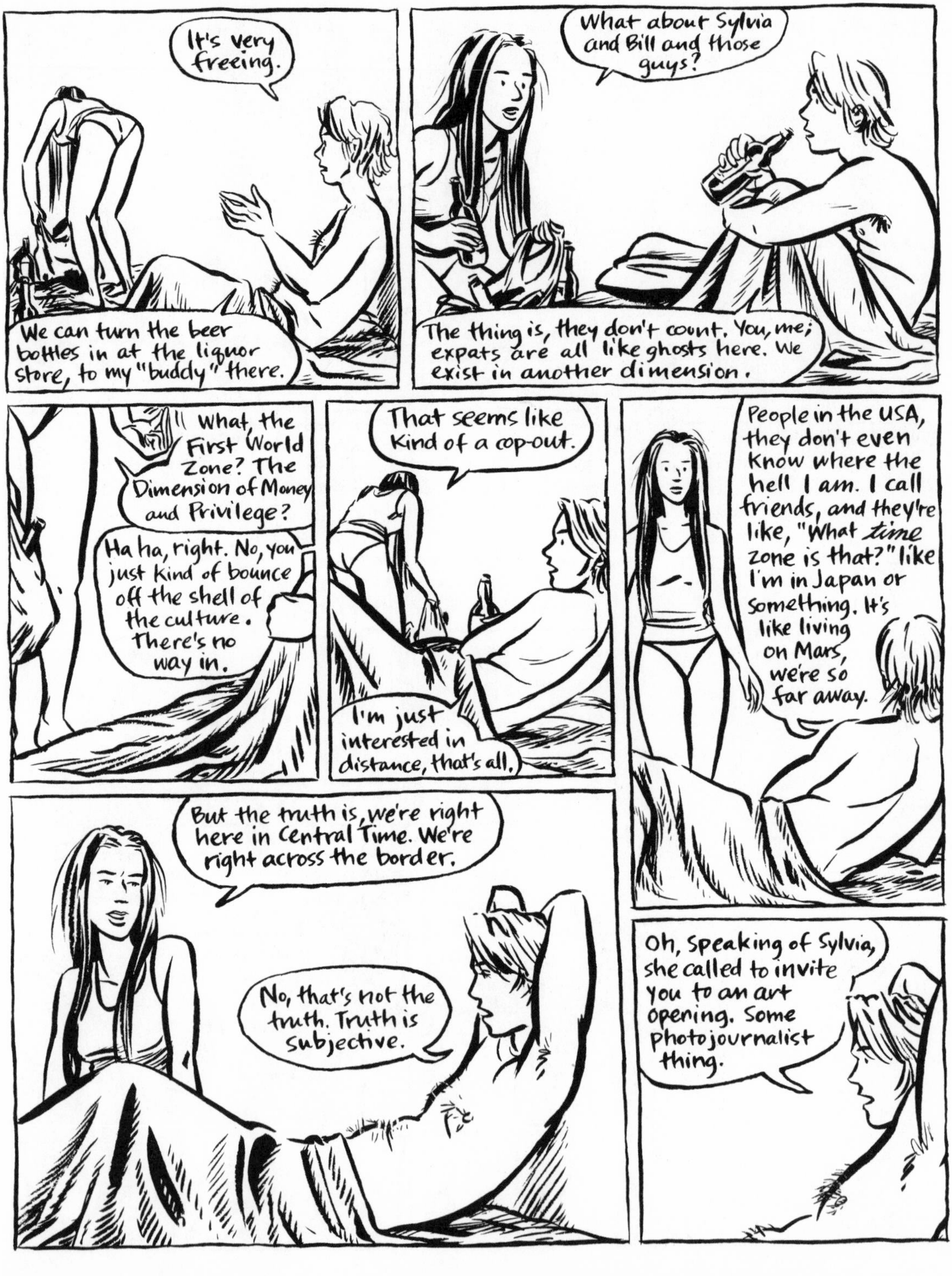
It's very freeing.
We can turn the beer bottles in at the liquor store, to my "buddy" there.
What about Sylvia and Bill and those guys?
The thing is, they don't count. You, me; expats are all like ghosts here. We exist in another dimension.
What, the First World Zone? The Dimension of Money and Privilege?
Ha ha, right. No, you just kind of bounce off the shell of the culture. There's no way in.
That seems like kind of a cop-out.
I'm just interested in distance, that's all.
People in the USA, they don't even know where the hell I am. I call friends, and they're like, "What *time* zone is that?" like I'm in Japan or something. It's like living on Mars, we're so far away.
But the truth is, we're right here in Central Time. We're right across the border.
No, that's not the truth. Truth is subjective.
Oh, speaking of Sylvia, she called to invite you to an art opening. Some photojournalist thing.

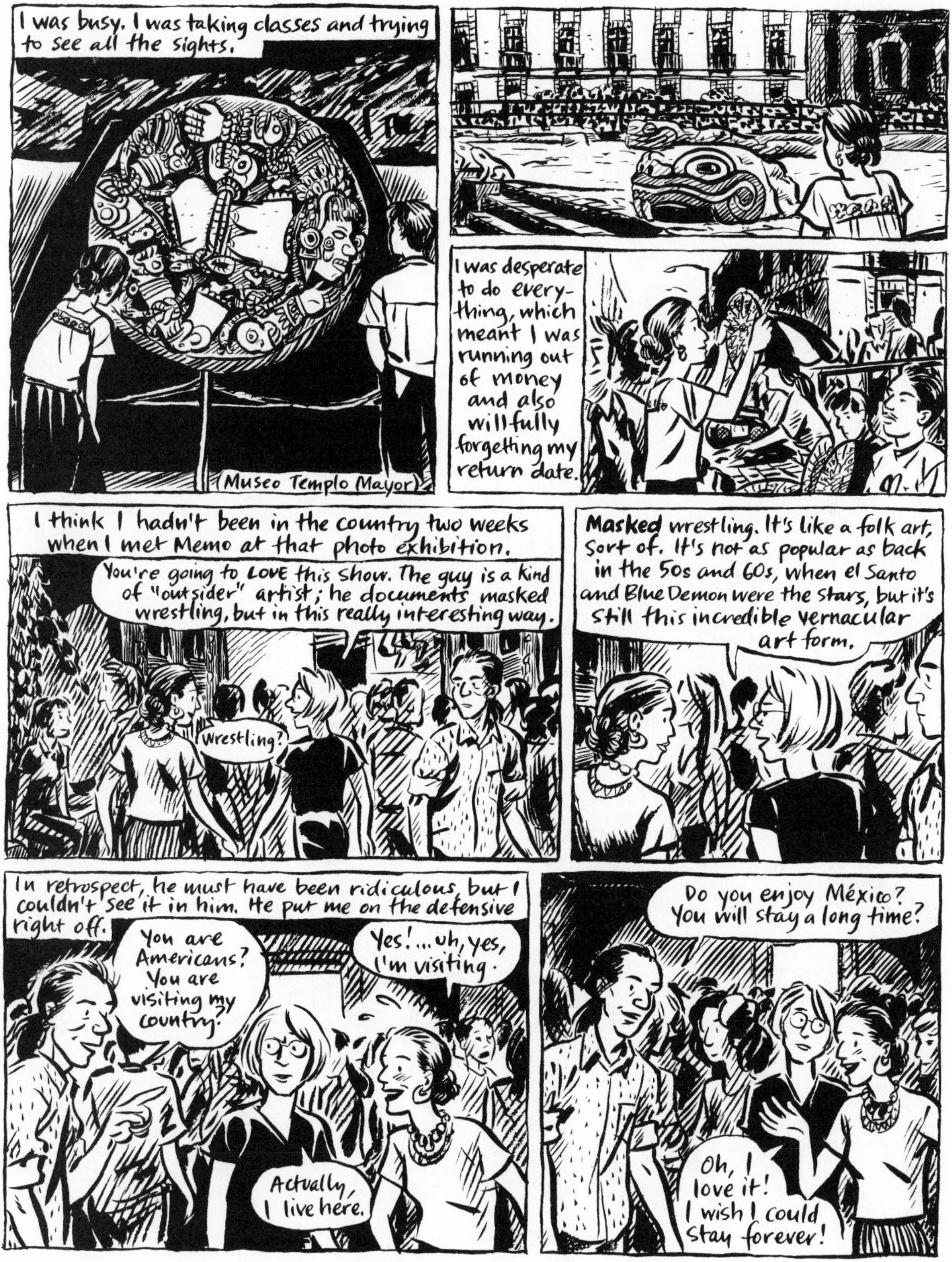
I was busy. I was taking classes and trying to see all the sights.
(Museo Templo Mayor)
I was desperate to do everything, which meant I was running out of money and also willfully forgetting my return date.
I think I hadn't been in the country two weeks when I met Memo at that photo exhibition.
You're going to LOVE this show. The guy is a kind of "outsider" artist; he documents masked wrestling, but in this really interesting way.
Wrestling?
Masked wrestling. It's like a folk art, sort of. It's not as popular as back in the 50s and 60s, when el Santo and Blue Demon were the stars, but it's still this incredible vernacular art form.
In retrospect, he must have been ridiculous, but I couldn't see it in him. He put me on the defensive right off.
You are Americans? You are visiting my country?
Yes!... uh, yes, I'm visiting.
Actually, I live here.
Do you enjoy México? You will stay a long time?
Oh, I love it! I wish I could stay forever!

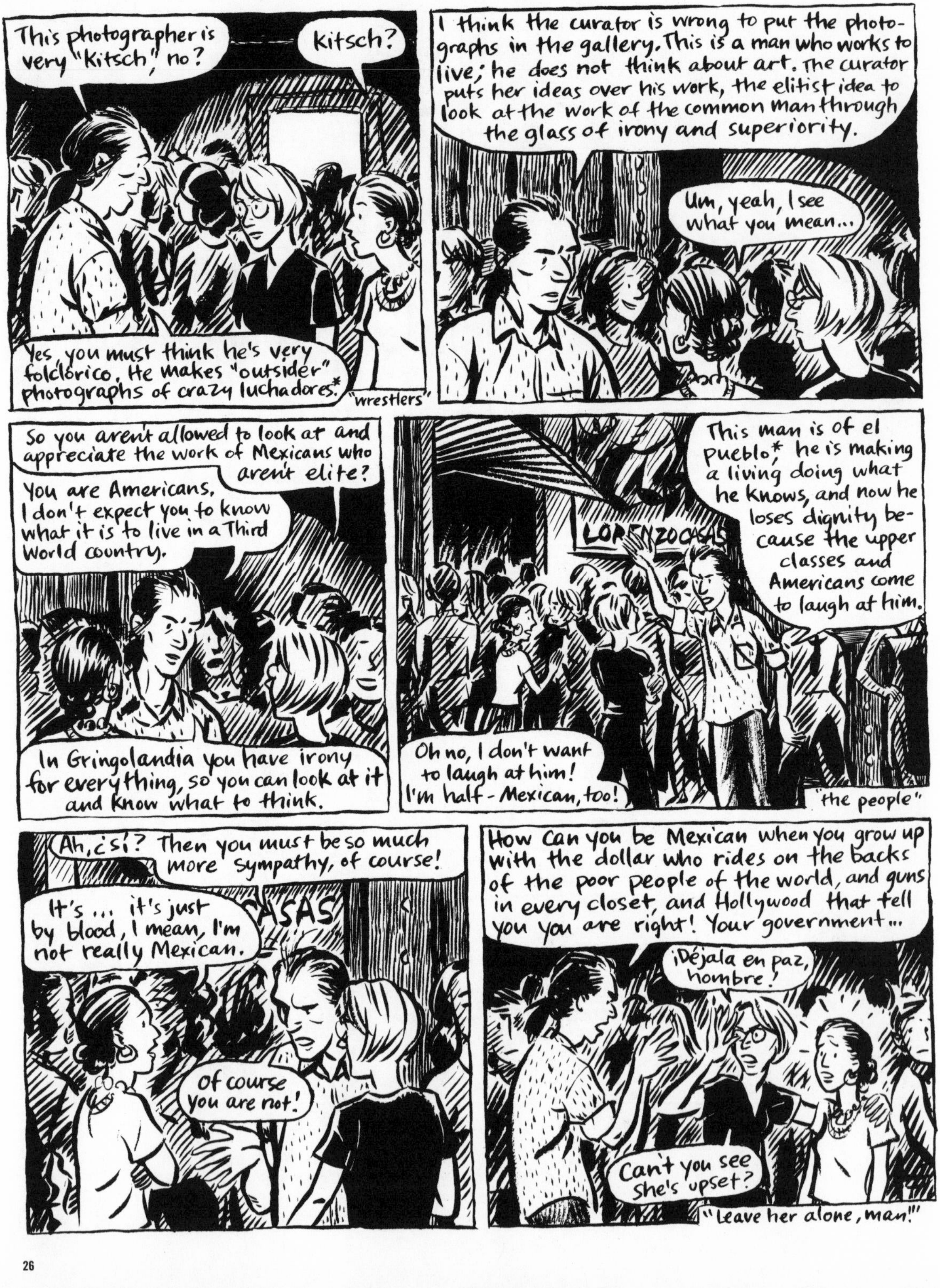
This photographer is very "Kitsch," no?
Kitsch?
Yes, you must think he's very folclórico. He makes "outsider" photographs of crazy luchadores.*
*"wrestlers"
I think the curator is wrong to put the photographs in the gallery. This is a man who works to live; he does not think about art. The curator puts her ideas over his work, the elitist idea to look at the work of the common man through the glass of irony and superiority.
Um, yeah, I see what you mean...
So you aren't allowed to look at and appreciate the work of Mexicans who aren't elite?
You are Americans. I don't expect you to know what it is to live in a Third World country.
In Gringolandia you have irony for everything, so you can look at it and know what to think.
This man is of el pueblo,* he is making a living doing what he knows, and now he loses dignity because the upper classes and Americans come to laugh at him.
LORENZO CASAS
Oh no, I don't want to laugh at him! I'm half-Mexican, too!
*"the people"
Ah, ¿sí? Then you must be so much more sympathy, of course!
It's ... it's just by blood, I mean, I'm not really Mexican.
CASAS
Of course you are not!
How can you be Mexican when you grow up with the dollar who rides on the backs of the poor people of the world, and guns in every closet, and Hollywood that tell you you are right! Your government...
¡Déjala en paz, hombre!*
Can't you see she's upset?
*"Leave her alone, man!"

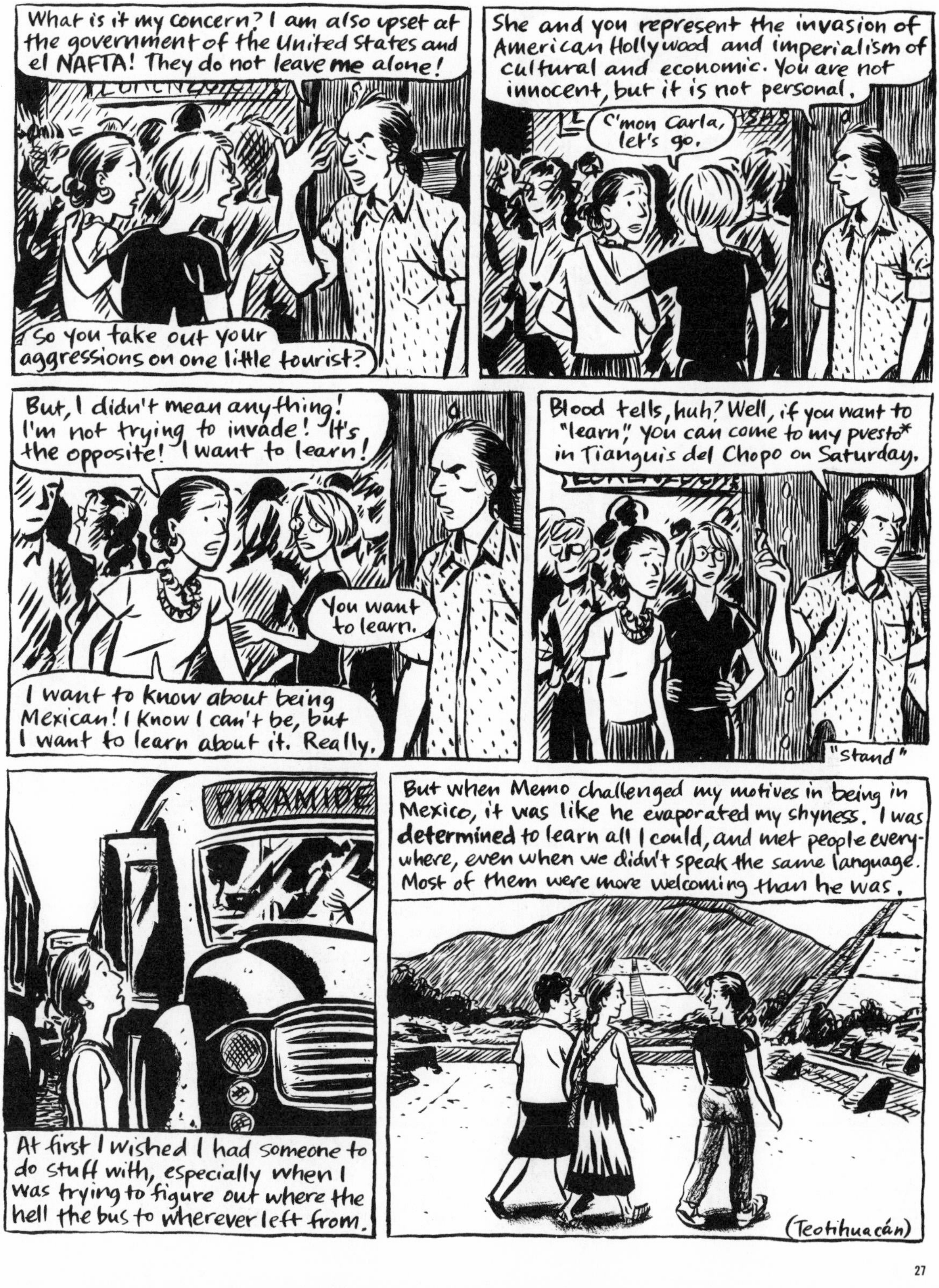

What is it my concern? I am also upset at the government of the United States and el NAFTA! They do not leave me alone!
So you take out your aggressions on one little tourist?
She and you represent the invasion of American Hollywood and imperialism of cultural and economic. You are not innocent, but it is not personal.
C'mon Carla, let's go.
But, I didn't mean anything! I'm not trying to invade! It's the opposite! I want to learn!
You want to learn.
I want to know about being Mexican! I know I can't be, but I want to learn about it. Really.
Blood tells, huh? Well, if you want to "learn," you can come to my puesto* in Tianguis del Chopo on Saturday.
*"stand"
PIRAMIDE
At first I wished I had someone to do stuff with, especially when I was trying to figure out where the hell the bus to wherever left from.
But when Memo challenged my motives in being in Mexico, it was like he evaporated my shyness. I was determined to learn all I could, and met people everywhere, even when we didn't speak the same language. Most of them were more welcoming than he was.
(Teotihuacán)

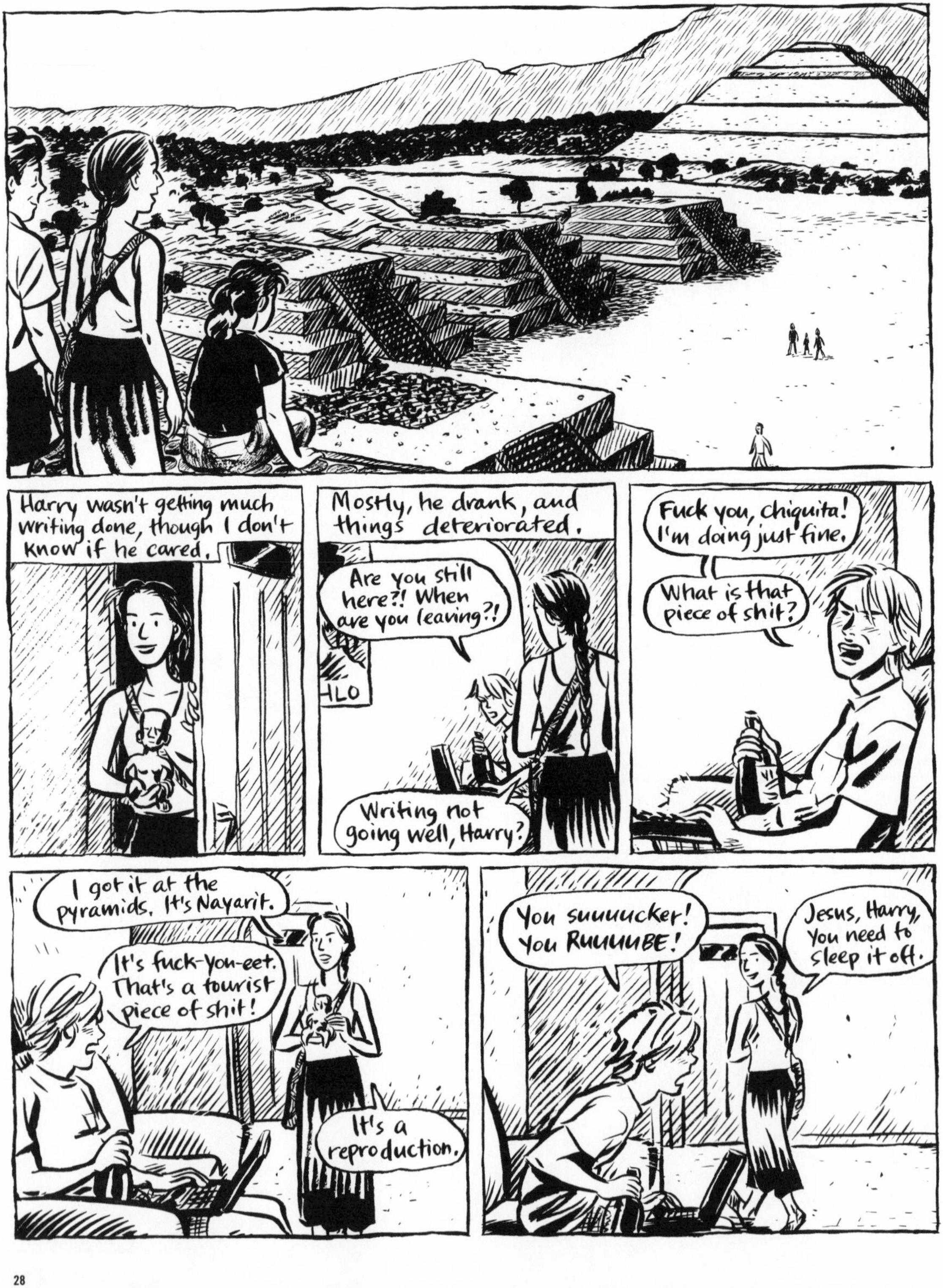

Harry wasn't getting much writing done, though I don't know if he cared.
Mostly, he drank, and things deteriorated.
Are you still here?! When are you leaving?!
HLO
Writing not going well, Harry?
Fuck you, chiquita! I'm doing just fine.
What is that piece of shit?
I got it at the pyramids. It's Nayarit.
It's fuck-you-eet. That's a tourist piece of shit!
It's a reproduction.
You suuuucker! You RUUUUBE!
Jesus, Harry, You need to sleep it off.

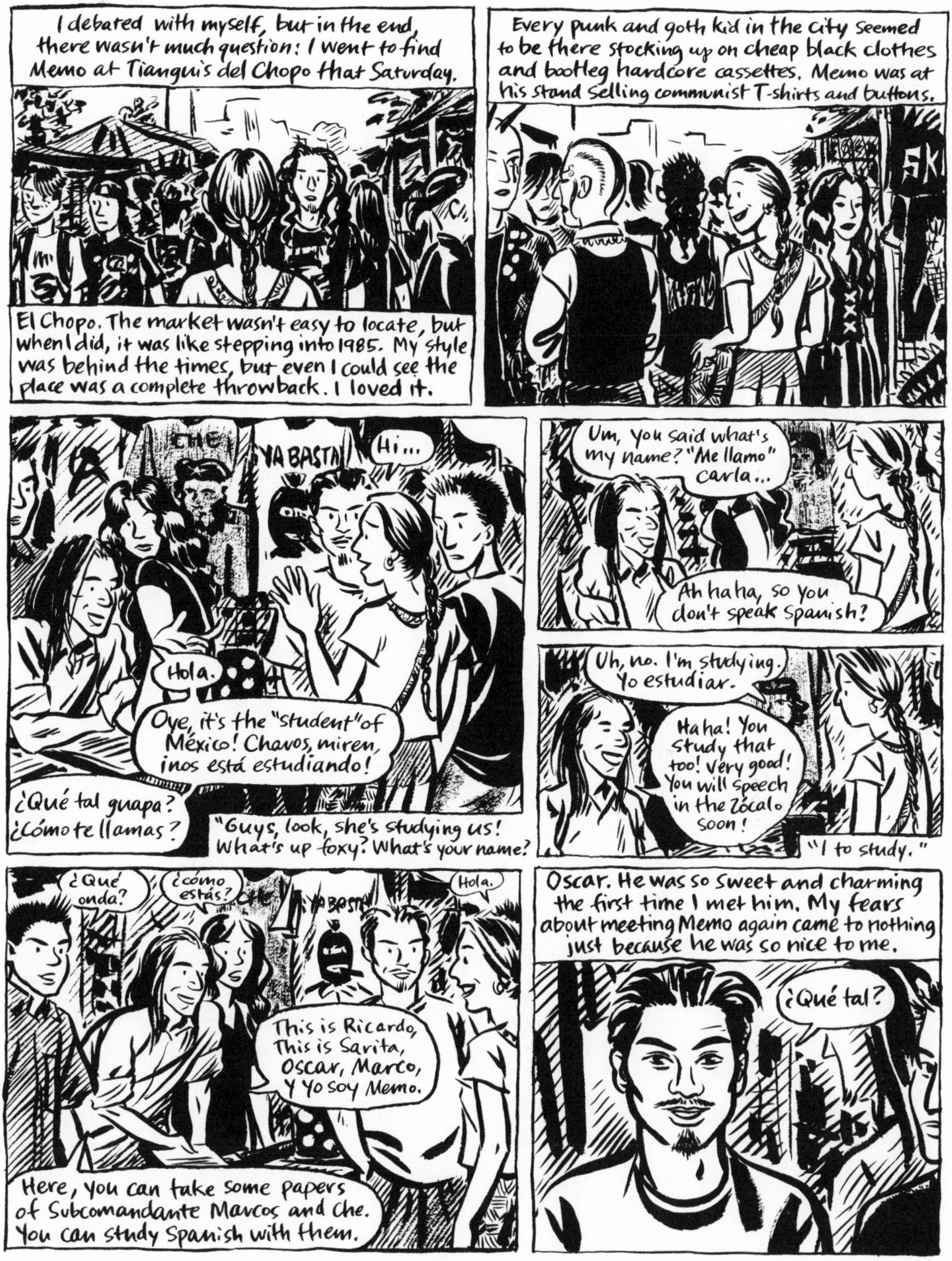
I debated with myself, but in the end, there wasn't much question: I went to find Memo at Tianguis del Chopo that Saturday.
El Chopo. The market wasn't easy to locate, but when I did, it was like stepping into 1985. My style was behind the times, but even I could see the place was a complete throwback. I loved it.
Every punk and goth kid in the city seemed to be there stocking up on cheap black clothes and bootleg hardcore cassettes. Memo was at his stand selling communist T-shirts and buttons.
CHE
YA BASTA
Hi...
Hola.
Oye, it's the "student" of México! Chavos, miren, ¡nos está estudiando!
¿Qué tal guapa? ¿Cómo te llamas?
"Guys, look, she's studying us! What's up foxy? What's your name?"
Um, you said what's my name? "Me llamo" Carla...
Ah ha ha, so you don't speak Spanish?
Uh, no. I'm studying. Yo estudiar.
Haha! You study that too! Very good! You will speech in the Zócalo soon!
"I to study."
¿Qué onda?
¿cómo estás?
Hola.
This is Ricardo, This is Sarita, Oscar, Marco, y yo soy Memo.
Here, you can take some papers of Subcomandante Marcos and Che. You can study Spanish with them.
Oscar. He was so sweet and charming the first time I met him. My fears about meeting Memo again came to nothing just because he was so nice to me.
¿Qué tal?

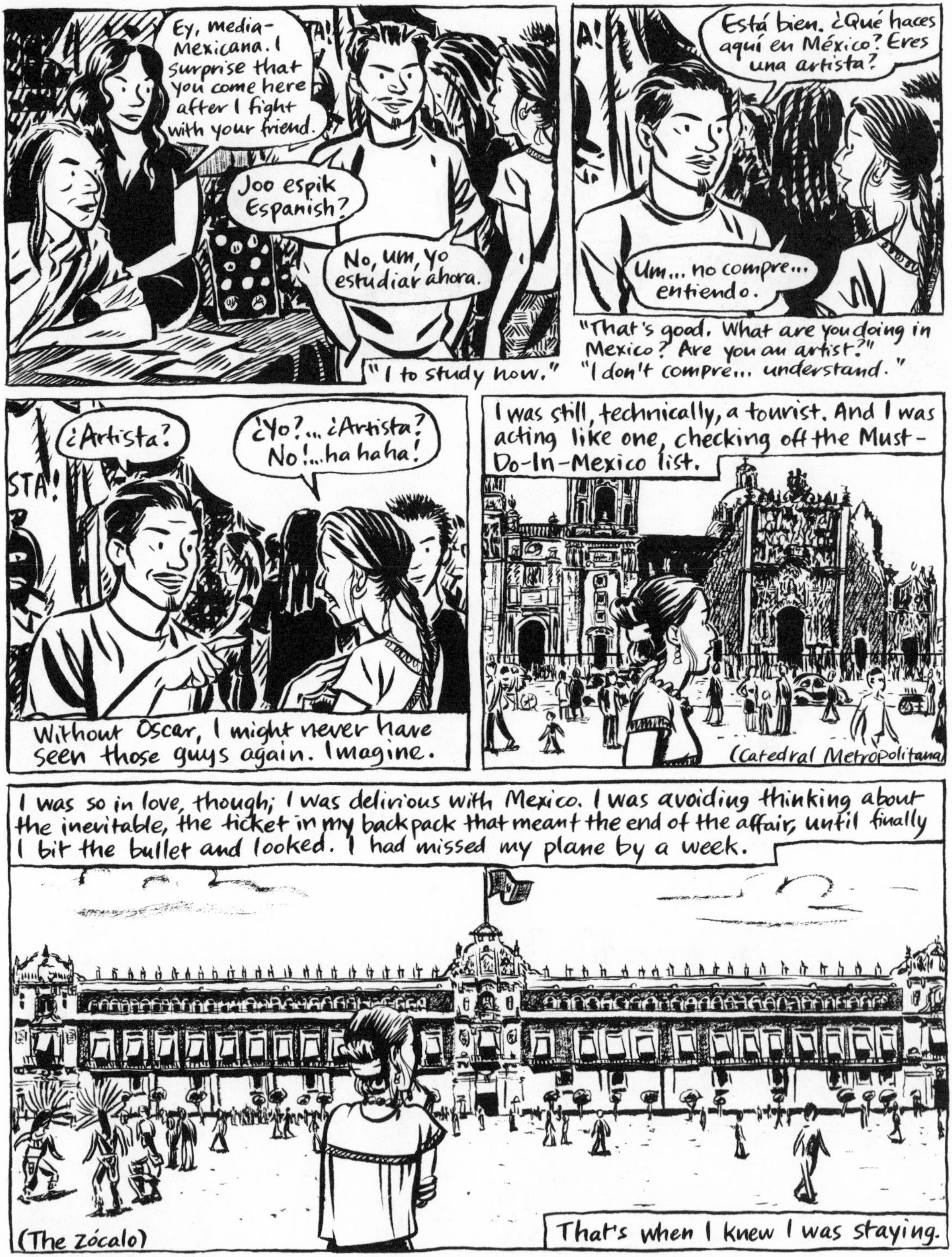
Ey, media-Mexicana. I surprise that you come here after I fight with your friend.
A!
Joo espik Espanish?
No, um, yo estudiar ahora.
"I to study now."
A!
Está bien. ¿Qué haces aquí en México? Eres una artista?
Um... no compre... entiendo.
"That's good. What are you doing in Mexico? Are you an artist?" "I don't compre... understand."
¿Artista?
¿Yo?... ¿Artista? No!... ha ha ha!
STA!
Without Oscar, I might never have seen those guys again. Imagine.
I was still, technically, a tourist. And I was acting like one, checking off the Must-Do-In-Mexico list.
(Catedral Metropolitana)
I was so in love, though; I was delirious with Mexico. I was avoiding thinking about the inevitable, the ticket in my backpack that meant the end of the affair, until finally I bit the bullet and looked. I had missed my plane by a week.
(The Zócalo)
That's when I knew I was staying.

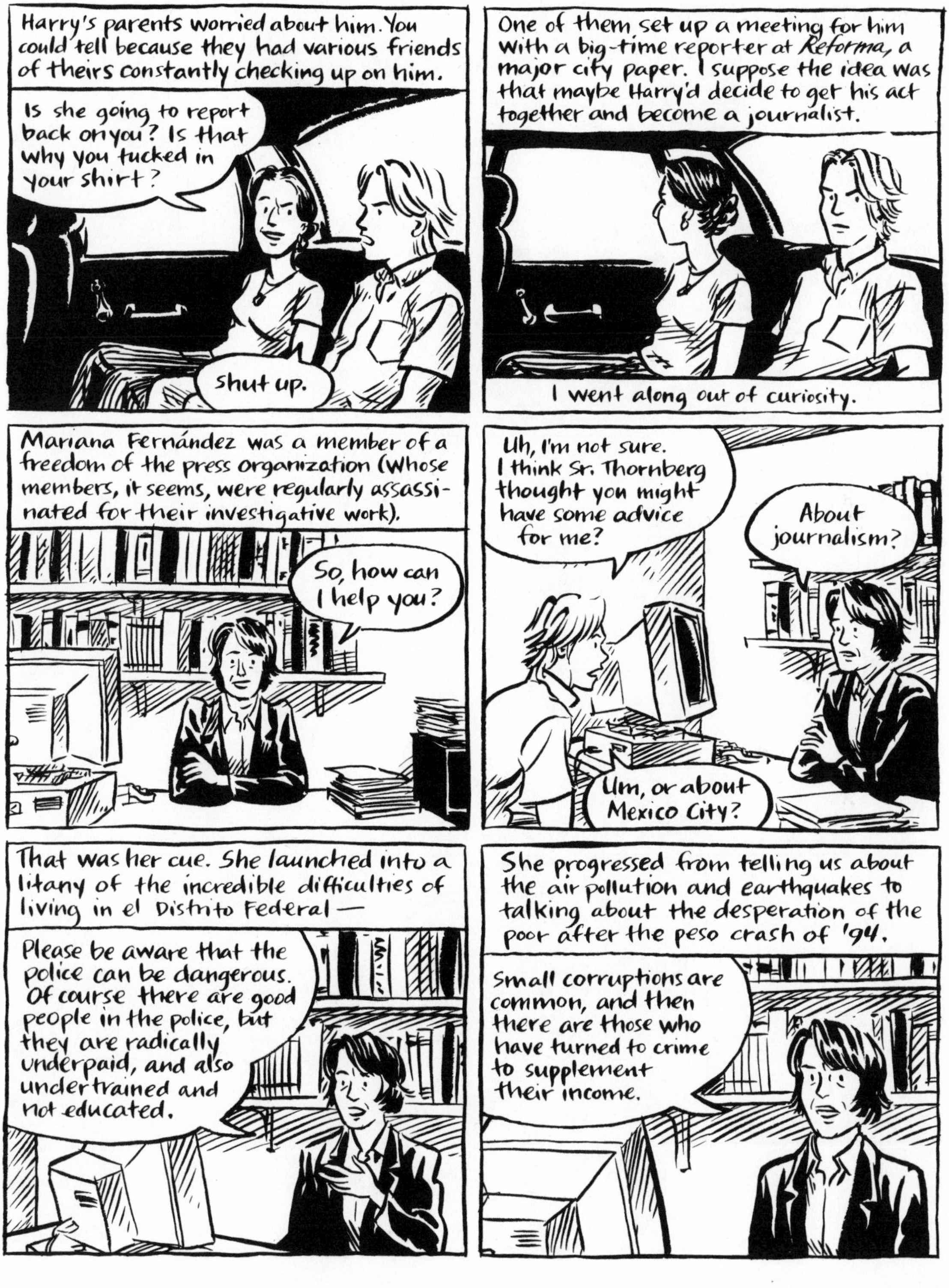
Harry's parents worried about him. You could tell because they had various friends of theirs constantly checking up on him.
Is she going to report back on you? Is that why you tucked in your shirt?
Shut up.
One of them set up a meeting for him with a big-time reporter at *Reforma*, a major city paper. I suppose the idea was that maybe Harry'd decide to get his act together and become a journalist.
I went along out of curiosity.
Mariana Fernández was a member of a freedom of the press organization (whose members, it seems, were regularly assassinated for their investigative work).
So, how can I help you?
Uh, I'm not sure. I think Sr. Thornberg thought you might have some advice for me?
About journalism?
Um, or about Mexico City?
That was her cue. She launched into a litany of the incredible difficulties of living in el Distrito Federal—
Please be aware that the police can be dangerous. Of course there are good people in the police, but they are radically underpaid, and also undertrained and not educated.
She progressed from telling us about the air pollution and earthquakes to talking about the desperation of the poor after the peso crash of '94.
Small corruptions are common, and then there are those who have turned to crime to supplement their income.

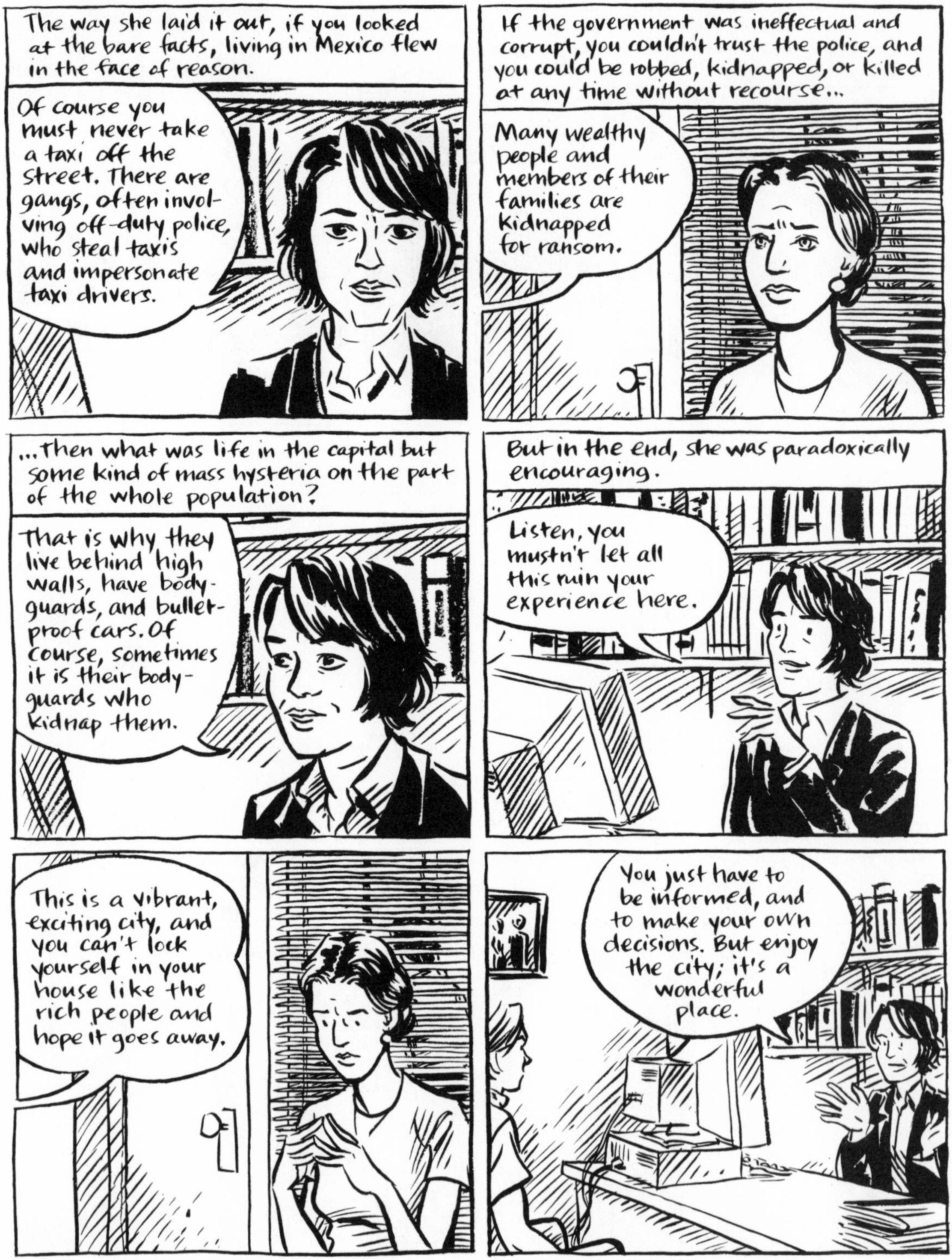
The way she laid it out, if you looked at the bare facts, living in Mexico flew in the face of reason.
Of course you must never take a taxi off the street. There are gangs, often involving off-duty police, who steal taxis and impersonate taxi drivers.
If the government was ineffectual and corrupt, you couldn't trust the police, and you could be robbed, kidnapped, or killed at any time without recourse...
Many wealthy people and members of their families are kidnapped for ransom.
...then what was life in the capital but some kind of mass hysteria on the part of the whole population?
That is why they live behind high walls, have bodyguards, and bulletproof cars. Of course, sometimes it is their bodyguards who kidnap them.
But in the end, she was paradoxically encouraging.
Listen, you mustn't let all this ruin your experience here.
This is a vibrant, exciting city, and you can't lock yourself in your house like the rich people and hope it goes away.
You just have to be informed, and to make your own decisions. But enjoy the city; it's a wonderful place.

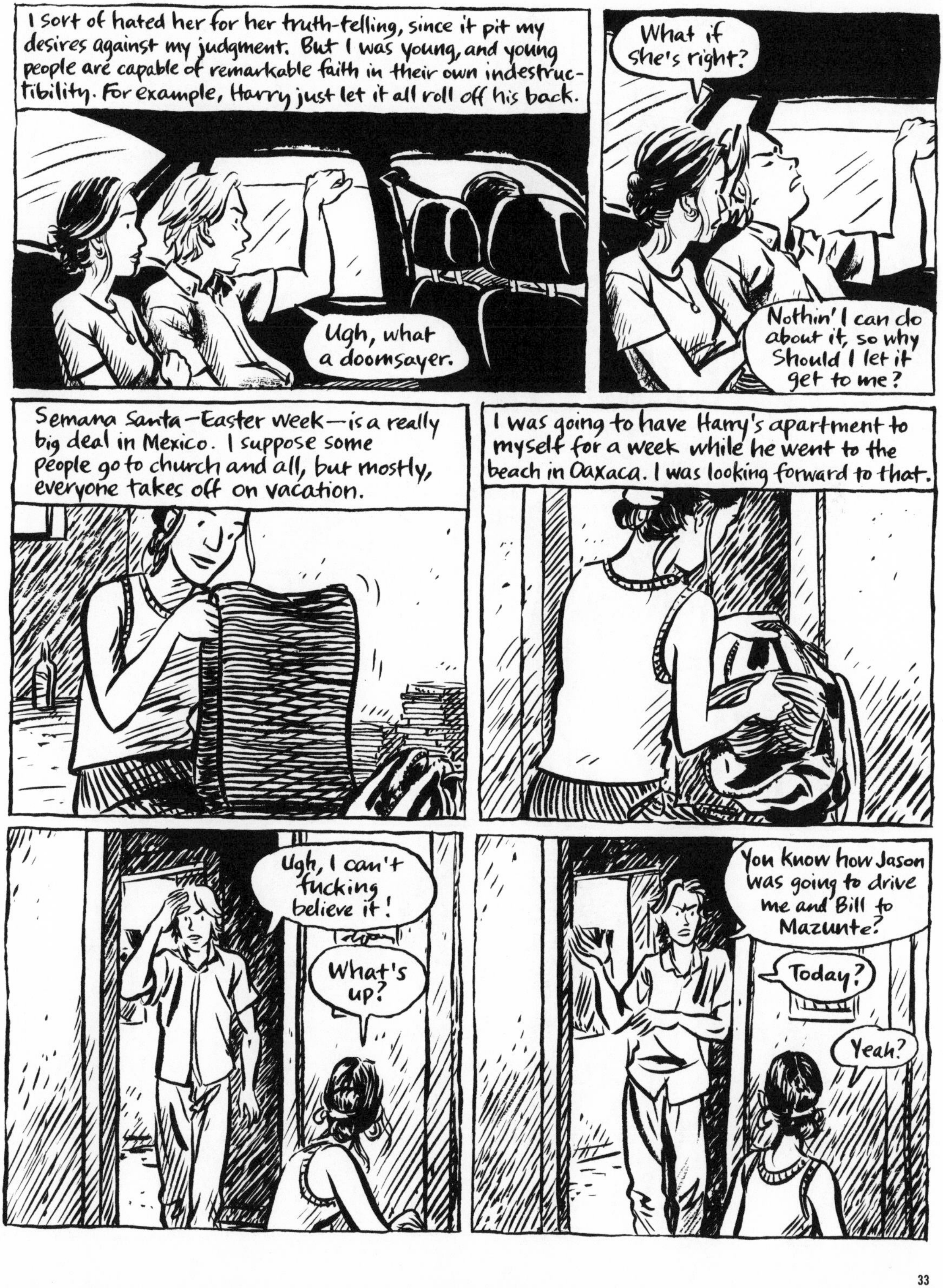
I sort of hated her for her truth-telling, since it pit my desires against my judgment. But I was young, and young people are capable of remarkable faith in their own indestructibility. For example, Harry just let it all roll off his back.
Ugh, what a doomsayer.
What if she's right?
Nothin' I can do about it, so why Should I let it get to me?
Semana Santa—Easter week—is a really big deal in Mexico. I suppose some people go to church and all, but mostly, everyone takes off on vacation.
I was going to have Harry's apartment to myself for a week while he went to the beach in Oaxaca. I was looking forward to that.
Ugh, I can't fucking believe it!
What's up?
You know how Jason was going to drive me and Bill to Mazunte?
Today?
Yeah?

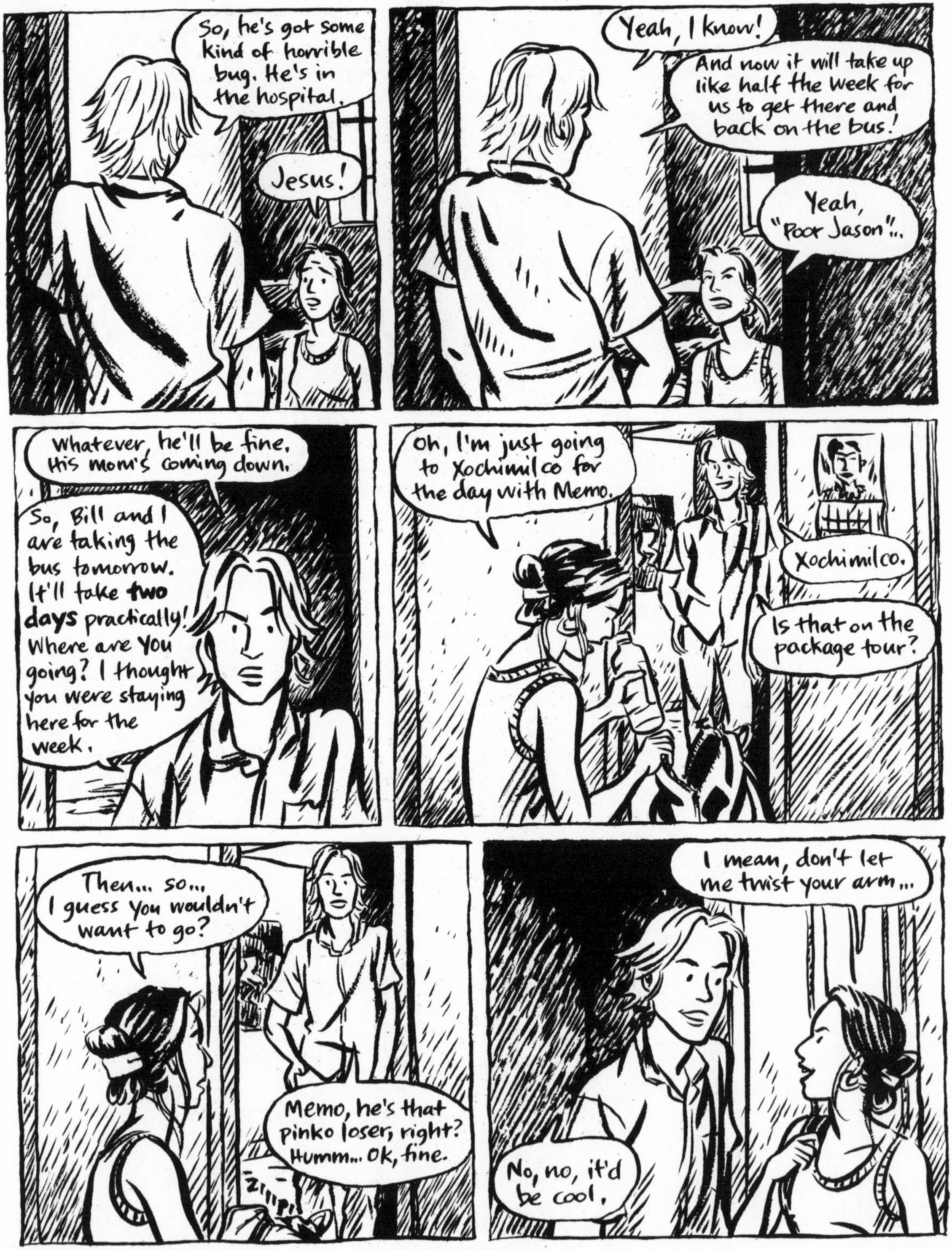

So, he's got some kind of horrible bug. He's in the hospital.
Jesus!
Yeah, I know!
And now it will take up like half the week for us to get there and back on the bus!
Yeah, "Poor Jason"...
Whatever, he'll be fine. His mom's coming down.
So, Bill and I are taking the bus tomorrow. It'll take **two days** practically! Where are you going? I thought you were staying here for the week.
Oh, I'm just going to Xochimilco for the day with Memo.
Xochimilco.
Is that on the package tour?
Then... so... I guess you wouldn't want to go?
Memo, he's that pinko loser, right? Humm... Ok, fine.
ZIPP!
I mean, don't let me twist your arm...
No, no, it'd be cool.

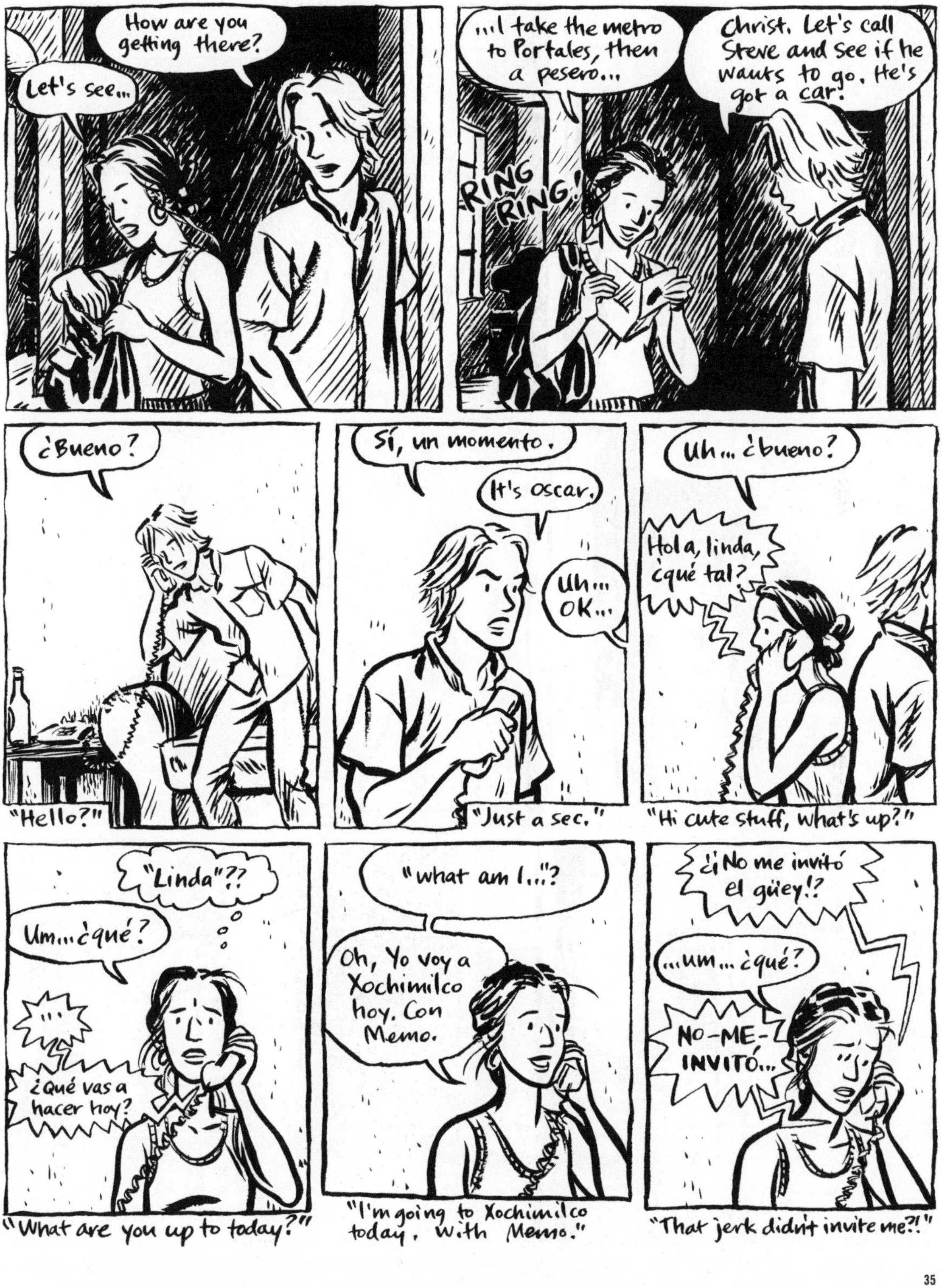
How are you getting there?
Let's see...
...I take the metro to Portales, then a pesero...
Christ. Let's call Steve and see if he wants to go. He's got a car.
RING RING!
¿Bueno?
"Hello?"
Sí, un momento.
It's oscar.
Uh... OK...
"Just a sec."
Uh... ¿bueno?
Hola, linda, ¿qué tal?
"Hi cute stuff, what's up?"
"Linda"??
Um... ¿qué?
...
¿Qué vas a hacer hoy?
"What are you up to today?"
"what am I..."?
Oh, Yo voy a Xochimilco hoy. Con Memo.
"I'm going to Xochimilco today. With Memo."
¿¡No me invitó el güey!?
...um... ¿qué?
NO-ME-INVITÓ...
"That jerk didn't invite me?!"

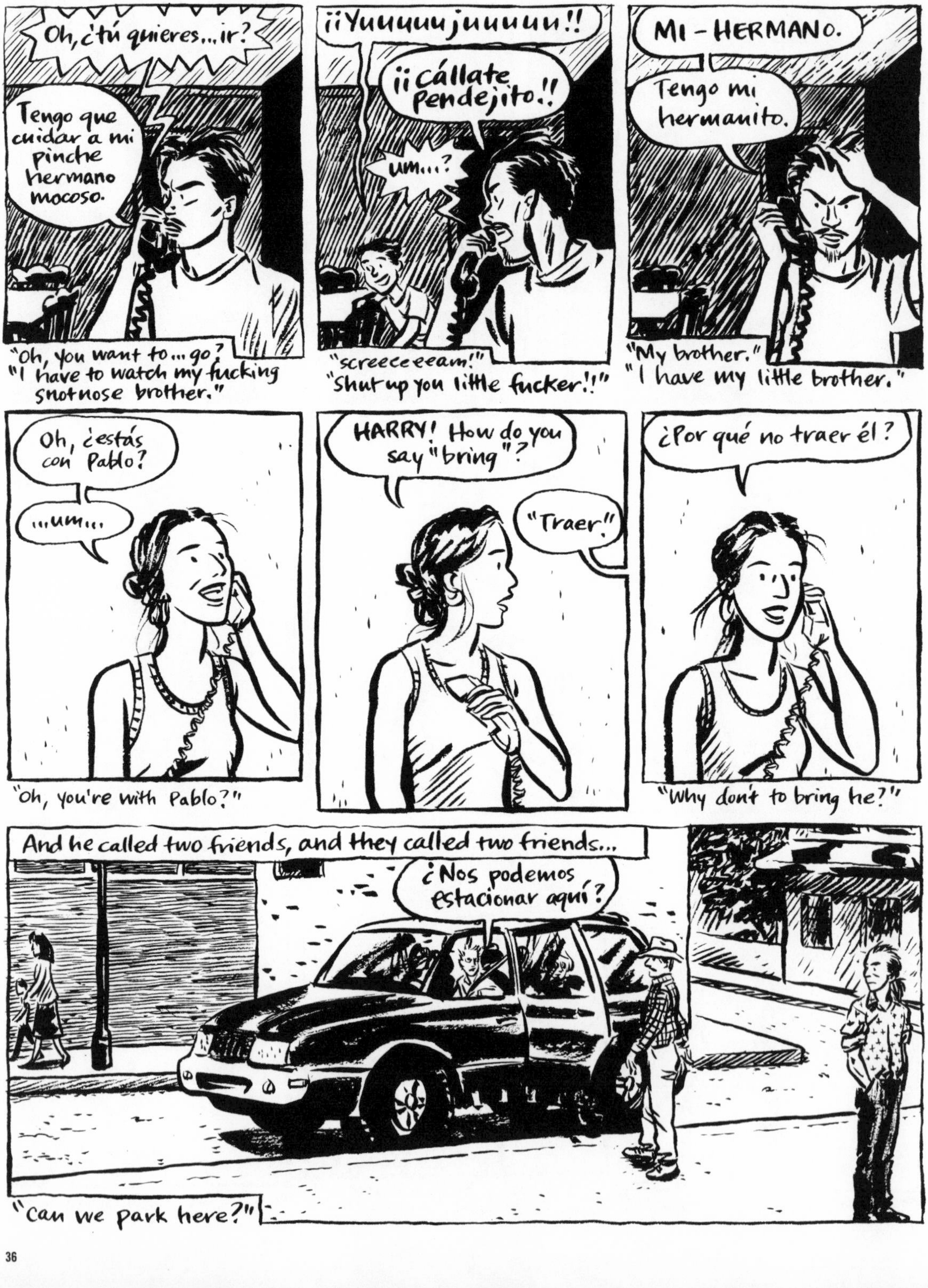

Oh, ¿tú quieres...ir?
Tengo que cuidar a mi pinche hermano mocoso.
"Oh, you want to... go?
"I have to watch my fucking snotnose brother."
¡¡Yuuuuujuuuuu!!
¡¡Cállate pendejito.!!
um...?
"screeeeeeam!"
"Shut up you little fucker!!"
MI - HERMANO.
Tengo mi hermanito.
"My brother."
"I have my little brother."
Oh, ¿estás con Pablo?
...um...
"Oh, you're with Pablo?"
HARRY! How do you say "bring"?
"Traer."
¿Por qué no traer él?
"Why don't to bring he?"
And he called two friends, and they called two friends...
¿Nos podemos estacionar aquí?
"Can we park here?"

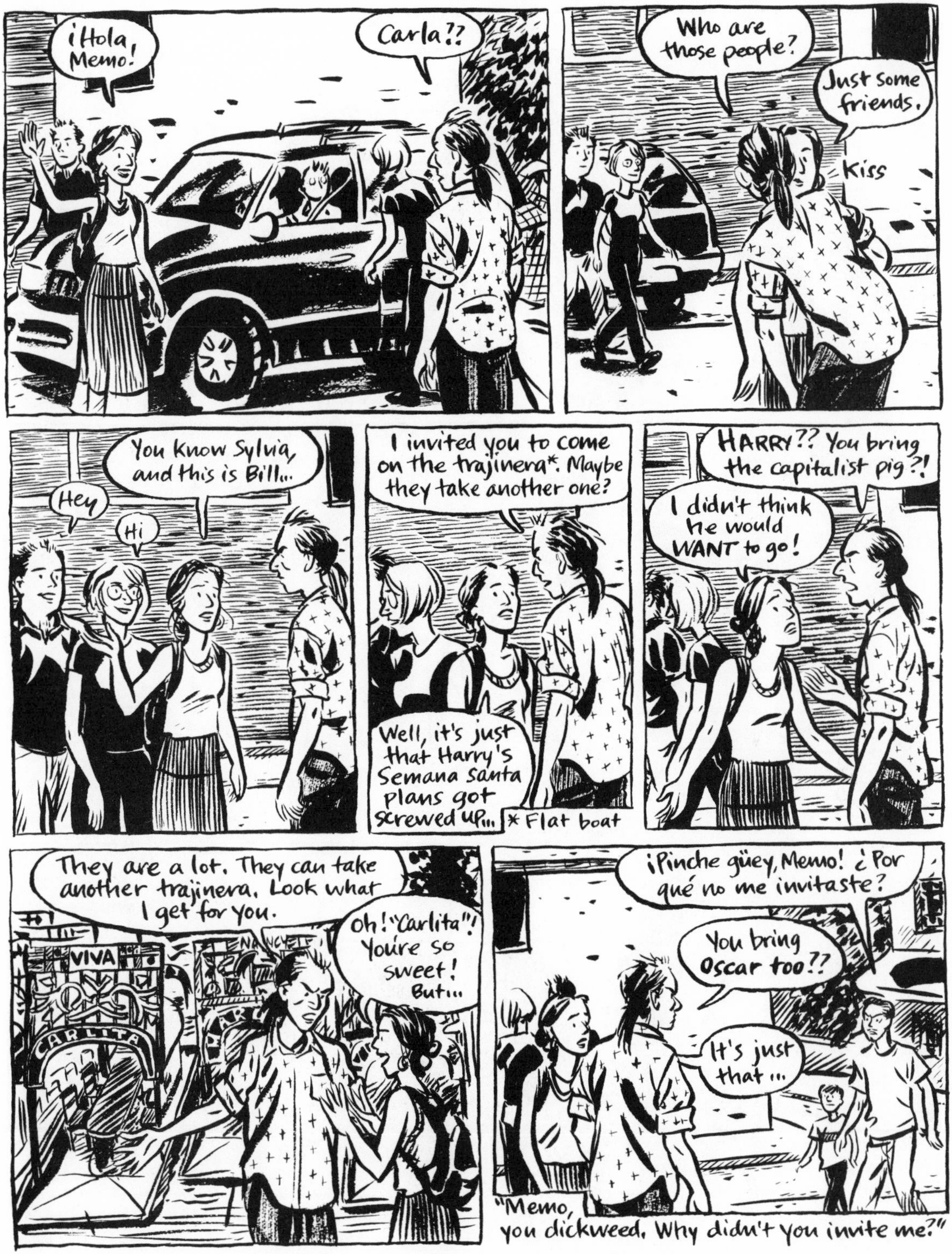
¡Hola, Memo!
Carla??
Who are those people?
Just some friends.
Kiss
You know Sylvia, and this is Bill...
Hey
Hi
I invited you to come on the trajinera*. Maybe they take another one?
Well, it's just that Harry's Semana Santa plans got screwed up...
* Flat boat
HARRY?? You bring the capitalist pig?!
I didn't think he would WANT to go!
They are a lot. They can take another trajinera. Look what I get for you.
VIVA
CARLITA
Oh! "Carlita"! You're so sweet! But...
¡Pinche güey, Memo! ¿Por qué no me invitaste?
You bring Oscar too??
It's just that...
"Memo, you dickweed. Why didn't you invite me?"

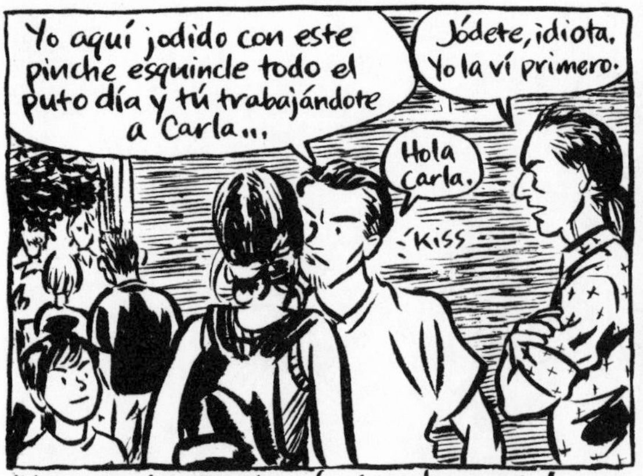
Yo aquí jodido con este pinche esquincle todo el puto día y tú trabajándote a Carla...
Jódete, idiota. Yo la ví primero.
Hola Carla.
Kiss

"I'm stuck with this fucking brat all day and you're off making the moves on Carla?" "Screw you, shitface. I saw her first."

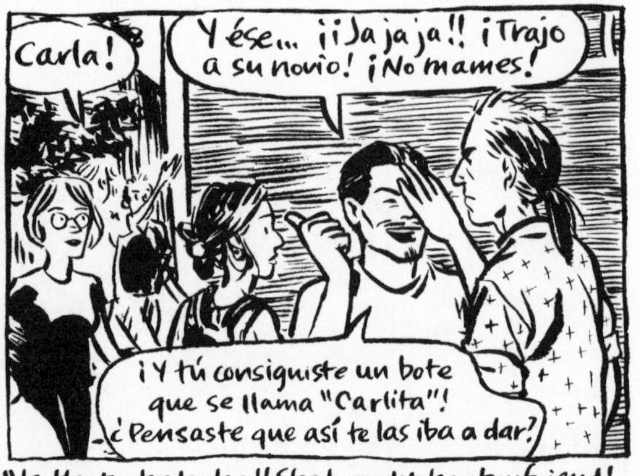
Carla!
Y ése... ¡¡Ja ja ja!! ¡Trajo a su novio! ¡No mames!
¡Y tú consiguiste un bote que se llama "Carlita"! ¿Pensaste que así te las iba a dar?

"Is that... ha ha ha!! She brought her boyfriend! That's priceless!" "...And you got a 'Carlita' boat! You thought that might get you in her pants??"

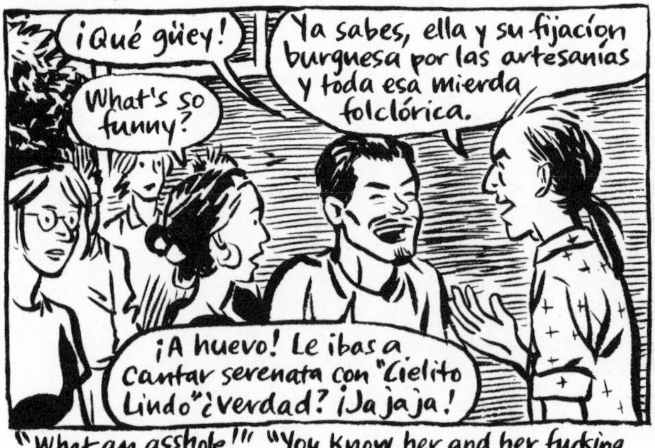
¡Qué güey!
Ya sabes, ella y su fijación burguesa por las artesanías y toda esa mierda folclórica.
What's so funny?
¡A huevo! Le ibas a cantar serenata con "Cielito Lindo" ¿verdad? ¡Ja ja ja!

"What an asshole!" "You know her and her fucking bourgeois attachment to artesanías and all that folkloric shit." "Oh yeah! You were going to serenade her with 'Cielito Lindo', right? Ha ha ha!

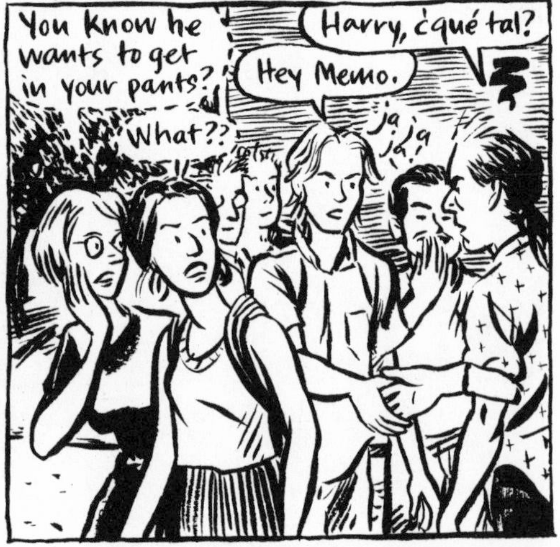
You know he wants to get in your pants?
Harry, ¿qué tal?
Hey Memo.
What??
ja ja ja!

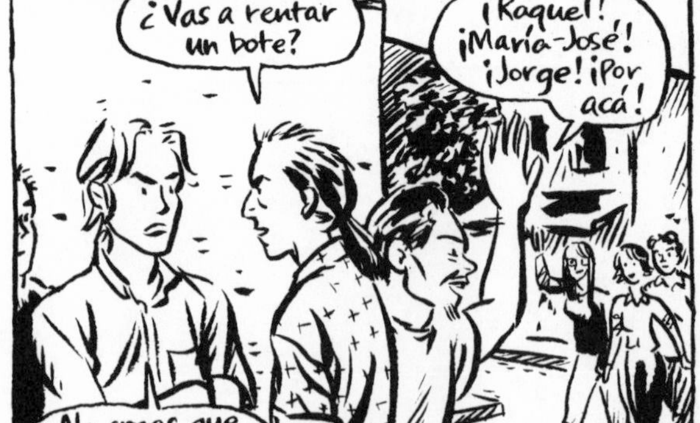
¿Vas a rentar un bote?
¡Raquel! ¡María-José! ¡Jorge! ¡Por acá!
No creas que yo voy a pagar solo yo.

"Are you going to rent a boat?" "I'm not paying for it alone, if that's what you mean."

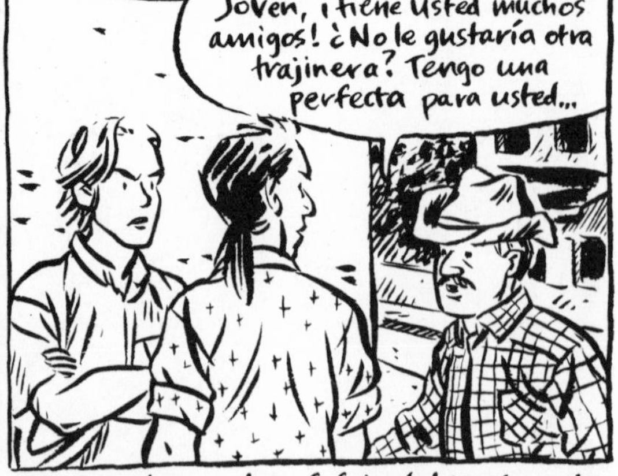
Joven, ¡tiene usted muchos amigos! ¿No le gustaría otra trajinera? Tengo una perfecta para usted...

"Sir, you have a lot of friends! Maybe you'd like another boat? I have the perfect one..."

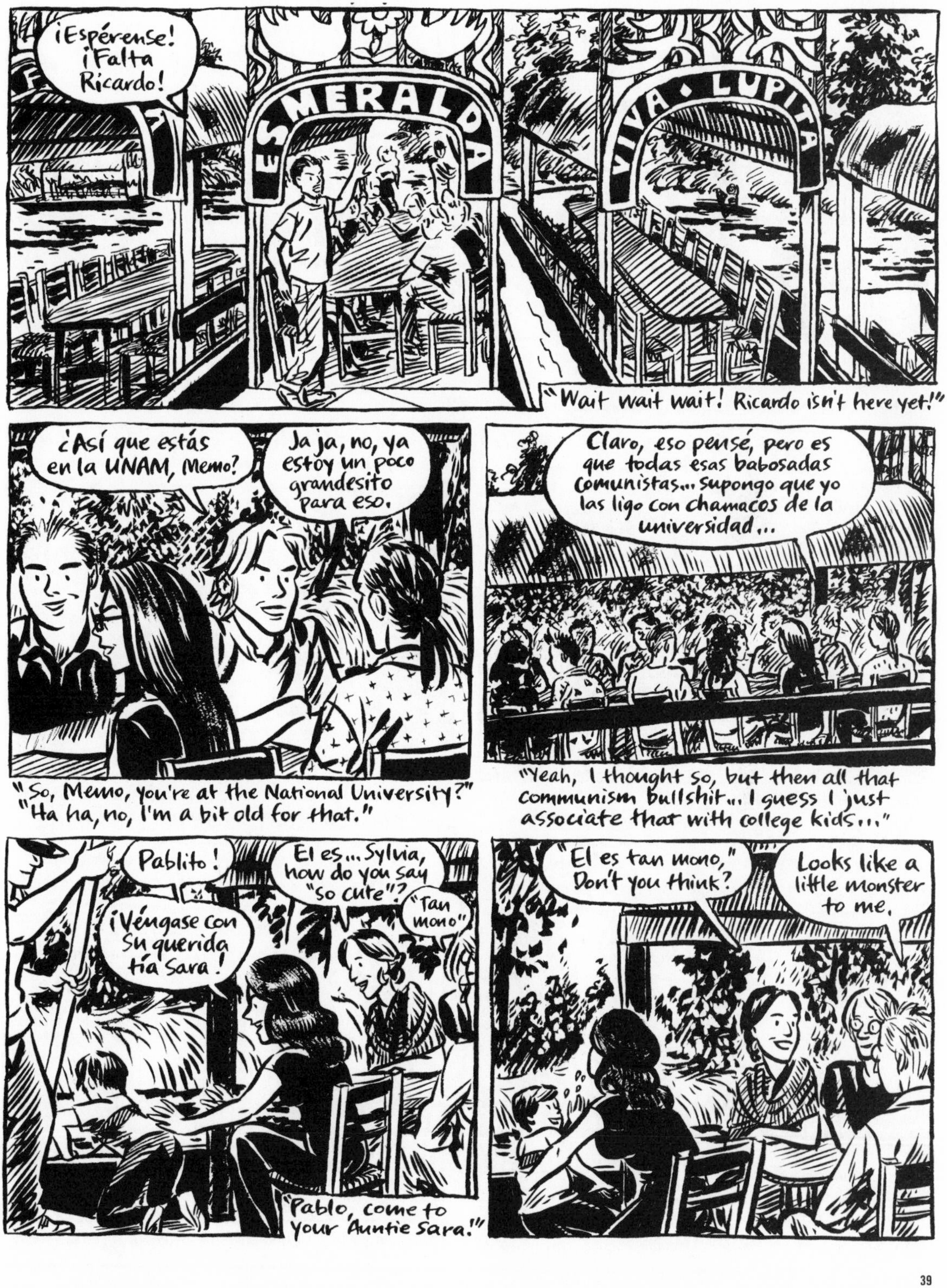
¡Espérense! ¡Falta Ricardo!
ESMERALDA
VIVA • LUPITA
"Wait wait wait! Ricardo isn't here yet!"
¿Así que estás en la UNAM, Memo?
Ja ja, no, ya estoy un poco grandesito para eso.
"So, Memo, you're at the National University?" "Ha ha, no, I'm a bit old for that."
Claro, eso pensé, pero es que todas esas babosadas comunistas... supongo que yo las ligo con chamacos de la universidad...
"Yeah, I thought so, but then all that communism bullshit... I guess I just associate that with college kids..."
Pablito!
¡Véngase con su querida tía Sara!
El es... Sylvia, how do you say "so cute"?
"Tan mono"
"Pablo, come to your Auntie Sara!"
"El es tan mono," Don't you think?
Looks like a little monster to me.

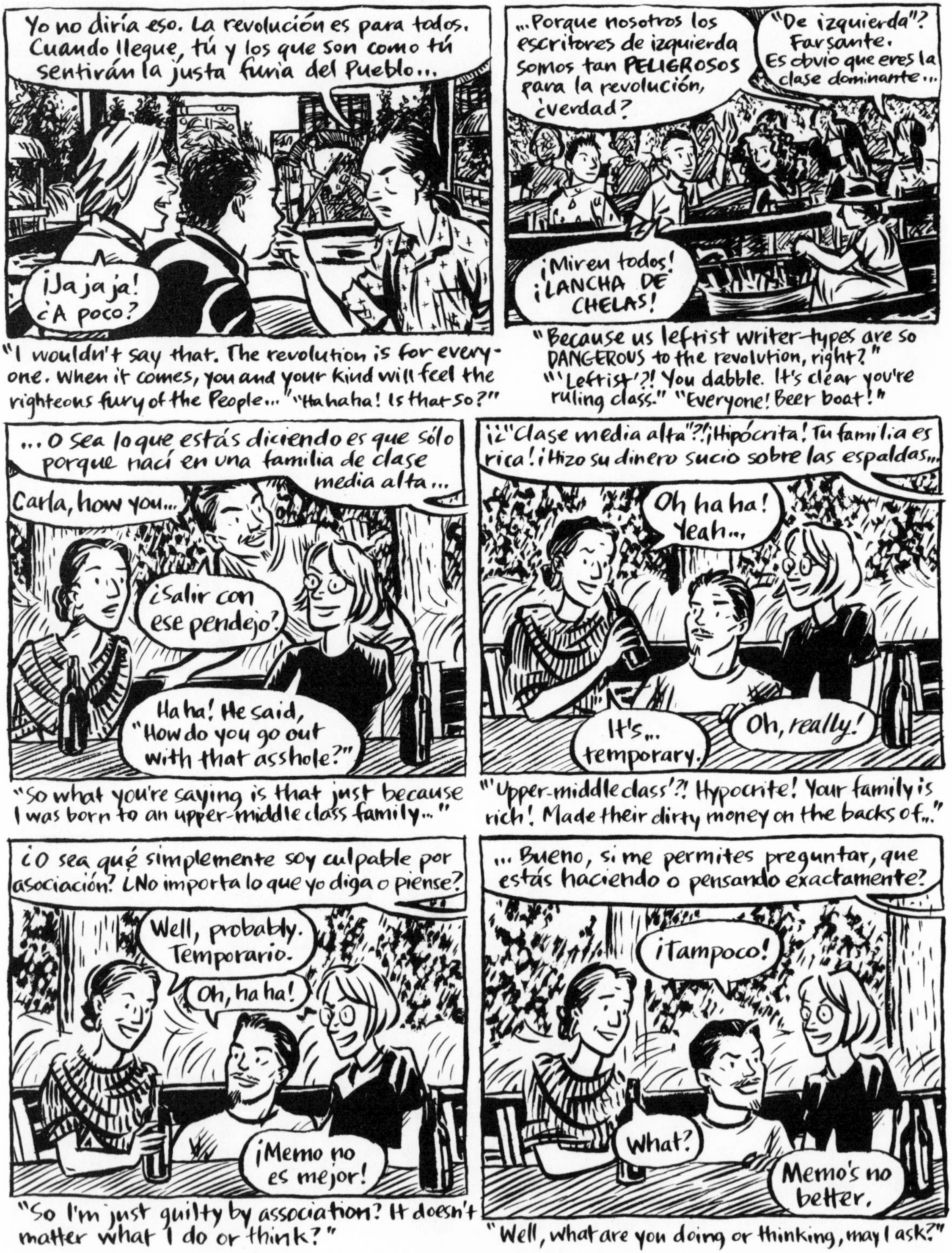
Yo no diría eso. La revolución es para todos. Cuando llegue, tú y los que son como tú sentirán la justa furia del Pueblo...
¡Ja ja ja! ¿A poco?
"I wouldn't say that. The revolution is for everyone. When it comes, you and your kind will feel the righteous fury of the People..." "Ha ha ha! Is that so?"
...Porque nosotros los escritores de izquierda somos tan PELIGROSOS para la revolución, ¿verdad?
"¿De izquierda"? Farsante. Es obvio que eres la clase dominante...
¡Miren todos! ¡LANCHA DE CHELAS!
"Because us leftist writer-types are so DANGEROUS to the revolution, right?" "'Leftist'?! You dabble. It's clear you're ruling class." "Everyone! Beer boat!"
...O sea lo que estás diciendo es que sólo porque nací en una familia de clase media alta...
Carla, how you...
¿Salir con ese pendejo?
Ha ha! He said, "How do you go out with that asshole?"
"So what you're saying is that just because I was born to an upper-middle class family..."
¡¿"Clase media alta"?! ¡Hipócrita! Tu familia es rica! ¡Hizo su dinero sucio sobre las espaldas...
Oh ha ha! Yeah...
It's... temporary.
Oh, really!
"'Upper-middle class'?! Hypocrite! Your family is rich! Made their dirty money on the backs of..."
¿O sea qué simplemente soy culpable por asociación? ¿No importa lo que yo diga o piense?
Well, probably. Temporario.
Oh, ha ha!
¡Memo no es mejor!
"So I'm just guilty by association? It doesn't matter what I do or think?"
...Bueno, si me permites preguntar, que estás haciendo o pensando exactamente?
¡Tampoco!
What?
Memo's no better.
"Well, what are you doing or thinking, may I ask?"

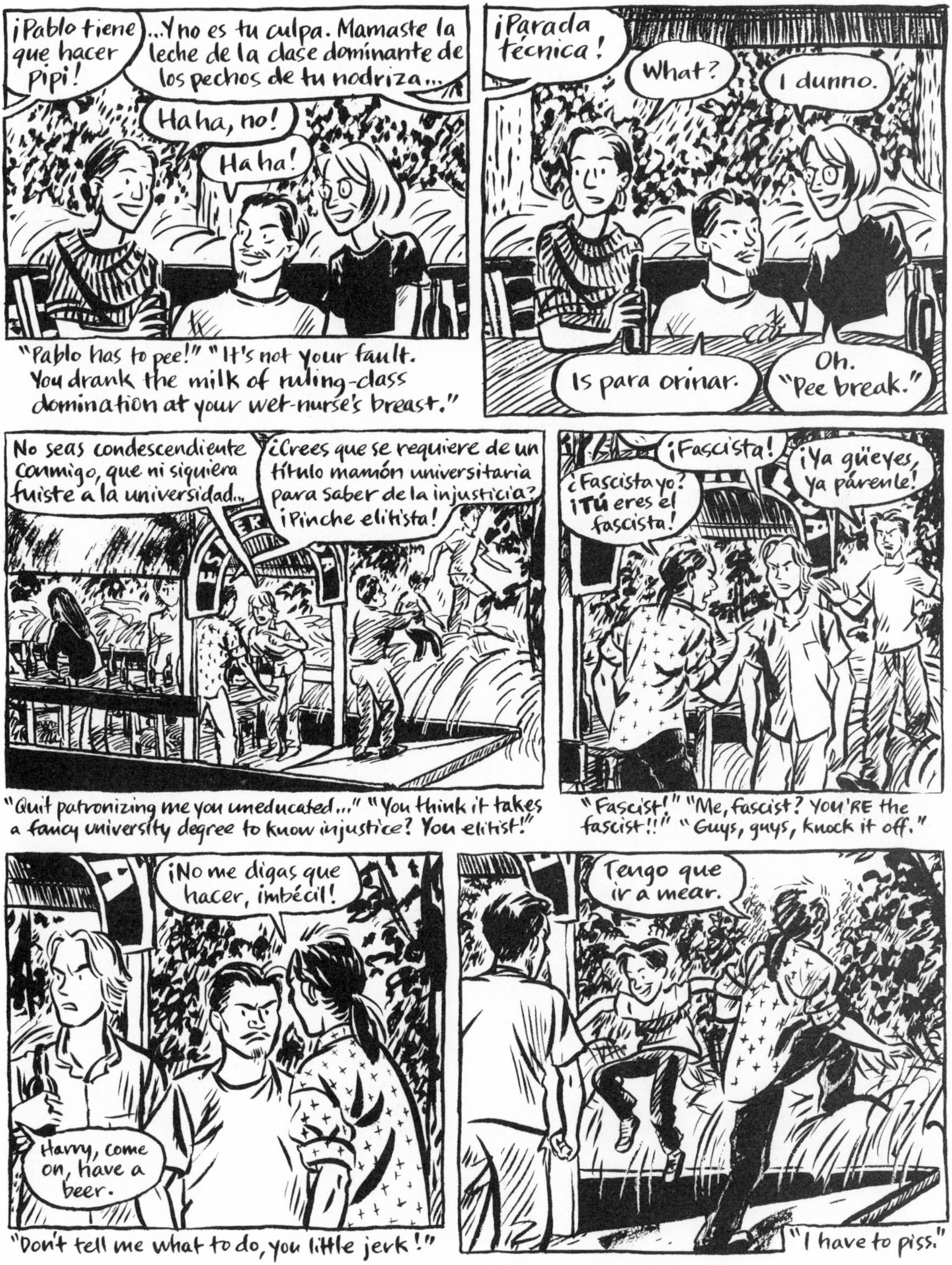
¡Pablo tiene que hacer pipi!
...Y no es tu culpa. Mamaste la leche de la clase dominante de los pechos de tu nodriza...
Ha ha, no!
Ha ha!
"Pablo has to pee!" "It's not your fault. You drank the milk of ruling-class domination at your wet-nurse's breast."
¡Parada técnica!
What?
I dunno.
Is para orinar.
Oh. "Pee break."
No seas condescendiente conmigo, que ni siquiera fuiste a la universidad...
¿Crees que se requiere de un título mamón universitaria para saber de la injusticia? ¡Pinche elitista!
"Quit patronizing me you uneducated..." "You think it takes a fancy university degree to know injustice? You elitist!"
¡Fascista!
¿Fascista yo? ¡TÚ eres el fascista!
¡Ya güeyes, ya párenle!
"Fascist!" "Me, fascist? You'RE the fascist!!" "Guys, guys, knock it off."
¡No me digas que hacer, imbécil!
Harry, come on, have a beer.
"Don't tell me what to do, you little jerk!"
Tengo que ir a mear.
"I have to piss."

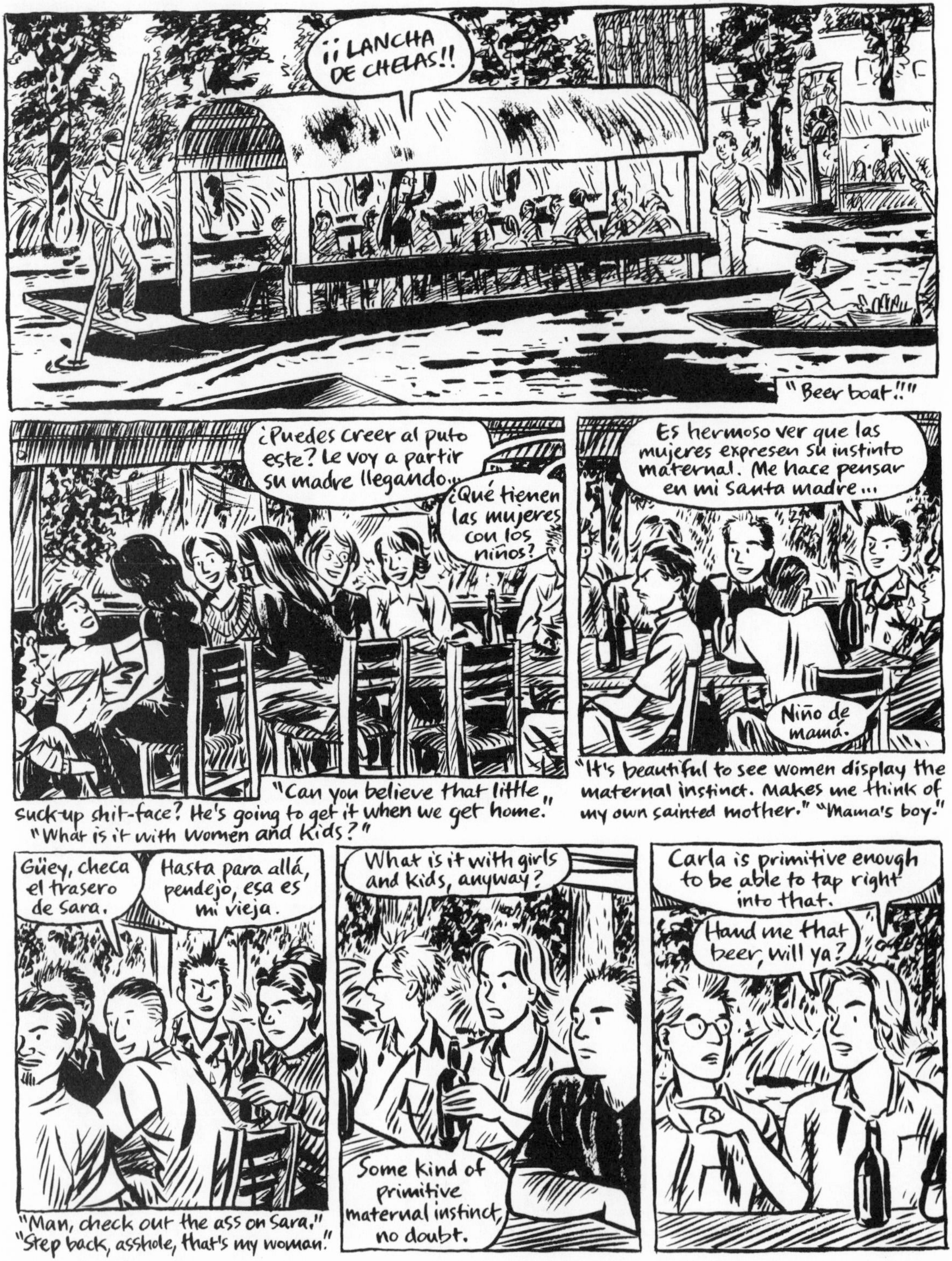
¡¡LANCHA DE CHELAS!!
"Beer boat!!"
¿Puedes creer al puto este? Le voy a partir su madre llegando...
¿Qué tienen las mujeres con los niños?
"Can you believe that little suck-up shit-face? He's going to get it when we get home." "What is it with women and kids?"
Es hermoso ver que las mujeres expresen su instinto maternal. Me hace pensar en mi santa madre...
Niño de mamá.
"It's beautiful to see women display the maternal instinct. Makes me think of my own sainted mother." "Mama's boy."
Güey, checa el trasero de Sara.
Hasta para allá, pendejo, esa es mi vieja.
"Man, check out the ass on Sara." "Step back, asshole, that's my woman."
What is it with girls and kids, anyway?
Some kind of primitive maternal instinct, no doubt.
Carla is primitive enough to be able to tap right into that.
Hand me that beer, will ya?

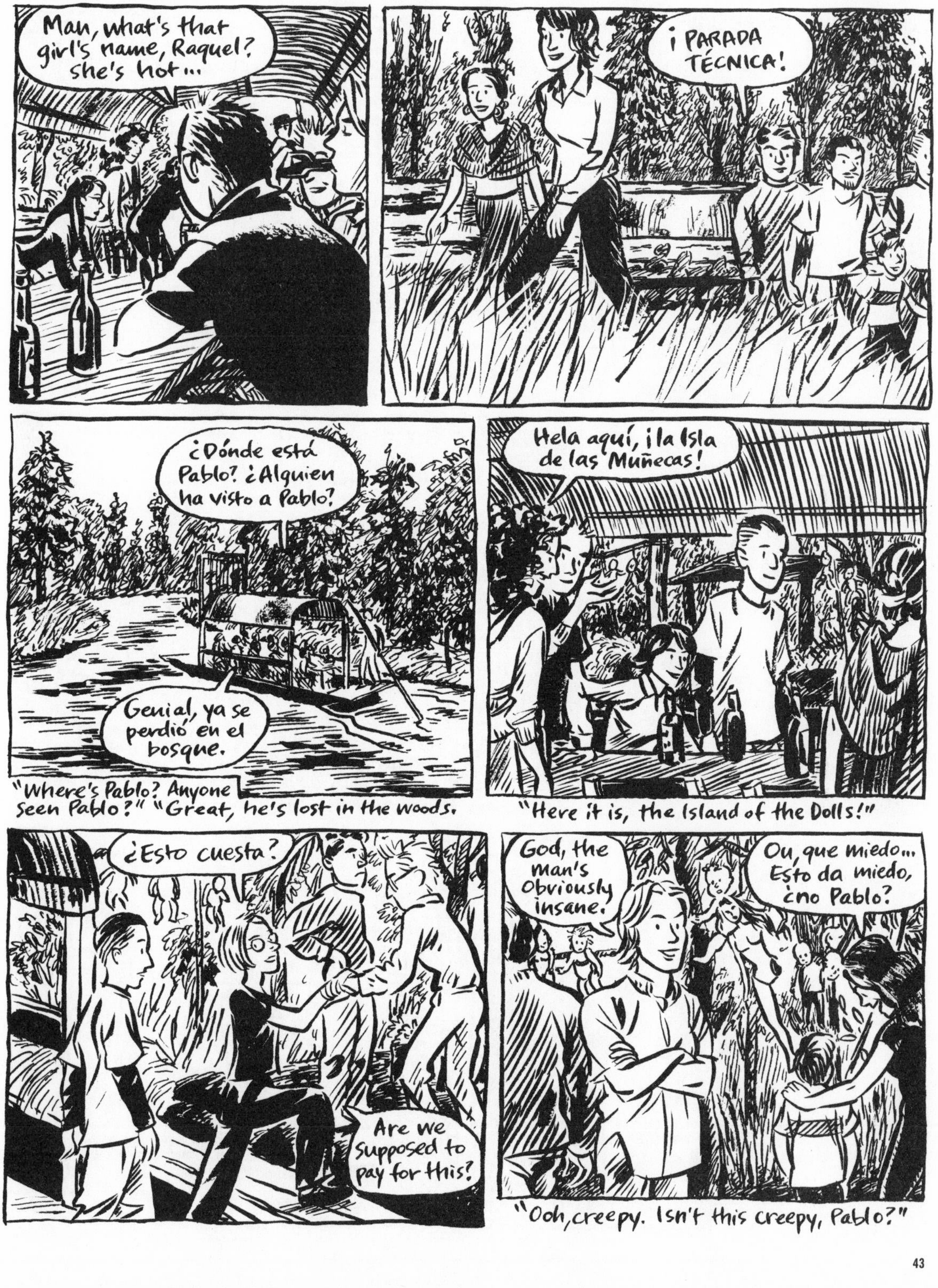

Man, what's that girl's name, Raquel? she's hot...
¡PARADA TÉCNICA!
¿Dónde está Pablo? ¿Alquien ha visto a Pablo?
Genial, ya se perdió en el bosque.
"Where's Pablo? Anyone seen Pablo?" "Great, he's lost in the woods.
Hela aquí, ¡la Isla de las Muñecas!
"Here it is, the Island of the Dolls!"
¿Esto cuesta?
Are we supposed to pay for this?
God, the man's Obviously insane.
Ou, que miedo... Esto da miedo, ¿no Pablo?
"Ooh, creepy. Isn't this creepy, Pablo?"

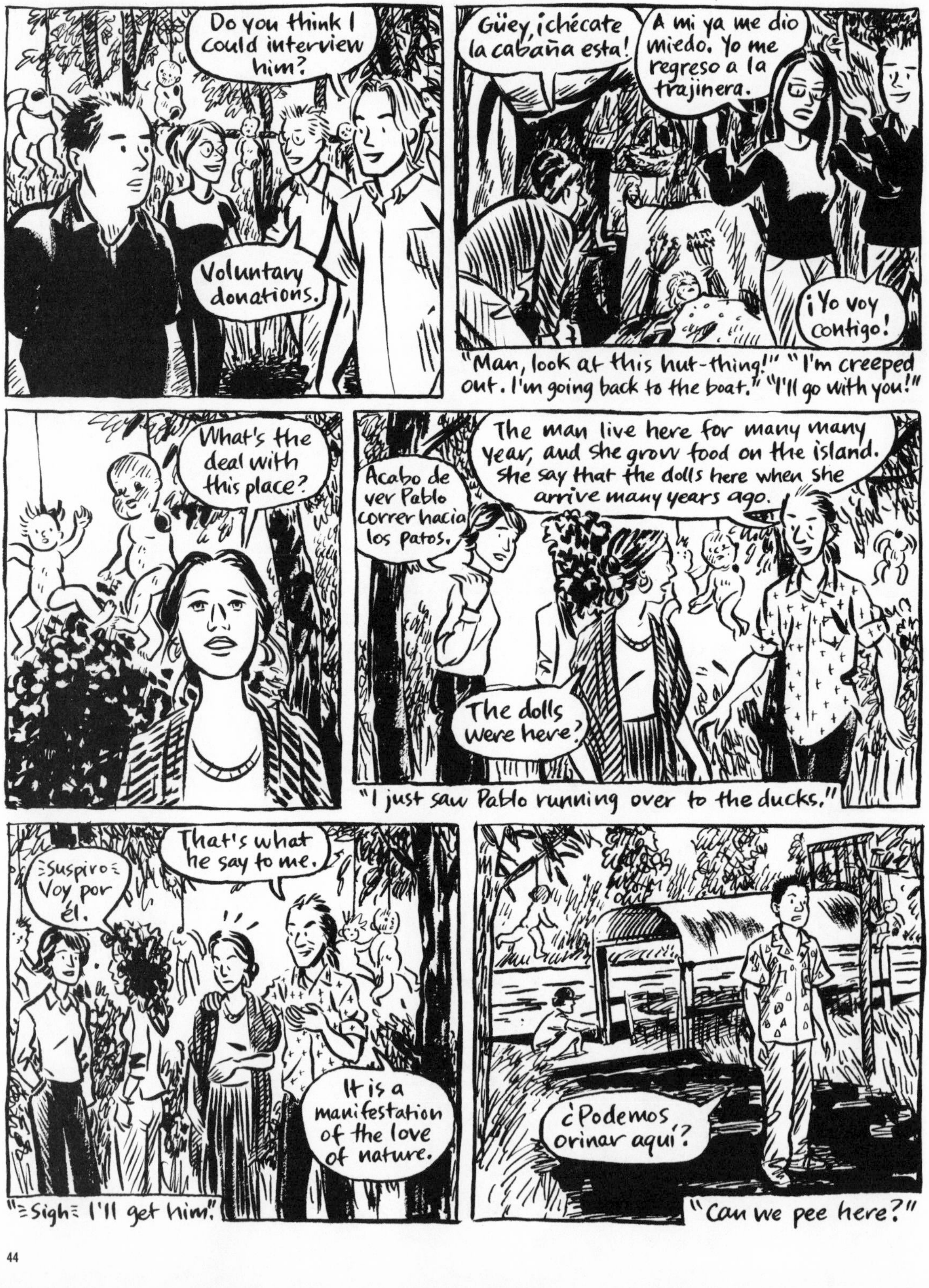
Do you think I could interview him?
Voluntary donations.
Güey, ¡chécate la cabaña esta!
A mi ya me dio miedo. Yo me regreso a la trajinera.
¡Yo voy contigo!
"Man, look at this hut-thing!" "I'm creeped out. I'm going back to the boat." "I'll go with you!"
What's the deal with this place?
Acabo de ver Pablo correr hacia los patos.
The man live here for many many year, and she grow food on the island. She say that the dolls here when she arrive many years ago.
The dolls were here?
"I just saw Pablo running over to the ducks."
≡Suspiro≡ Voy por él.
That's what he say to me.
It is a manifestation of the love of nature.
"≡Sigh≡ I'll get him."
¿Podemos orinar aquí?
"Can we pee here?"

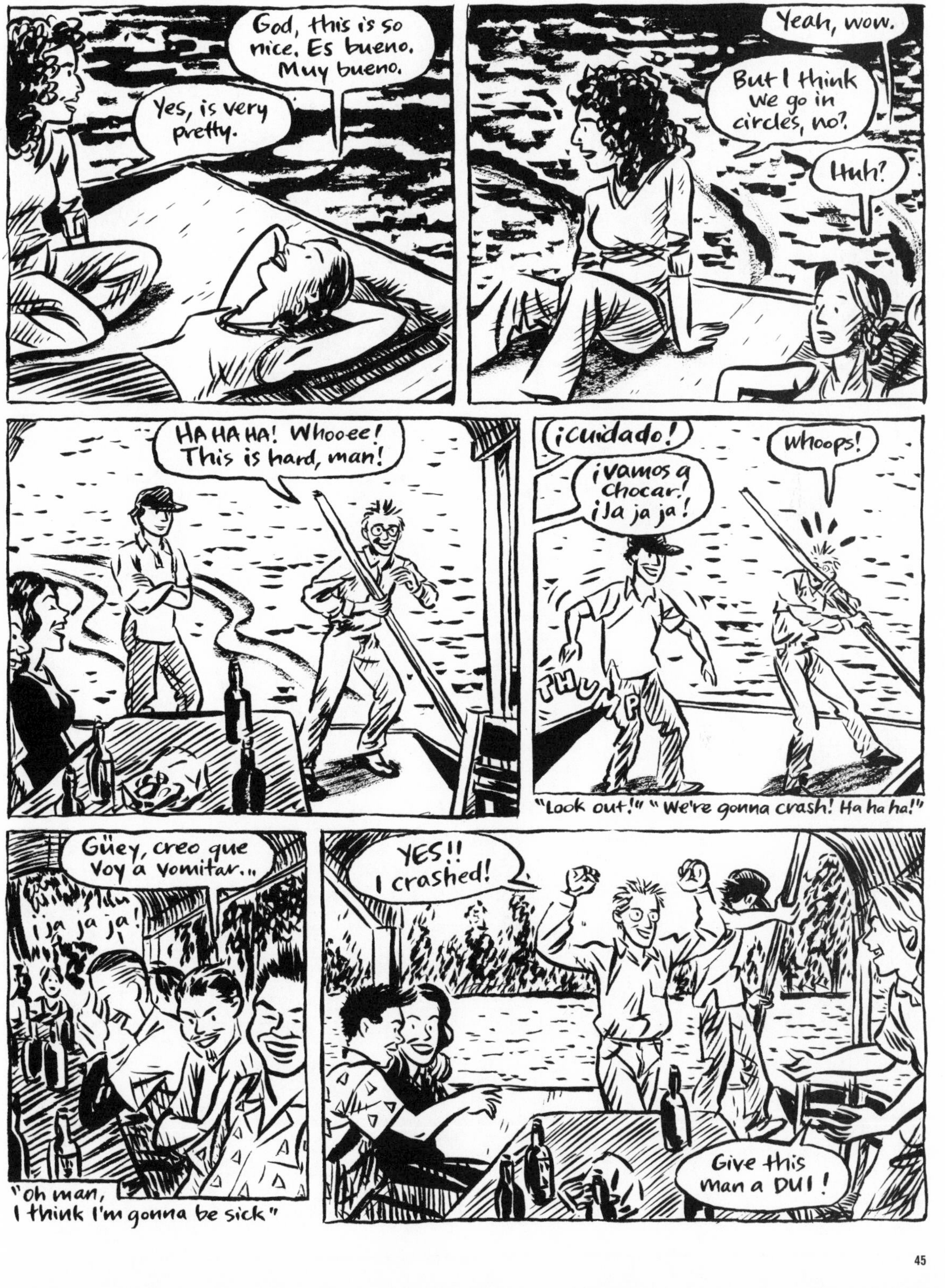
God, this is so nice. Es bueno. Muy bueno.
Yes, is very pretty.
Yeah, wow.
But I think we go in circles, no?
Huh?
HA HA HA! Whooee! This is hard, man!
¡Cuidado!
¡Vamos a chocar! ¡Ja ja ja!
Whoops!
THUMP
"Look out!" "We're gonna crash! Ha ha ha!"
Güey, creo que voy a vomitar..
¡Ja ja ja!
"oh man, I think I'm gonna be sick"
YES!! I crashed!
Give this man a DUI!

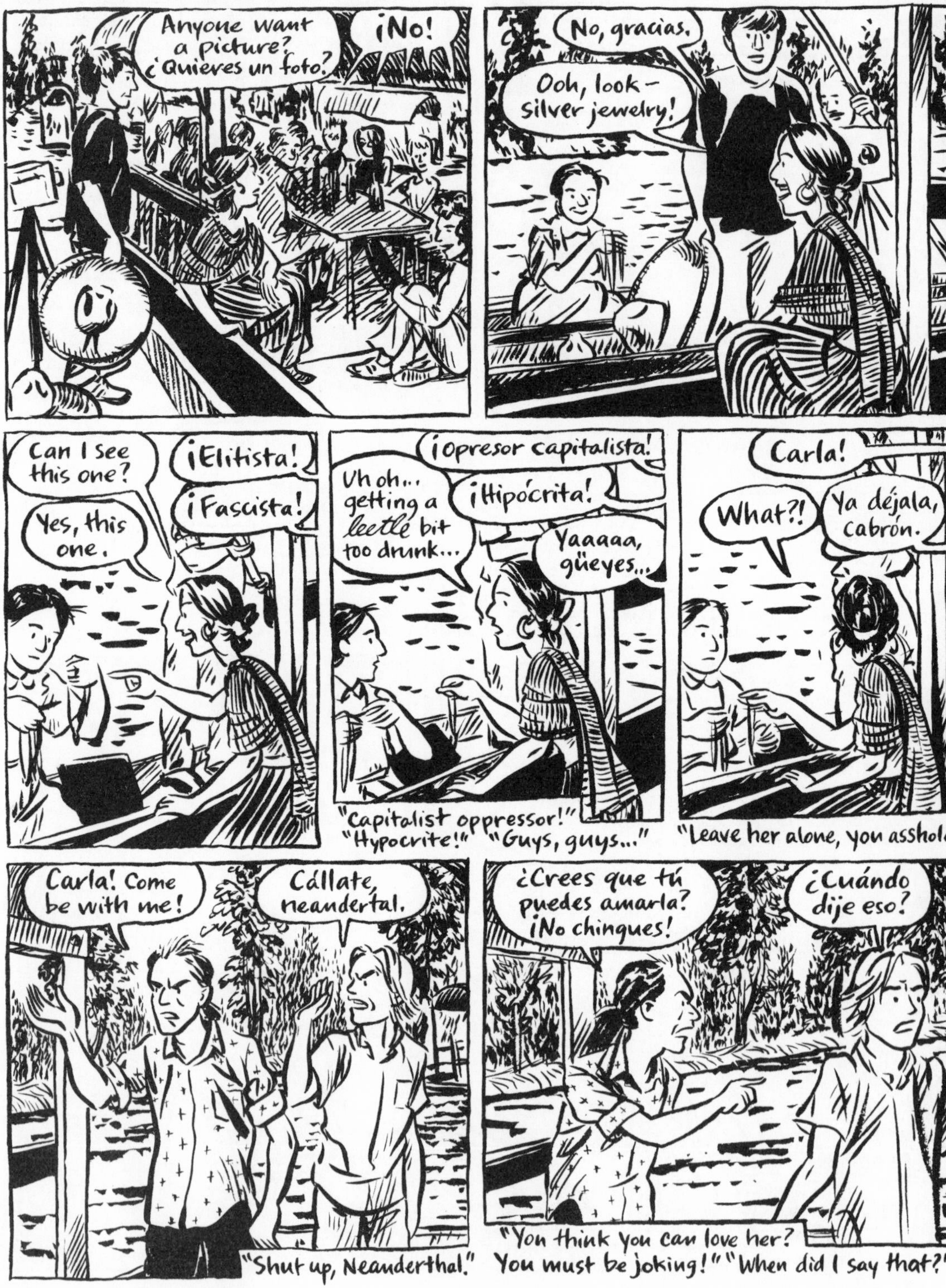

Anyone want a picture? ¿Quieres un foto?
¡No!
No, gracias.
Ooh, look – Silver jewelry!
Can I see this one?
Yes, this one.
¡Elitista!
¡Fascista!
¡Opresor capitalista!
Uh oh... getting a leetle bit too drunk...
¡Hipócrita!
Yaaaaa, güeyes...
"Capitalist oppressor!" "Hypocrite!" "Guys, guys..."
Carla!
What?!
Ya déjala, cabrón.
"Leave her alone, you asshole."
Carla! Come be with me!
Cállate, neandertal.
"Shut up, Neanderthal."
¿Crees que tú puedes amarla? ¡No chingues!
¿Cuándo dije eso?
"You think you can love her? You must be joking!" "When did I say that?"

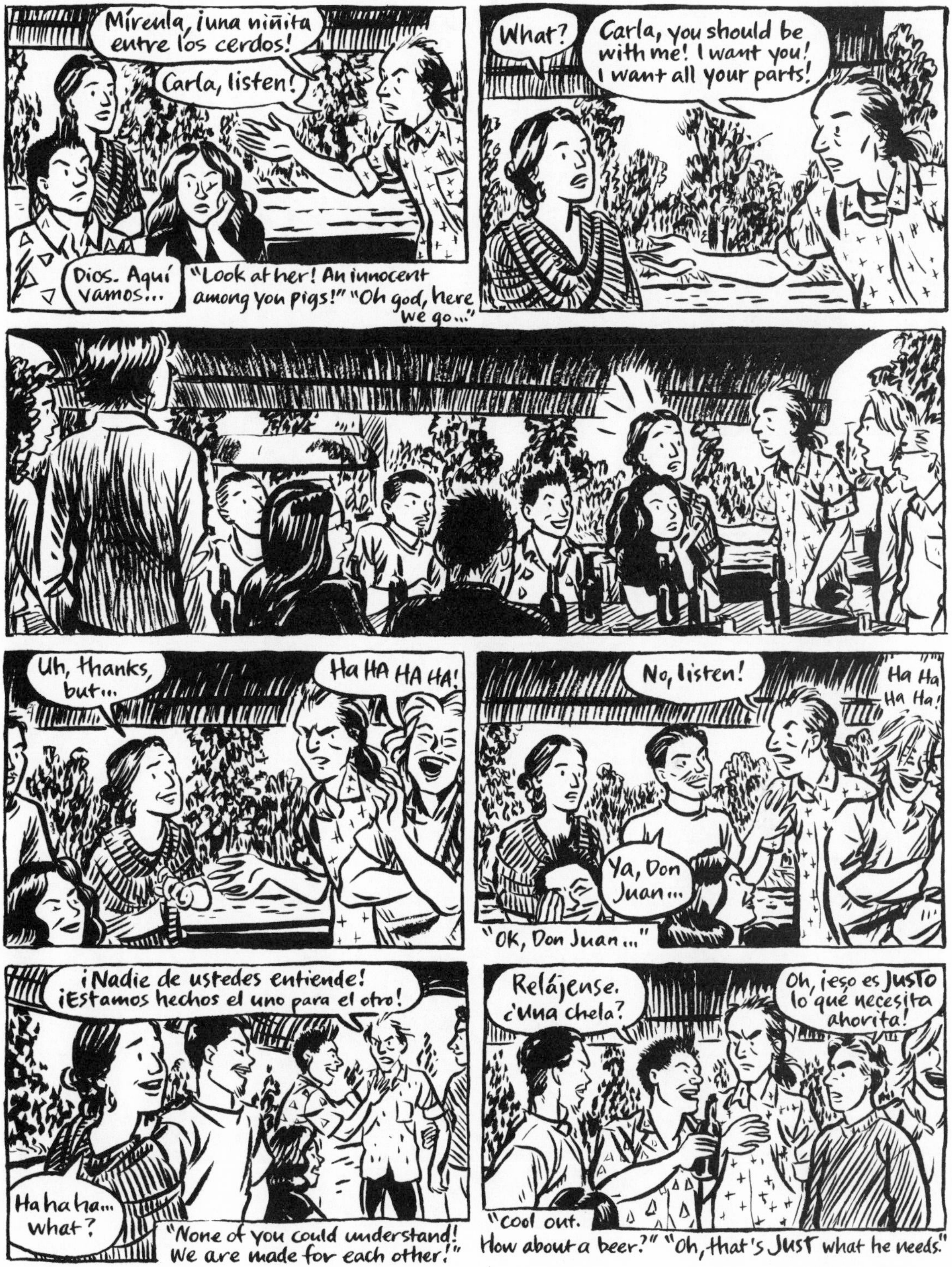
Mírenla, ¡una niñita entre los cerdos!
Carla, listen!
Dios. Aquí vamos...
"Look at her! An innocent among you pigs!" "Oh god, here we go..."
What?
Carla, you should be with me! I want you! I want all your parts!
Uh, thanks, but...
Ha HA HA HA!
No, listen!
Ha Ha Ha Ha!
Ya, Don Juan...
"OK, Don Juan..."
¡Nadie de ustedes entiende! ¡Estamos hechos el uno para el otro!
Ha ha ha... what?
"None of you could understand! We are made for each other!"
Relájense. ¿Una chela?
Oh, ¡eso es JUSTO lo qué necesita ahorita!
"Cool out. How about a beer?" "Oh, that's JUST what he needs."

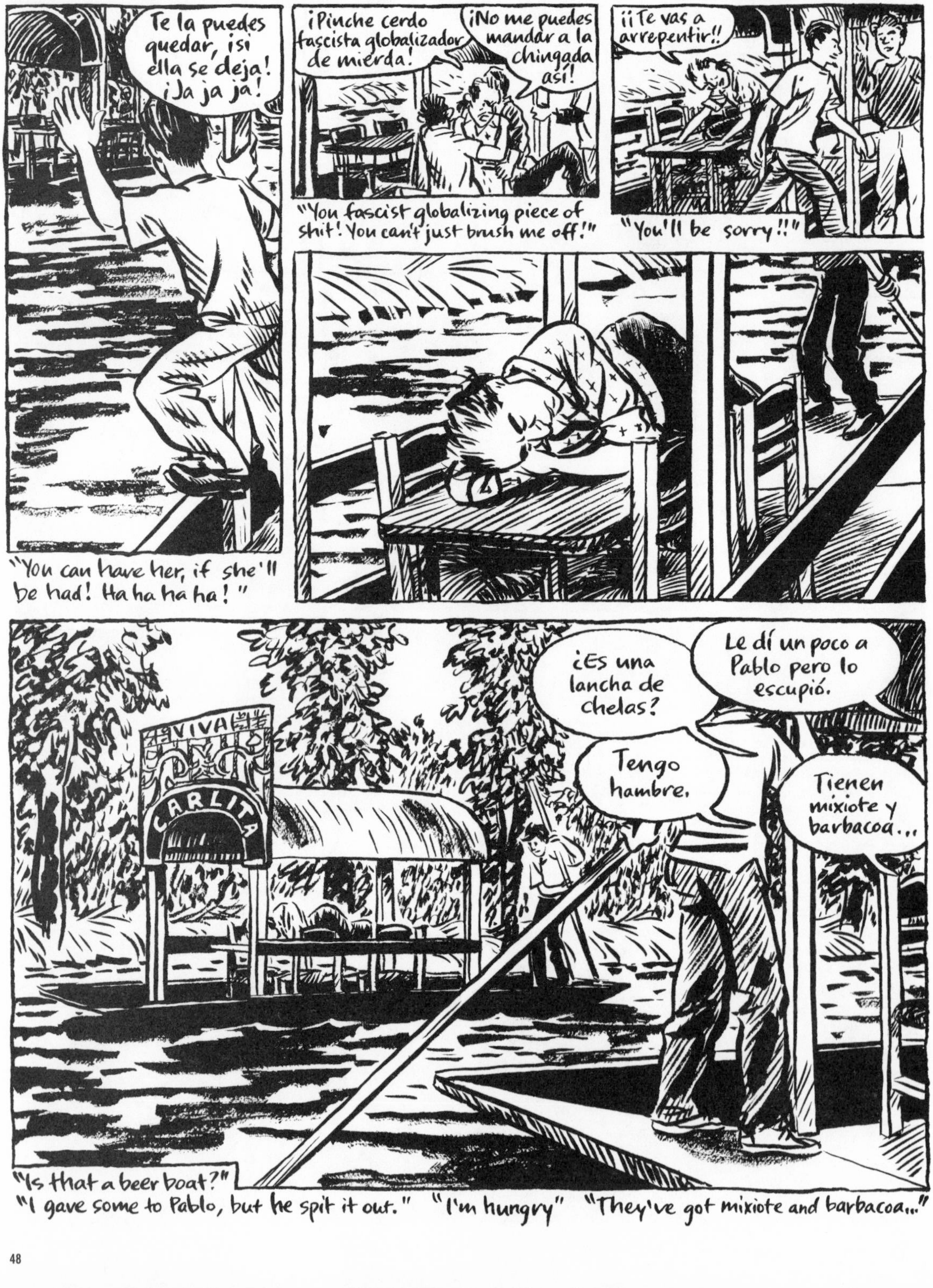
Te la puedes quedar, ¡si ella se deja! ¡Ja ja ja!
"You can have her, if she'll be had! Ha ha ha ha!"
¡Pinche cerdo fascista globalizador de mierda!
¡No me puedes mandar a la chingada así!
"You fascist globalizing piece of shit! You can't just brush me off!"
¡¡Te vas a arrepentir!!
"You'll be sorry!!"
VIVA
CARLITA
¿Es una lancha de chelas?
Le dí un poco a Pablo pero lo escupió.
Tengo hambre.
Tienen mixiote y barbacoa...
"Is that a beer boat?"
"I gave some to Pablo, but he spit it out."
"I'm hungry"
"They've got mixiote and barbacoa..."

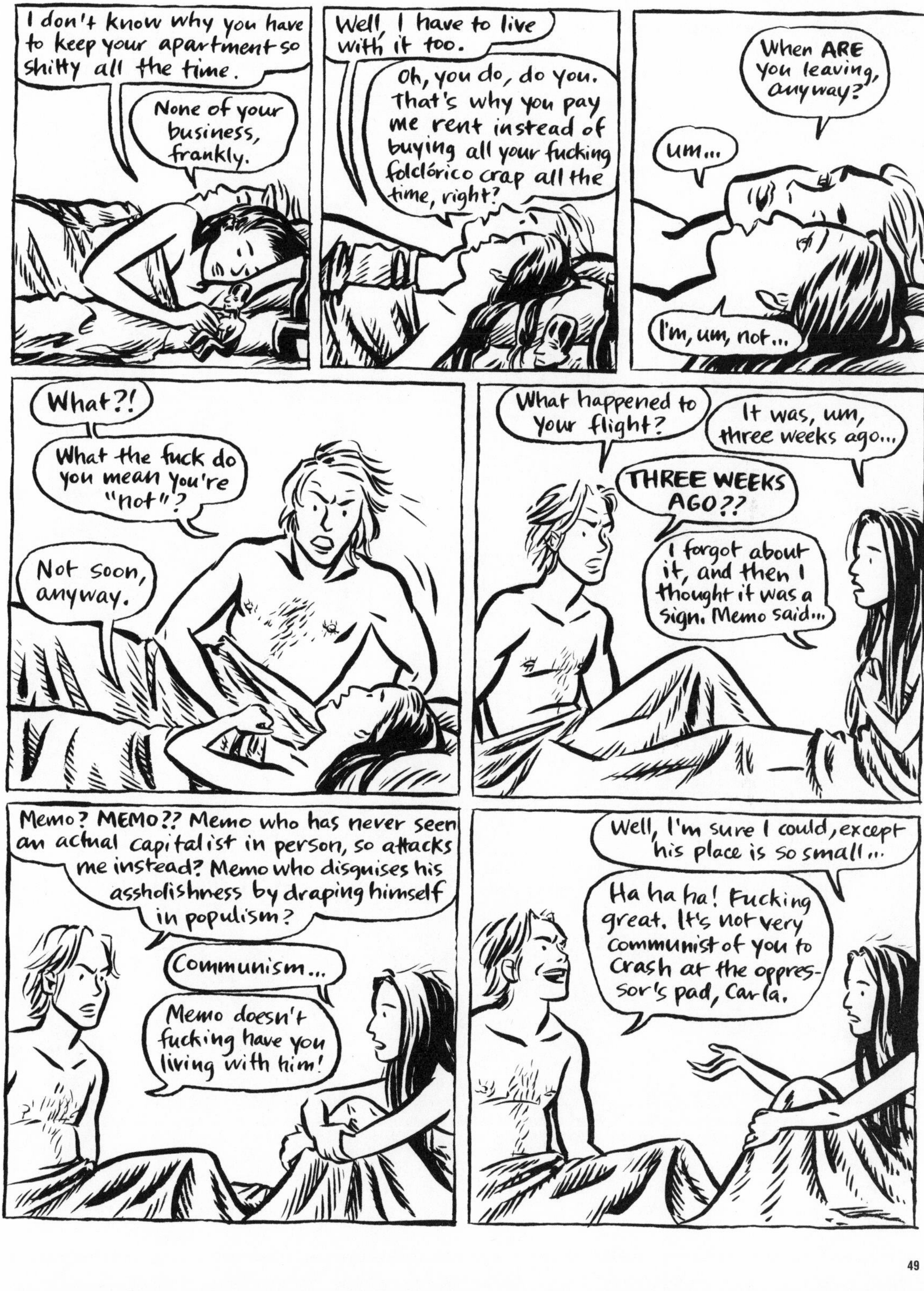

I don't know why you have to keep your apartment so shitty all the time.
None of your business, frankly.
Well, I have to live with it too.
Oh, you do, do you. That's why you pay me rent instead of buying all your fucking folclórico crap all the time, right?
When ARE you leaving, anyway?
Um...
I'm, um, not...
What?!
What the fuck do you mean you're "not"?
Not soon, anyway.
What happened to your flight?
It was, um, three weeks ago...
THREE WEEKS AGO??
I forgot about it, and then I thought it was a sign. Memo said...
Memo? MEMO?? Memo who has never seen an actual capitalist in person, so attacks me instead? Memo who disguises his assholishness by draping himself in populism?
Communism...
Memo doesn't fucking have you living with him!
Well, I'm sure I could, except his place is so small...
Ha ha ha! Fucking great. It's not very communist of you to crash at the oppressor's pad, Carla.

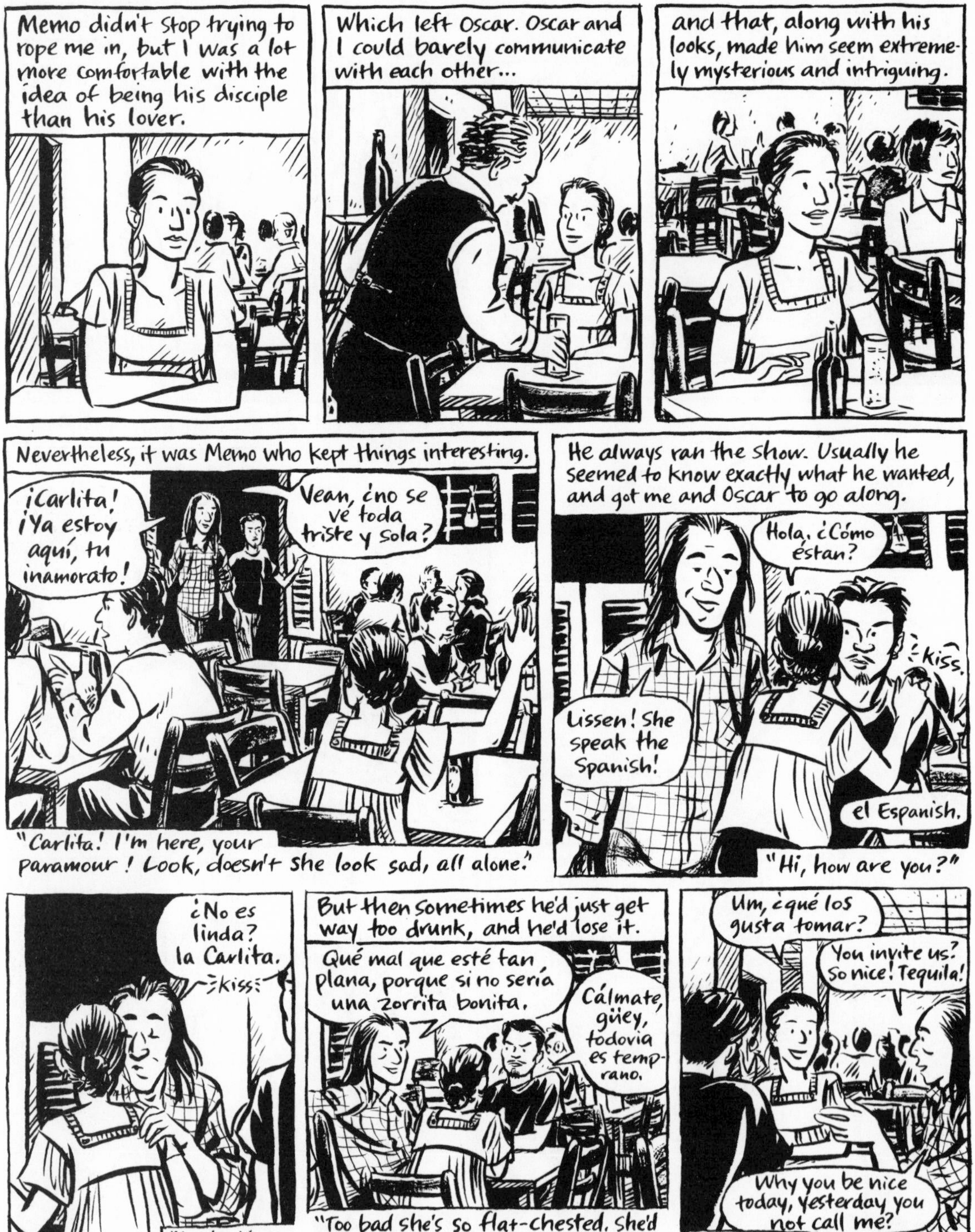

Memo didn't stop trying to rope me in, but I was a lot more comfortable with the idea of being his disciple than his lover.
Which left Oscar. Oscar and I could barely communicate with each other...
and that, along with his looks, made him seem extremely mysterious and intriguing.
Nevertheless, it was Memo who kept things interesting.
¡Carlita! ¡Ya estoy aquí, tu inamorato!
Vean, ¿no se vé toda triste y sola?
"Carlita! I'm here, your paramour! Look, doesn't she look sad, all alone."
He always ran the show. Usually he seemed to know exactly what he wanted, and got me and Oscar to go along.
Hola, ¿Cómo éstan?
Kiss.
Lissen! She speak the Spanish!
el Espanish.
"Hi, how are you?"
¿No es linda? la Carlita.
kiss
"Isn't that cute? Our little Carla."
But then sometimes he'd just get way too drunk, and he'd lose it.
Qué mal que esté tan plana, porque si no sería una zorrita bonita.
Cálmate, güey, todovia es temprano.
"Too bad she's so flat-chested. She'd be pretty otherwise. Little vixen."
"Cool out, man, it's early still."
Um, ¿qué los gusta tomar?
You invite us? So nice! Tequila!
Why you be nice today, yesterday you not call me?
"What likes to have you to drink?"

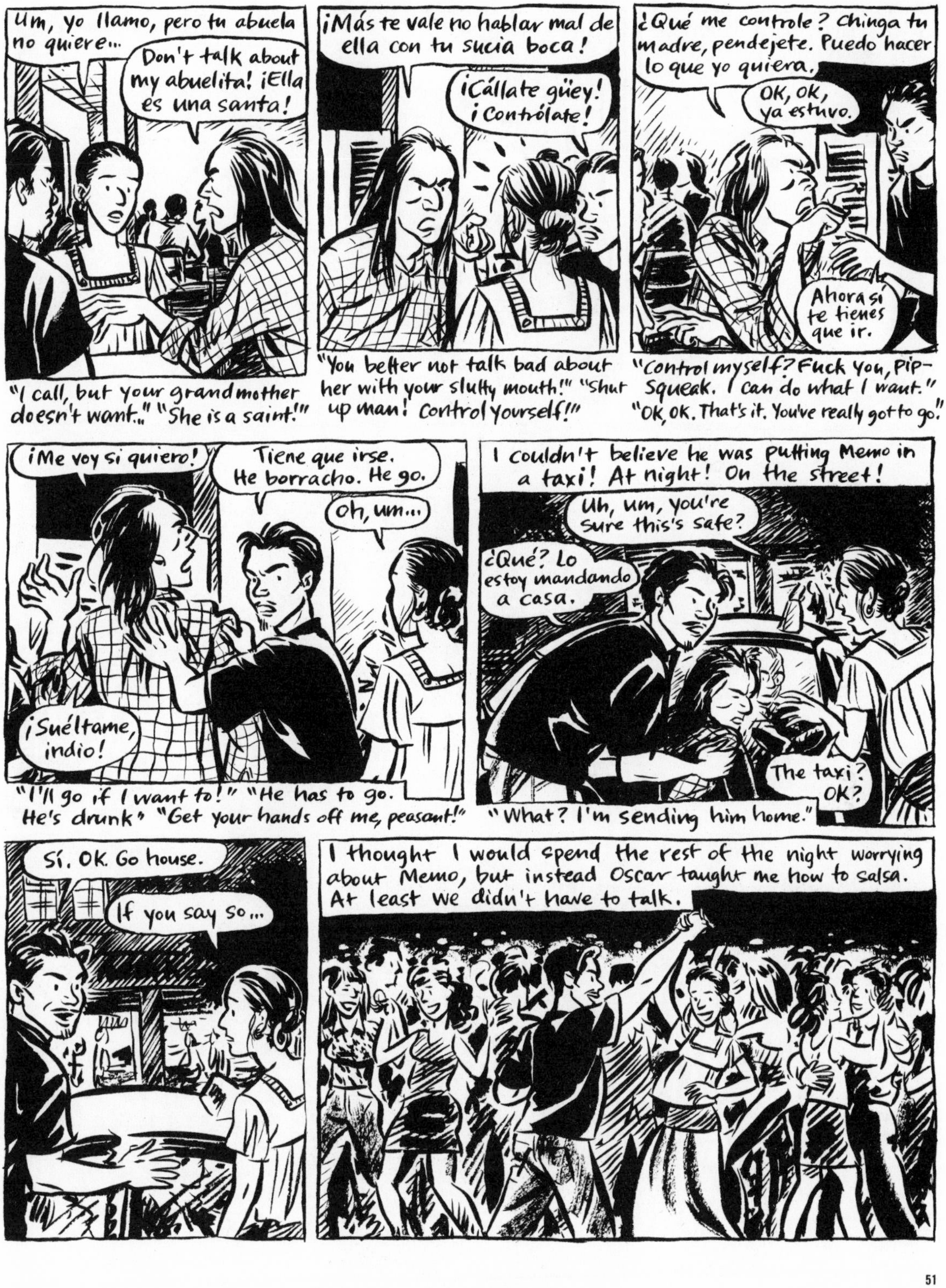

Um, yo llamo, pero tu abuela no quiere...
Don't talk about my abuelita! ¡Ella es una santa!
"I call, but your grandmother doesn't want..." "She is a saint!"
¡Más te vale no hablar mal de ella con tu sucia boca!
¡Cállate güey! ¡Contrólate!
"You better not talk bad about her with your slutty mouth!" "Shut up man! Control yourself!"
¿Qué me controle? Chinga tu madre, pendejete. Puedo hacer lo que yo quiera.
OK, OK, ya estuvo.
Ahora sí te tienes que ir.
"Control myself? Fuck you, Pip-Squeak. I can do what I want." "OK, OK. That's it. You've really got to go."
¡Me voy si quiero!
Tiene que irse. He borracho. He go.
Oh, um...
¡Suéltame, indio!
"I'll go if I want to!" "He has to go. He's drunk" "Get your hands off me, peasant!"
I couldn't believe he was putting Memo in a taxi! At night! On the street!
Uh, um, you're sure this's safe?
¿Qué? Lo estoy mandando a casa.
The taxi? OK?
"What? I'm sending him home."
Sí. OK. Go house.
If you say so...
I thought I would spend the rest of the night worrying about Memo, but instead Oscar taught me how to salsa. At least we didn't have to talk.

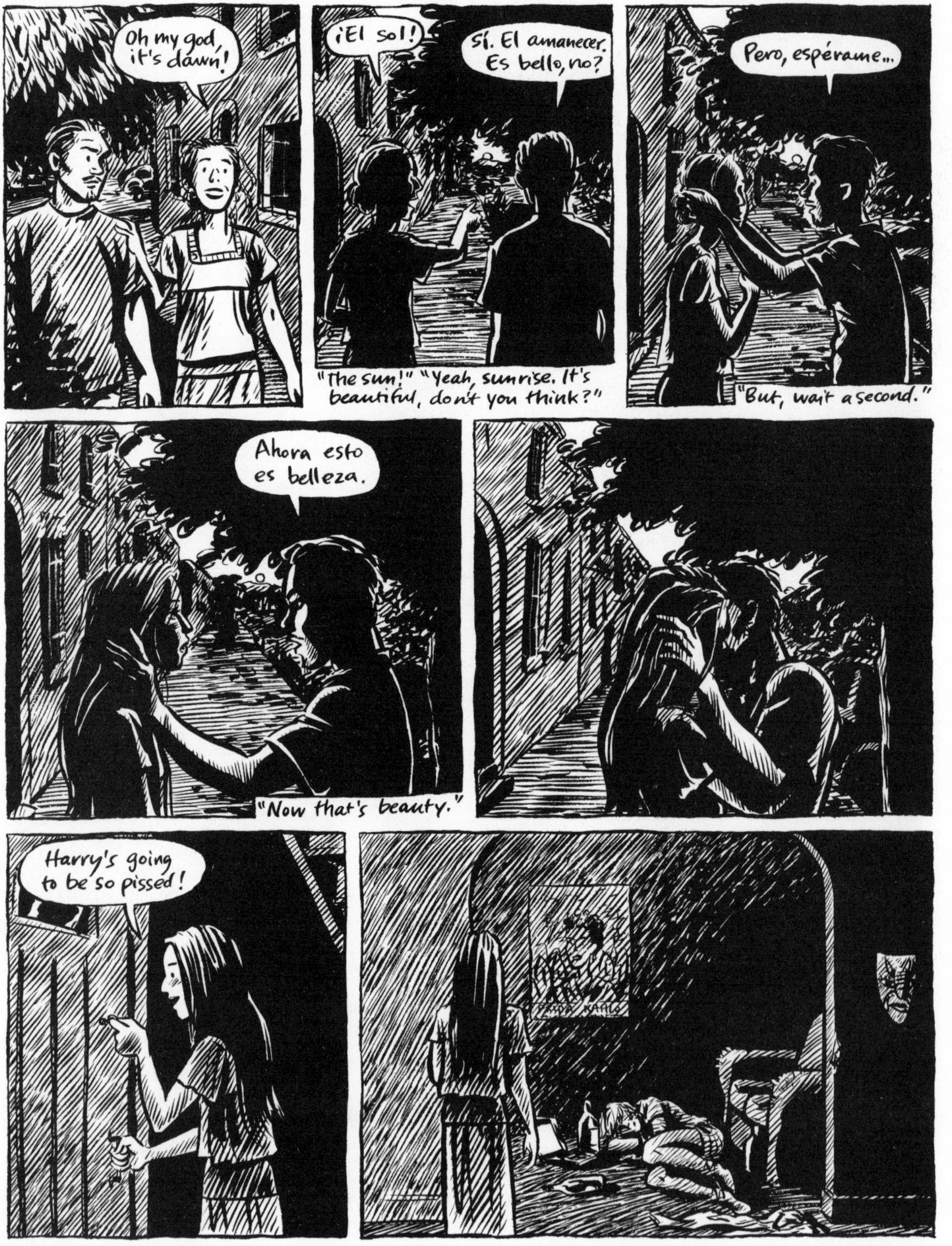
Oh my god, it's dawn!
¡El sol!
Sí. El amanecer. Es bello, no?
"The sun!" "Yeah, sunrise. It's beautiful, don't you think?"
Pero, espérame...
"But, wait a second."
Ahora esto es belleza.
"Now that's beauty."
Harry's going to be so pissed!
FRIDA KAHLO

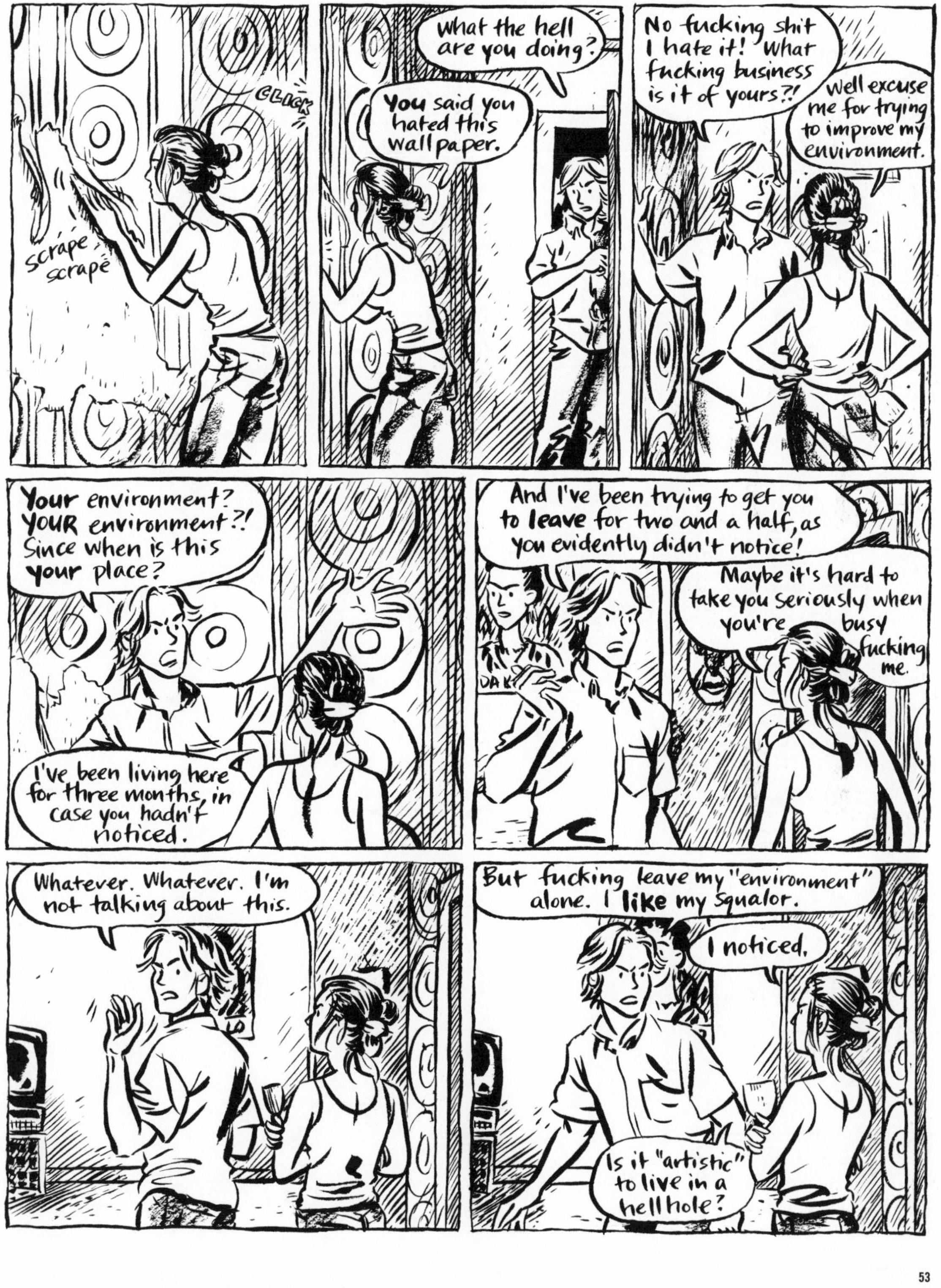

SCRAPE SCRAPE
CLICK
What the hell are you doing?
You said you hated this wallpaper.
No fucking shit I hate it! What fucking business is it of yours?!
Well excuse me for trying to improve my environment.
Your environment? YOUR environment?! Since when is this your place?
I've been living here for three months, in case you hadn't noticed.
And I've been trying to get you to leave for two and a half, as you evidently didn't notice!
Maybe it's hard to take you seriously when you're busy fucking me.
Whatever. Whatever. I'm not talking about this.
But fucking leave my "environment" alone. I like my squalor.
I noticed.
Is it "artistic" to live in a hellhole?

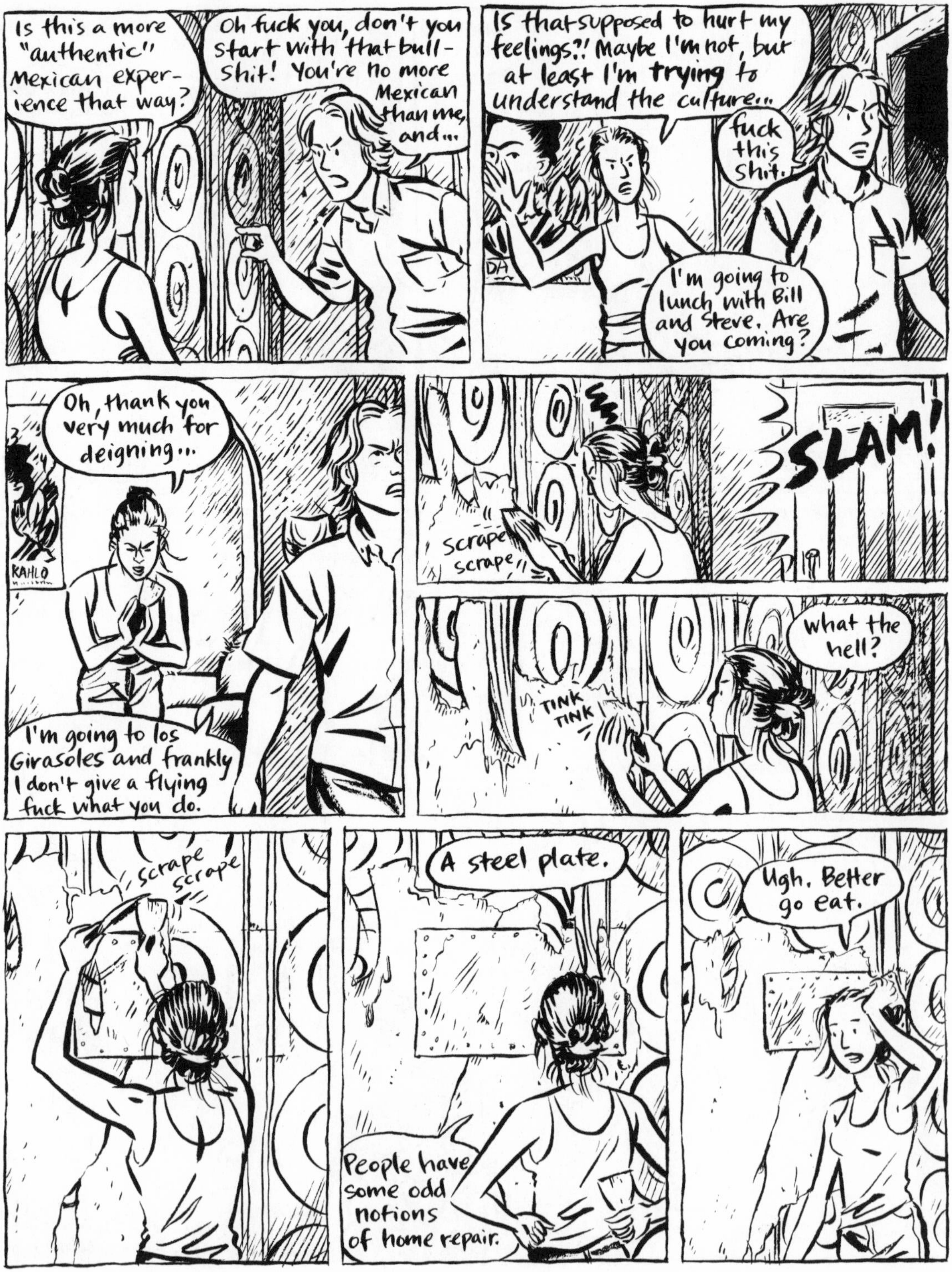
Is this a more "authentic" Mexican experience that way?
Oh fuck you, don't you start with that bullshit! You're no more Mexican than me, and...
Is that supposed to hurt my feelings?! Maybe I'm not, but at least I'm trying to understand the culture...
fuck this shit.
DH
I'm going to lunch with Bill and Steve. Are you coming?
Oh, thank you very much for deigning...
KAHLO
I'm going to los Girasoles and frankly I don't give a flying fuck what you do.
scrape scrape
SLAM!
what the hell?
TINK TINK
scrape scrape
A steel plate.
People have some odd notions of home repair.
Ugh. Better go eat.

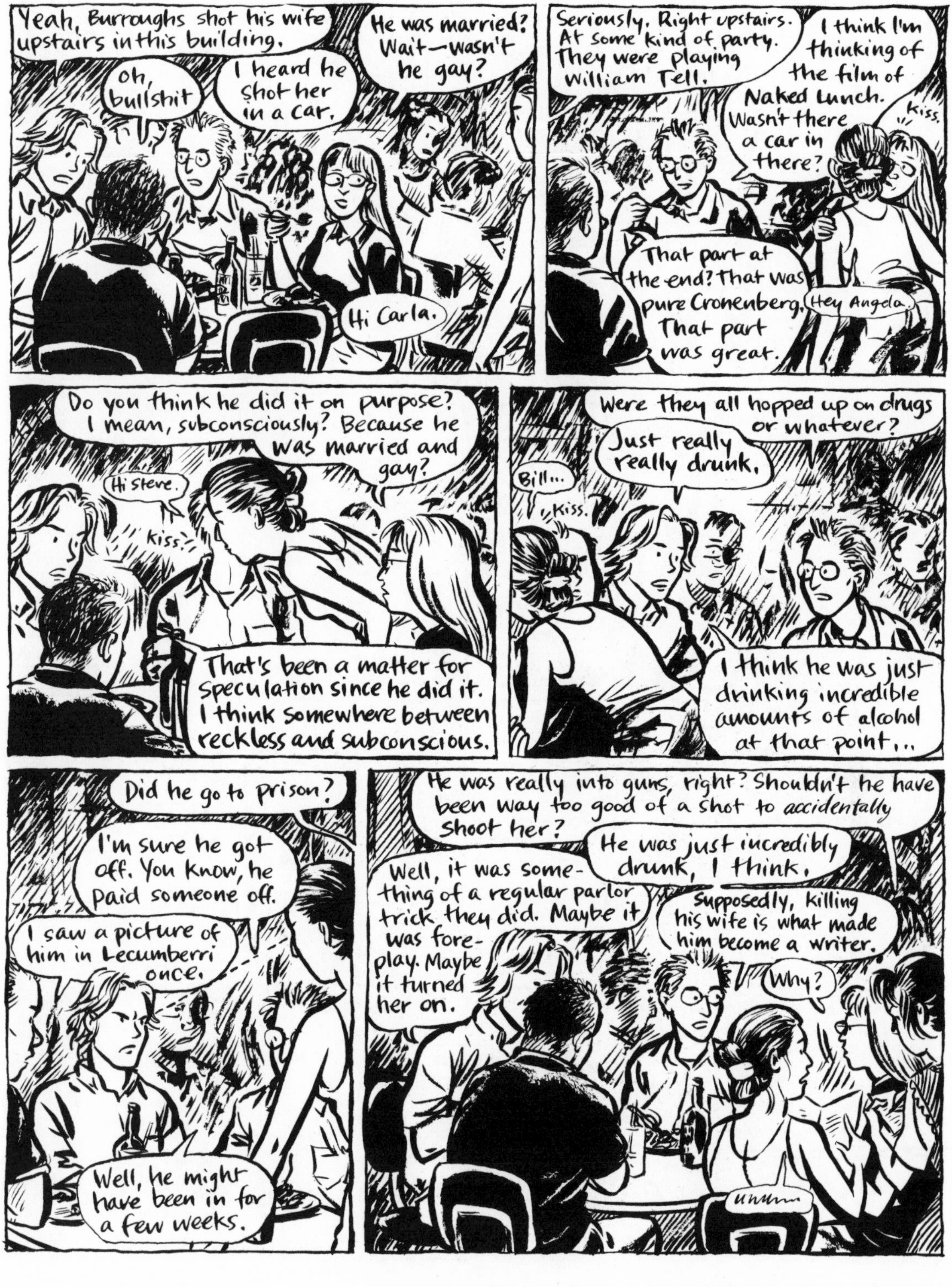
Yeah, Burroughs shot his wife upstairs in this building.
Oh, bullshit
I heard he shot her in a car.
He was married? Wait—wasn't he gay?
Hi Carla.
Seriously. Right upstairs. At some kind of party. They were playing William Tell.
I think I'm thinking of the film of Naked Lunch. Wasn't there a car in there?
Kiss.
That part at the end? That was pure Cronenberg. That part was great.
Hey Angela.
Do you think he did it on purpose? I mean, subconsciously? Because he was married and gay?
Hi Steve.
Kiss.
That's been a matter for speculation since he did it. I think somewhere between reckless and subconscious.
Were they all hopped up on drugs or whatever?
Just really really drunk.
Bill...
Kiss.
I think he was just drinking incredible amounts of alcohol at that point...
Did he go to prison?
I'm sure he got off. You know, he paid someone off.
I saw a picture of him in Lecumberri once.
Well, he might have been in for a few weeks.
He was really into guns, right? Shouldn't he have been way too good of a shot to accidentally shoot her?
He was just incredibly drunk, I think.
Well, it was something of a regular parlor trick they did. Maybe it was foreplay. Maybe it turned her on.
Supposedly, killing his wife is what made him become a writer.
Why?
Uhhhm

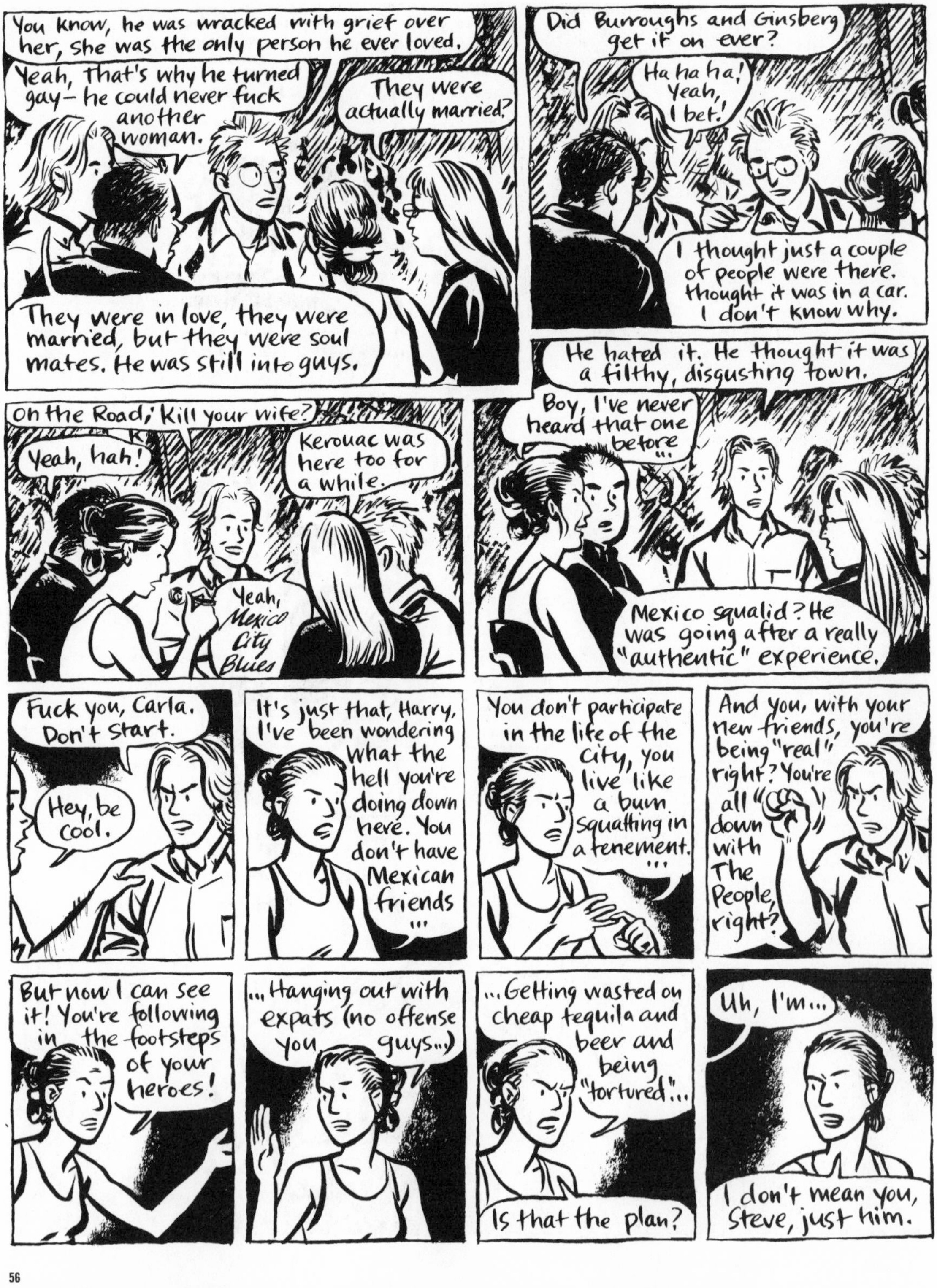

You know, he was wracked with grief over her, she was the only person he ever loved.
Yeah, that's why he turned gay– he could never fuck another woman.
They were actually married?
They were in love, they were married, but they were soul mates. He was still into guys.
Did Burroughs and Ginsberg get it on ever?
Ha ha ha! Yeah, I bet!
I thought just a couple of people were there. thought it was in a car. I don't know why.
On the Road, 'Kill your wife?'
Yeah, hah!
Kerouac was here too for a while.
Yeah, Mexico City Blues
He hated it. He thought it was a filthy, disgusting town.
Boy, I've never heard that one before...
Mexico squalid? He was going after a really "authentic" experience.
Fuck you, Carla. Don't start.
Hey, be cool.
It's just that, Harry, I've been wondering what the hell you're doing down here. You don't have Mexican friends...
You don't participate in the life of the city, you live like a bum squatting in a tenement...
And you, with your new friends, you're being "real" right? You're all "down" with The People, right?
But now I can see it! You're following in the footsteps of your heroes!
...Hanging out with expats (no offense you guys...)
...Getting wasted on cheap tequila and beer and being "tortured"...
Is that the plan?
Uh, I'm...
I don't mean you, Steve, just him.

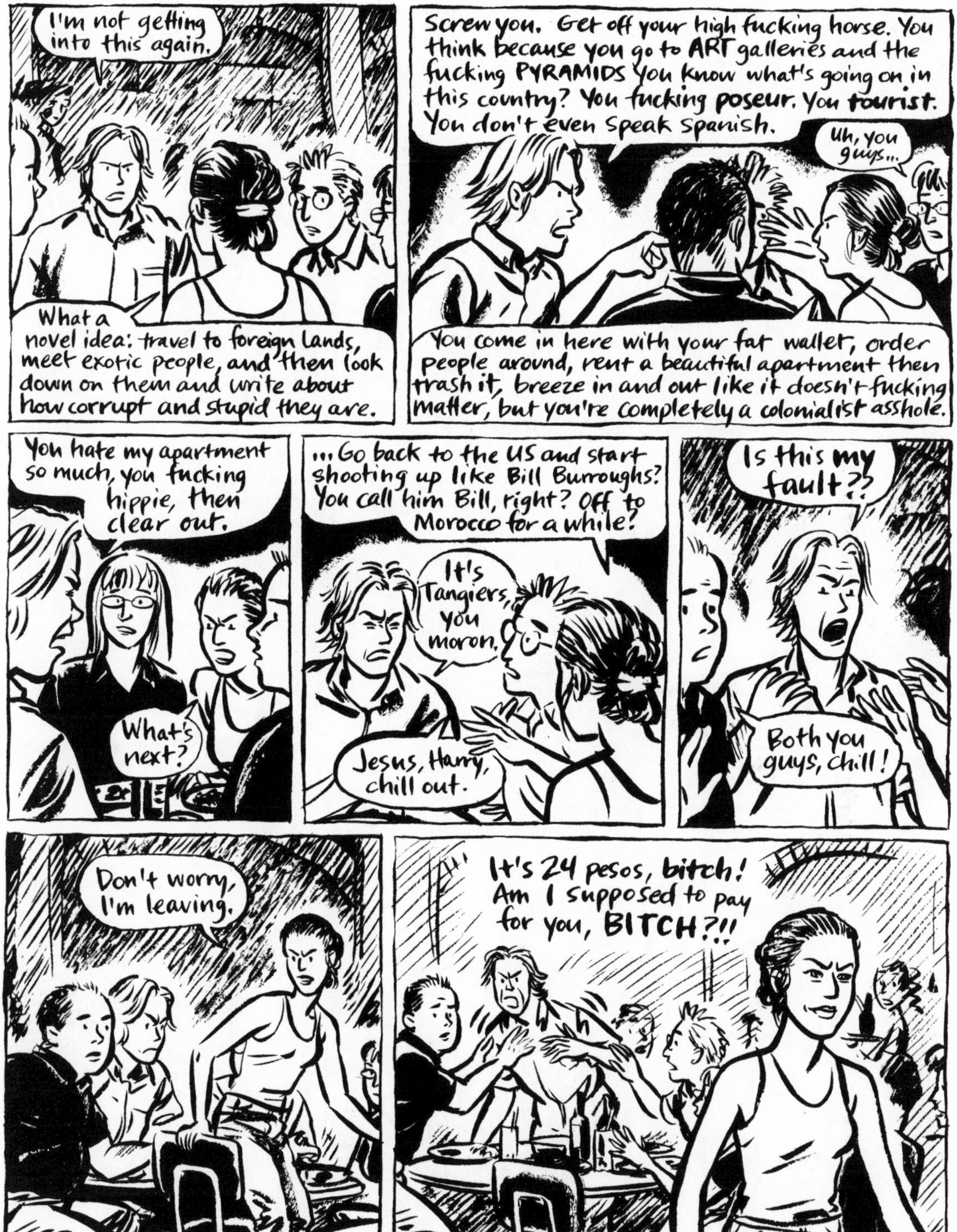
I'm not getting into this again.
What a novel idea: travel to foreign lands, meet exotic people, and then look down on them and write about how corrupt and stupid they are.
Screw you. Get off your high fucking horse. You think because you go to ART galleries and the fucking PYRAMIDS you know what's going on in this country? You fucking poseur. You tourist. You don't even speak spanish.
Uh, you guys...
You come in here with your fat wallet, order people around, rent a beautiful apartment then trash it, breeze in and out like it doesn't fucking matter, but you're completely a colonialist asshole.
You hate my apartment so much, you fucking hippie, then clear out.
What's next?
...Go back to the US and start shooting up like Bill Burroughs? You call him Bill, right? Off to Morocco for a while?
It's Tangiers, you moron.
Jesus, Harry, chill out.
Is this my fault??
Both you guys, chill!
Don't worry, I'm leaving.
It's 24 pesos, bitch! Am I supposed to pay for you, BITCH?!!

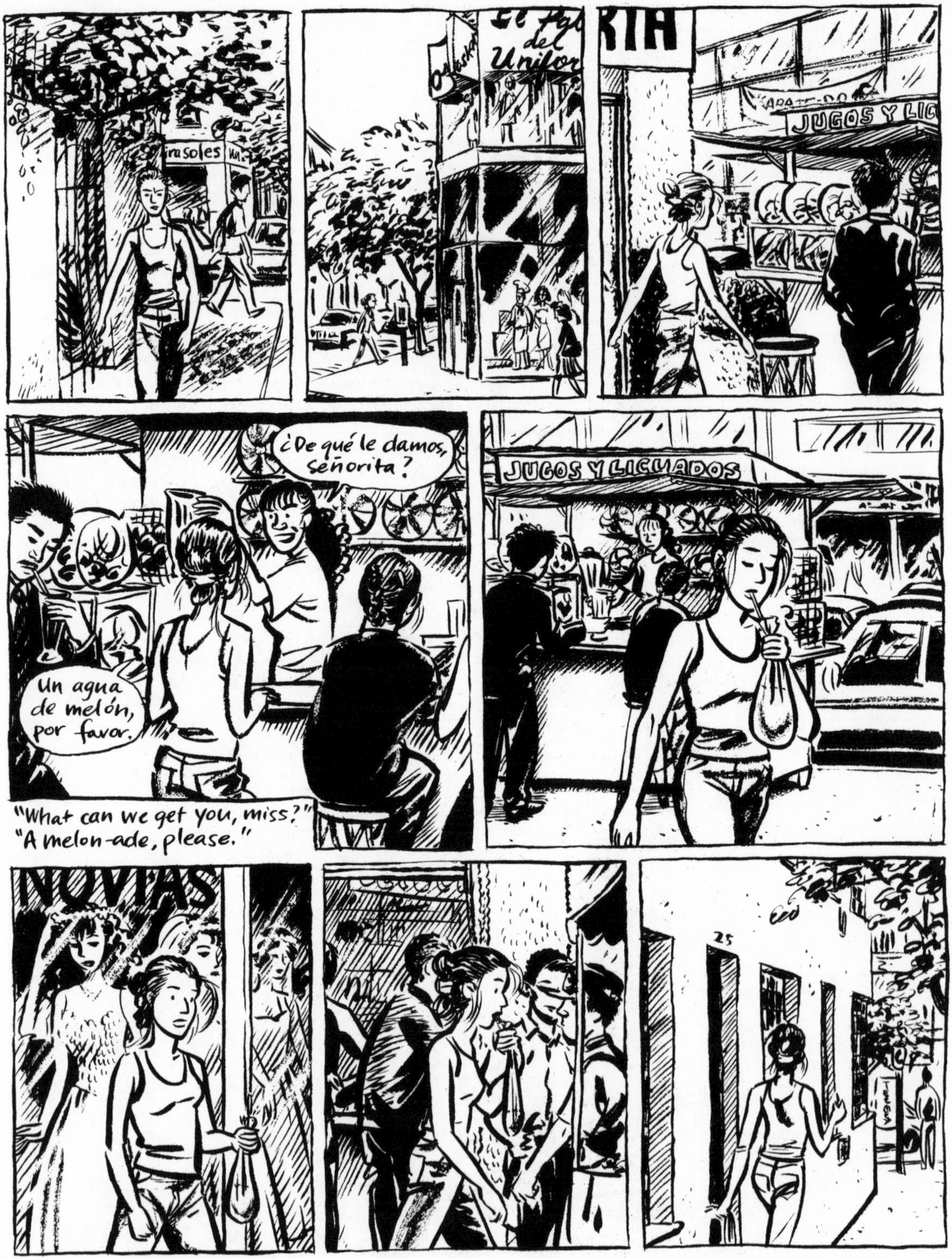
JUGOS Y LIC
¿De qué le damos, señorita?
Un agua de melón, por favor.
"What can we get you, miss?"
"A melon-ade, please."
JUGOS Y LICUADOS
NOVIAS
25

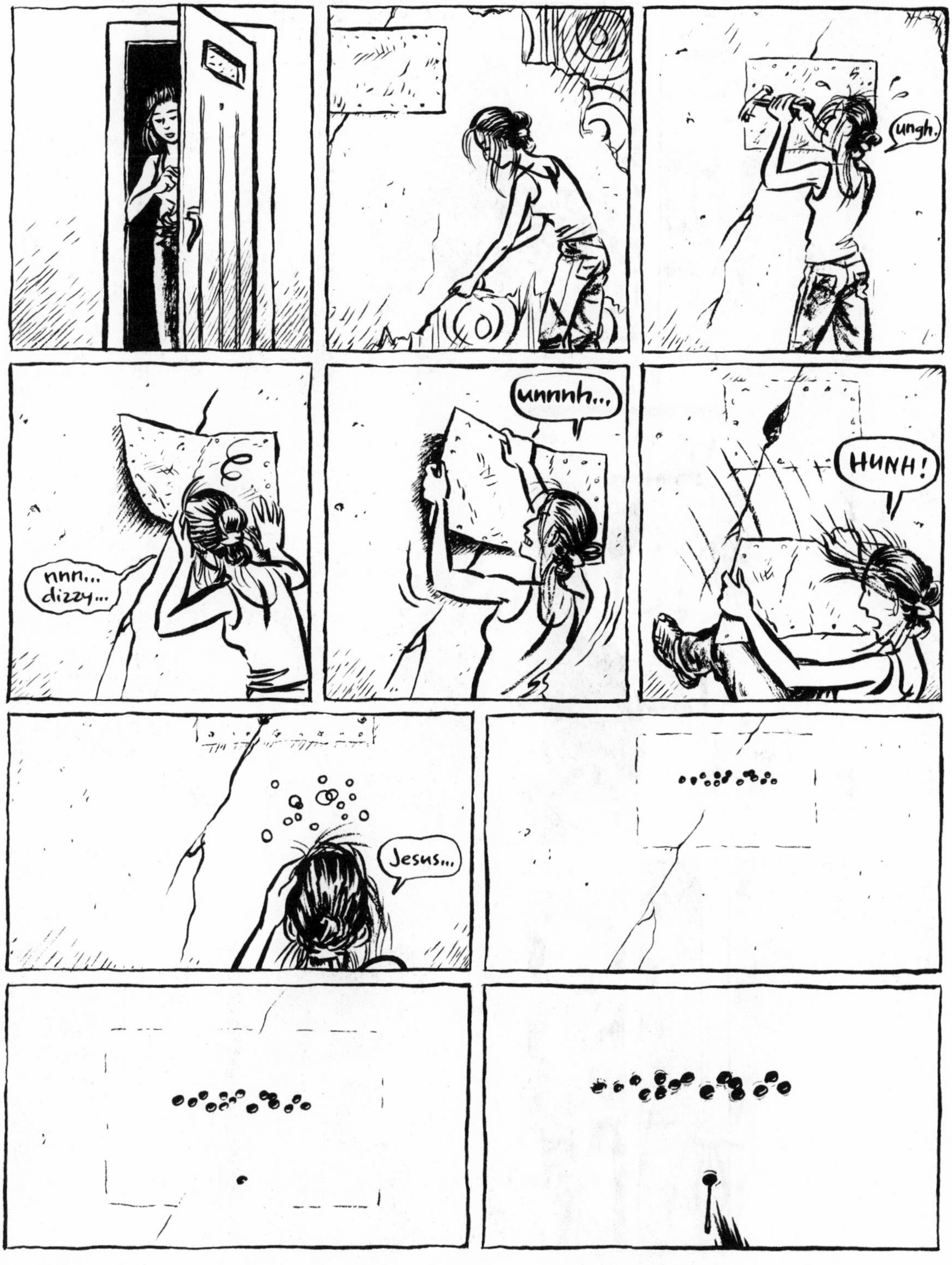
ungh.
nnn... dizzy...
unnnh...
HUNH!
Jesus...

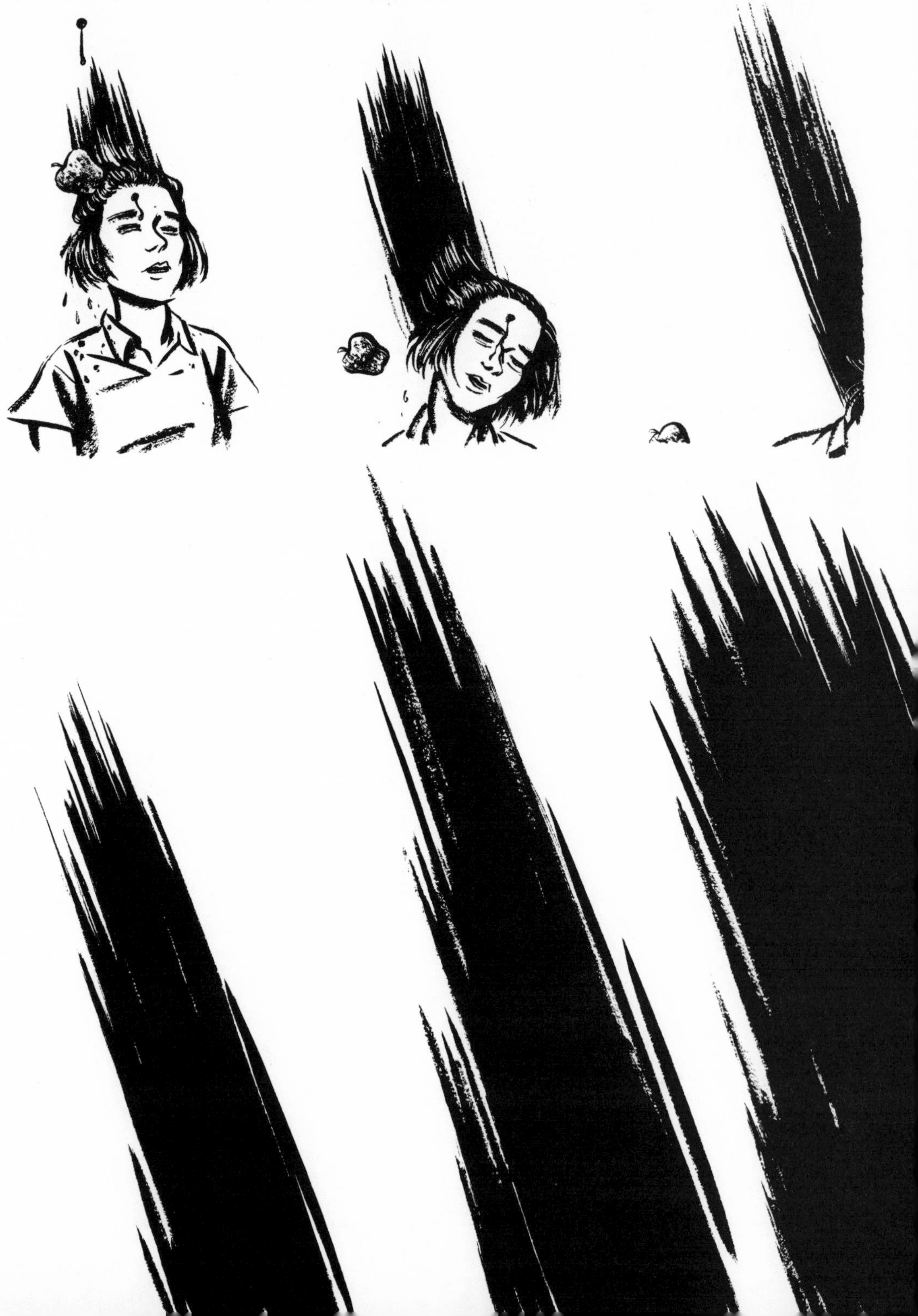

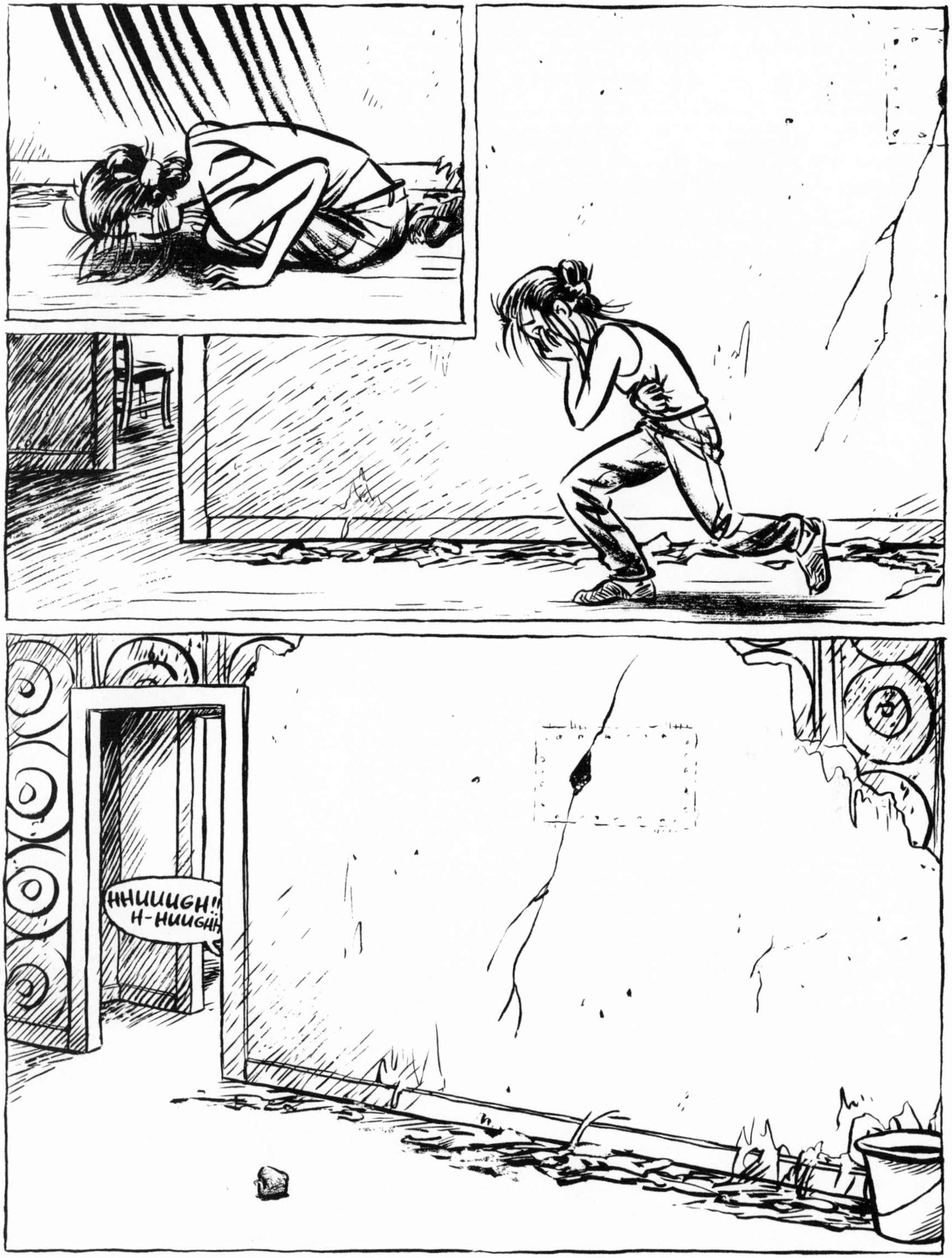
HHUUUGH!!
H-HUUGHH

From this point forward, dialogue spoken in English
will be indicated with < arrow brackets >.

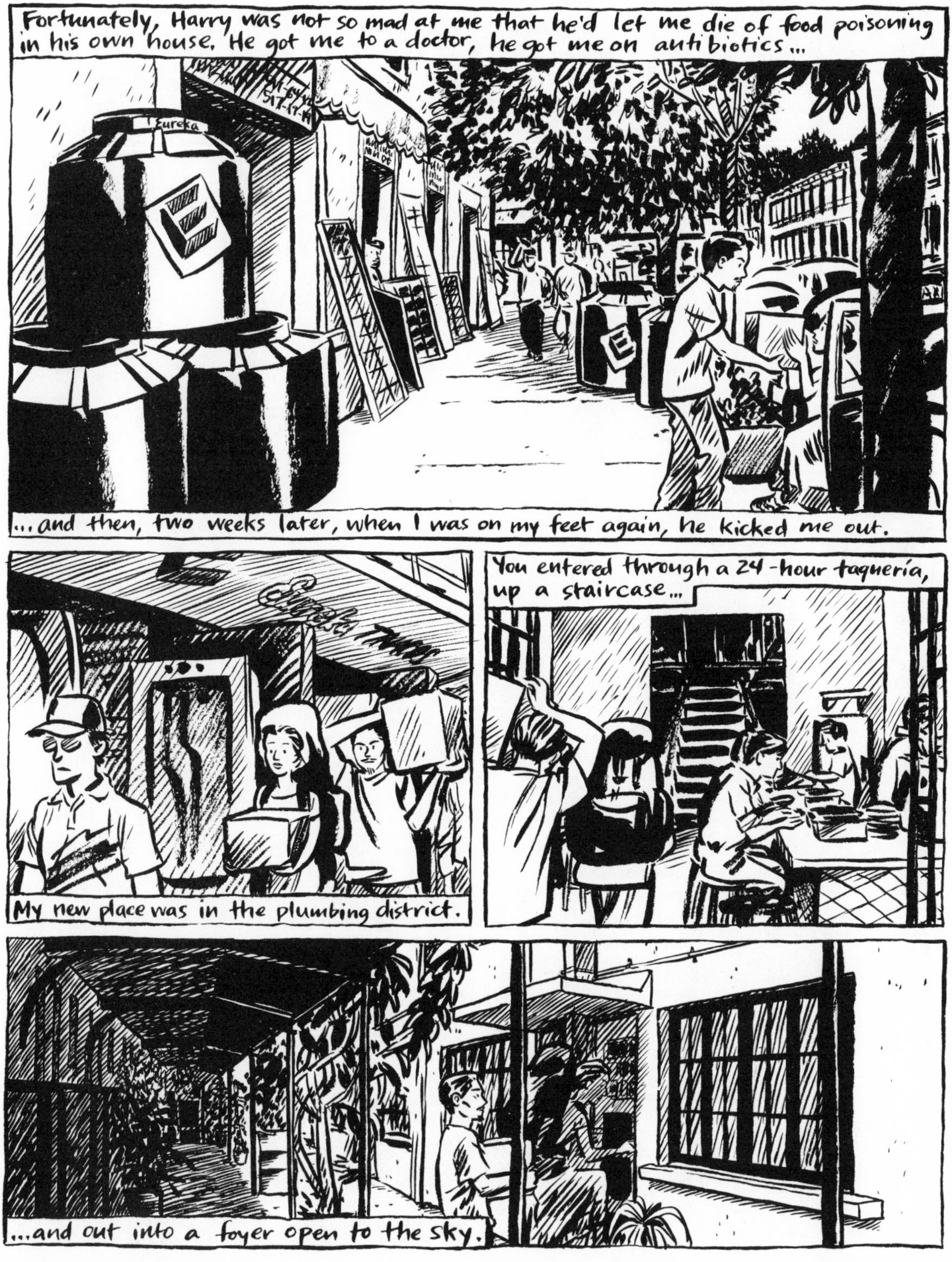

Fortunately, Harry was not so mad at me that he'd let me die of food poisoning in his own house. He got me to a doctor, he got me on antibiotics...
Eureka
...and then, two weeks later, when I was on my feet again, he kicked me out.
My new place was in the plumbing district.
You entered through a 24-hour taquería, up a staircase...
...and out into a foyer open to the sky.

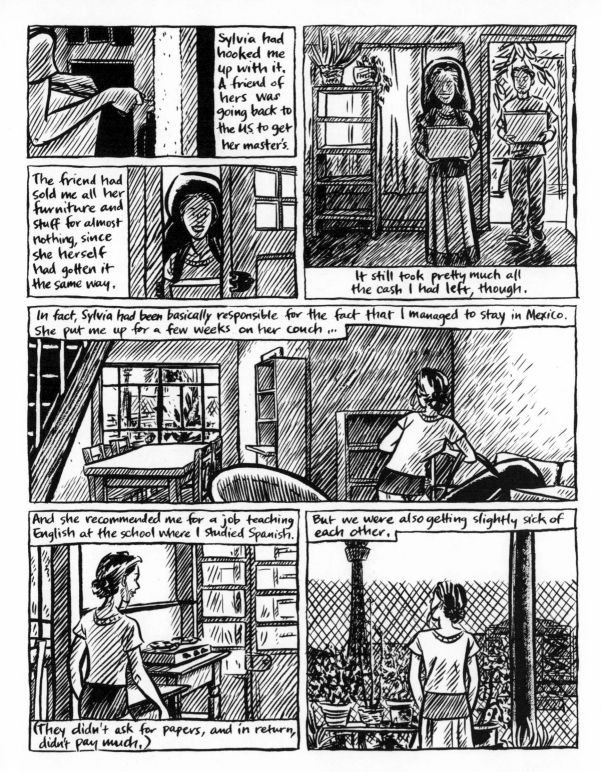

Sylvia had hooked me up with it. A friend of hers was going back to the U.S. to get her master's.

The friend had sold me all her furniture and stuff for almost nothing, since she herself had gotten it the same way.

It still took pretty much all the cash I had left, though.

In fact, Sylvia had been basically responsible for the fact that I managed to stay in Mexico. She put me up for a few weeks on her couch ...

And she recommended me for a job teaching English at the school where I studied Spanish.

(They didn't ask for papers, and in return, didn't pay much.)

But we were also getting slightly sick of each other.

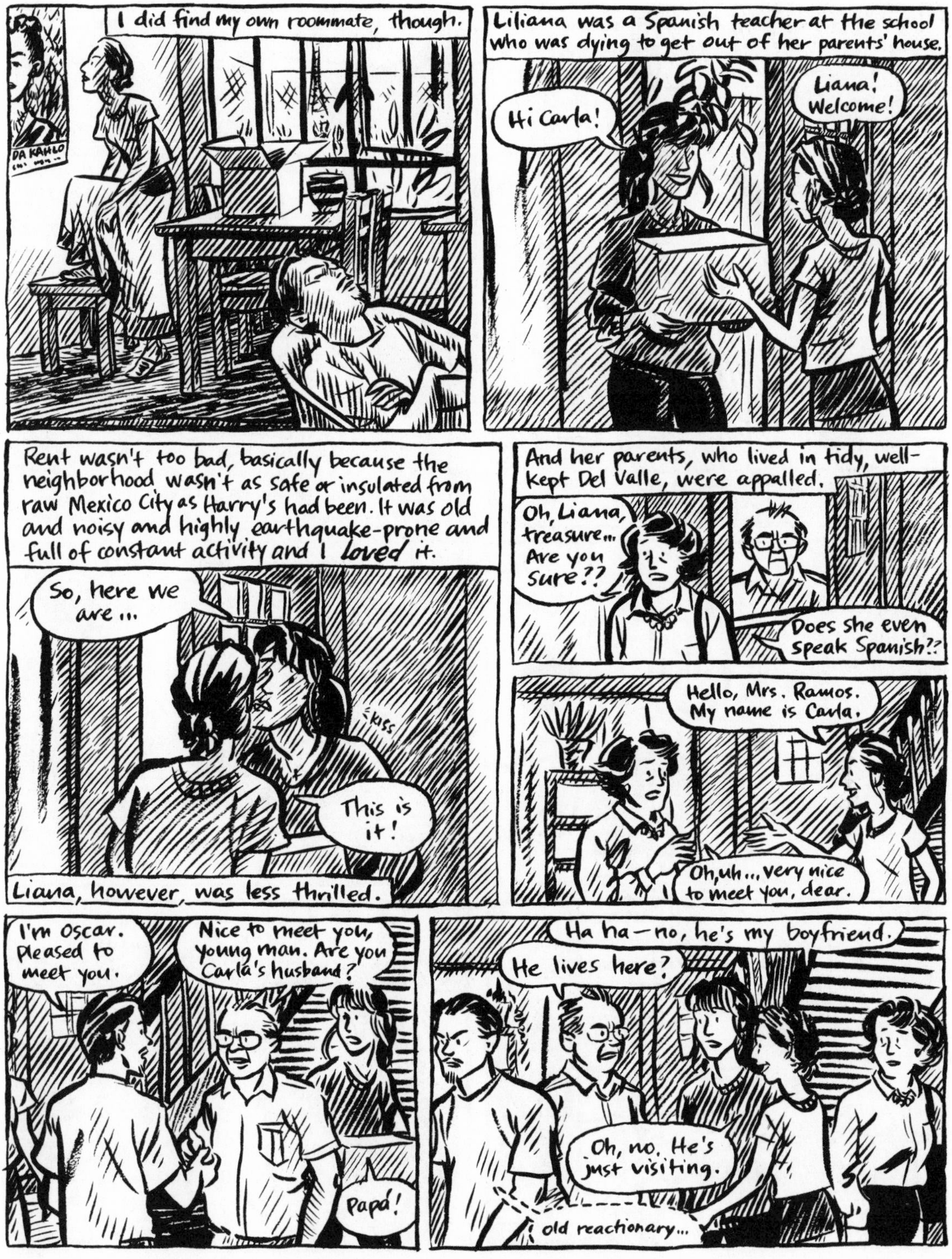

I did find my own roommate, though.
FRIDA KAHLO
Liliana was a Spanish teacher at the school who was dying to get out of her parents' house.
Hi Carla!
Liana! Welcome!
Rent wasn't too bad, basically because the neighborhood wasn't as safe or insulated from raw Mexico City as Harry's had been. It was old and noisy and highly earthquake-prone and full of constant activity and I loved it.
So, here we are...
kiss
This is it!
Liana, however, was less thrilled.
And her parents, who lived in tidy, well-kept Del Valle, were appalled.
Oh, Liana, treasure... Are you sure??
Does she even speak Spanish??
Hello, Mrs. Ramos. My name is Carla.
Oh, uh... very nice to meet you, dear.
I'm Oscar. Pleased to meet you.
Nice to meet you, young man. Are you Carla's husband?
Papá!
Ha ha—no, he's my boyfriend.
He lives here?
Oh, no. He's just visiting.
old reactionary...

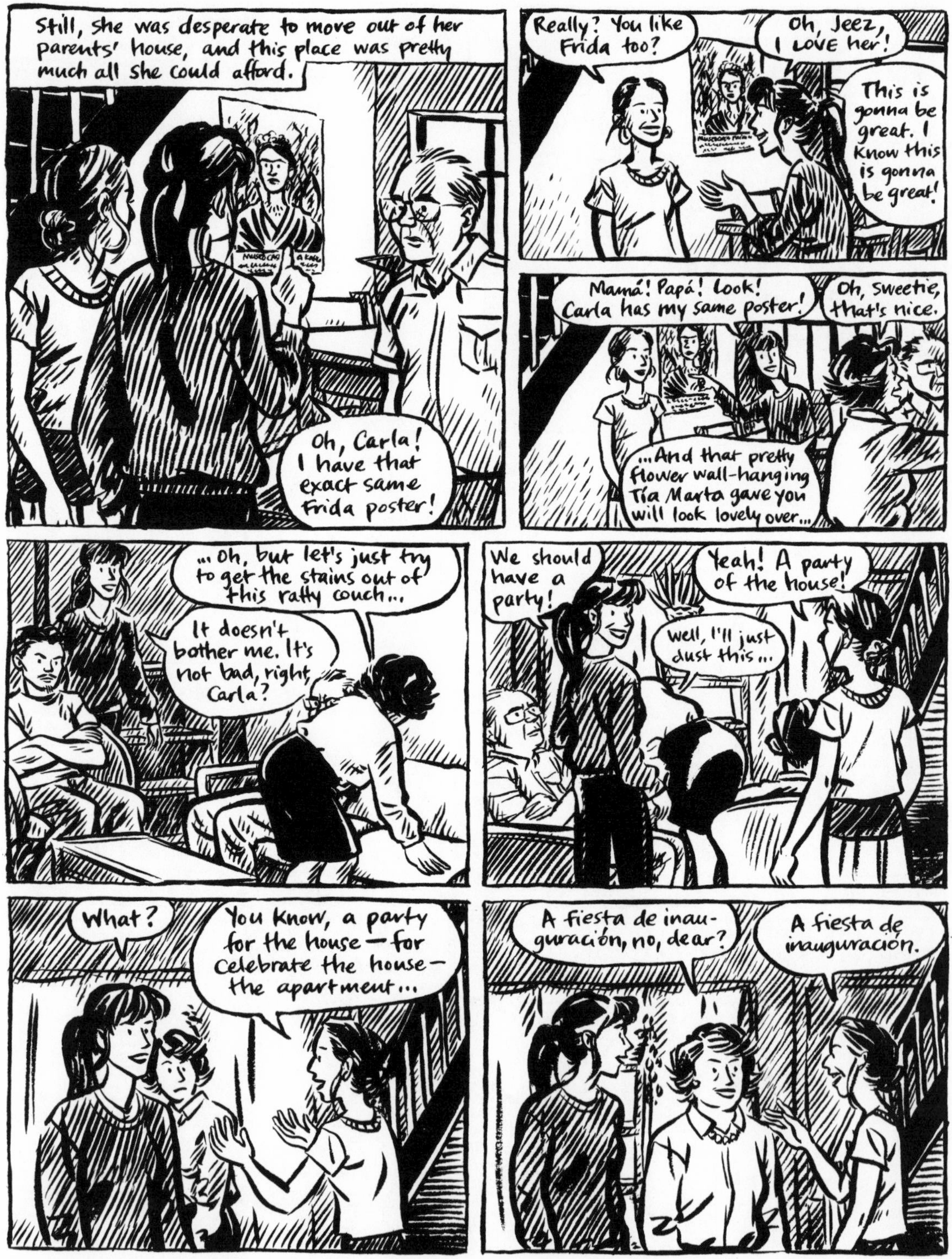
Still, she was desperate to move out of her parents' house, and this place was pretty much all she could afford.
Oh, Carla! I have that exact same Frida poster!
Really? You like Frida too?
Oh, Jeez, I LOVE her!
This is gonna be great. I know this is gonna be great!
Mamá! Papá! Look! Carla has my same poster!
Oh, sweetie, that's nice.
...And that pretty flower wall-hanging Tía Marta gave you will look lovely over...
...Oh, but let's just try to get the stains out of this ratty couch...
It doesn't bother me. It's not bad, right, Carla?
We should have a party!
Yeah! A party of the house!
Well, I'll just dust this...
What?
You know, a party for the house — for celebrate the house — the apartment...
A fiesta de inauguración, no, dear?
A fiesta de inauguración.

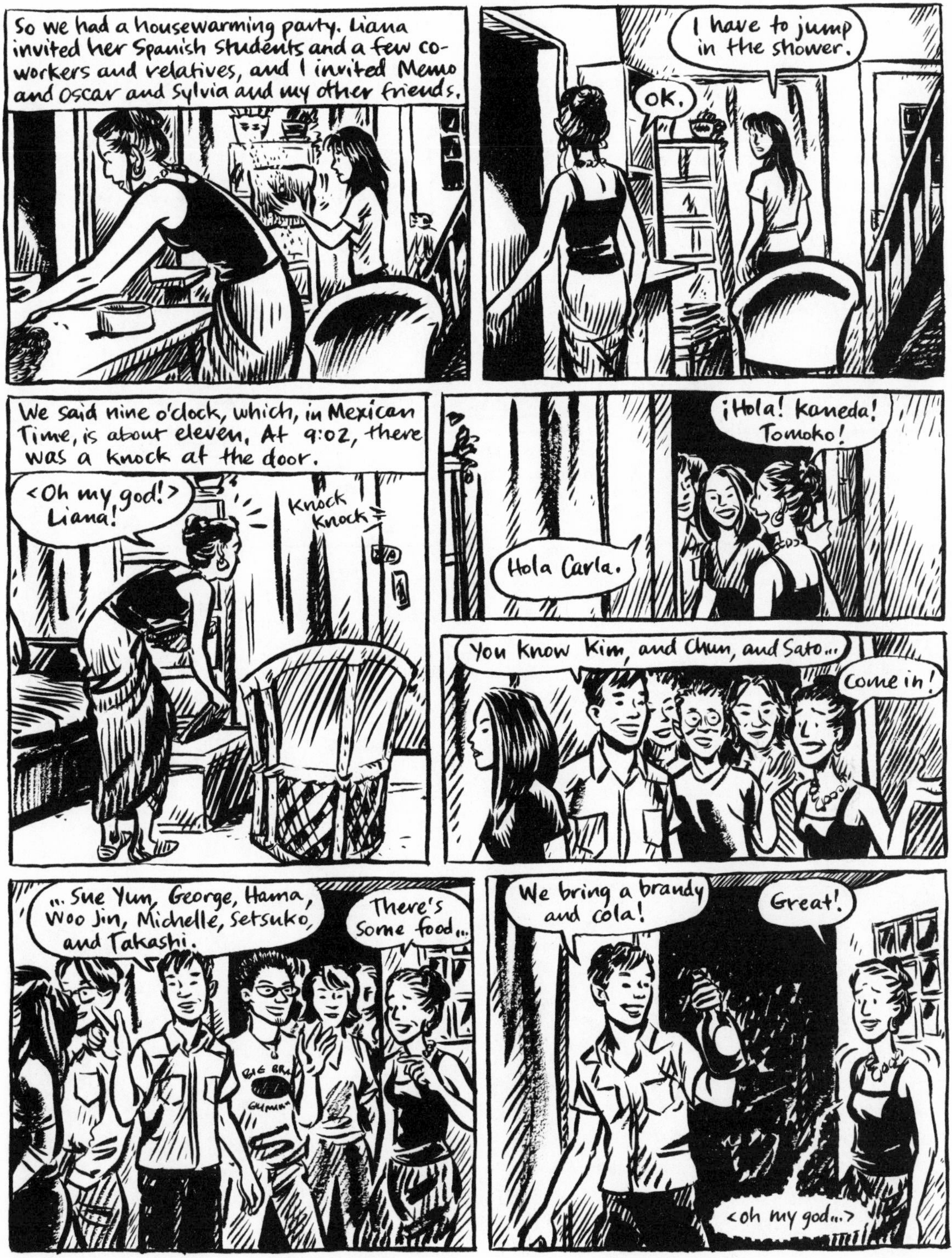

So we had a housewarming party. Liana invited her Spanish students and a few co-workers and relatives, and I invited Memo and Oscar and Sylvia and my other friends.
I have to jump in the shower.
Ok.
We said nine o'clock, which, in Mexican Time, is about eleven. At 9:02, there was a knock at the door.
<Oh my god!> Liana!
Knock Knock
¡Hola! Kaneda! Tomoko!
Hola Carla.
You know Kim, and Chun, and Sato...
Come in!
... Sue Yun, George, Hama, Woo Jin, Michelle, Setsuko, and Takashi.
There's some food...
We bring a brandy and cola!
Great!
<oh my god...>

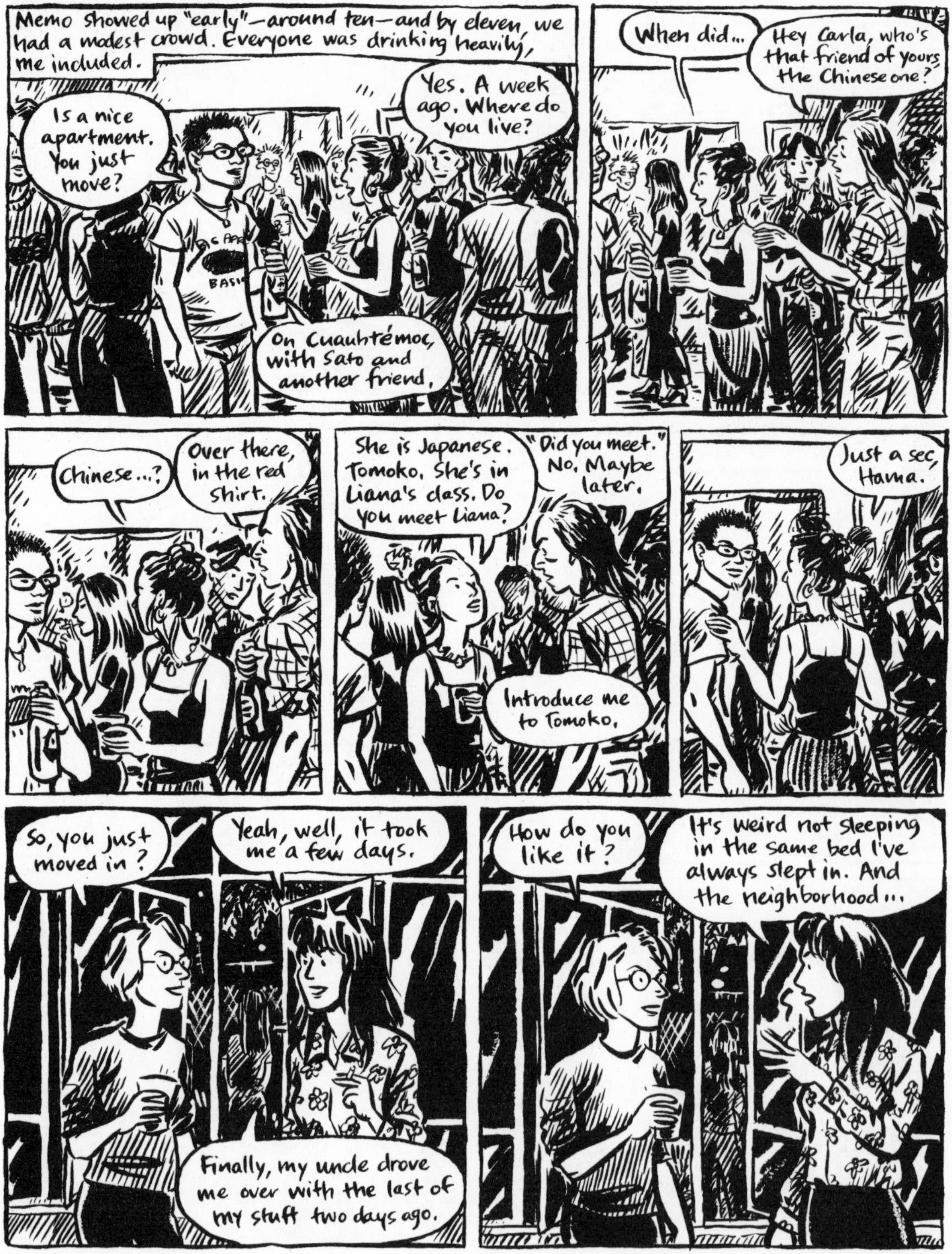
Memo showed up "early"—around ten—and by eleven, we had a modest crowd. Everyone was drinking heavily, me included.
Is a nice apartment. You just move?
Yes. A week ago. Where do you live?
On Cuauhtémoc, with Sato and another friend.
When did...
Hey Carla, who's that friend of yours the Chinese one?
Chinese...?
Over there, in the red shirt.
She is Japanese. Tomoko. She's in Liana's class. Do you meet Liana?
"Did you meet." No. Maybe later.
Introduce me to Tomoko.
Just a sec, Hama.
So, you just moved in?
Yeah, well, it took me a few days.
Finally, my uncle drove me over with the last of my stuff two days ago.
How do you like it?
It's weird not sleeping in the same bed I've always slept in. And the neighborhood...

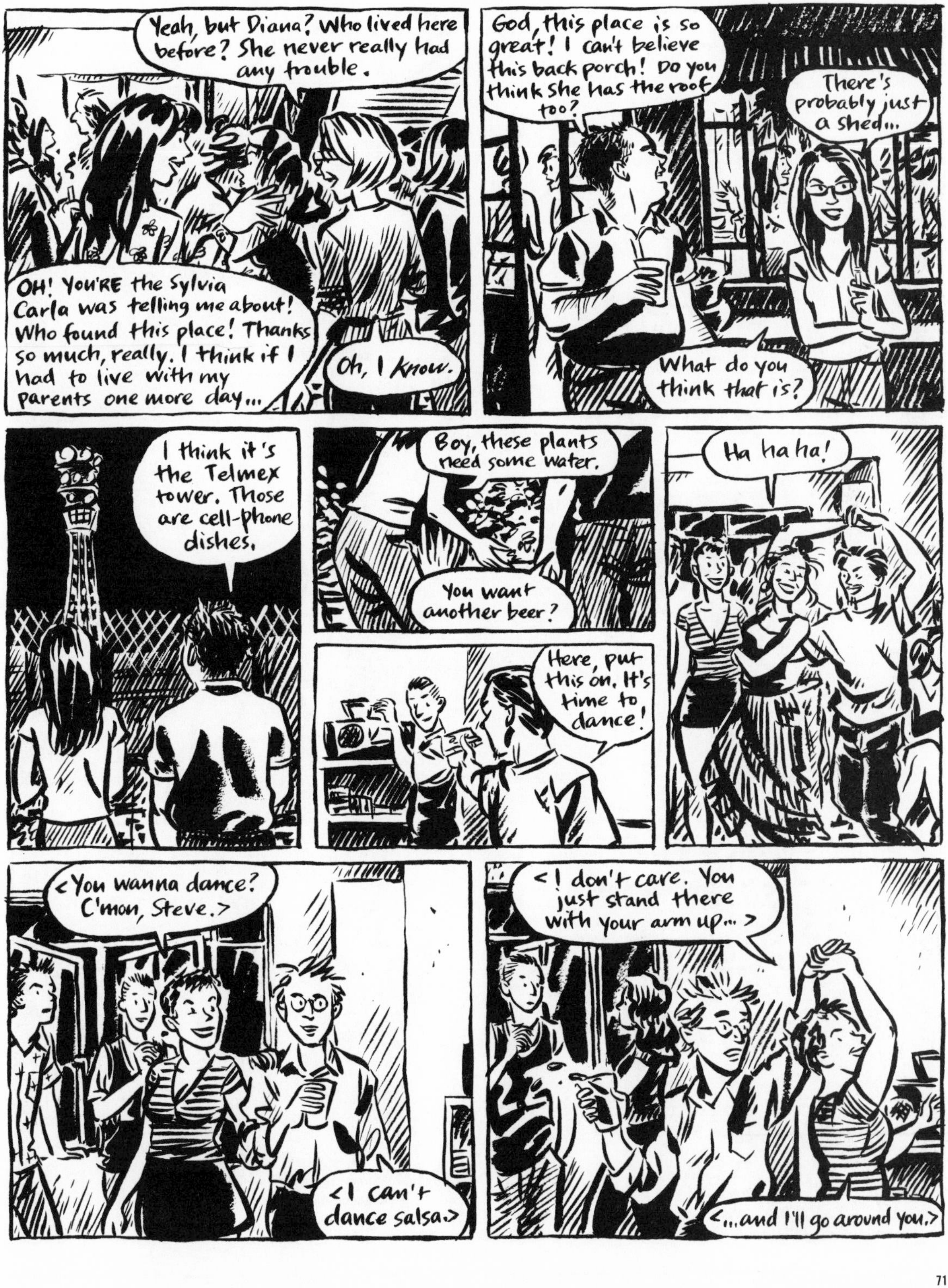
Yeah, but Diana? Who lived here before? She never really had any trouble.
OH! YOU'RE the Sylvia Carla was telling me about! Who found this place! Thanks so much, really. I think if I had to live with my parents one more day...
Oh, I know.
God, this place is so great! I can't believe this back porch! Do you think she has the roof too?
There's probably just a shed...
What do you think that is?
I think it's the Telmex tower. Those are cell-phone dishes.
Boy, these plants need some water.
You want another beer?
Here, put this on. It's time to dance!
Ha ha ha!
<You wanna dance? C'mon, Steve.>
<I can't dance salsa.>
<I don't care. You just stand there with your arm up...>
<...and I'll go around you.>

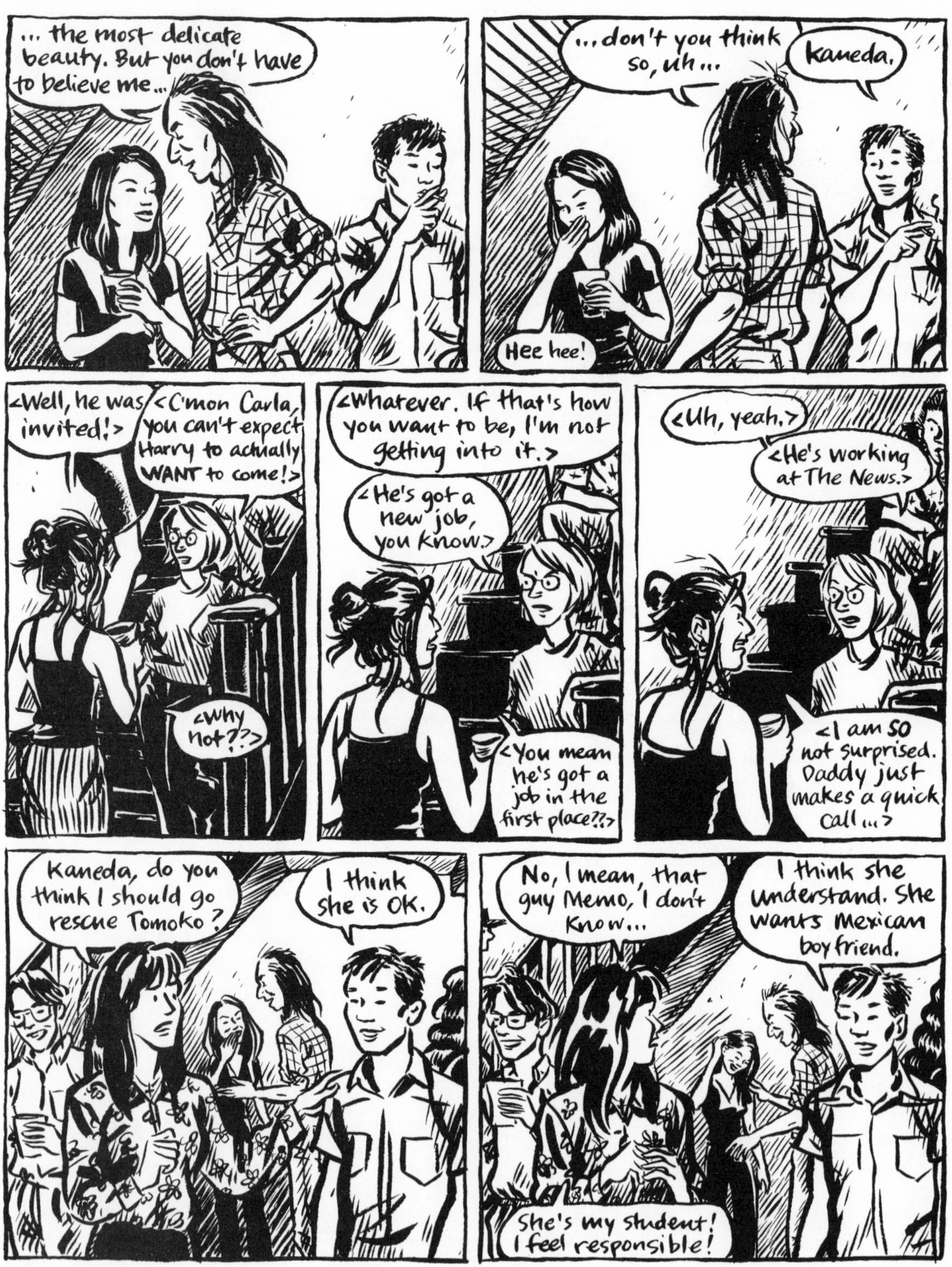
... the most delicate beauty. But you don't have to believe me...
... don't you think so, uh...
Kaneda.
Hee hee!
<Well, he was invited!>
<C'mon Carla, you can't expect Harry to actually WANT to come!>
<Why not??>
<Whatever. If that's how you want to be, I'm not getting into it.>
<He's got a new job, you know.>
<You mean he's got a job in the first place??>
<Uh, yeah.>
<He's working at The News.>
<I am SO not surprised. Daddy just makes a quick call...>
Kaneda, do you think I should go rescue Tomoko?
I think she is OK.
No, I mean, that guy Memo, I don't know...
I think she understand. She wants Mexican boy friend.
She's my student! I feel responsible!

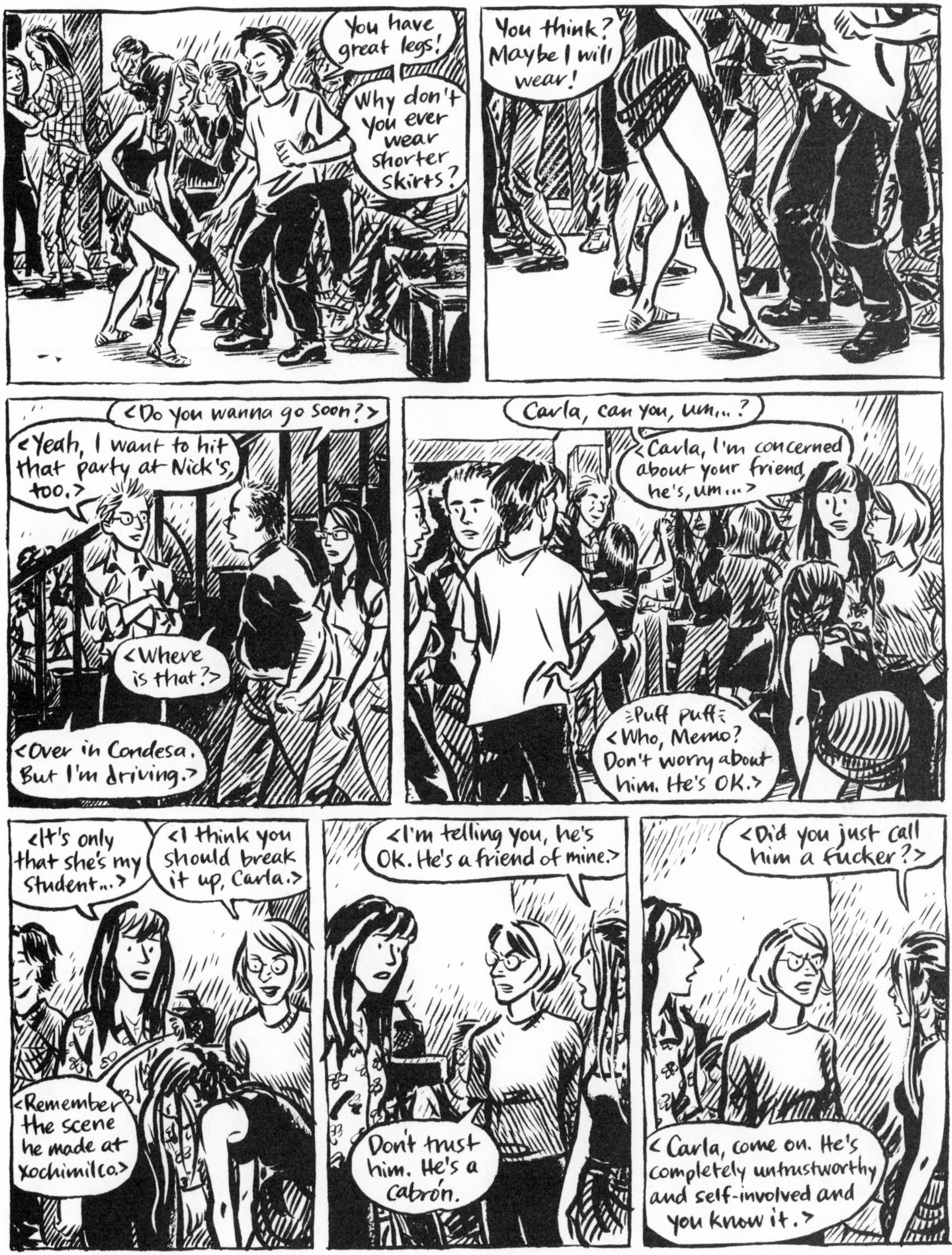
You have great legs!
Why don't you ever wear shorter skirts?
You think? Maybe I will wear!
<Do you wanna go soon?>
<Yeah, I want to hit that party at Nick's, too.>
<Where is that?>
<Over in Condesa. But I'm driving.>
Carla, can you, um...?
<Carla, I'm concerned about your friend, he's, um...>
Puff puff
<Who, Memo? Don't worry about him. He's OK.>
<It's only that she's my student...>
<I think you should break it up, Carla.>
<Remember the scene he made at Xochimilco.>
<I'm telling you, he's OK. He's a friend of mine.>
Don't trust him. He's a cabrón.
<Did you just call him a fucker?>
<Carla, come on. He's completely untrustworthy and self-involved and you know it.>

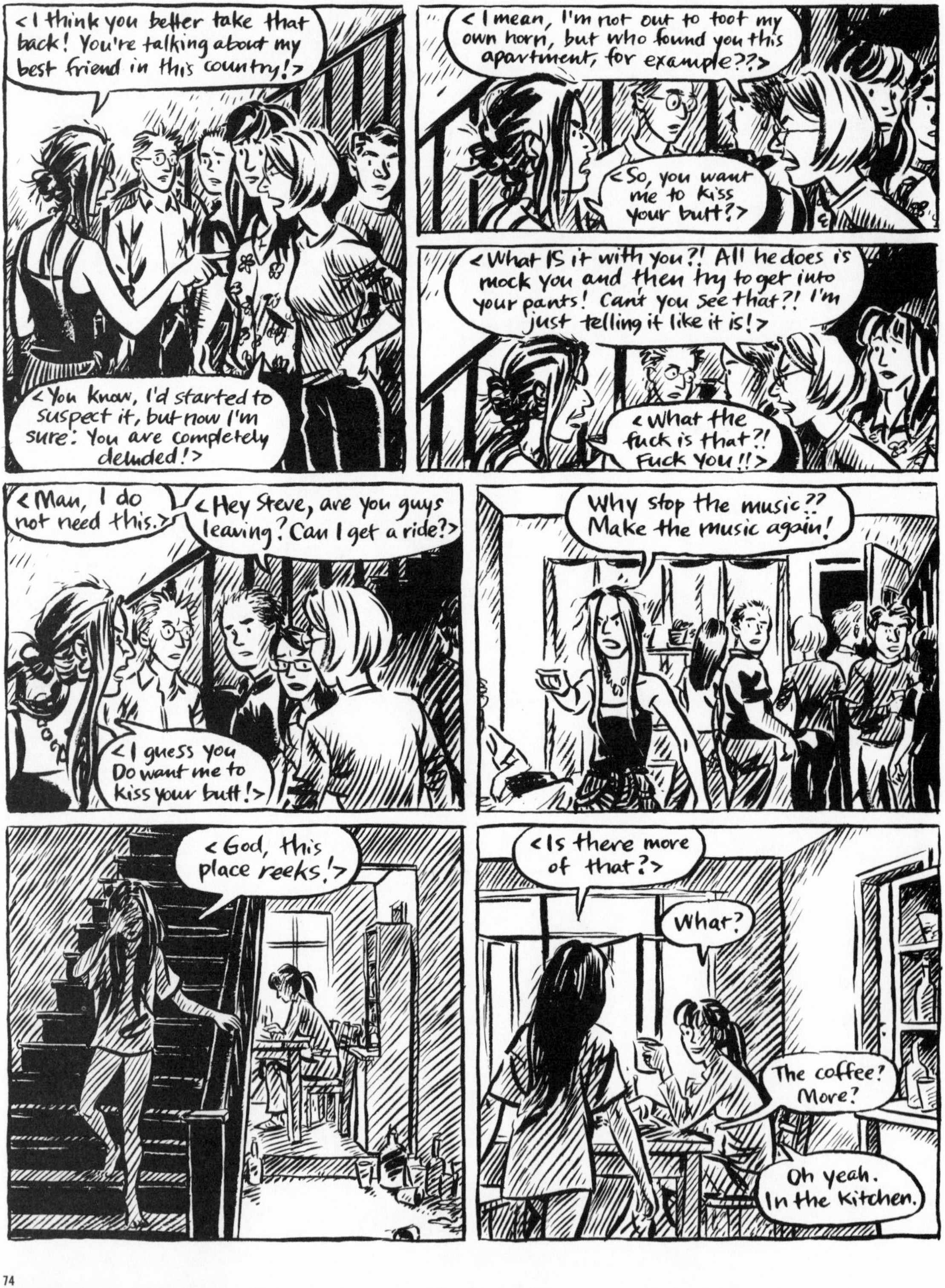
<I think you better take that back! You're talking about my best friend in this country!>
<You know, I'd started to suspect it, but now I'm sure: You are completely deluded!>
<I mean, I'm not out to toot my own horn, but who found you this apartment, for example??>
<So, you want me to kiss your butt?>
<What IS it with you?! All he does is mock you and then try to get into your pants! Can't you see that?! I'm just telling it like it is!>
<What the fuck is that?! Fuck you!!>
<Man, I do not need this.>
<Hey Steve, are you guys leaving? Can I get a ride?>
<I guess you Do want me to kiss your butt!>
Why stop the music?? Make the music again!
<God, this place reeks!>
<Is there more of that?>
What?
The coffee? More?
Oh yeah. In the kitchen.

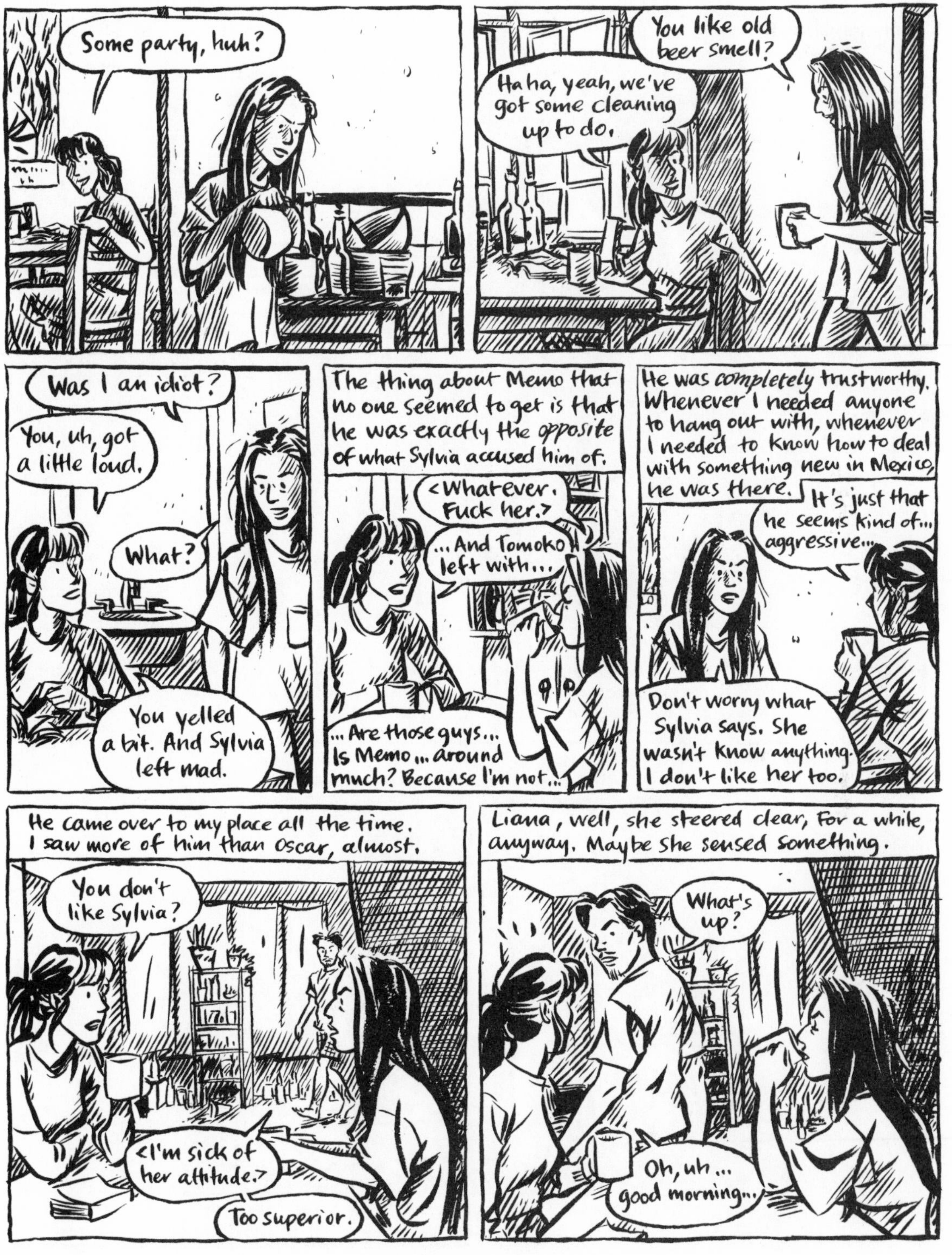

Some party, huh?
You like old beer smell?
Ha ha, yeah, we've got some cleaning up to do.
Was I an idiot?
You, uh, got a little loud.
What?
You yelled a bit. And Sylvia left mad.
The thing about Memo that no one seemed to get is that he was exactly the *opposite* of what Sylvia accused him of.
<Whatever. Fuck her.>
...And Tomoko left with...
...Are those guys... Is Memo... around much? Because I'm not...
He was *completely* trustworthy. Whenever I needed anyone to hang out with, whenever I needed to know how to deal with something new in Mexico, he was there.
It's just that he seems kind of... aggressive...
Don't worry what Sylvia says. She wasn't know anything. I don't like her too.
He came over to my place all the time. I saw more of him than Oscar, almost.
You don't like Sylvia?
<I'm sick of her attitude.>
Too superior.
Liana, well, she steered clear, for a while, anyway. Maybe she sensed something.
What's up?
Oh, uh... good morning...

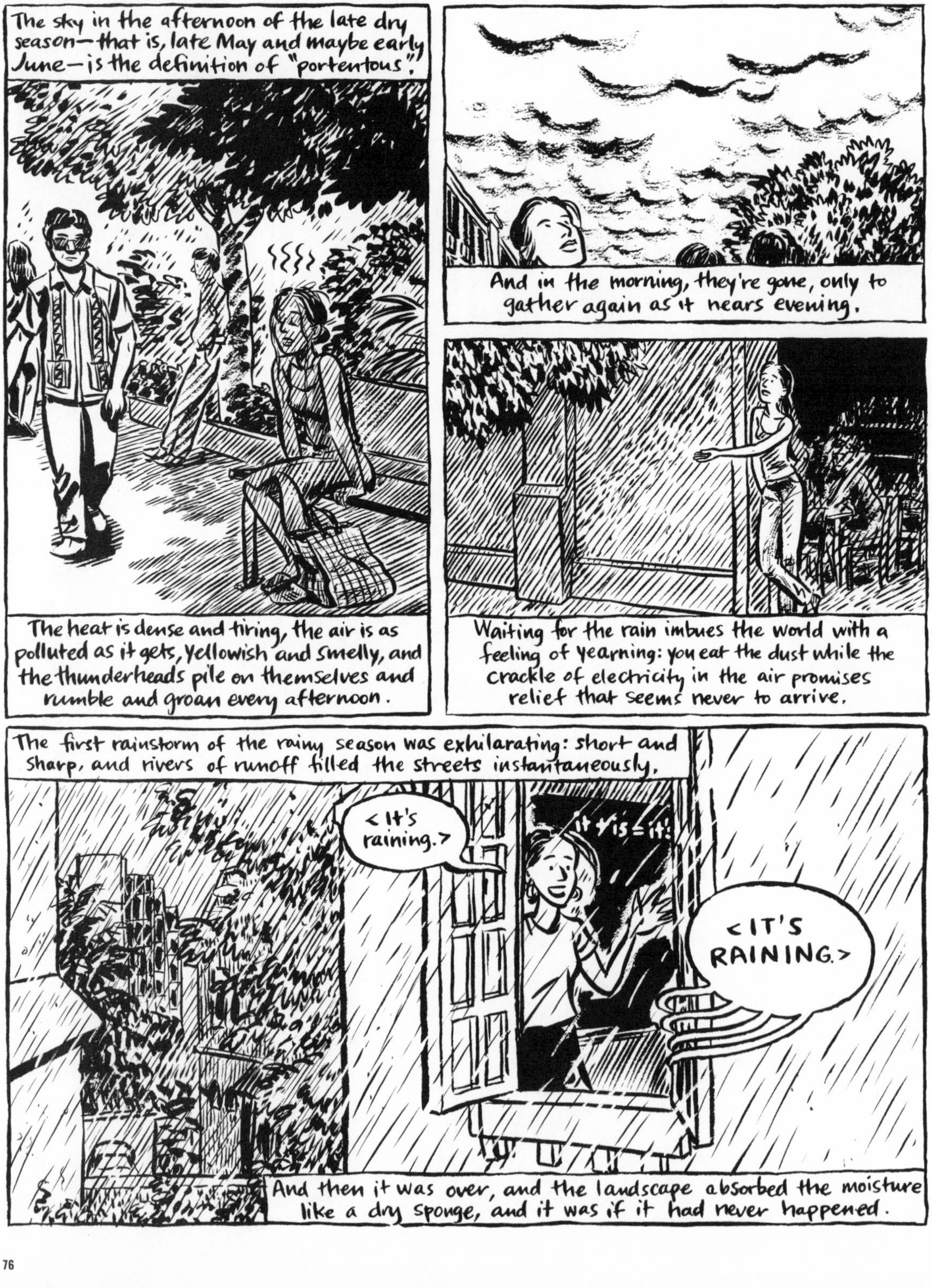
The sky in the afternoon of the late dry season—that is, late May and maybe early June—is the definition of "portentous".
The heat is dense and tiring, the air is as polluted as it gets, yellowish and smelly, and the thunderheads pile on themselves and rumble and groan every afternoon.
And in the morning, they're gone, only to gather again as it nears evening.
Waiting for the rain imbues the world with a feeling of yearning: you eat the dust while the crackle of electricity in the air promises relief that seems never to arrive.
The first rainstorm of the rainy season was exhilarating: short and sharp, and rivers of runoff filled the streets instantaneously.
<It's raining.>
<IT'S RAINING.>
And then it was over, and the landscape absorbed the moisture like a dry sponge, and it was if it had never happened.

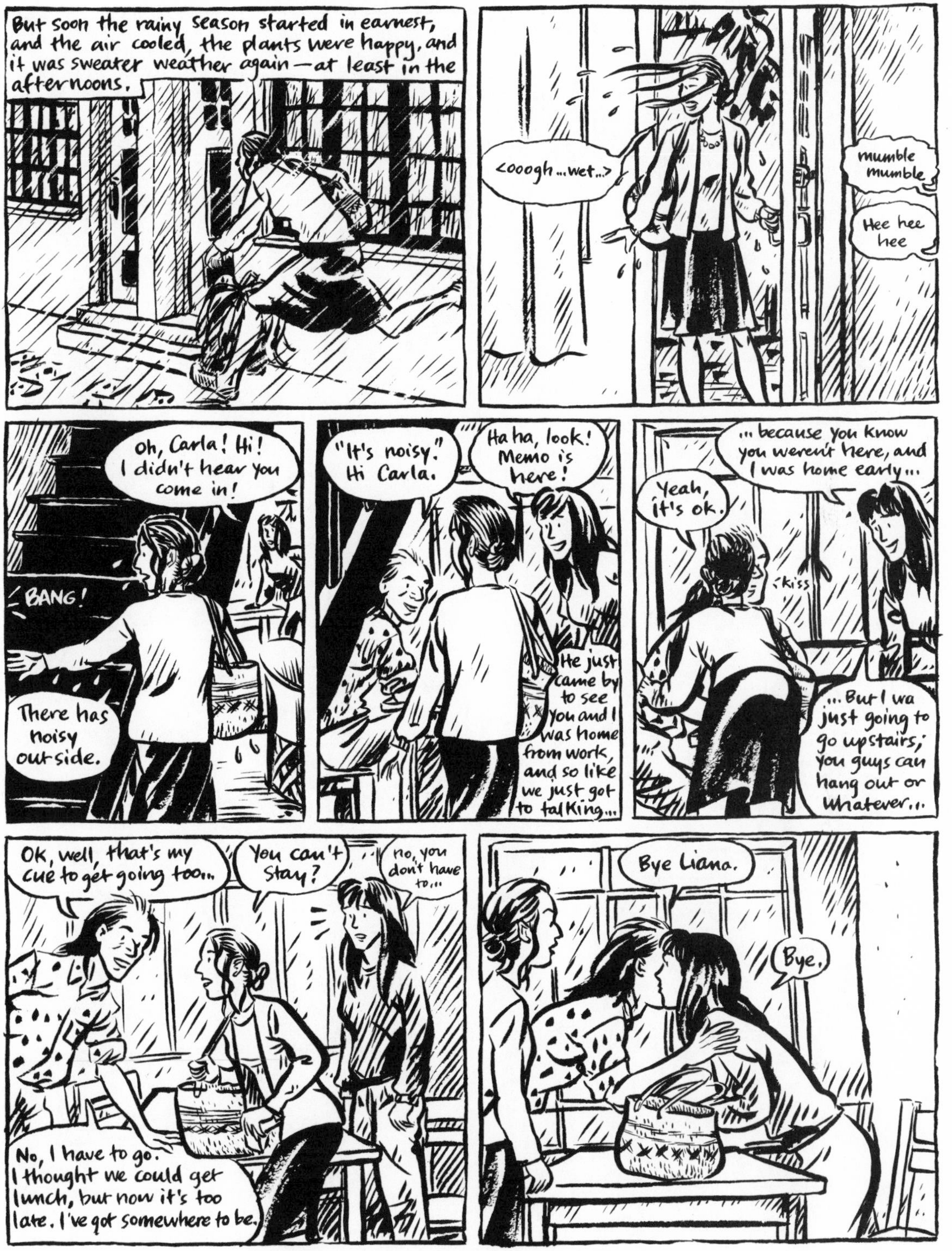
But soon the rainy season started in earnest, and the air cooled, the plants were happy, and it was sweater weather again—at least in the afternoons.
<ooogh...wet...>
mumble mumble
Hee hee hee
Oh, Carla! Hi! I didn't hear you come in!
BANG!
There has noisy outside.
"It's noisy." Hi Carla.
Ha ha, look! Memo is here!
He just came by to see you and I was home from work, and so like we just got to talking...
... because you know you weren't here, and I was home early...
Yeah, it's ok.
kiss
... But I wa just going to go upstairs; you guys can hang out or whatever...
Ok, well, that's my cue to get going too...
You can't stay?
no, you don't have to...
No, I have to go. I thought we could get lunch, but now it's too late. I've got somewhere to be.
Bye Liana.
Bye.

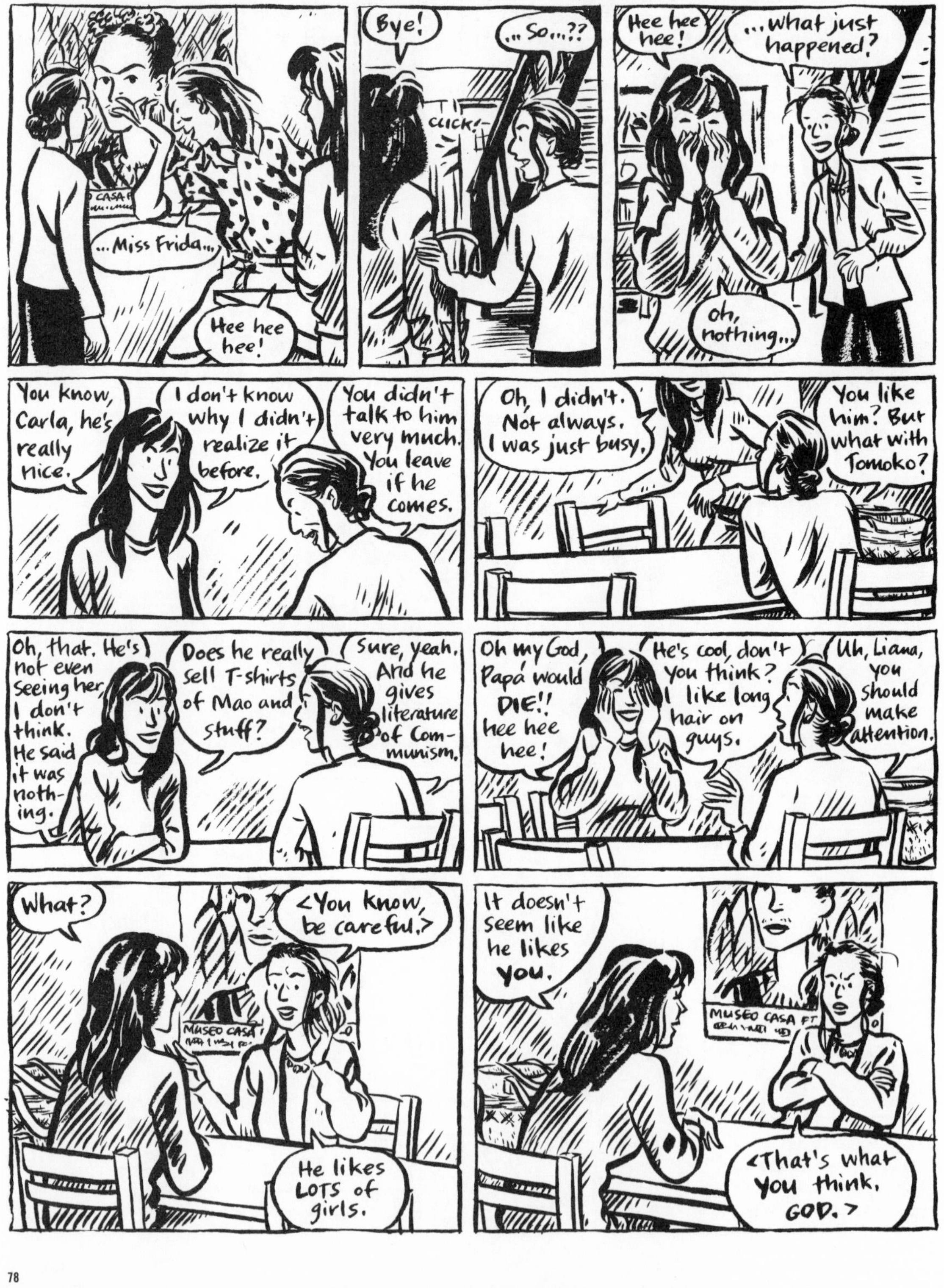
...Miss Frida...
Hee hee hee!
Bye!
...So...??
CLICK!
Hee hee hee!
...what just happened?
oh, nothing...
You know, Carla, he's really nice.
I don't know why I didn't realize it before.
You didn't talk to him very much. You leave if he comes.
Oh, I didn't. Not always. I was just busy.
You like him? But what with Tomoko?
Oh, that. He's not even seeing her, I don't think. He said it was nothing.
Does he really sell T-shirts of Mao and stuff?
Sure, yeah. And he gives literature of Communism.
Oh my God, Papá would DIE!! hee hee hee!
He's cool, don't you think? I like long hair on guys.
Uh, Liana, you should make attention.
What?
<You know, be careful.>
He likes LOTS of girls.
MUSEO CASA
It doesn't seem like he likes you.
MUSEO CASA
<That's what you think, GOD.>

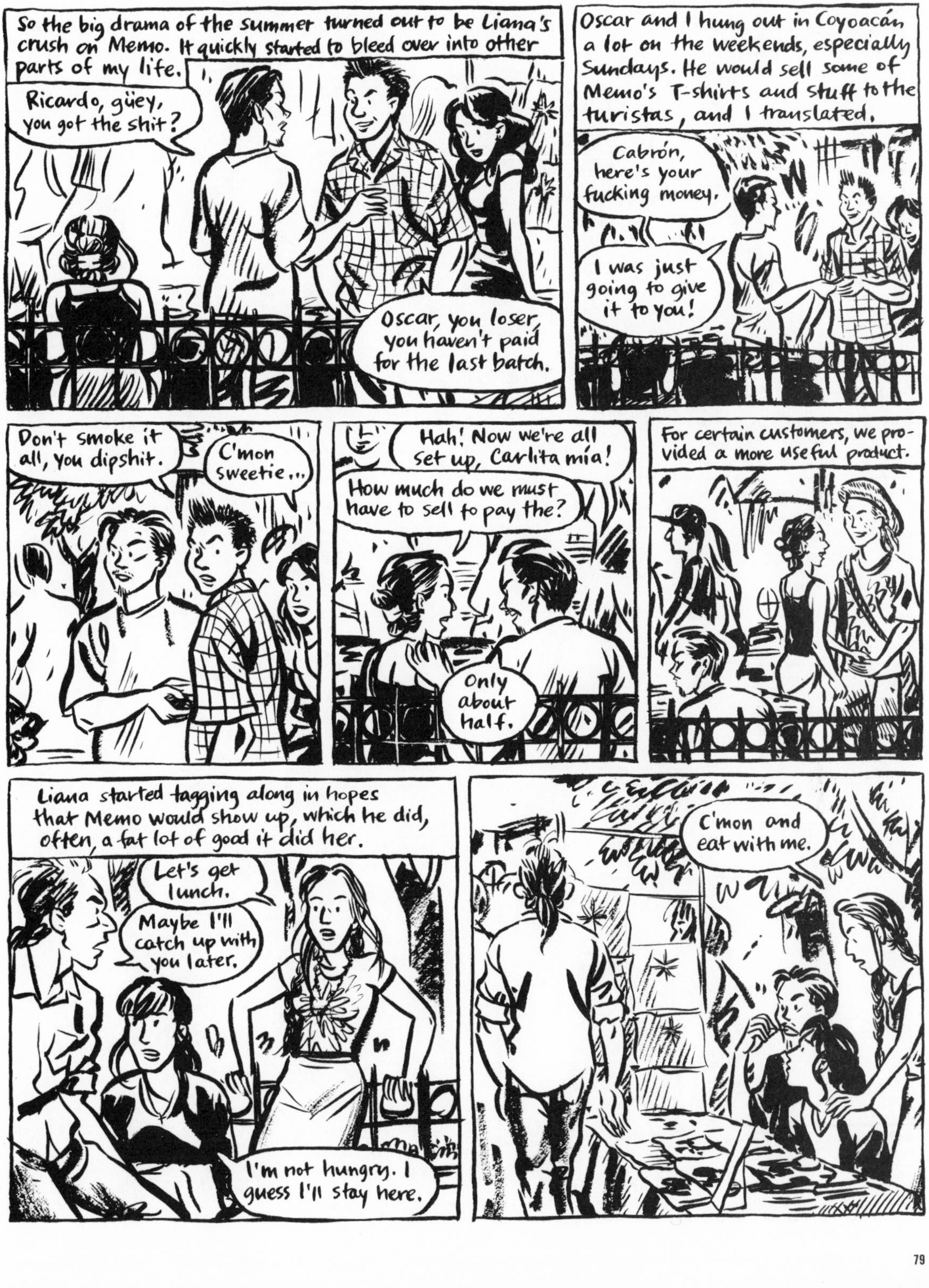
So the big drama of the summer turned out to be Liana's crush on Memo. It quickly started to bleed over into other parts of my life.
Ricardo, güey, you got the shit?
Oscar, you loser, you haven't paid for the last batch.
Oscar and I hung out in Coyoacán a lot on the weekends, especially Sundays. He would sell some of Memo's T-shirts and stuff to the turistas, and I translated.
Cabrón, here's your fucking money.
I was just going to give it to you!
Don't smoke it all, you dipshit.
C'mon sweetie...
Hah! Now we're all set up, Carlita mía!
How much do we must have to sell to pay the?
Only about half.
For certain customers, we provided a more useful product.
Liana started tagging along in hopes that Memo would show up, which he did, often, a fat lot of good it did her.
Let's get lunch.
Maybe I'll catch up with you later.
I'm not hungry. I guess I'll stay here.
C'mon and eat with me.

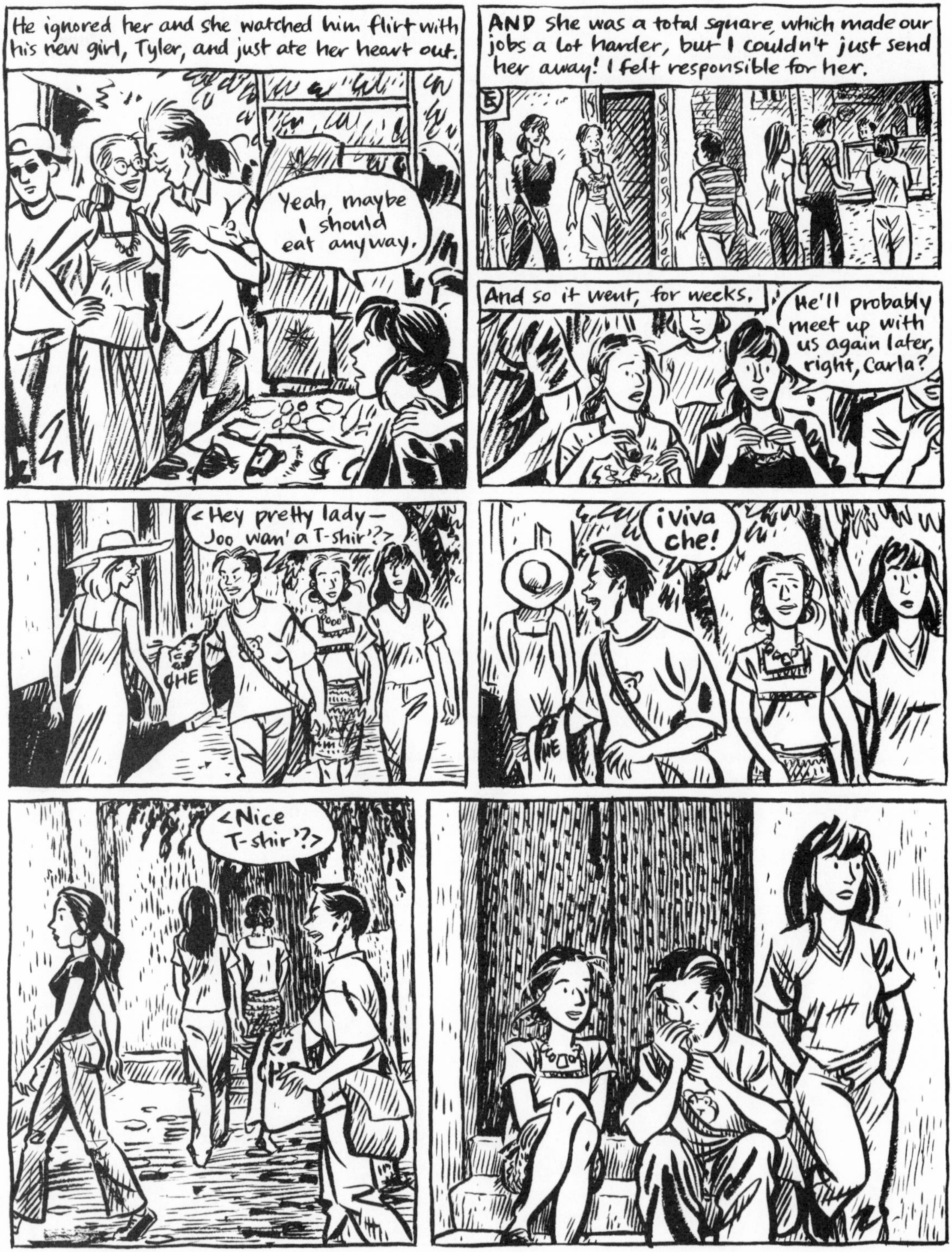
He ignored her and she watched him flirt with his new girl, Tyler, and just ate her heart out.
Yeah, maybe I should eat anyway.
AND she was a total square, which made our jobs a lot harder, but I couldn't just send her away! I felt responsible for her.
And so it went, for weeks.
He'll probably meet up with us again later, right, Carla?
<Hey pretty lady— Joo wan' a T-shir'?>
CHE
¡Viva che!
<Nice T-shir'?>

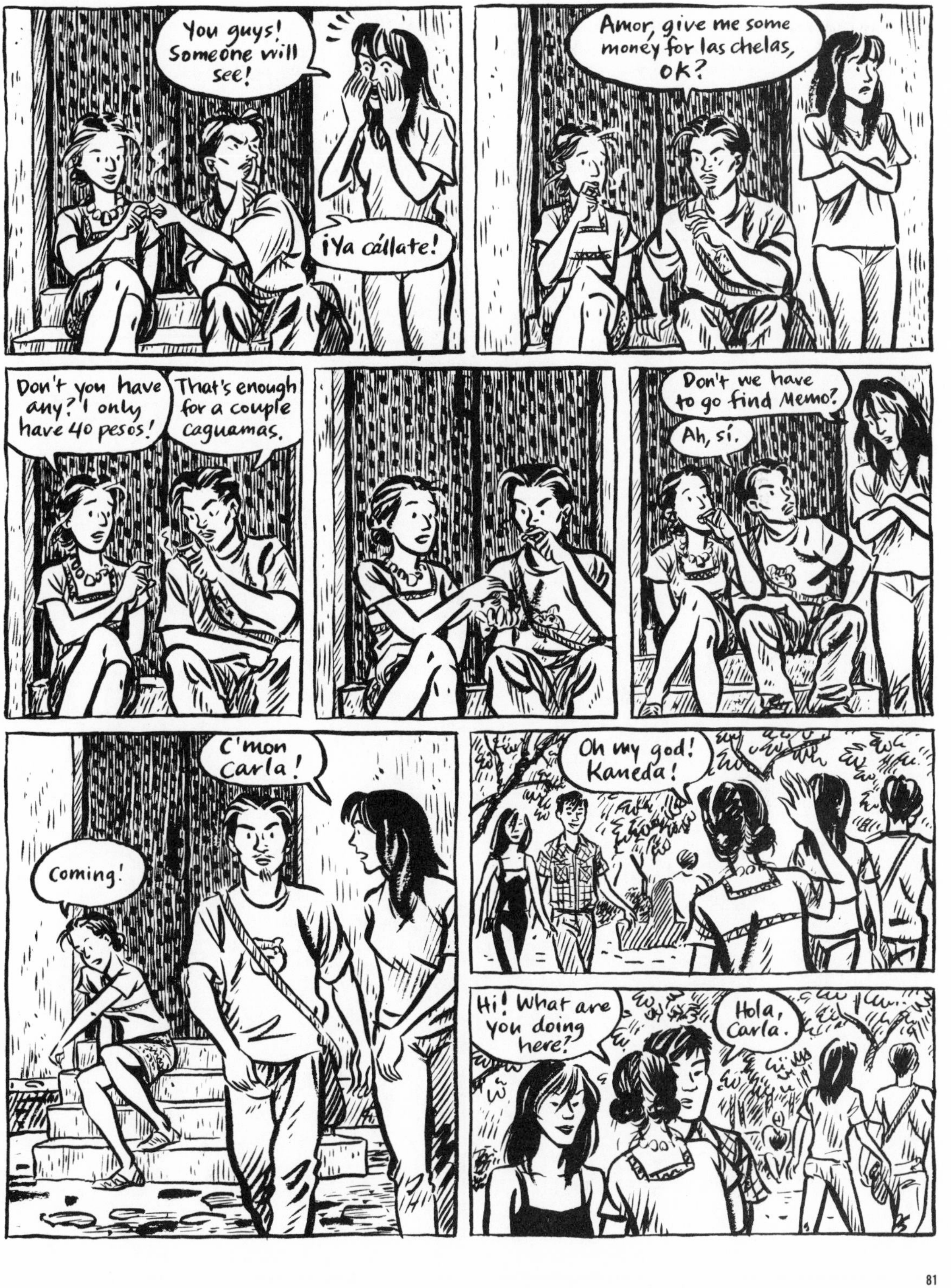
You guys! Someone will see!
¡Ya cállate!
Amor, give me some money for las chelas, OK?
Don't you have any? I only have 40 pesos!
That's enough for a couple caguamas.
Don't we have to go find Memo?
Ah, sí.
C'mon Carla!
Coming!
Oh my god! Kaneda!
Hi! What are you doing here?
Hola, Carla.

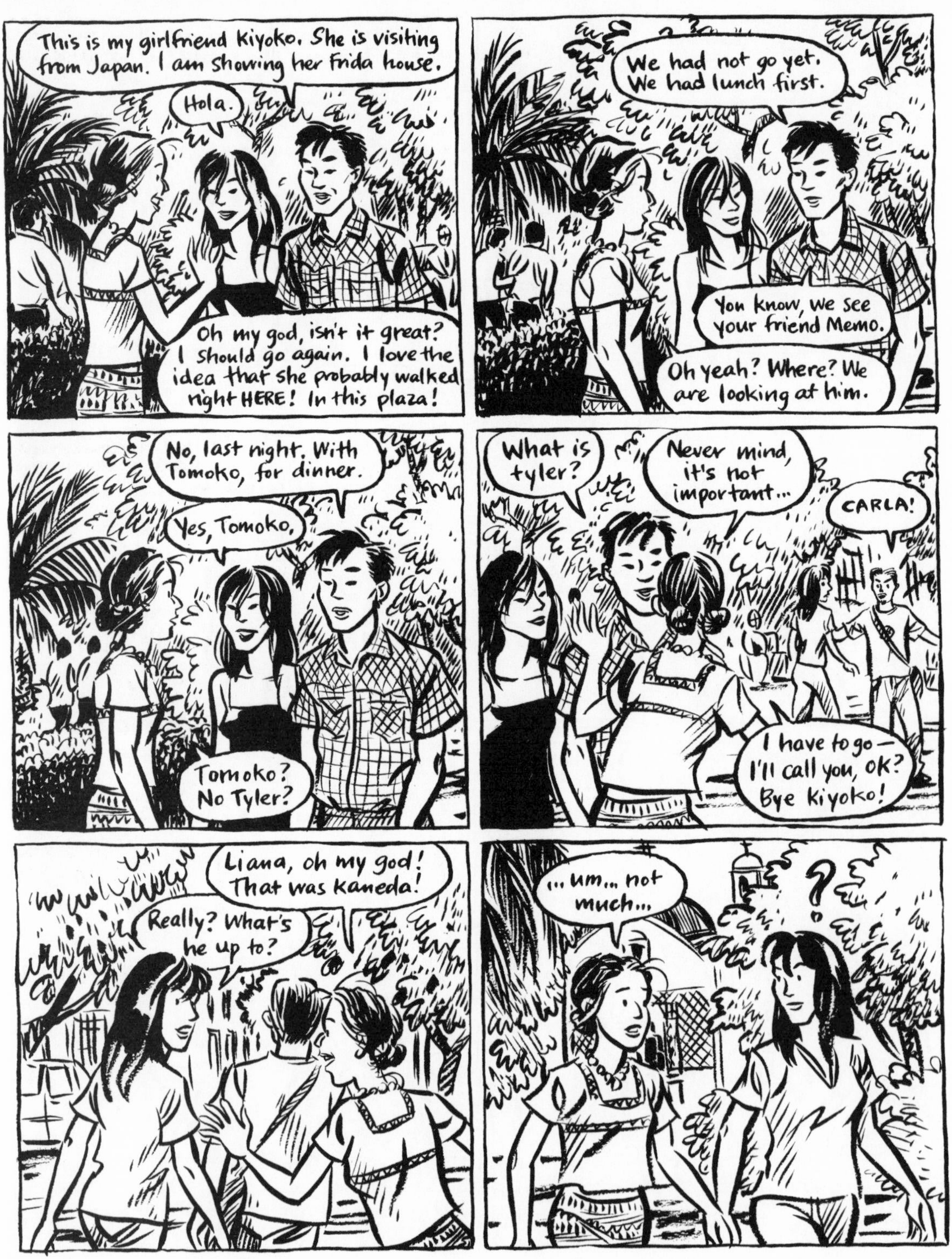

This is my girlfriend Kiyoko. She is visiting from Japan. I am showing her Frida house.
Hola.
Oh my god, isn't it great? I should go again. I love the idea that she probably walked right HERE! In this plaza!
We had not go yet. We had lunch first.
You know, we see your friend Memo.
Oh yeah? Where? We are looking at him.
No, last night. With Tomoko, for dinner.
Yes, Tomoko.
Tomoko? No Tyler?
What is tyler?
Never mind, it's not important...
CARLA!
I have to go— I'll call you, OK? Bye Kiyoko!
Liana, oh my god! That was Kaneda!
Really? What's he up to?
...um... not much...
?

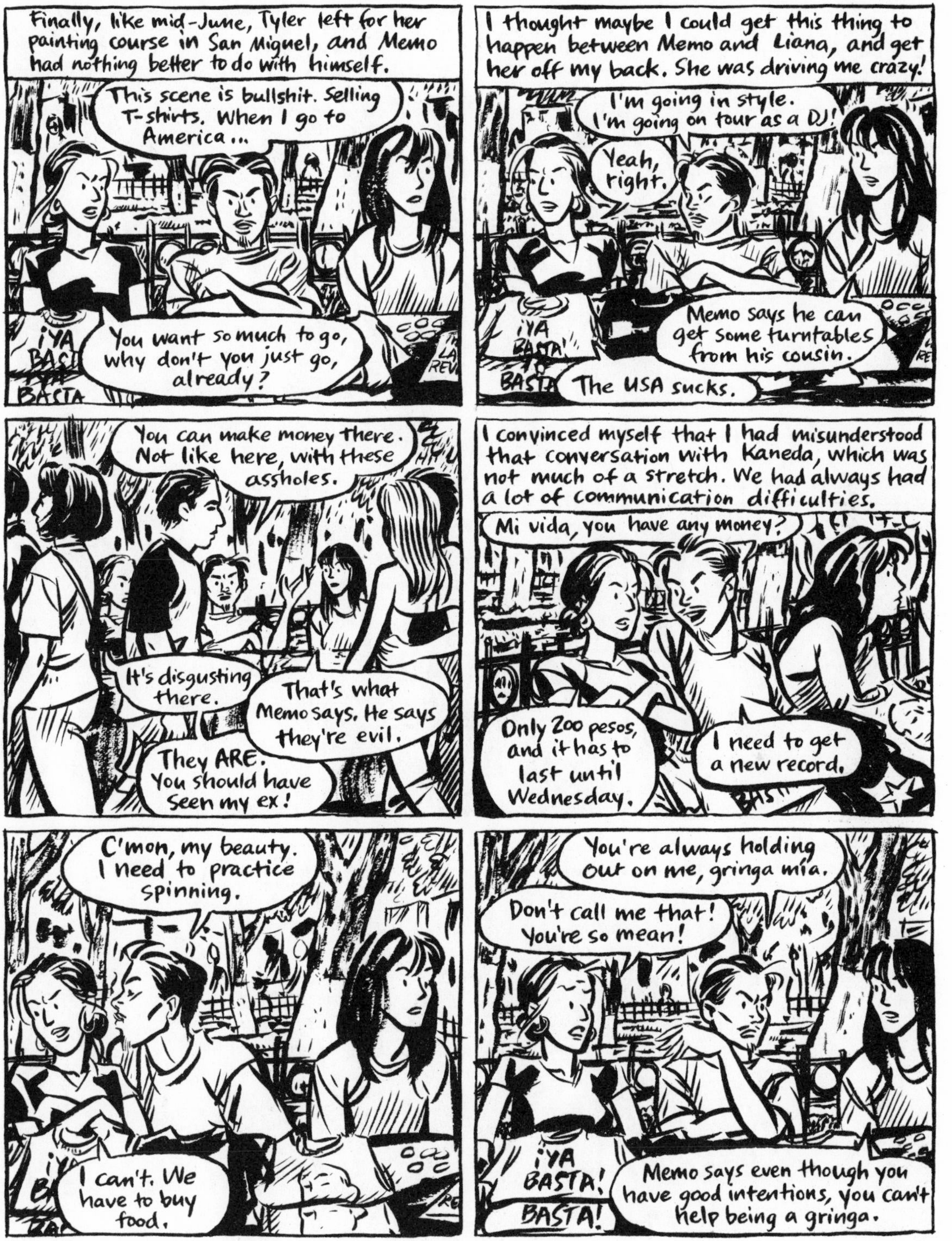
Finally, like mid-June, Tyler left for her painting course in San Miguel, and Memo had nothing better to do with himself.
This scene is bullshit. Selling T-shirts. When I go to America...
You want so much to go, why don't you just go, already?
¡YA BASTA
BASTA
I thought maybe I could get this thing to happen between Memo and Liana, and get her off my back. She was driving me crazy!
I'm going in style. I'm going on tour as a DJ!
Yeah, right.
Memo says he can get some turntables from his cousin.
The USA sucks.
You can make money there. Not like here, with these assholes.
It's disgusting there.
That's what Memo says. He says they're evil.
They ARE. You should have seen my ex!
I convinced myself that I had misunderstood that conversation with Kaneda, which was not much of a stretch. We had always had a lot of communication difficulties.
Mi vida, you have any money?
Only 200 pesos, and it has to last until Wednesday.
I need to get a new record.
C'mon, my beauty. I need to practice spinning.
I can't. We have to buy food.
You're always holding out on me, gringa mía.
Don't call me that! You're so mean!
¡YA BASTA!
BASTA!
Memo says even though you have good intentions, you can't help being a gringa.

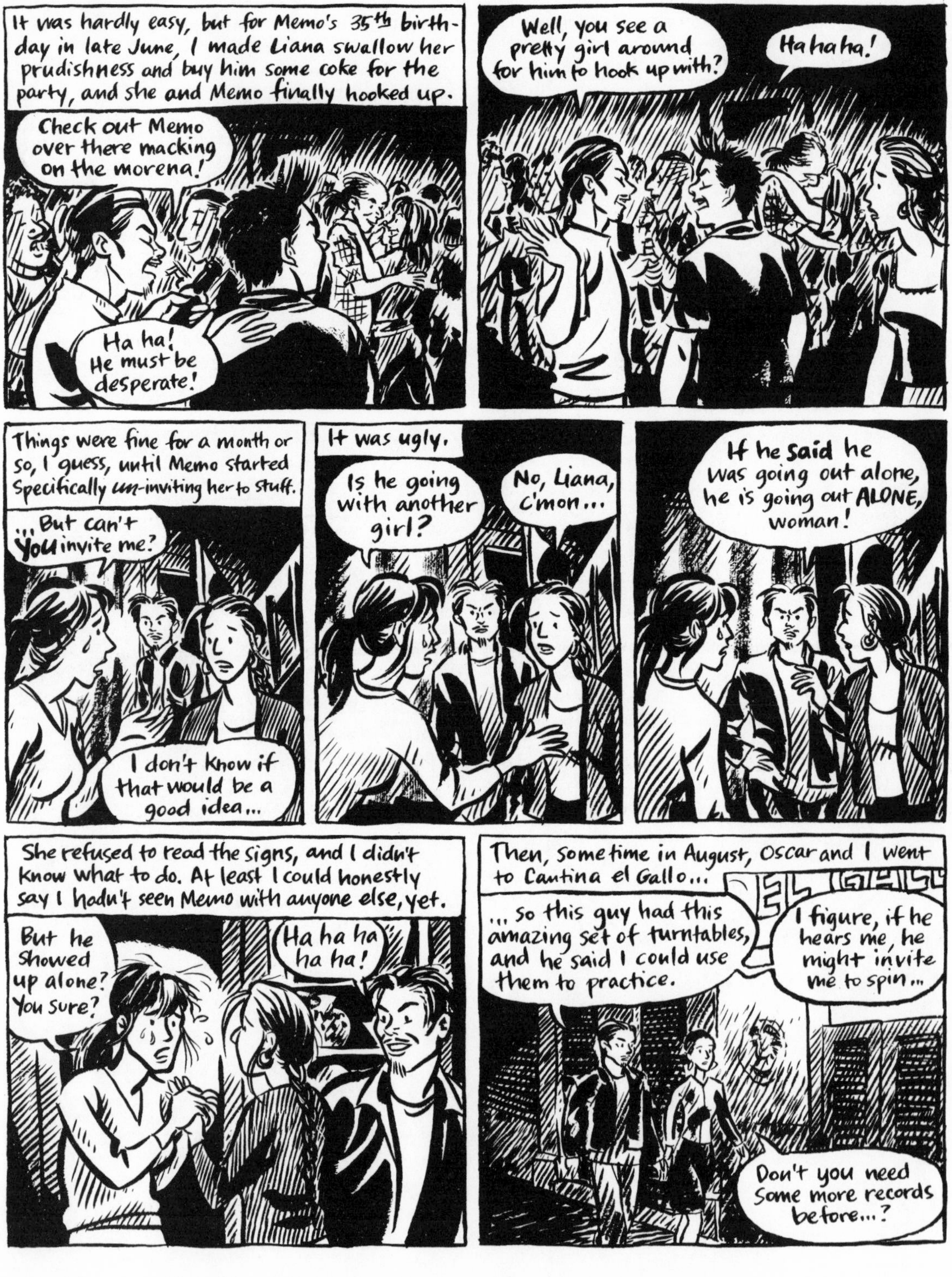
It was hardly easy, but for Memo's 35th birthday in late June, I made Liana swallow her prudishness and buy him some coke for the party, and she and Memo finally hooked up.
Check out Memo over there macking on the morena!
Ha ha! He must be desperate!
Well, you see a pretty girl around for him to hook up with?
Ha ha ha!
Things were fine for a month or so, I guess, until Memo started specifically un-inviting her to stuff.
... But can't YOU invite me?
I don't know if that would be a good idea...
It was ugly.
Is he going with another girl?
No, Liana, c'mon...
If he SAID he was going out alone, he is going out ALONE, woman!
She refused to read the signs, and I didn't know what to do. At least I could honestly say I hadn't seen Memo with anyone else, yet.
But he showed up alone? You sure?
Ha ha ha ha ha!
Then, some time in August, Oscar and I went to Cantina el Gallo...
... So this guy had this amazing set of turntables, and he said I could use them to practice.
I figure, if he hears me, he might invite me to spin...
Don't you need some more records before...?

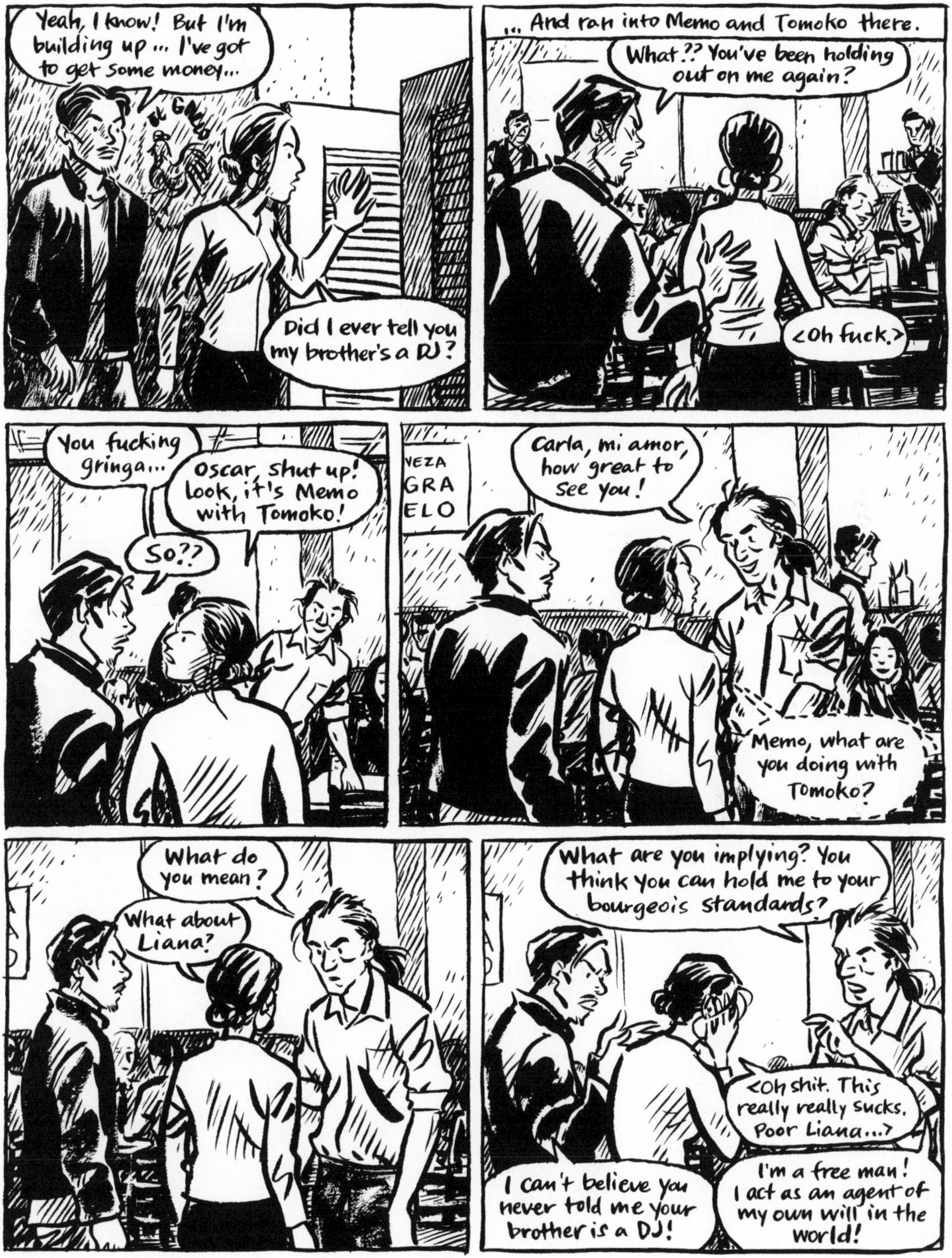
Yeah, I know! But I'm building up... I've got to get some money...
Did I ever tell you my brother's a DJ?
... And ran into Memo and Tomoko there.
What?? You've been holding out on me again?
<Oh fuck.>
You fucking gringa...
Oscar, shut up! look, it's Memo with Tomoko!
So??
VEZA
GRA
ELO
Carla, mi amor, how great to see you!
Memo, what are you doing with Tomoko?
What do you mean?
What about Liana?
What are you implying? You think you can hold me to your bourgeois standards?
<Oh shit. This really really sucks. Poor Liana...>
I can't believe you never told me your brother is a DJ!
I'm a free man! I act as an agent of my own will in the world!

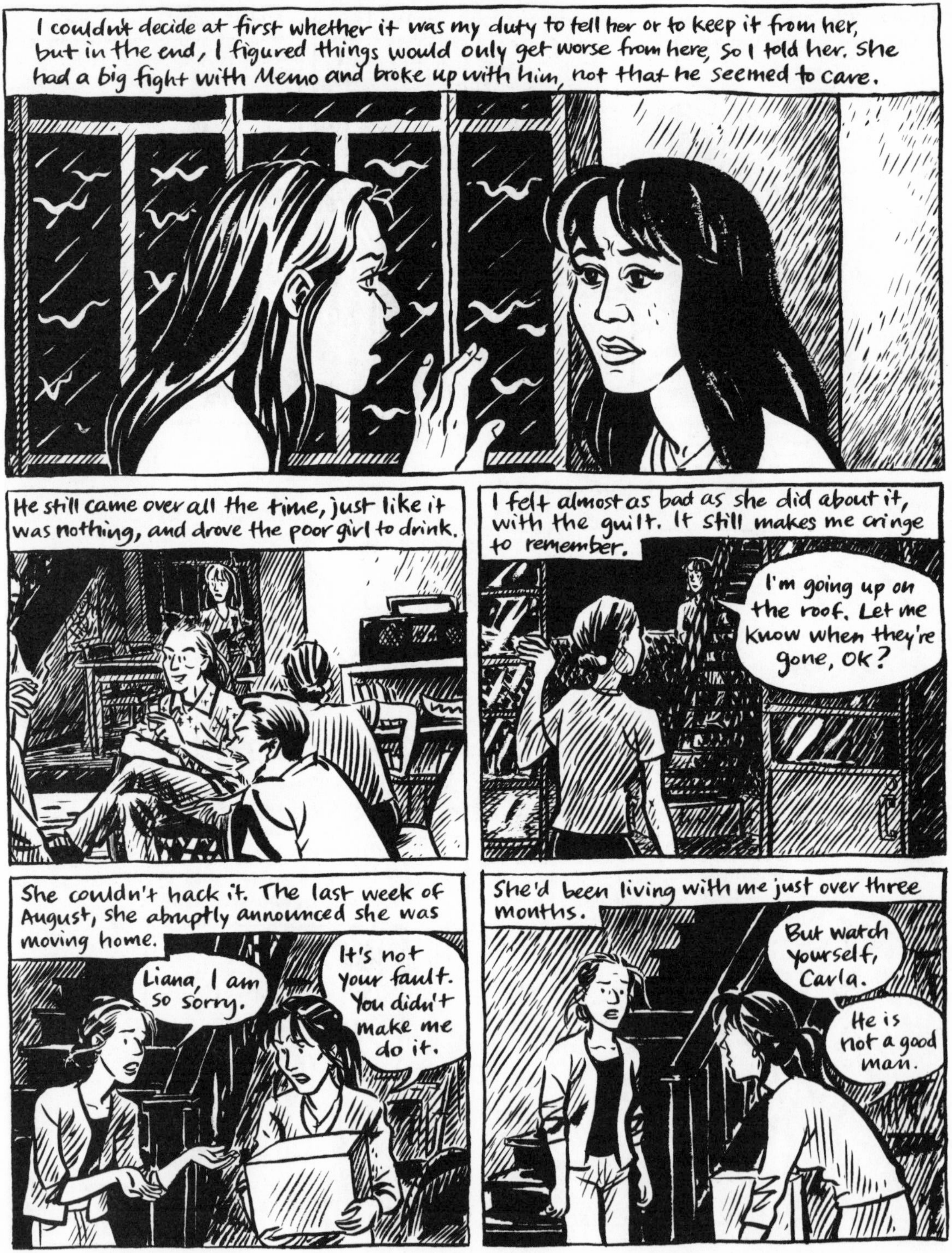
I couldn't decide at first whether it was my duty to tell her or to keep it from her, but in the end, I figured things would only get worse from here, so I told her. She had a big fight with Memo and broke up with him, not that he seemed to care.
He still came over all the time, just like it was nothing, and drove the poor girl to drink.
I felt almost as bad as she did about it, with the guilt. It still makes me cringe to remember.
I'm going up on the roof. Let me know when they're gone, OK?
She couldn't hack it. The last week of August, she abruptly announced she was moving home.
Liana, I am so sorry.
It's not your fault. You didn't make me do it.
She'd been living with me just over three months.
But watch yourself, Carla.
He is not a good man.

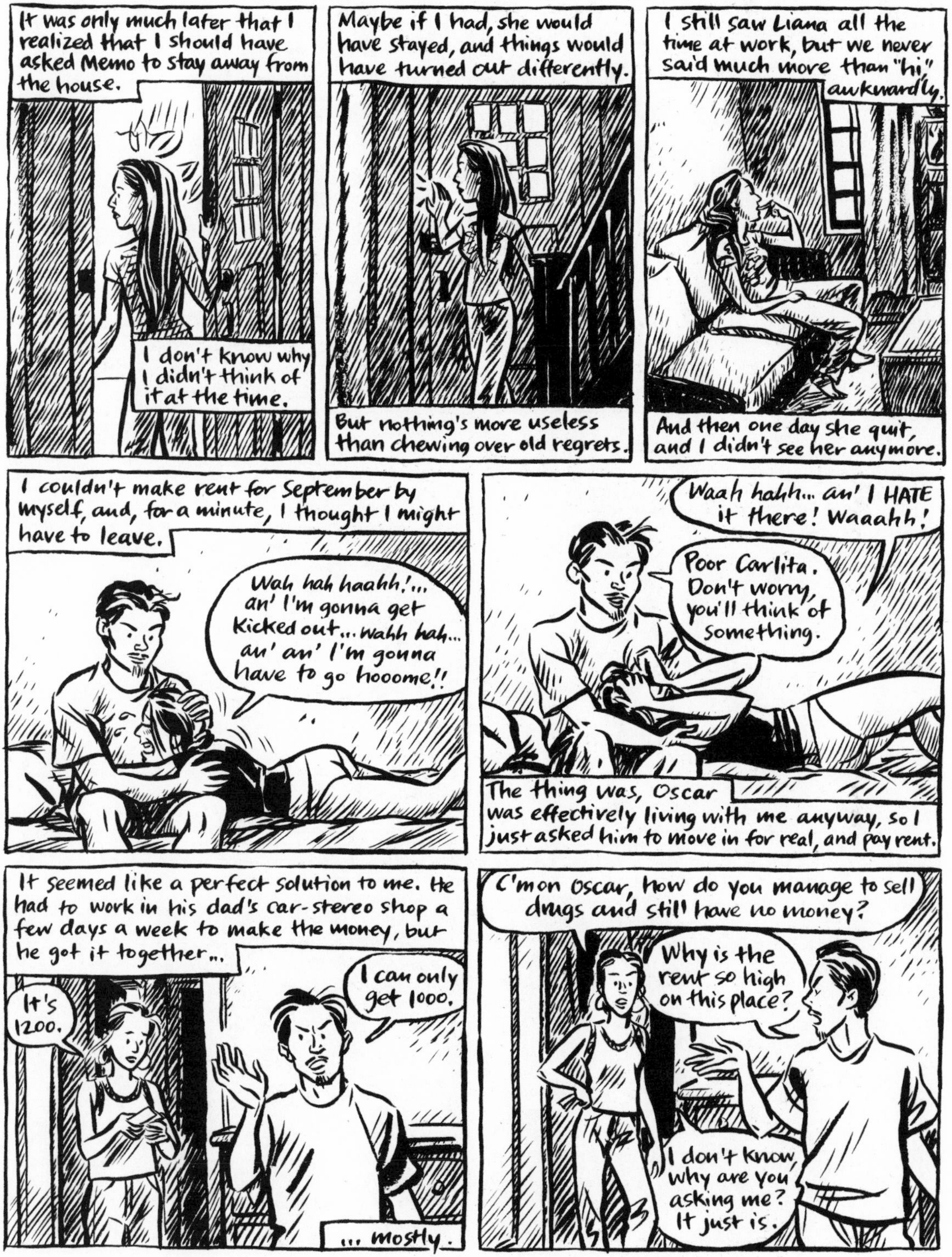
It was only much later that I realized that I should have asked Memo to stay away from the house.
I don't know why I didn't think of it at the time.
Maybe if I had, she would have stayed, and things would have turned out differently.
But nothing's more useless than chewing over old regrets.
I still saw Liana all the time at work, but we never said much more than "hi," awkwardly.
And then one day she quit, and I didn't see her anymore.
I couldn't make rent for September by myself, and, for a minute, I thought I might have to leave.
Wah hah haahh!... an' I'm gonna get kicked out... wahh hah... an' an' I'm gonna have to go hooome!!
Waah hahh... an' I HATE it there! Waaahh!
Poor Carlita. Don't worry, you'll think of something.
The thing was, Oscar was effectively living with me anyway, so I just asked him to move in for real, and pay rent.
It seemed like a perfect solution to me. He had to work in his dad's car-stereo shop a few days a week to make the money, but he got it together...
It's 1200.
I can only get 1000.
... mostly.
C'mon Oscar, how do you manage to sell drugs and still have no money?
Why is the rent so high on this place?
I don't know, why are you asking me? It just is.

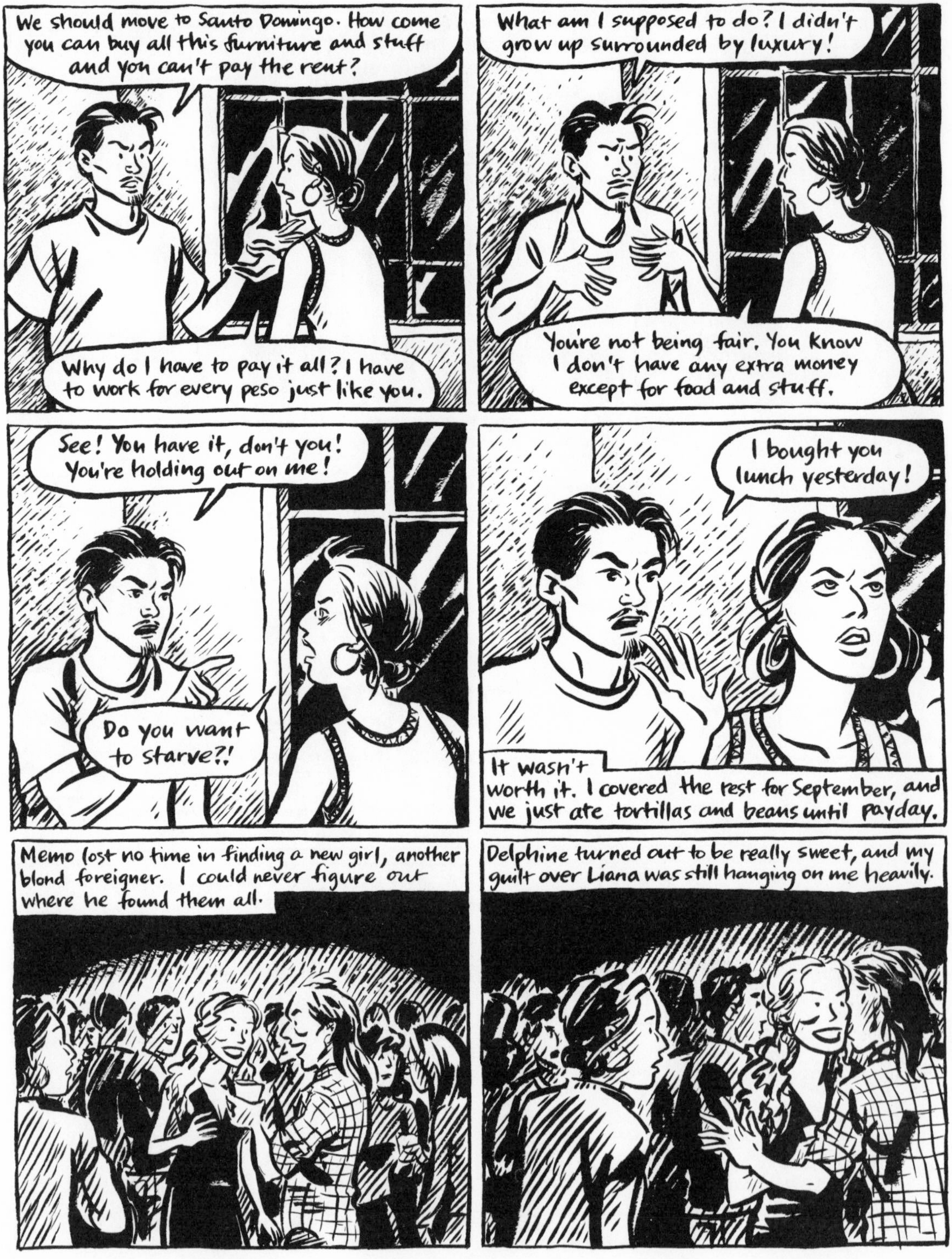

We should move to Santo Domingo. How come you can buy all this furniture and stuff and you can't pay the rent?
Why do I have to pay it all? I have to work for every peso just like you.
What am I supposed to do? I didn't grow up surrounded by luxury!
You're not being fair. You know I don't have any extra money except for food and stuff.
See! You have it, don't you! You're holding out on me!
Do you want to starve?!
I bought you lunch yesterday!
It wasn't worth it. I covered the rest for September, and we just ate tortillas and beans until payday.
Memo lost no time in finding a new girl, another blond foreigner. I could never figure out where he found them all.
Delphine turned out to be really sweet, and my guilt over Liana was still hanging on me heavily.

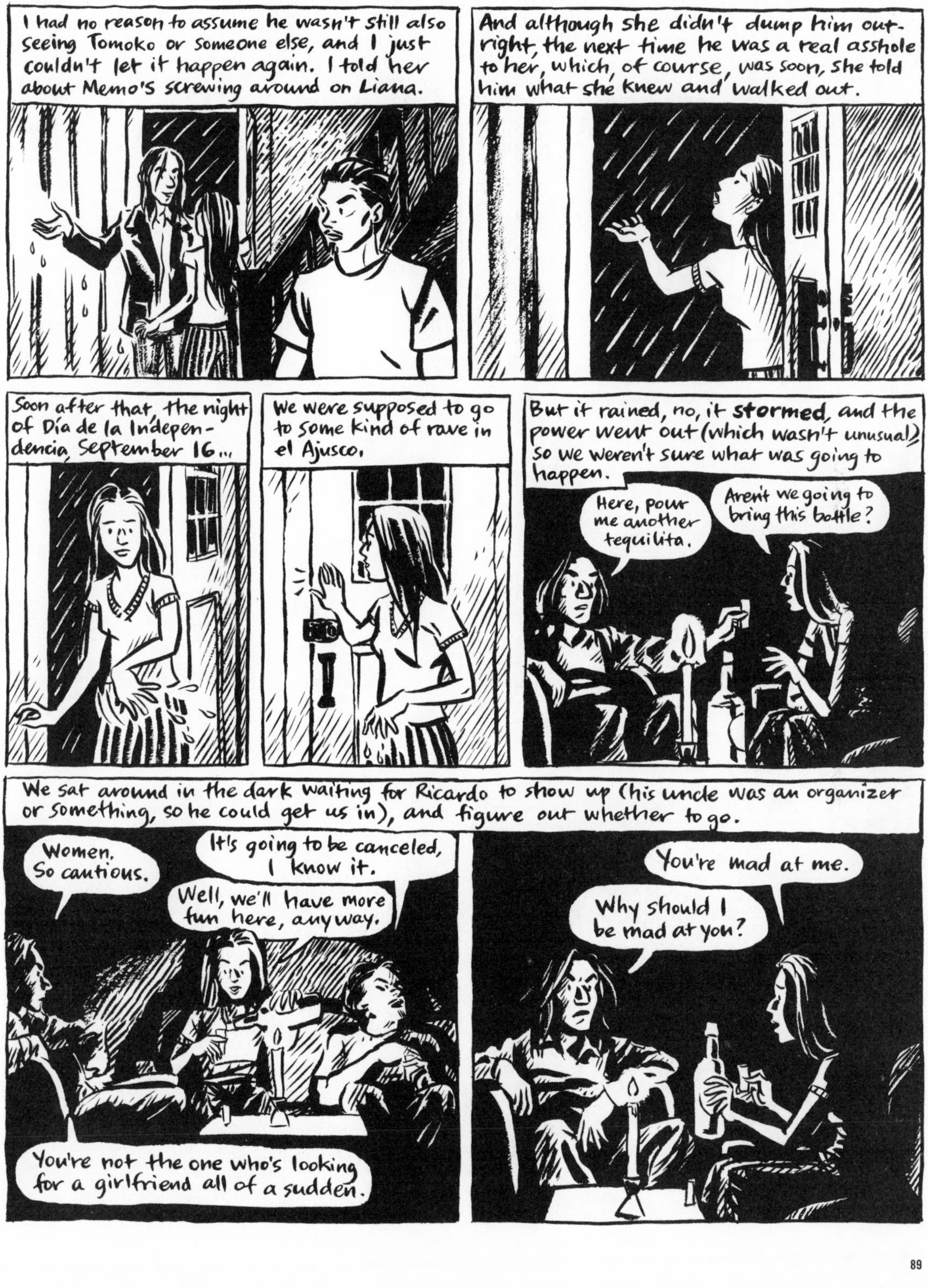
I had no reason to assume he wasn't still also seeing Tomoko or someone else, and I just couldn't let it happen again. I told her about Memo's screwing around on Liana.
And although she didn't dump him outright, the next time he was a real asshole to her, which, of course, was soon, she told him what she knew and walked out.
Soon after that, the night of Día de la Independencia, September 16...
We were supposed to go to some kind of rave in el Ajusco,
But it rained, no, it stormed, and the power went out (which wasn't unusual) so we weren't sure what was going to happen.
Here, pour me another tequilita.
Aren't we going to bring this bottle?
We sat around in the dark waiting for Ricardo to show up (his uncle was an organizer or something, so he could get us in), and figure out whether to go.
Women. So cautious.
It's going to be canceled, I know it.
Well, we'll have more fun here, anyway.
You're not the one who's looking for a girlfriend all of a sudden.
You're mad at me.
Why should I be mad at you?

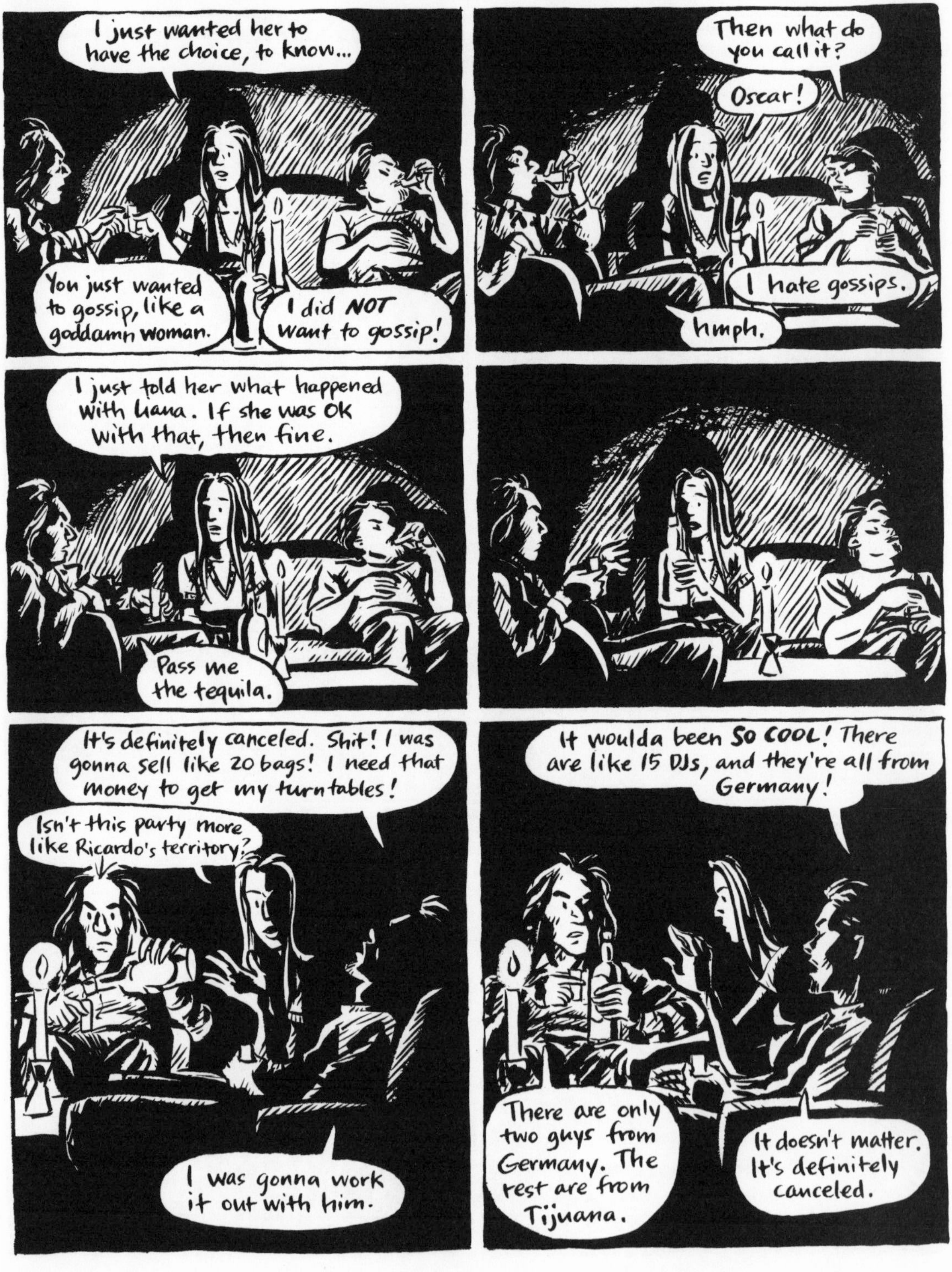
I just wanted her to have the choice, to know...
You just wanted to gossip, like a goddamn woman.
I did NOT want to gossip!
Then what do you call it?
Oscar!
I hate gossips.
hmph.
I just told her what happened with Liana. If she was OK with that, then fine.
Pass me the tequila.
It's definitely canceled. Shit! I was gonna sell like 20 bags! I need that money to get my turntables!
Isn't this party more like Ricardo's territory?
I was gonna work it out with him.
It woulda been SO COOL! There are like 15 DJs, and they're all from Germany!
There are only two guys from Germany. The rest are from Tijuana.
It doesn't matter. It's definitely canceled.

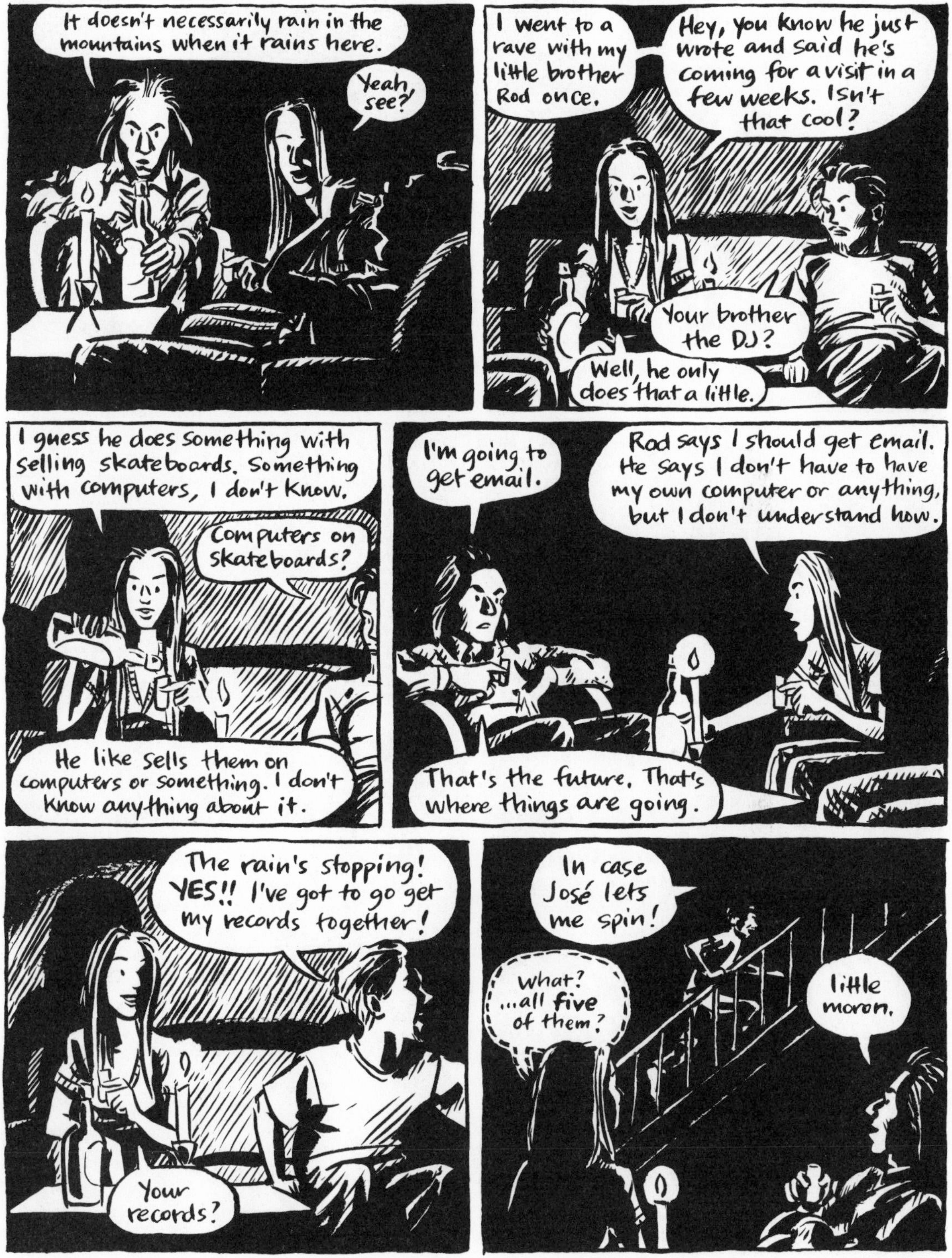

It doesn't necessarily rain in the mountains when it rains here.
Yeah, see?
I went to a rave with my little brother Rod once.
Hey, you know he just wrote and said he's coming for a visit in a few weeks. Isn't that cool?
Your brother the DJ?
Well, he only does that a little.
I guess he does something with selling skateboards. Something with computers, I don't know.
Computers on skateboards?
He like sells them on computers or something. I don't know anything about it.
I'm going to get email.
Rod says I should get email. He says I don't have to have my own computer or anything, but I don't understand how.
That's the future. That's where things are going.
The rain's stopping! YES!! I've got to go get my records together!
Your records?
In case José lets me spin!
what? ...all five of them?
little moron.

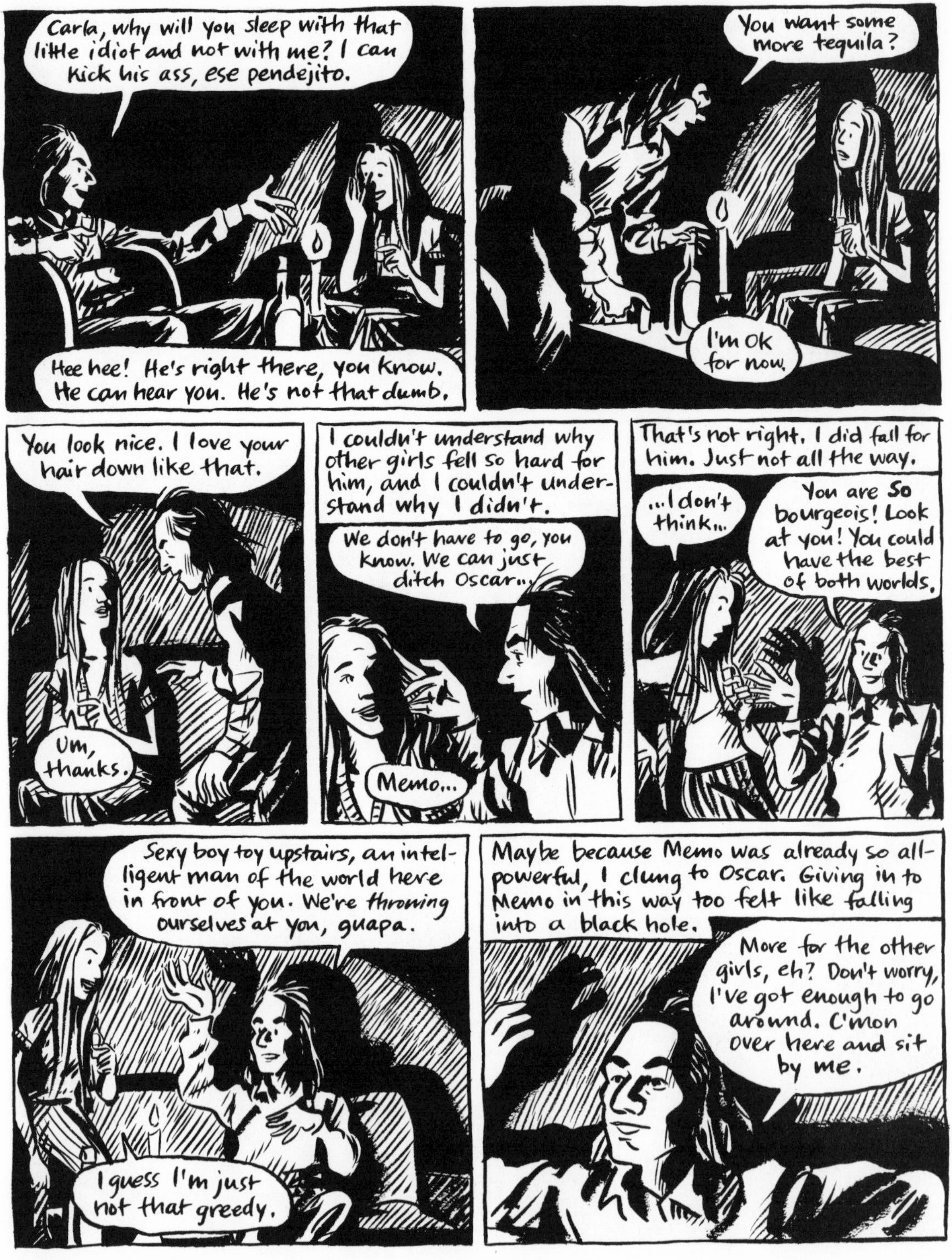

Carla, why will you sleep with that little idiot and not with me? I can kick his ass, ese pendejito.
Hee hee! He's right there, you know. He can hear you. He's not that dumb.
You want some more tequila?
I'm OK for now.
You look nice. I love your hair down like that.
Um, thanks.
I couldn't understand why other girls fell so hard for him, and I couldn't understand why I didn't.
We don't have to go, you know. We can just ditch Oscar...
Memo...
That's not right. I did fall for him. Just not all the way.
...I don't think...
You are SO bourgeois! Look at you! You could have the best of both worlds.
Sexy boy toy upstairs, an intelligent man of the world here in front of you. We're *throwing* ourselves at you, guapa.
I guess I'm just not that greedy.
Maybe because Memo was already so all-powerful, I clung to Oscar. Giving in to Memo in this way too felt like falling into a black hole.
More for the other girls, eh? Don't worry, I've got enough to go around. C'mon over here and sit by me.

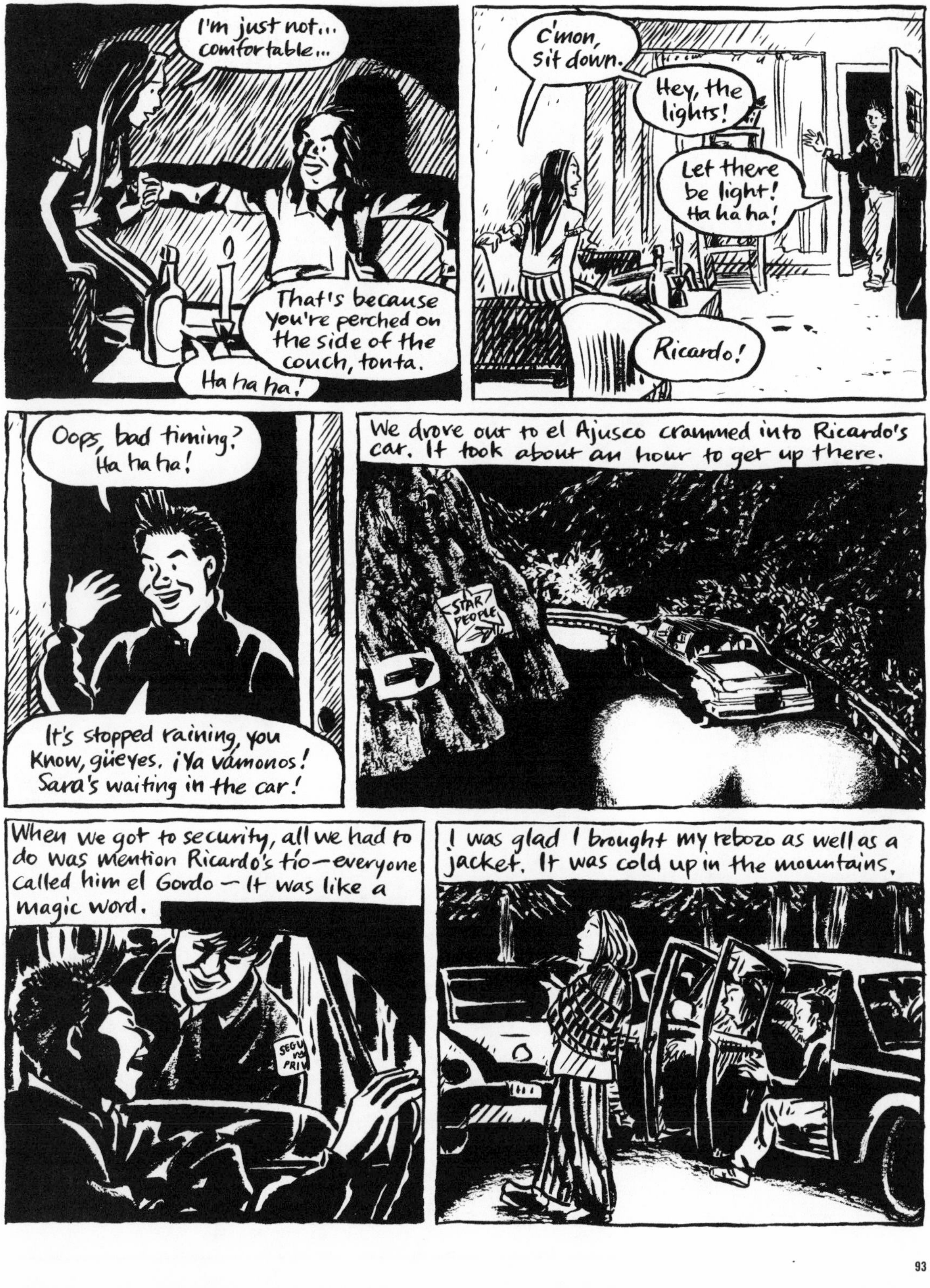
I'm just not... comfortable...
That's because you're perched on the side of the couch, tonta.
Ha ha ha!
C'mon, sit down.
Hey, the lights!
Let there be light! Ha ha ha!
Ricardo!
Oops, bad timing? Ha ha ha!
It's stopped raining, you know, güeyes. ¡Ya vámonos! Sara's waiting in the car!
We drove out to el Ajusco crammed into Ricardo's car. It took about an hour to get up there.
STAR PEOPLE
When we got to security, all we had to do was mention Ricardo's tío—everyone called him el Gordo—It was like a magic word.
I was glad I brought my rebozo as well as a jacket. It was cold up in the mountains.

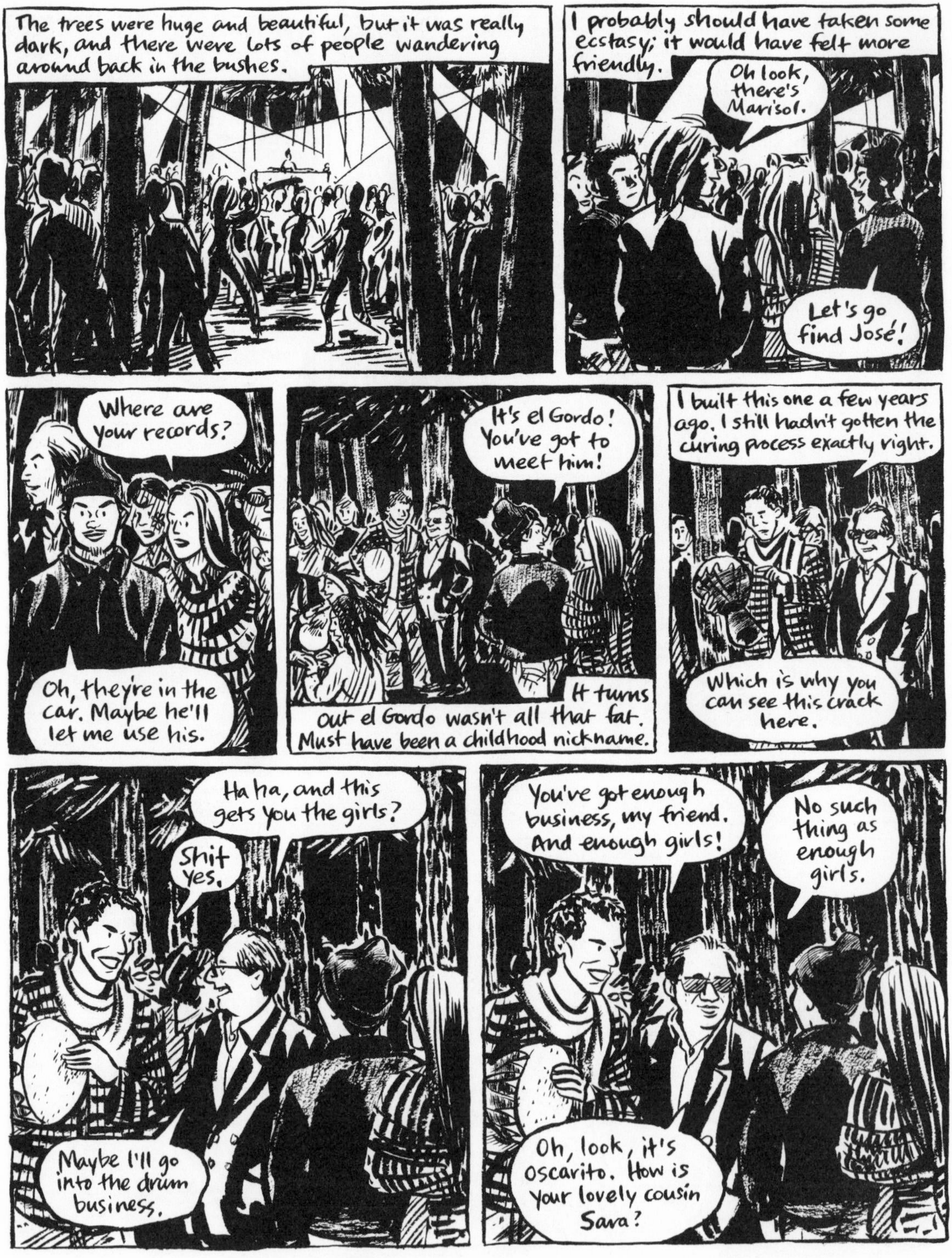
The trees were huge and beautiful, but it was really dark, and there were lots of people wandering around back in the bushes.
I probably should have taken some ecstasy; it would have felt more friendly.
Oh look, there's Marisol.
Let's go find José!
Where are your records?
Oh, they're in the car. Maybe he'll let me use his.
It's el Gordo! You've got to meet him!
It turns out el Gordo wasn't all that fat. Must have been a childhood nickname.
I built this one a few years ago. I still hadn't gotten the curing process exactly right.
Which is why you can see this crack here.
Ha ha, and this gets you the girls?
Shit yes.
Maybe I'll go into the drum business.
You've got enough business, my friend. And enough girls!
No such thing as enough girls.
Oh, look, it's Oscarito. How is your lovely cousin Sara?

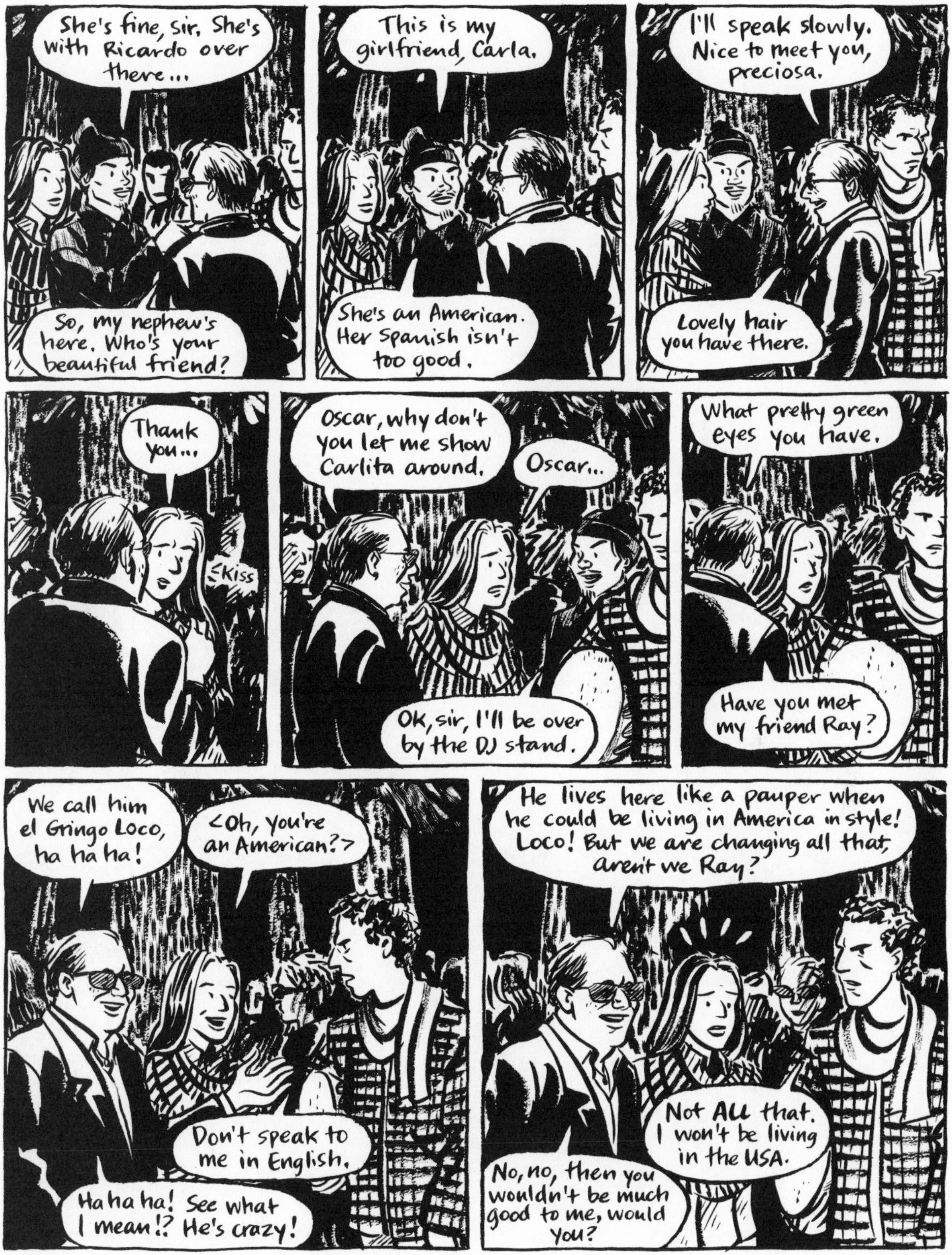
She's fine, sir. She's with Ricardo over there...
So, my nephew's here. Who's your beautiful friend?
This is my girlfriend, Carla.
She's an American. Her Spanish isn't too good.
I'll speak slowly. Nice to meet you, preciosa.
Lovely hair you have there.
Thank you...
<Kiss
Oscar, why don't you let me show Carlita around.
Oscar...
Ok, sir, I'll be over by the DJ stand.
What pretty green eyes you have.
Have you met my friend Ray?
We call him el Gringo Loco, ha ha ha!
<Oh, you're an American?>
Don't speak to me in English.
Ha ha ha! See what I mean!? He's crazy!
He lives here like a pauper when he could be living in America in style! Loco! But we are changing all that, aren't we Ray?
Not ALL that. I won't be living in the USA.
No, no, then you wouldn't be much good to me, would you?

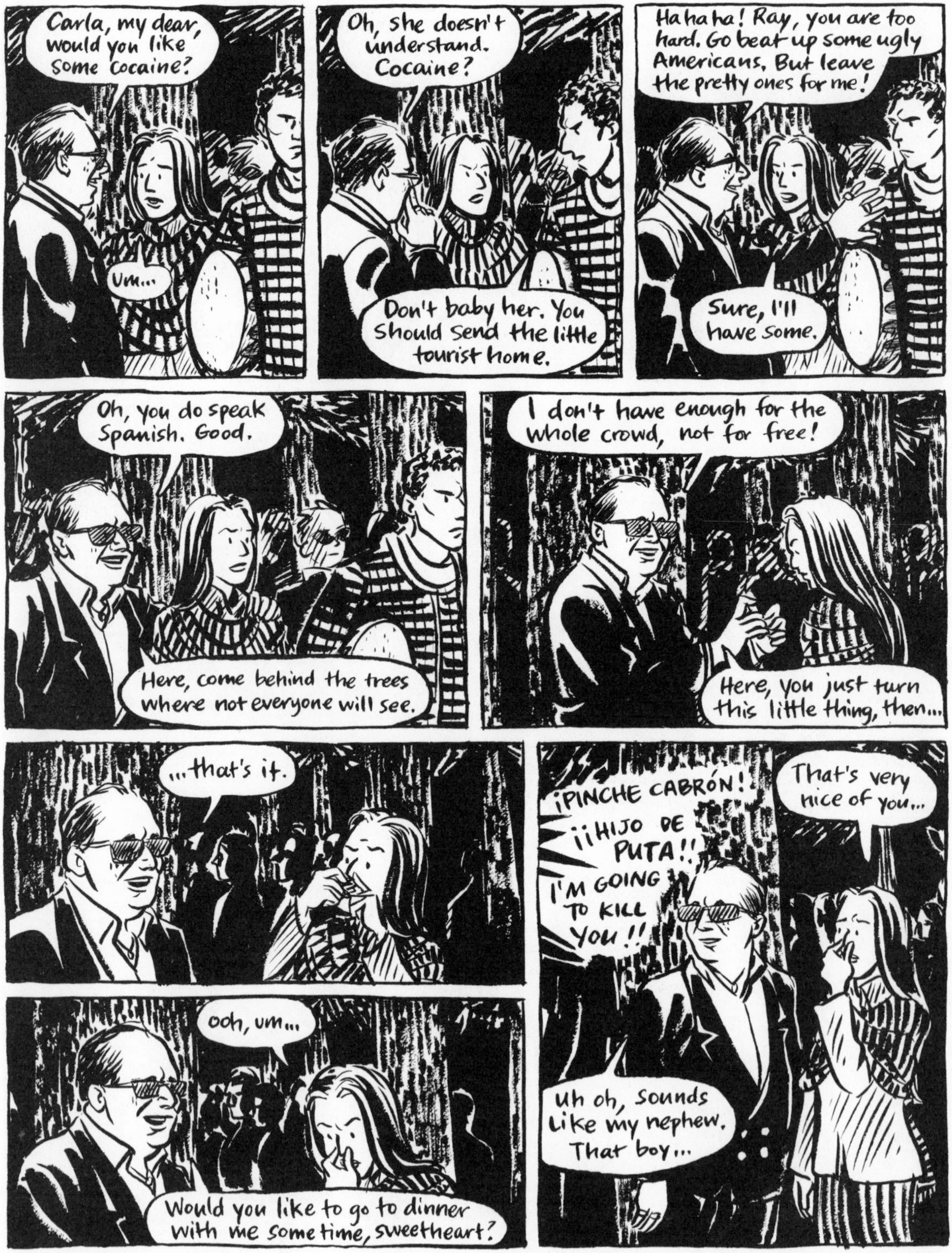
Carla, my dear, would you like some cocaine?
Um...
Oh, she doesn't understand. Cocaine?
Don't baby her. You should send the little tourist home.
Hahaha! Ray, you are too hard. Go beat up some ugly Americans. But leave the pretty ones for me!
Sure, I'll have some.
Oh, you do speak Spanish. Good.
Here, come behind the trees where not everyone will see.
I don't have enough for the whole crowd, not for free!
Here, you just turn this little thing, then...
...that's it.
ooh, um...
Would you like to go to dinner with me some time, sweetheart?
That's very nice of you...
¡PINCHE CABRÓN!
¡¡HIJO DE PUTA!!
I'M GOING TO KILL YOU!!
Uh oh, sounds like my nephew. That boy...

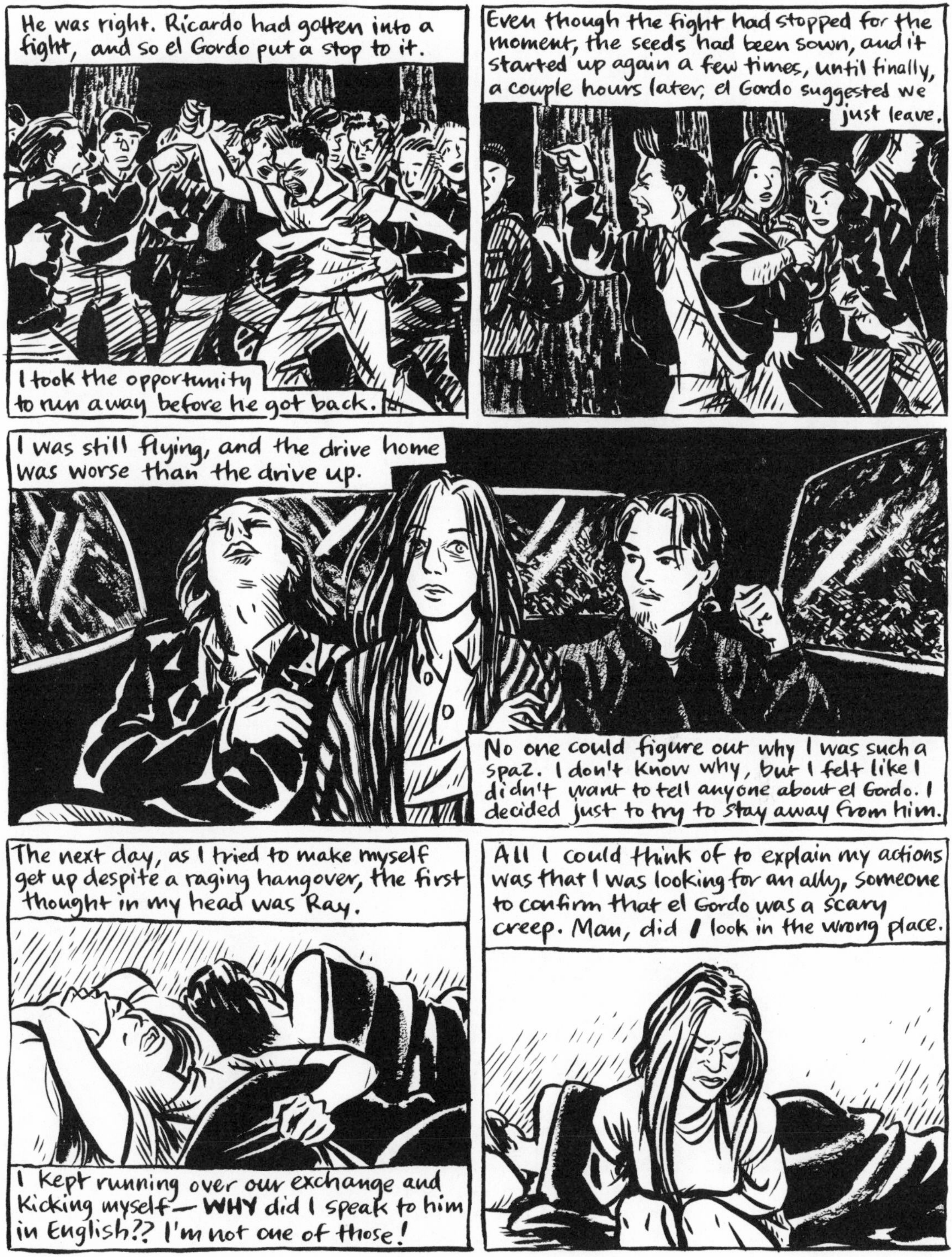
He was right. Ricardo had gotten into a fight, and so el Gordo put a stop to it.
I took the opportunity to run away before he got back.
Even though the fight had stopped for the moment, the seeds had been sown, and it started up again a few times, until finally, a couple hours later, el Gordo suggested we just leave.
I was still flying, and the drive home was worse than the drive up.
No one could figure out why I was such a spaz. I don't know why, but I felt like I didn't want to tell anyone about el Gordo. I decided just to try to stay away from him.
The next day, as I tried to make myself get up despite a raging hangover, the first thought in my head was Ray.
I kept running over our exchange and kicking myself— WHY did I speak to him in English?? I'm not one of those!
All I could think of to explain my actions was that I was looking for an ally, someone to confirm that el Gordo was a scary creep. Man, did I look in the wrong place.

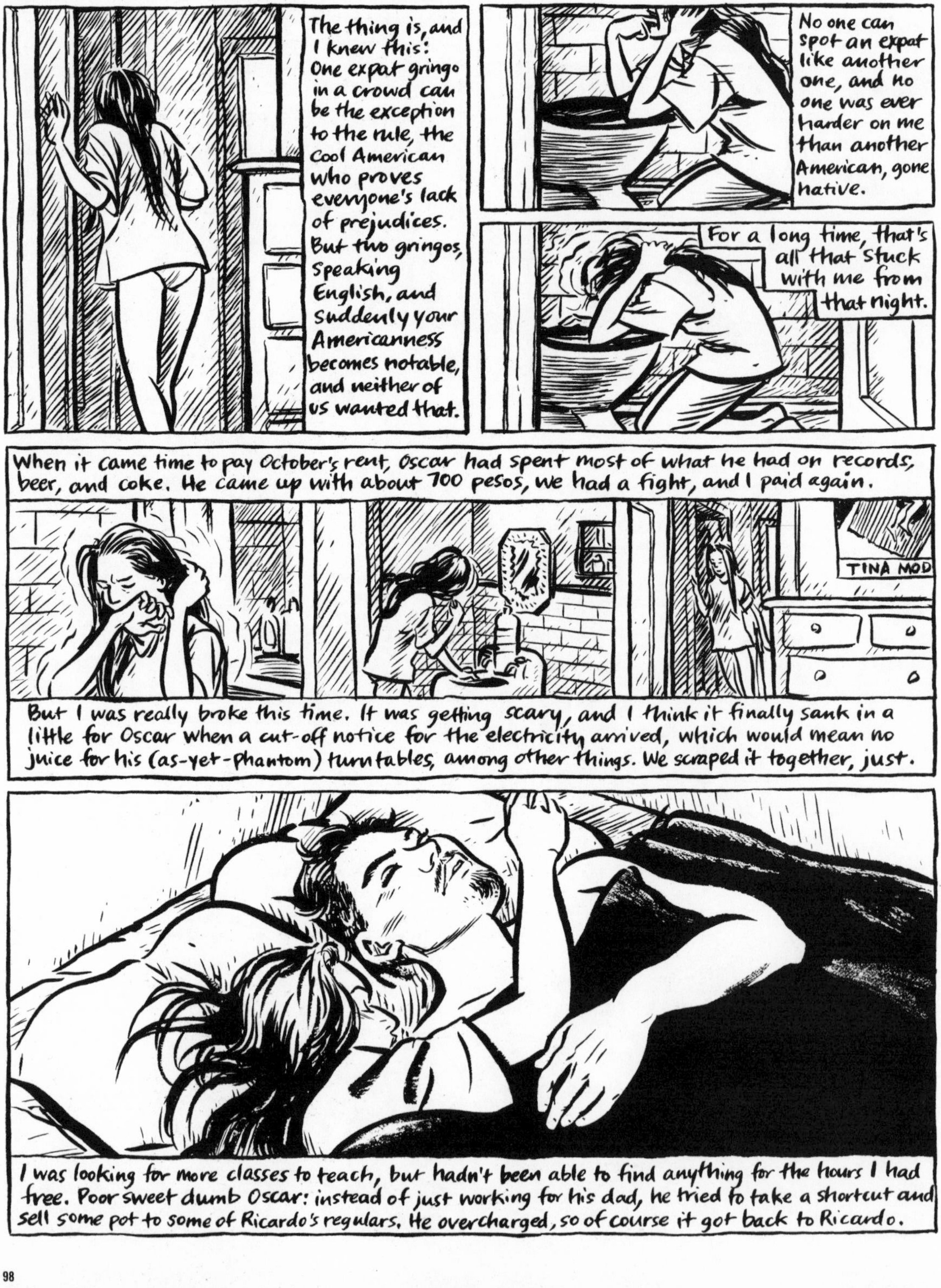

The thing is, and I knew this: One expat gringo in a crowd can be the exception to the rule, the cool American who proves everyone's lack of prejudices. But two gringos, speaking English, and suddenly your Americanness becomes notable, and neither of us wanted that.
No one can spot an expat like another one, and no one was ever harder on me than another American, gone native.
For a long time, that's all that stuck with me from that night.
When it came time to pay October's rent, Oscar had spent most of what he had on records, beer, and coke. He came up with about 700 pesos, we had a fight, and I paid again.
TINA MOD
But I was really broke this time. It was getting scary, and I think it finally sank in a little for Oscar when a cut-off notice for the electricity arrived, which would mean no juice for his (as-yet-phantom) turntables, among other things. We scraped it together, just.
I was looking for more classes to teach, but hadn't been able to find anything for the hours I had free. Poor sweet dumb Oscar: instead of just working for his dad, he tried to take a shortcut and sell some pot to some of Ricardo's regulars. He overcharged, so of course it got back to Ricardo.

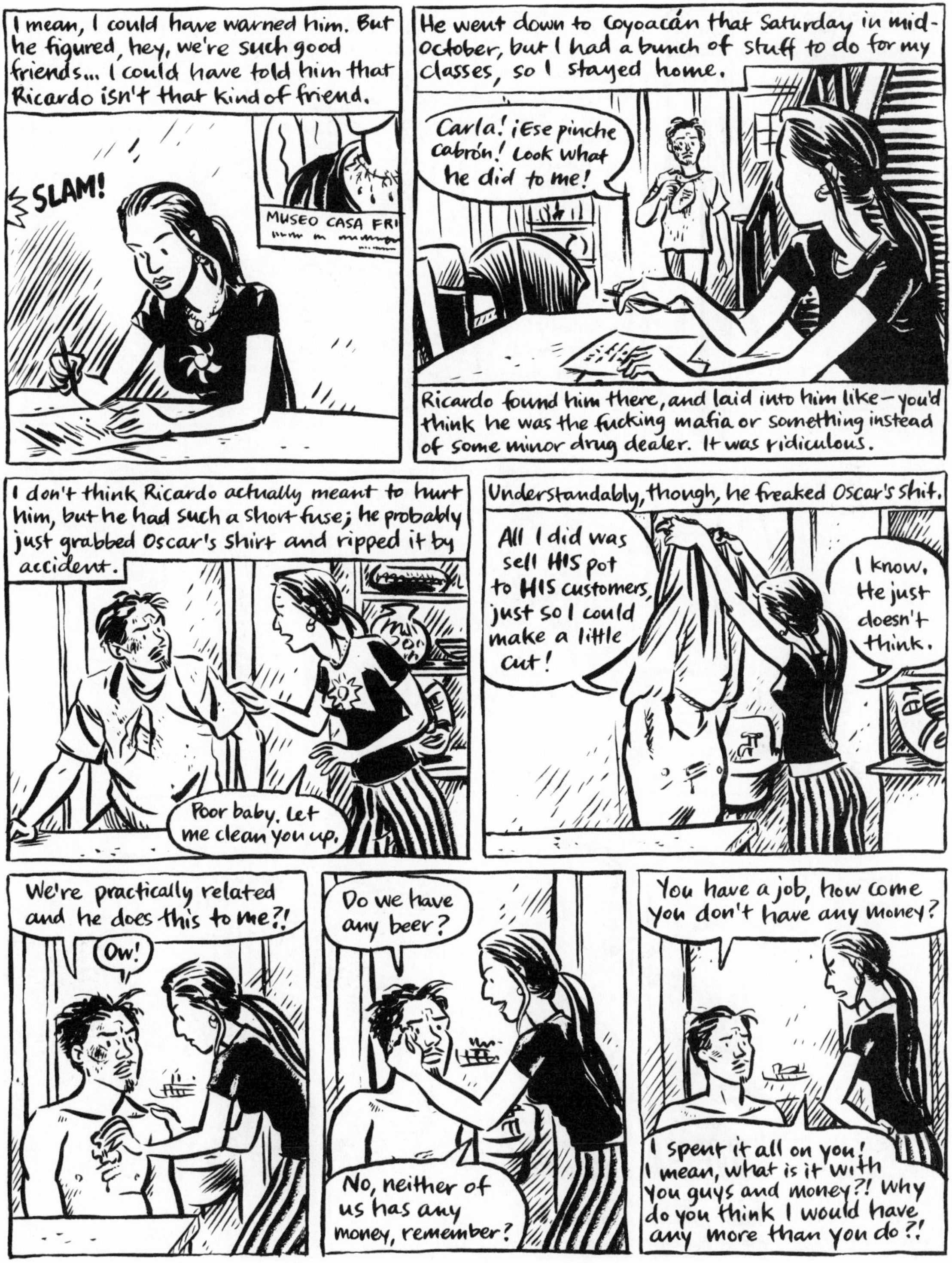
I mean, I could have warned him. But he figured, hey, we're such good friends... I could have told him that Ricardo isn't that kind of friend.
SLAM!
MUSEO CASA FRI
He went down to Coyoacán that Saturday in mid-October, but I had a bunch of stuff to do for my classes, so I stayed home.
Carla! ¡Ese pinche cabrón! Look what he did to me!
Ricardo found him there, and laid into him like—you'd think he was the fucking mafia or something instead of some minor drug dealer. It was ridiculous.
I don't think Ricardo actually meant to hurt him, but he had such a short fuse; he probably just grabbed Oscar's shirt and ripped it by accident.
Poor baby. Let me clean you up.
Understandably, though, he freaked Oscar's shit.
All I did was sell HIS pot to HIS customers, just so I could make a little cut!
I know. He just doesn't think.
We're practically related and he does this to me?!
Ow!
Do we have any beer?
No, neither of us has any money, remember?
You have a job, how come you don't have any money?
I spent it all on you! I mean, what is it with you guys and money?! Why do you think I would have any more than you do?!

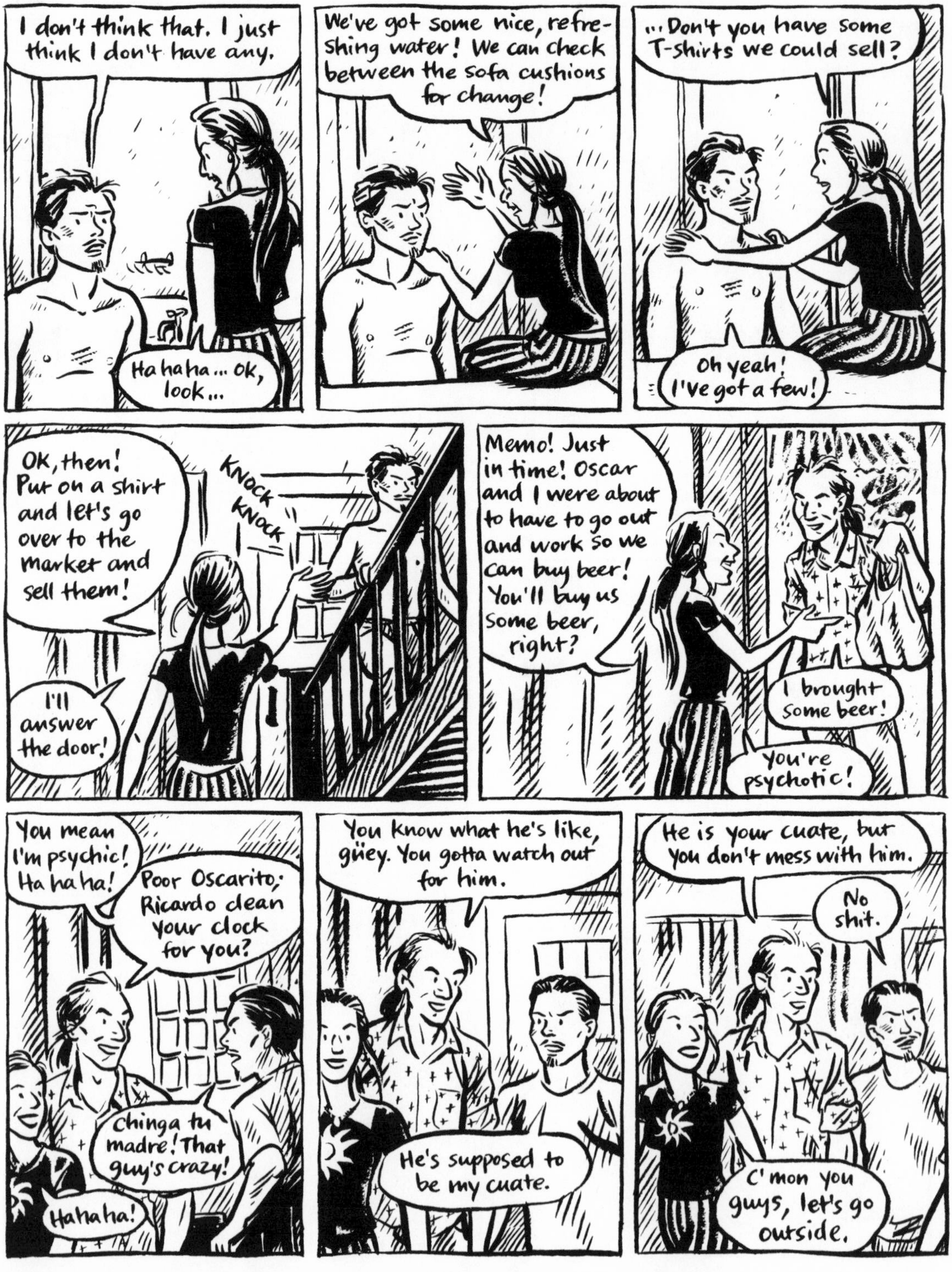

I don't think that. I just think I don't have any.
Ha ha ha... ok, look...
We've got some nice, refreshing water! We can check between the sofa cushions for change!
...Don't you have some T-shirts we could sell?
Oh yeah! I've got a few!
Ok, then! Put on a shirt and let's go over to the market and sell them!
KNOCK KNOCK
I'll answer the door!
Memo! Just in time! Oscar and I were about to have to go out and work so we can buy beer! You'll buy us some beer, right?
I brought some beer!
You're psychotic!
You mean I'm psychic! Ha ha ha!
Poor Oscarito; Ricardo clean your clock for you?
Chinga tu madre! That guy's crazy!
Ha ha ha!
You know what he's like, güey. You gotta watch out for him.
He's supposed to be my cuate.
He is your cuate, but you don't mess with him.
No shit.
C'mon you guys, let's go outside.

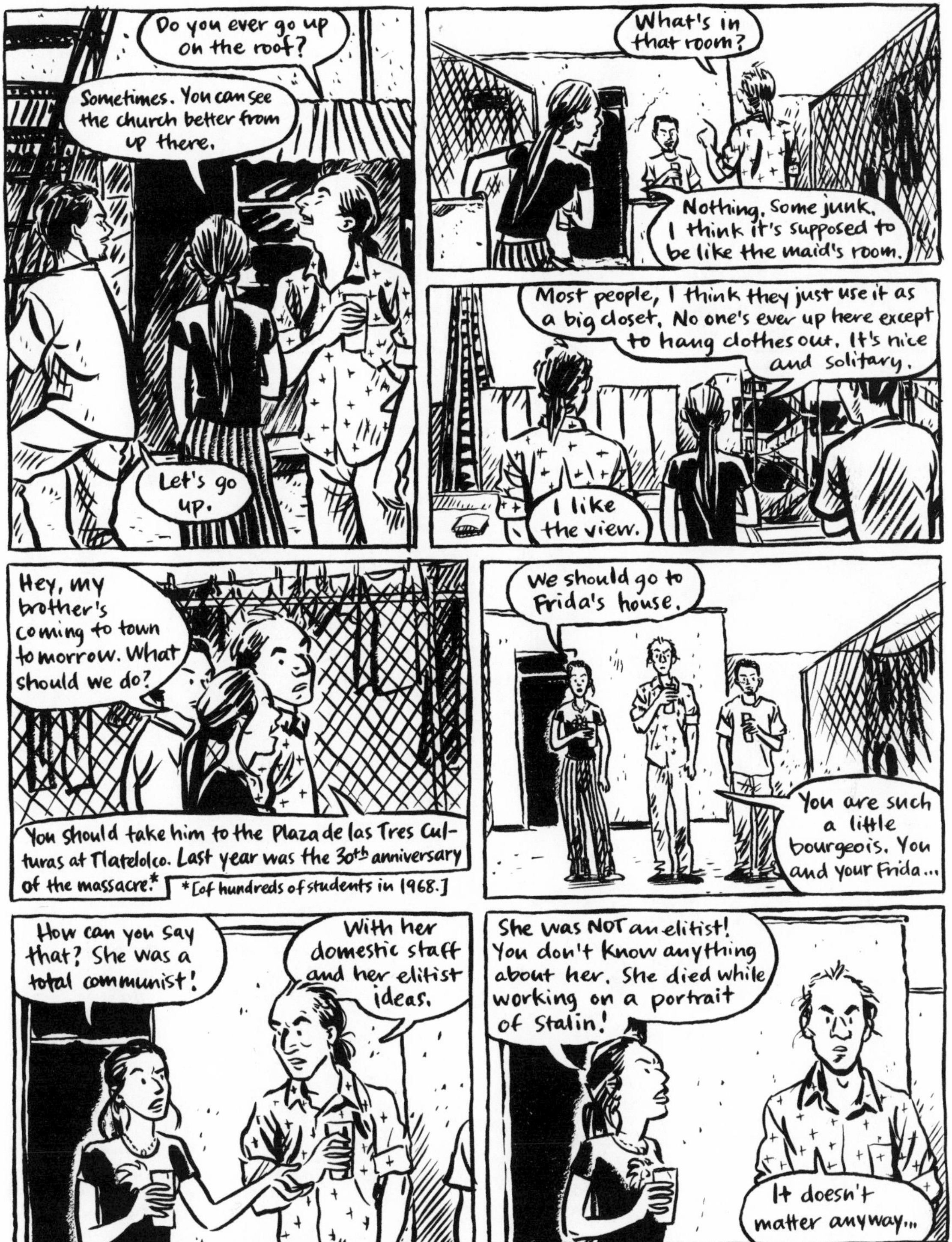

Do you ever go up on the roof?
Sometimes. You can see the church better from up there.
Let's go up.
What's in that room?
Nothing. Some junk. I think it's supposed to be like the maid's room.
Most people, I think they just use it as a big closet. No one's ever up here except to hang clothes out. It's nice and solitary.
I like the view.
Hey, my brother's coming to town tomorrow. What should we do?
You should take him to the Plaza de las Tres Culturas at Tlatelolco. Last year was the 30th anniversary of the massacre.*
*[of hundreds of students in 1968.]
We should go to Frida's house.
You are such a little bourgeois. You and your Frida...
How can you say that? She was a total communist!
With her domestic staff and her elitist ideas.
She was NOT an elitist! You don't know anything about her. She died while working on a portrait of Stalin!
It doesn't matter anyway...

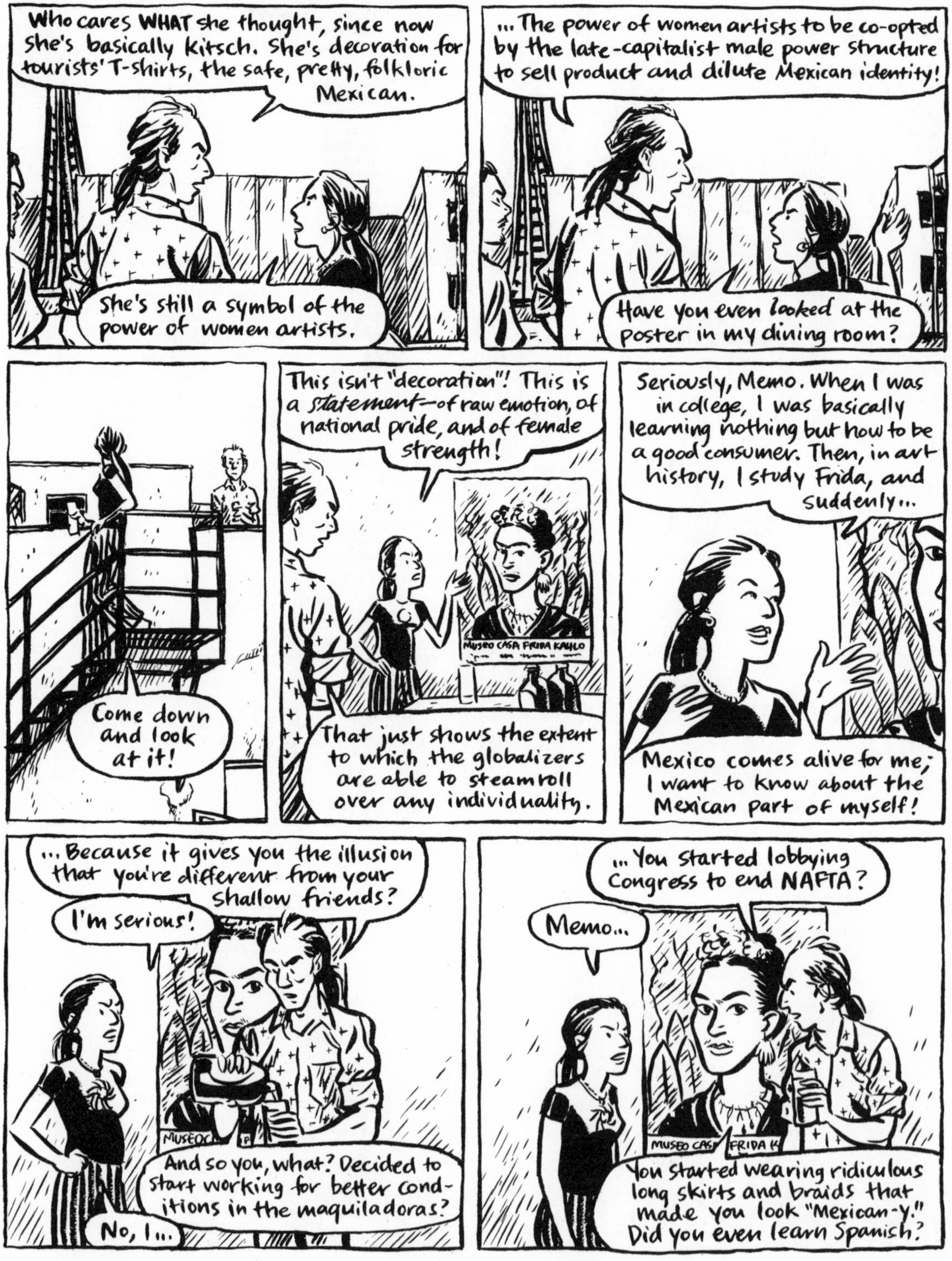
Who cares WHAT she thought, since now she's basically kitsch. She's decoration for tourists' T-shirts, the safe, pretty, folkloric Mexican.
She's still a symbol of the power of women artists.
...The power of women artists to be co-opted by the late-capitalist male power structure to sell product and dilute Mexican identity!
Have you even looked at the poster in my dining room?
Come down and look at it!
This isn't "decoration"! This is a statement—of raw emotion, of national pride, and of female strength!
MUSEO CASA FRIDA KAHLO
That just shows the extent to which the globalizers are able to steamroll over any individuality.
Seriously, Memo. When I was in college, I was basically learning nothing but how to be a good consumer. Then, in art history, I study Frida, and suddenly...
Mexico comes alive for me; I want to know about the Mexican part of myself!
...Because it gives you the illusion that you're different from your shallow friends?
I'm serious!
And so you, what? Decided to start working for better conditions in the maquiladoras?
No, I...
...You started lobbying Congress to end NAFTA?
Memo...
You started wearing ridiculous long skirts and braids that made you look "Mexican-y." Did you even learn Spanish?

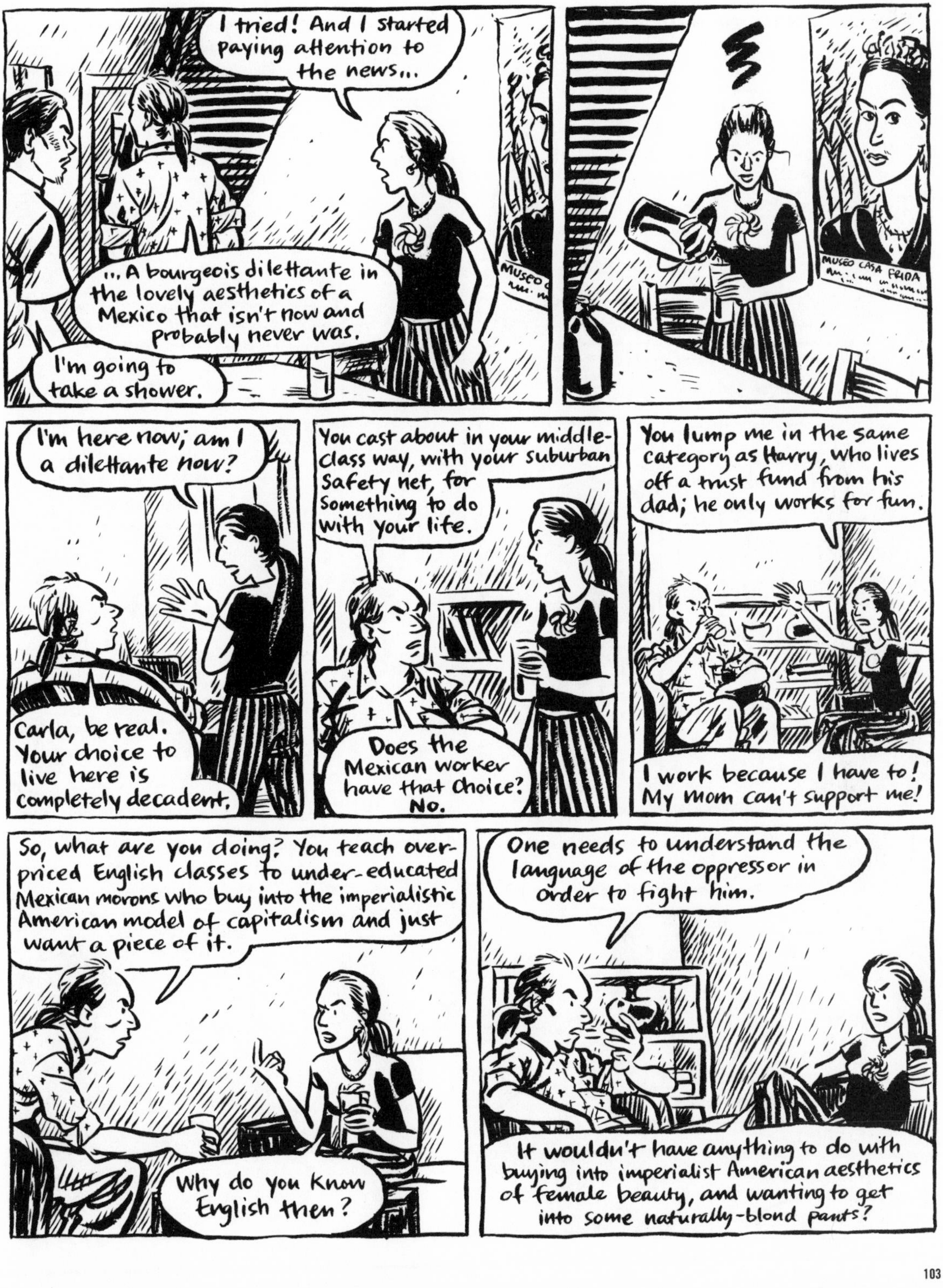
I tried! And I started paying attention to the news...
...A bourgeois dilettante in the lovely aesthetics of a Mexico that isn't now and probably never was.
I'm going to take a shower.
MUSEO CASA FRIDA
I'm here now; am I a dilettante now?
Carla, be real. Your choice to live here is completely decadent.
You cast about in your middle-class way, with your suburban safety net, for something to do with your life.
Does the Mexican worker have that choice? No.
You lump me in the same category as Harry, who lives off a trust fund from his dad; he only works for fun.
I work because I have to! My mom can't support me!
So, what are you doing? You teach over-priced English classes to under-educated Mexican morons who buy into the imperialistic American model of capitalism and just want a piece of it.
Why do you know English then?
One needs to understand the language of the oppressor in order to fight him.
It wouldn't have anything to do with buying into imperialist American aesthetics of female beauty, and wanting to get into some naturally-blond pants?

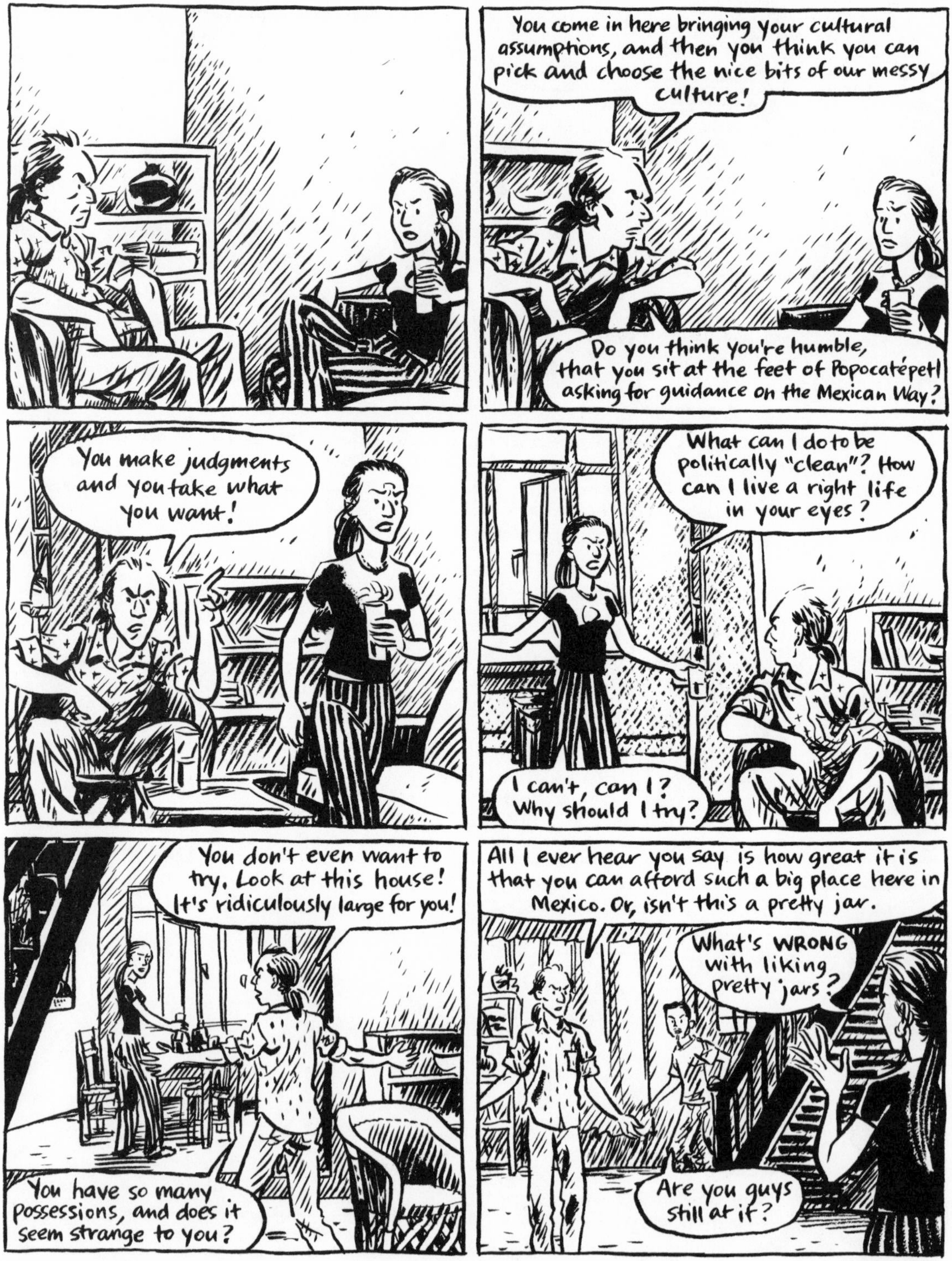
You come in here bringing your cultural assumptions, and then you think you can pick and choose the nice bits of our messy culture!
Do you think you're humble, that you sit at the feet of Popocatépetl asking for guidance on the Mexican Way?
You make judgments and you take what you want!
What can I do to be politically "clean"? How can I live a right life in your eyes?
I can't, can I? Why should I try?
You don't even want to try. Look at this house! It's ridiculously large for you!
You have so many possessions, and does it seem strange to you?
All I ever hear you say is how great it is that you can afford such a big place here in Mexico. Or, isn't this a pretty jar.
What's WRONG with liking pretty jars?
Are you guys still at it?

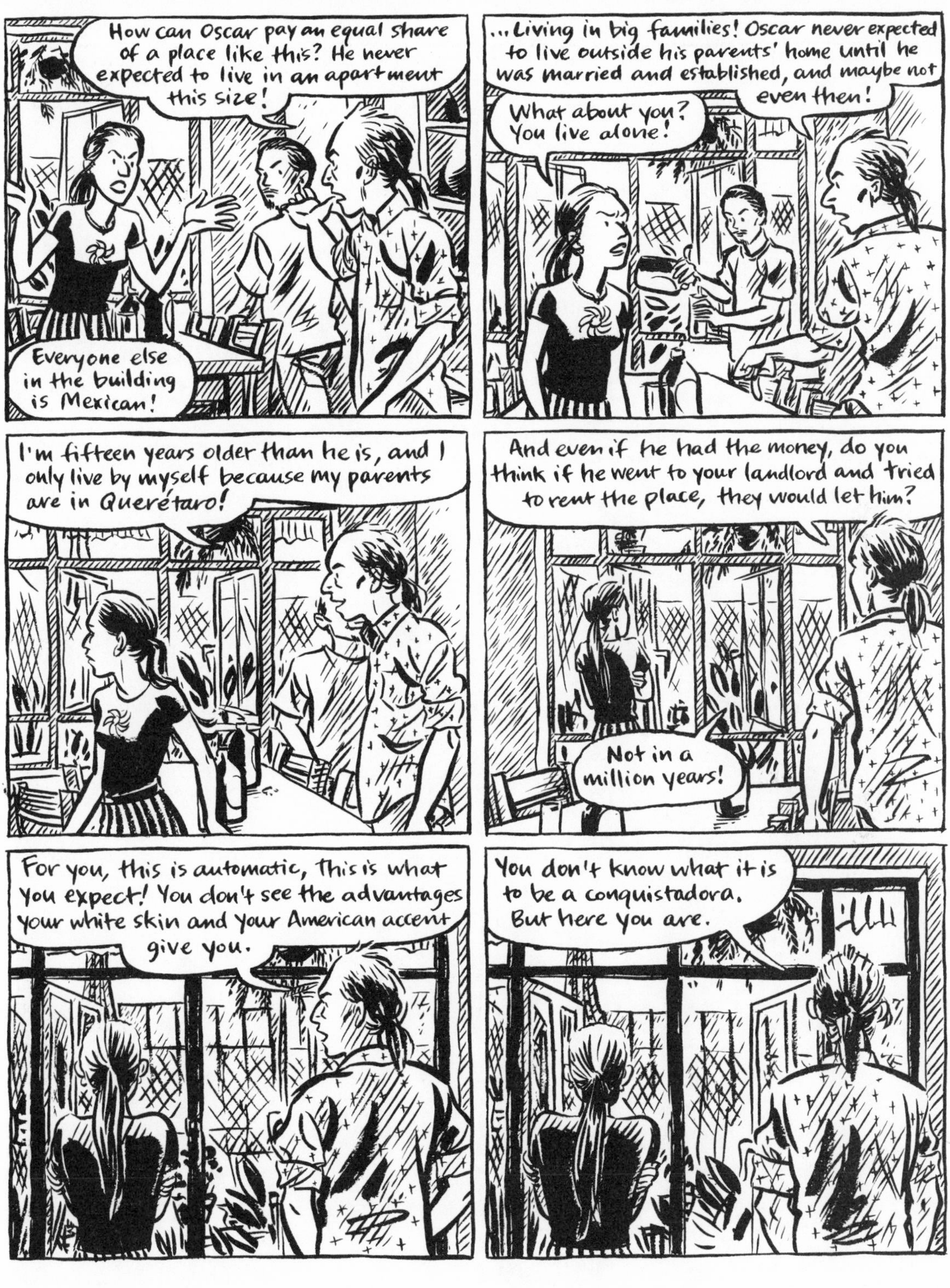
How can Oscar pay an equal share of a place like this? He never expected to live in an apartment this size!
Everyone else in the building is Mexican!
...Living in big families! Oscar never expected to live outside his parents' home until he was married and established, and maybe not even then!
What about you? You live alone!
I'm fifteen years older than he is, and I only live by myself because my parents are in Querétaro!
And even if he had the money, do you think if he went to your landlord and tried to rent the place, they would let him?
Not in a million years!
For you, this is automatic, this is what you expect! You don't see the advantages your white skin and your American accent give you.
You don't know what it is to be a conquistadora. But here you are.

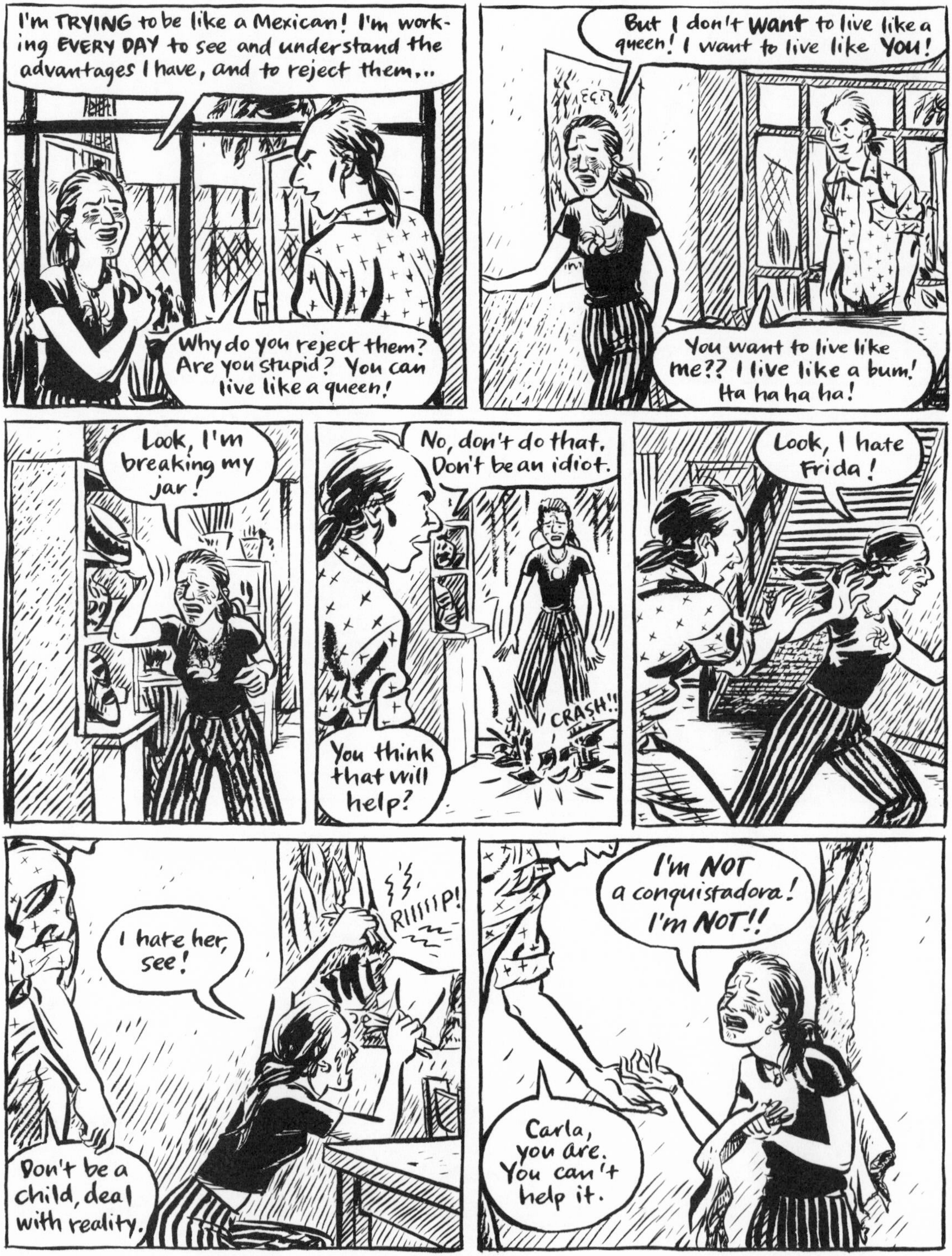
I'm TRYING to be like a Mexican! I'm working EVERY DAY to see and understand the advantages I have, and to reject them...
Why do you reject them? Are you stupid? You can live like a queen!
But I don't WANT to live like a queen! I want to live like YOU!
You want to live like me?? I live like a bum! Ha ha ha ha!
Look, I'm breaking my jar!
No, don't do that. Don't be an idiot.
CRASH!!
You think that will help?
Look, I hate Frida!
RIIIIIP!
I hate her, see!
Don't be a child, deal with reality.
I'm NOT a conquistadora! I'm NOT!!
Carla, you are. You can't help it.

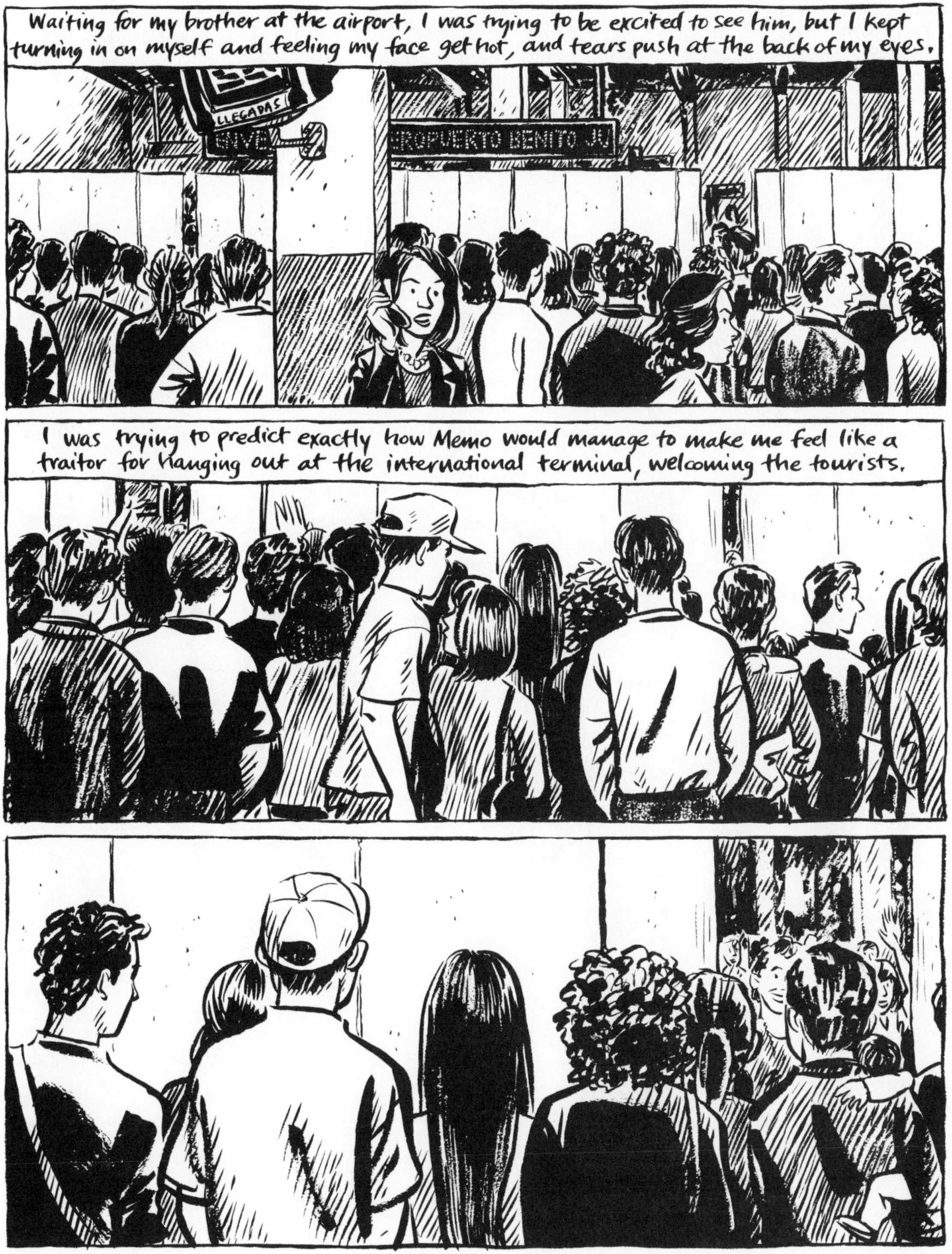
Waiting for my brother at the airport, I was trying to be excited to see him, but I kept turning in on myself and feeling my face get hot, and tears push at the back of my eyes.
LLEGADAS
ROPUERTO BENITO JU
I was trying to predict exactly how Memo would manage to make me feel like a traitor for hanging out at the international terminal, welcoming the tourists.

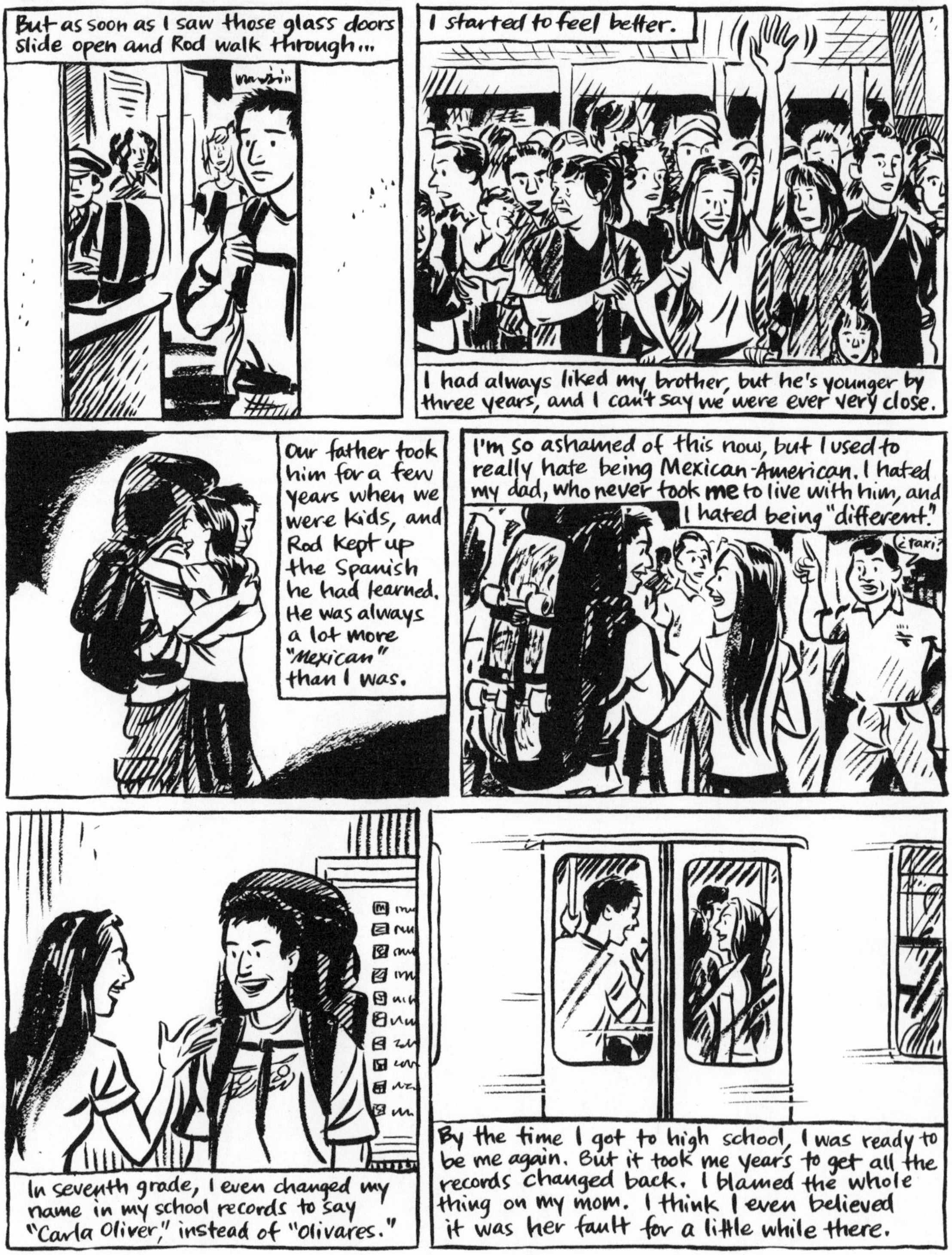

But as soon as I saw those glass doors slide open and Rod walk through...
I started to feel better.
I had always liked my brother, but he's younger by three years, and I can't say we were ever very close.
Our father took him for a few years when we were kids, and Rod kept up the Spanish he had learned. He was always a lot more "Mexican" than I was.
I'm so ashamed of this now, but I used to really hate being Mexican-American. I hated my dad, who never took **me** to live with him, and I hated being "different."
¿Taxi?
In seventh grade, I even changed my name in my school records to say "Carla Oliver," instead of "Olivares."
By the time I got to high school, I was ready to be me again. But it took me years to get all the records changed back. I blamed the whole thing on my mom. I think I even believed it was her fault for a little while there.

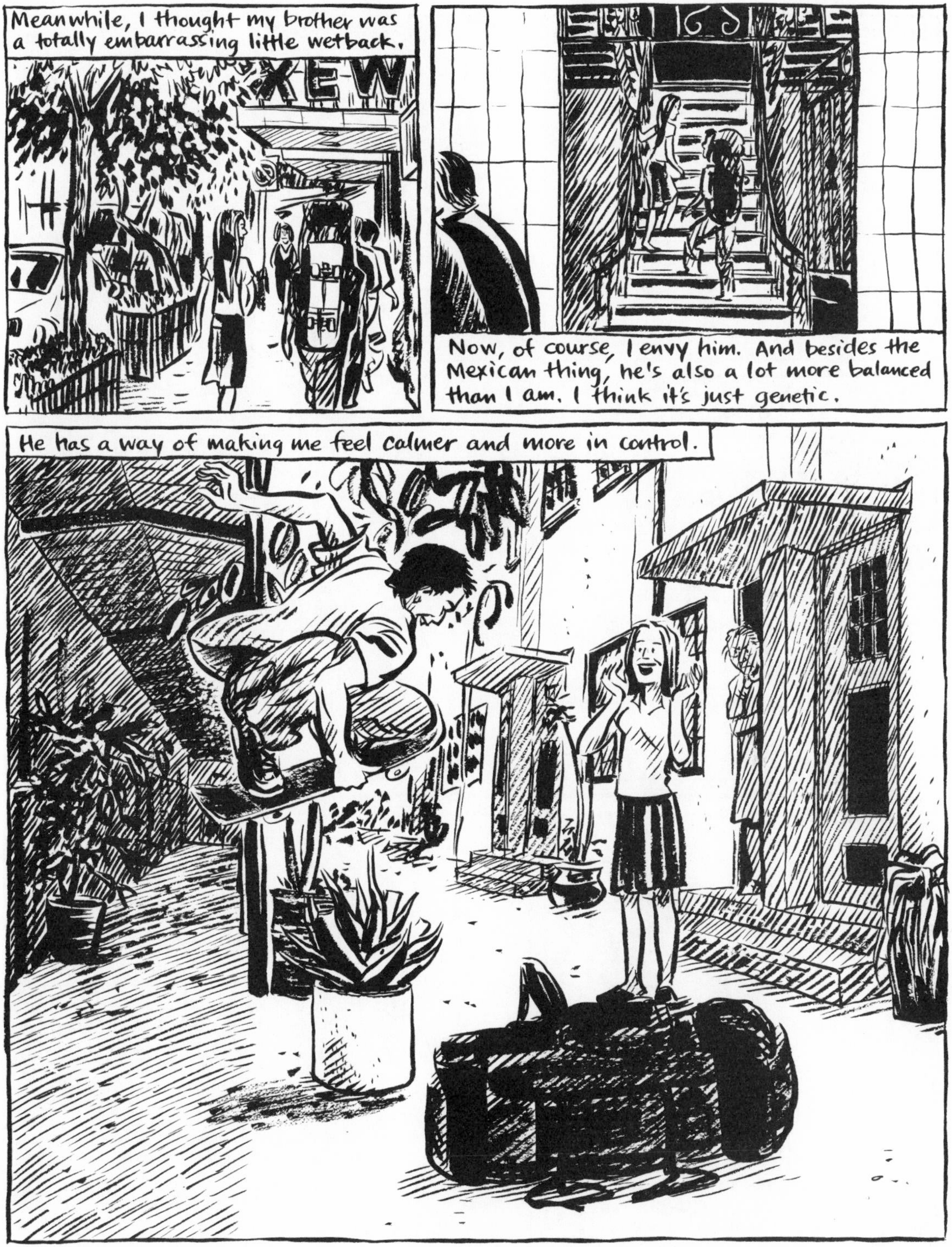
Meanwhile, I thought my brother was a totally embarrassing little wetback.
XEW
Now, of course, I envy him. And besides the Mexican thing, he's also a lot more balanced than I am. I think it's just genetic.
He has a way of making me feel calmer and more in control.

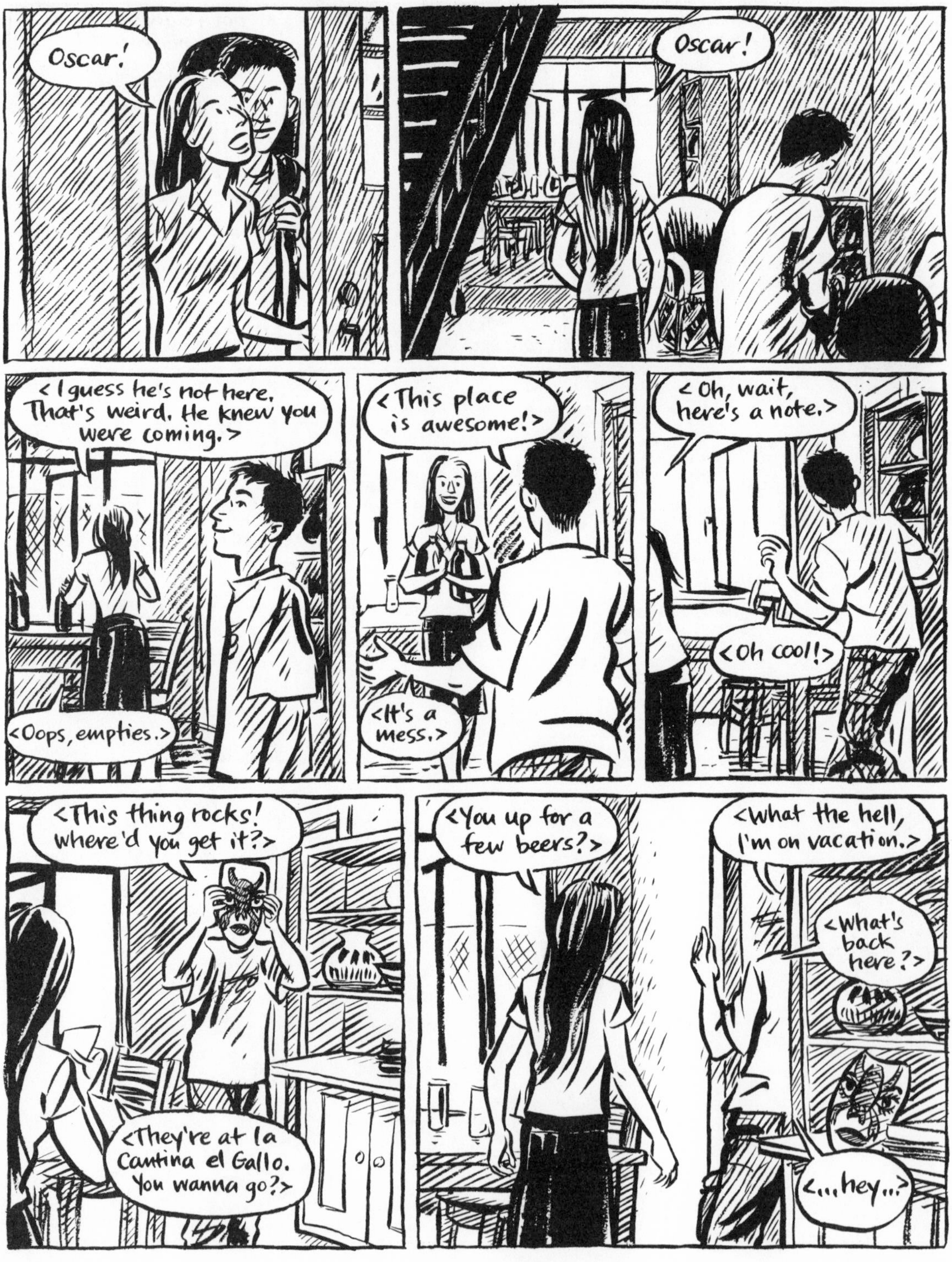
Oscar!
Oscar!
<I guess he's not here. That's weird. He knew you were coming.>
<Oops, empties.>
<This place is awesome!>
<It's a mess.>
<Oh, wait, here's a note.>
<Oh cool!>
<This thing rocks! Where'd you get it?>
<They're at la Cantina el Gallo. You wanna go?>
<You up for a few beers?>
<What the hell, I'm on vacation.>
<What's back here?>
<...hey...>

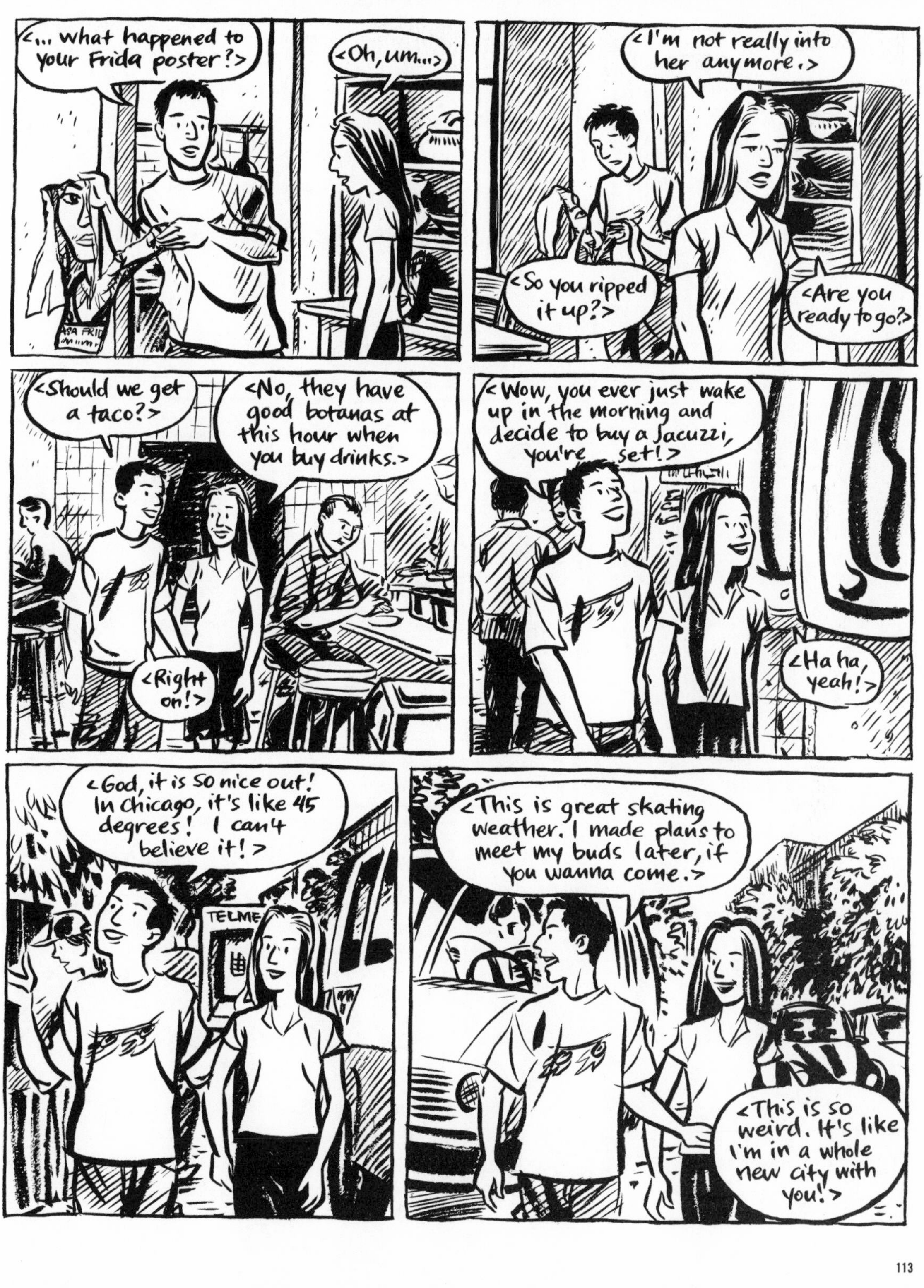
<... what happened to your Frida poster?>
<Oh, um...>
<I'm not really into her anymore.>
<So you ripped it up?>
<Are you ready to go?>
<Should we get a taco?>
<No, they have good botanas at this hour when you buy drinks.>
<Right on!>
<Wow, you ever just wake up in the morning and decide to buy a Jacuzzi, you're set!>
<Ha ha, yeah!>
<God, it is so nice out! In Chicago, it's like 45 degrees! I can't believe it!>
TELME
<This is great skating weather. I made plans to meet my buds later, if you wanna come.>
<This is so weird. It's like I'm in a whole new city with you!>

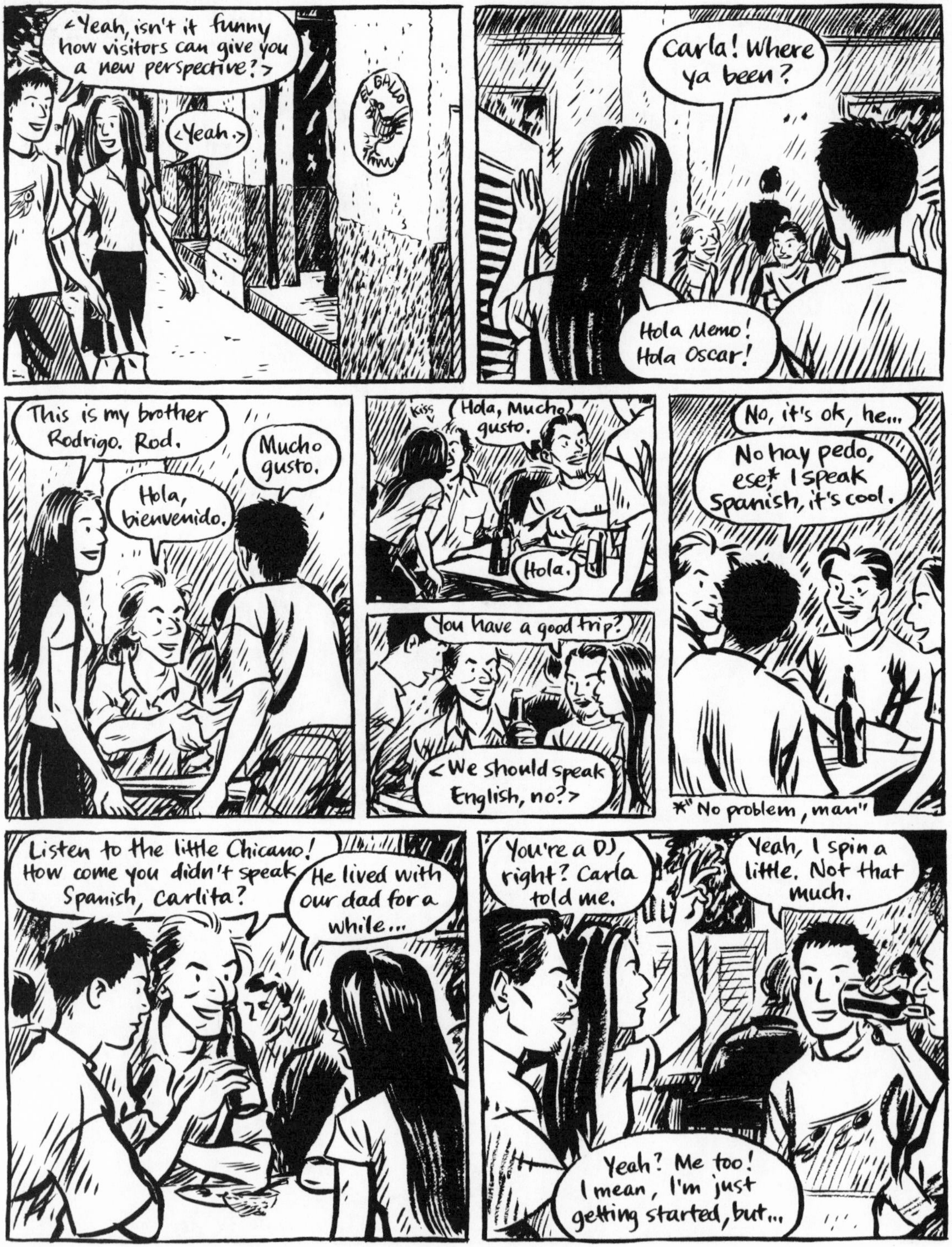

<Yeah, isn't it funny how visitors can give you a new perspective?>
<Yeah.>
EL GALLO
Carla! Where ya been?
Hola Memo! Hola Oscar!
This is my brother Rodrigo. Rod.
Hola, bienvenido.
Mucho gusto.
KISS
Hola, Mucho gusto.
Hola.
You have a good trip?
<We should speak English, no?>
No, it's ok, he...
No hay pedo, ese* I speak Spanish, it's cool.
*"No problem, man"
Listen to the little Chicano! How come you didn't speak Spanish, Carlita?
He lived with our dad for a while...
You're a DJ right? Carla told me.
Yeah, I spin a little. Not that much.
Yeah? Me too! I mean, I'm just getting started, but...

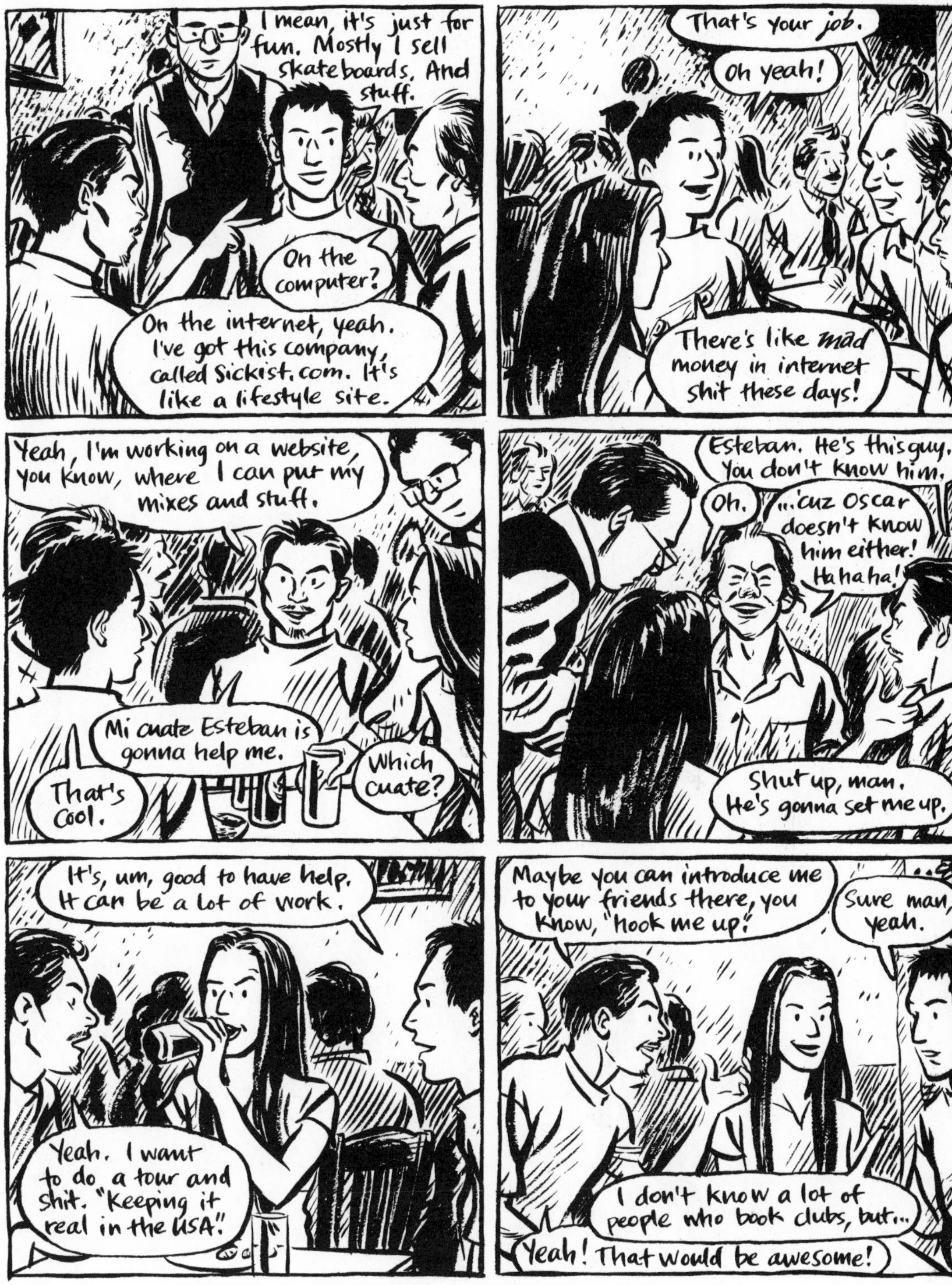
I mean, it's just for fun. Mostly I sell skateboards. And stuff.
On the computer?
On the internet, yeah. I've got this company, called Sickist.com. It's like a lifestyle site.
That's your job.
Oh yeah!
There's like mad money in internet shit these days!
Yeah, I'm working on a website, you know, where I can put my mixes and stuff.
Mi cuate Esteban is gonna help me.
That's cool.
Which cuate?
Esteban. He's this guy. You don't know him.
Oh.
...'cuz Oscar doesn't know him either! Hahaha!
Shut up, man. He's gonna set me up.
It's, um, good to have help. It can be a lot of work.
Yeah. I want to do a tour and shit. "Keeping it real in the USA."
Maybe you can introduce me to your friends there, you know, "hook me up."
Sure man, yeah.
I don't know a lot of people who book clubs, but...
Yeah! That would be awesome!

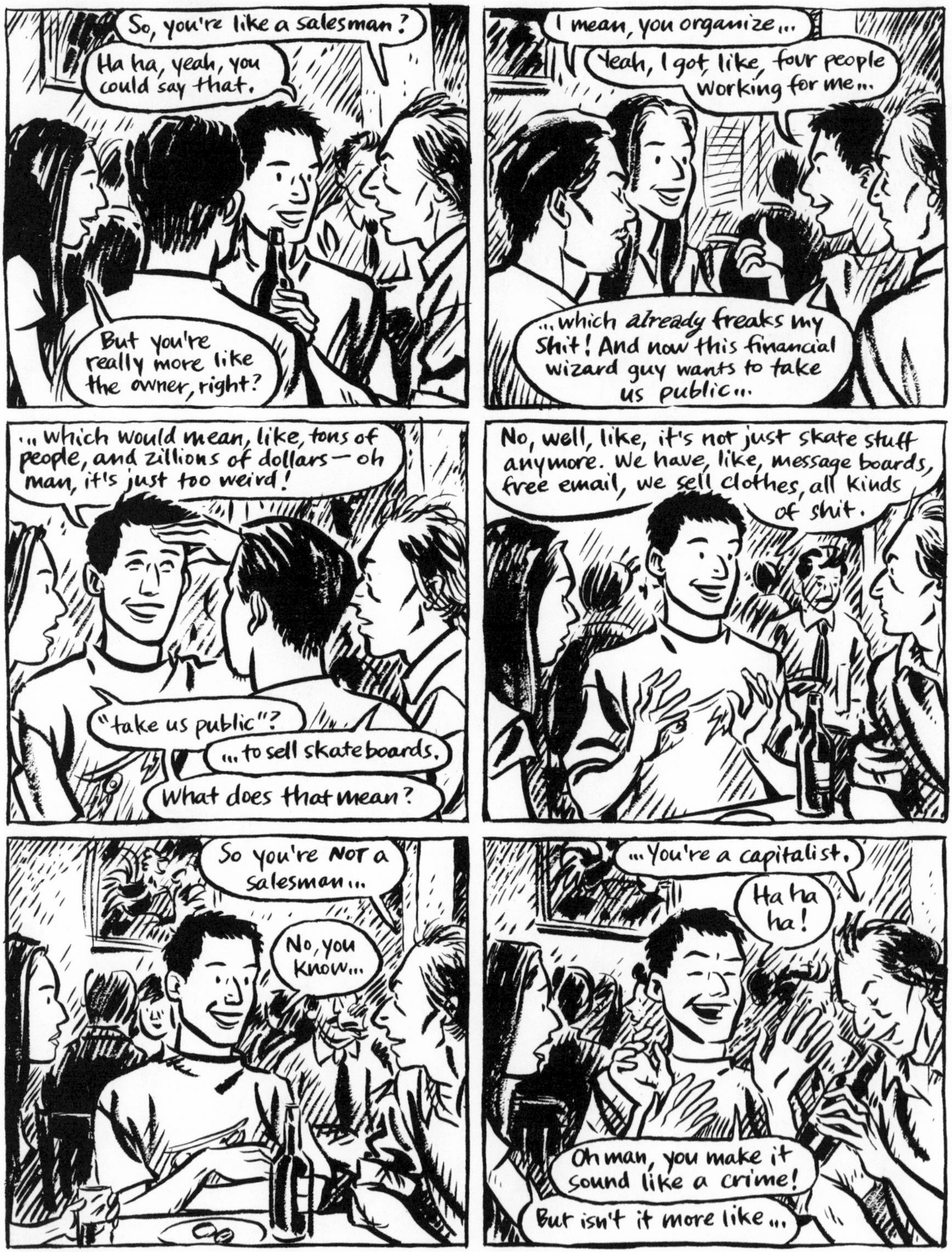
So, you're like a salesman?
Ha ha, yeah, you could say that.
But you're really more like the owner, right?
I mean, you organize...
Yeah, I got, like, four people working for me...
...which *already* freaks my shit! And now this financial wizard guy wants to take us public...
...which would mean, like, tons of people, and zillions of dollars—oh man, it's just too weird!
"take us public"?
...to sell skateboards.
What does that mean?
No, well, like, it's not just skate stuff anymore. We have, like, message boards, free email, we sell clothes, all kinds of shit.
So you're **NOT** a salesman...
No, you know...
...You're a capitalist.
Ha ha ha!
Oh man, you make it sound like a crime!
But isn't it more like...

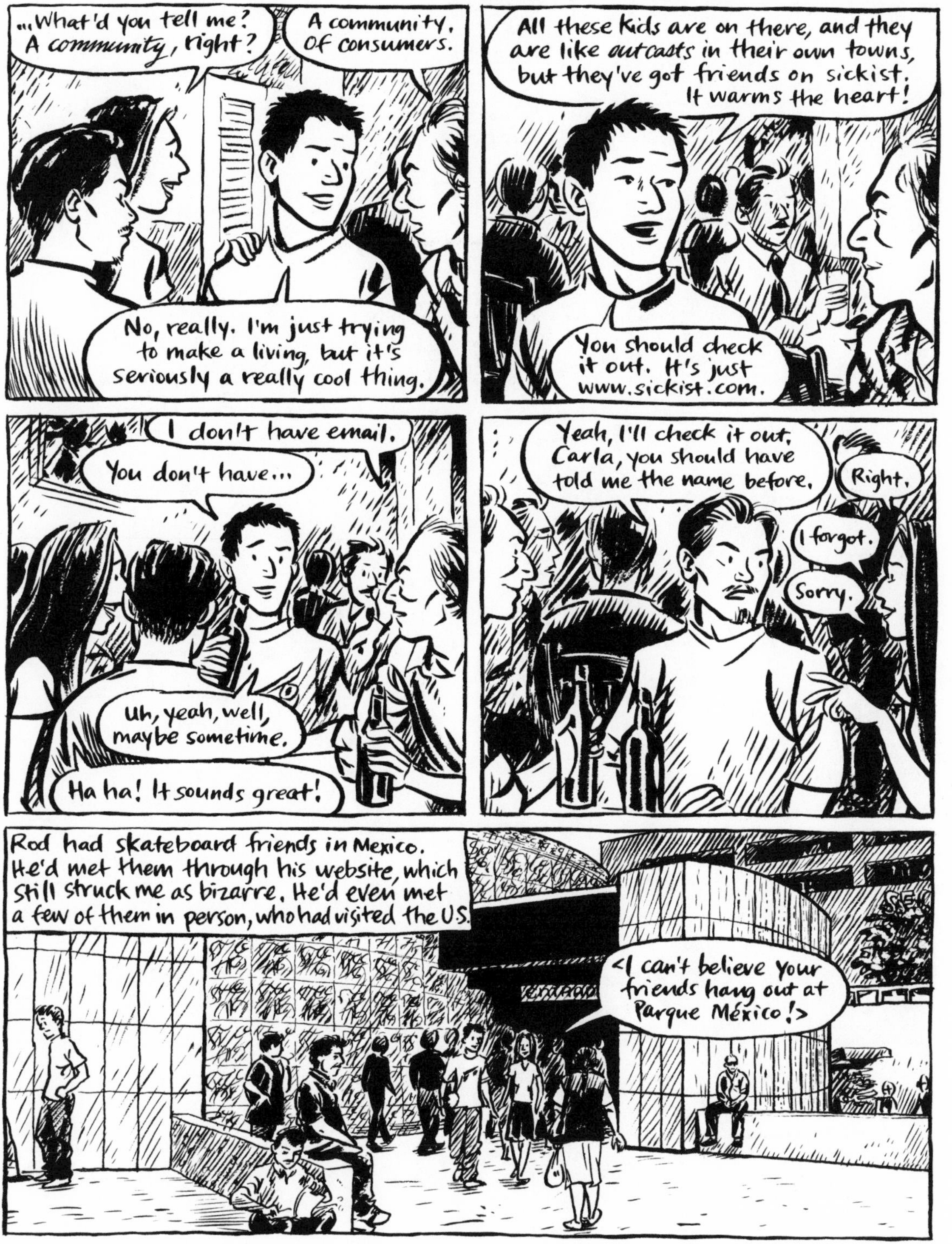

...What'd you tell me? A community, right?
A community. Of consumers.
No, really. I'm just trying to make a living, but it's seriously a really cool thing.
All these kids are on there, and they are like outcasts in their own towns, but they've got friends on sickist. It warms the heart!
You should check it out. It's just www.sickist.com.
I don't have email.
You don't have...
Uh, yeah, well, maybe sometime.
Ha ha! It sounds great!
Yeah, I'll check it out. Carla, you should have told me the name before.
Right.
I forgot.
Sorry.
Rod had skateboard friends in Mexico. He'd met them through his website, which still struck me as bizarre. He'd even met a few of them in person, who had visited the U.S.
<I can't believe your friends hang out at Parque México!>

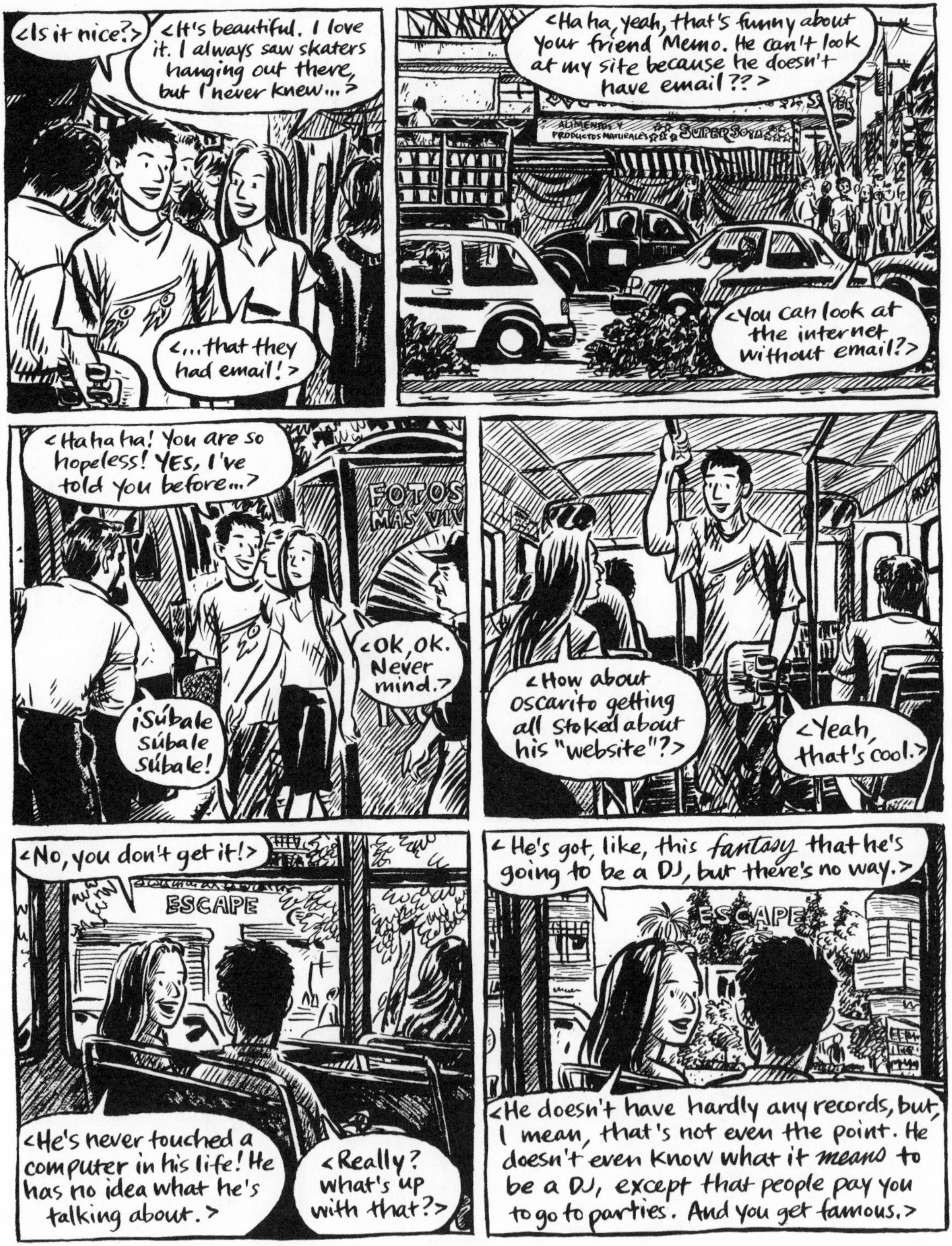
<Is it nice?>
<It's beautiful. I love it. I always saw skaters hanging out there, but I never knew...>
<...that they had email!>
<Ha ha, yeah, that's funny about your friend Memo. He can't look at my site because he doesn't have email??>
ALIMENTOS Y PRODUCTOS NATURALES SUPERSOYA
<You can look at the internet without email?>
<Ha ha ha! You are so hopeless! YES, I've told you before...>
FOTOS MAS VIV
¡Súbale súbale súbale!
<OK, OK. Never mind.>
<How about Oscarito getting all stoked about his "website"?>
<Yeah, that's cool.>
<No, you don't get it!>
ESCAPE
<He's never touched a computer in his life! He has no idea what he's talking about.>
<Really? What's up with that?>
<He's got, like, this *fantasy* that he's going to be a DJ, but there's no way.>
ESCAPE
<He doesn't have hardly any records, but, I mean, that's not even the point. He doesn't even know what it *means* to be a DJ, except that people pay you to go to parties. And you get famous.>

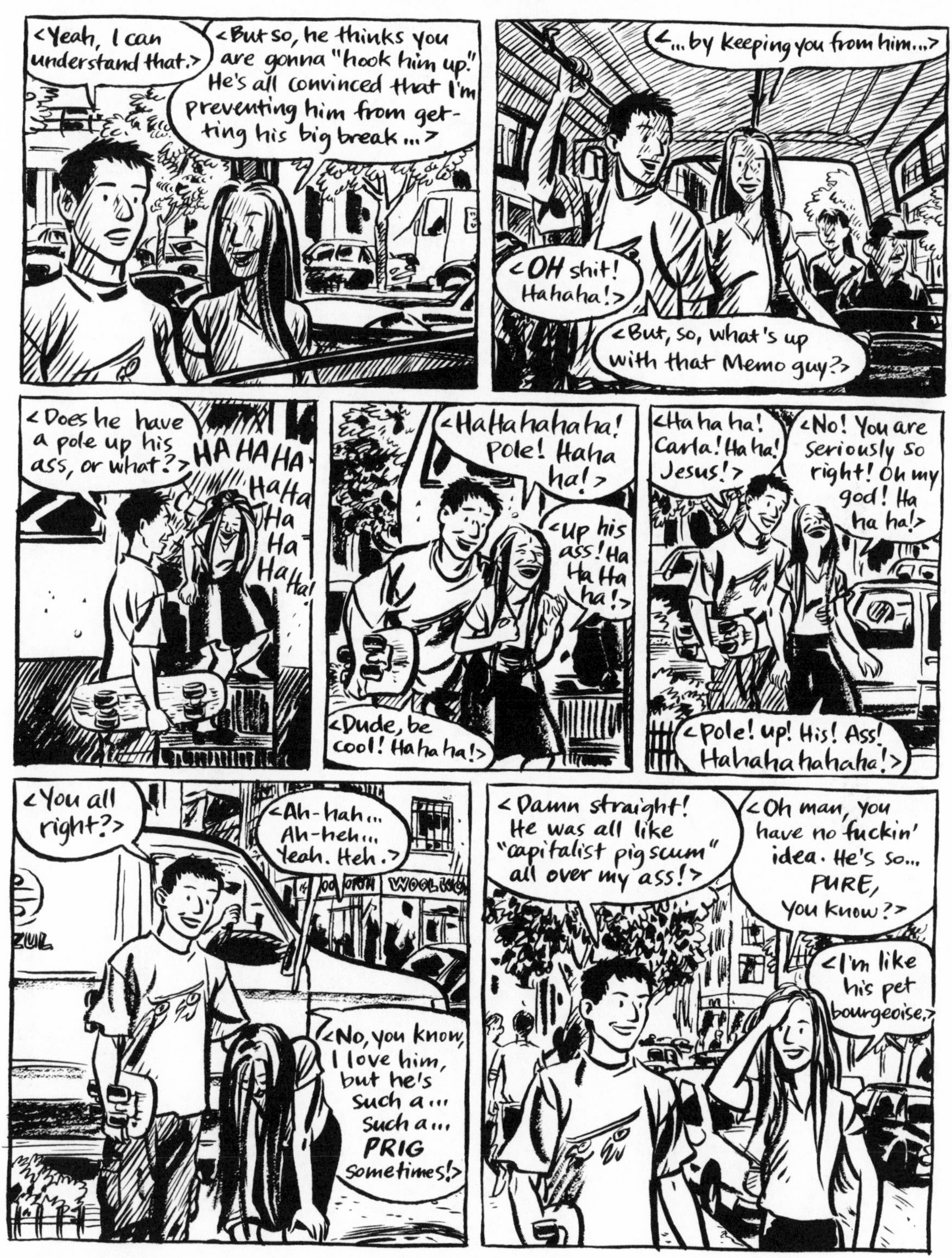

<Yeah, I can understand that.>
<But so, he thinks you are gonna "hook him up." He's all convinced that I'm preventing him from getting his big break...>
<...by keeping you from him...>
<OH shit! Hahaha!>
<But, so, what's up with that Memo guy?>
<Does he have a pole up his ass, or what?>
HAHAHA HaHa Ha Ha HaHa!
<HaHahahaha! Pole! Haha ha!>
<Up his ass! Ha HaHa ha!>
<Dude, be cool! Hahaha!>
<Ha ha ha! Carla! Haha! Jesus!>
<No! You are seriously so right! Oh my god! Ha ha ha!>
<Pole! Up! His! Ass! Hahahahahaha!>
<You all right?>
<Ah-hah... Ah-heh... Yeah. Heh.>
<No, you know, I love him, but he's such a... such a... PRIG sometimes!>
<Damn straight! He was all like "capitalist pigscum" all over my ass!>
<Oh man, you have no fuckin' idea. He's so... PURE, you know?>
<I'm like his pet bourgeoise.>

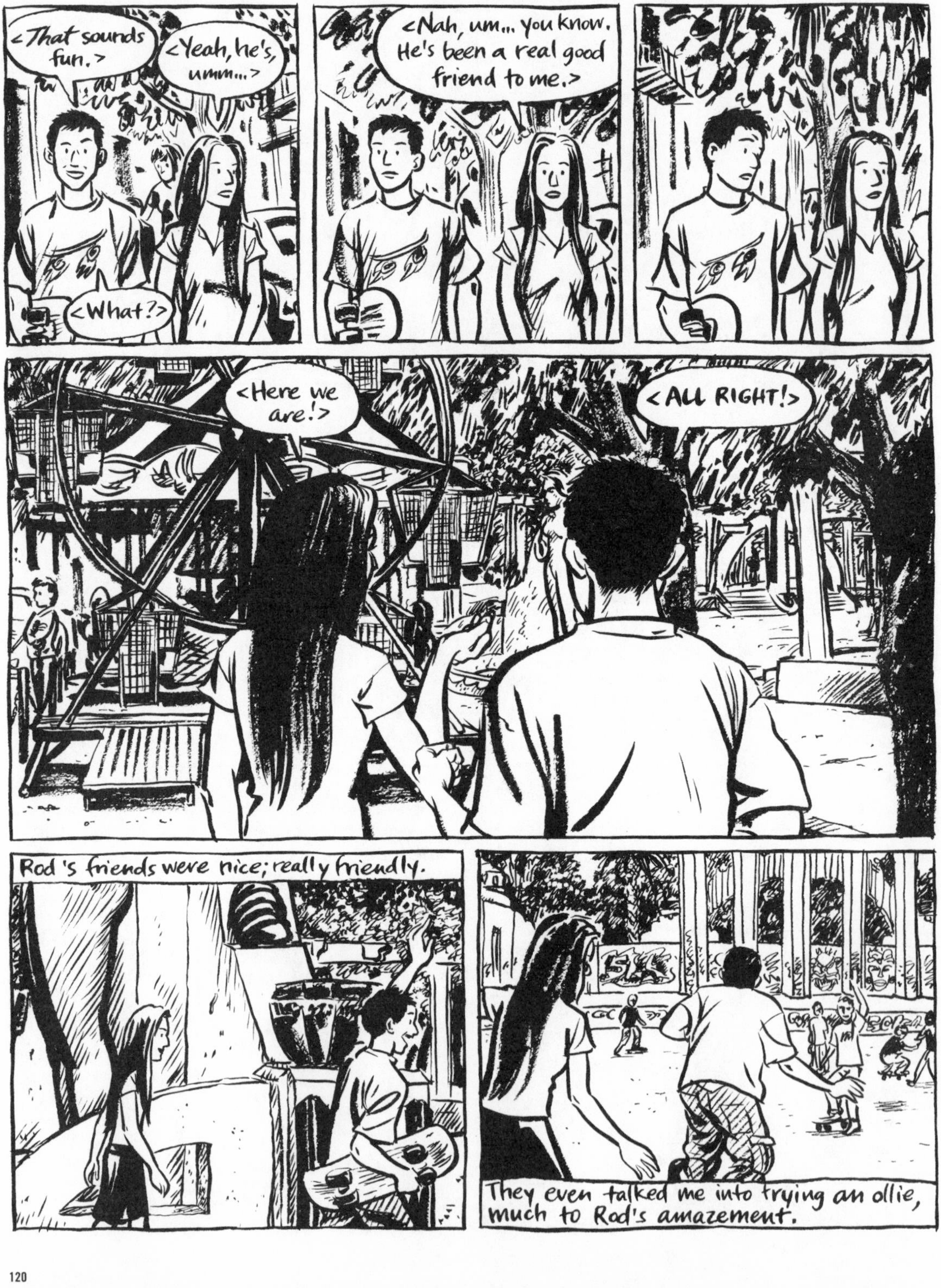

<That sounds fun.>
<Yeah, he's, umm...>
<What?>
<Nah, um... you know. He's been a real good friend to me.>
<Here we are!>
<ALL RIGHT!>
Rod's friends were nice; really friendly.
They even talked me into trying an ollie, much to Rod's amazement.

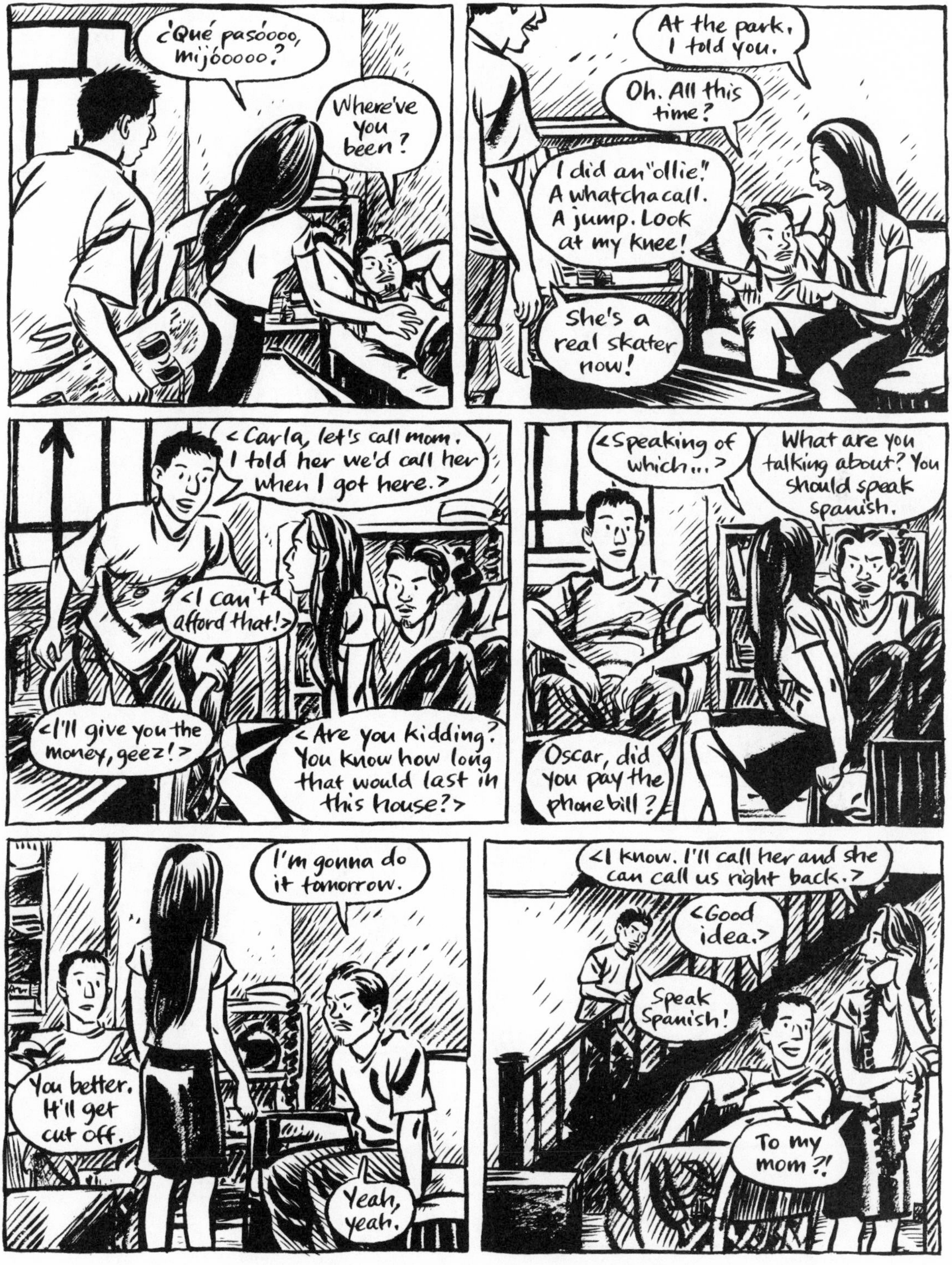
¿Qué pasóooo, mijóoooo?
Where've you been?
At the park, I told you.
Oh. All this time?
I did an "ollie." A whatchacall. A jump. Look at my knee!
She's a real skater now!
<Carla, let's call mom. I told her we'd call her when I got here.>
<I can't afford that!>
<I'll give you the money, geez!>
<Are you kidding? You know how long that would last in this house?>
<Speaking of which...>
What are you talking about? You should speak spanish.
Oscar, did you pay the phone bill?
I'm gonna do it tomorrow.
You better. It'll get cut off.
Yeah, yeah.
<I know. I'll call her and she can call us right back.>
<Good idea.>
Speak Spanish!
To my mom?!

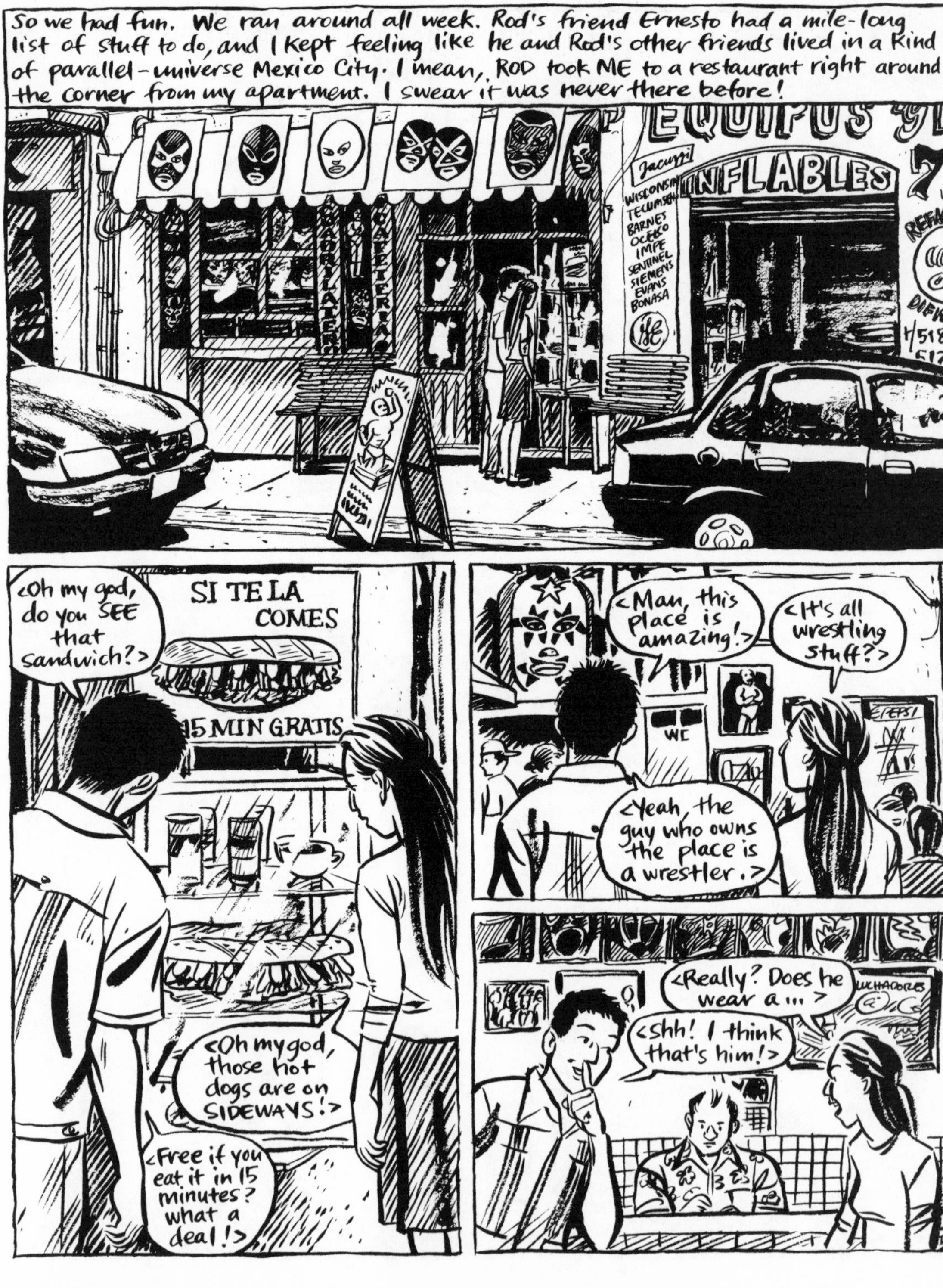
So we had fun. We ran around all week. Rod's friend Ernesto had a mile-long list of stuff to do, and I kept feeling like he and Rod's other friends lived in a kind of parallel-universe Mexico City. I mean, ROD took ME to a restaurant right around the corner from my apartment. I swear it was never there before!
INFLABLES
Jacuzzi
WISCONSIN
TECUMSEH
BARNES
IMPE
SENTINEL
SIEMENS
EVANS
BONASA
SI TE LA COMES
15 MIN GRATIS
<Oh my god, do you SEE that sandwich?>
<Oh my god, those hot dogs are on SIDEWAYS!>
<Free if you eat it in 15 minutes? what a deal!>
<Man, this place is amazing!>
<It's all wrestling stuff?>
<Yeah, the guy who owns the place is a wrestler.>
<Really? Does he wear a ...>
<Shh! I think that's him!>

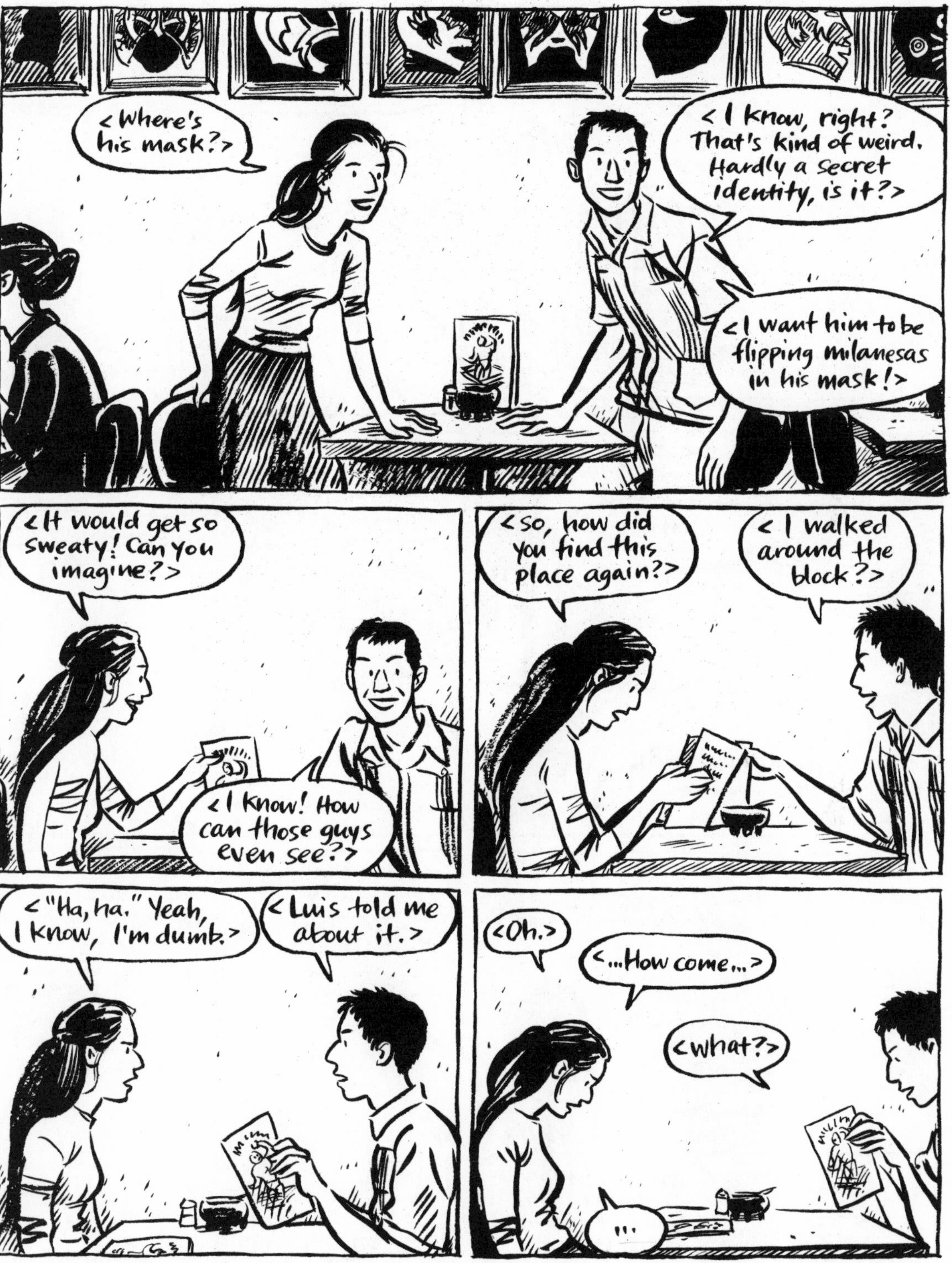
<Where's his mask?>
<I know, right? That's kind of weird. Hardly a secret identity, is it?>
<I want him to be flipping milanesas in his mask!>
<It would get so sweaty! Can you imagine?>
<I know! How can those guys even see?>
<So, how did you find this place again?>
<I walked around the block?>
<"Ha, ha." Yeah, I know, I'm dumb.>
<Luis told me about it.>
<Oh.>
<...How come...>
<What?>

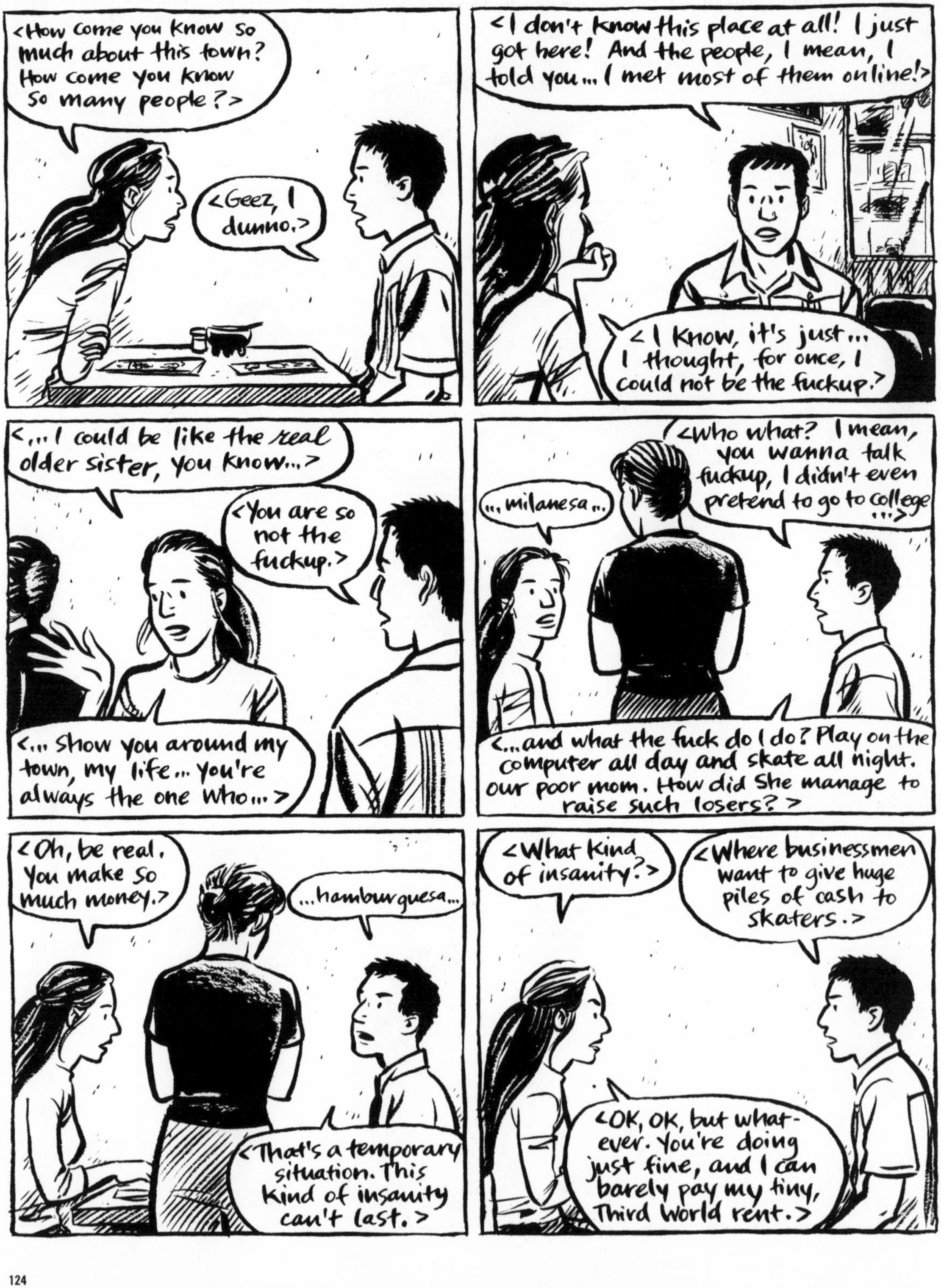

<How come you know so much about this town? How come you know so many people?>
<Geez, I dunno.>
<I don't know this place at all! I just got here! And the people, I mean, I told you... I met most of them online!>
<I know, it's just... I thought, for once, I could not be the fuckup.>
<...I could be like the *real* older sister, you know...>
<You are so not the fuckup.>
<... show you around my town, my life... you're always the one who...>
<Who what? I mean, you wanna talk fuckup, I didn't even pretend to go to college...>
...milanesa...
<...and what the fuck do I do? Play on the computer all day and skate all night. Our poor mom. How did she manage to raise such losers?>
<Oh, be real. You make so much money.>
...hamburguesa...
<That's a temporary situation. This kind of insanity can't last.>
<What kind of insanity?>
<Where businessmen want to give huge piles of cash to skaters.>
<OK, OK, but whatever. You're doing just fine, and I can barely pay my tiny, Third World rent.>

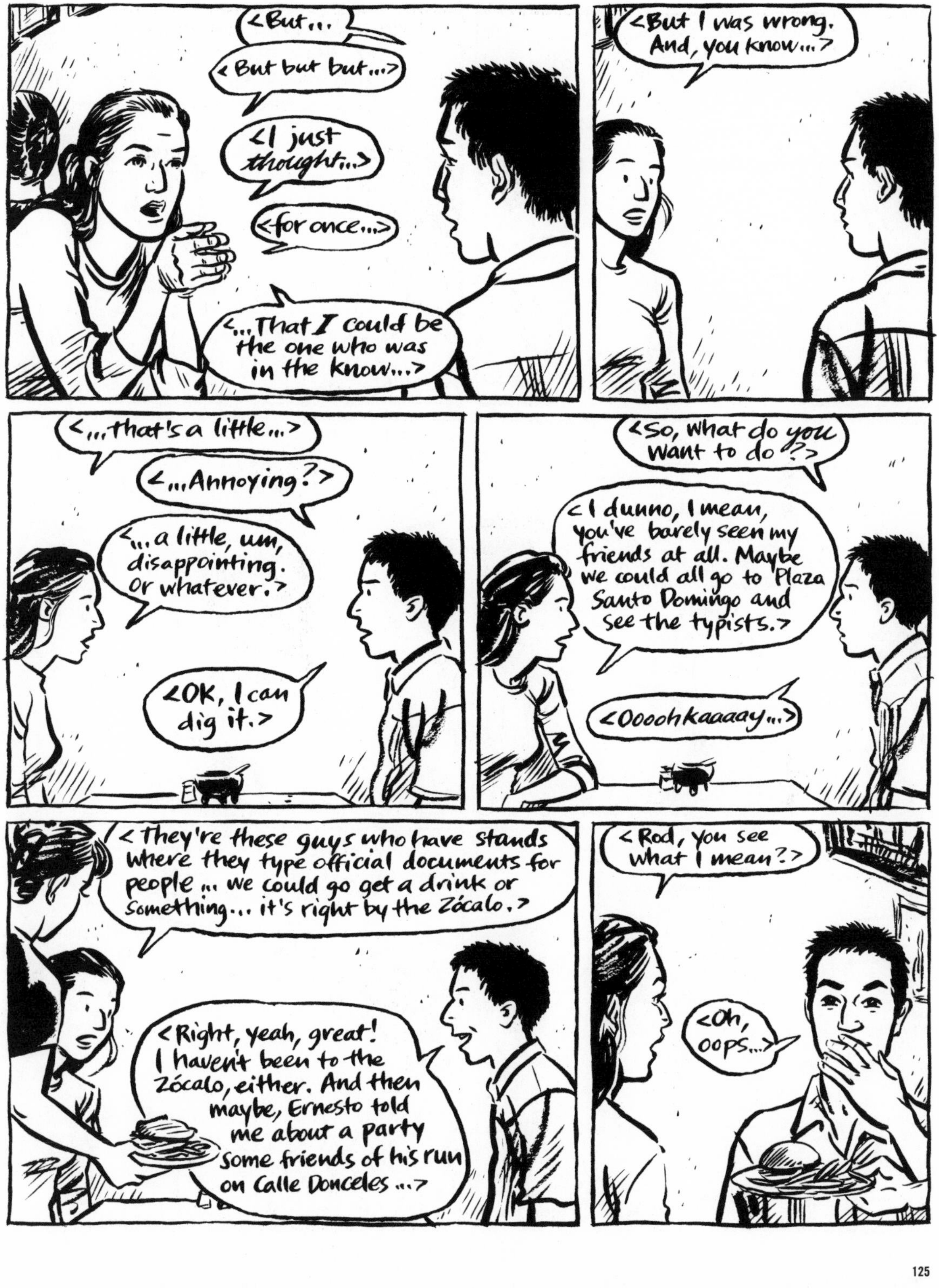

<But...
<But but but...>
<I just *thought*...>
<for once...>
<...That *I* could be the one who was in the know...>
<But I was wrong. And, you know...>
<...that's a little...>
<...Annoying?>
<...a little, um, disappointing. Or whatever.>
<OK, I can dig it.>
<So, what do you want to do?>
<I dunno, I mean, you've barely seen my friends at all. Maybe we could all go to Plaza Santo Domingo and see the typists.>
<Ooooh kaaaay...>
<They're these guys who have stands where they type official documents for people ... we could go get a drink or something... it's right by the Zócalo.>
<Right, yeah, great! I haven't been to the Zócalo, either. And then maybe, Ernesto told me about a party some friends of his run on Calle Donceles ...>
<Rod, you see what I mean?>
<Oh, oops...>

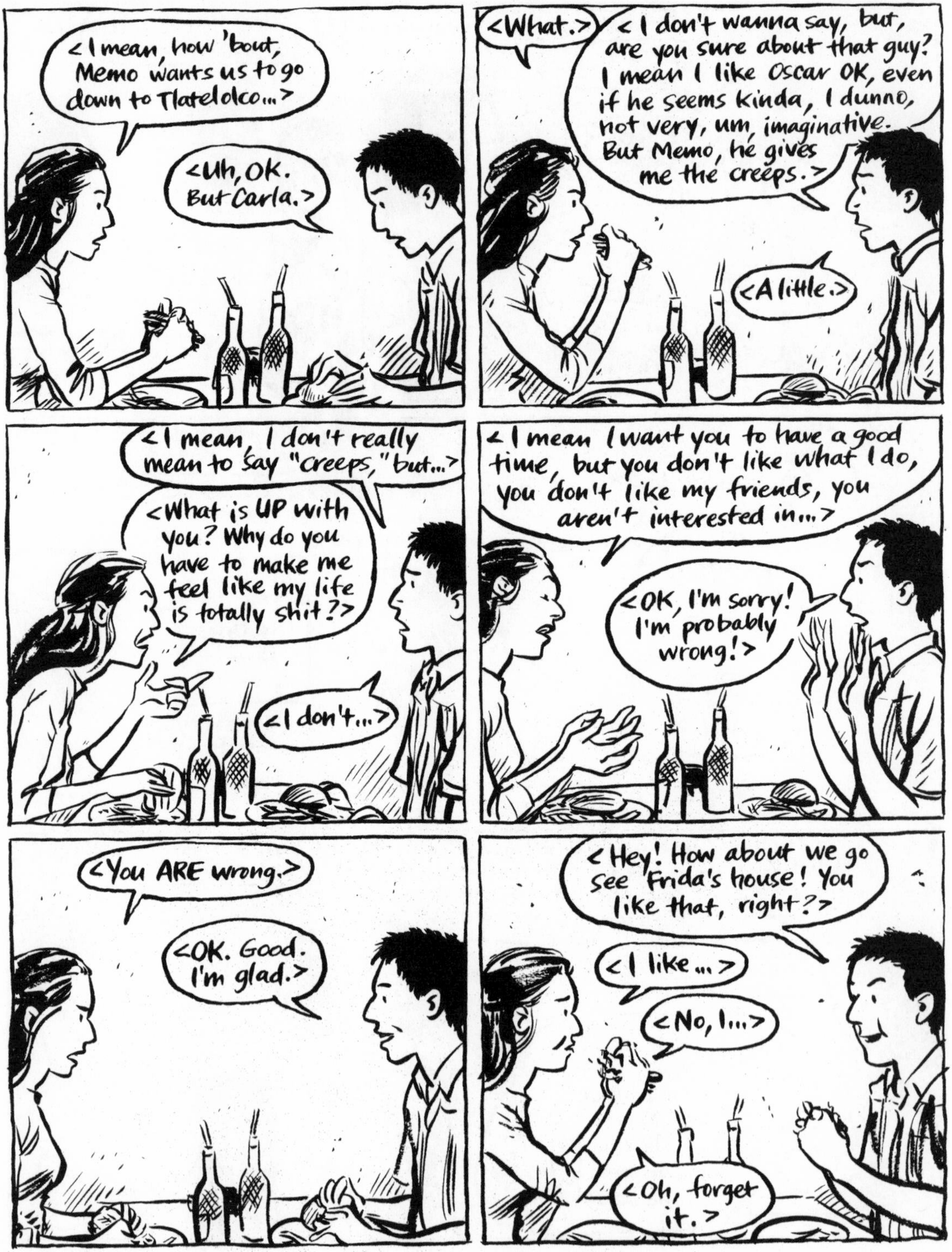
<I mean, how 'bout, Memo wants us to go down to Tlatelolco...>
<Uh, OK. But Carla.>
<What.>
<I don't wanna say, but, are you sure about that guy? I mean I like Oscar OK, even if he seems kinda, I dunno, not very, um, imaginative. But Memo, he gives me the creeps.>
<A little.>
<I mean, I don't really mean to say "creeps," but...>
<What is UP with you? Why do you have to make me feel like my life is totally shit?>
<I don't...>
<I mean I want you to have a good time, but you don't like what I do, you don't like my friends, you aren't interested in...>
<OK, I'm sorry! I'm probably wrong!>
<You ARE wrong.>
<OK. Good. I'm glad.>
<Hey! How about we go see Frida's house! You like that, right?>
<I like...>
<No, I...>
<Oh, forget it.>

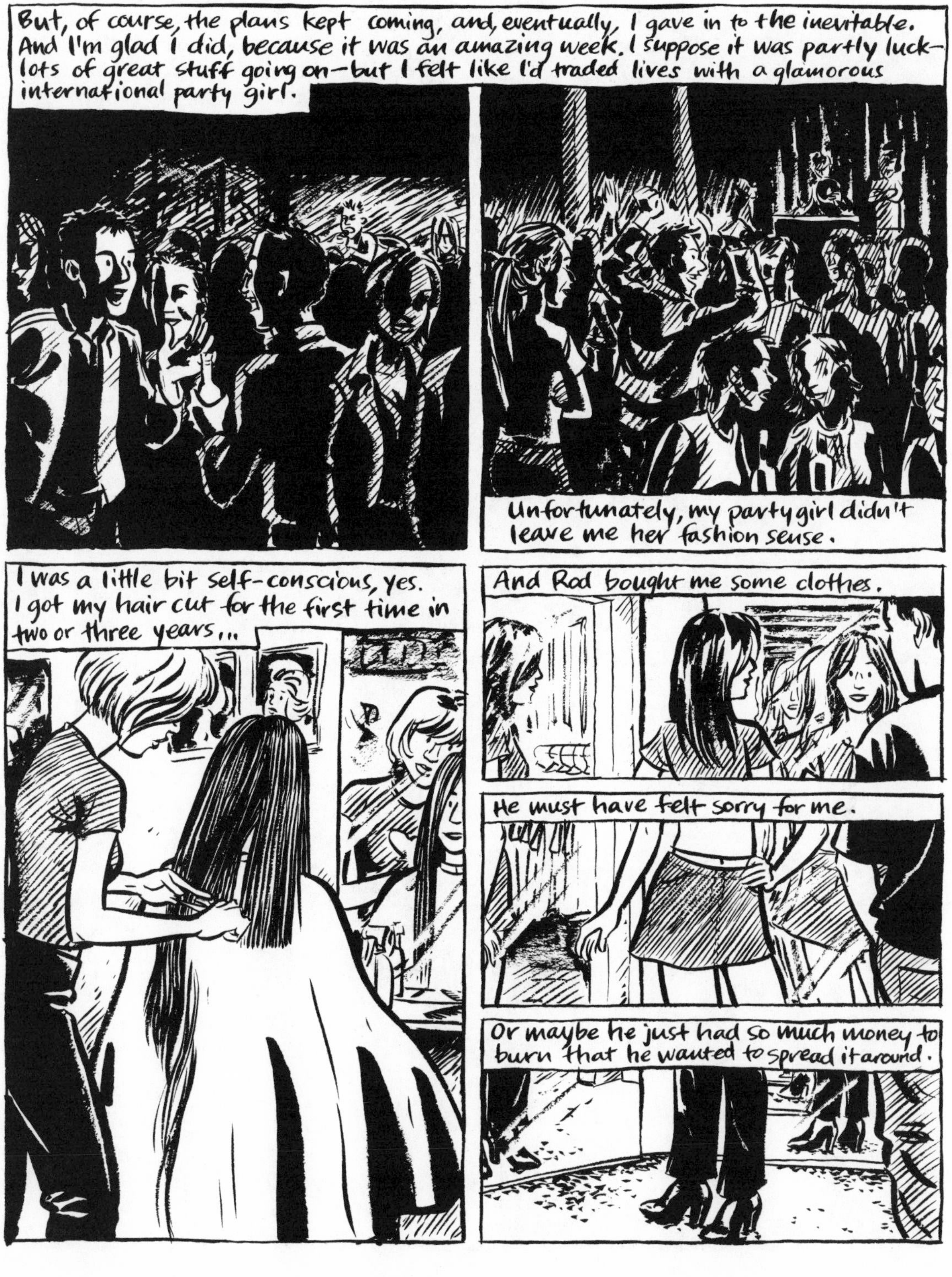
But, of course, the plans kept coming, and, eventually, I gave in to the inevitable. And I'm glad I did, because it was an amazing week. I suppose it was partly luck-lots of great stuff going on—but I felt like I'd traded lives with a glamorous international party girl.
Unfortunately, my party girl didn't leave me her fashion sense.
I was a little bit self-conscious, yes. I got my hair cut for the first time in two or three years...
And Rod bought me some clothes.
He must have felt sorry for me.
Or maybe he just had so much money to burn that he wanted to spread it around.

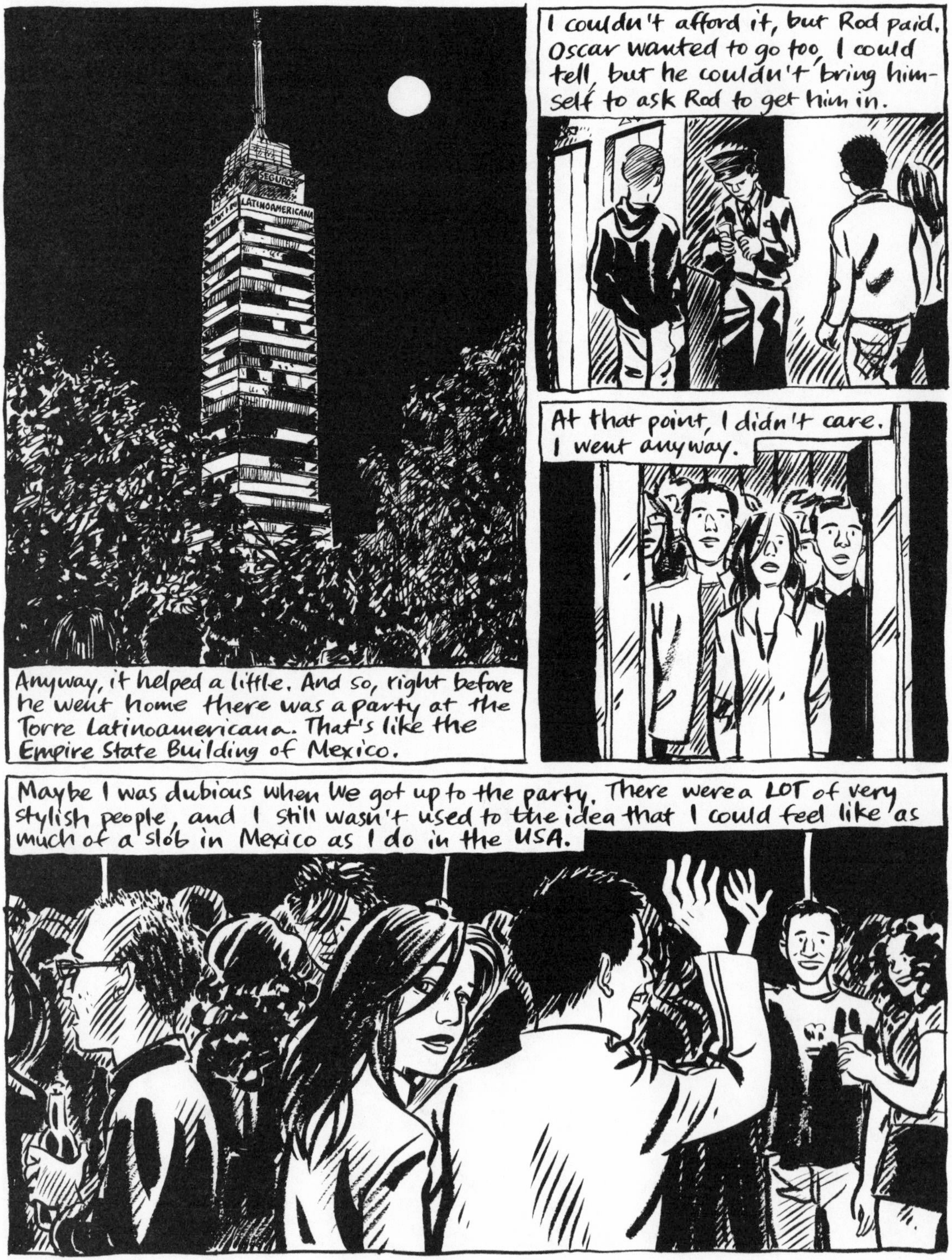
SEGUROS
LATINOAMERICANA
Anyway, it helped a little. And so, right before he went home there was a party at the Torre Latinoamericana. That's like the Empire State Building of Mexico.
I couldn't afford it, but Rod paid. Oscar wanted to go too, I could tell, but he couldn't bring himself to ask Rod to get him in.
At that point, I didn't care. I went anyway.
Maybe I was dubious when we got up to the party. There were a LOT of very stylish people, and I still wasn't used to the idea that I could feel like as much of a slob in Mexico as I do in the USA.

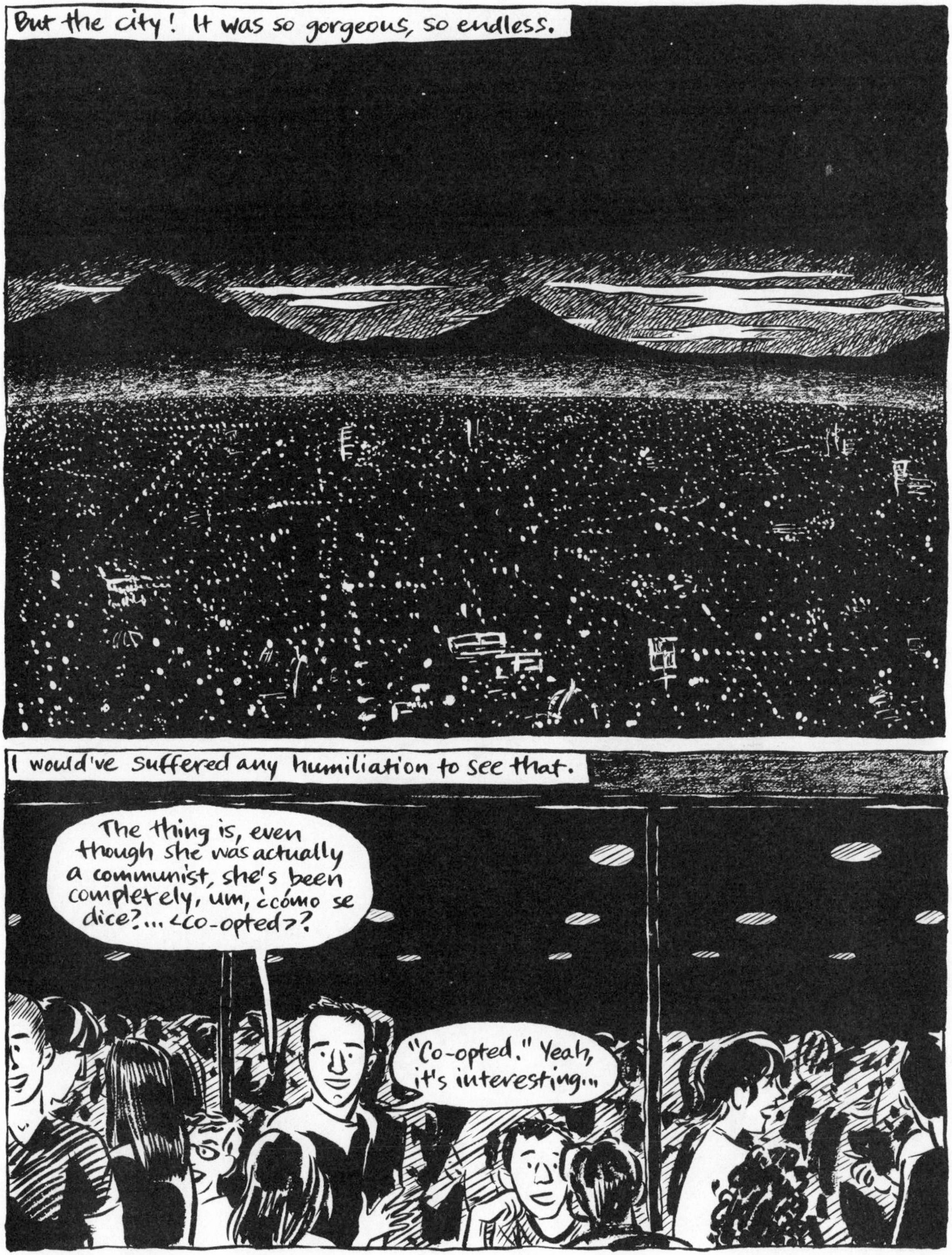
But the city! It was so gorgeous, so endless.
I would've suffered any humiliation to see that.
The thing is, even though she was actually a communist, she's been completely, um, ¿cómo se dice?... <co-opted>?
"Co-opted." Yeah, it's interesting...

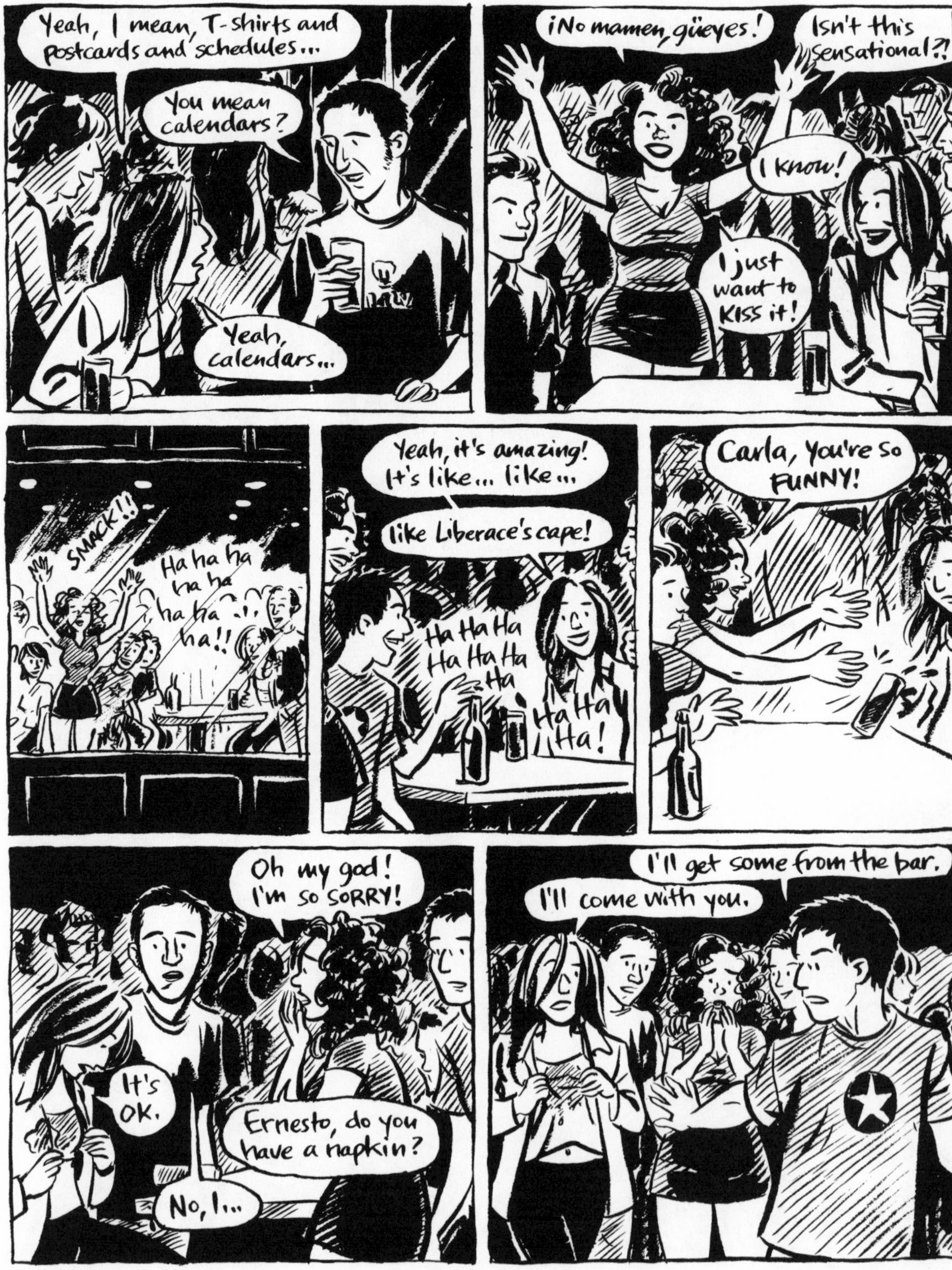

Yeah, I mean, T-shirts and postcards and schedules...
You mean calendars?
Yeah, calendars...
¡No mamen, güeyes!
Isn't this sensational?!
I know!
I just want to KISS it!
SMACK!!
Ha ha ha ha ha ha ha ha!!
Yeah, it's amazing! It's like... like...
like Liberace's cape!
Ha Ha Ha Ha Ha Ha Ha
Ha Ha Ha!
Carla, you're so FUNNY!
Oh my god! I'm so SORRY!
It's OK.
Ernesto, do you have a napkin?
No, I...
I'll get some from the bar.
I'll come with you.

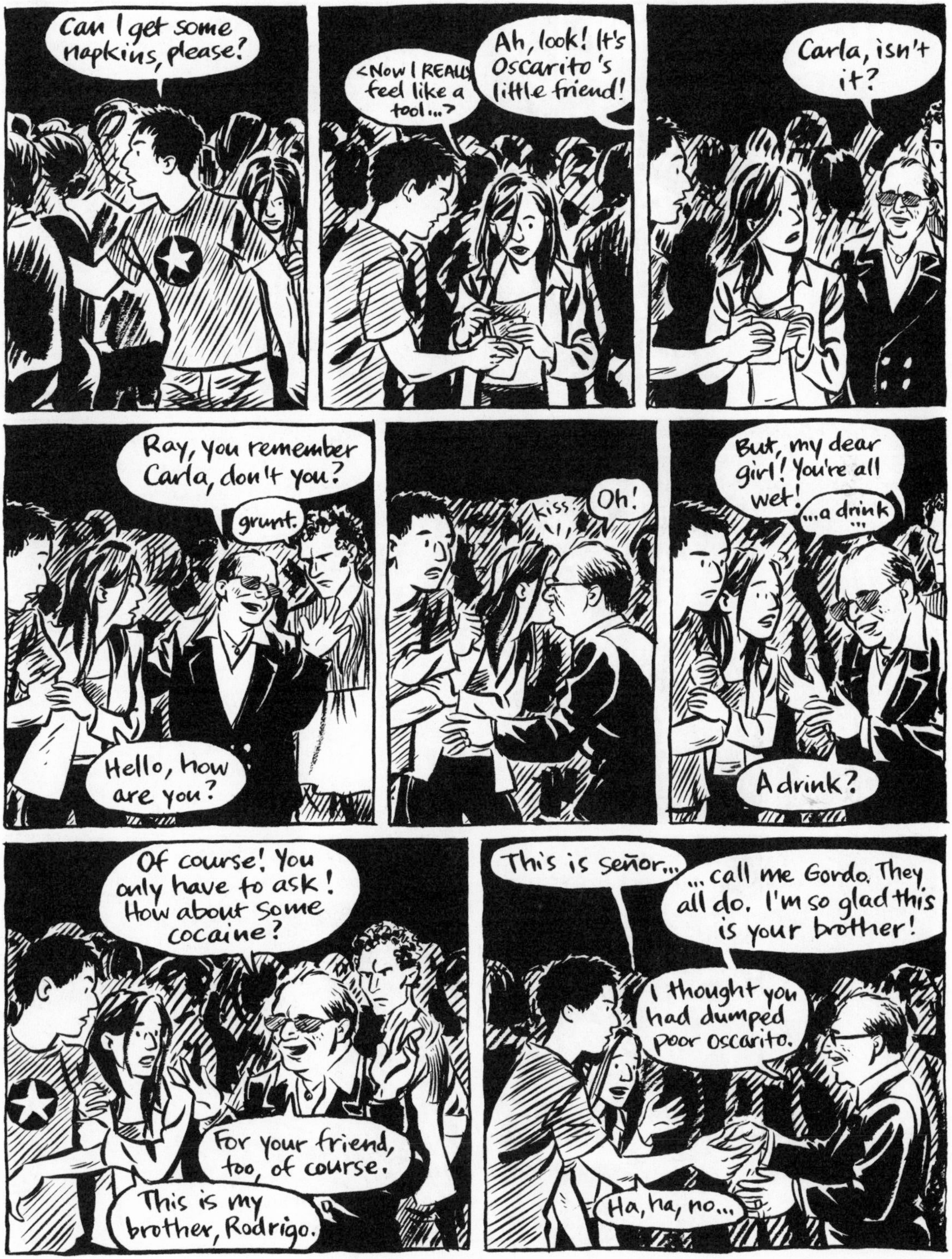

Can I get some napkins, please?
<Now I REALLY feel like a tool...>
Ah, look! It's Oscarito's little friend!
Carla, isn't it?
Ray, you remember Carla, don't you?
grunt.
Hello, how are you?
kiss
Oh!
But, my dear girl! You're all wet!
...a drink...
A drink?
Of course! You only have to ask! How about some cocaine?
For your friend, too, of course.
This is my brother, Rodrigo.
This is señor...
...call me Gordo. They all do. I'm so glad this is your brother!
I thought you had dumped poor Oscarito.
Ha, ha, no...

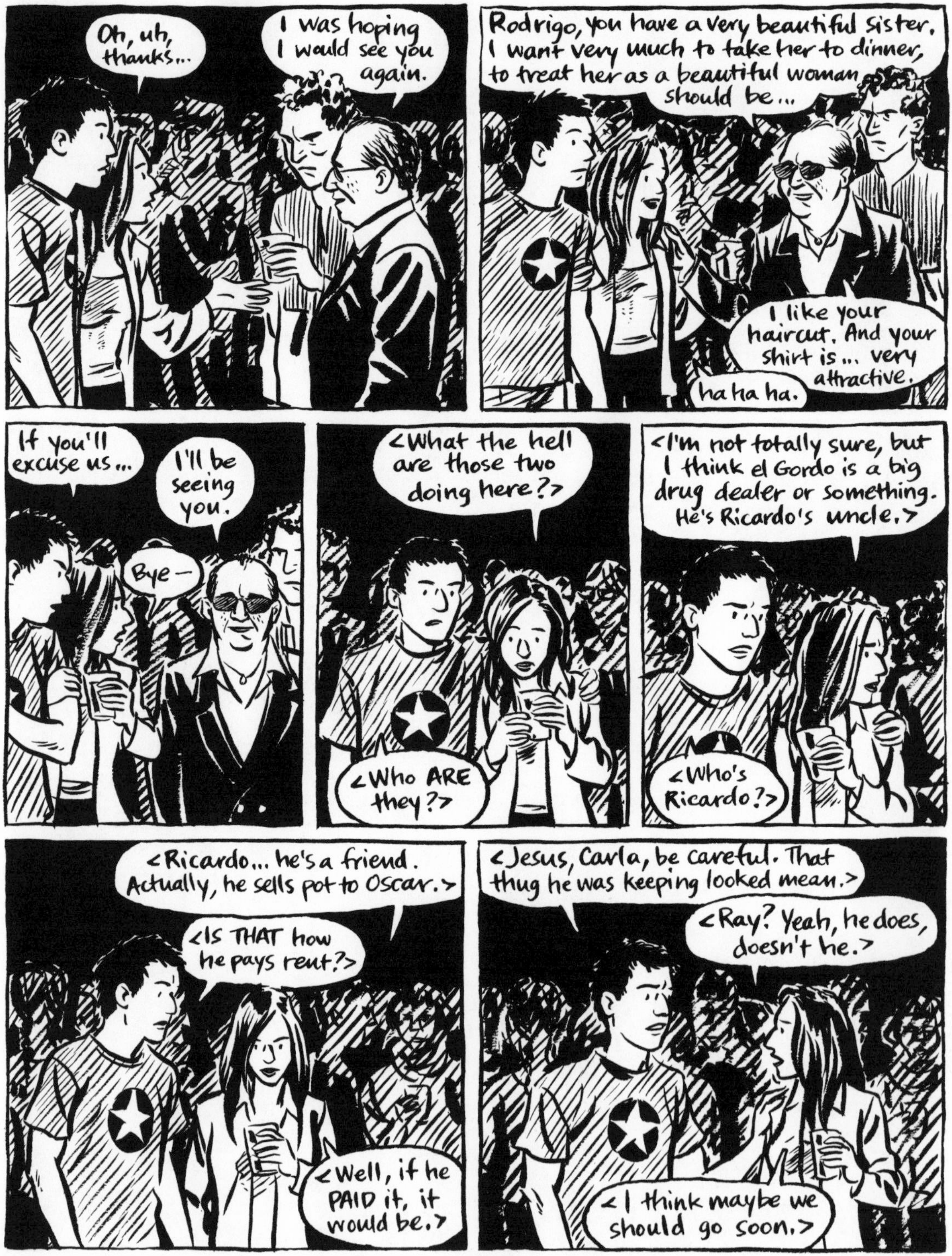
Oh, uh, thanks...
I was hoping I would see you again.
Rodrigo, you have a very beautiful Sister. I want very much to take her to dinner, to treat her as a beautiful woman should be...
I like your haircut. And your shirt is... very attractive.
ha ha ha.
If you'll excuse us...
I'll be seeing you.
Bye—
<What the hell are those two doing here?>
<Who ARE they?>
<I'm not totally sure, but I think el Gordo is a big drug dealer or something. He's Ricardo's uncle.>
<Who's Ricardo?>
<Ricardo... he's a friend. Actually, he sells pot to Oscar.>
<IS THAT how he pays rent?>
<Well, if he PAID it, it would be.>
<Jesus, Carla, be careful. That thug he was keeping looked mean.>
<Ray? Yeah, he does, doesn't he.>
<I think maybe we should go soon.>

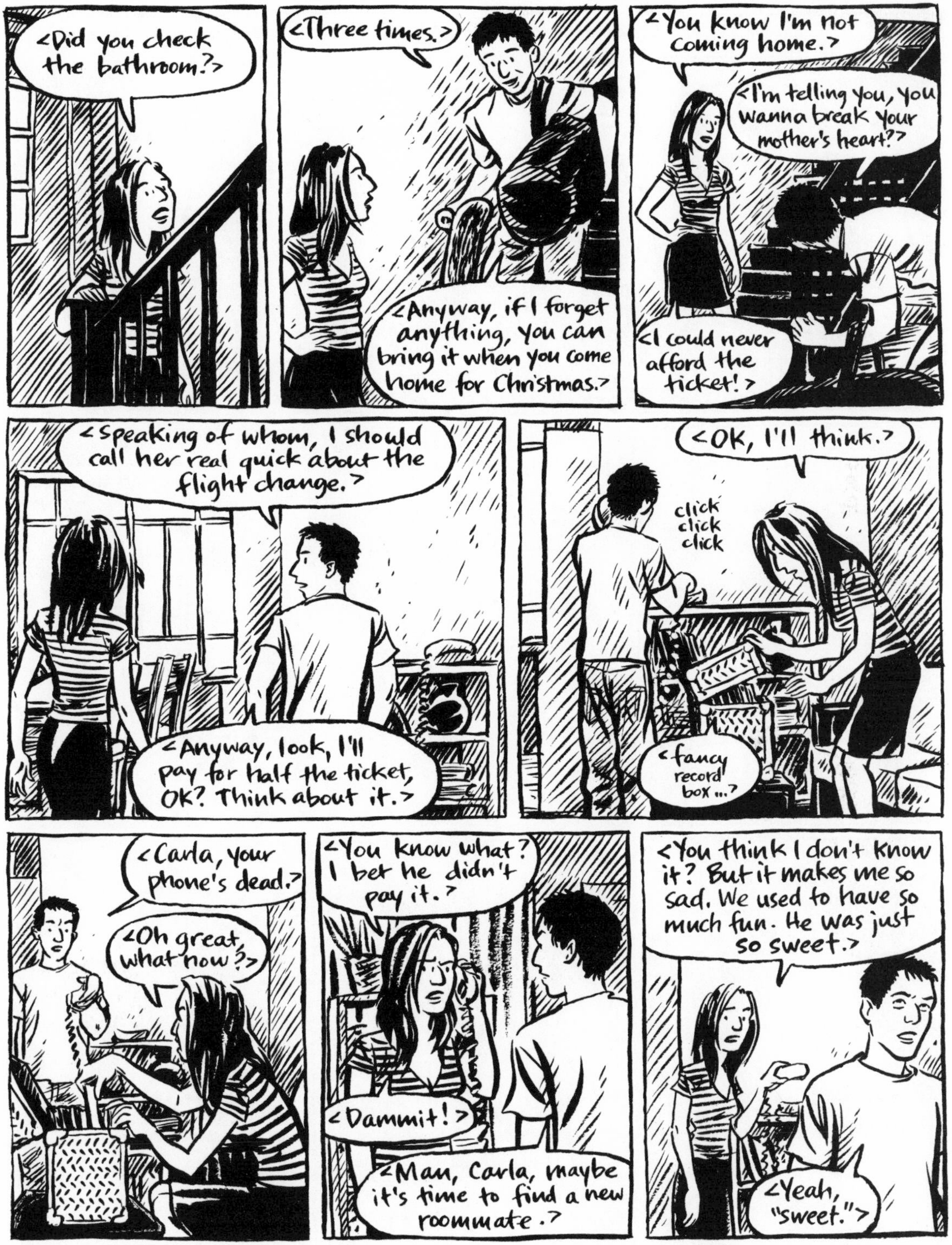

<Did you check the bathroom?>
<Three times.>
<Anyway, if I forget anything, you can bring it when you come home for Christmas.>
<You know I'm not coming home.>
<I'm telling you, you wanna break your mother's heart?>
<I could never afford the ticket!>
<Speaking of whom, I should call her real quick about the flight change.>
<Anyway, look, I'll pay for half the ticket, OK? Think about it.>
<OK, I'll think.>
click
click
click
<fancy record box...>
<Carla, your phone's dead.>
<Oh great, what now?>
<You know what? I bet he didn't pay it.>
<Dammit!>
<Man, Carla, maybe it's time to find a new roommate.>
<You think I don't know it? But it makes me so sad. We used to have so much fun. He was just so sweet.>
<Yeah, "sweet.">

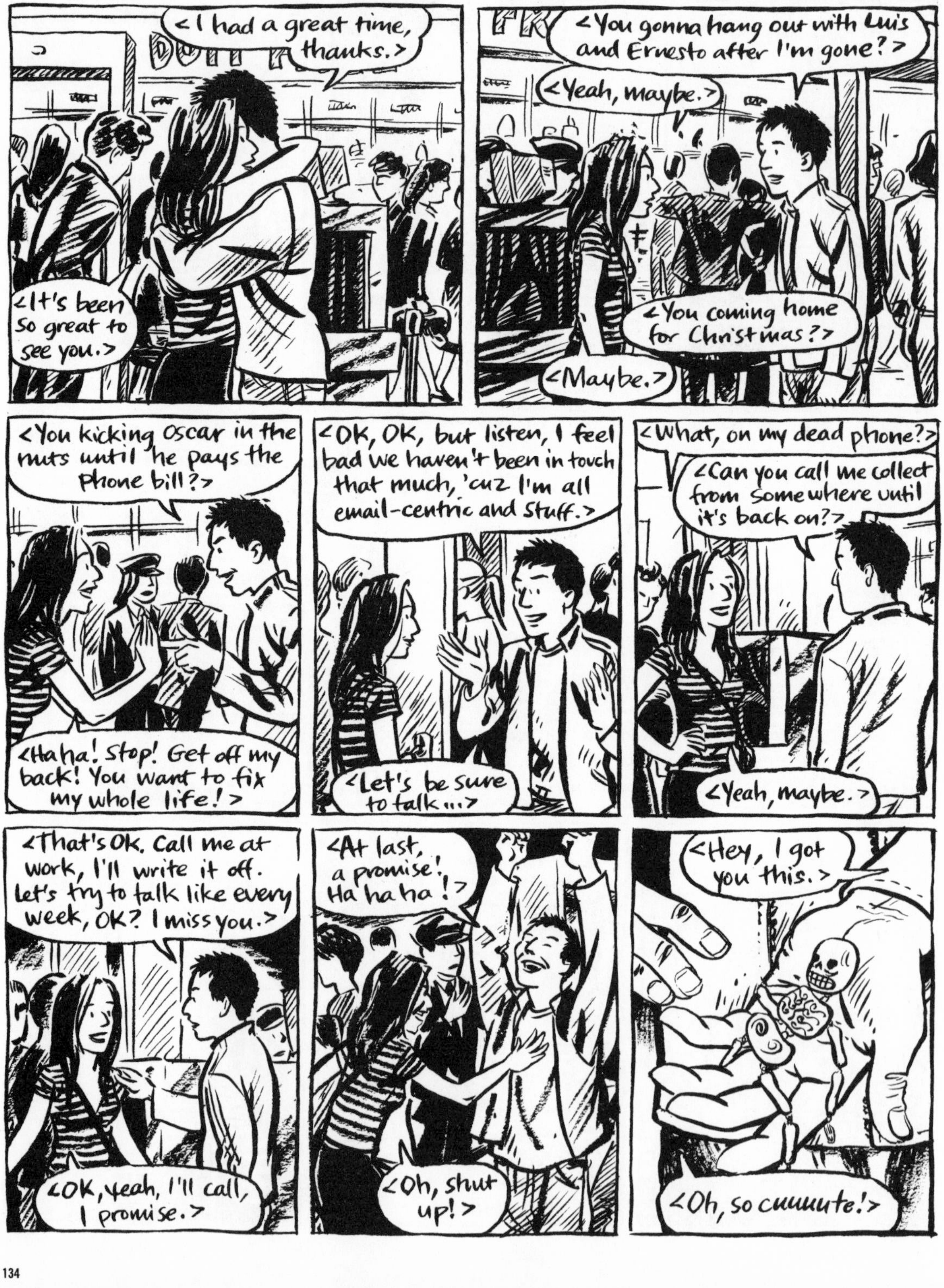
<I had a great time, thanks.>
<It's been so great to see you.>
<You gonna hang out with Luis and Ernesto after I'm gone?>
<Yeah, maybe.>
<You coming home for Christmas?>
<Maybe.>
<You kicking Oscar in the nuts until he pays the phone bill?>
<Ha ha! Stop! Get off my back! You want to fix my whole life!>
<OK, OK, but listen, I feel bad we haven't been in touch that much, 'cuz I'm all email-centric and stuff.>
<Let's be sure to talk...>
<What, on my dead phone?>
<Can you call me collect from somewhere until it's back on?>
<Yeah, maybe.>
<That's OK. Call me at work, I'll write it off. Let's try to talk like every week, OK? I miss you.>
<OK, yeah, I'll call, I promise.>
<At last, a promise! Ha ha ha!>
<Oh, shut up!>
<Hey, I got you this.>
<Oh, so cuuuute!>

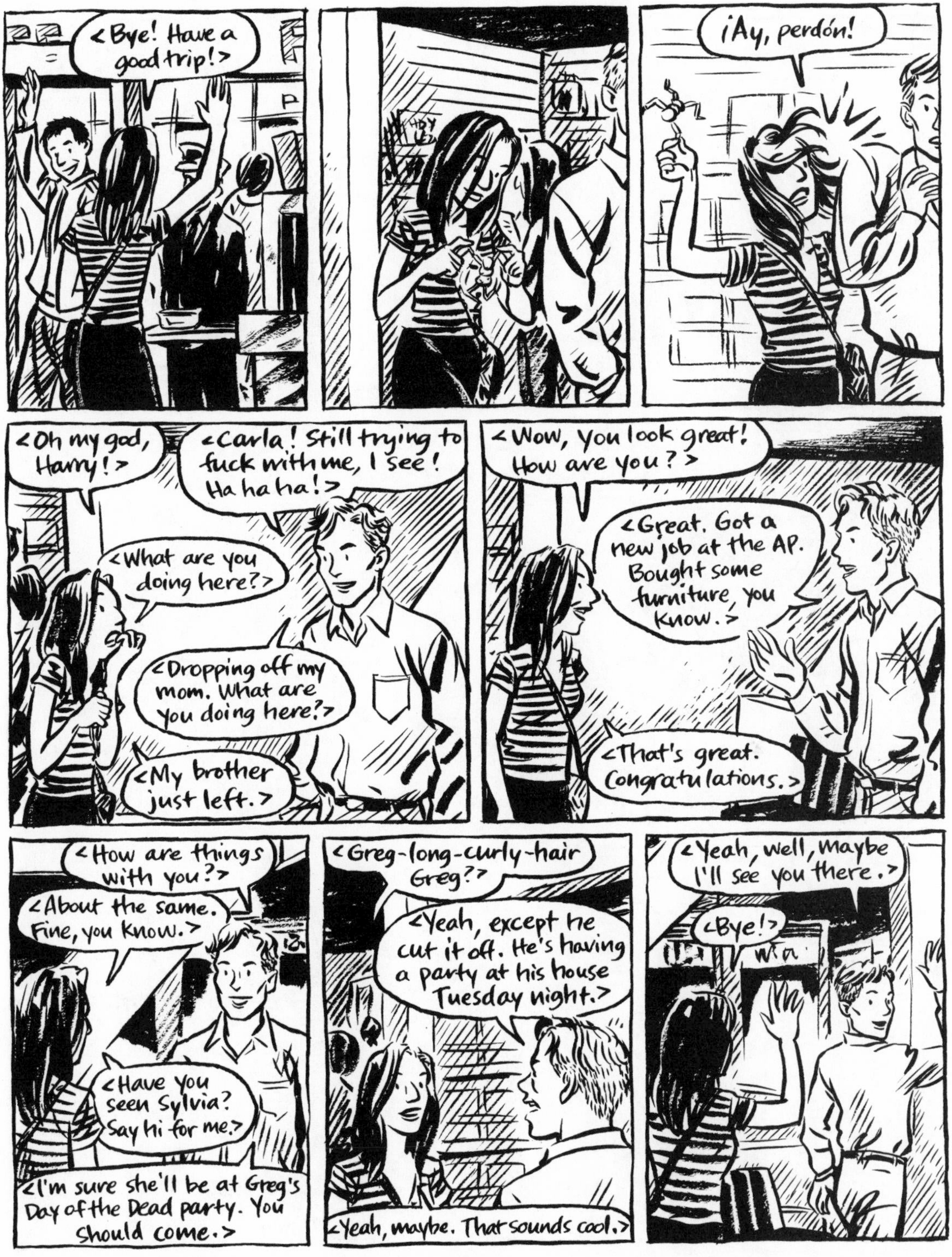
<Bye! Have a good trip!>
¡Ay, perdón!
<Oh my god, Harry!>
<Carla! Still trying to fuck with me, I see! Ha ha ha!>
<What are you doing here?>
<Dropping off my mom. What are you doing here?>
<My brother just left.>
<Wow, you look great! How are you?>
<Great. Got a new job at the AP. Bought some furniture, you know.>
<That's great. Congratulations.>
<How are things with you?>
<About the same. Fine, you know.>
<Have you seen Sylvia? Say hi for me.>
<I'm sure she'll be at Greg's Day of the Dead party. You should come.>
<Greg-long-curly-hair Greg?>
<Yeah, except he cut it off. He's having a party at his house Tuesday night.>
<Yeah, maybe. That sounds cool.>
<Yeah, well, maybe I'll see you there.>
<Bye!>

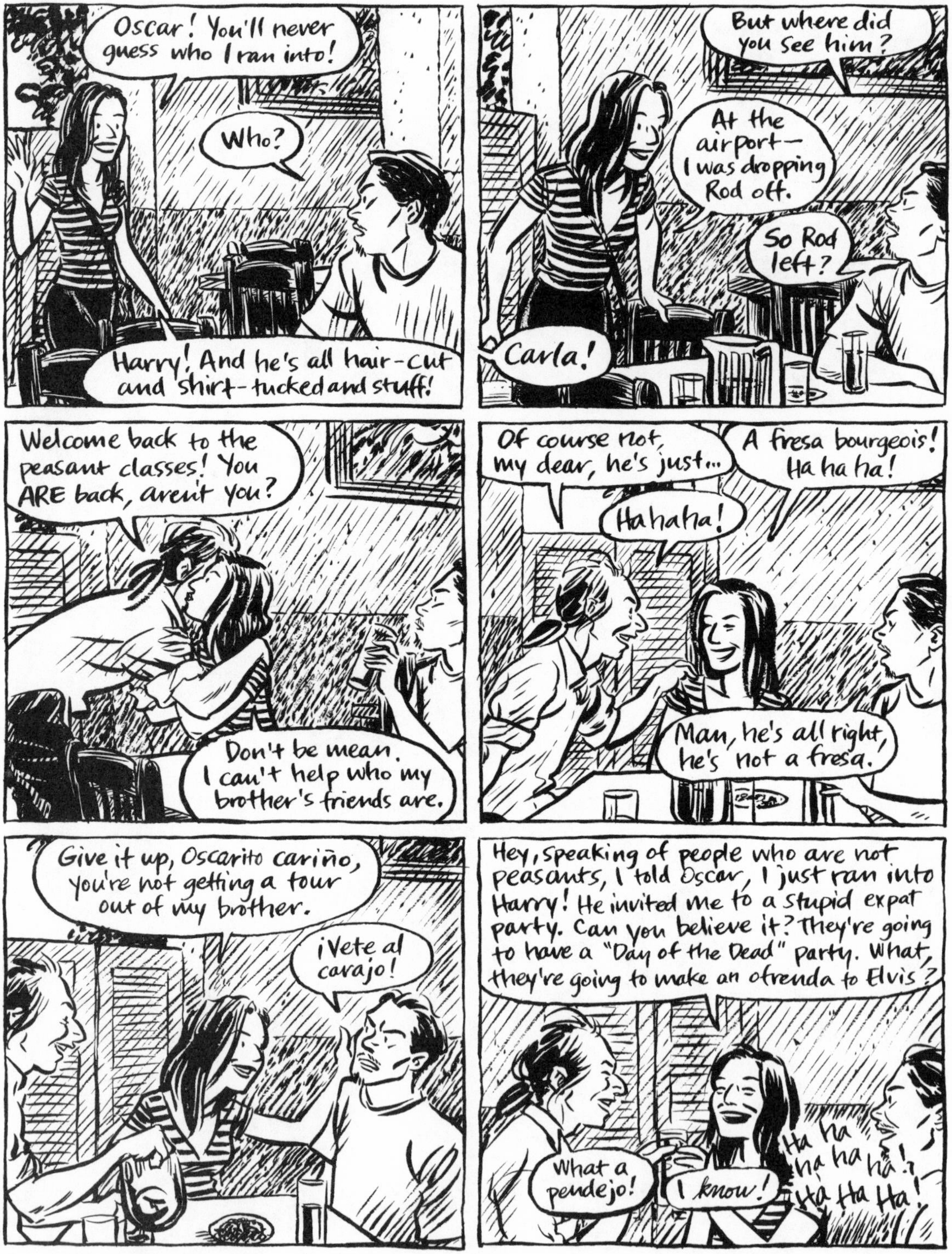
Oscar! You'll never guess who I ran into!
Who?
Harry! And he's all hair-cut and shirt-tucked and stuff!
But where did you see him?
At the airport— I was dropping Rod off.
So Rod left?
Carla!
Welcome back to the peasant classes! You ARE back, aren't you?
Don't be mean. I can't help who my brother's friends are.
Of course not, my dear, he's just...
A fresa bourgeois! Ha ha ha!
Hahaha!
Man, he's all right, he's not a fresa.
Give it up, Oscarito cariño, you're not getting a tour out of my brother.
¡Vete al carajo!
Hey, speaking of people who are not peasants, I told Oscar, I just ran into Harry! He invited me to a stupid expat party. Can you believe it? They're going to have a "Day of the Dead" party. What, they're going to make an ofrenda to Elvis?
What a pendejo!
I know!
Ha ha ha ha ha! Ha Ha Ha!

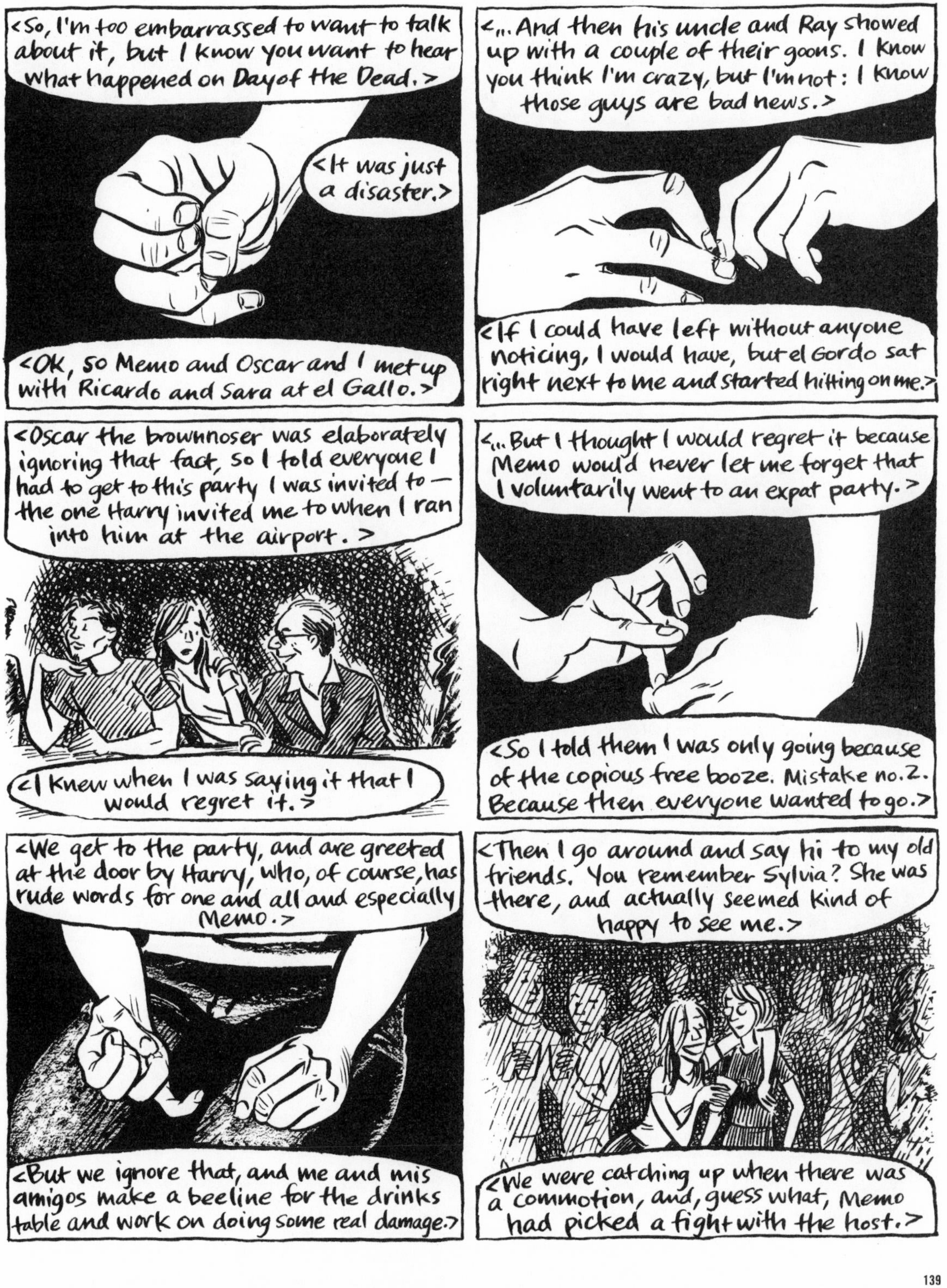
<So, I'm too embarrassed to want to talk about it, but I know you want to hear what happened on Day of the Dead.>
<It was just a disaster.>
<OK, so Memo and Oscar and I met up with Ricardo and Sara at el Gallo.>
<... And then his uncle and Ray showed up with a couple of their goons. I know you think I'm crazy, but I'm not: I know those guys are bad news.>
<If I could have left without anyone noticing, I would have, but el Gordo sat right next to me and started hitting on me.>
<Oscar the brownnoser was elaborately ignoring that fact, so I told everyone I had to get to this party I was invited to— the one Harry invited me to when I ran into him at the airport.>
<I knew when I was saying it that I would regret it.>
<... But I thought I would regret it because Memo would never let me forget that I voluntarily went to an expat party.>
<So I told them I was only going because of the copious free booze. Mistake no. 2. Because then everyone wanted to go.>
<We get to the party, and are greeted at the door by Harry, who, of course, has rude words for one and all and especially Memo.>
<But we ignore that, and me and mis amigos make a beeline for the drinks table and work on doing some real damage.>
<Then I go around and say hi to my old friends. You remember Sylvia? She was there, and actually seemed kind of happy to see me.>
<We were catching up when there was a commotion, and, guess what, Memo had picked a fight with the host.>

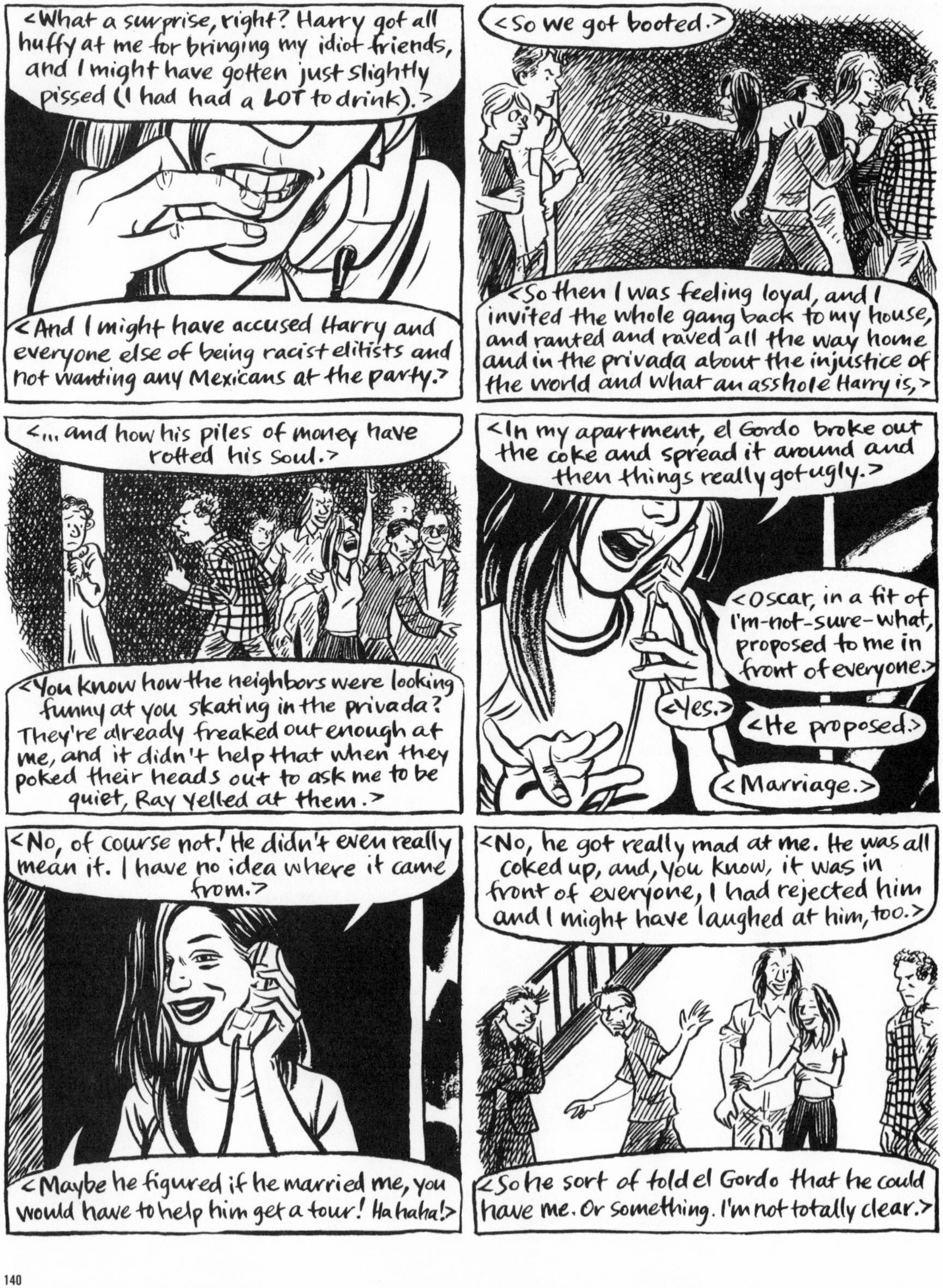
<What a surprise, right? Harry got all huffy at me for bringing my idiot friends, and I might have gotten just slightly pissed (I had had a LOT to drink).>
<And I might have accused Harry and everyone else of being racist elitists and not wanting any Mexicans at the party.>
<So we got booted.>
<So then I was feeling loyal, and I invited the whole gang back to my house, and ranted and raved all the way home and in the privada about the injustice of the world and what an asshole Harry is,>
<... and how his piles of money have rotted his soul.>
<You know how the neighbors were looking funny at you skating in the privada? They're already freaked out enough at me, and it didn't help that when they poked their heads out to ask me to be quiet, Ray yelled at them.>
<In my apartment, el Gordo broke out the coke and spread it around and then things really got ugly.>
<Oscar, in a fit of I'm-not-sure-what, proposed to me in front of everyone.>
<Yes.>
<He proposed.>
<Marriage.>
<No, of course not! He didn't even really mean it. I have no idea where it came from.>
<Maybe he figured if he married me, you would have to help him get a tour! Ha haha!>
<No, he got really mad at me. He was all coked up, and, you know, it was in front of everyone, I had rejected him and I might have laughed at him, too.>
<So he sort of told el Gordo that he could have me. Or something. I'm not totally clear.>

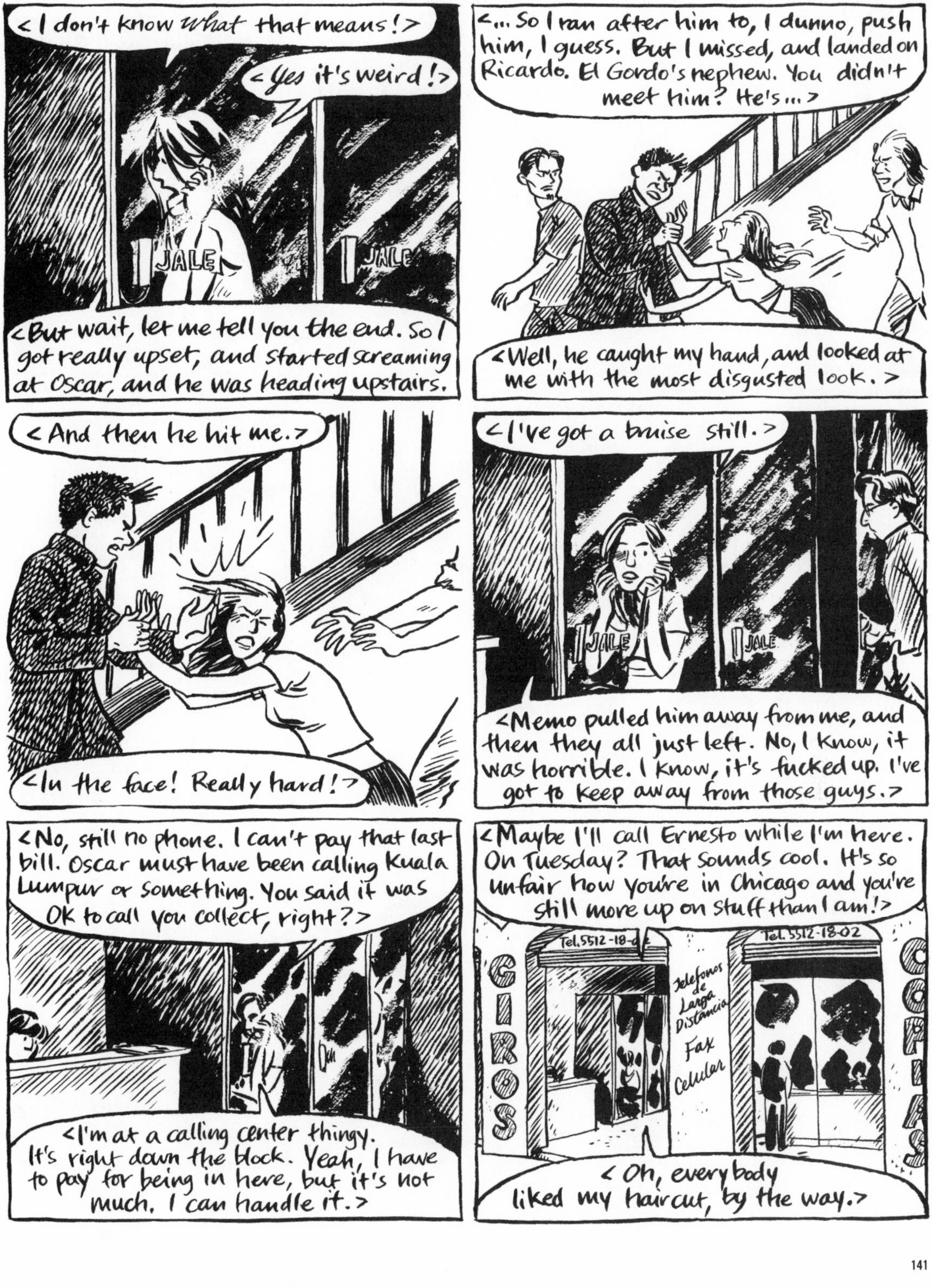
<I don't know what that means!>
<Yes it's weird!>
JALE
JALE
<But wait, let me tell you the end. So I got really upset, and started screaming at Oscar, and he was heading upstairs.
<... So I ran after him to, I dunno, push him, I guess. But I missed, and landed on Ricardo. El Gordo's nephew. You didn't meet him? He's...>
<Well, he caught my hand, and looked at me with the most disgusted look.>
<And then he hit me.>
<In the face! Really hard!>
<I've got a bruise still.>
JALE
JALE
<Memo pulled him away from me, and then they all just left. No, I know, it was horrible. I know, it's fucked up. I've got to keep away from those guys.>
<No, still no phone. I can't pay that last bill. Oscar must have been calling Kuala Lumpur or something. You said it was OK to call you collect, right?>
<I'm at a calling center thingy. It's right down the block. Yeah, I have to pay for being in here, but it's not much. I can handle it.>
<Maybe I'll call Ernesto while I'm here. On Tuesday? That sounds cool. It's so unfair how you're in Chicago and you're still more up on stuff than I am!>
Tel. 5512-18-02
GIROS
Telefonos de Larga Distancia
Fax
Celular
COPIAS
<Oh, everybody liked my haircut, by the way.>

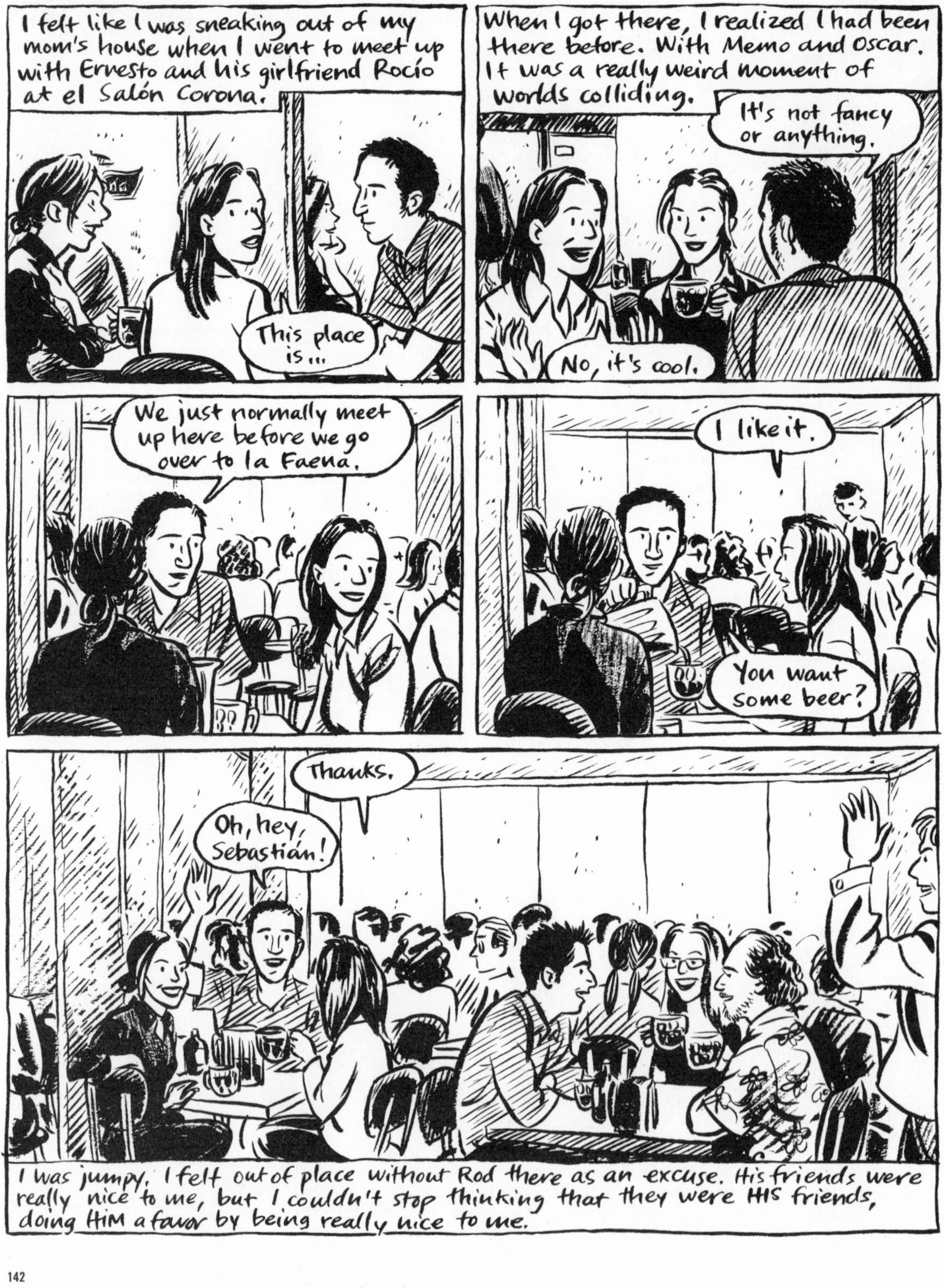

I felt like I was sneaking out of my mom's house when I went to meet up with Ernesto and his girlfriend Rocío at el Salón Corona.
This place is...
When I got there, I realized I had been there before. With Memo and Oscar. It was a really weird moment of worlds colliding.
It's not fancy or anything.
No, it's cool.
We just normally meet up here before we go over to la Faena.
I like it.
You want some beer?
Thanks.
Oh, hey, Sebastián!
I was jumpy. I felt out of place without Rod there as an excuse. His friends were really nice to me, but I couldn't stop thinking that they were HIS friends, doing HIM a favor by being really nice to me.

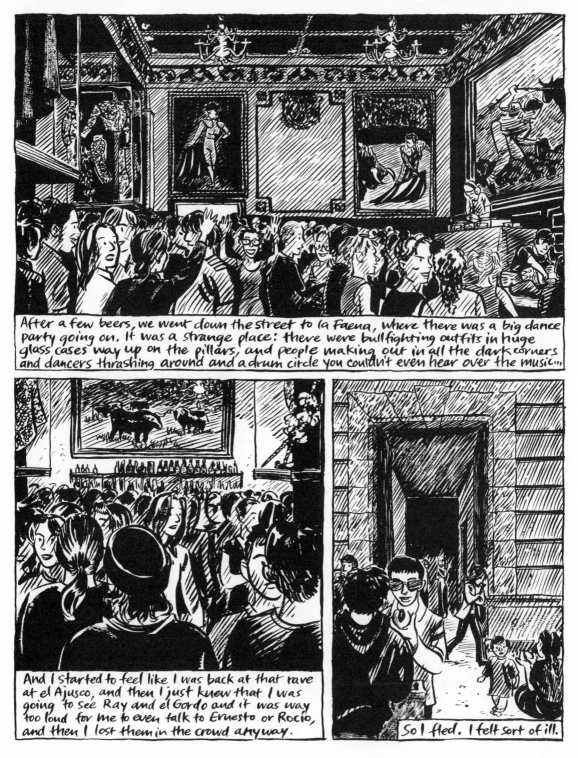

After a few beers, we went down the street to la Faena, where there was a big dance party going on. It was a strange place: there were bullfighting outfits in huge glass cases way up on the pillars, and people making out in all the dark corners and dancers thrashing around and a drum circle you couldn't even hear over the music...

And I started to feel like I was back at that rave at el Ajusco, and then I just knew that I was going to see Ray and el Gordo and it was way too loud for me to even talk to Ernesto or Rocío, and then I lost them in the crowd anyway.

So I fled. I felt sort of ill.

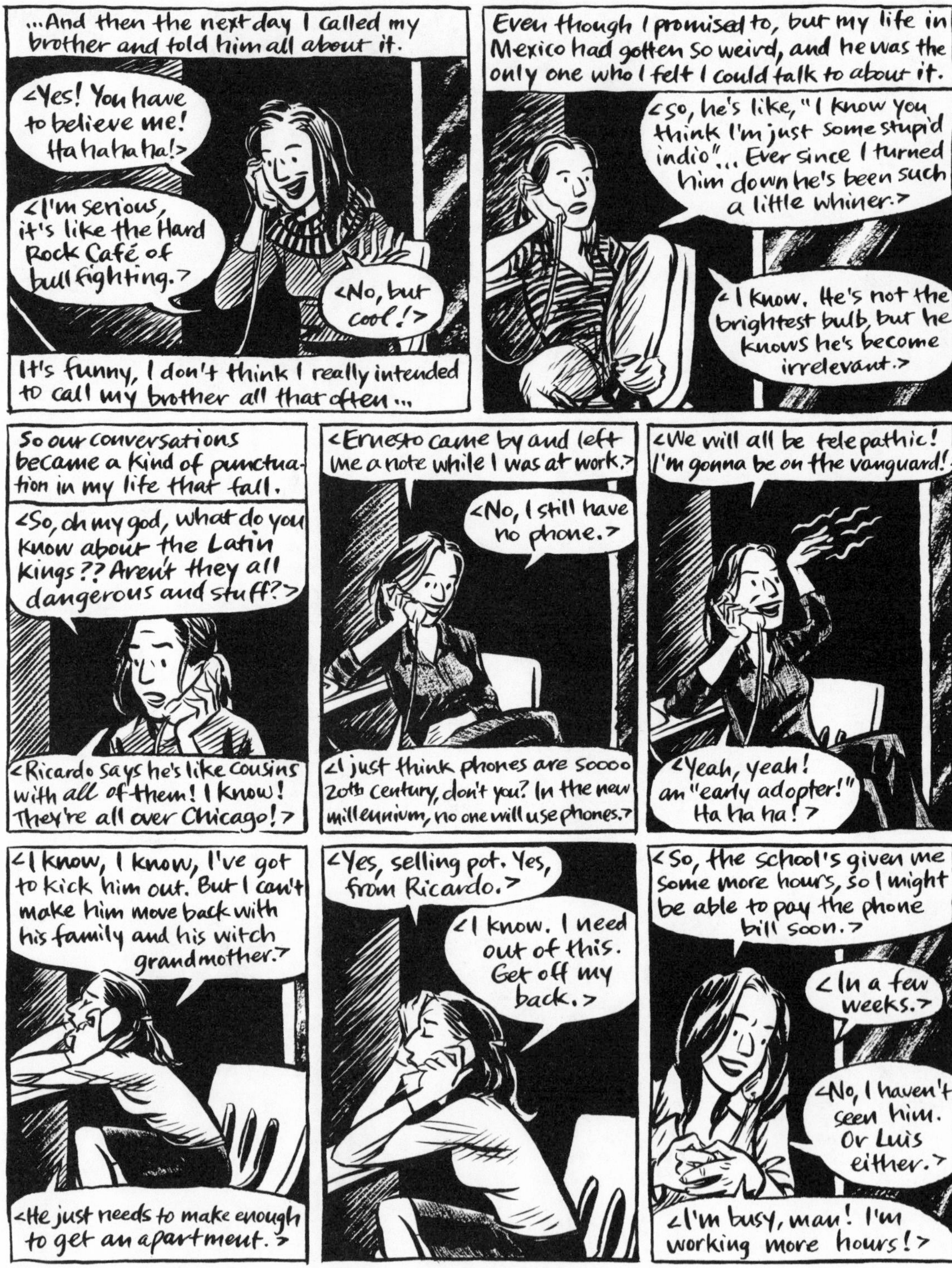
...And then the next day I called my brother and told him all about it.
<Yes! You have to believe me! Hahahaha!>
<I'm serious, it's like the Hard Rock Café of bullfighting.>
<No, but cool!>
It's funny, I don't think I really intended to call my brother all that often...
Even though I promised to, but my life in Mexico had gotten so weird, and he was the only one who I felt I could talk to about it.
<So, he's like, "I know you think I'm just some stupid indio"... Ever since I turned him down he's been such a little whiner.>
<I know. He's not the brightest bulb, but he knows he's become irrelevant.>
So our conversations became a kind of punctuation in my life that fall.
<So, oh my god, what do you know about the Latin Kings?? Aren't they all dangerous and stuff?>
<Ricardo says he's like cousins with all of them! I know! They're all over Chicago!>
<Ernesto came by and left me a note while I was at work.>
<No, I still have no phone.>
<I just think phones are soooo 20th century, don't you? In the new millennium, no one will use phones.>
<We will all be telepathic! I'm gonna be on the vanguard!>
<Yeah, yeah! an "early adopter!" Ha ha ha!>
<I know, I know, I've got to kick him out. But I can't make him move back with his family and his witch grandmother.>
<He just needs to make enough to get an apartment.>
<Yes, selling pot. Yes, from Ricardo.>
<I know. I need out of this. Get off my back.>
<So, the school's given me some more hours, so I might be able to pay the phone bill soon.>
<In a few weeks.>
<No, I haven't seen him. Or Luis either.>
<I'm busy, man! I'm working more hours!>

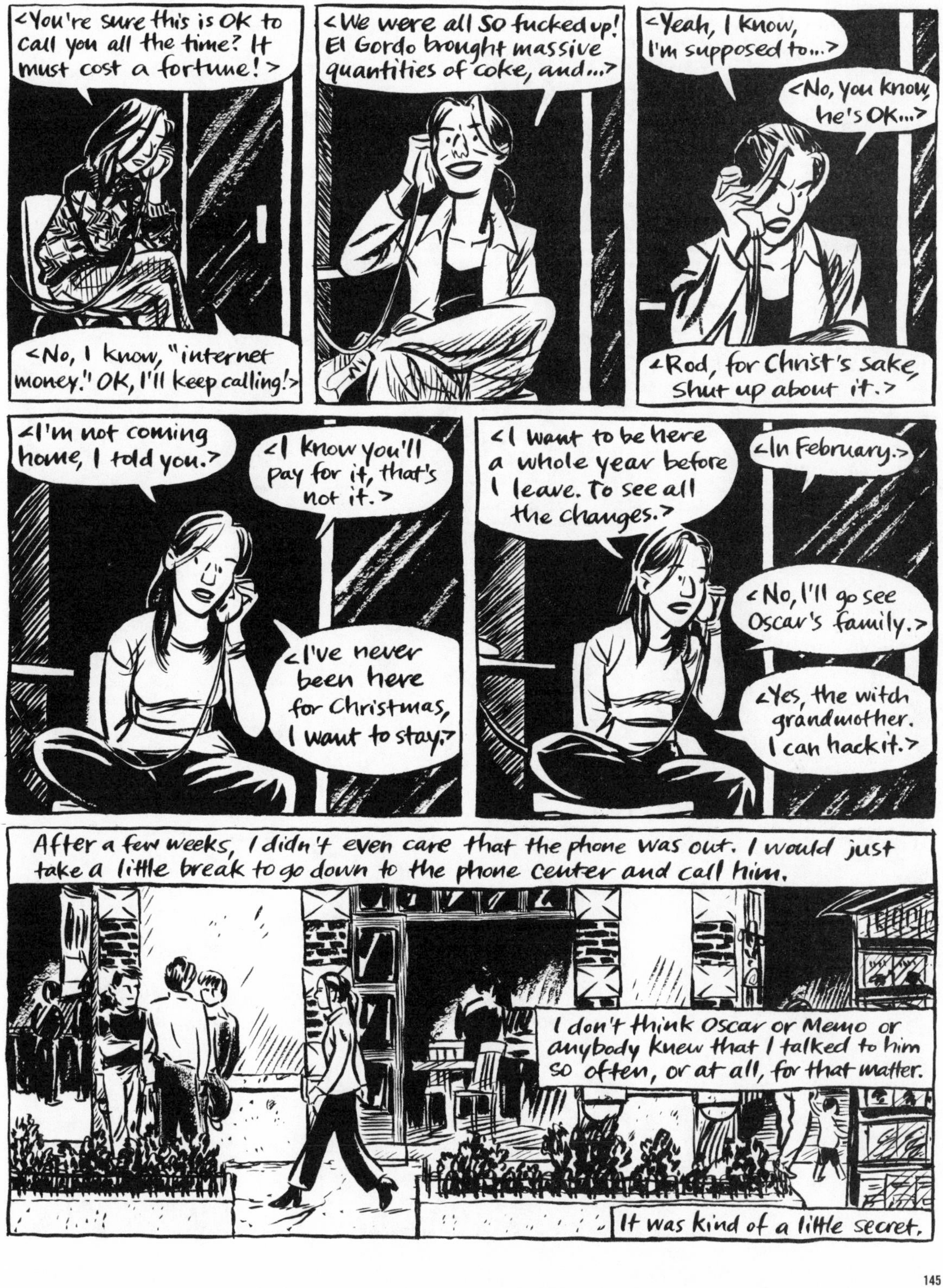

<You're sure this is OK to call you all the time? It must cost a fortune!>
<No, I know, "internet money." OK, I'll keep calling!>
<We were all so fucked up! El Gordo brought massive quantities of coke, and...>
<Yeah, I know, I'm supposed to...>
<No, you know, he's OK...>
<Rod, for Christ's sake, shut up about it.>
<I'm not coming home, I told you.>
<I know you'll pay for it, that's not it.>
<I've never been here for Christmas, I want to stay.>
<I want to be here a whole year before I leave. To see all the changes.>
<In February.>
<No, I'll go see Oscar's family.>
<Yes, the witch grandmother. I can hack it.>
After a few weeks, I didn't even care that the phone was out. I would just take a little break to go down to the phone center and call him.
I don't think Oscar or Memo or anybody knew that I talked to him so often, or at all, for that matter.
It was kind of a little secret.

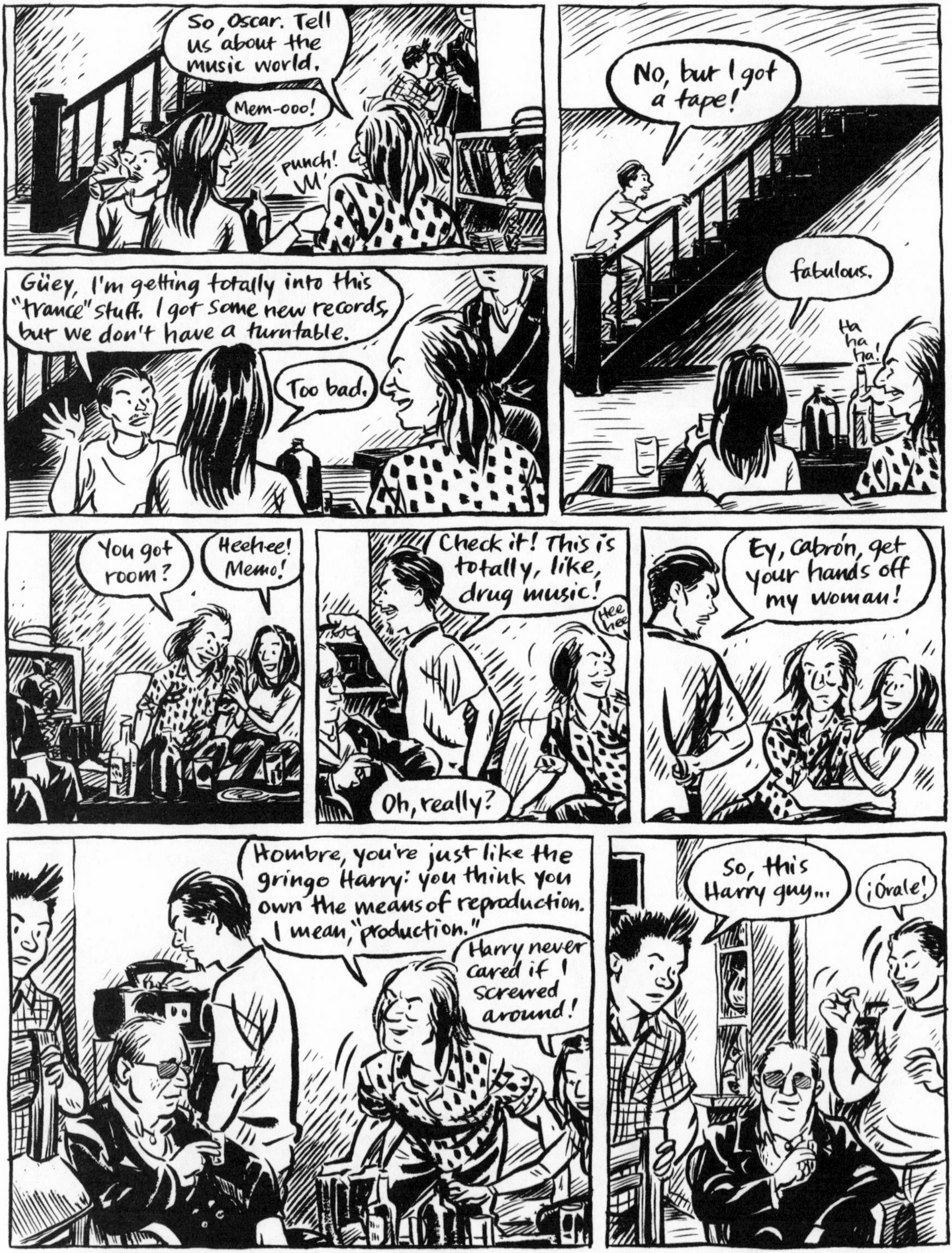
So, Oscar. Tell us about the music world.
Mem-ooo!
punch!
No, but I got a tape!
Güey, I'm getting totally into this "trance" stuff. I got some new records, but we don't have a turntable.
Too bad.
fabulous.
Ha ha ha!
You got room?
Heehee! Memo!
Check it! This is totally, like, drug music!
Hee hee
Oh, really?
Ey, cabrón, get your hands off my woman!
Hombre, you're just like the gringo Harry: you think you own the means of reproduction. I mean, "production."
Harry never cared if I screwed around!
So, this Harry guy...
¡Órale!

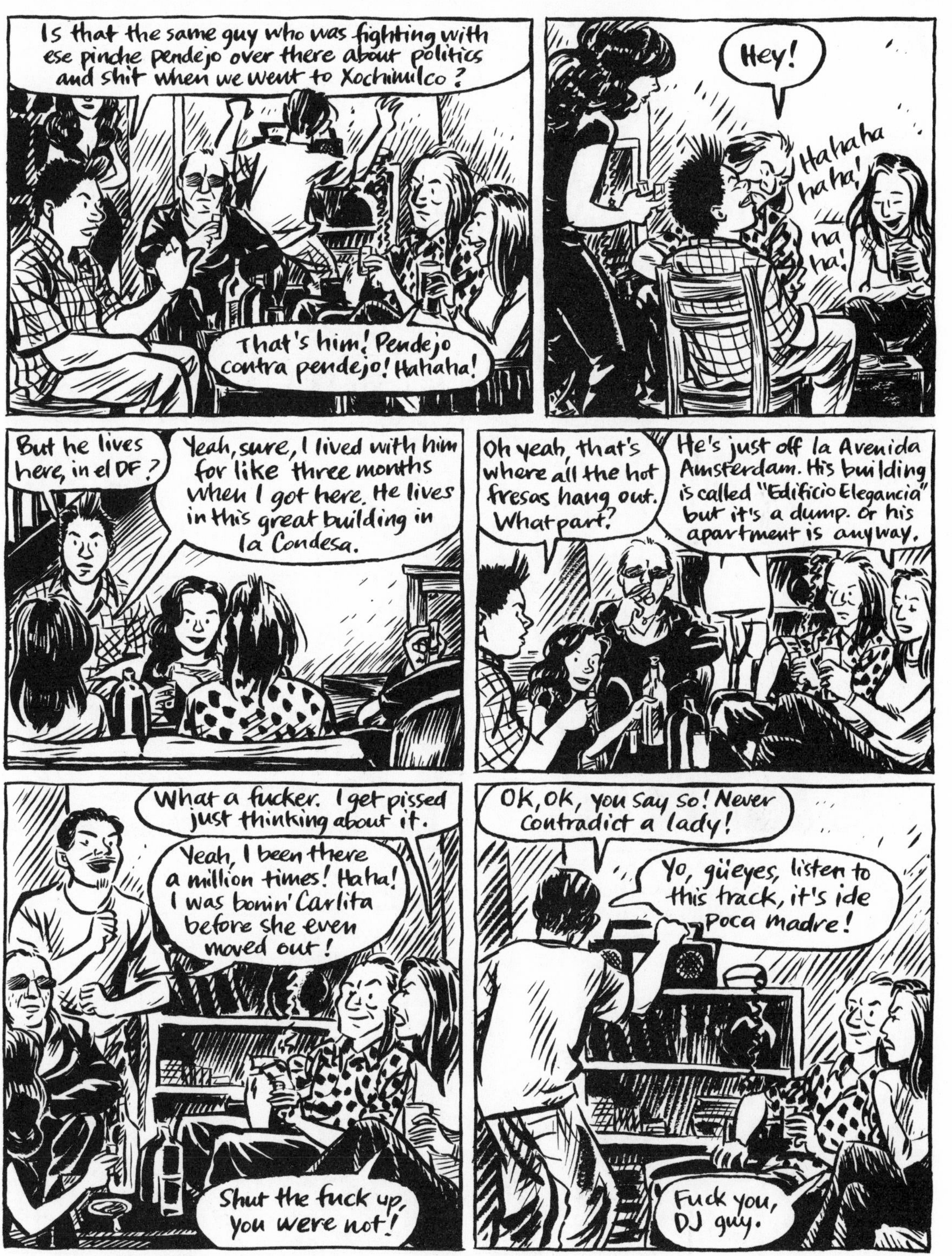
Is that the same guy who was fighting with ese pinche pendejo over there about politics and shit when we went to Xochimilco?
That's him! Pendejo contra pendejo! Hahaha!
Hey!
Hahaha haha!
ha ha!
But he lives here, in el DF?
Yeah, sure, I lived with him for like three months when I got here. He lives in this great building in la Condesa.
Oh yeah, that's where all the hot fresas hang out. What part?
He's just off la Avenida Amsterdam. His building is called "Edificio Elegancia" but it's a dump. Or his apartment is anyway.
What a fucker. I get pissed just thinking about it.
Yeah, I been there a million times! Haha! I was bonin' Carlita before she even moved out!
Shut the fuck up, you were not!
Ok, ok, you say so! Never contradict a lady!
Yo, güeyes, listen to this track, it's ide poca madre!
Fuck you, DJ guy.

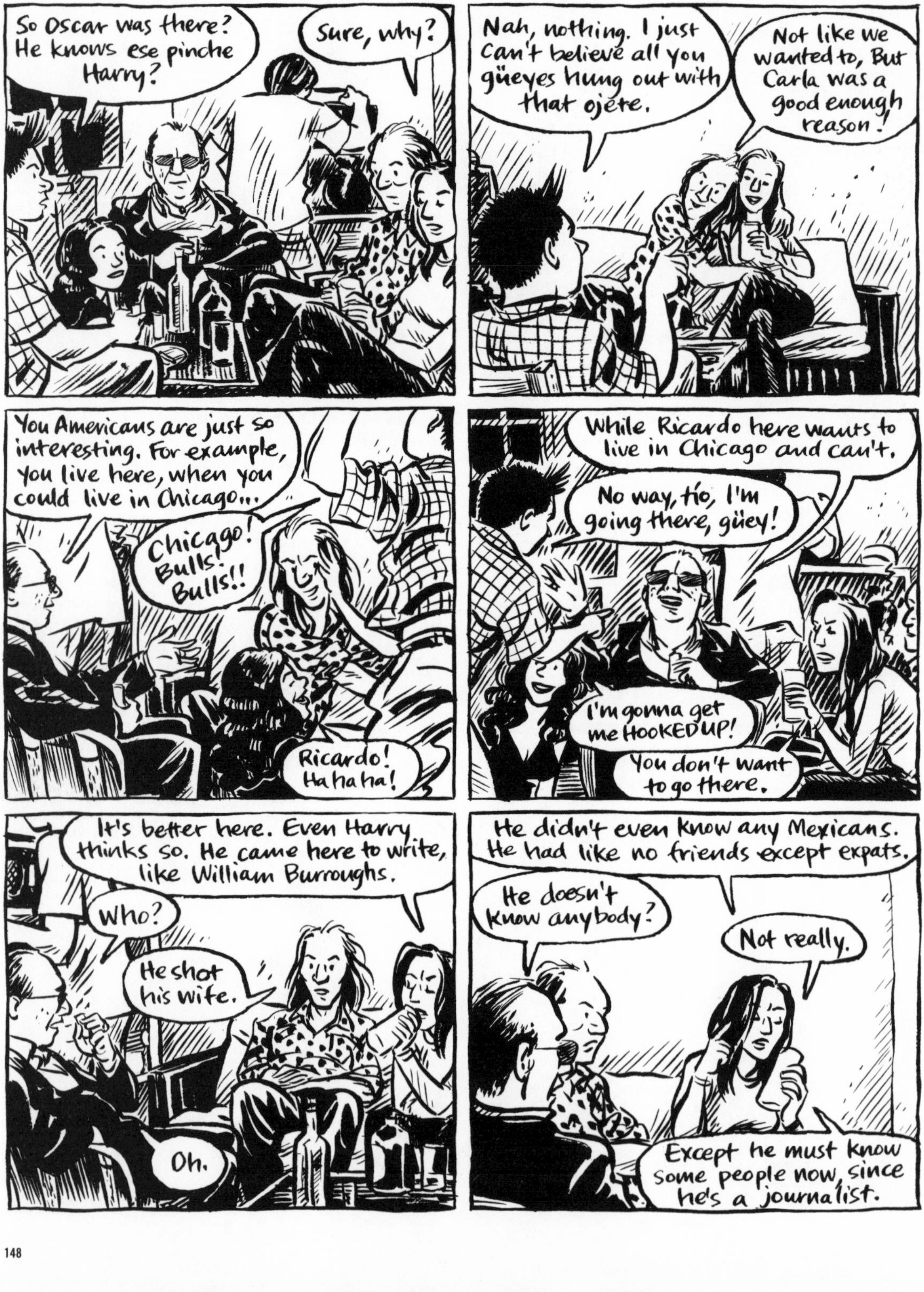
So Oscar was there? He knows ese pinche Harry?
Sure, why?
Nah, nothing. I just can't believe all you güeyes hung out with that ojete.
Not like we wanted to, But Carla was a good enough reason!
You Americans are just so interesting. For example, you live here, when you could live in Chicago...
Chicago! Bulls! Bulls!!
Ricardo! Ha ha ha!
While Ricardo here wants to live in Chicago and can't.
No way, tío, I'm going there, güey!
I'm gonna get me HOOKED UP!
You don't want to go there.
It's better here. Even Harry thinks so. He came here to write, like William Burroughs.
Who?
He shot his wife.
Oh.
He didn't even know any Mexicans. He had like no friends except expats.
He doesn't know anybody?
Not really.
Except he must know some people now, since he's a journalist.

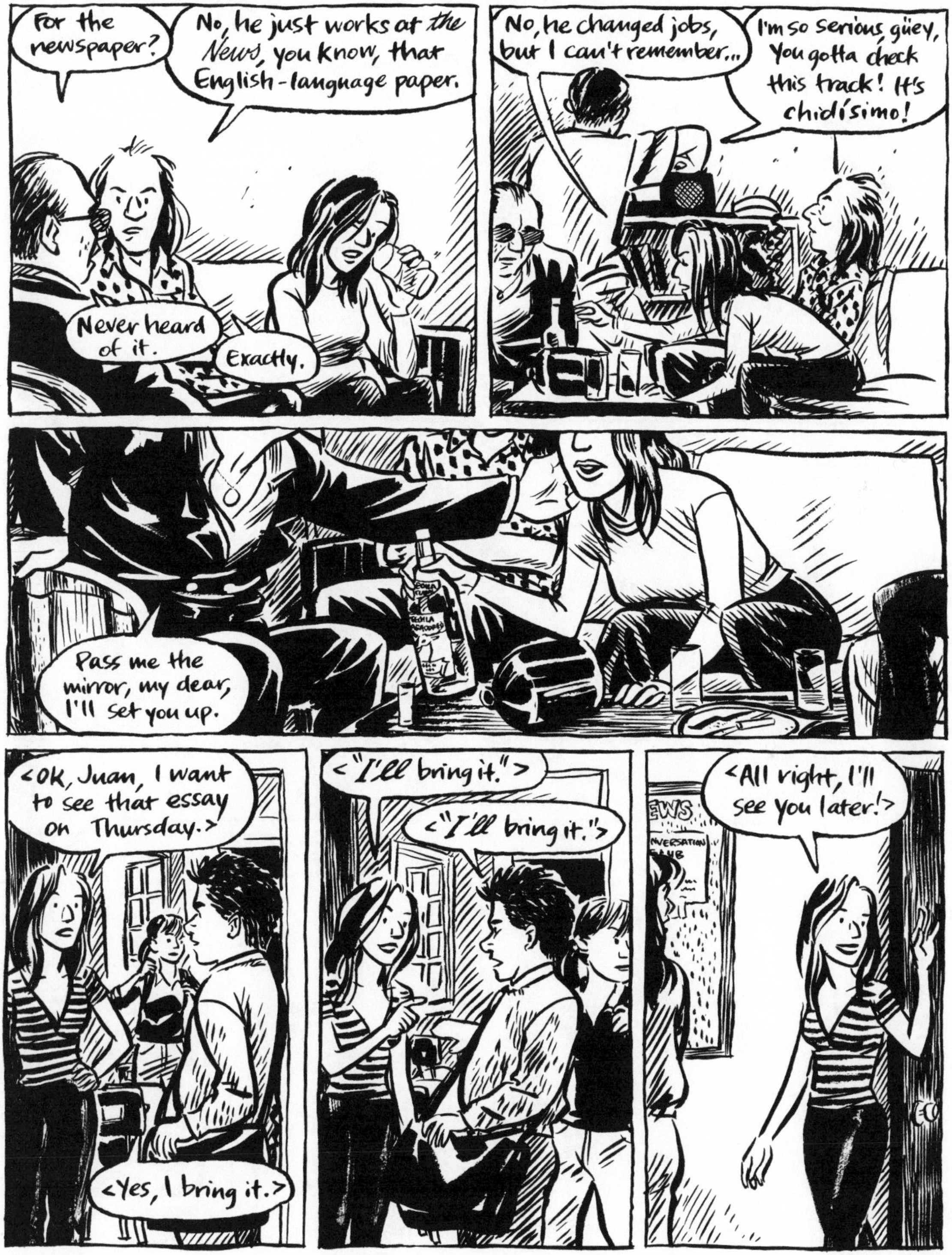
For the newspaper?
No, he just works at the *News*, you know, that English-language paper.
Never heard of it.
Exactly.
No, he changed jobs, but I can't remember...
I'm so serious güey, You gotta check this track! It's chidísimo!
Pass me the mirror, my dear, I'll set you up.
<OK, Juan, I want to see that essay on Thursday.>
<Yes, I bring it.>
<"I'll bring it.">
<"I'll bring it.">
<All right, I'll see you later!>

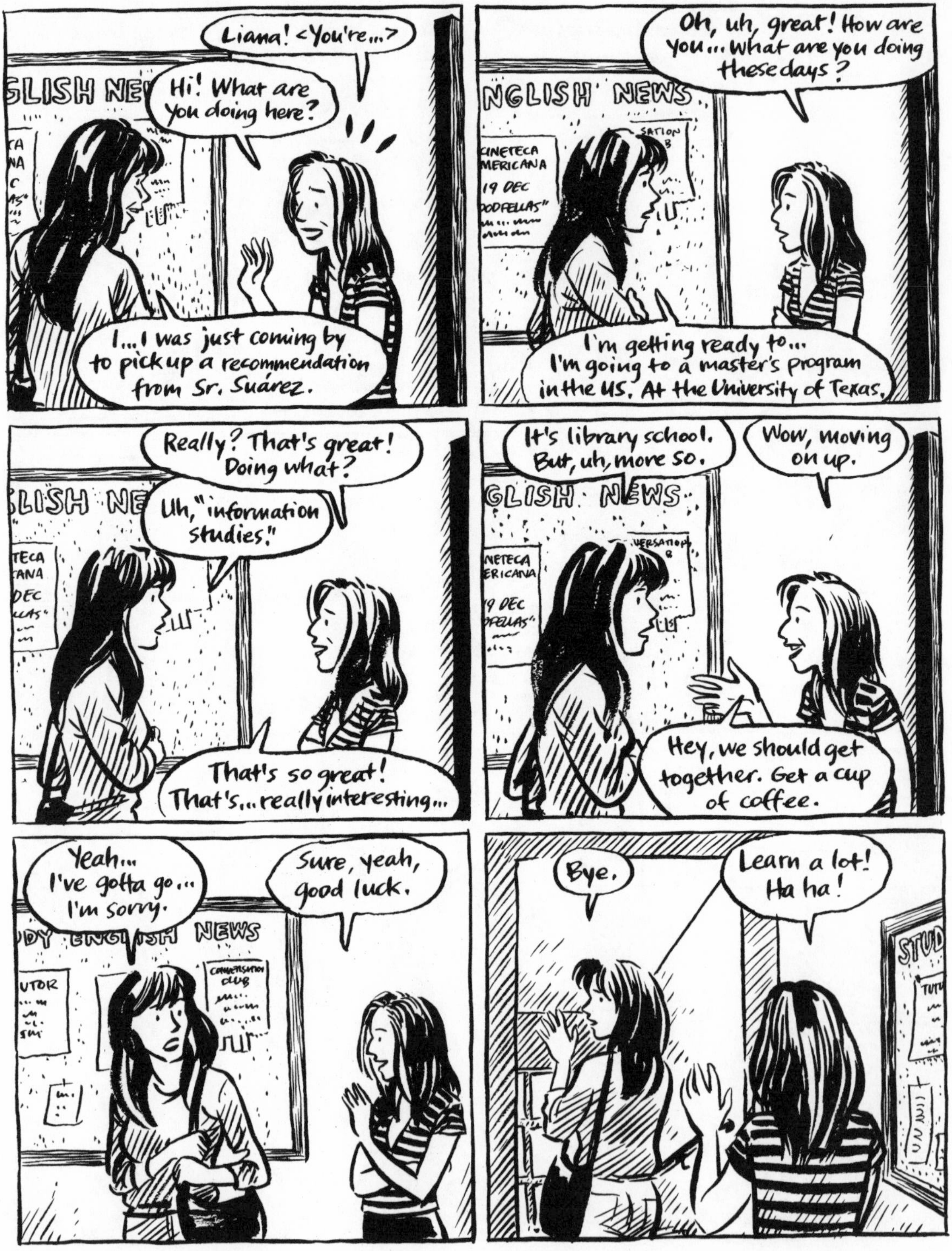
Liana! <You're...>
Hi! What are you doing here?
I... I was just coming by to pick up a recommendation from Sr. Suárez.
Oh, uh, great! How are you... what are you doing these days?
I'm getting ready to... I'm going to a master's program in the US. At the University of Texas.
Really? That's great! Doing what?
Uh, "information studies."
That's so great! That's... really interesting...
It's library school. But, uh, more so.
Wow, moving on up.
Hey, we should get together. Get a cup of coffee.
Yeah... I've gotta go... I'm sorry.
Sure, yeah, good luck.
Bye.
Learn a lot! Ha ha!

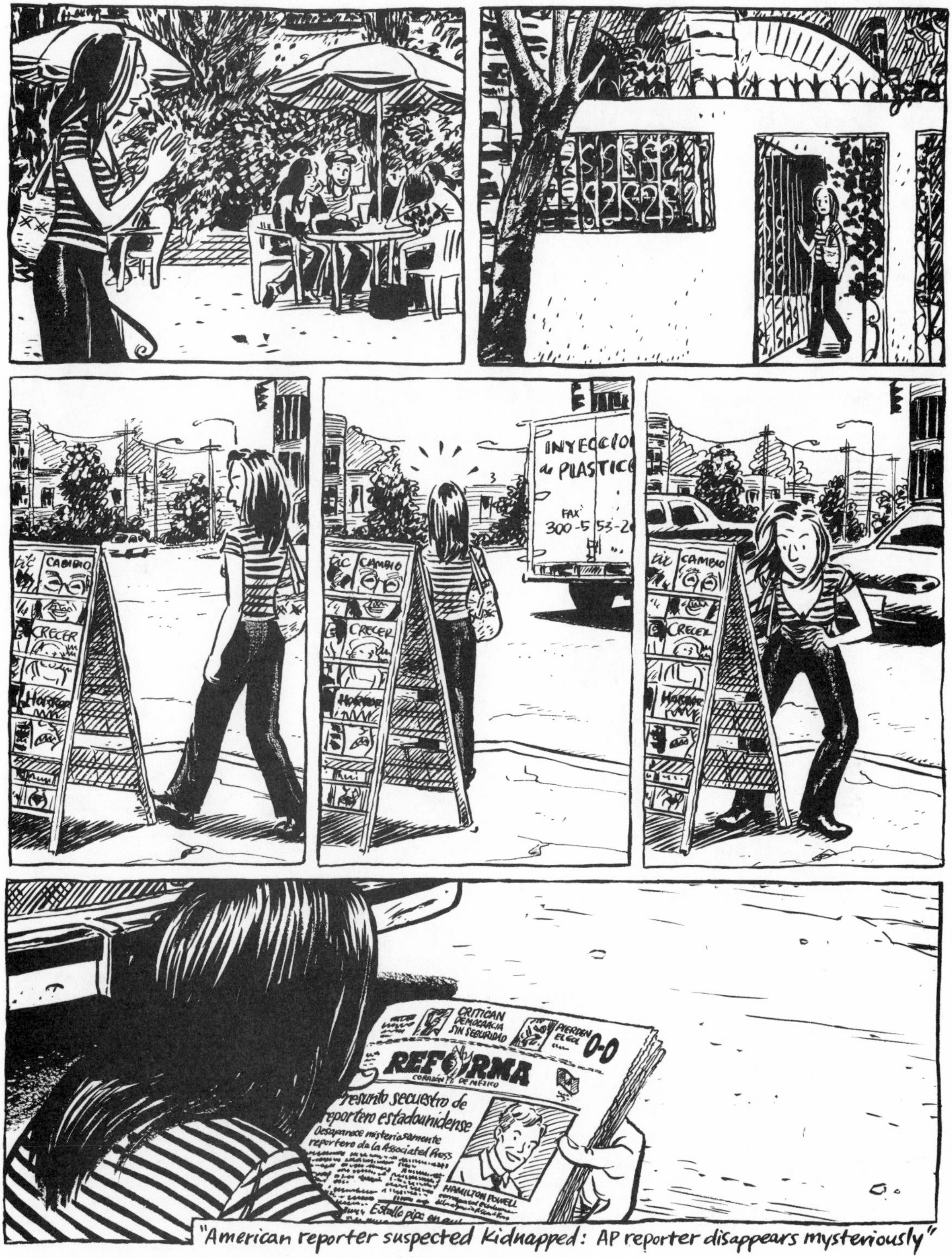
INYECCIO
de PLASTIC
FAX
300-5 53-2
tic
CAMBIO
CRECER
HORROR
CRITICAN
DEMOCRACIA
SIN SEGURIDAD
PIERDEN
EL GOL
0-0
REFORMA
CORAZÓN DE MÉXICO
Presunto secuestro de
reportero estadounidense
Desaparece misteriosamente
reportero de la Associated Press
HAMILTON POWELL
Estalla pipa en
"American reporter suspected Kidnapped: AP reporter disappears mysteriously"

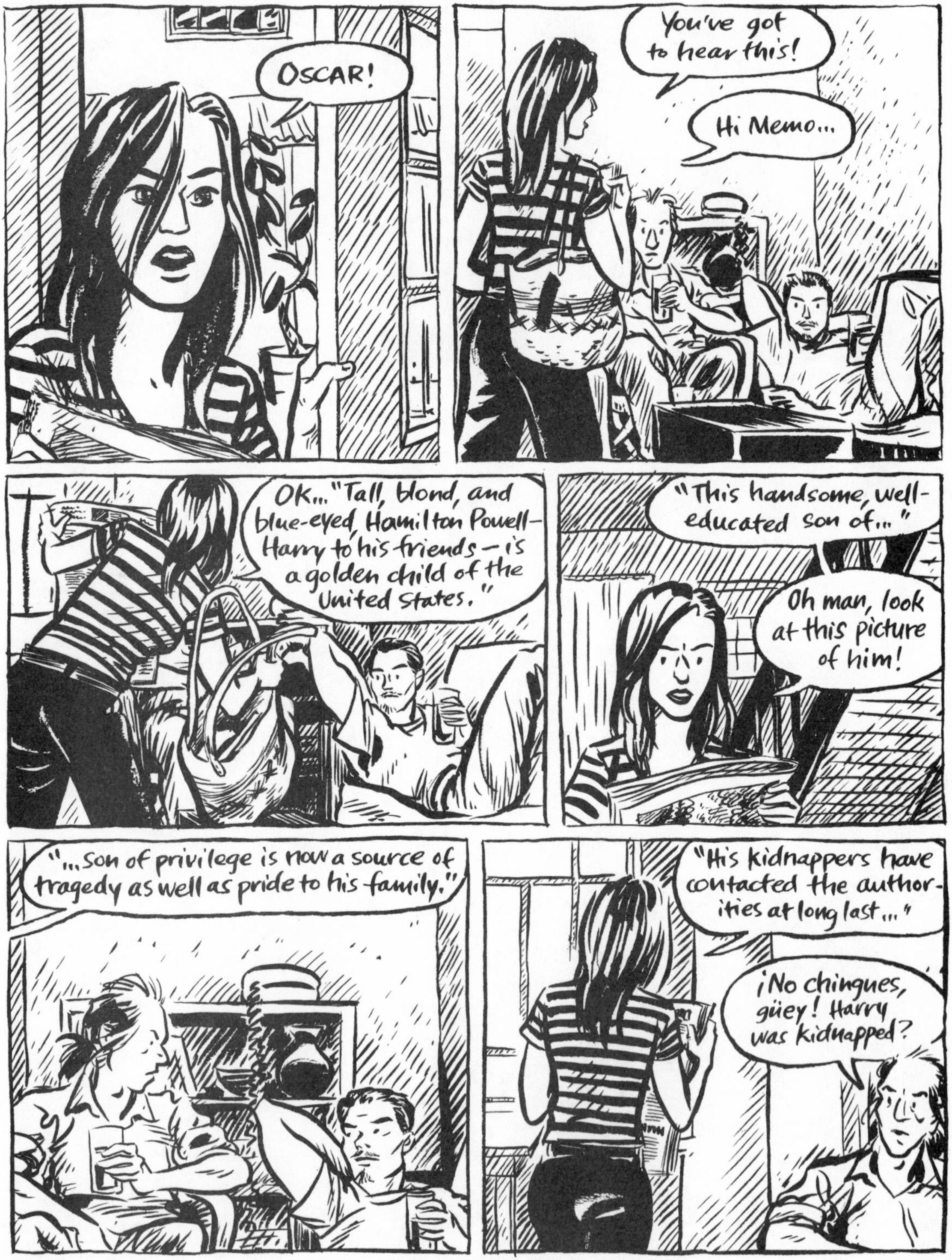
OSCAR!
You've got to hear this!
Hi Memo...
OK... "Tall, blond, and blue-eyed, Hamilton Powell- Harry to his friends — is a golden child of the United States."
"This handsome, well-educated son of..."
Oh man, look at this picture of him!
"...son of privilege is now a source of tragedy as well as pride to his family."
"His kidnappers have contacted the authorities at long last..."
¡No chingues, güey! Harry was kidnapped?

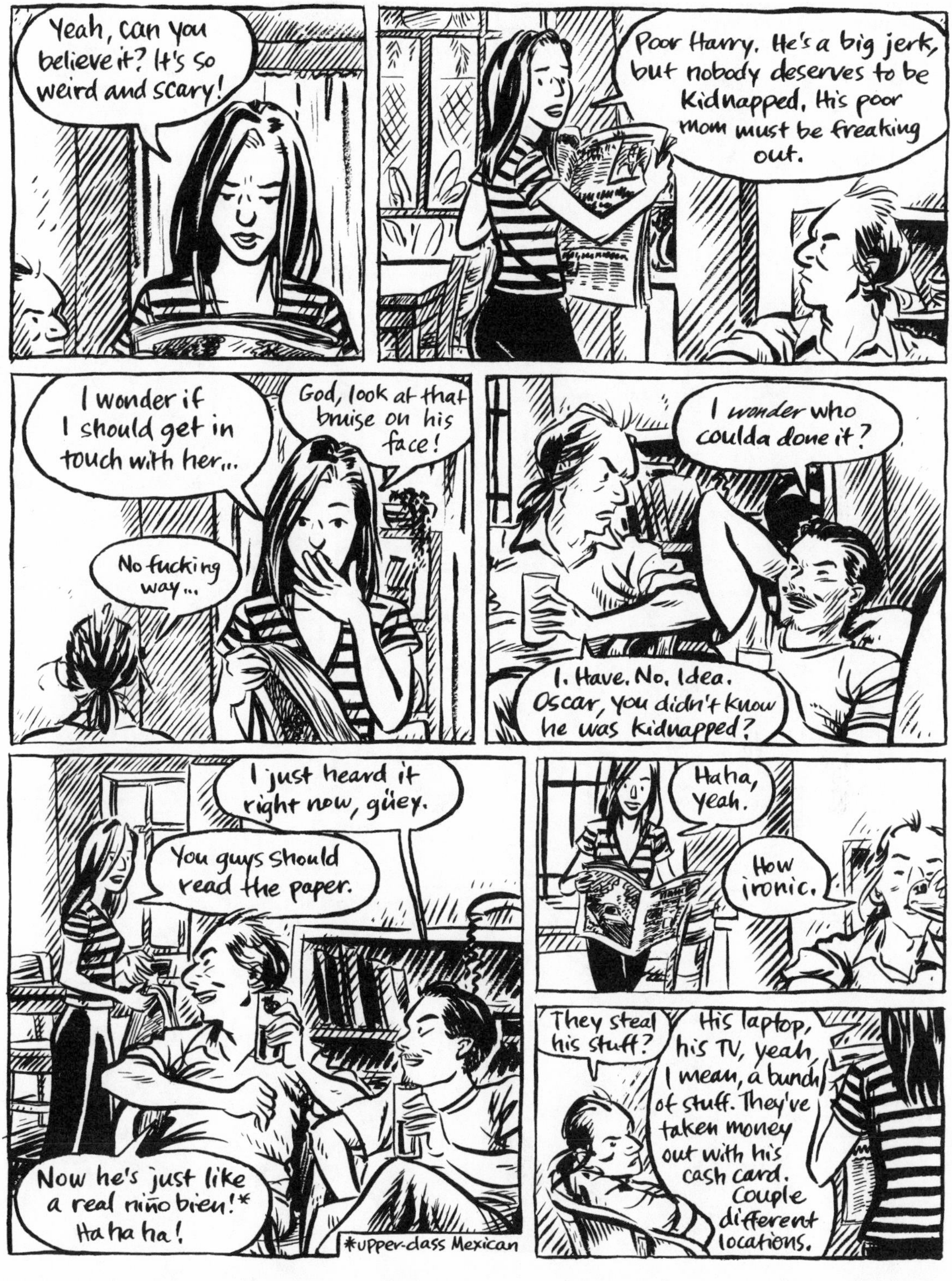
Yeah, can you believe it? It's so weird and scary!
Poor Harry. He's a big jerk, but nobody deserves to be Kidnapped. His poor mom must be freaking out.
I wonder if I should get in touch with her...
God, look at that bruise on his face!
No fucking way...
I wonder who coulda done it?
I. Have. No. Idea. Oscar, you didn't know he was kidnapped?
I just heard it right now, güey.
You guys should read the paper.
Now he's just like a real niño bien!* Ha ha ha!
*upper-class Mexican
Haha, yeah.
How ironic.
They steal his stuff?
His laptop, his TV, yeah, I mean, a bunch of stuff. They've taken money out with his cash card. Couple different locations.

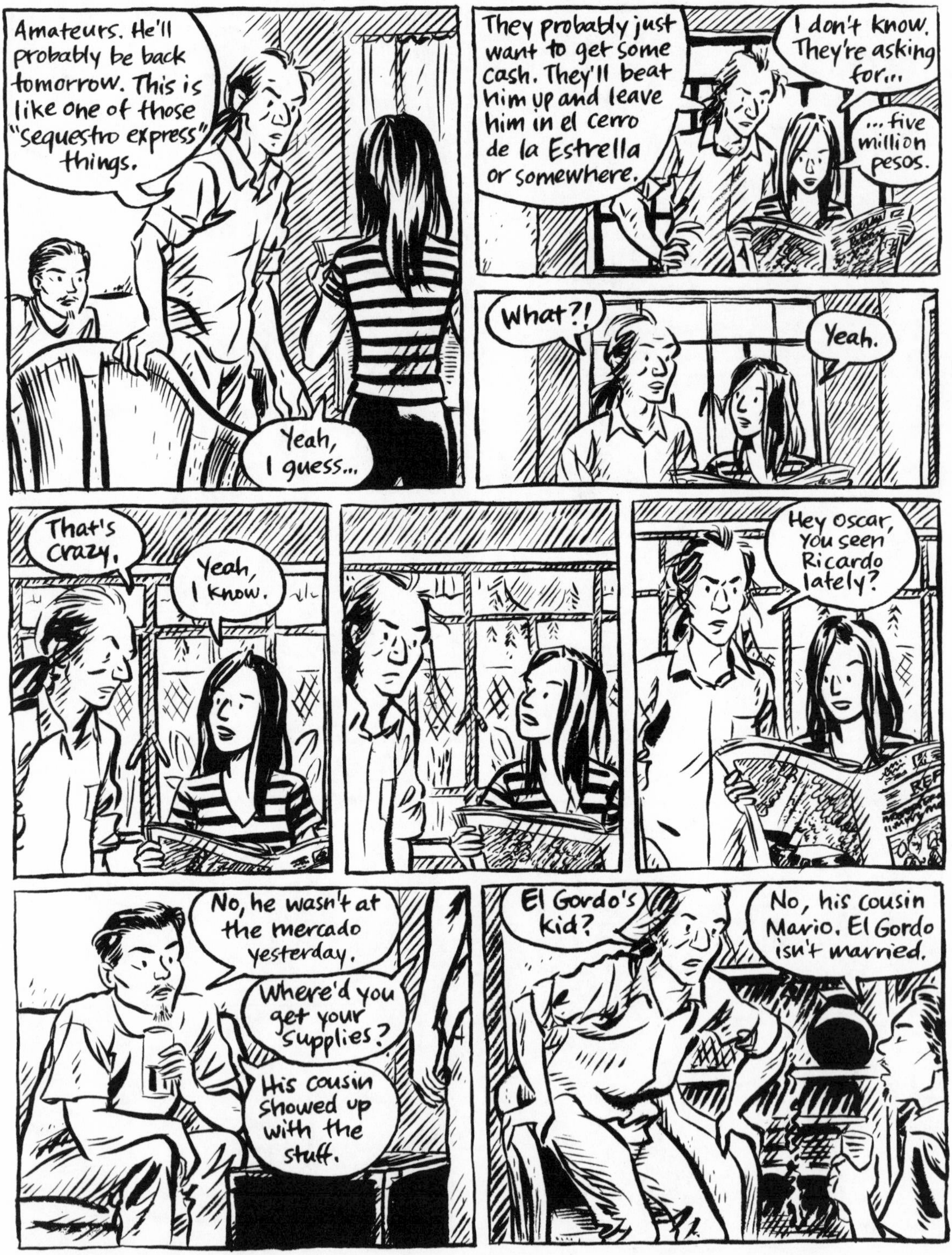

Amateurs. He'll probably be back tomorrow. This is like one of those "sequestro express" things.
Yeah, I guess...
They probably just want to get some cash. They'll beat him up and leave him in el cerro de la Estrella or somewhere.
I don't know. They're asking for...
...five million pesos.
What?!
Yeah.
That's Crazy.
Yeah, I know.
Hey Oscar, You seen Ricardo lately?
No, he wasn't at the mercado yesterday.
Where'd you get your supplies?
His cousin showed up with the stuff.
El Gordo's kid?
No, his cousin Mario. El Gordo isn't married.

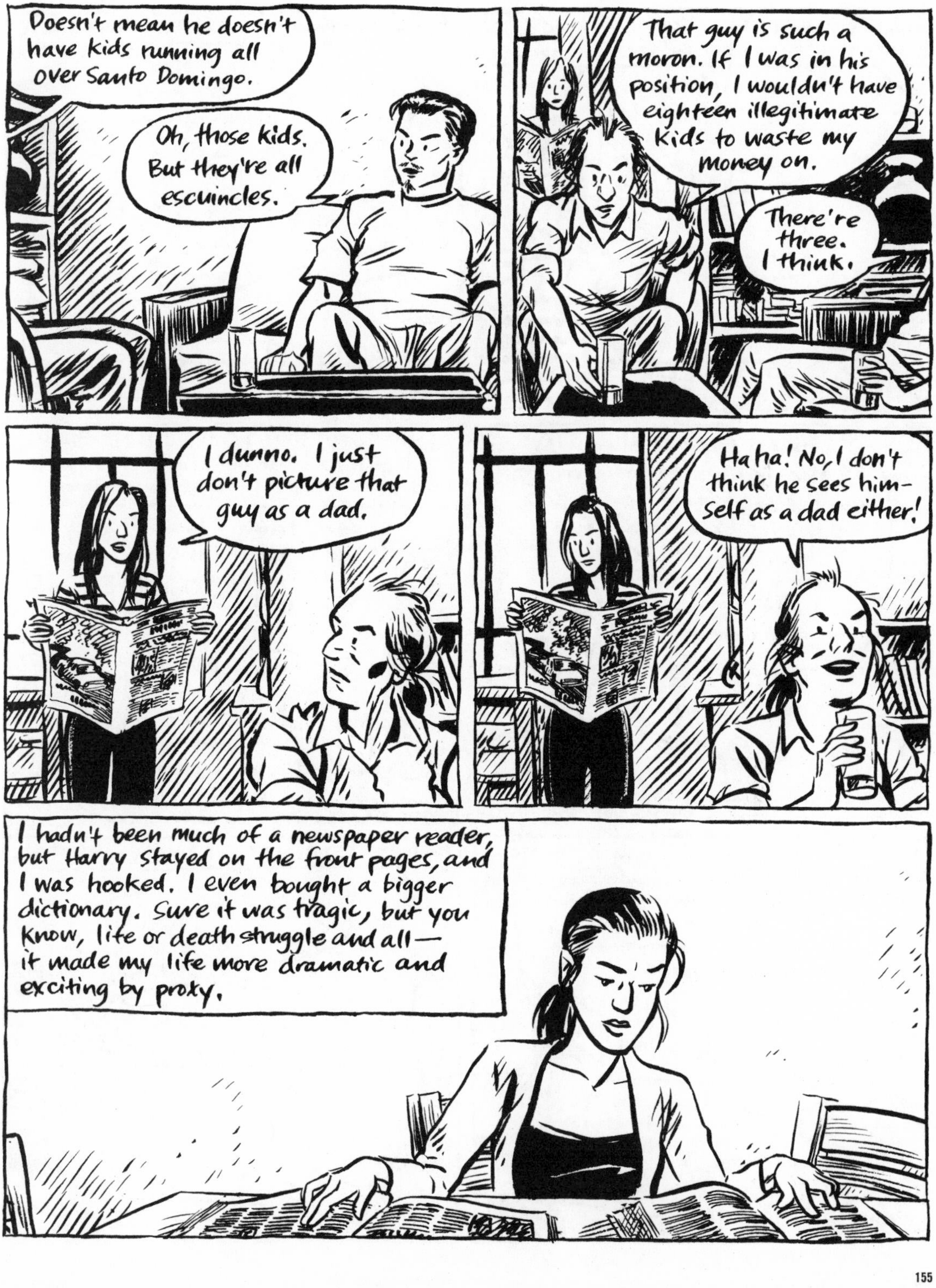
Doesn't mean he doesn't have kids running all over Santo Domingo.
Oh, those kids. But they're all escuincles.
That guy is such a moron. If I was in his position, I wouldn't have eighteen illegitimate kids to waste my money on.
There're three. I think.
I dunno. I just don't picture that guy as a dad.
Ha ha! No, I don't think he sees himself as a dad either!
I hadn't been much of a newspaper reader, but Harry stayed on the front pages, and I was hooked. I even bought a bigger dictionary. Sure it was tragic, but you know, life or death struggle and all— it made my life more dramatic and exciting by proxy.

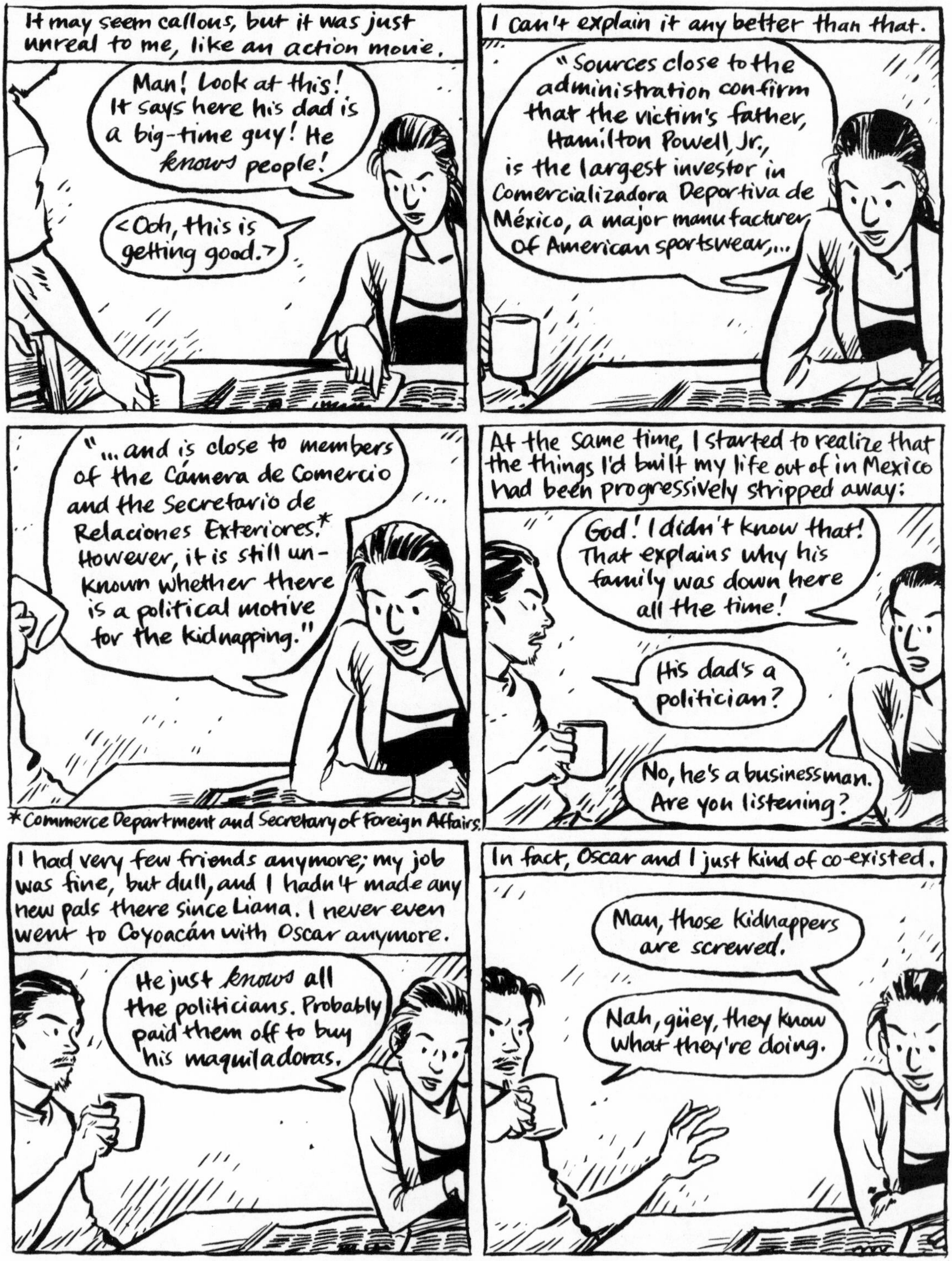
It may seem callous, but it was just unreal to me, like an action movie.
Man! Look at this! It says here his dad is a big-time guy! He *knows* people!
<Ooh, this is getting good.>
I can't explain it any better than that.
"Sources close to the administration confirm that the victim's father, Hamilton Powell, Jr., is the largest investor in Comercializadora Deportiva de México, a major manufacturer of American sportswear,...
"... and is close to members of the Cámera de Comercio and the Secretario de Relaciones Exteriores.* However, it is still unknown whether there is a political motive for the kidnapping."
*Commerce Department and Secretary of Foreign Affairs.
At the same time, I started to realize that the things I'd built my life out of in Mexico had been progressively stripped away:
God! I didn't know that! That explains why his family was down here all the time!
His dad's a politician?
No, he's a businessman. Are you listening?
I had very few friends anymore; my job was fine, but dull, and I hadn't made any new pals there since Liana. I never even went to Coyoacán with Oscar anymore.
He just *knows* all the politicians. Probably paid them off to buy his maquiladoras.
In fact, Oscar and I just kind of co-existed.
Man, those kidnappers are screwed.
Nah, güey, they know what they're doing.

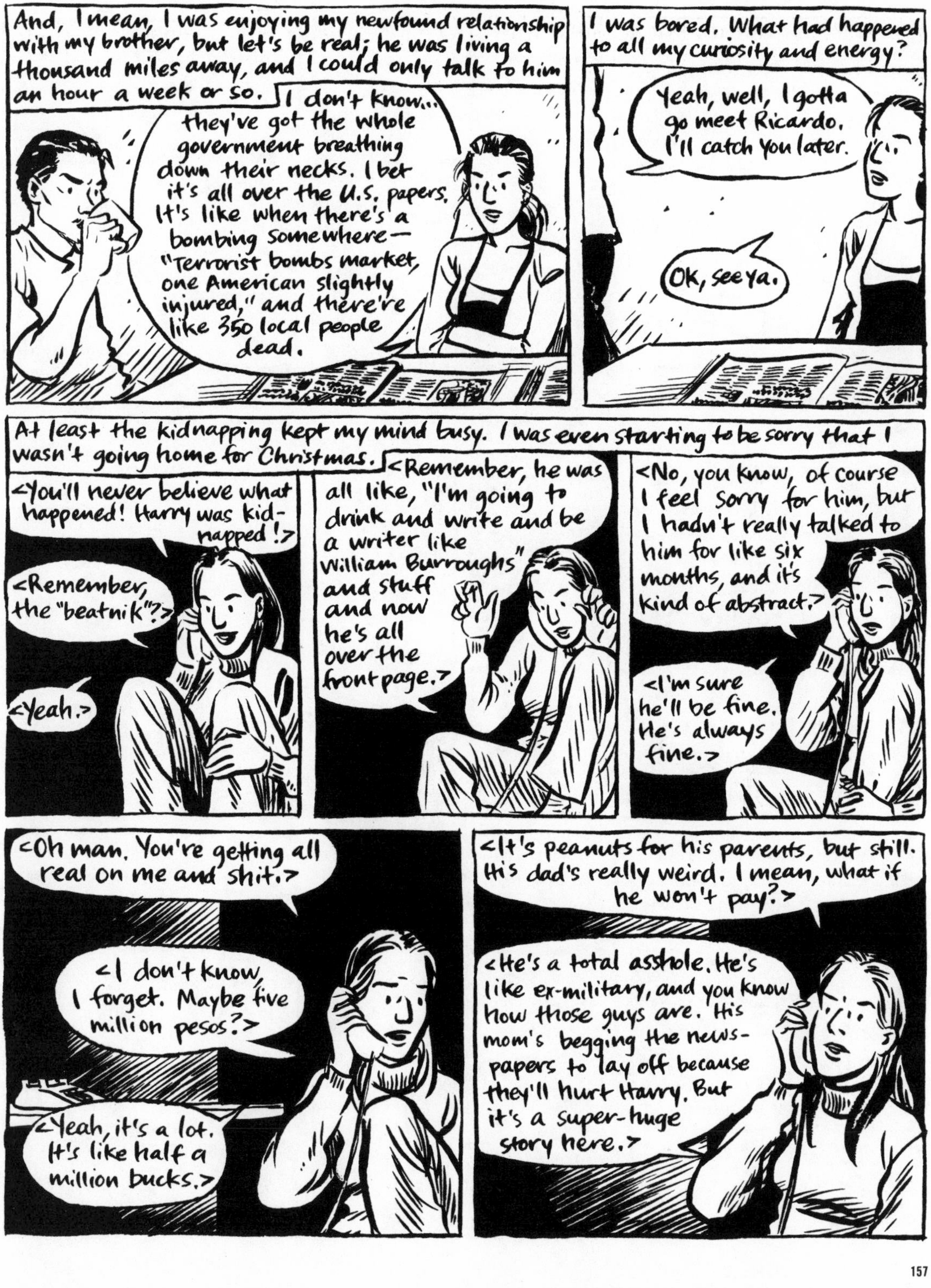

And, I mean, I was enjoying my newfound relationship with my brother, but let's be real; he was living a thousand miles away, and I could only talk to him an hour a week or so.
I don't know... they've got the whole government breathing down their necks. I bet it's all over the U.S. papers. It's like when there's a bombing somewhere— "Terrorist bombs market, one American slightly injured," and there're like 350 local people dead.
I was bored. What had happened to all my curiosity and energy?
Yeah, well, I gotta go meet Ricardo. I'll catch you later.
Ok, see ya.
At least the kidnapping kept my mind busy. I was even starting to be sorry that I wasn't going home for Christmas.
<You'll never believe what happened! Harry was kidnapped!>
<Remember, the "beatnik"?>
<Yeah.>
<Remember, he was all like, "I'm going to drink and write and be a writer like William Burroughs" and stuff and now he's all over the front page.>
<No, you know, of course I feel sorry for him, but I hadn't really talked to him for like six months, and it's kind of abstract.>
<I'm sure he'll be fine. He's always fine.>
<Oh man. You're getting all real on me and shit.>
<I don't know, I forget. Maybe five million pesos?>
<Yeah, it's a lot. It's like half a million bucks.>
<It's peanuts for his parents, but still. His dad's really weird. I mean, what if he won't pay?>
<He's a total asshole. He's like ex-military, and you know how those guys are. His mom's begging the newspapers to lay off because they'll hurt Harry. But it's a super-huge story here.>

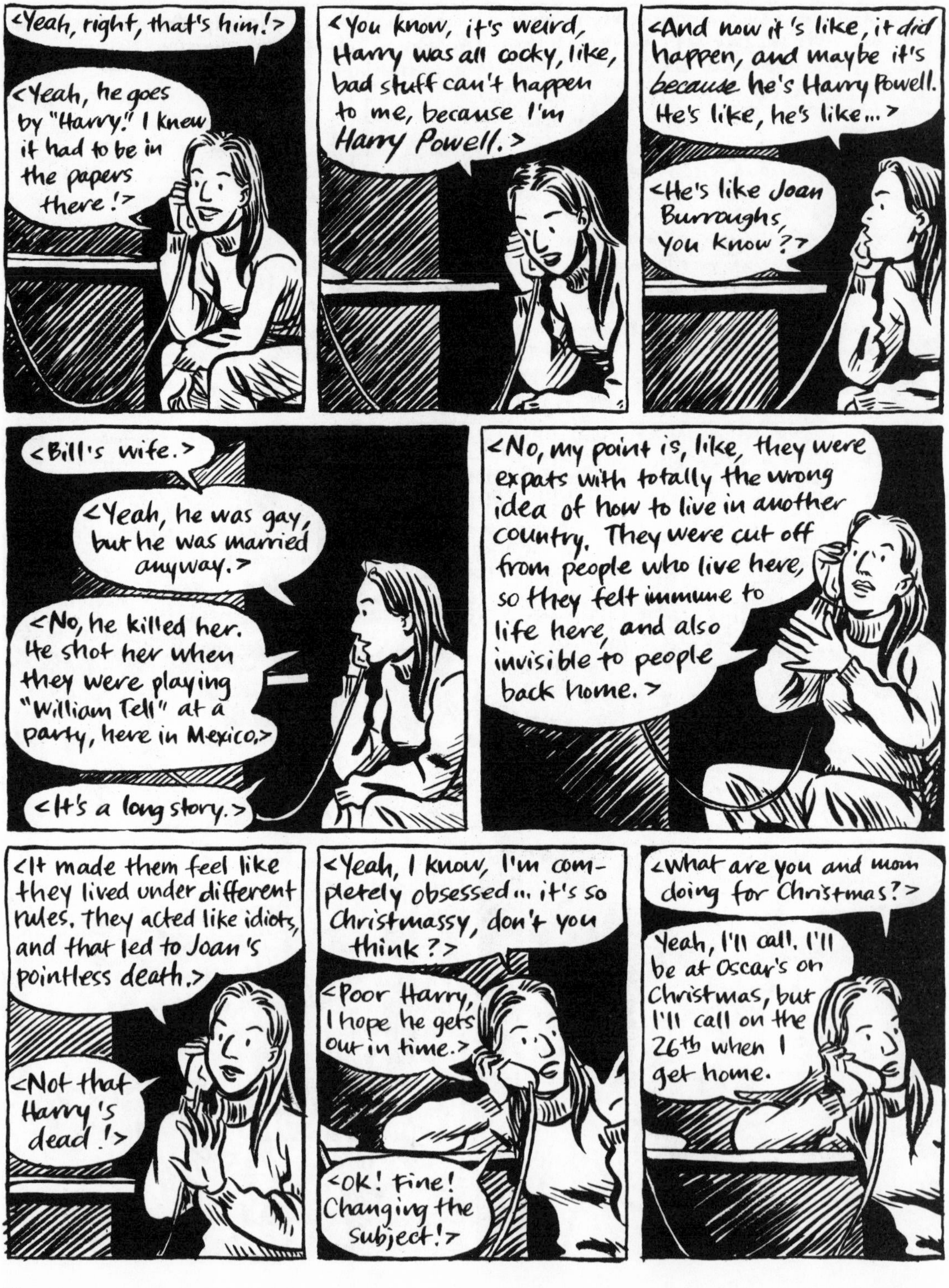

<Yeah, right, that's him!>
<Yeah, he goes by "Harry." I knew it had to be in the papers there!>
<You know, it's weird, Harry was all cocky, like, bad stuff can't happen to me, because I'm Harry Powell.>
<And now it's like, it *did* happen, and maybe it's *because* he's Harry Powell. He's like, he's like...>
<He's like Joan Burroughs, you know?>
<Bill's wife.>
<Yeah, he was gay, but he was married anyway.>
<No, he killed her. He shot her when they were playing "William Tell" at a party, here in Mexico.>
<It's a long story.>
<No, my point is, like, they were expats with totally the wrong idea of how to live in another country. They were cut off from people who live here, so they felt immune to life here, and also invisible to people back home.>
<It made them feel like they lived under different rules. they acted like idiots, and that led to Joan's pointless death.>
<Not that Harry's dead!>
<Yeah, I know, I'm completely obsessed... it's so Christmassy, don't you think?>
<Poor Harry, I hope he gets out in time.>
<OK! Fine! Changing the subject!>
<What are you and mom doing for Christmas?>
Yeah, I'll call. I'll be at Oscar's on Christmas, but I'll call on the 26th when I get home.

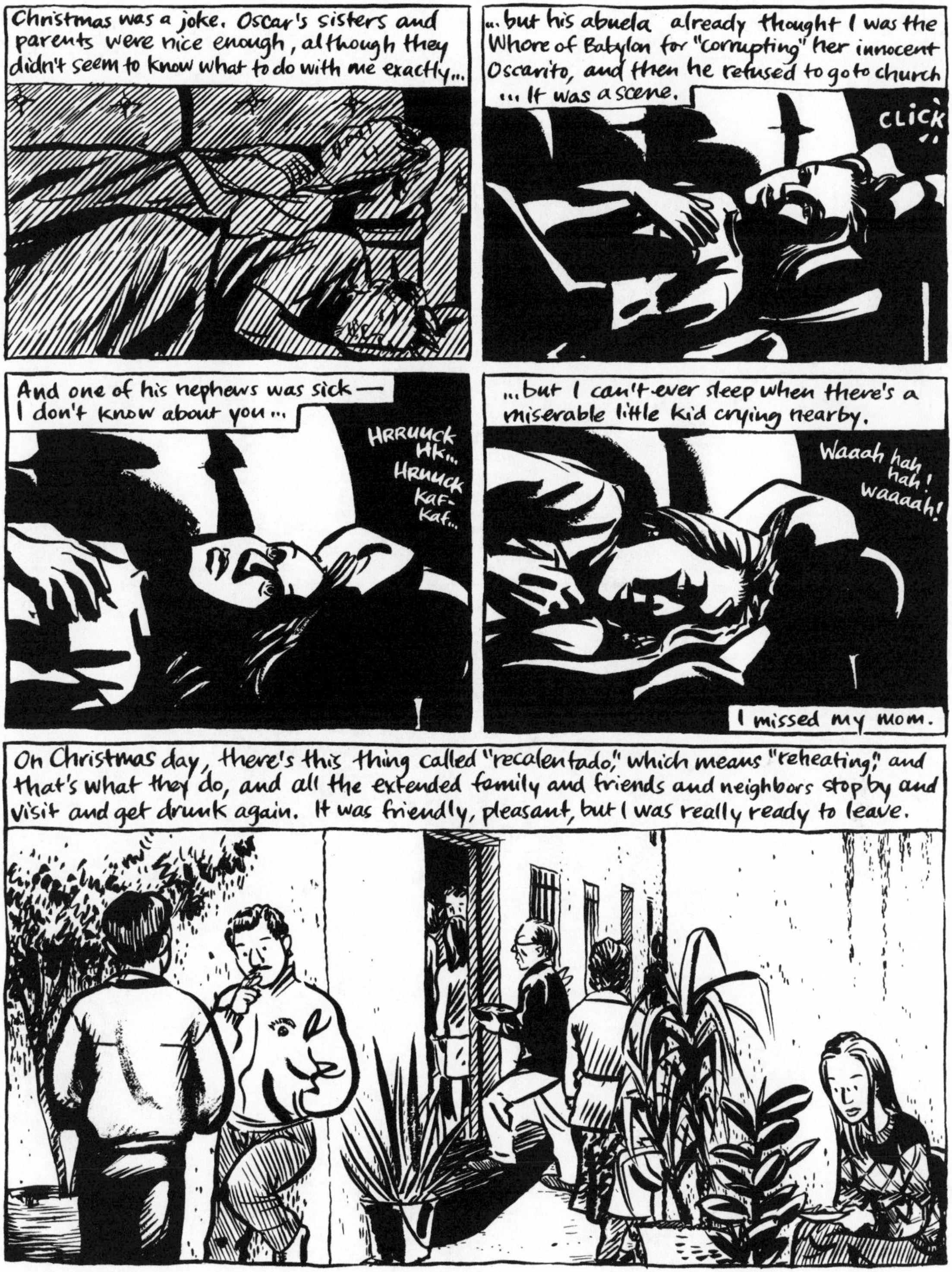

Christmas was a joke. Oscar's sisters and parents were nice enough, although they didn't seem to know what to do with me exactly...
...but his abuela already thought I was the Whore of Babylon for "corrupting" her innocent Oscarito, and then he refused to go to church ... It was a scene.
CLICK
And one of his nephews was sick — I don't know about you...
HRRUUCK HK... HRUUCK KAF-KAF...
...but I can't ever sleep when there's a miserable little kid crying nearby.
Waaah hah hah! waaaah!
I missed my mom.
On Christmas day, there's this thing called "recalentado," which means "reheating," and that's what they do, and all the extended family and friends and neighbors stop by and visit and get drunk again. It was friendly, pleasant, but I was really ready to leave.

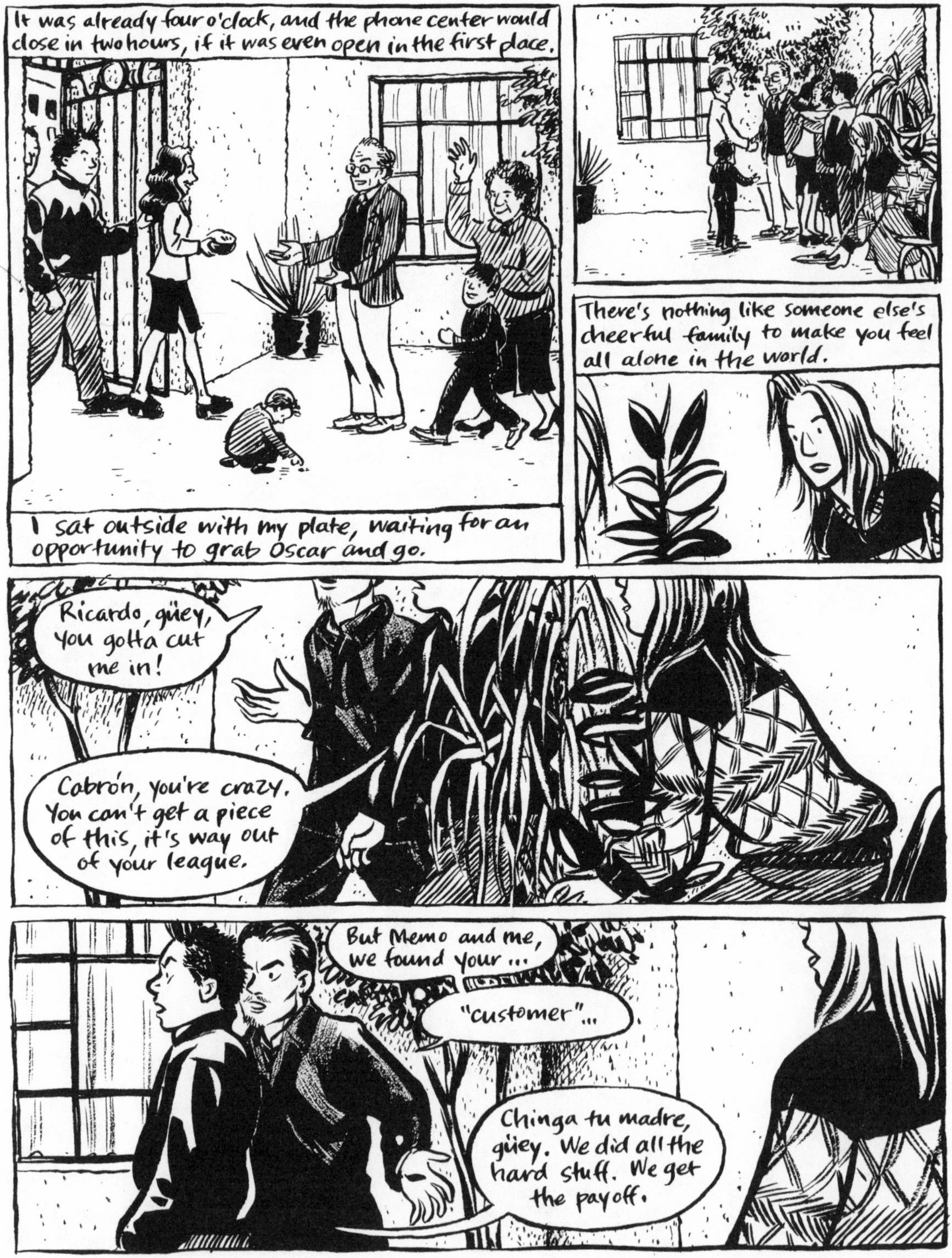
It was already four o'clock, and the phone center would close in two hours, if it was even open in the first place.
I sat outside with my plate, waiting for an opportunity to grab Oscar and go.
There's nothing like someone else's cheerful family to make you feel all alone in the world.
Ricardo, güey, you gotta cut me in!
Cabrón, you're crazy. You can't get a piece of this, it's way out of your league.
But Memo and me, we found your ...
"customer"...
Chinga tu madre, güey. We did all the hard stuff. We get the payoff.

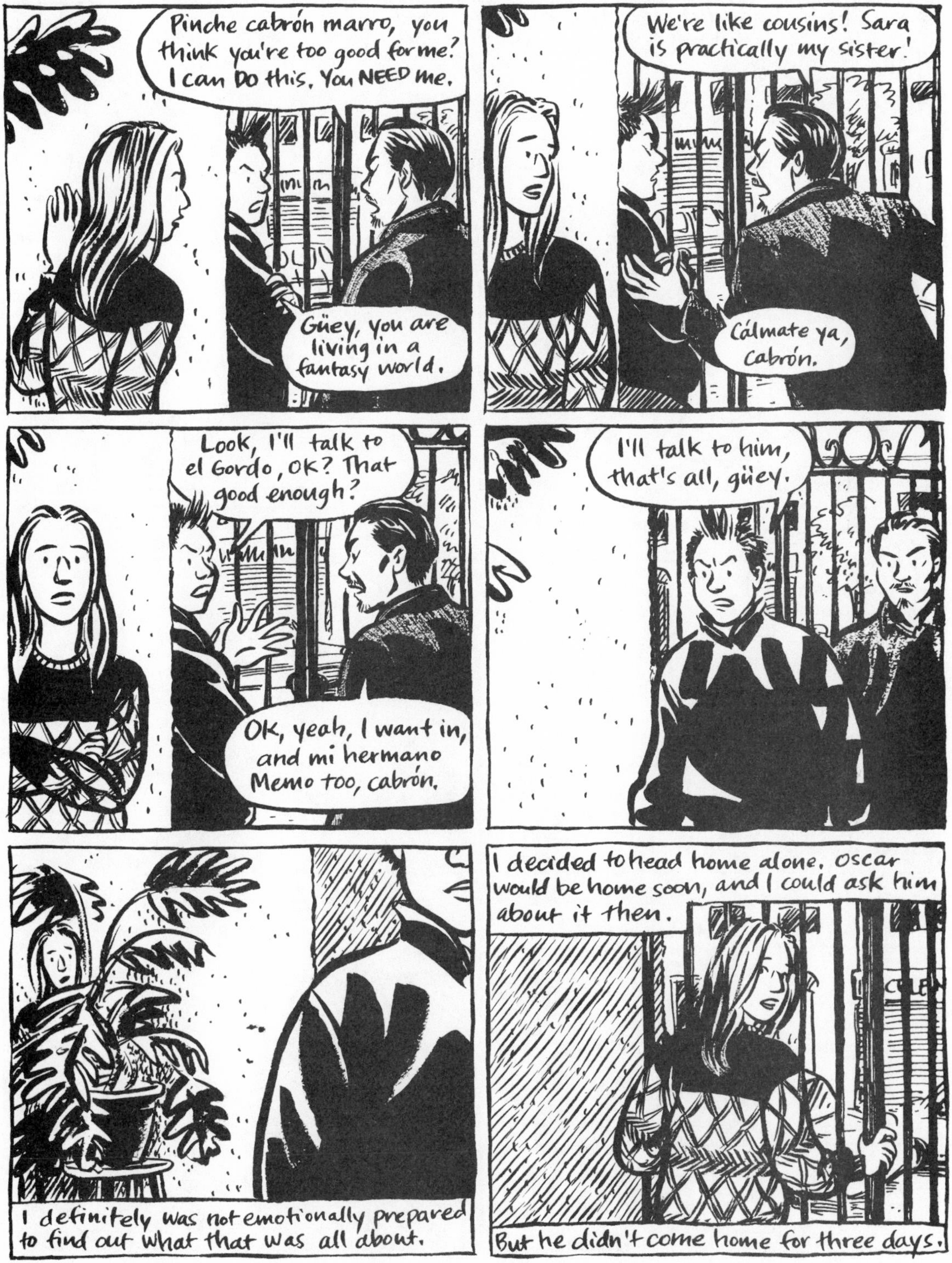
Pinche cabrón marro, you think you're too good for me? I can DO this. You NEED me.
Güey, you are living in a fantasy world.
We're like cousins! Sara is practically my sister!
Cálmate ya, cabrón.
Look, I'll talk to el Gordo, OK? That good enough?
OK, yeah, I want in, and mi hermano Memo too, cabrón.
I'll talk to him, that's all, güey.
I definitely was not emotionally prepared to find out what that was all about.
I decided to head home alone. Oscar would be home soon, and I could ask him about it then.
But he didn't come home for three days.

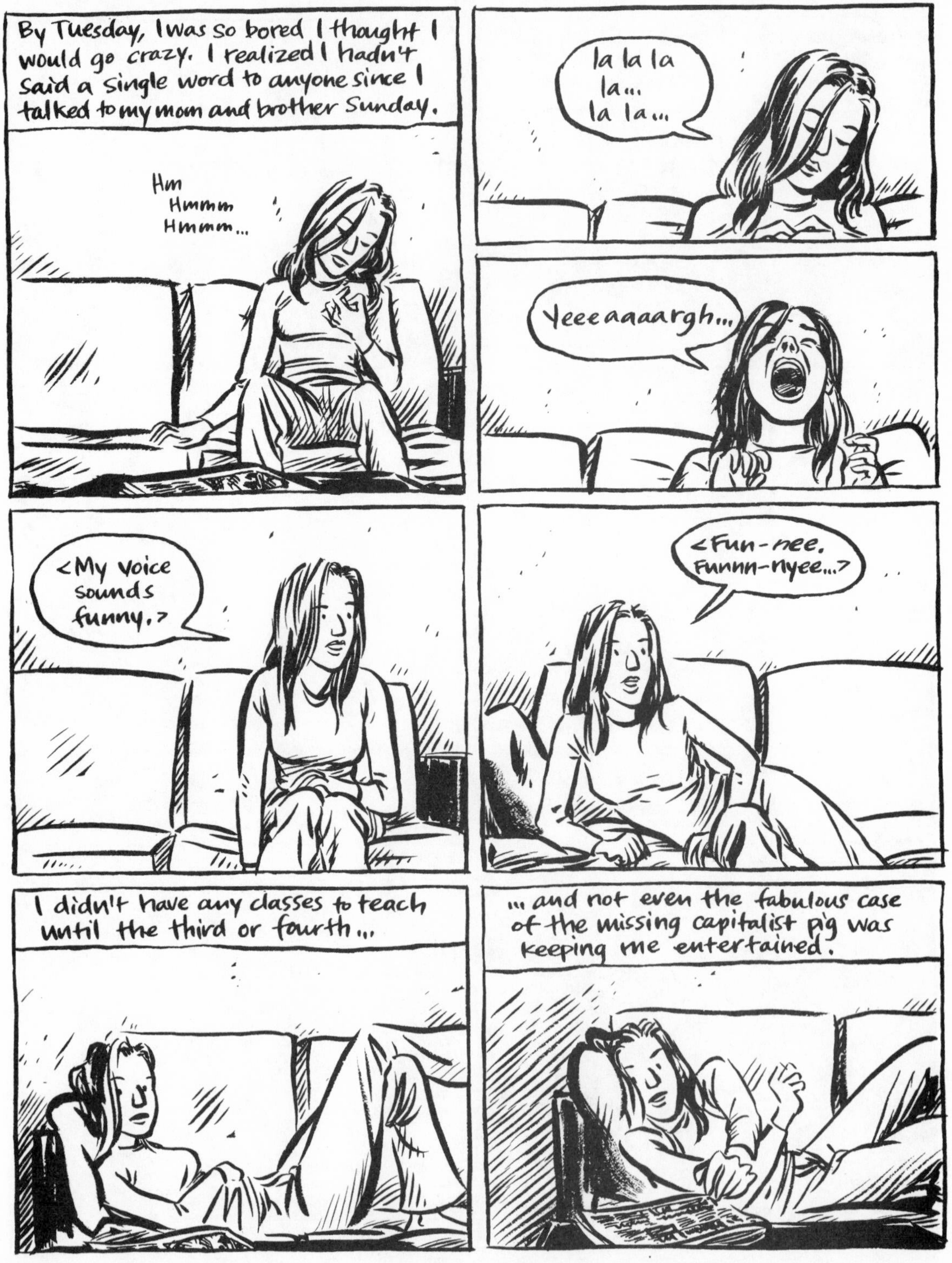

By Tuesday, I was so bored I thought I would go crazy. I realized I hadn't said a single word to anyone since I talked to my mom and brother Sunday.
Hm Hmmm Hmmm...
la la la la... la la...
Yeeeaaaargh...
<My voice sounds funny.>
<Fun-nee. Funnn-nyee...>
I didn't have any classes to teach until the third or fourth...
... and not even the fabulous case of the missing capitalist pig was keeping me entertained.

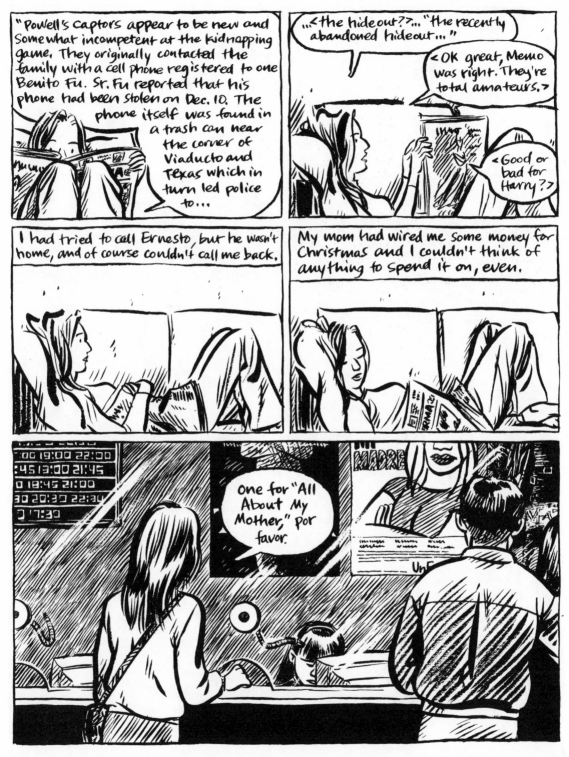

"Powell's captors appear to be new and somewhat incompetent at the kidnapping game. They originally contacted the family with a cell phone registered to one Benito Fu. Sr. Fu reported that his phone had been stolen on Dec. 10. The phone itself was found in a trash can near the corner of Viaducto and Texas which in turn led police to..."

"...<the hideout?>..." the recently abandoned hideout..."

<OK great, Memo was right. They're total amateurs.>

<Good or bad for Harry?>

I had tried to call Ernesto, but he wasn't home, and of course couldn't call me back.

My mom had wired me some money for Christmas and I couldn't think of anything to spend it on, even.

One for "All About My Mother," por favor.

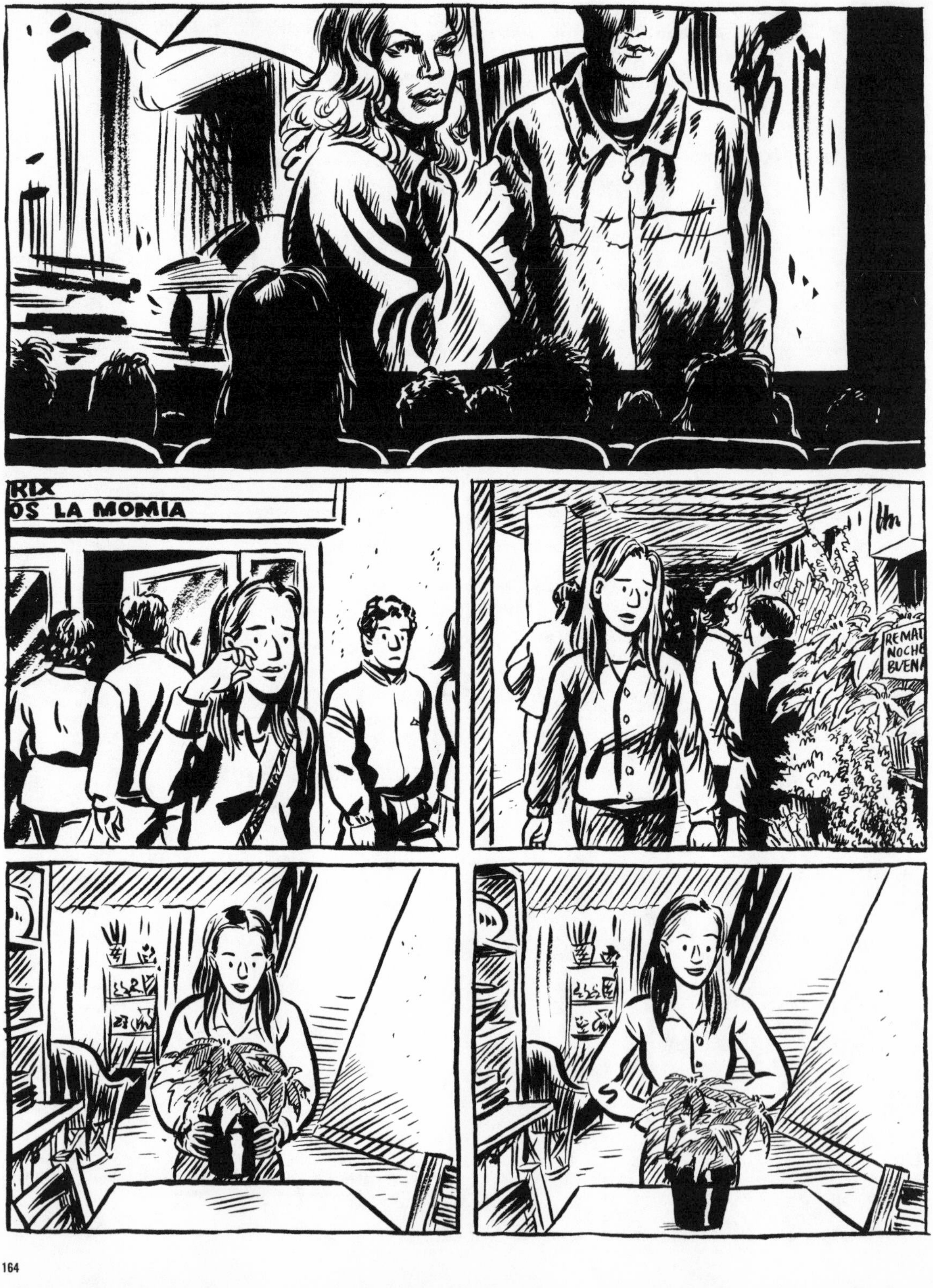
RIX
OS LA MOMIA
REMAT
NOCHE
BUENA

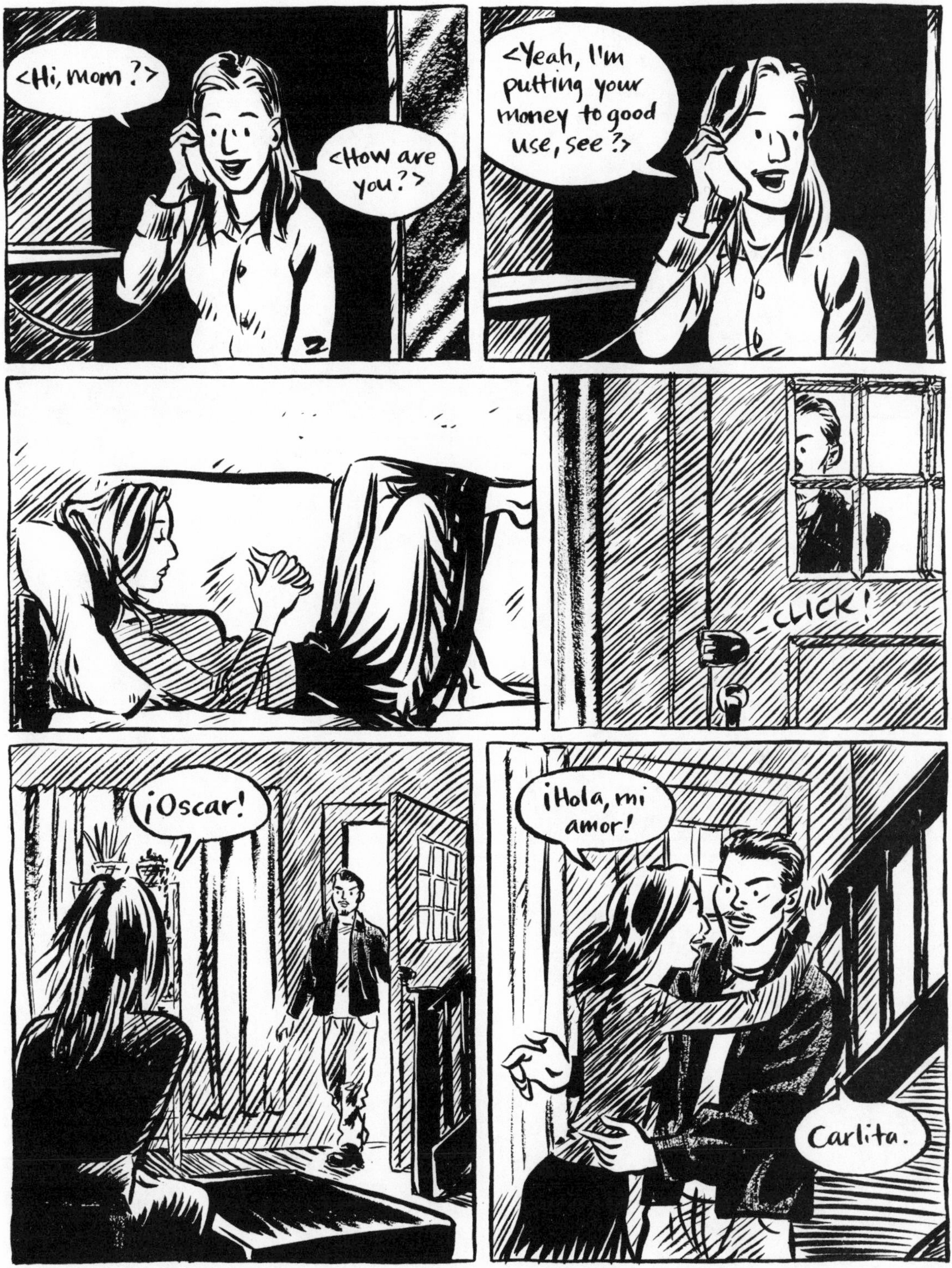
<Hi, mom?>
<How are you?>
<Yeah, I'm putting your money to good use, see?>
CLICK!
¡Oscar!
¡Hola, mi amor!
Carlita.

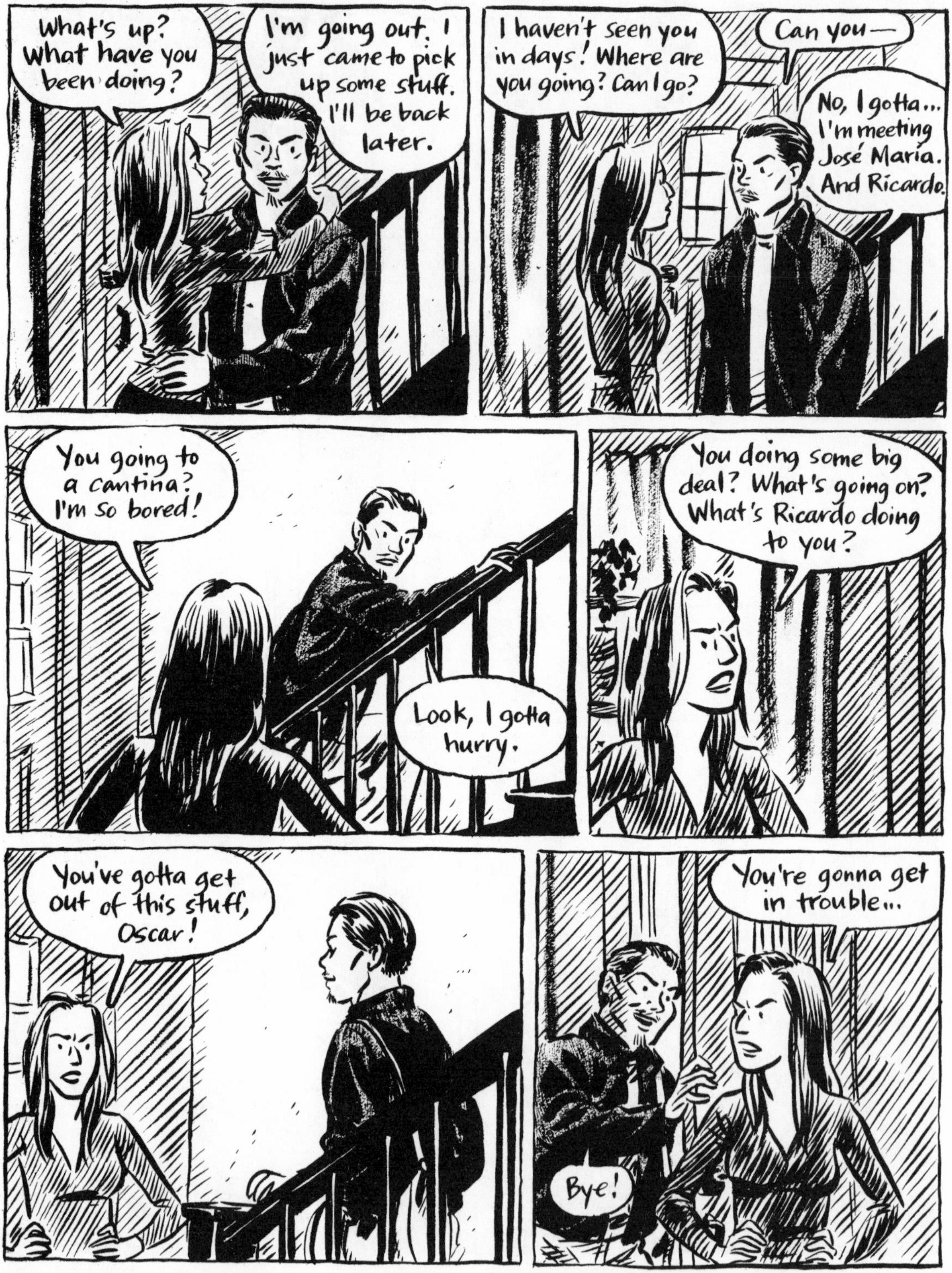
What's up? What have you been doing?
I'm going out. I just came to pick up some stuff. I'll be back later.
I haven't seen you in days! Where are you going? Can I go?
Can you—
No, I gotta... I'm meeting José María. And Ricardo.
You going to a cantina? I'm so bored!
Look, I gotta hurry.
You doing some big deal? What's going on? What's Ricardo doing to you?
You've gotta get out of this stuff, Oscar!
You're gonna get in trouble...
Bye!

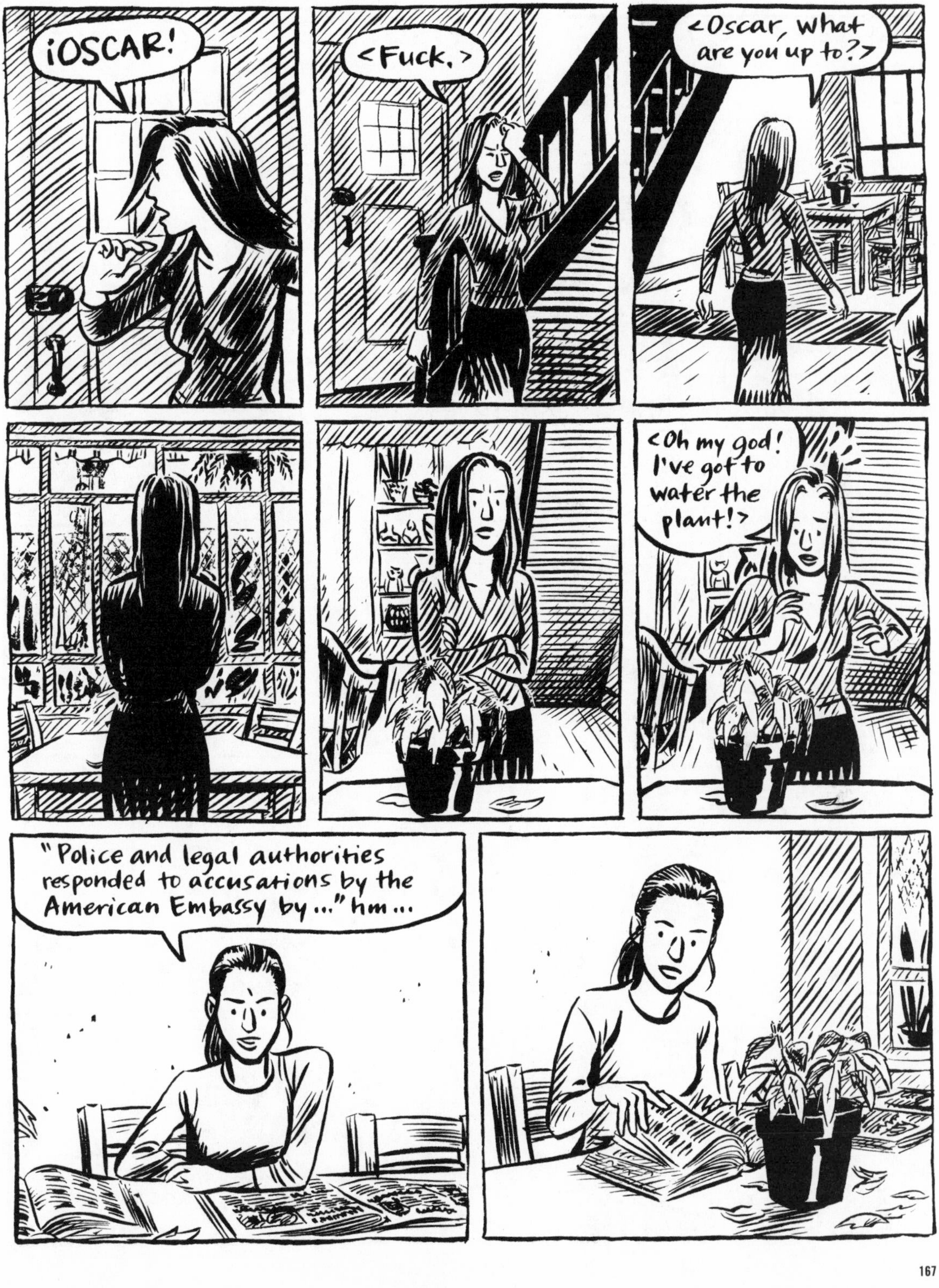

¡OSCAR!
<Fuck.>
<Oscar, what are you up to?>
<Oh my god! I've got to water the plant!>
"Police and legal authorities responded to accusations by the American Embassy by..." hm...

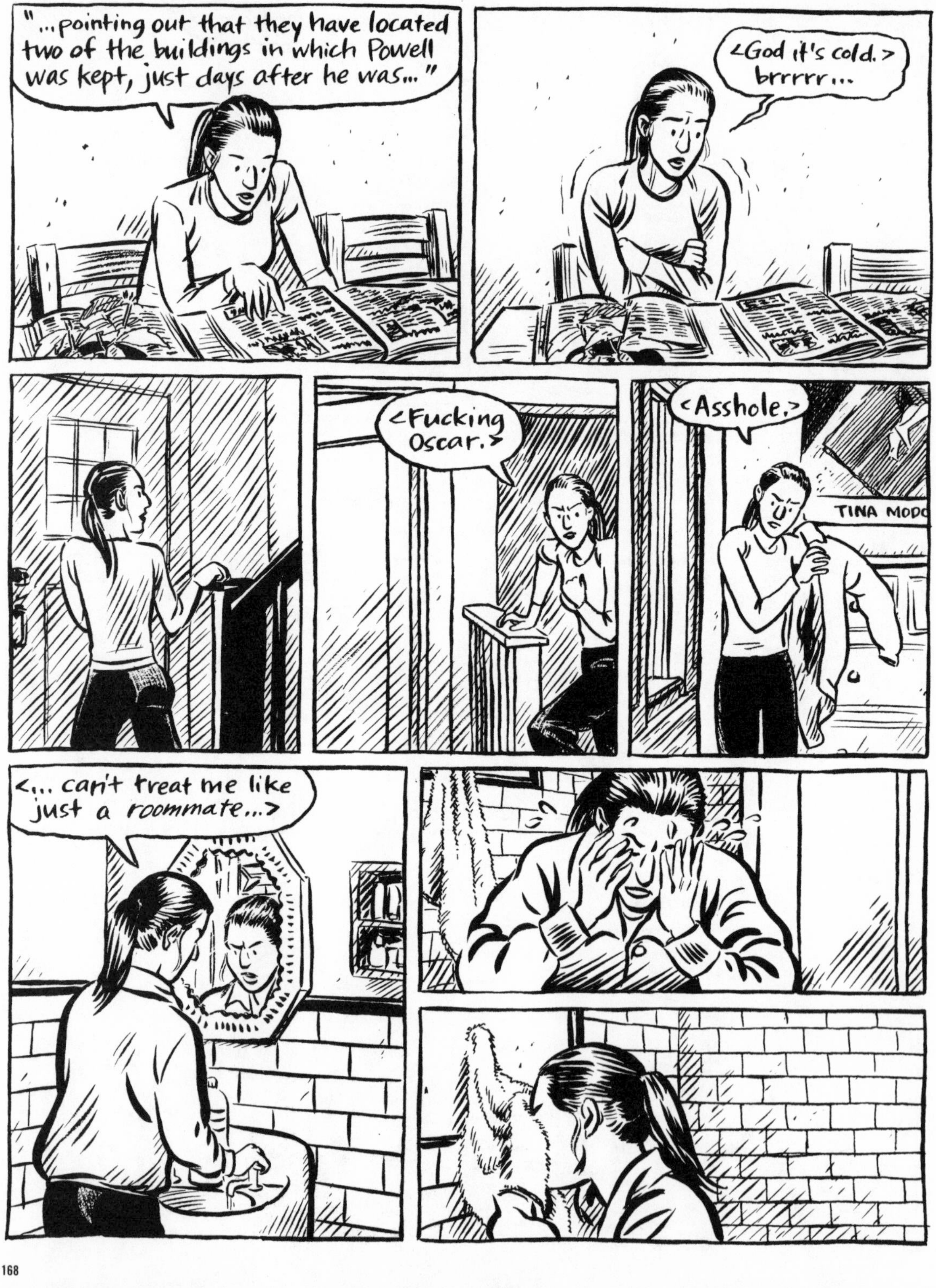
"...pointing out that they have located two of the buildings in which Powell was kept, just days after he was..."
<God it's cold.> brrrrr...
<Fucking Oscar.>
<Asshole.>
TINA MODO
<... can't treat me like just a roommate...>

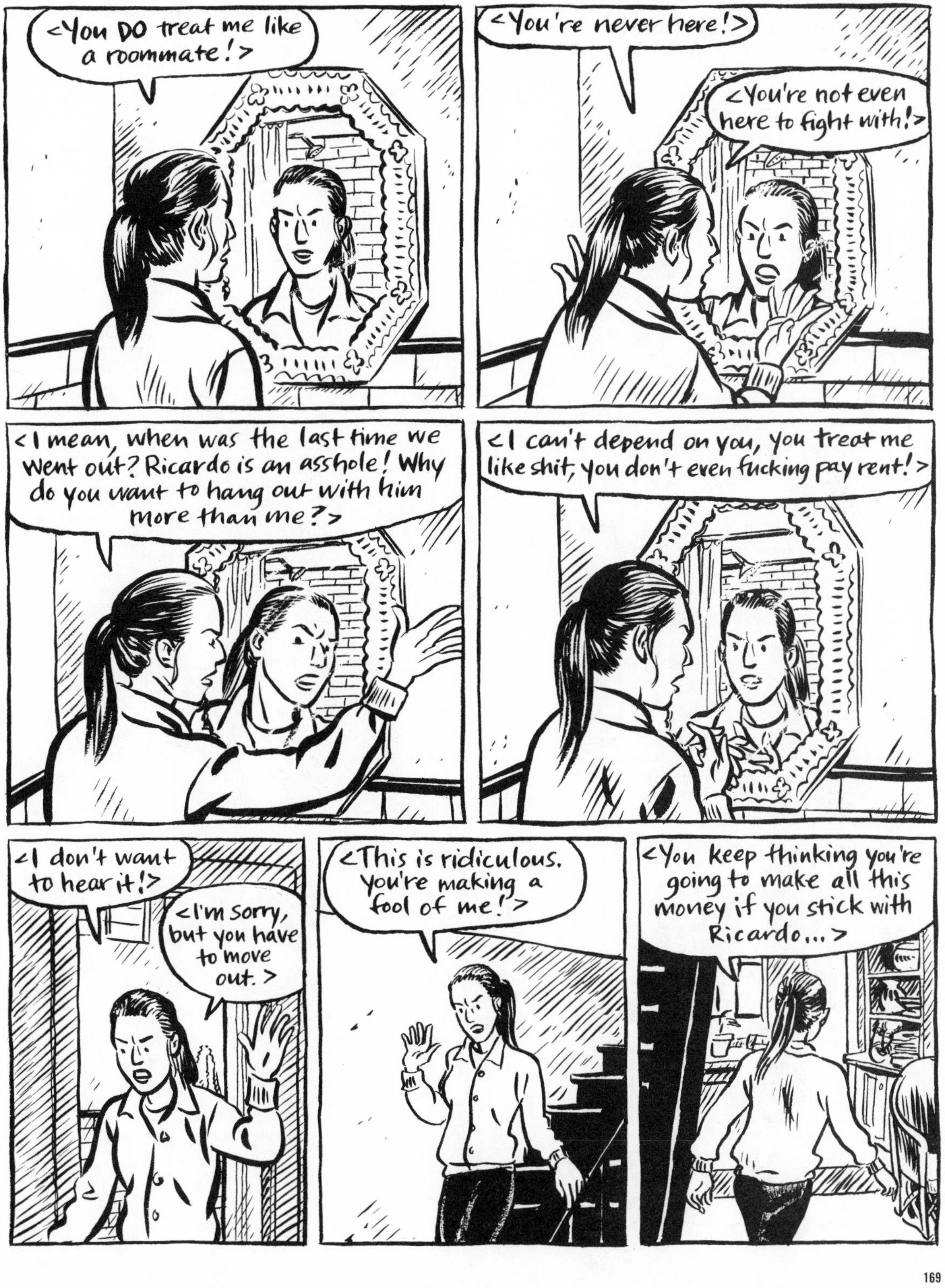
<You DO treat me like a roommate!>
<You're never here!>
<You're not even here to fight with!>
<I mean, when was the last time we went out? Ricardo is an asshole! Why do you want to hang out with him more than me?>
<I can't depend on you, you treat me like shit, you don't even fucking pay rent!>
<I don't want to hear it!>
<I'm sorry, but you have to move out.>
<This is ridiculous. You're making a fool of me!>
<You keep thinking you're going to make all this money if you stick with Ricardo...>

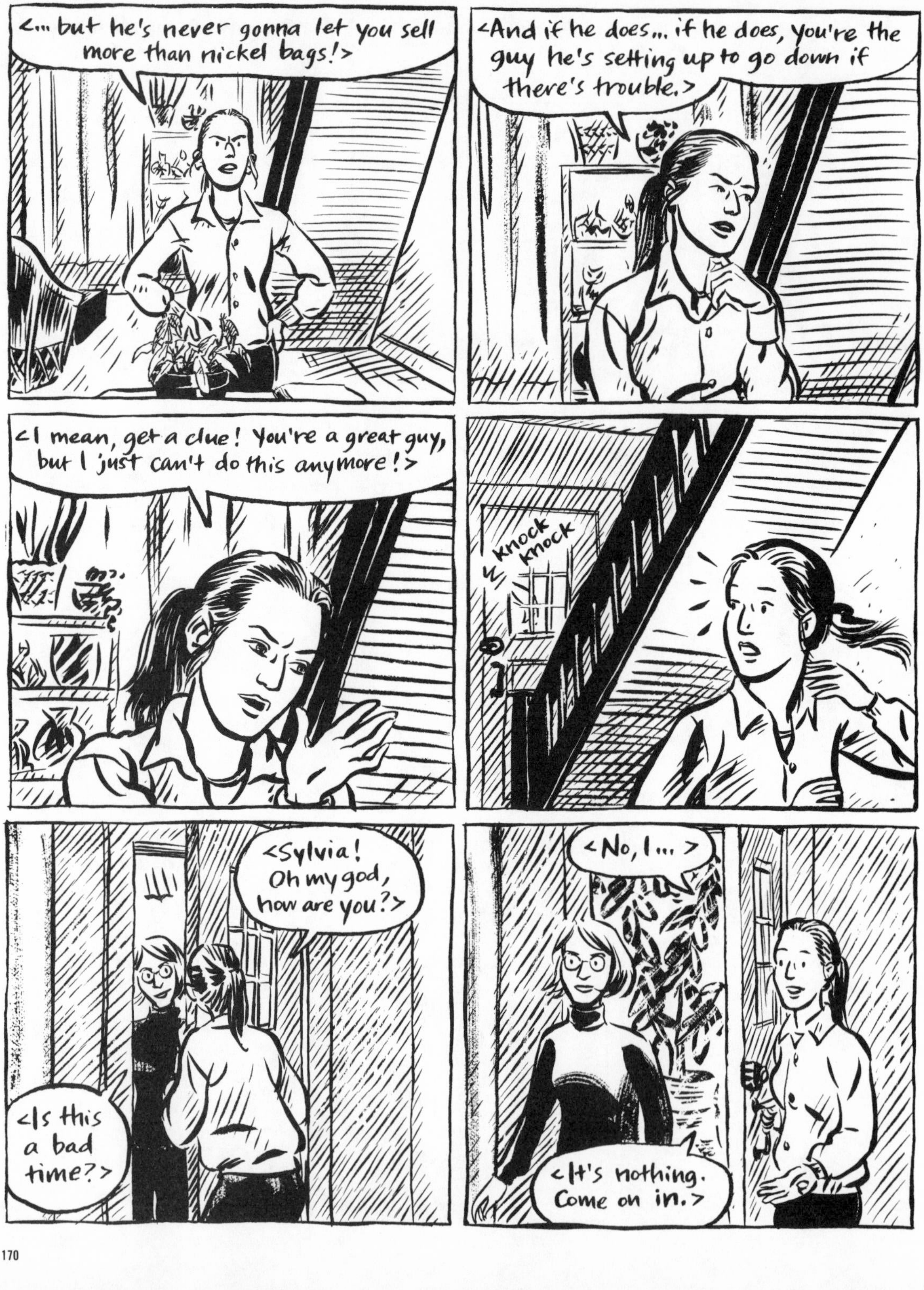
<... but he's never gonna let you sell more than nickel bags!>
<And if he does... if he does, you're the guy he's setting up to go down if there's trouble.>
<I mean, get a clue! You're a great guy, but I just can't do this anymore!>
KNOCK KNOCK
<Sylvia! Oh my god, how are you?>
<Is this a bad time?>
<No, I... >
<It's nothing. Come on in.>

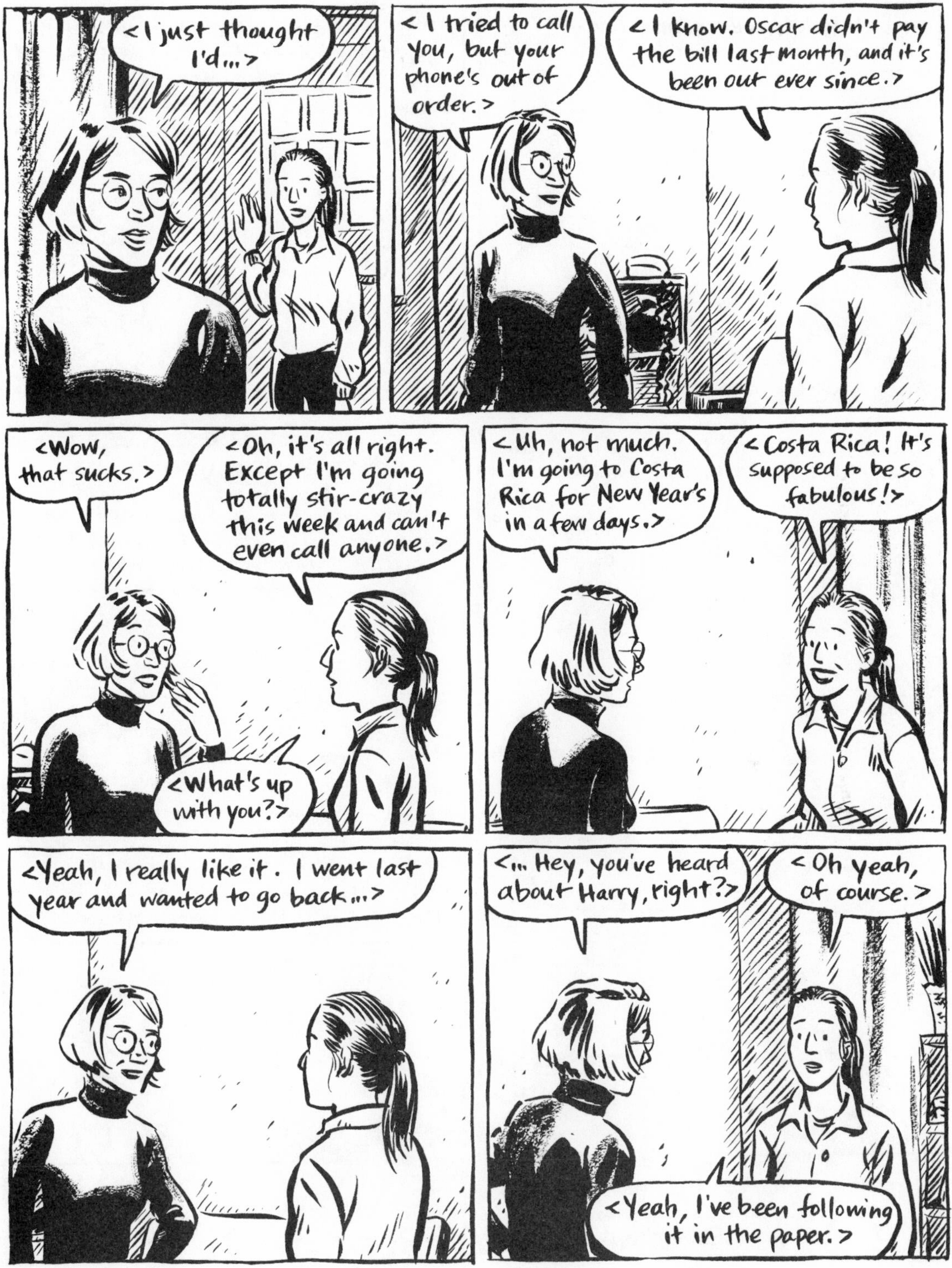
<I just thought I'd...>
<I tried to call you, but your phone's out of order.>
<I know. Oscar didn't pay the bill last month, and it's been out ever since.>
<Wow, that sucks.>
<Oh, it's all right. Except I'm going totally stir-crazy this week and can't even call anyone.>
<What's up with you?>
<Uh, not much. I'm going to Costa Rica for New Year's in a few days.>
<Costa Rica! It's supposed to be so fabulous!>
<Yeah, I really like it. I went last year and wanted to go back...>
<... Hey, you've heard about Harry, right?>
<Oh yeah, of course.>
<Yeah, I've been following it in the paper.>

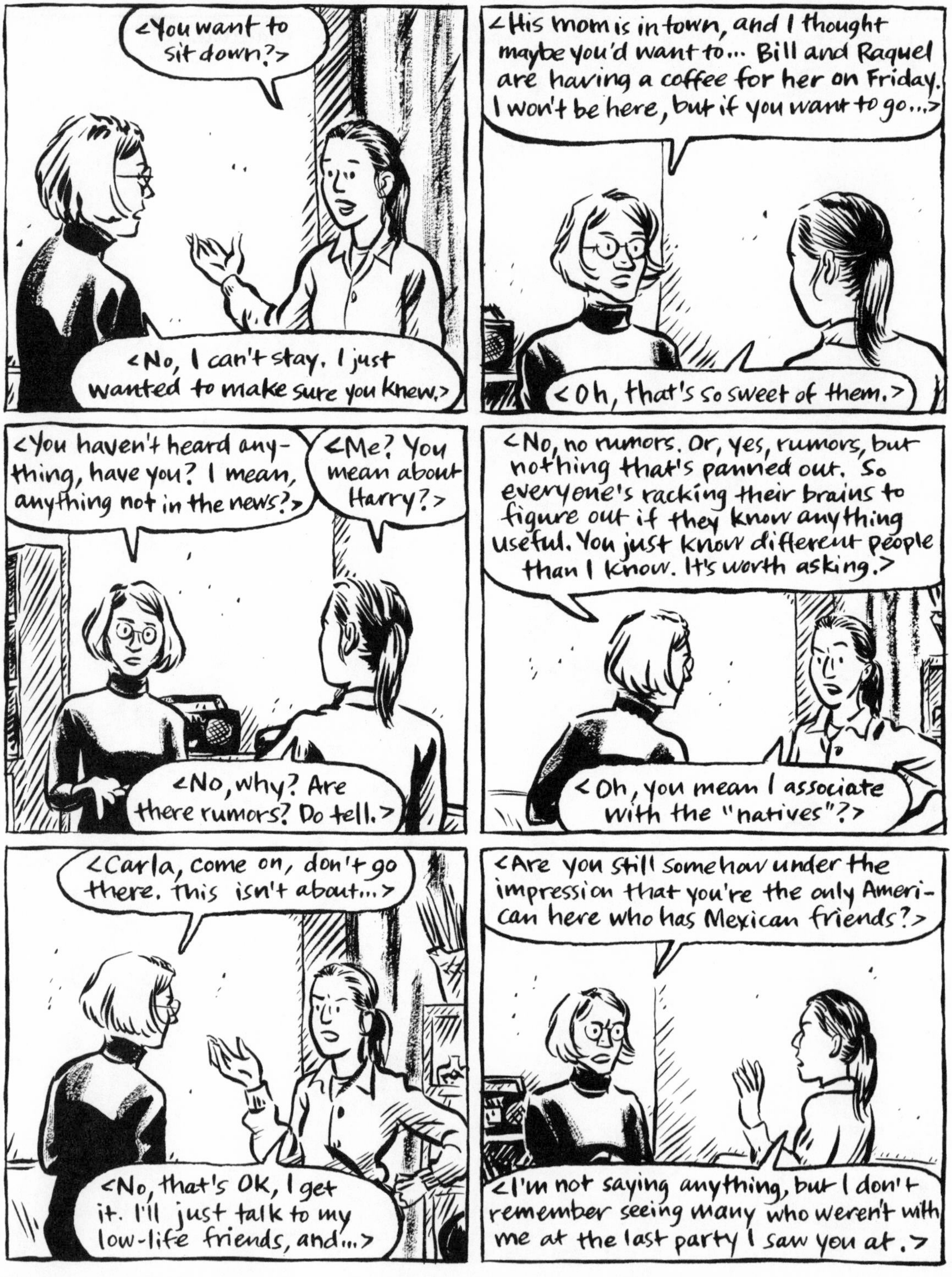
<You want to sit down?>
<No, I can't stay. I just wanted to make sure you knew.>
<His mom is in town, and I thought maybe you'd want to... Bill and Raquel are having a coffee for her on Friday. I won't be here, but if you want to go...>
<Oh, that's so sweet of them.>
<You haven't heard anything, have you? I mean, anything not in the news?>
<Me? You mean about Harry?>
<No, why? Are there rumors? Do tell.>
<No, no rumors. Or, yes, rumors, but nothing that's panned out. So everyone's racking their brains to figure out if they know anything useful. You just know different people than I know. It's worth asking.>
<Oh, you mean I associate with the "natives"?>
<Carla, come on, don't go there. This isn't about...>
<No, that's OK, I get it. I'll just talk to my low-life friends, and...>
<Are you still somehow under the impression that you're the only American here who has Mexican friends?>
<I'm not saying anything, but I don't remember seeing many who weren't with me at the last party I saw you at.>

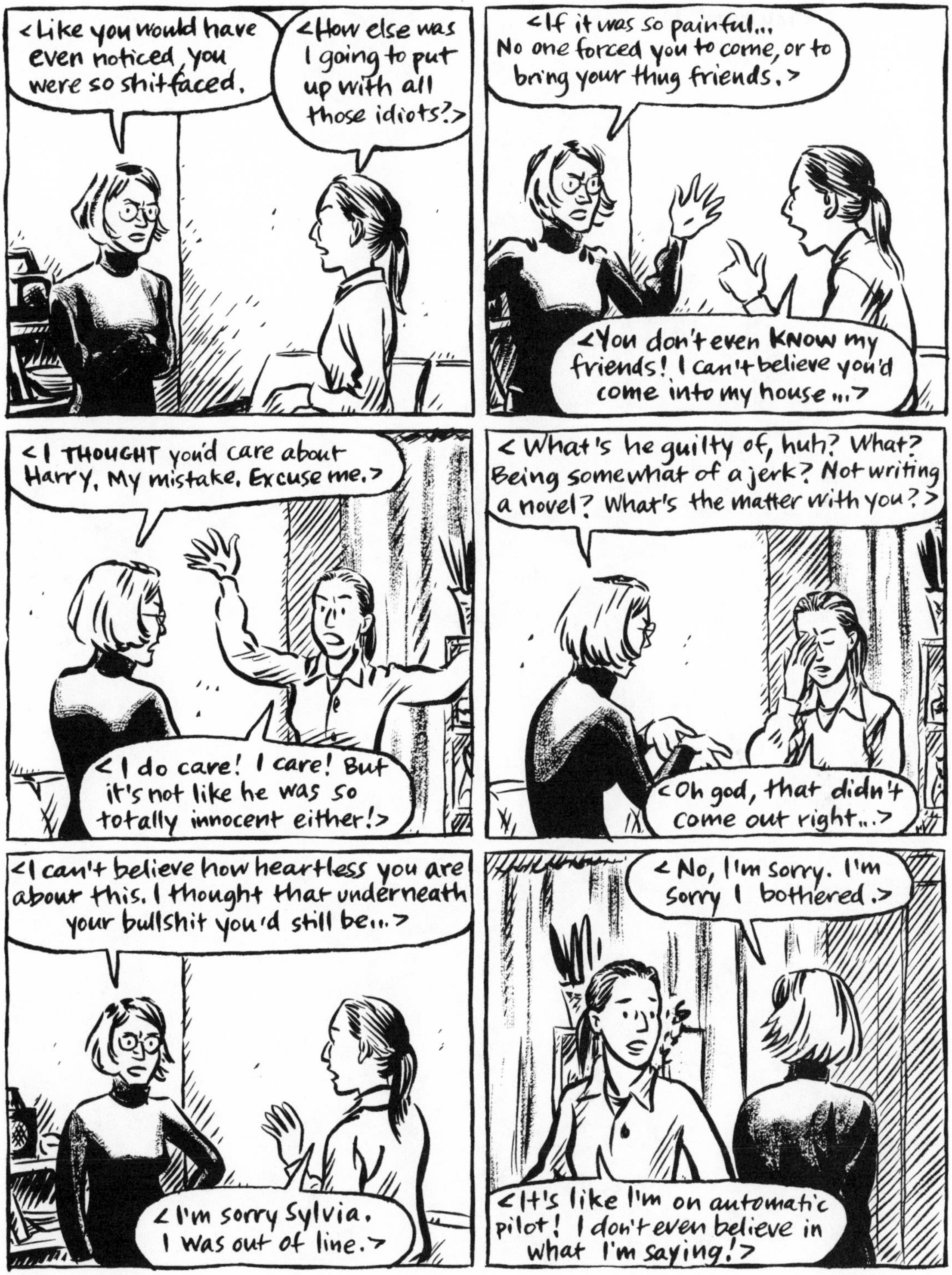
<Like you would have even noticed, you were so shitfaced.
<How else was I going to put up with all those idiots?>
<If it was so painful... No one forced you to come, or to bring your thug friends.>
<You don't even KNOW my friends! I can't believe you'd come into my house...>
<I THOUGHT you'd care about Harry. My mistake. Excuse me.>
...
<I do care! I care! But it's not like he was so totally innocent either!>
<What's he guilty of, huh? What? Being somewhat of a jerk? Not writing a novel? What's the matter with you?>
<Oh god, that didn't come out right...>
<I can't believe how heartless you are about this. I thought that underneath your bullshit you'd still be...>
<I'm sorry Sylvia. I was out of line.>
<No, I'm sorry. I'm sorry I bothered.>
<It's like I'm on automatic pilot! I don't even believe in what I'm saying!>

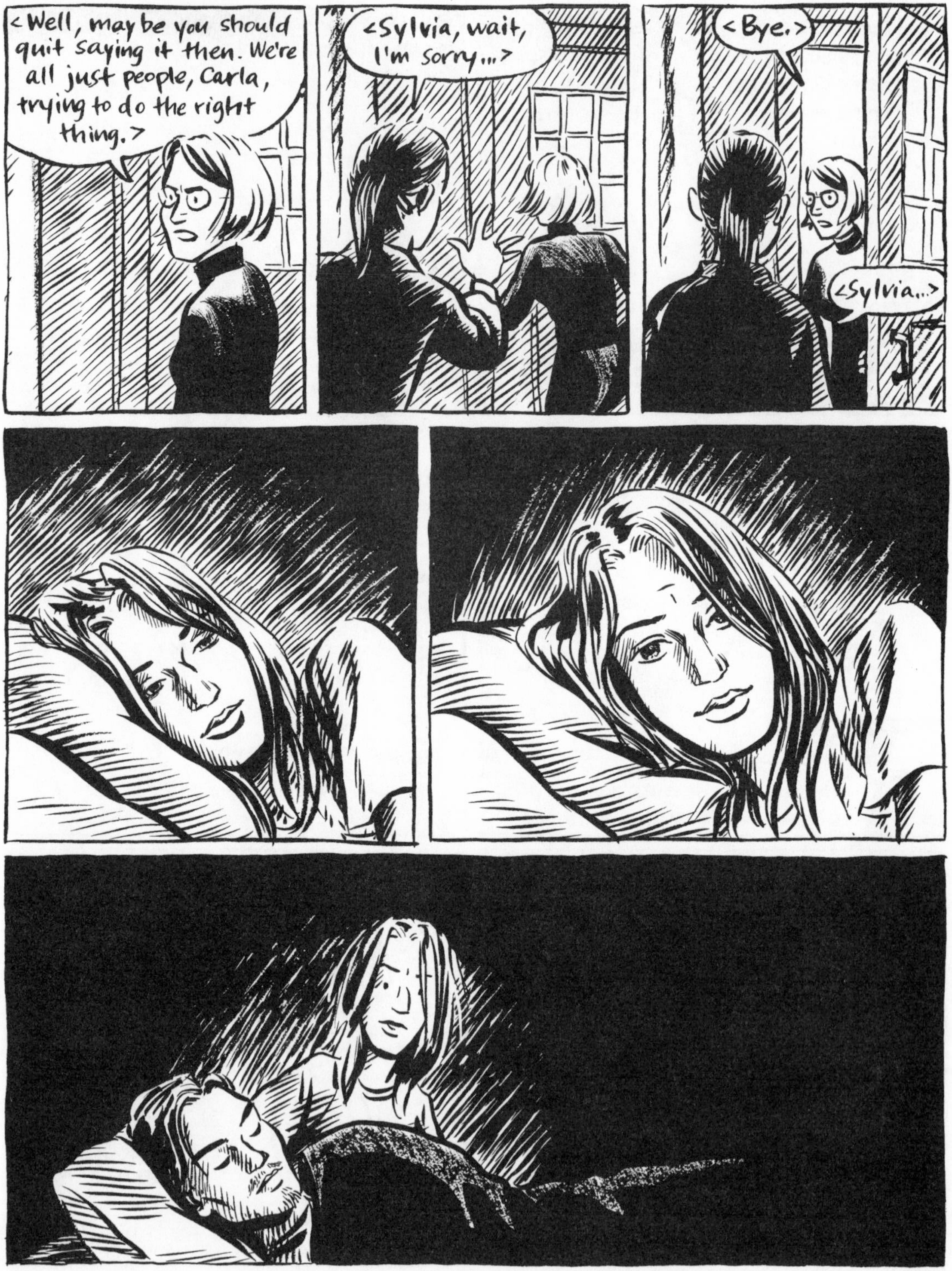
<Well, maybe you should quit saying it then. We're all just people, Carla, trying to do the right thing.>
<Sylvia, wait, I'm sorry...>
<Bye.>
<Sylvia...>

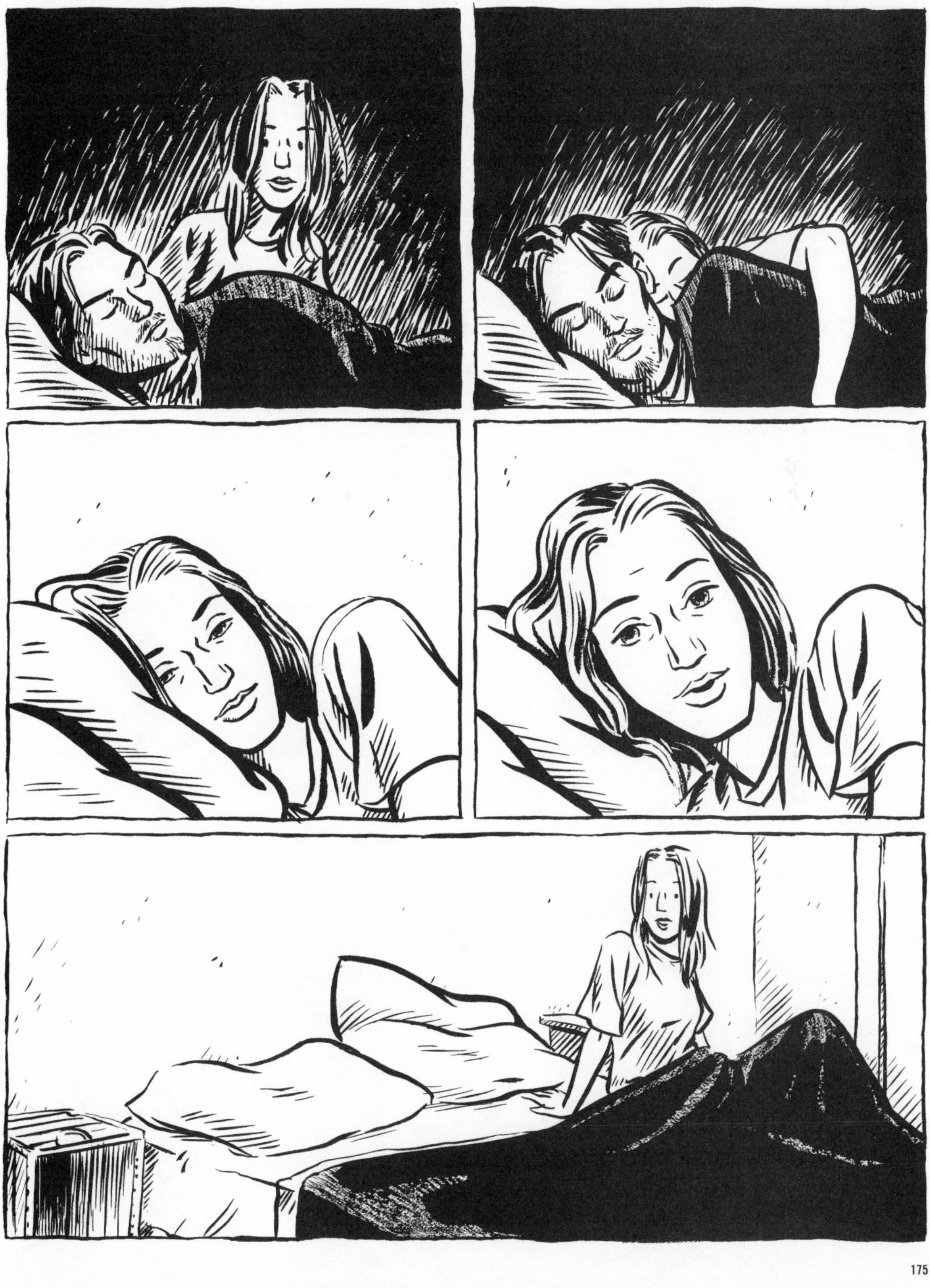

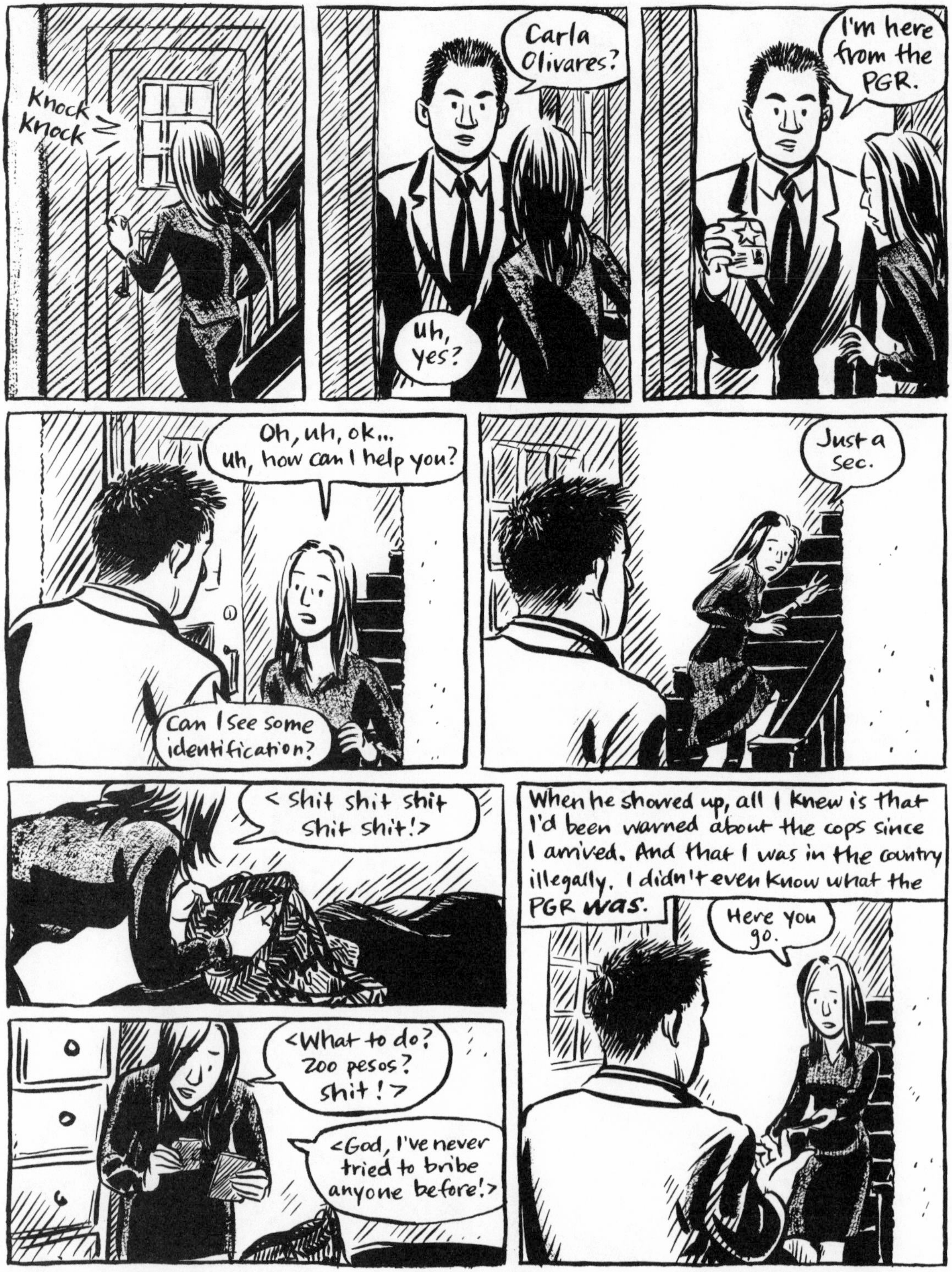
Knock knock
Carla Olivares?
Uh, yes?
I'm here from the PGR.
Oh, uh, ok... Uh, how can I help you?
Can I see some identification?
Just a sec.
< Shit shit shit shit shit!>
<What to do? 200 pesos? shit!>
<God, I've never tried to bribe anyone before!>
When he showed up, all I knew is that I'd been warned about the cops since I arrived. And that I was in the country illegally. I didn't even know what the PGR *was*.
Here you go.

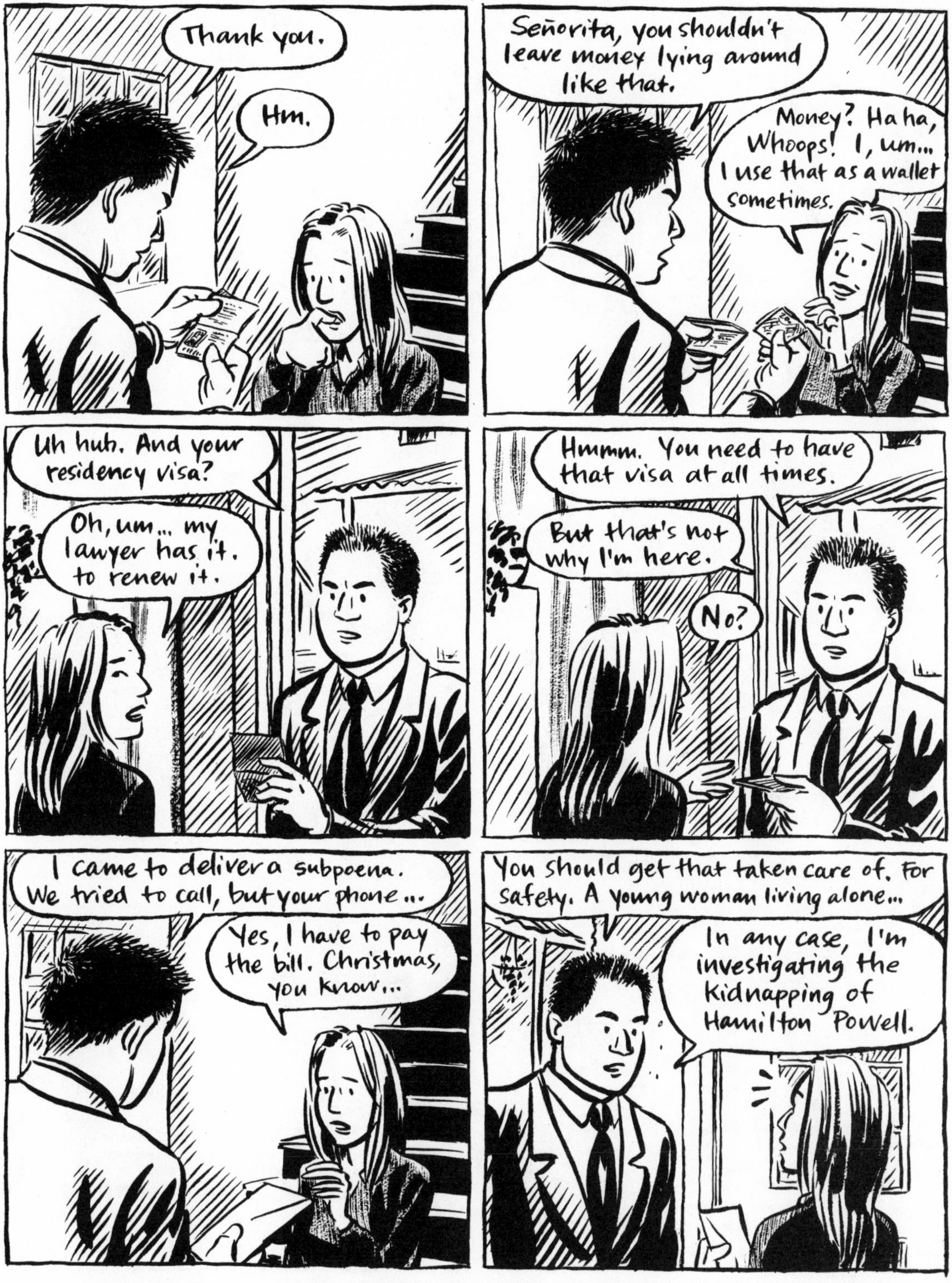
Thank you.
Hm.
Señorita, you shouldn't leave money lying around like that.
Money? Ha ha, Whoops! I, um... I use that as a wallet sometimes.
Uh huh. And your residency visa?
Oh, um... my lawyer has it. to renew it.
Hmmm. You need to have that visa at all times.
But that's not why I'm here.
No?
I came to deliver a subpoena. We tried to call, but your phone...
Yes, I have to pay the bill. Christmas, you know...
You should get that taken care of. For safety. A young woman living alone...
In any case, I'm investigating the kidnapping of Hamilton Powell.

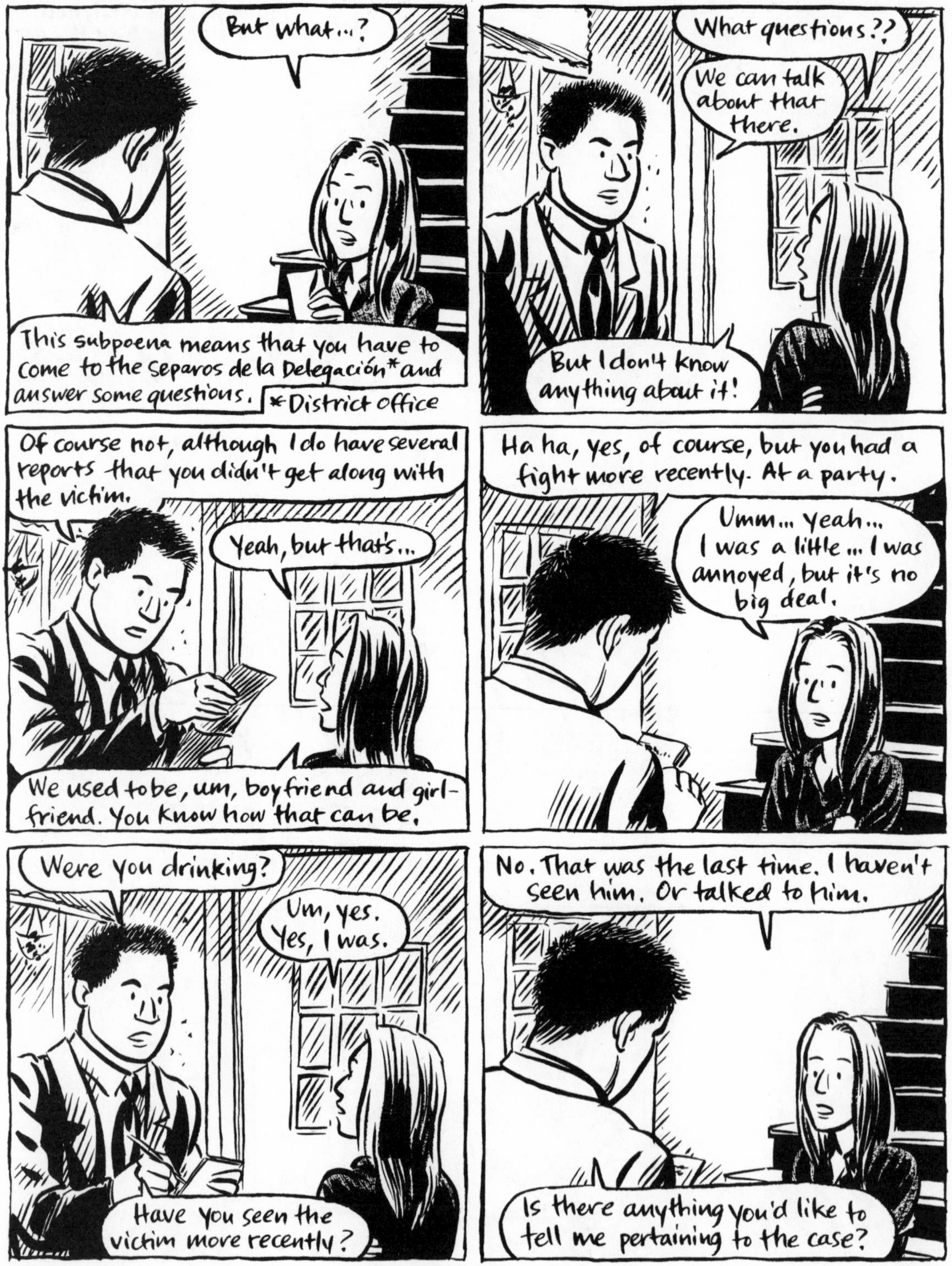
But what...?
This subpoena means that you have to come to the separos de la Delegación* and answer some questions.
*District office
What questions??
We can talk about that there.
But I don't know anything about it!
Of course not, although I do have several reports that you didn't get along with the victim.
Yeah, but that's...
We used to be, um, boyfriend and girl-friend. You know how that can be.
Ha ha, yes, of course, but you had a fight more recently. At a party.
Umm... yeah... I was a little ... I was annoyed, but it's no big deal.
Were you drinking?
Um, yes. Yes, I was.
Have you seen the victim more recently?
No. That was the last time. I haven't seen him. Or talked to him.
Is there anything you'd like to tell me pertaining to the case?

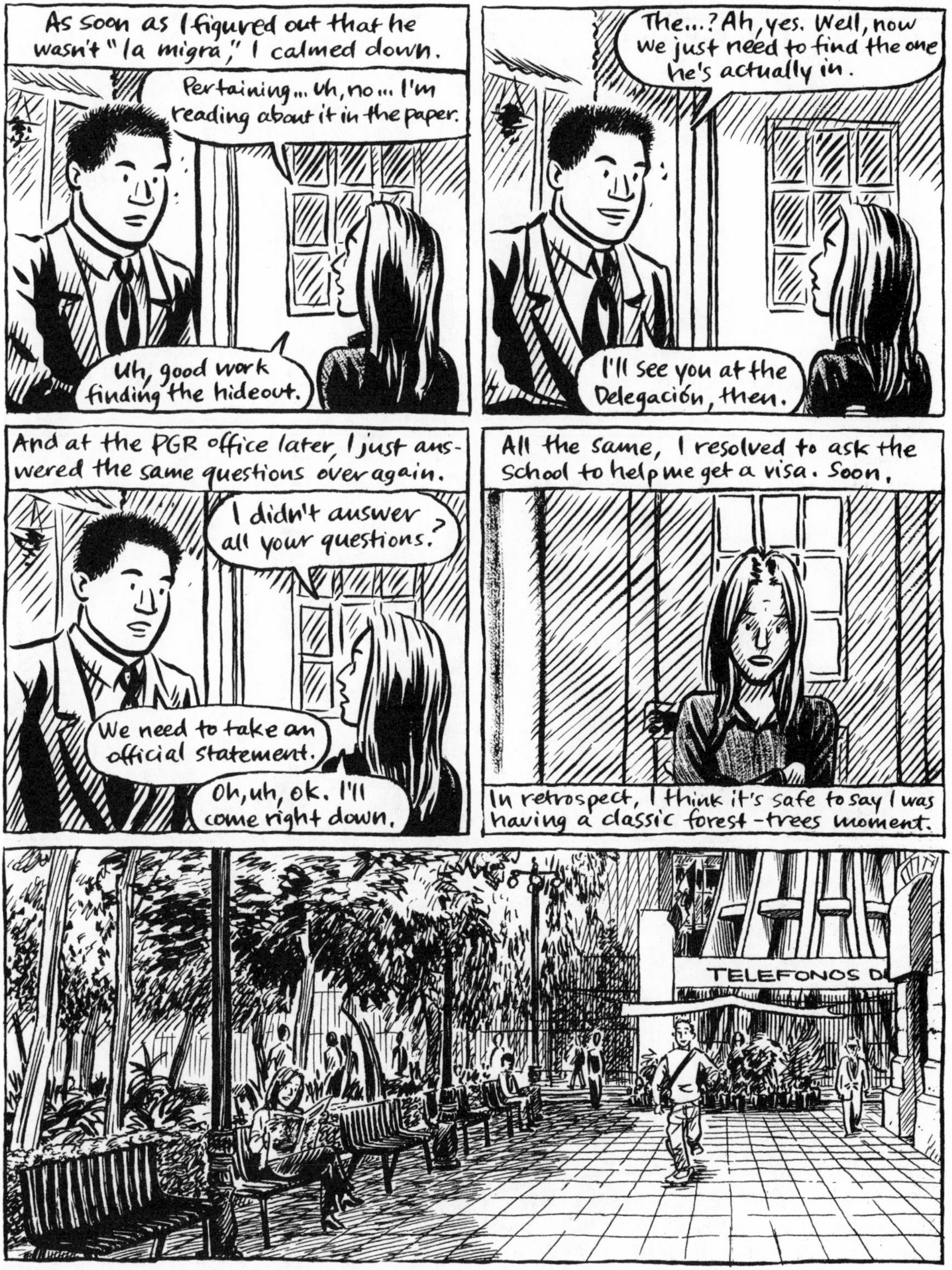

As soon as I figured out that he wasn't "la migra," I calmed down.
Pertaining... uh, no... I'm reading about it in the paper.
Uh, good work finding the hideout.
The...? Ah, yes. Well, now we just need to find the one he's actually in.
I'll see you at the Delegación, then.
And at the PGR office later, I just answered the same questions over again.
I didn't answer all your questions?
We need to take an official statement.
Oh, uh, ok. I'll come right down.
All the same, I resolved to ask the school to help me get a visa. Soon.
In retrospect, I think it's safe to say I was having a classic forest-trees moment.
TELEFONOS D

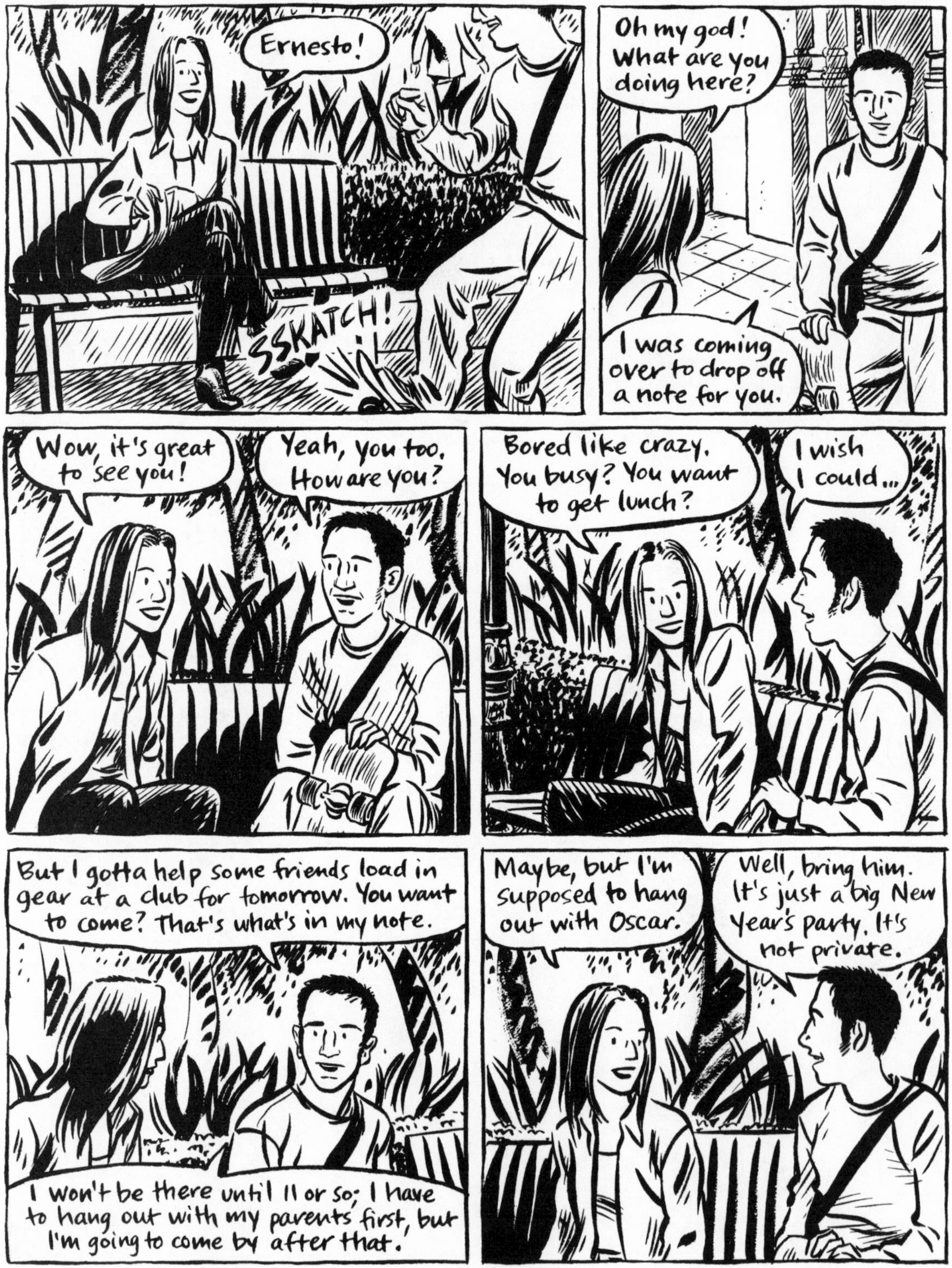
Ernesto!
SSKATCH!
Oh my god! What are you doing here?
I was coming over to drop off a note for you.
Wow, it's great to see you!
Yeah, you too. How are you?
Bored like crazy. You busy? You want to get lunch?
I wish I could...
But I gotta help some friends load in gear at a club for tomorrow. You want to come? That's what's in my note.
I won't be there until 11 or so; I have to hang out with my parents first, but I'm going to come by after that.
Maybe, but I'm supposed to hang out with Oscar.
Well, bring him. It's just a big New Year's party. It's not private.

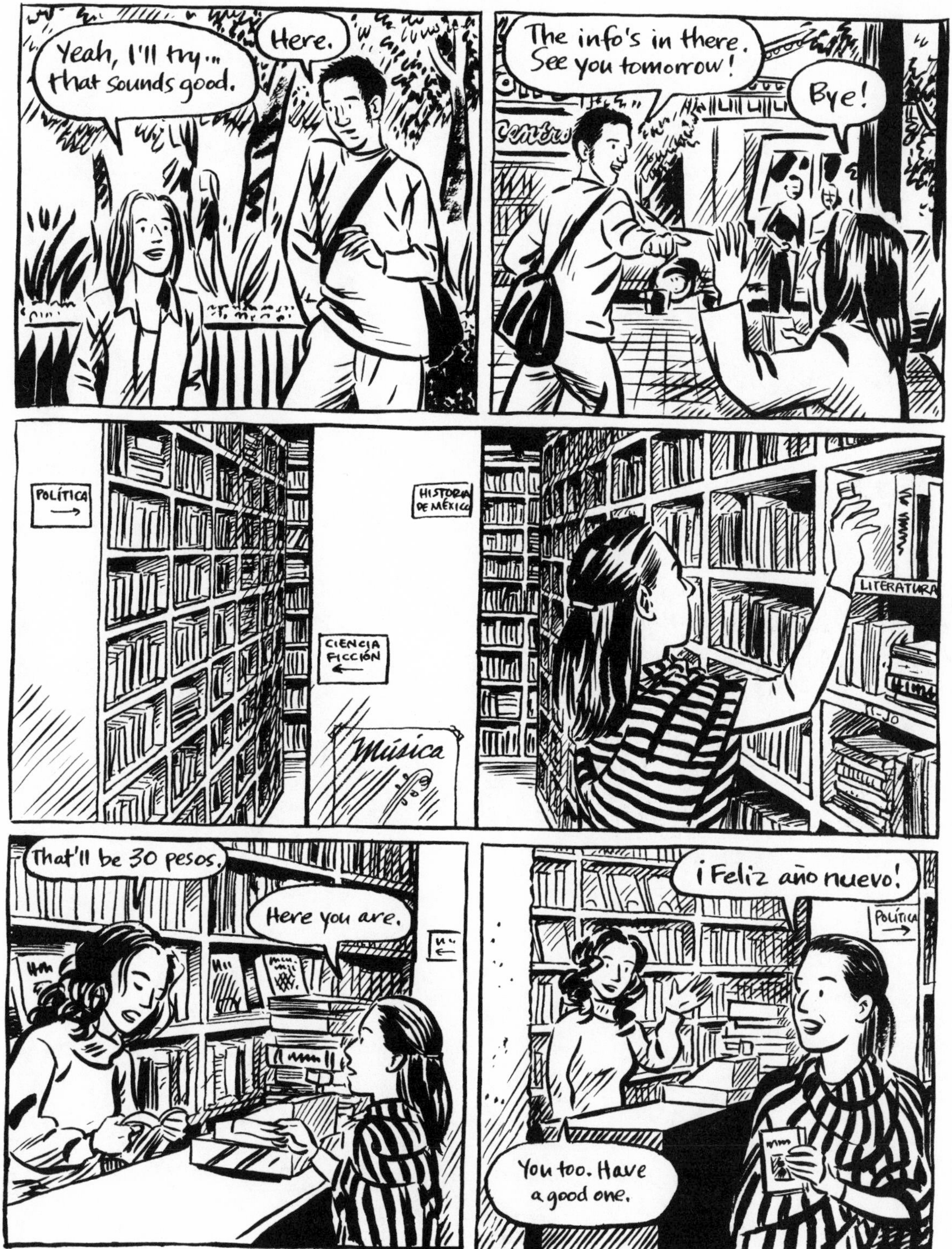

Yeah, I'll try... that sounds good.
Here.
The info's in there. See you tomorrow!
Bye!
POLÍTICA →
HISTORIA DE MÉXICO
CIENCIA FICCIÓN ←
Música
LITERATURA
That'll be 30 pesos.
Here you are.
¡Feliz año nuevo!
POLÍTICA →
You too. Have a good one.

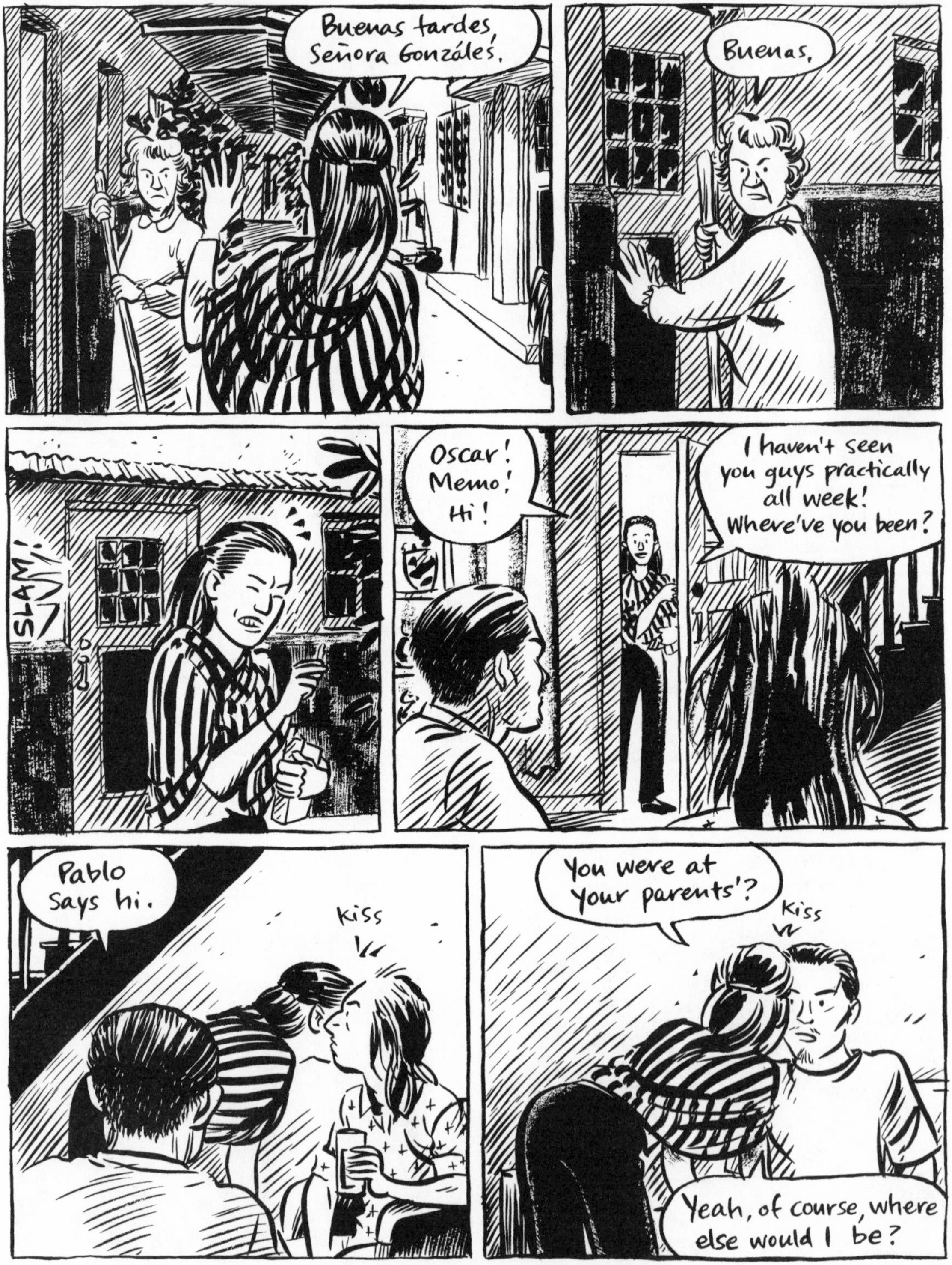
Buenas tardes, Señora Gonzáles.
Buenas.
SLAM!
Oscar! Memo! Hi!
I haven't seen you guys practically all week! Where've you been?
Pablo says hi.
kiss
You were at your parents'?
kiss
Yeah, of course, where else would I be?

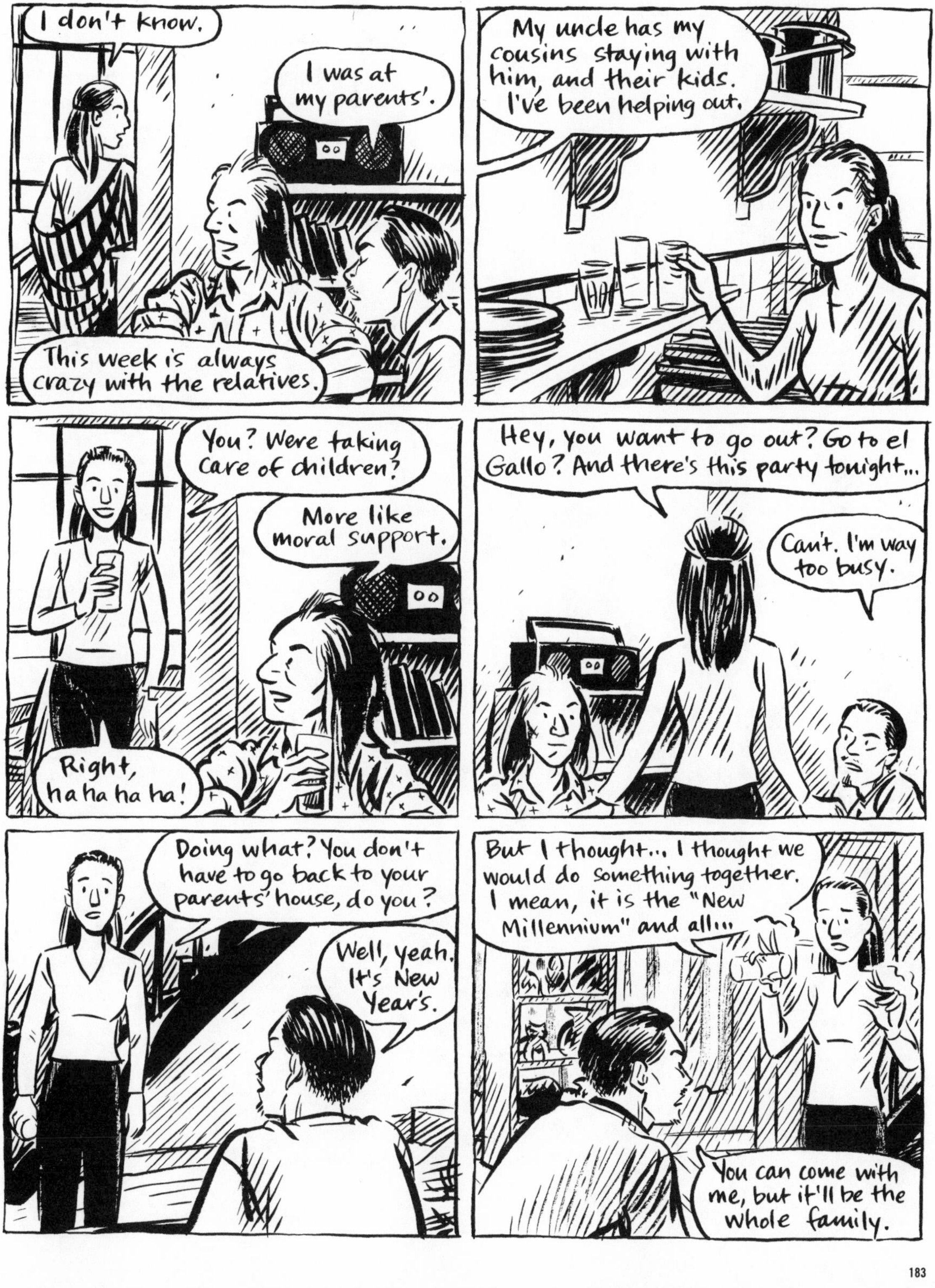
I don't know.
I was at my parents'.
This week is always crazy with the relatives.
My uncle has my cousins staying with him, and their kids. I've been helping out.
You? Were taking care of children?
More like moral support.
Right, ha ha ha ha!
Hey, you want to go out? Go to el Gallo? And there's this party tonight...
Can't. I'm way too busy.
Doing what? You don't have to go back to your parents' house, do you?
Well, yeah. It's New Year's.
But I thought... I thought we would do something together. I mean, it is the "New Millennium" and all...
You can come with me, but it'll be the whole family.

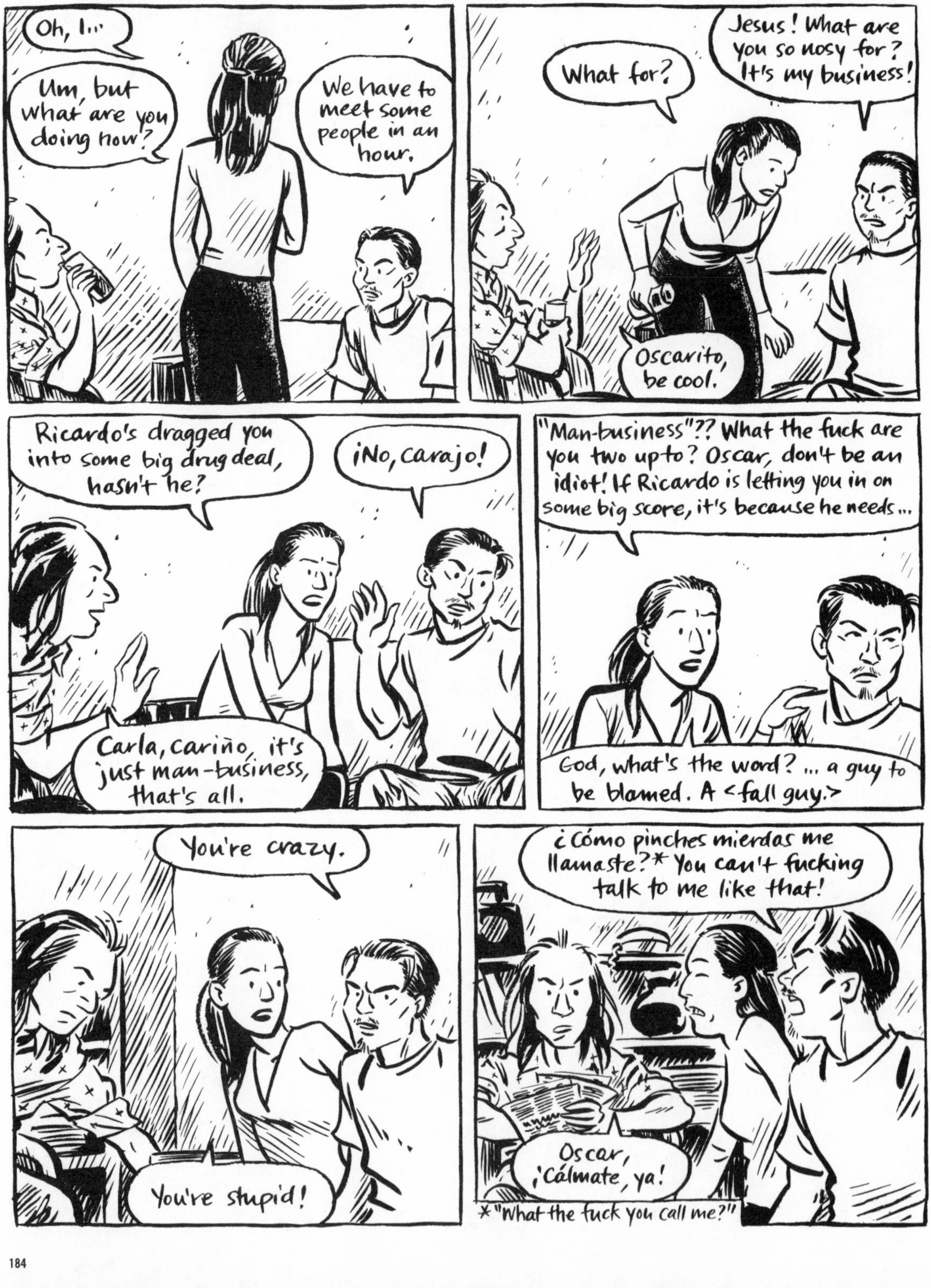
Oh, I...
Um, but what are you doing now?
We have to meet some people in an hour.
What for?
Jesus! What are you so nosy for? It's my business!
Oscarito, be cool.
Ricardo's dragged you into some big drug deal, hasn't he?
¡No, carajo!
Carla, cariño, it's just man-business, that's all.
"Man-business"?? What the fuck are you two up to? Oscar, don't be an idiot! If Ricardo is letting you in on some big score, it's because he needs...
God, what's the word? ... a guy to be blamed. A <fall guy.>
You're crazy.
You're stupid!
¿Cómo pinches mierdas me llamaste?* You can't fucking talk to me like that!
Oscar, ¡Cálmate, ya!
*"What the fuck you call me?"

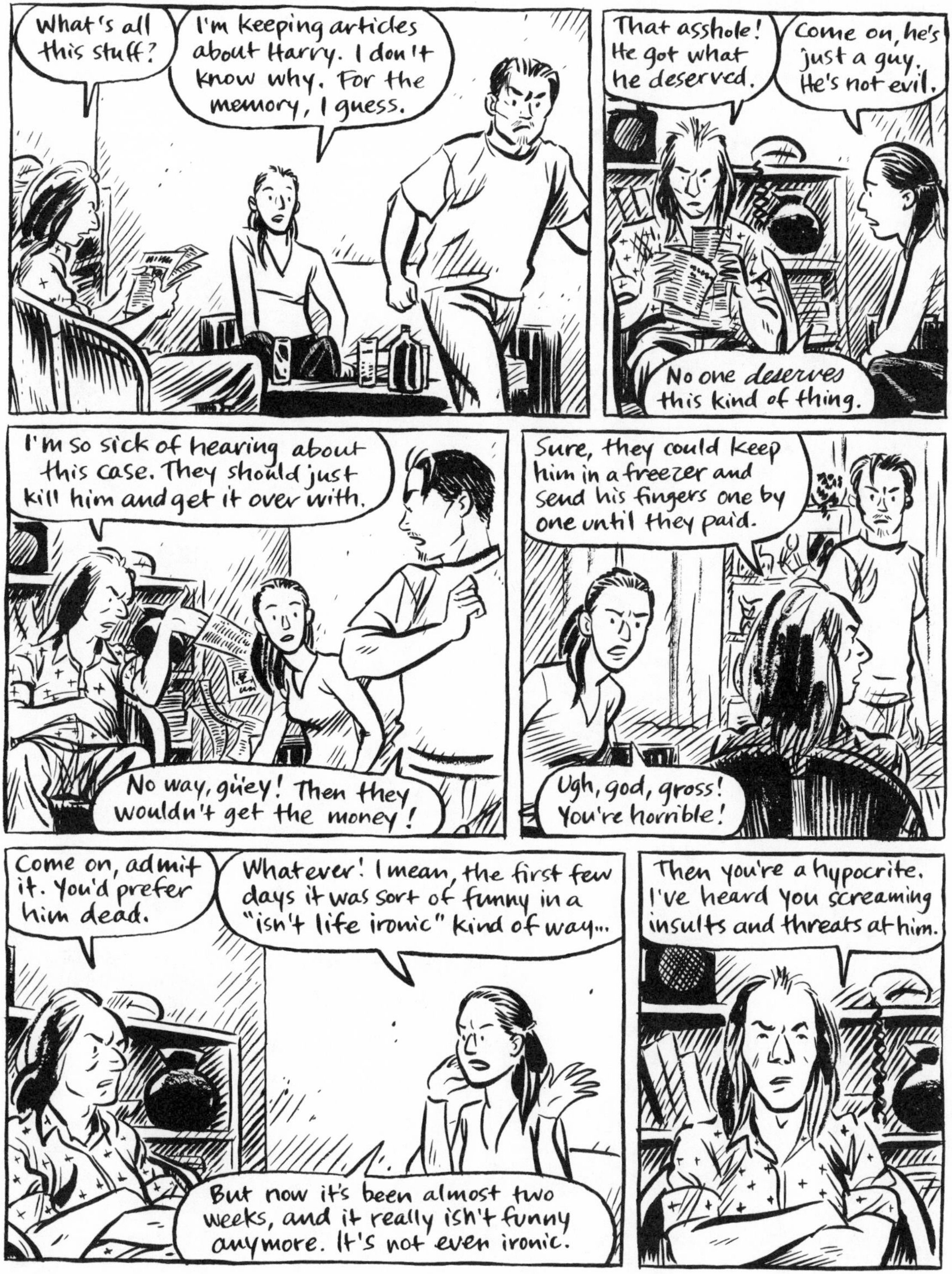
What's all this stuff?
I'm keeping articles about Harry. I don't know why. For the memory, I guess.
That asshole! He got what he deserved.
Come on, he's just a guy. He's not evil.
No one deserves this kind of thing.
I'm so sick of hearing about this case. They should just kill him and get it over with.
No way, güey! Then they wouldn't get the money!
Sure, they could keep him in a freezer and send his fingers one by one until they paid.
Ugh, god, gross! You're horrible!
Come on, admit it. You'd prefer him dead.
Whatever! I mean, the first few days it was sort of funny in a "isn't life ironic" kind of way...
But now it's been almost two weeks, and it really isn't funny anymore. It's not even ironic.
Then you're a hypocrite. I've heard you screaming insults and threats at him.

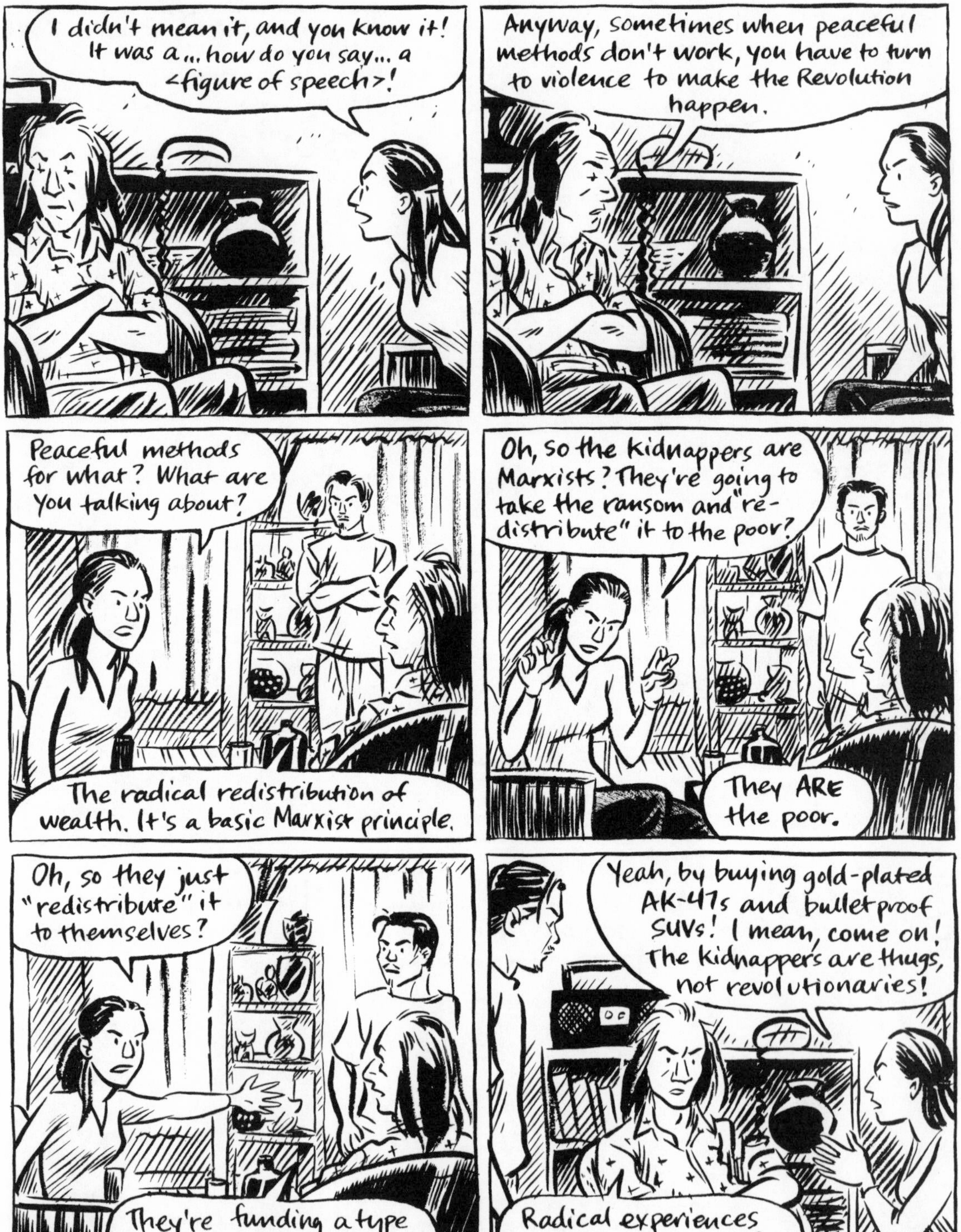
I didn't mean it, and you know it! It was a... how do you say... a <figure of speech>!
Anyway, sometimes when peaceful methods don't work, you have to turn to violence to make the Revolution happen.
Peaceful methods for what? What are you talking about?
The radical redistribution of wealth. It's a basic Marxist principle.
Oh, so the kidnappers are Marxists? They're going to take the ransom and "re-distribute" it to the poor?
They ARE the poor.
Oh, so they just "redistribute" it to themselves?
They're funding a type of armed insurrection.
Yeah, by buying gold-plated AK-47s and bulletproof SUVs! I mean, come on! The kidnappers are thugs, not revolutionaries!
Radical experiences can transform people.

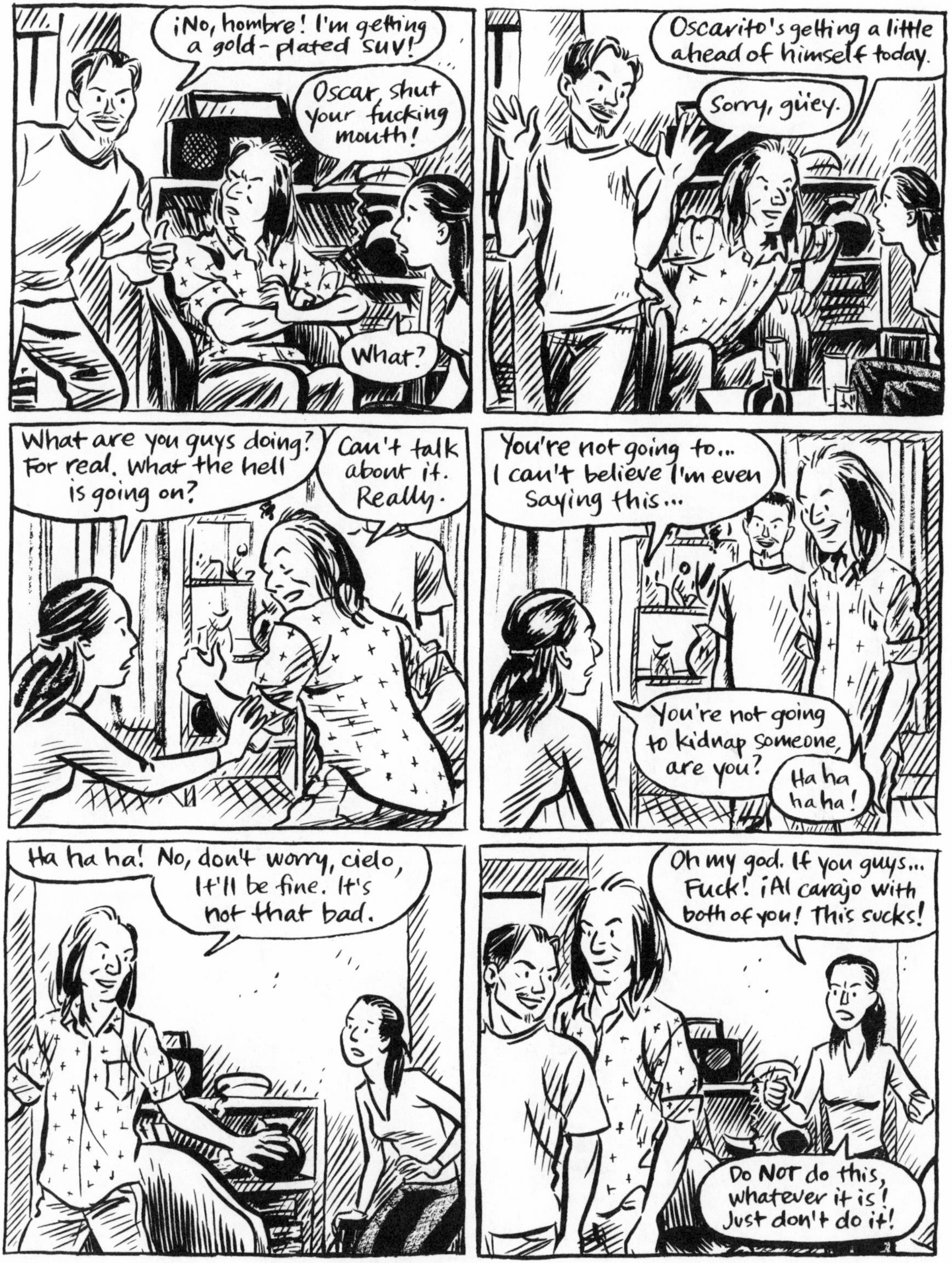
¡No, hombre! I'm getting a gold-plated SUV!
Oscar, shut your fucking mouth!
What?
Oscarito's getting a little ahead of himself today.
Sorry, güey.
What are you guys doing? For real. What the hell is going on?
Can't talk about it. Really.
You're not going to... I can't believe I'm even saying this...
You're not going to kidnap someone, are you?
Ha ha ha ha!
Ha ha ha! No, don't worry, cielo, It'll be fine. It's not that bad.
Oh my god. If you guys... Fuck! ¡Al carajo with both of you! This sucks!
Do NOT do this, whatever it is! Just don't do it!

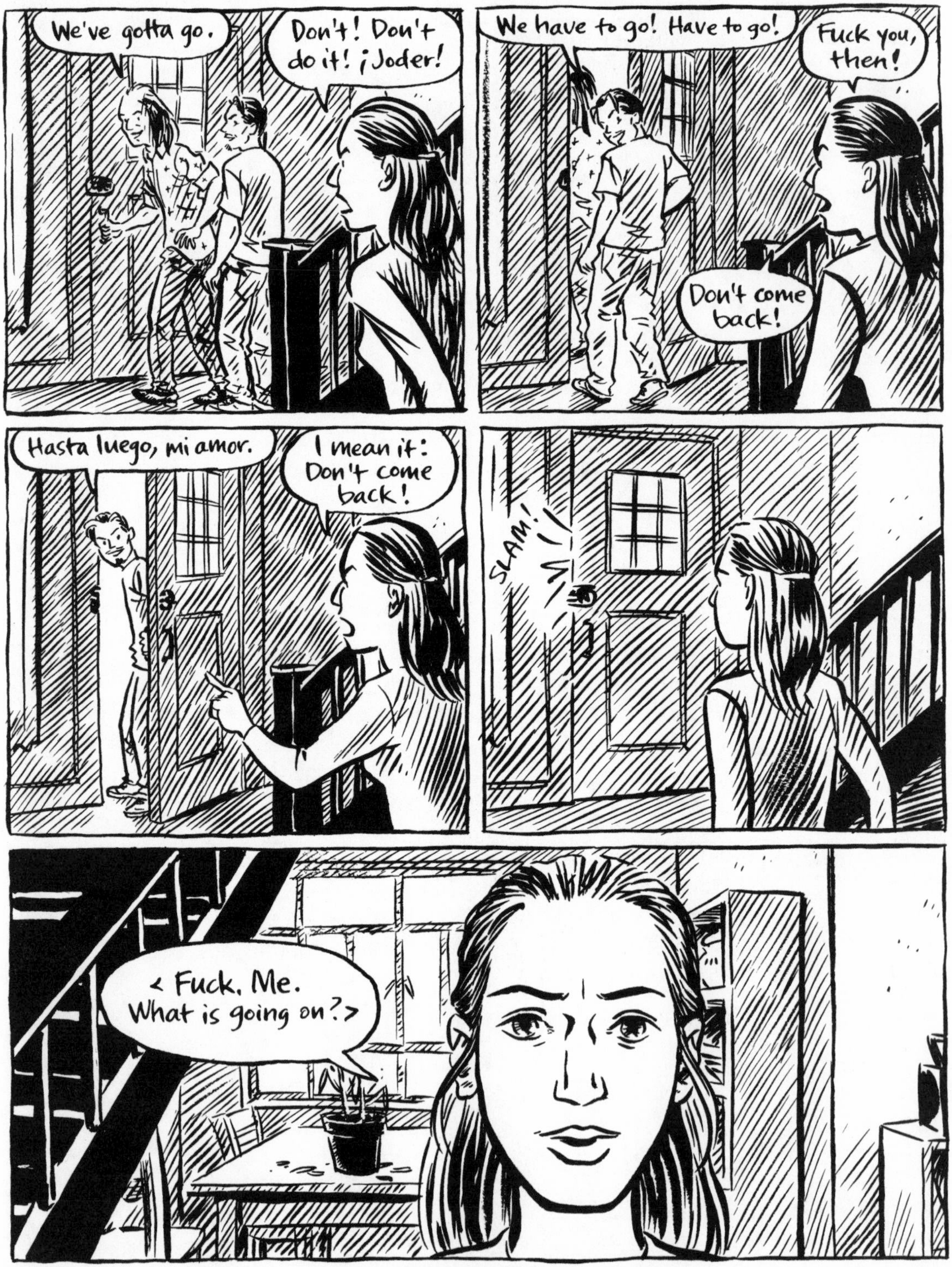
We've gotta go.
Don't! Don't do it! ¡Joder!
We have to go! Have to go!
Fuck you, then!
Don't come back!
Hasta luego, mi amor.
I mean it: Don't come back!
SLAM!
< Fuck. Me. What is going on? >

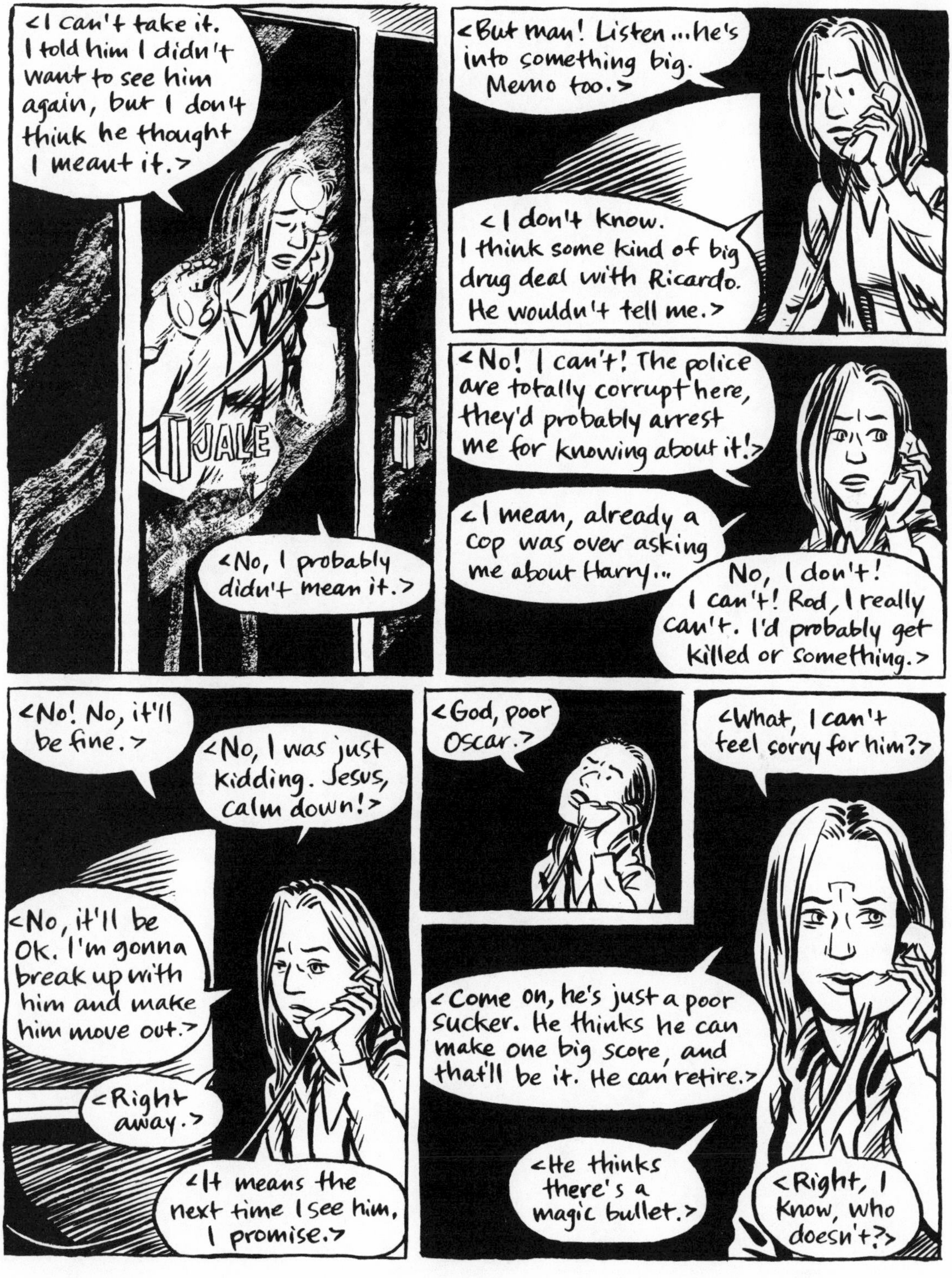
<I can't take it. I told him I didn't want to see him again, but I don't think he thought I meant it.>
JALE
<No, I probably didn't mean it.>
<But man! Listen...he's into something big. Memo too.>
<I don't know. I think some kind of big drug deal with Ricardo. He wouldn't tell me.>
<No! I can't! The police are totally corrupt here, they'd probably arrest me for knowing about it!>
<I mean, already a cop was over asking me about Harry...
No, I don't! I can't! Rod, I really can't. I'd probably get killed or something.>
<No! No, it'll be fine.>
<No, I was just kidding. Jesus, calm down!>
<No, it'll be Ok. I'm gonna break up with him and make him move out.>
<Right away.>
<It means the next time I see him, I promise.>
<God, poor Oscar.>
<What, I can't feel sorry for him?>
<Come on, he's just a poor sucker. He thinks he can make one big score, and that'll be it. He can retire.>
<He thinks there's a magic bullet.>
<Right, I know, who doesn't?>

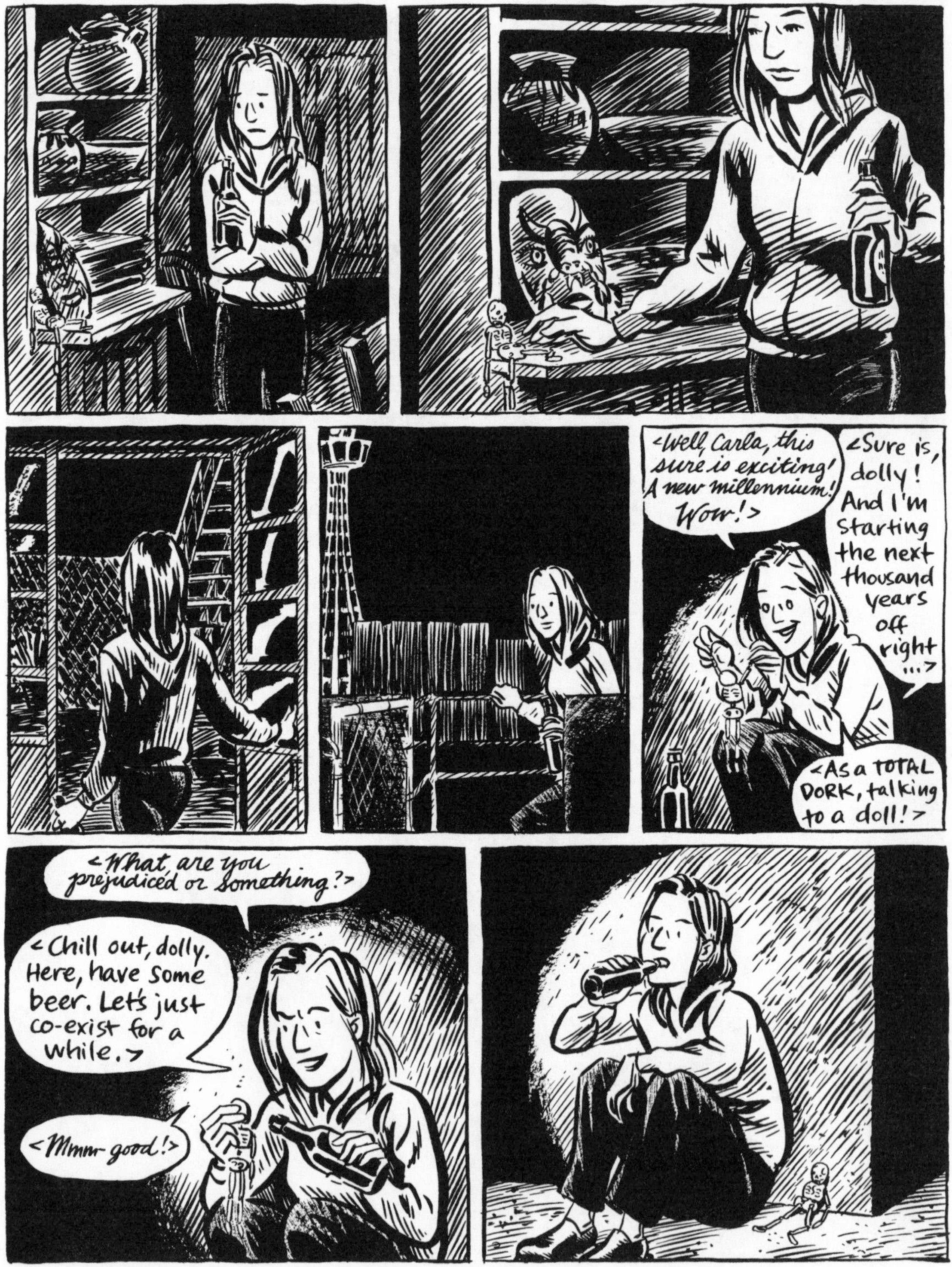

<Well, Carla, this sure is exciting! A new millennium! Wow!>
<Sure is, dolly! And I'm starting the next thousand years off right ...>
<As a TOTAL DORK, talking to a doll!>
<What, are you prejudiced or something?>
<Chill out, dolly. Here, have some beer. Let's just co-exist for a while.>
<Mmm-good!>

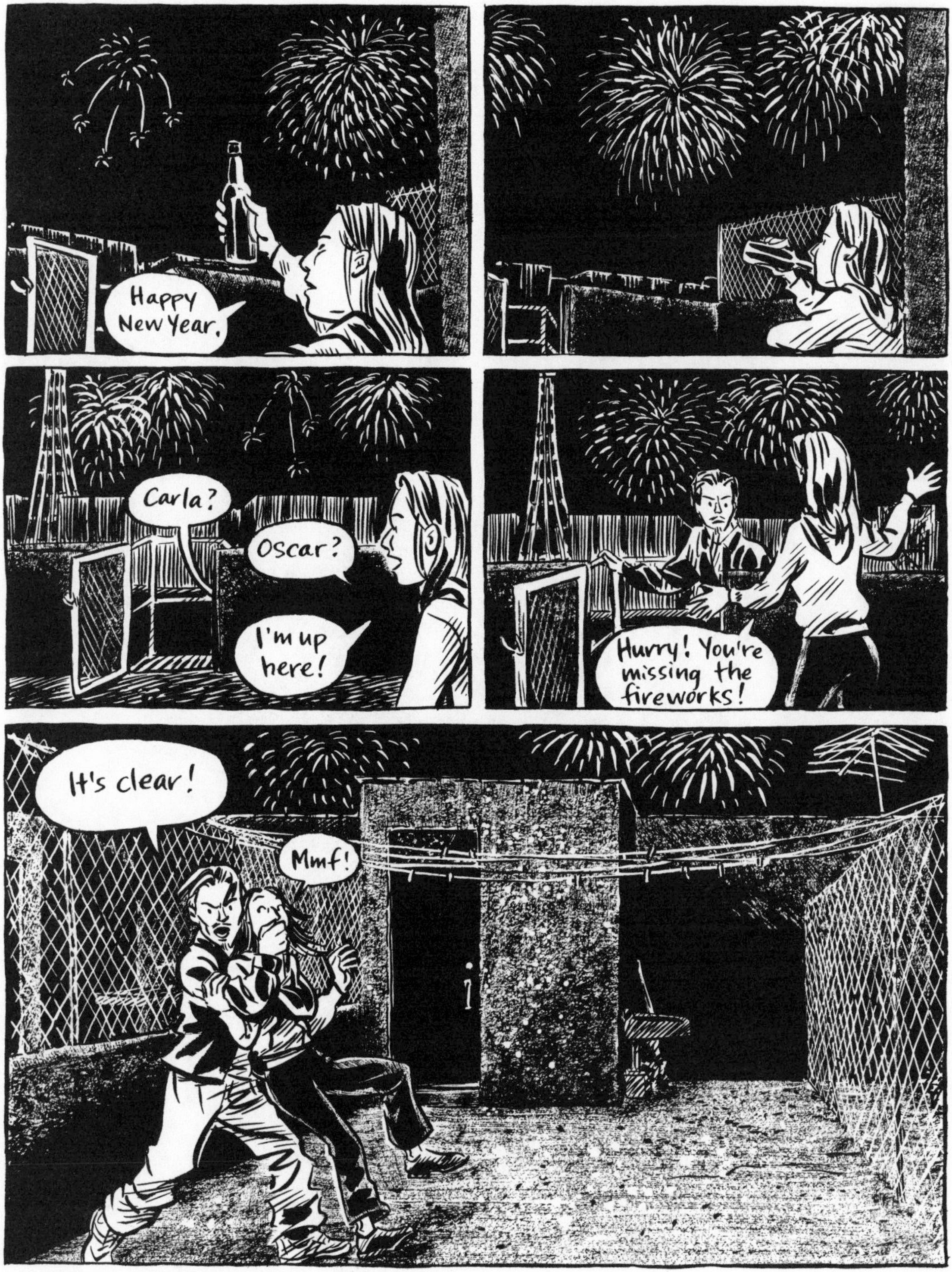
Happy New Year.
Carla?
Oscar?
I'm up here!
Hurry! You're missing the fireworks!
It's clear!
Mmf!

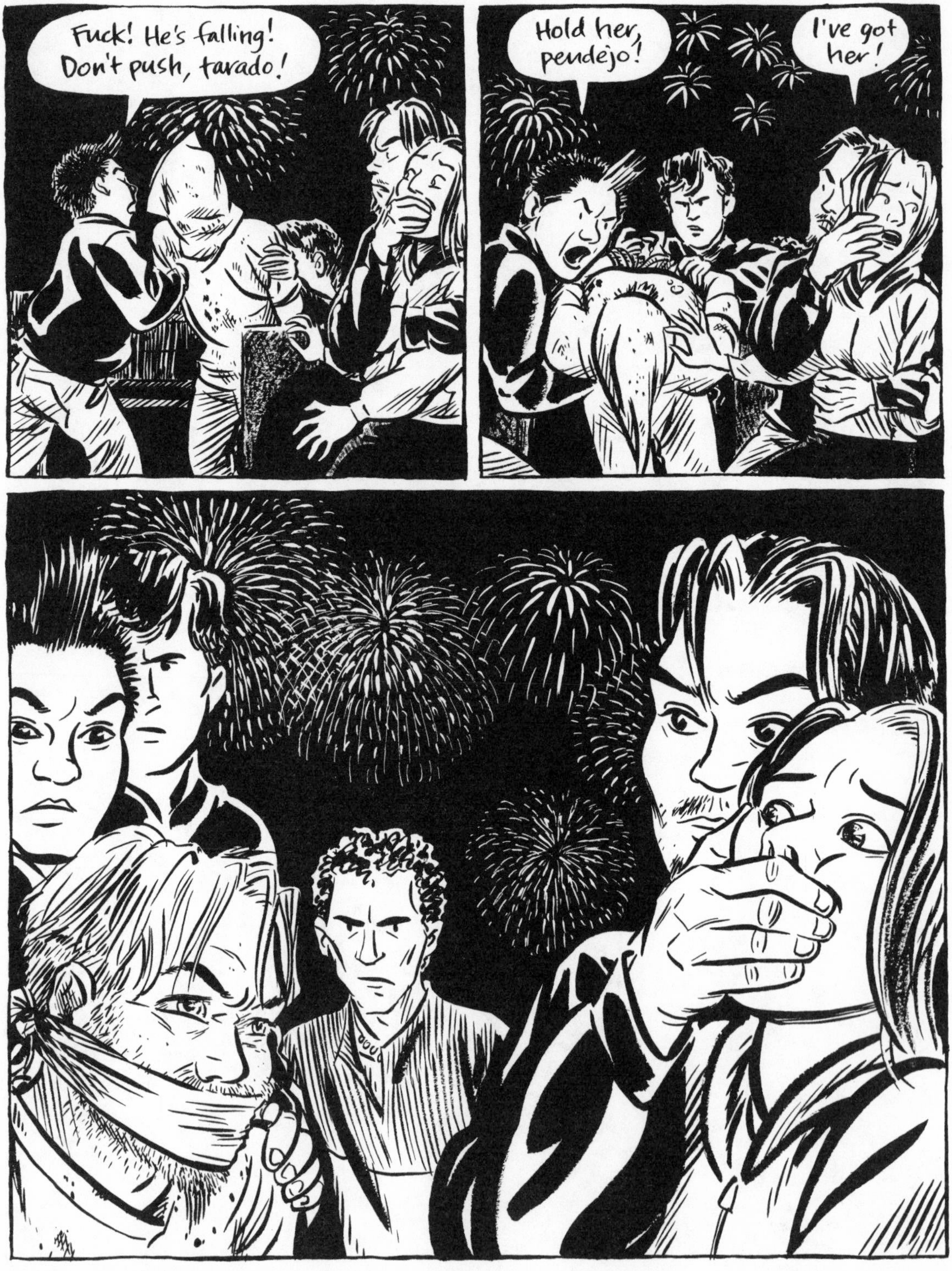
Fuck! He's falling! Don't push, tarado!
Hold her, pendejo!
I've got her!

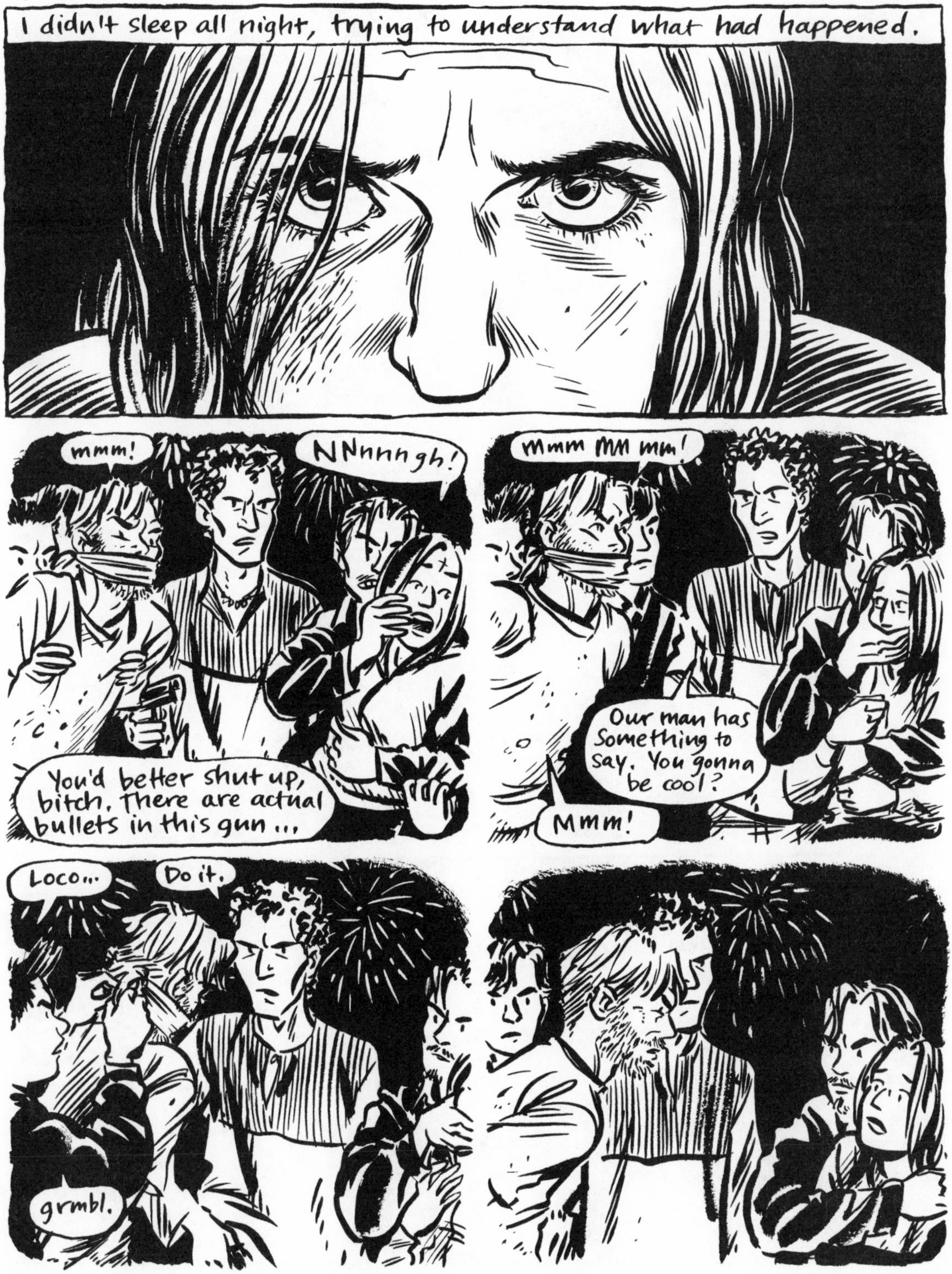
I didn't sleep all night, trying to understand what had happened.
mmm!
NNnnngh!
You'd better shut up, bitch. There are actual bullets in this gun ...
mmm MM mm!
Our man has something to say. You gonna be cool?
Mmm!
Loco...
Do it.
grmbl.

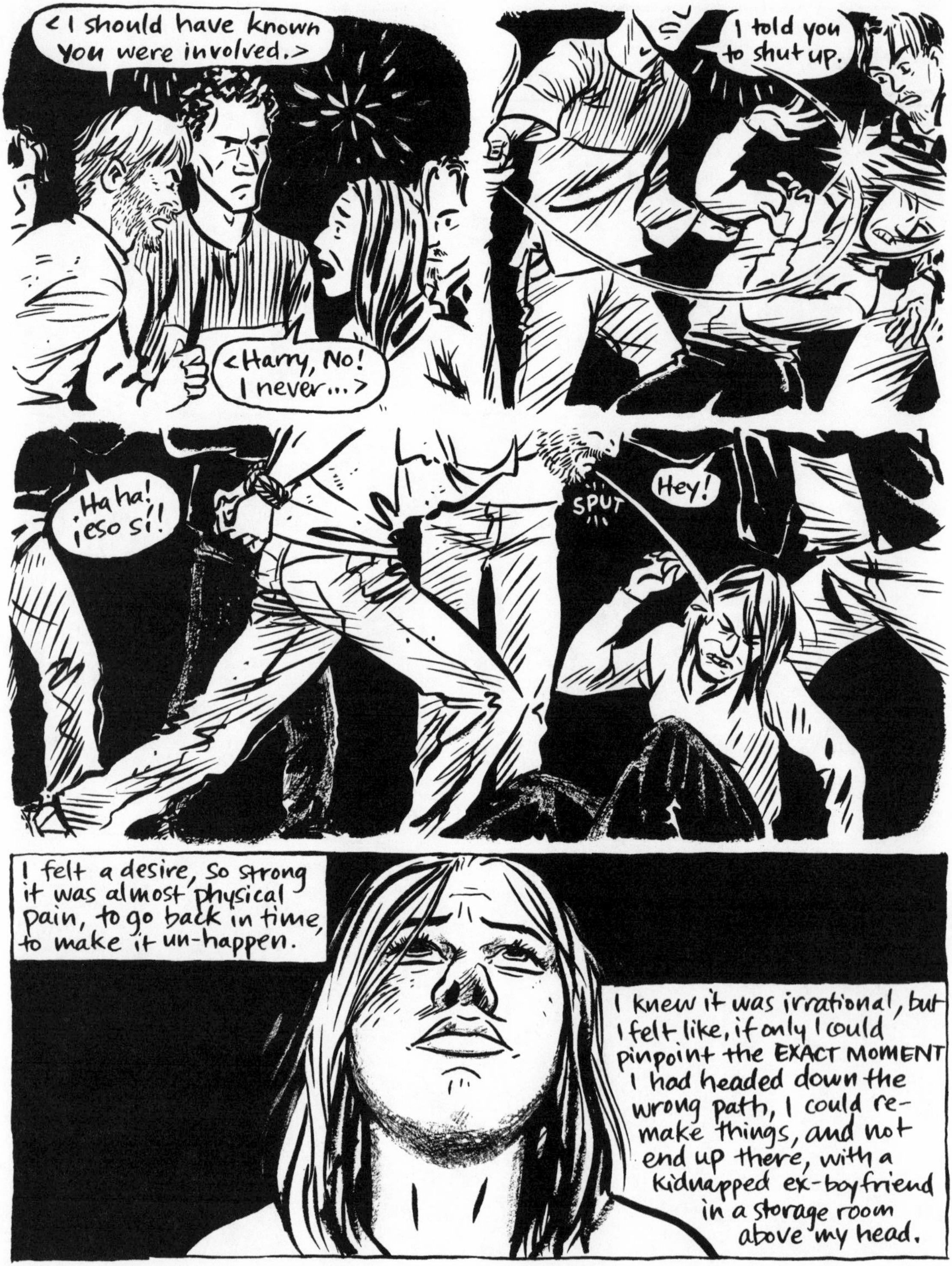
<I should have known you were involved.>
<Harry, No! I never...>
I told you to shut up.
Ha ha! ¡eso sí!
SPUT
Hey!
I felt a desire, so strong it was almost physical pain, to go back in time, to make it un-happen.
I knew it was irrational, but I felt like, if only I could pinpoint the EXACT MOMENT I had headed down the wrong path, I could re-make things, and not end up there, with a kidnapped ex-boyfriend in a storage room above my head.

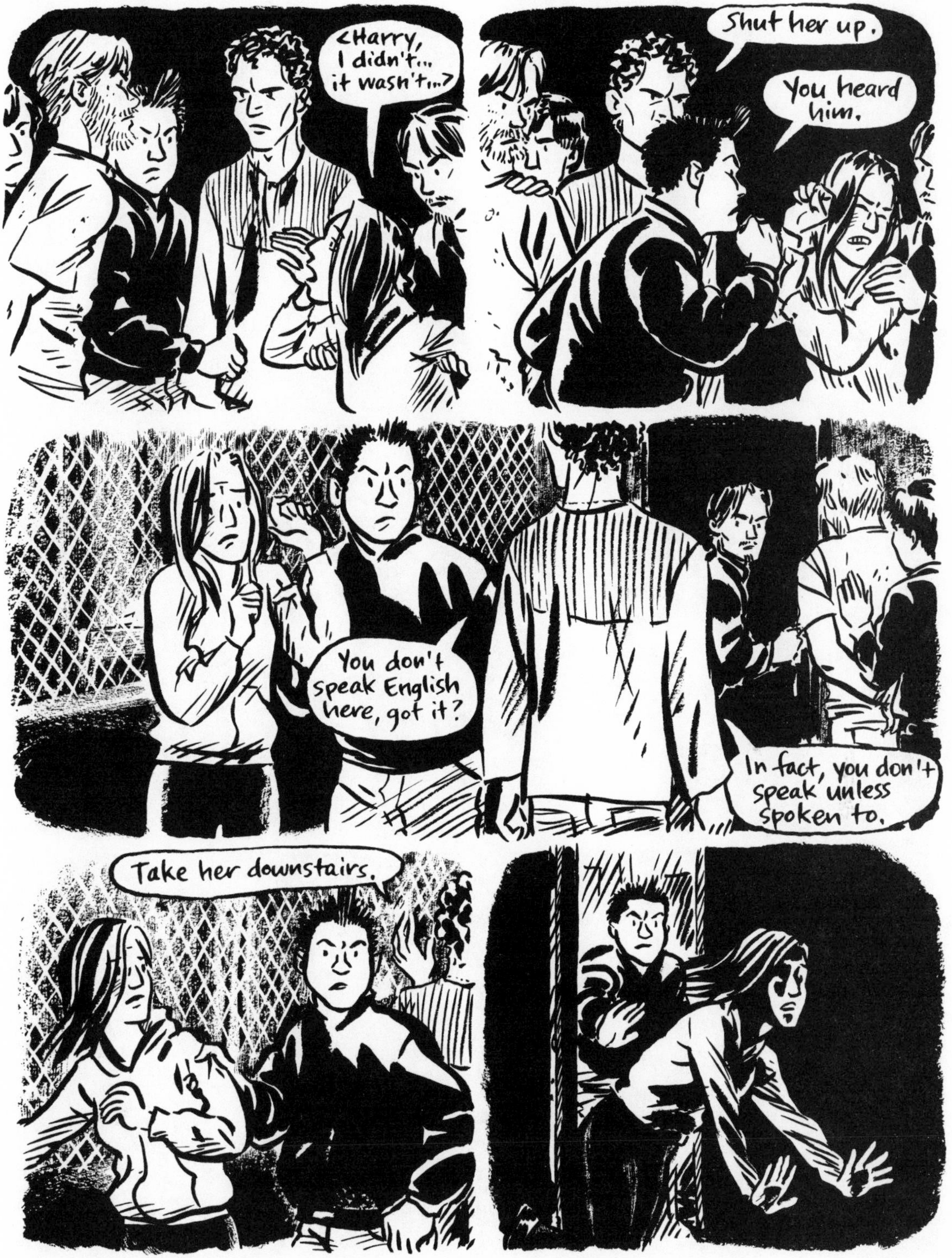
<Harry, I didn't... it wasn't...>
Shut her up.
You heard him.
You don't speak English here, got it?
In fact, you don't speak unless spoken to.
Take her downstairs.

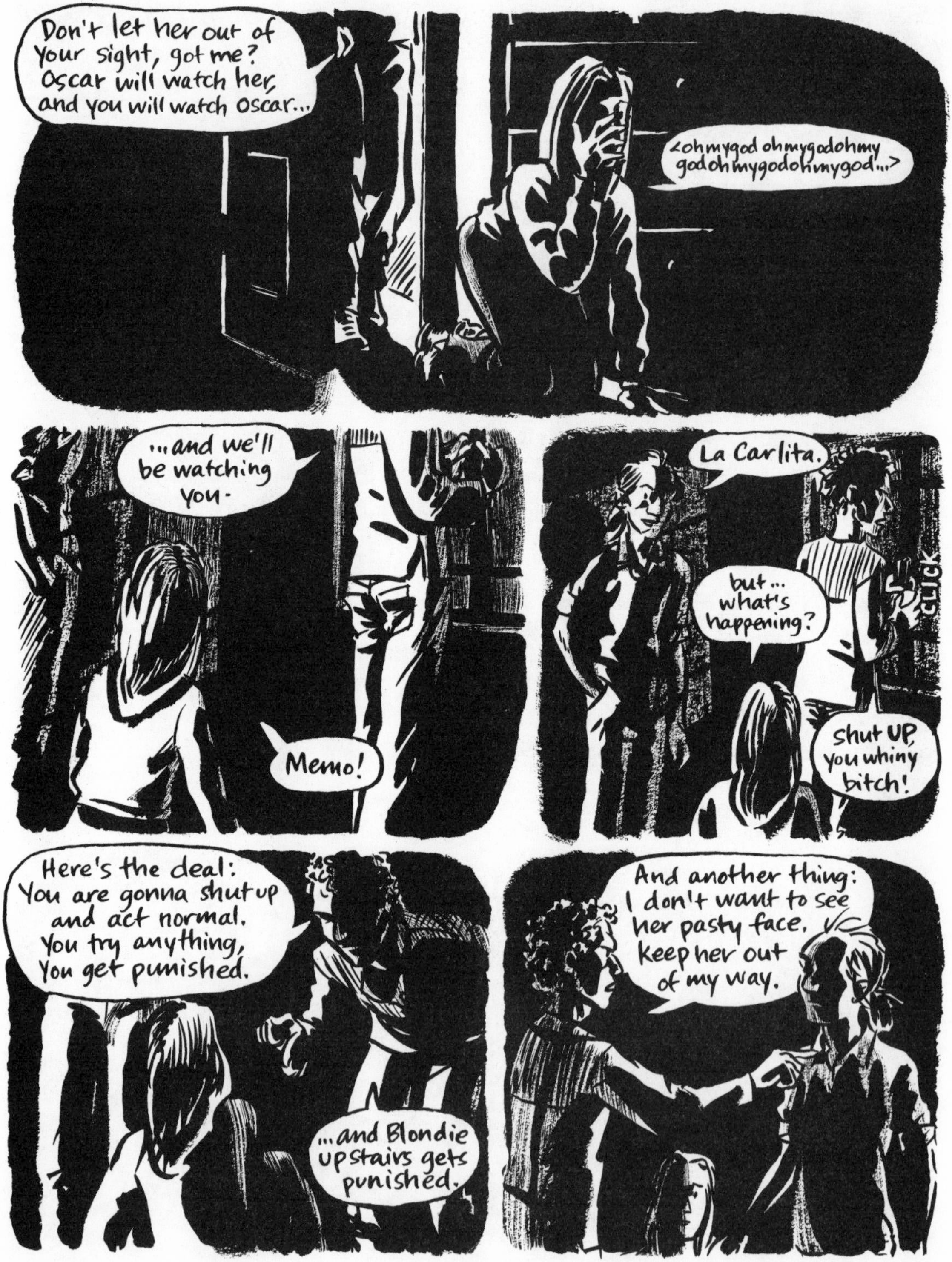
Don't let her out of your sight, got me? Oscar will watch her, and you will watch Oscar...
<ohmygod ohmygodohmy godohmygodohmygod...>
...and we'll be watching you-
Memo!
La Carlita.
but... what's happening?
CLICK
shut UP, you whiny bitch!
Here's the deal: You are gonna shut up and act normal. You try anything, You get punished.
...and Blondie upstairs gets punished.
And another thing: I don't want to see her pasty face. keep her out of my way.

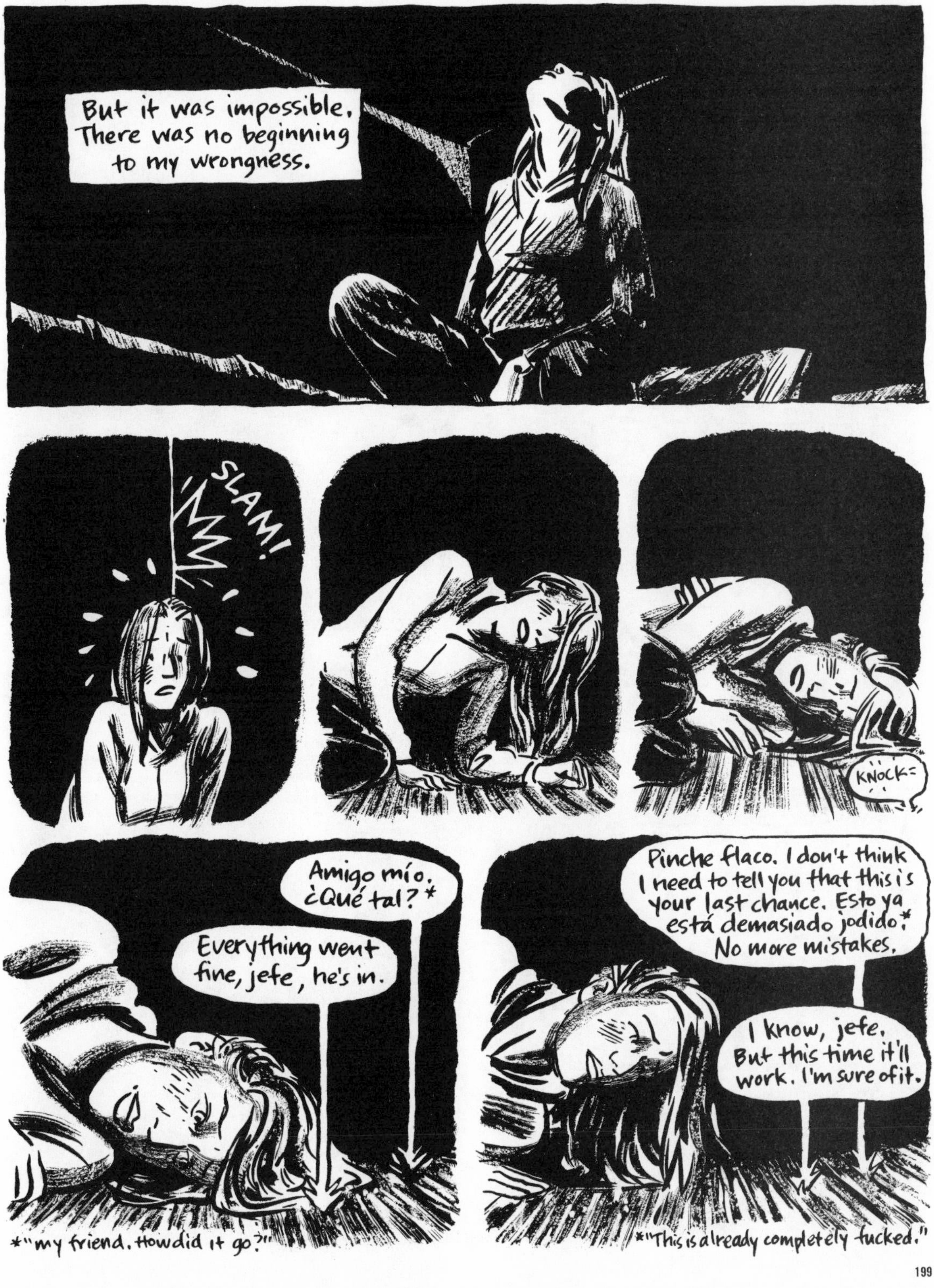

But it was impossible. There was no beginning to my wrongness.
SLAM!
KNOCK=
Amigo mío. ¿Qué tal?*
Everything went fine, jefe, he's in.
Pinche flaco. I don't think I need to tell you that this is your last chance. Esto ya está demasiado jodido.* No more mistakes.
I know, jefe. But this time it'll work. I'm sure of it.
*"my friend. How did it go?"
*"This is already completely fucked."

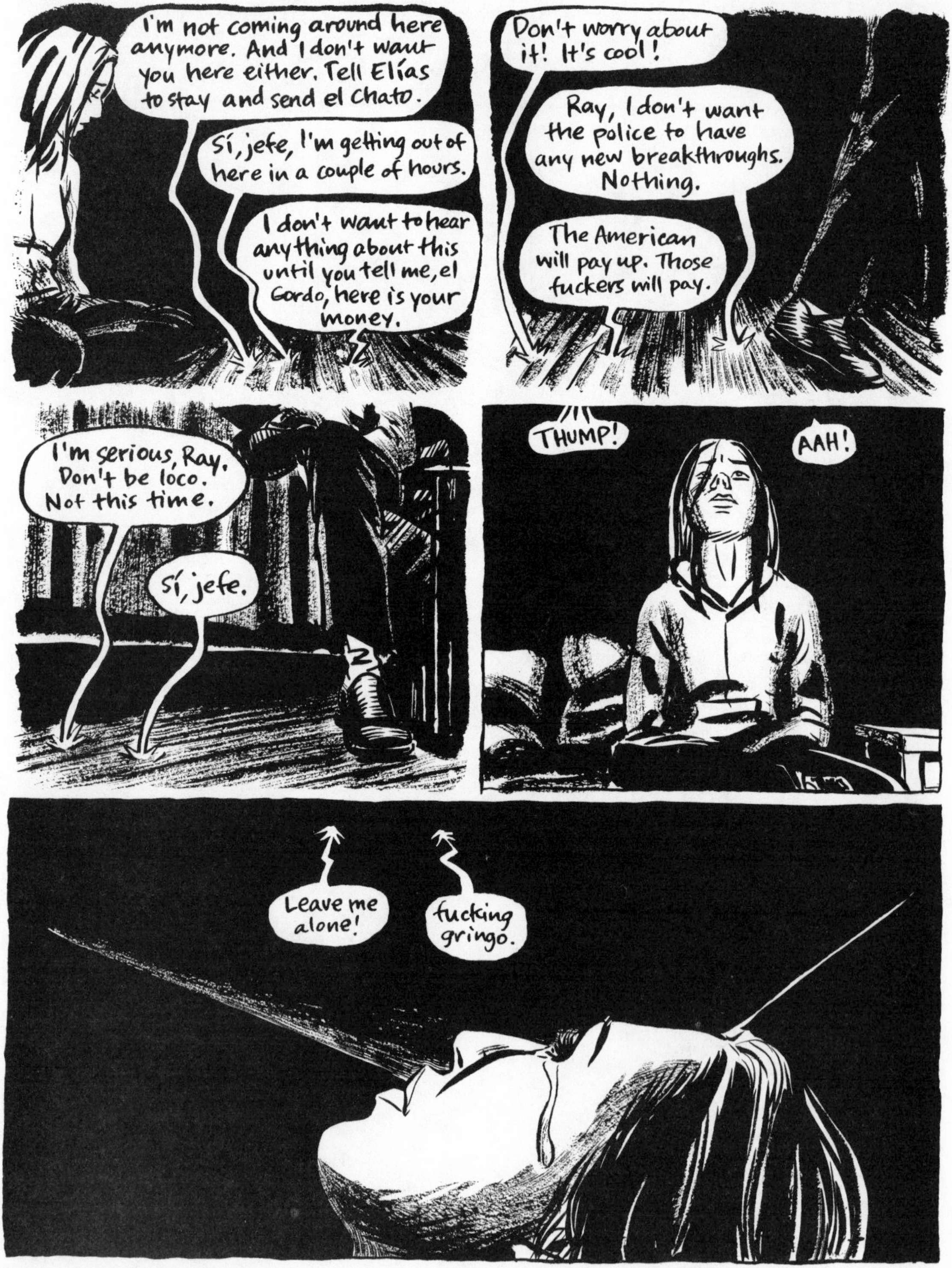
I'm not coming around here anymore. And I don't want you here either. Tell Elías to stay and send el Chato.
Sí, jefe, I'm getting out of here in a couple of hours.
I don't want to hear anything about this until you tell me, el Gordo, here is your money.
Don't worry about it! It's cool!
Ray, I don't want the police to have any new breakthroughs. Nothing.
The American will pay up. Those fuckers will pay.
I'm serious, Ray. Don't be loco. Not this time.
Sí, jefe.
THUMP!
AAH!
Leave me alone!
fucking gringo.

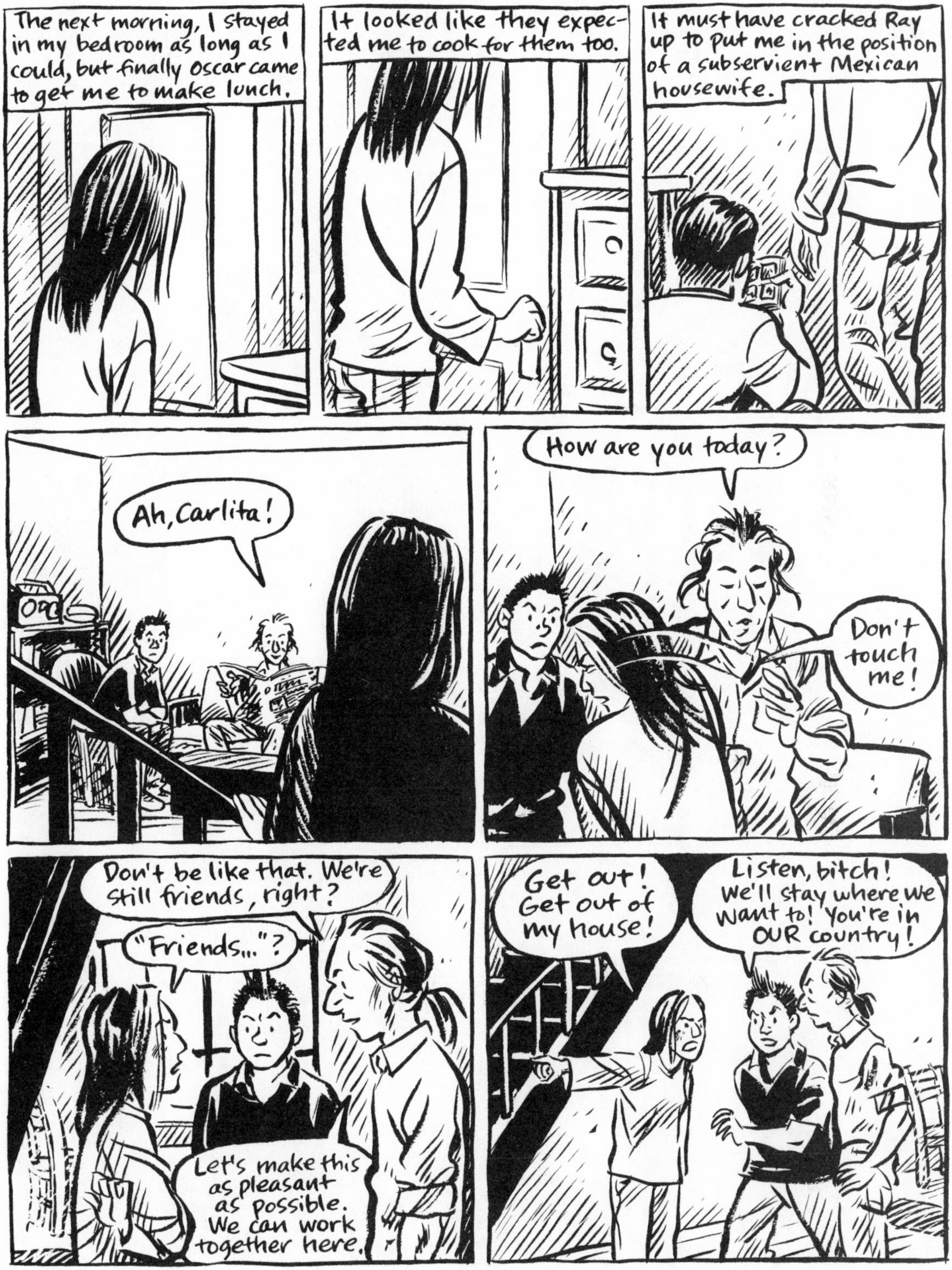
The next morning, I stayed in my bedroom as long as I could, but finally Oscar came to get me to make lunch.
It looked like they expected me to cook for them too.
It must have cracked Ray up to put me in the position of a subservient Mexican housewife.
Ah, Carlita!
How are you today?
Don't touch me!
Don't be like that. We're still friends, right?
"Friends..."?
Let's make this as pleasant as possible. We can work together here.
Get out! Get out of my house!
Listen, bitch! We'll stay where we want to! You're in OUR country!

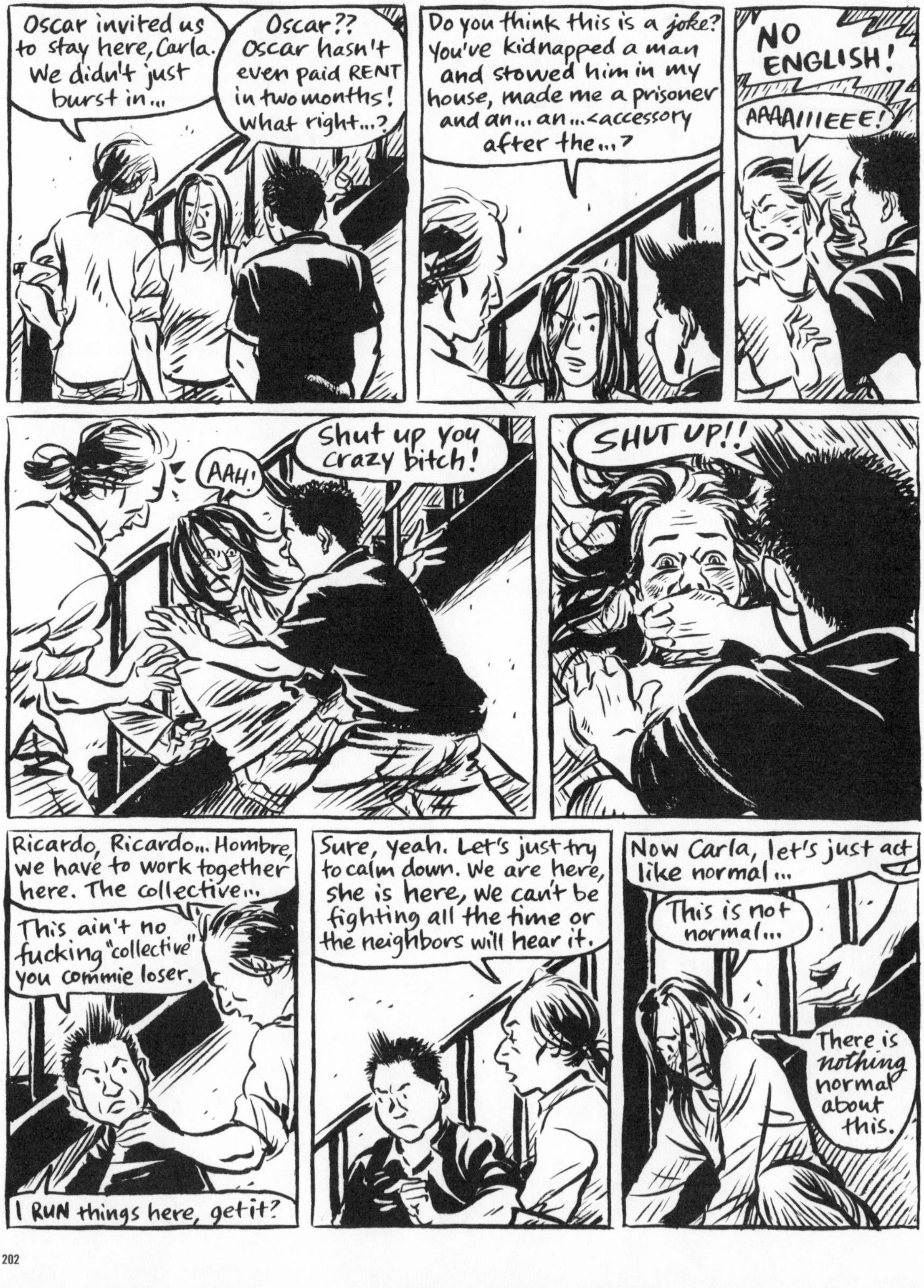

Oscar invited us to stay here, Carla. We didn't just burst in...
Oscar?? Oscar hasn't even paid RENT in two months! What right...?
Do you think this is a *joke*? You've kidnapped a man and stowed him in my house, made me a prisoner and an... an... <accessory after the...?
NO ENGLISH!
AAAAIIIEEE!
AAH!
Shut up you crazy bitch!
SHUT UP!!
Ricardo, Ricardo... Hombre, we have to work together here. The collective...
This ain't no fucking "collective" you commie loser.
I RUN things here, get it?
Sure, yeah. Let's just try to calm down. We are here, she is here, we can't be fighting all the time or the neighbors will hear it.
Now Carla, let's just act like normal...
This is not normal...
There is *nothing* normal about this.

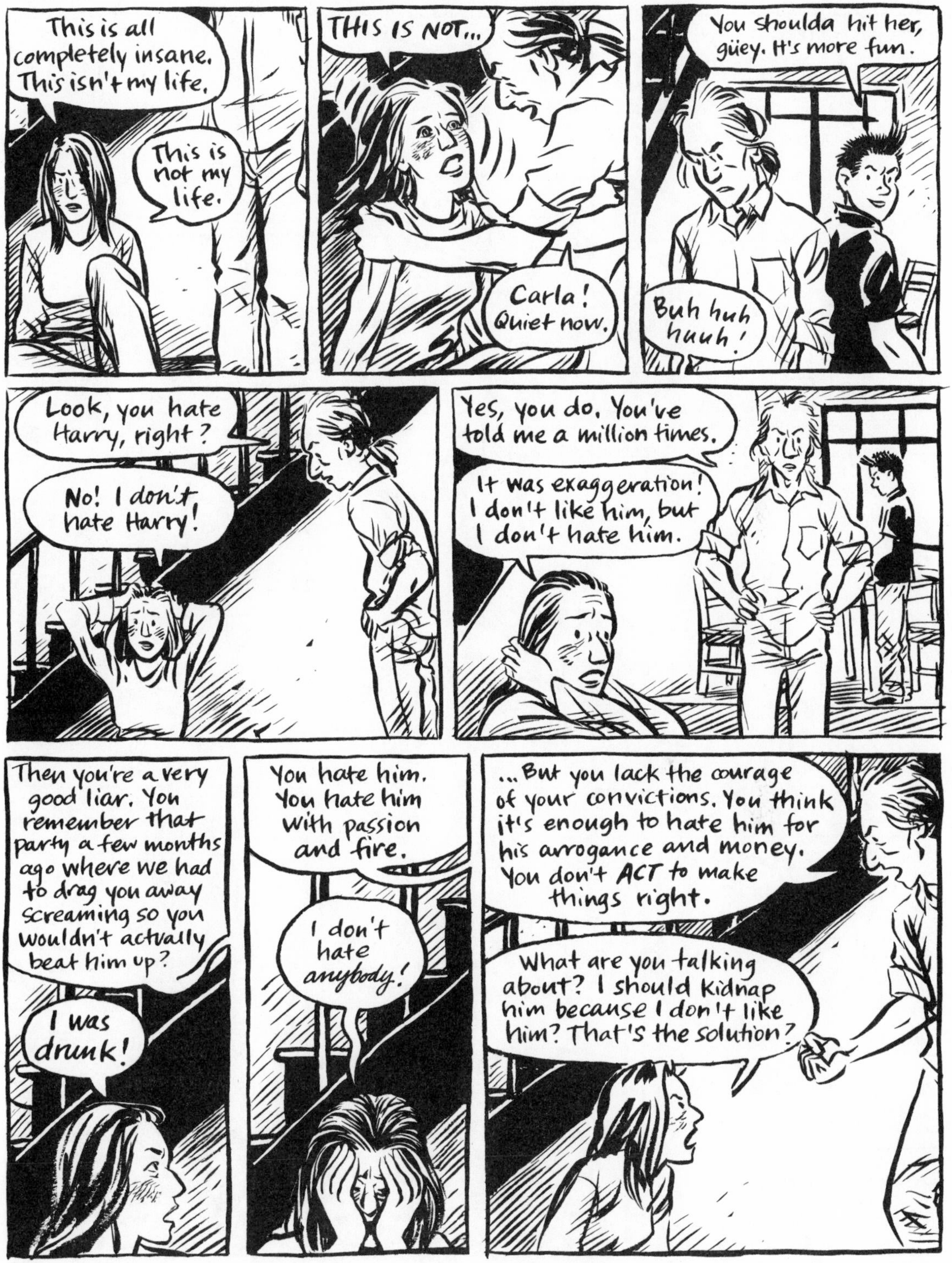
This is all completely insane. This isn't my life.
This is not my life.
THIS IS NOT...
Carla! Quiet now.
You shoulda hit her, güey. It's more fun.
Buh huh huuh!
Look, you hate Harry, right?
No! I don't hate Harry!
Yes, you do. You've told me a million times.
It was exaggeration! I don't like him, but I don't hate him.
Then you're a very good liar. You remember that party a few months ago where we had to drag you away screaming so you wouldn't actually beat him up?
I was drunk!
You hate him. You hate him with passion and fire.
I don't hate anybody!
...But you lack the courage of your convictions. You think it's enough to hate him for his arrogance and money. You don't ACT to make things right.
What are you talking about? I should kidnap him because I don't like him? That's the solution?

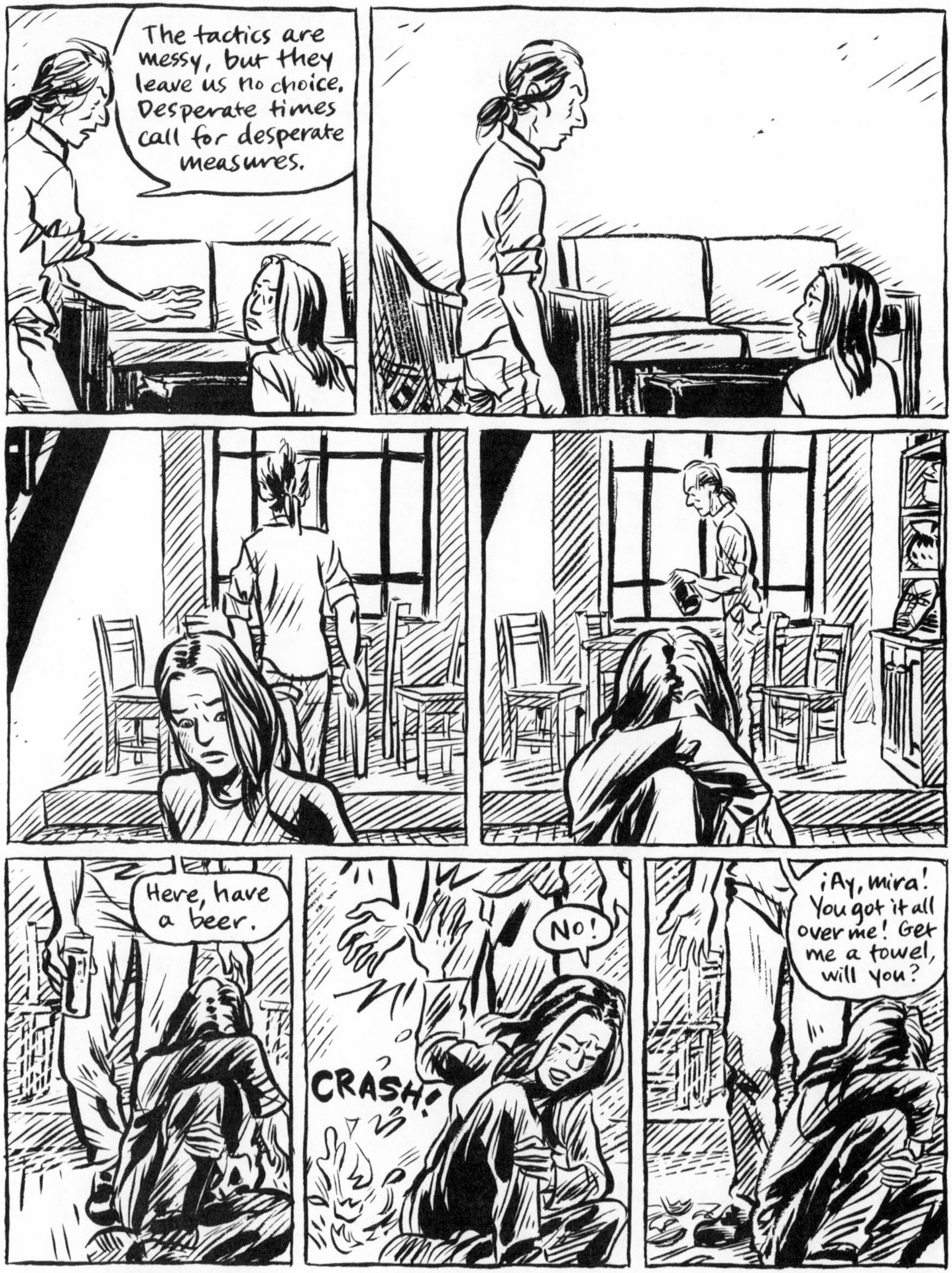
The tactics are messy, but they leave us no choice. Desperate times call for desperate measures.
Here, have a beer.
No!
CRASH!
¡Ay, mira! You got it all over me! Get me a towel, will you?

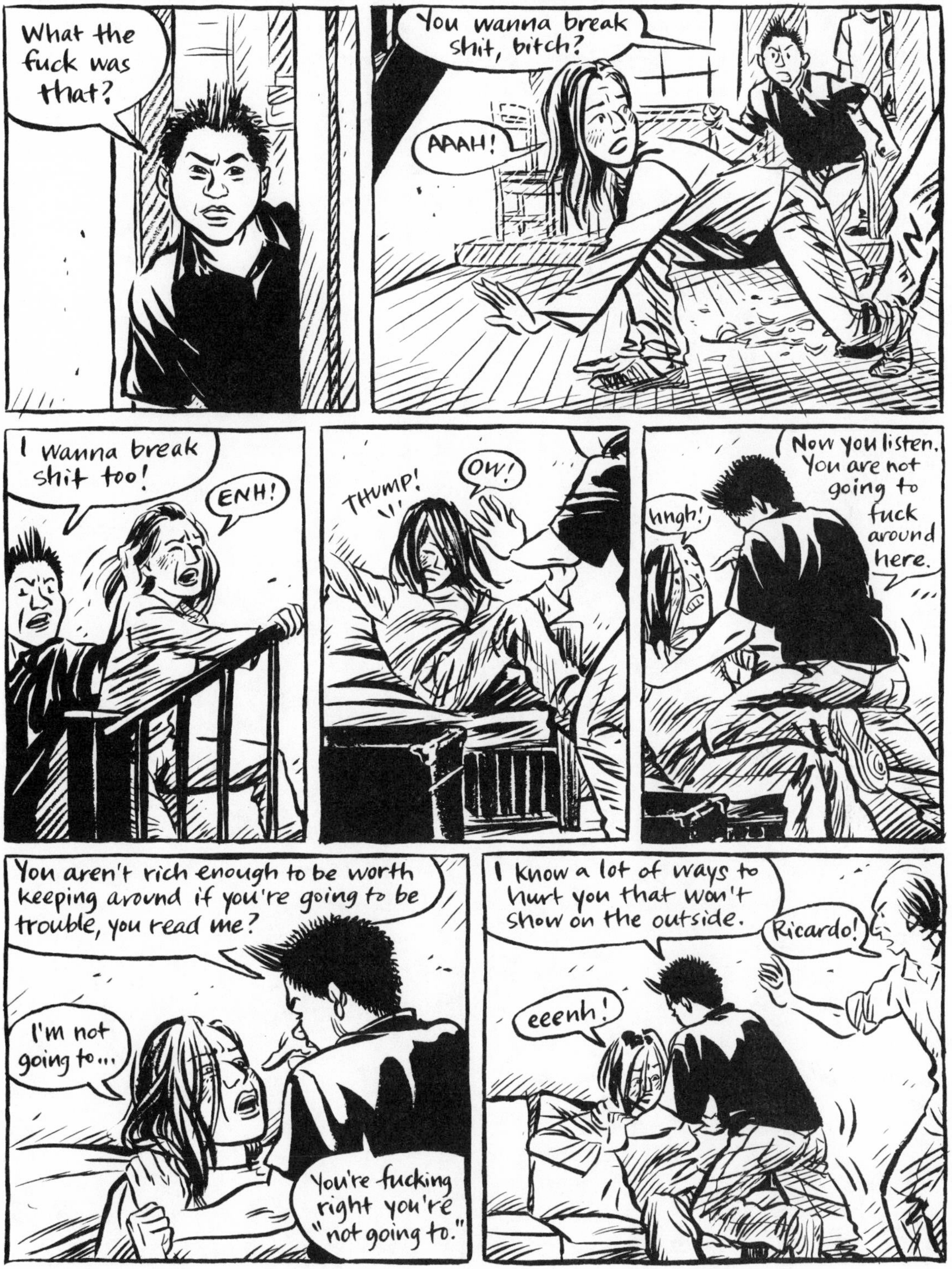
What the fuck was that?
You wanna break shit, bitch?
AAAH!
I wanna break shit too!
ENH!
THUMP!
OW!
hngh!
Now you listen. You are not going to fuck around here.
You aren't rich enough to be worth keeping around if you're going to be trouble, you read me?
I'm not going to...
You're fucking right you're "not going to."
I know a lot of ways to hurt you that won't show on the outside.
eeenh!
Ricardo!

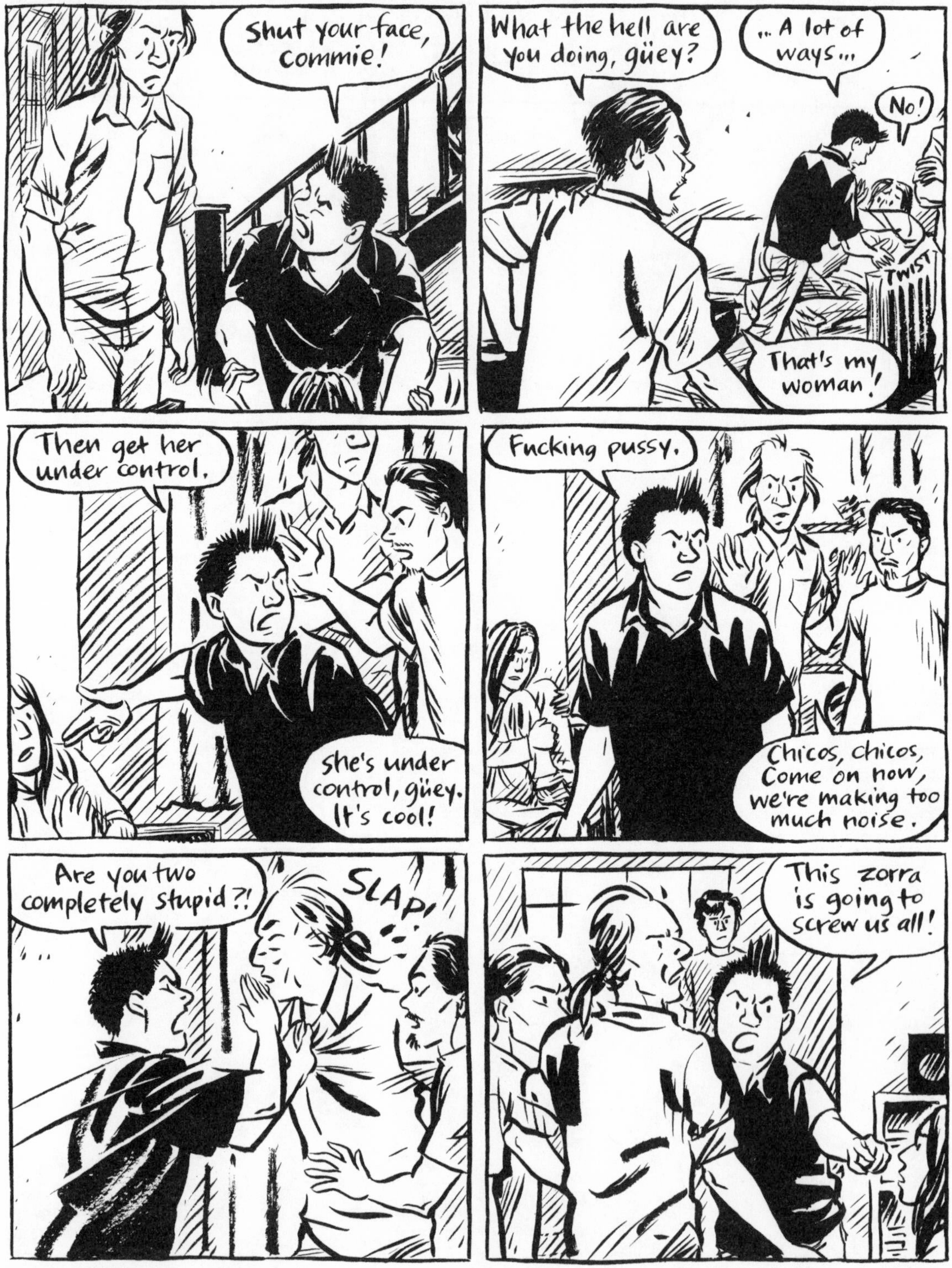
Shut your face, commie!
What the hell are you doing, güey?
... A lot of ways...
No!
TWIST
That's my woman!
Then get her under control.
She's under control, güey. It's cool!
Fucking pussy.
Chicos, chicos, Come on now, we're making too much noise.
Are you two completely stupid?!
SLAP!
This zorra is going to screw us all!

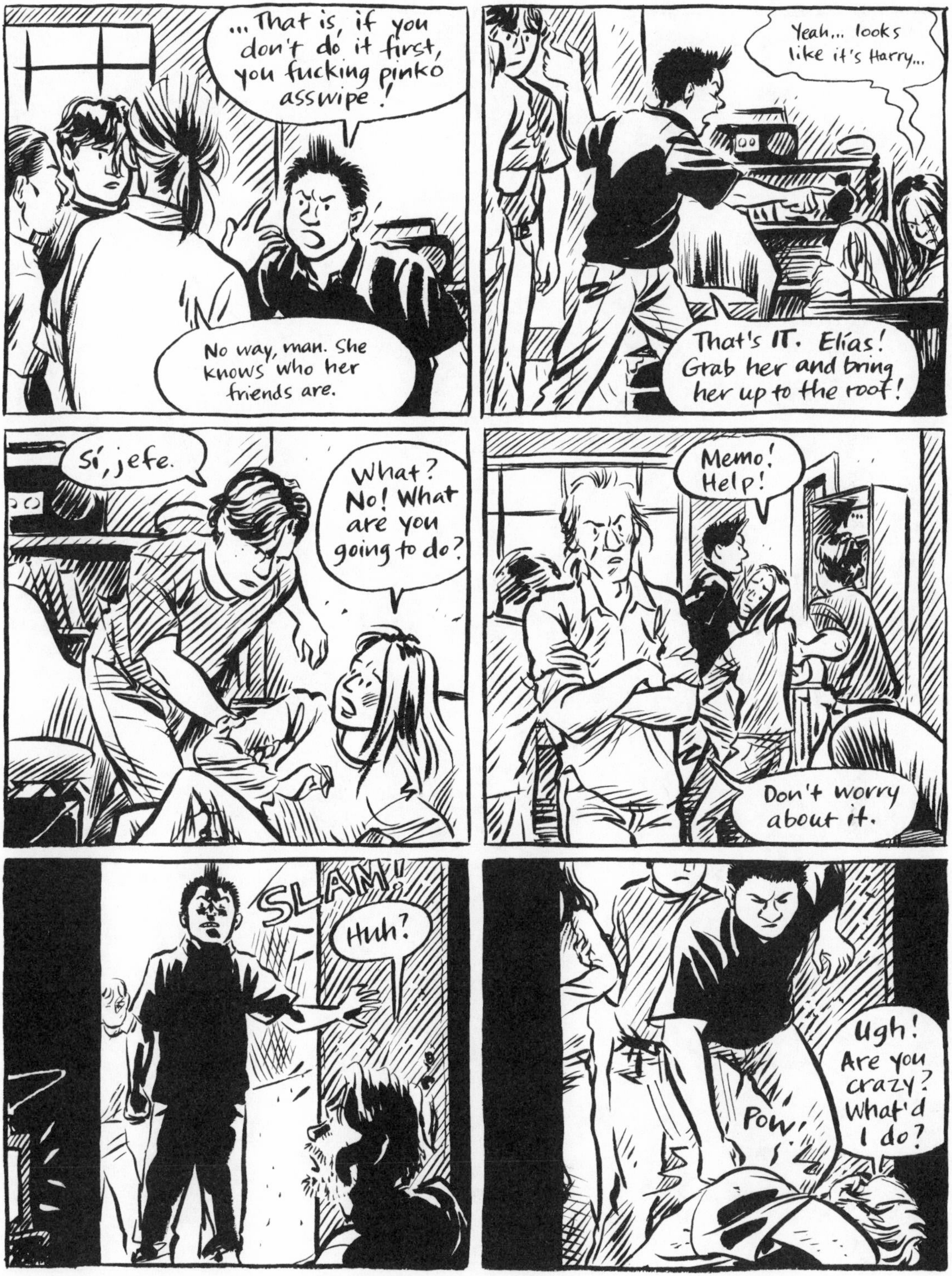
...That is, if you don't do it first, you fucking pinko asswipe!
No way, man. She knows who her friends are.
Yeah... looks like it's Harry...
That's IT. Elias! Grab her and bring her up to the roof!
Sí, jefe.
What? No! What are you going to do?
Memo! Help!
Don't worry about it.
SLAM!
Huh?
POW!
Ugh! Are you crazy? What'd I do?

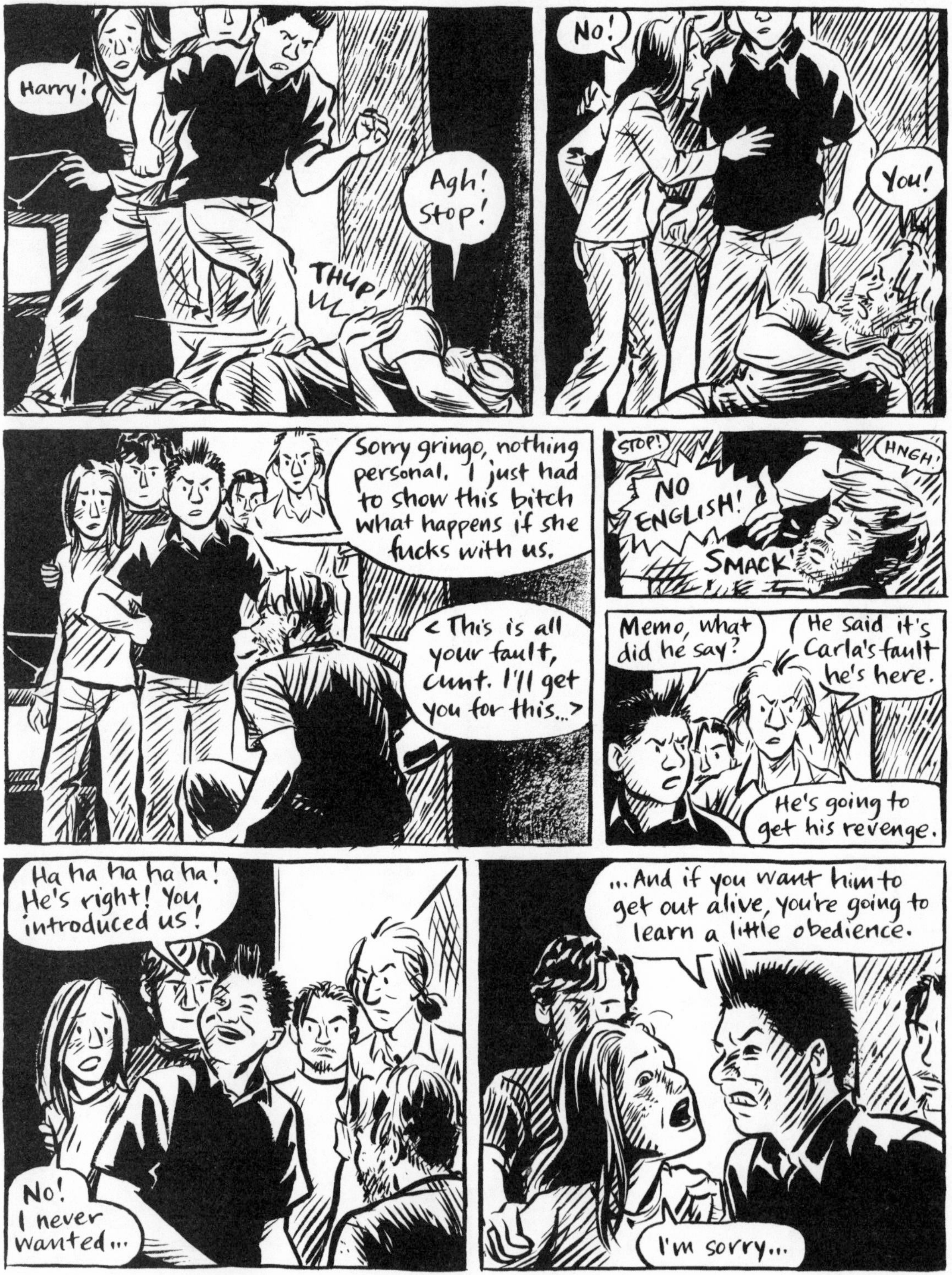
Harry!
Agh! Stop!
THUP!
No!
You!
Sorry gringo, nothing personal. I just had to show this bitch what happens if she fucks with us.
<This is all your fault, cunt. I'll get you for this...>
STOP!
HNGH!
NO ENGLISH!
SMACK!
Memo, what did he say?
He said it's Carla's fault he's here.
He's going to get his revenge.
Ha ha ha ha ha! He's right! You introduced us!
No! I never wanted...
...And if you want him to get out alive, you're going to learn a little obedience.
I'm sorry...

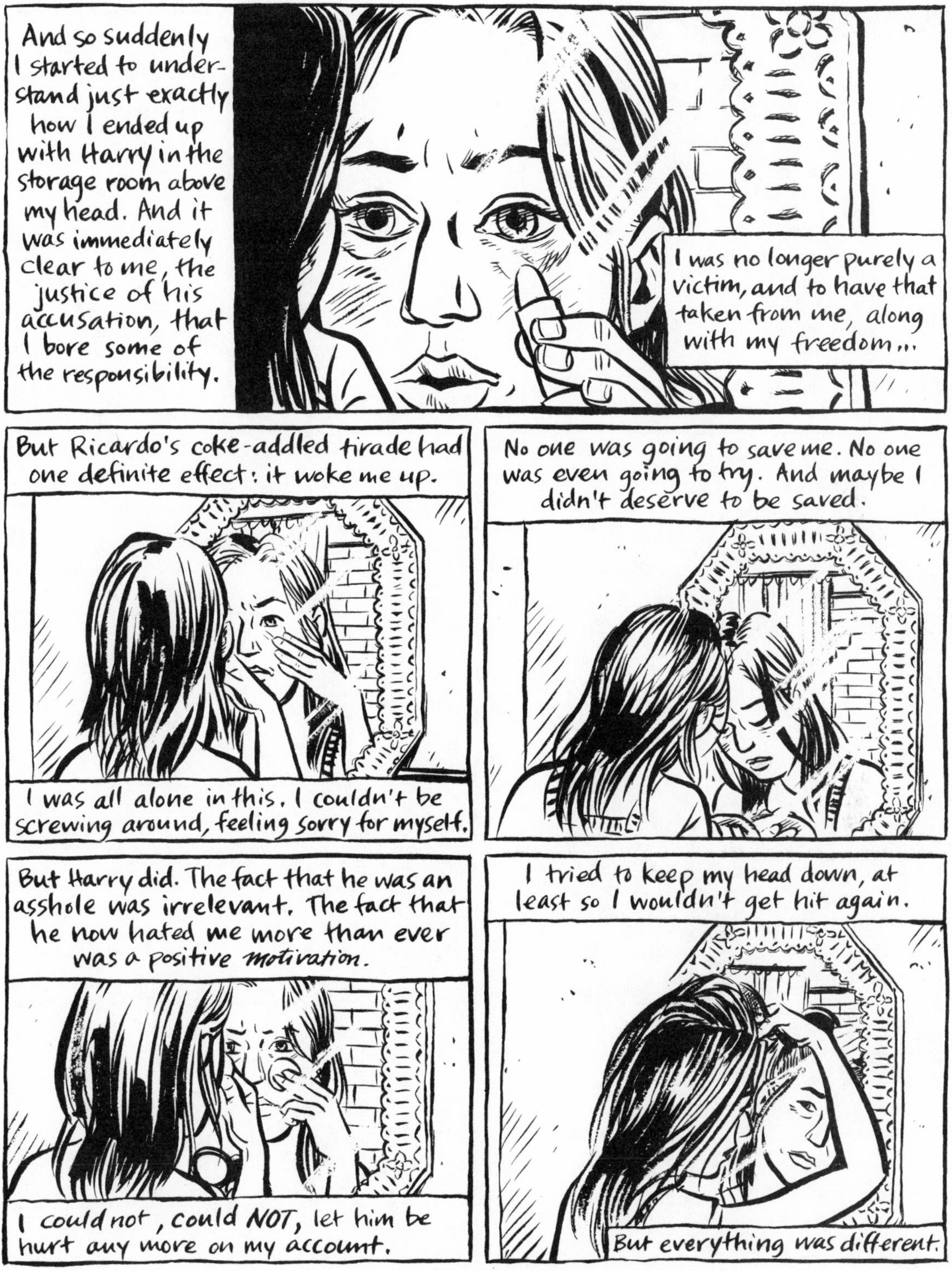

And so suddenly I started to understand just exactly how I ended up with Harry in the storage room above my head. And it was immediately clear to me, the justice of his accusation, that I bore some of the responsibility.
I was no longer purely a victim, and to have that taken from me, along with my freedom...
But Ricardo's coke-addled tirade had one definite effect: it woke me up.
I was all alone in this. I couldn't be screwing around, feeling sorry for myself.
No one was going to save me. No one was even going to try. And maybe I didn't deserve to be saved.
But Harry did. The fact that he was an asshole was irrelevant. The fact that he now hated me more than ever was a positive *motivation*.
I could not, could NOT, let him be hurt any more on my account.
I tried to keep my head down, at least so I wouldn't get hit again.
But everything was different.

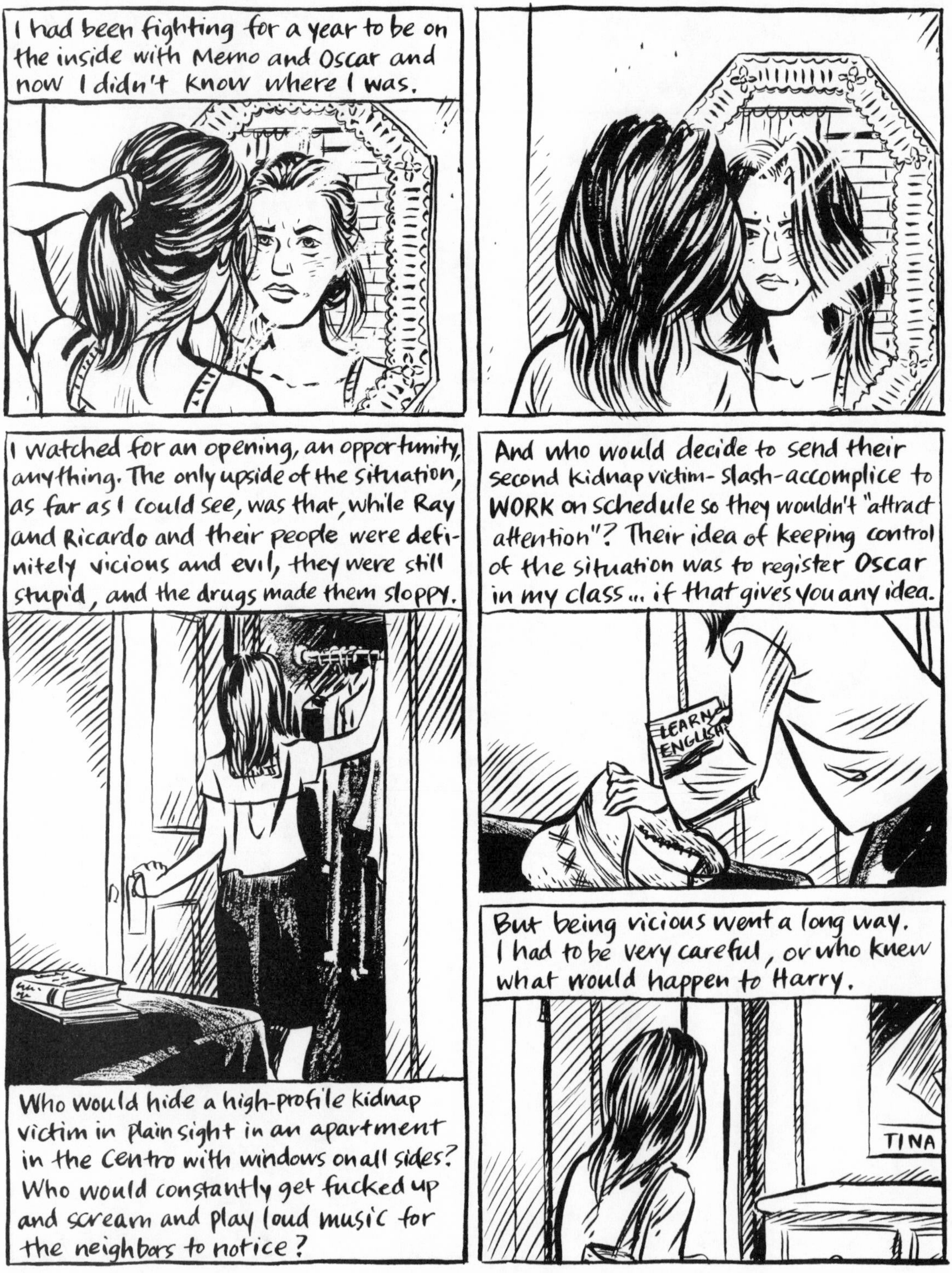

I had been fighting for a year to be on the inside with Memo and Oscar and now I didn't know where I was.
I watched for an opening, an opportunity, anything. The only upside of the situation, as far as I could see, was that, while Ray and Ricardo and their people were definitely vicious and evil, they were still stupid, and the drugs made them sloppy.
Who would hide a high-profile kidnap victim in plain sight in an apartment in the Centro with windows on all sides? Who would constantly get fucked up and scream and play loud music for the neighbors to notice?
And who would decide to send their second kidnap victim-slash-accomplice to WORK on schedule so they wouldn't "attract attention"? Their idea of keeping control of the situation was to register Oscar in my class... if that gives you any idea.
LEARN ENGLISH
But being vicious went a long way. I had to be very careful, or who knew what would happen to Harry.
TINA

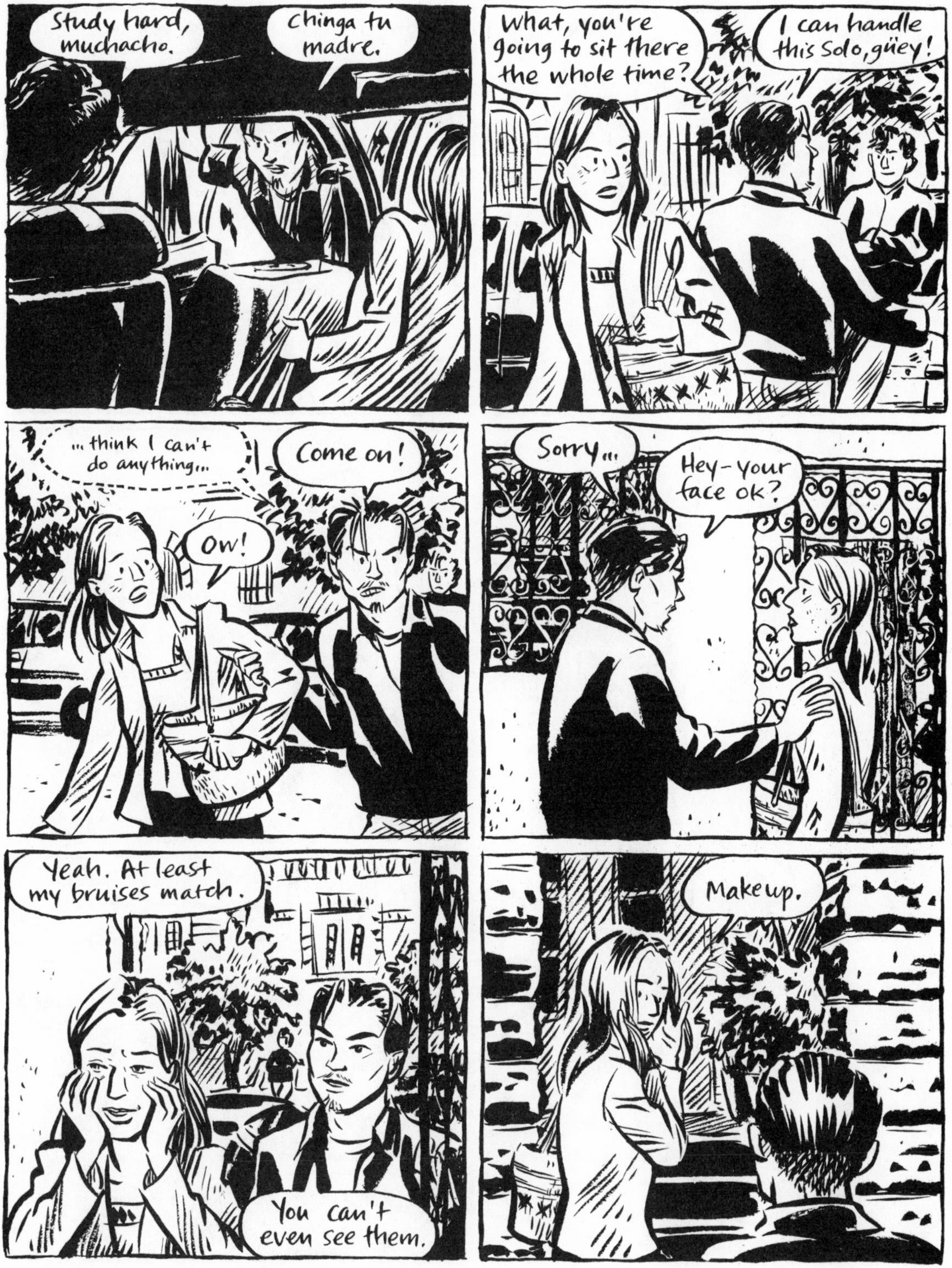
Study hard, muchacho.
Chinga tu madre.
What, you're going to sit there the whole time?
I can handle this solo, güey!
...think I can't do anything...
Come on!
Ow!
Sorry...
Hey-your face ok?
Yeah. At least my bruises match.
You can't even see them.
Makeup.

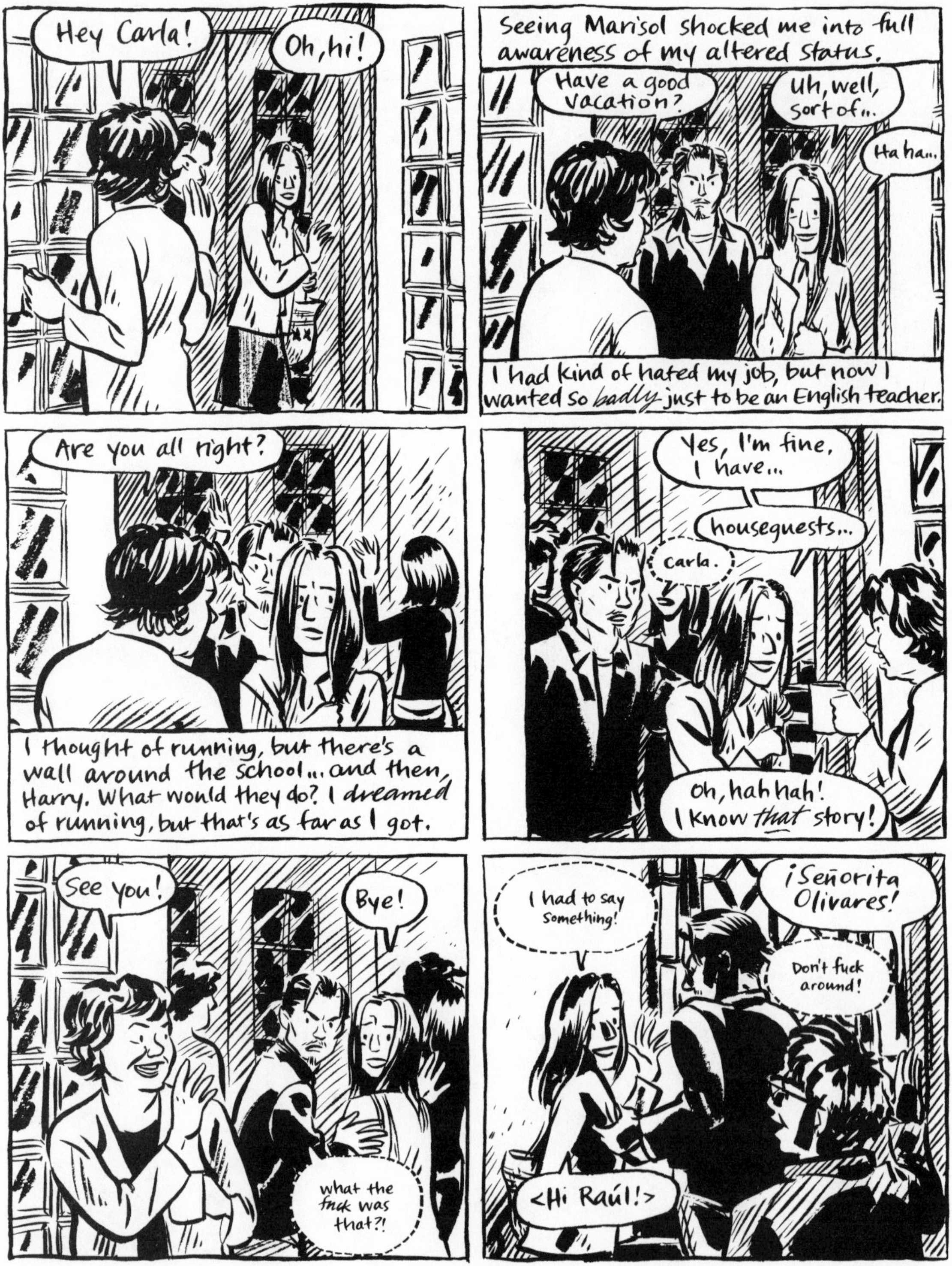

Hey Carla!
Oh, hi!
Seeing Marisol shocked me into full awareness of my altered status.
Have a good vacation?
Uh, well, sort of...
Ha ha...
I had kind of hated my job, but now I wanted so *badly* just to be an English teacher.
Are you all right?
I thought of running, but there's a wall around the school... and then, Harry. What would they do? I *dreamed* of running, but that's as far as I got.
Yes, I'm fine, I have...
houseguests...
Carla.
Oh, hah hah! I know *that* story!
See you!
Bye!
what the fuck was that?!
I had to say something!
¡Señorita Olivares!
Don't fuck around!
<Hi Raúl!>

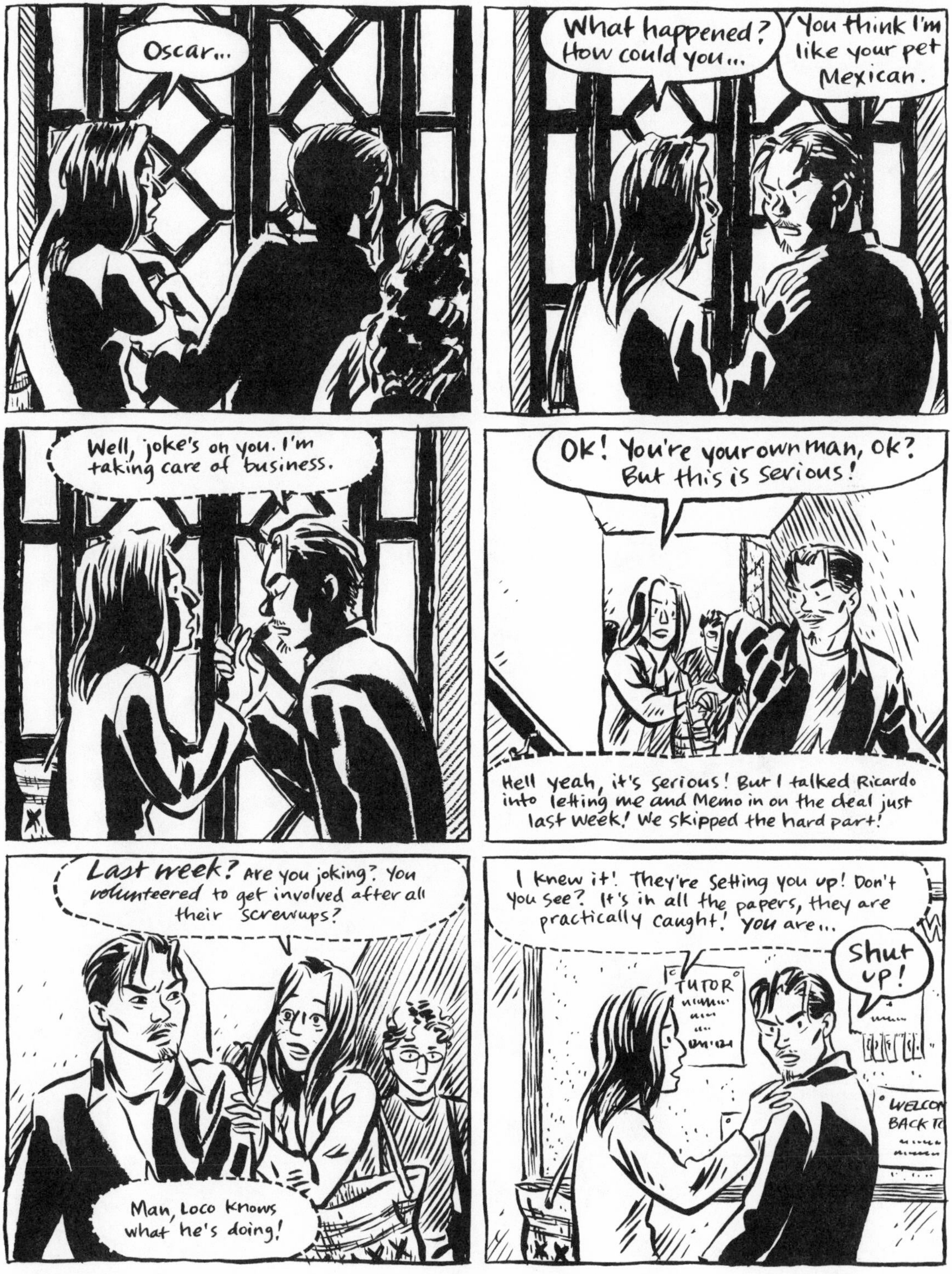
Oscar...
What happened? How could you...
You think I'm like your pet Mexican.
Well, joke's on you. I'm taking care of business.
OK! You're your own man, OK? But this is serious!
Hell yeah, it's serious! But I talked Ricardo into letting me and Memo in on the deal just last week! We skipped the hard part!
Last week? Are you joking? You volunteered to get involved after all their screwups?
Man, Loco knows what he's doing!
I knew it! They're setting you up! Don't you see? It's in all the papers, they are practically caught! You are...
Shut up!
TUTOR
WELCO
BACK TO

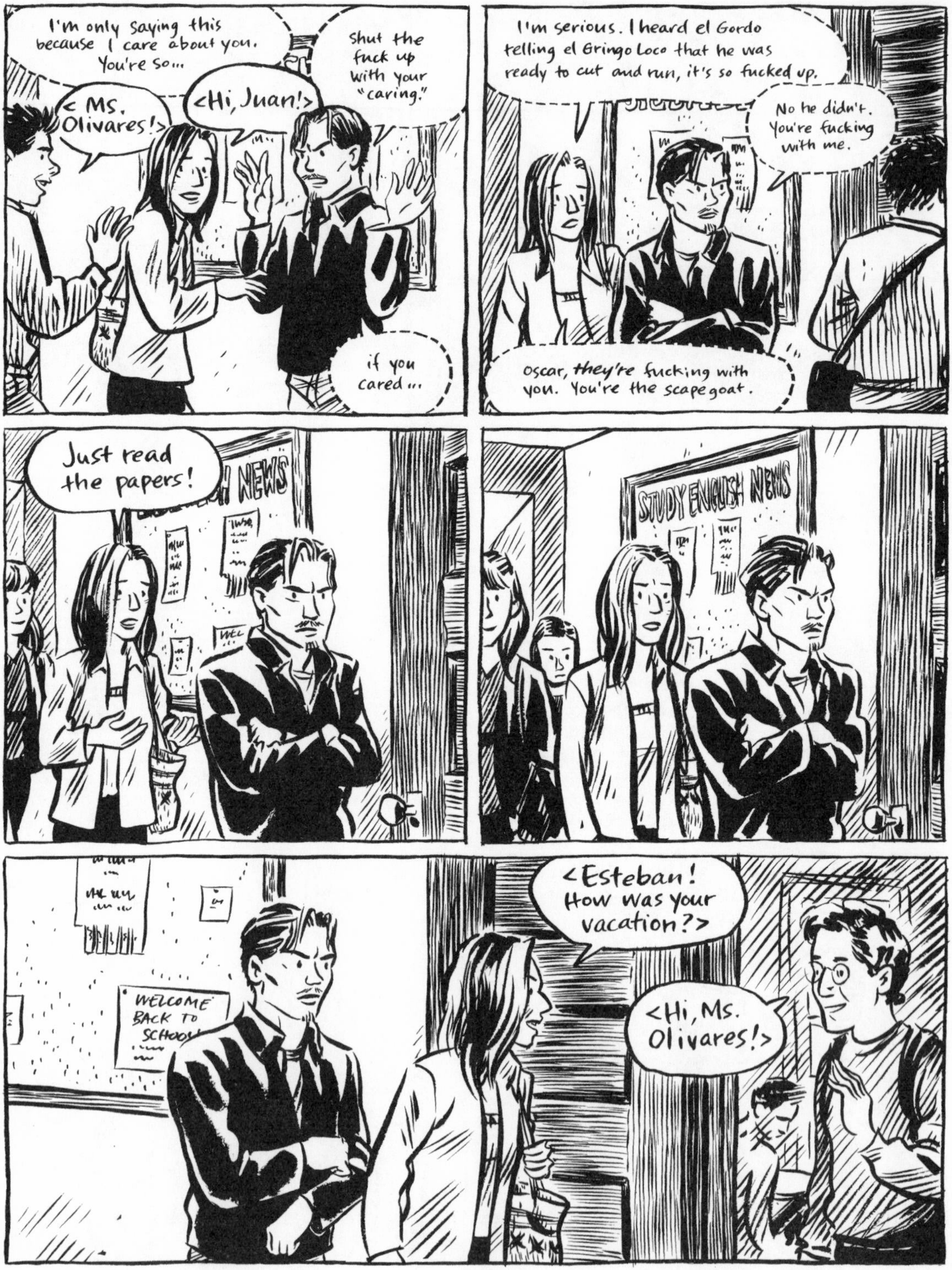
I'm only saying this because I care about you. You're so...
Shut the fuck up with your "caring."
< Ms. Olivares!>
<Hi, Juan!>
if you cared...
I'm serious. I heard el Gordo telling el Gringo Loco that he was ready to cut and run, it's so fucked up.
No he didn't. You're fucking with me.
Oscar, they're fucking with you. You're the scapegoat.
Just read the papers!
STUDY ENGLISH NEWS
<Esteban! How was your vacation?>
WELCOME BACK TO SCHOO
<Hi, Ms. Olivares!>

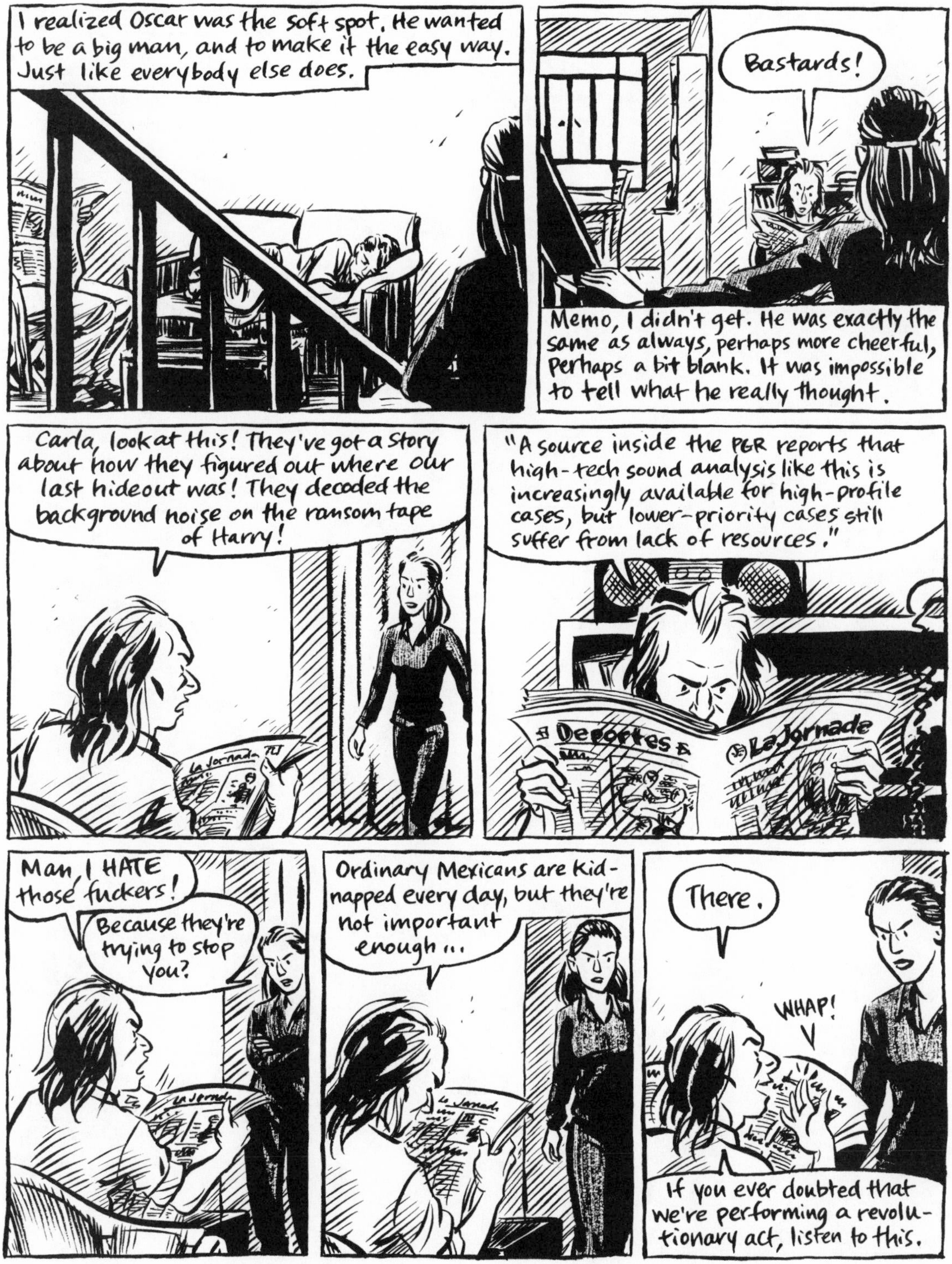
I realized Oscar was the soft spot. He wanted to be a big man, and to make it the easy way. Just like everybody else does.
Bastards!
Memo, I didn't get. He was exactly the same as always, perhaps more cheerful, perhaps a bit blank. It was impossible to tell what he really thought.
Carla, look at this! They've got a story about how they figured out where our last hideout was! They decoded the background noise on the ransom tape of Harry!
"A source inside the PGR reports that high-tech sound analysis like this is increasingly available for high-profile cases, but lower-priority cases still suffer from lack of resources."
Deportes
La Jornada
Man, I HATE those fuckers!
Because they're trying to stop you?
Ordinary Mexicans are kid-napped every day, but they're not important enough...
There.
WHAP!
If you ever doubted that we're performing a revolu-tionary act, listen to this.

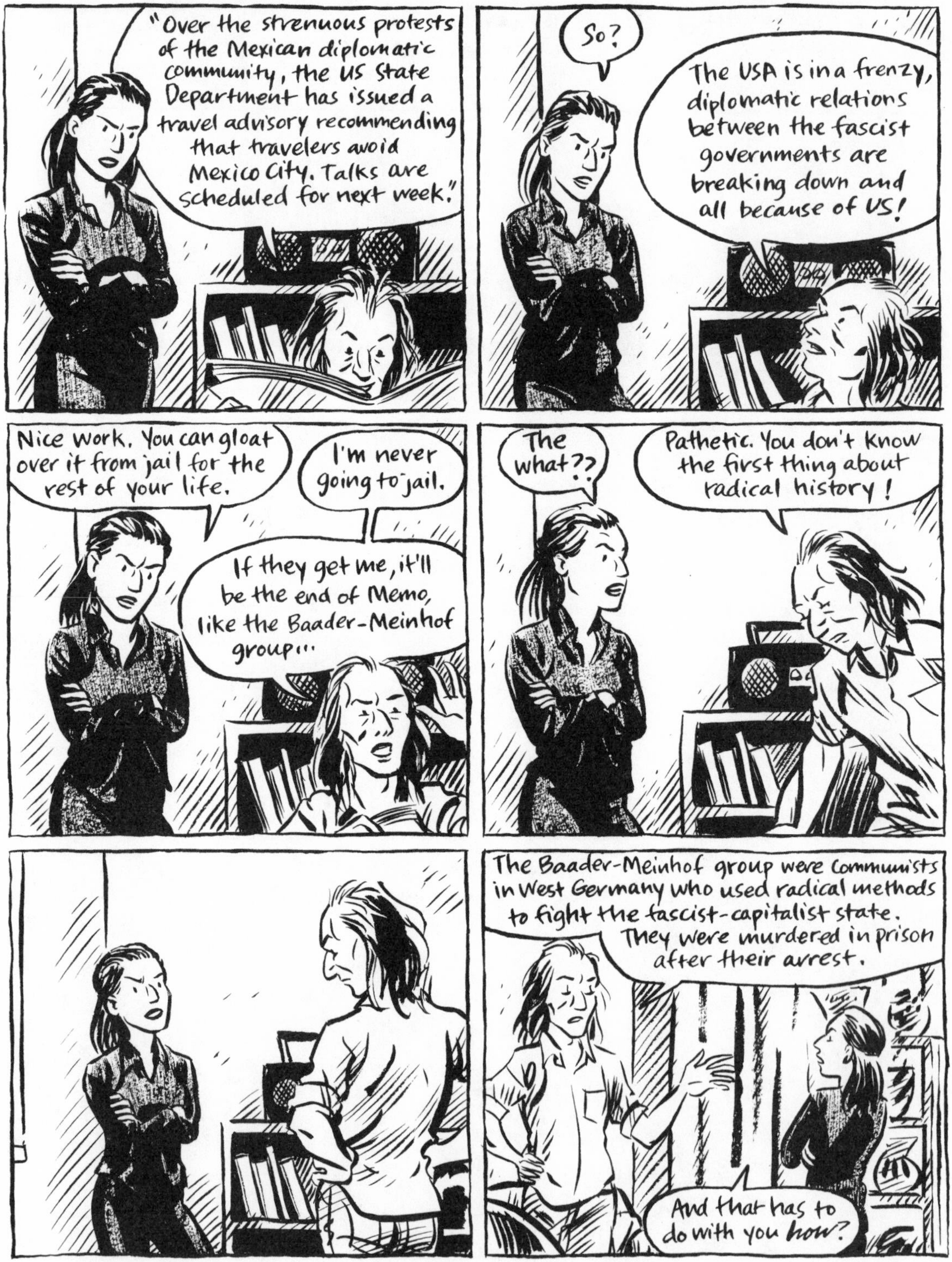
"Over the strenuous protests of the Mexican diplomatic community, the US State Department has issued a travel advisory recommending that travelers avoid Mexico City. Talks are scheduled for next week."
So?
The USA is in a frenzy, diplomatic relations between the fascist governments are breaking down and all because of US!
Nice work. You can gloat over it from jail for the rest of your life.
I'm never going to jail.
If they get me, it'll be the end of Memo, like the Baader-Meinhof group...
The what??
Pathetic. You don't know the first thing about radical history!
The Baader-Meinhof group were Communists in West Germany who used radical methods to fight the fascist-capitalist state.
They were murdered in prison after their arrest.
And that has to do with you *how*?

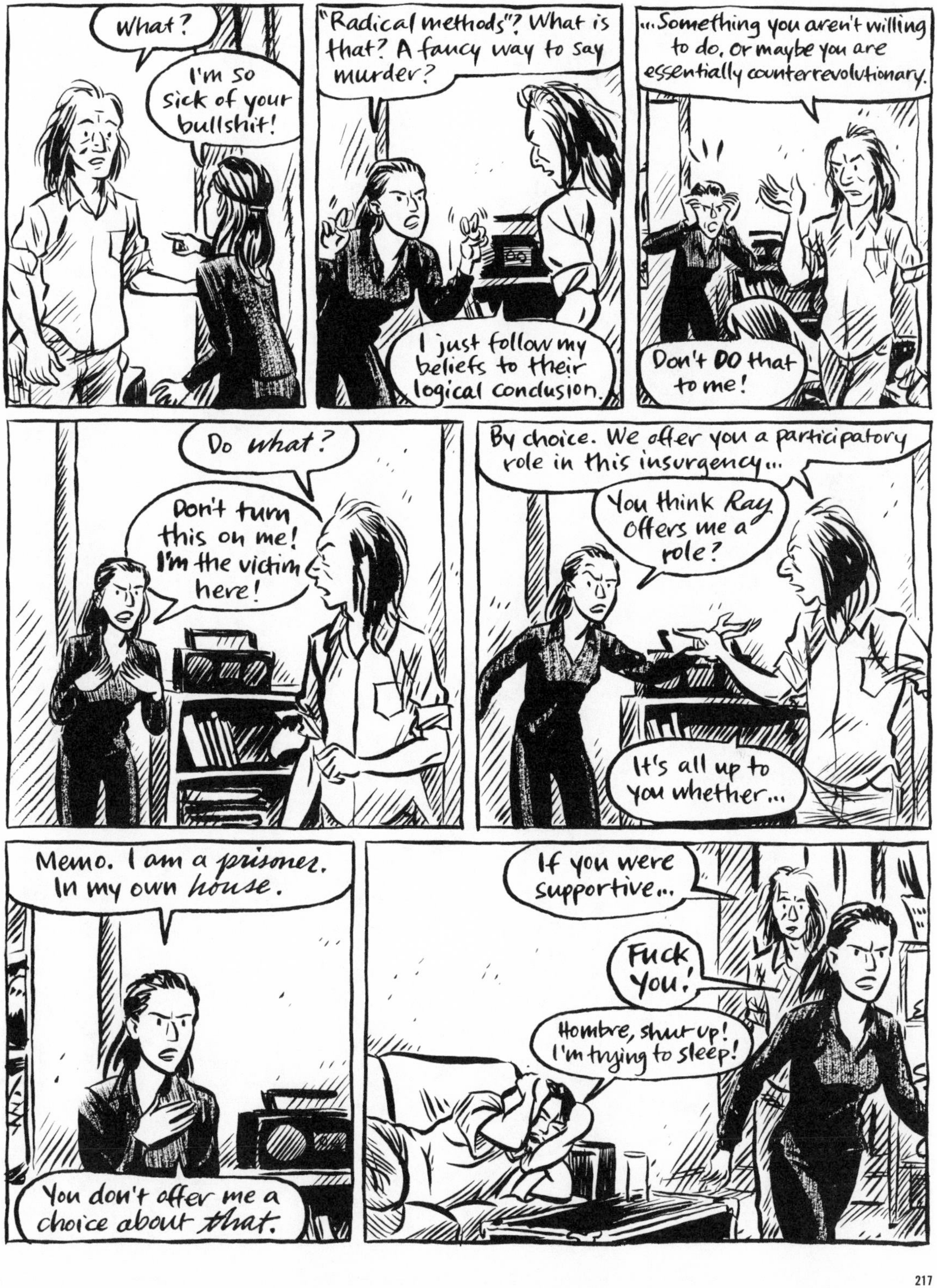
What?
I'm so sick of your bullshit!
"Radical methods"? What is that? A fancy way to say murder?
I just follow my beliefs to their logical conclusion.
...Something you aren't willing to do, or maybe you are essentially counterrevolutionary.
Don't DO that to me!
Do what?
Don't turn this on me! I'm the victim here!
By choice. We offer you a participatory role in this insurgency...
You think Ray offers me a role?
It's all up to you whether...
Memo. I am a prisoner. In my own house.
You don't offer me a choice about that.
If you were supportive...
Fuck you!
Hombre, shut up! I'm trying to sleep!

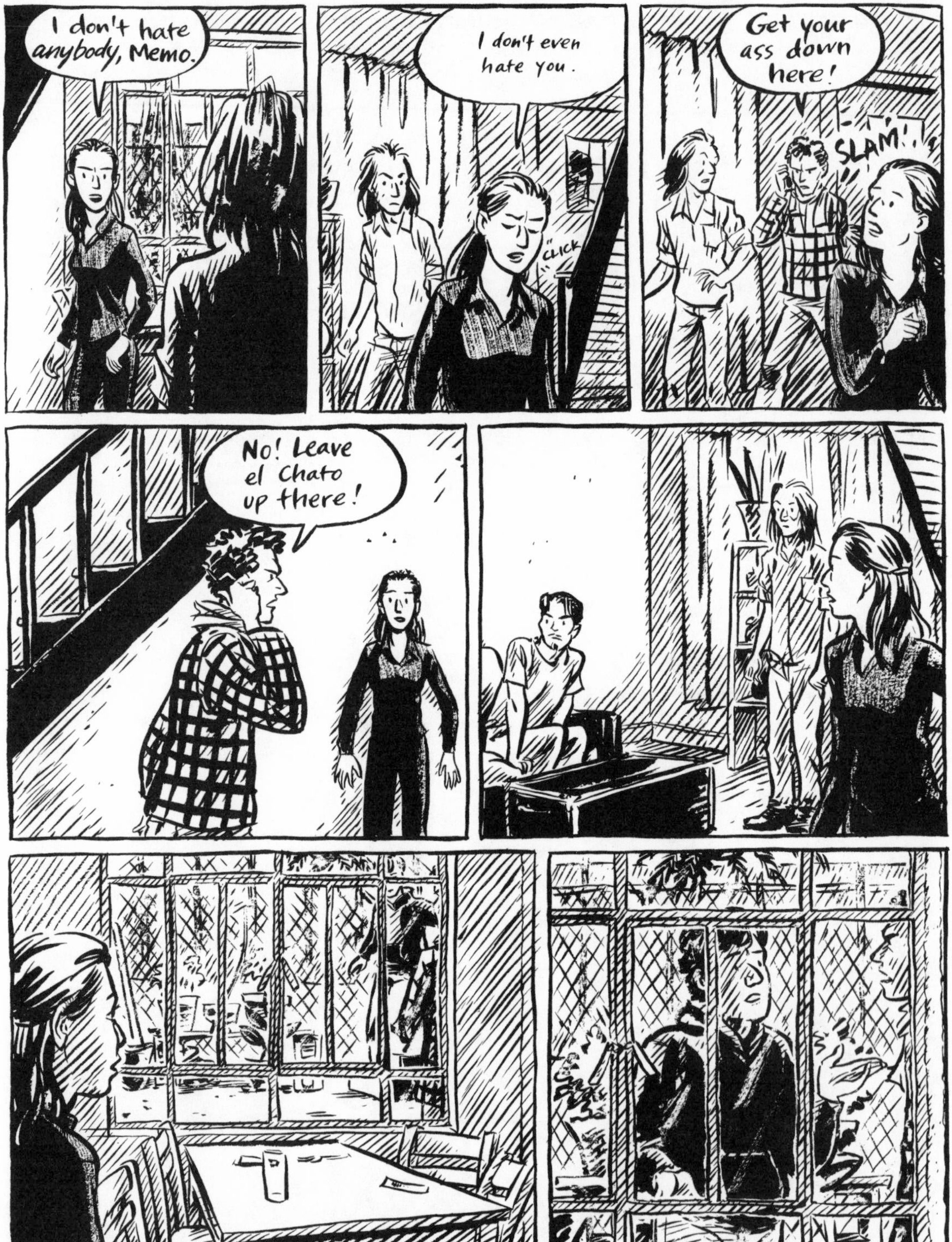
I don't hate anybody, Memo.
I don't even hate you.
CLICK
Get your ass down here!
SLAM!
No! Leave el Chato up there!

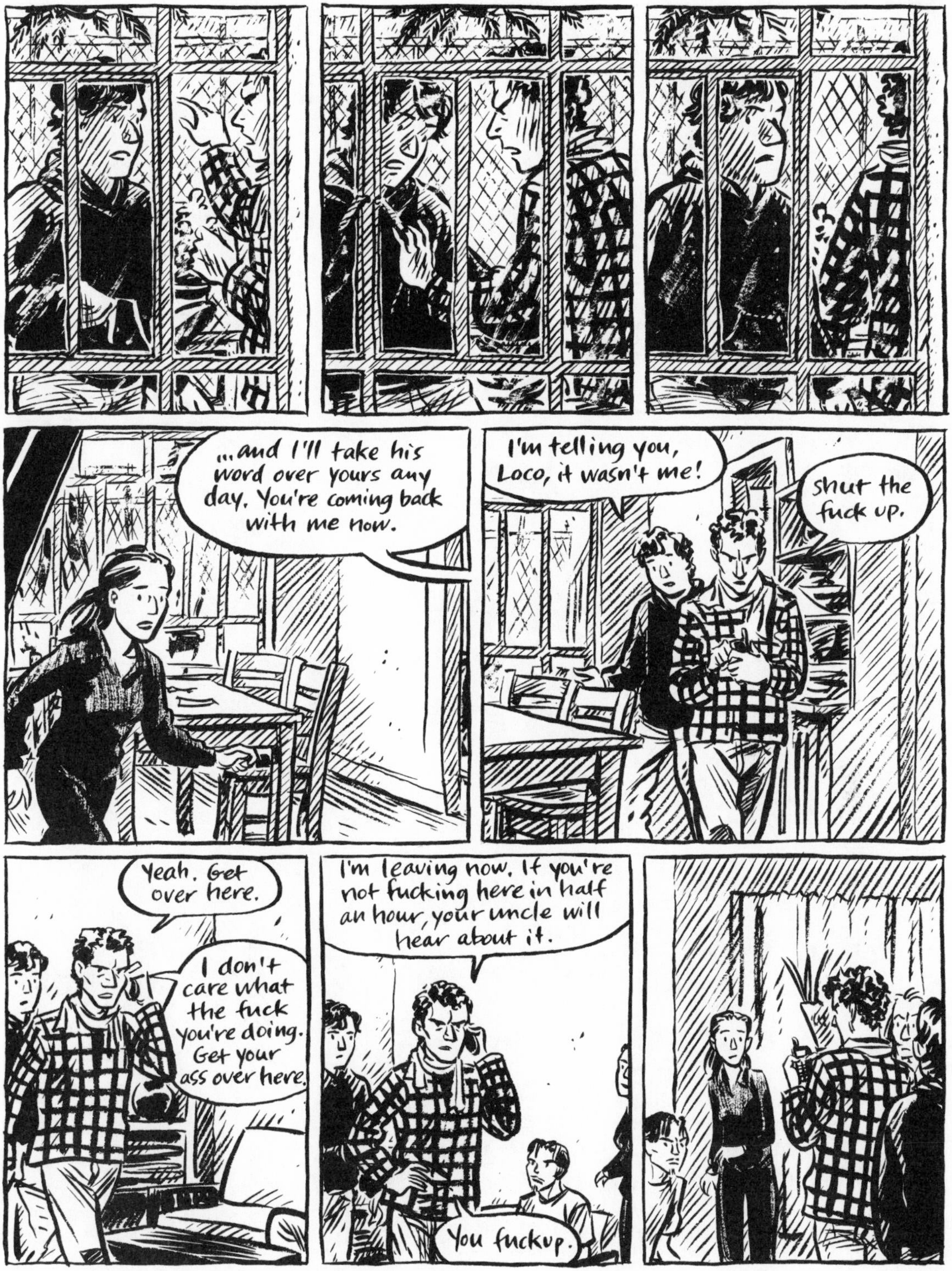
...and I'll take his word over yours any day. You're coming back with me now.
I'm telling you, Loco, it wasn't me!
Shut the fuck up.
Yeah. Get over here.
I don't care what the fuck you're doing. Get your ass over here.
I'm leaving now. If you're not fucking here in half an hour, your uncle will hear about it.
You fuckup.

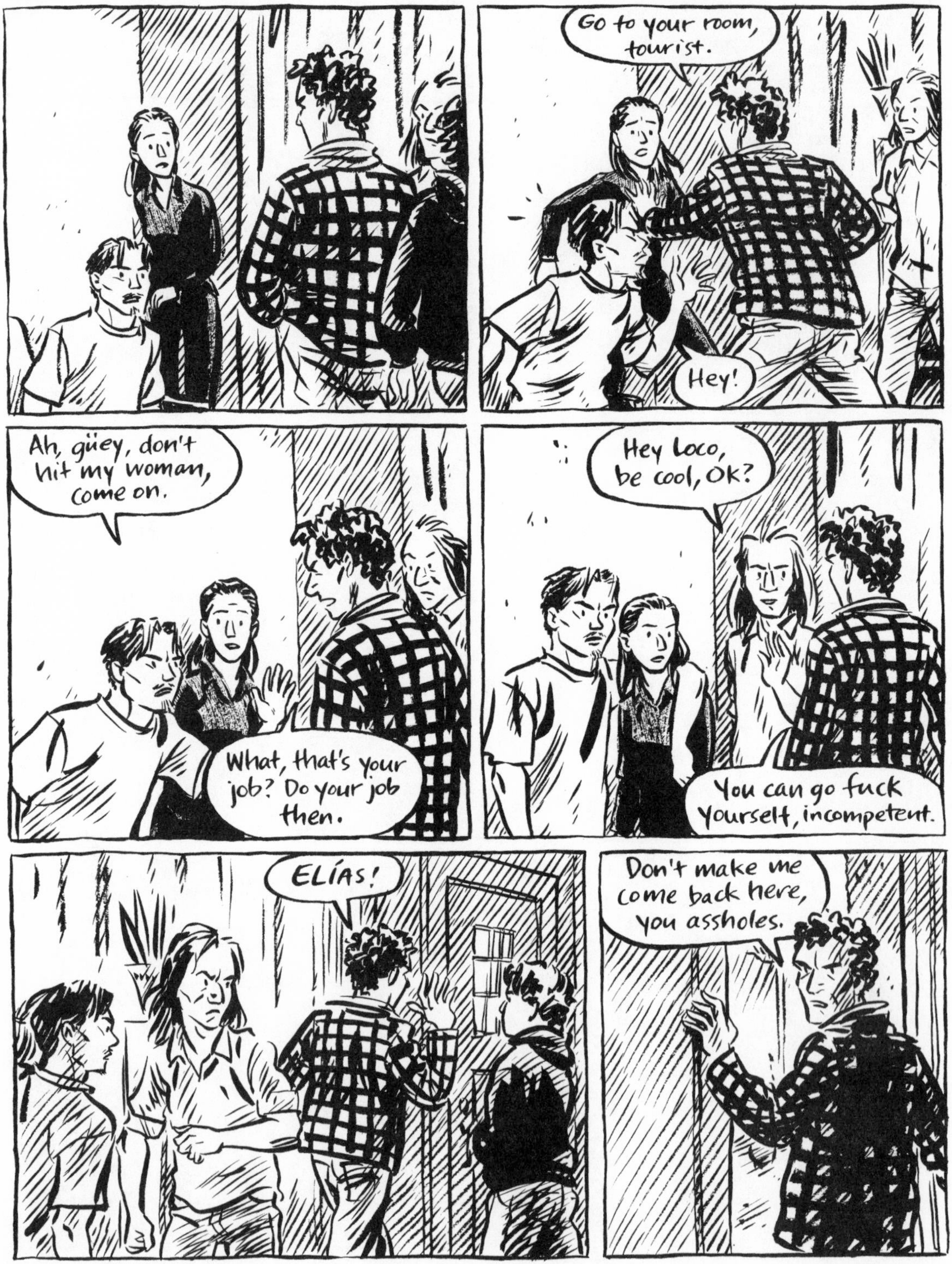
Go to your room, tourist.
Hey!
Ah, güey, don't hit my woman, come on.
What, that's your job? Do your job then.
Hey loco, be cool, OK?
You can go fuck yourself, incompetent.
ELÍAS!
Don't make me come back here, you assholes.

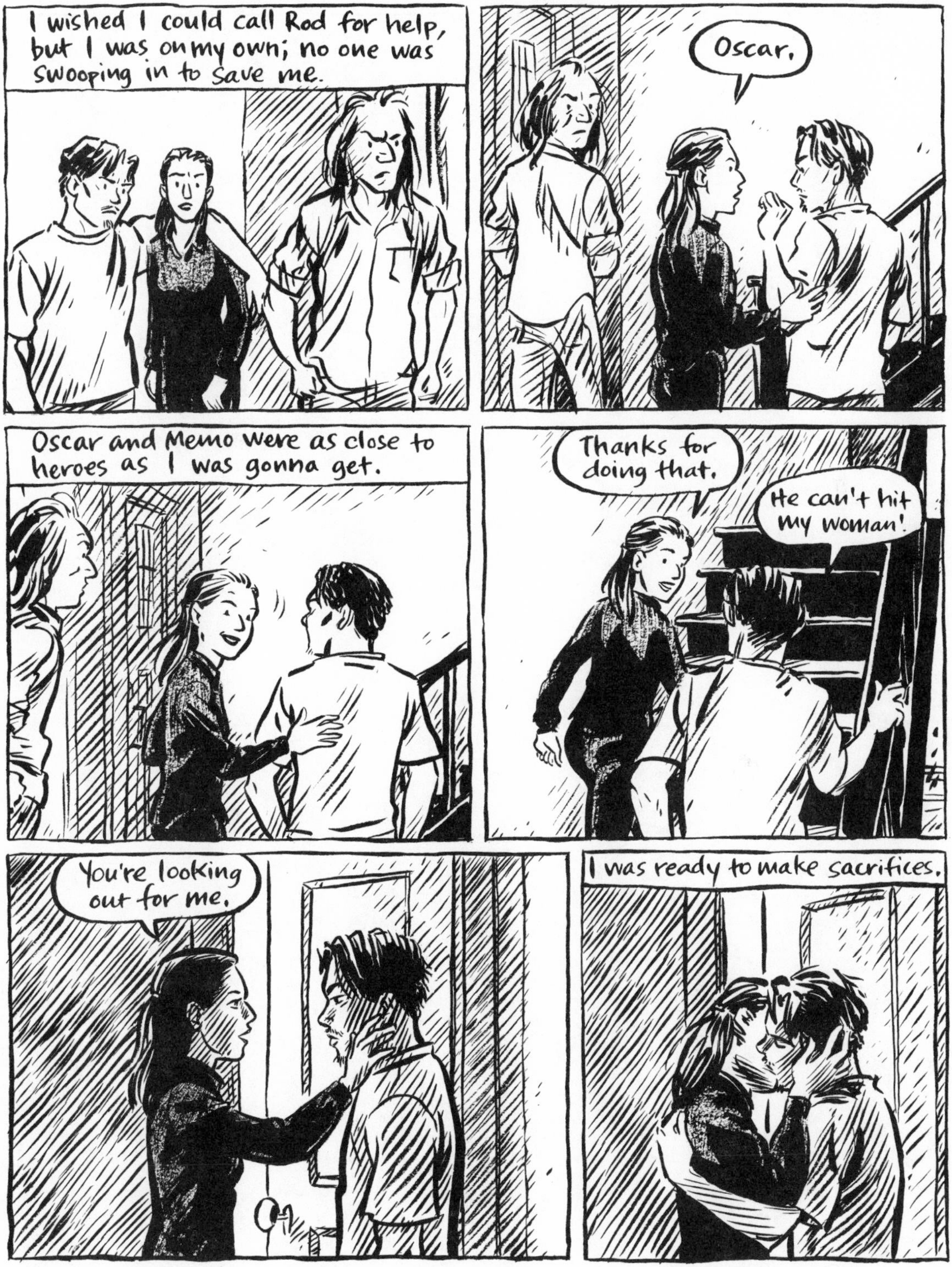
I wished I could call Rod for help, but I was on my own; no one was swooping in to save me.
Oscar.
Oscar and Memo were as close to heroes as I was gonna get.
Thanks for doing that.
He can't hit my woman!
You're looking out for me.
I was ready to make sacrifices.

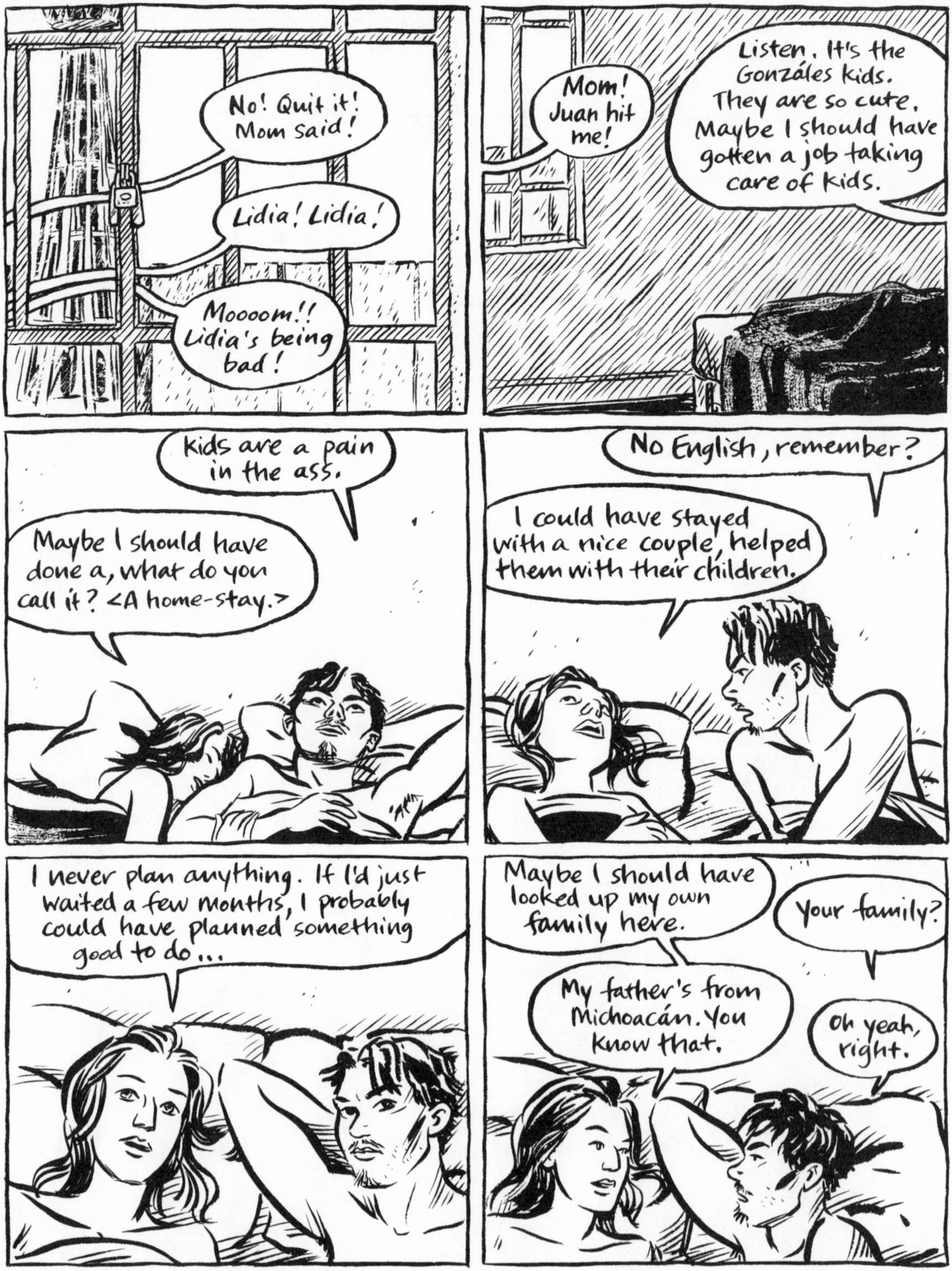
No! Quit it! Mom said!
Lidia! Lidia!
Moooom!! Lidia's being bad!
Mom! Juan hit me!
Listen. It's the Gonzáles kids. They are so cute. Maybe I should have gotten a job taking care of kids.
Kids are a pain in the ass.
Maybe I should have done a, what do you call it? <A home-stay.>
No English, remember?
I could have stayed with a nice couple, helped them with their children.
I never plan anything. If I'd just waited a few months, I probably could have planned something good to do...
Maybe I should have looked up my own family here.
Your family?
My father's from Michoacán. You know that.
Oh yeah, right.

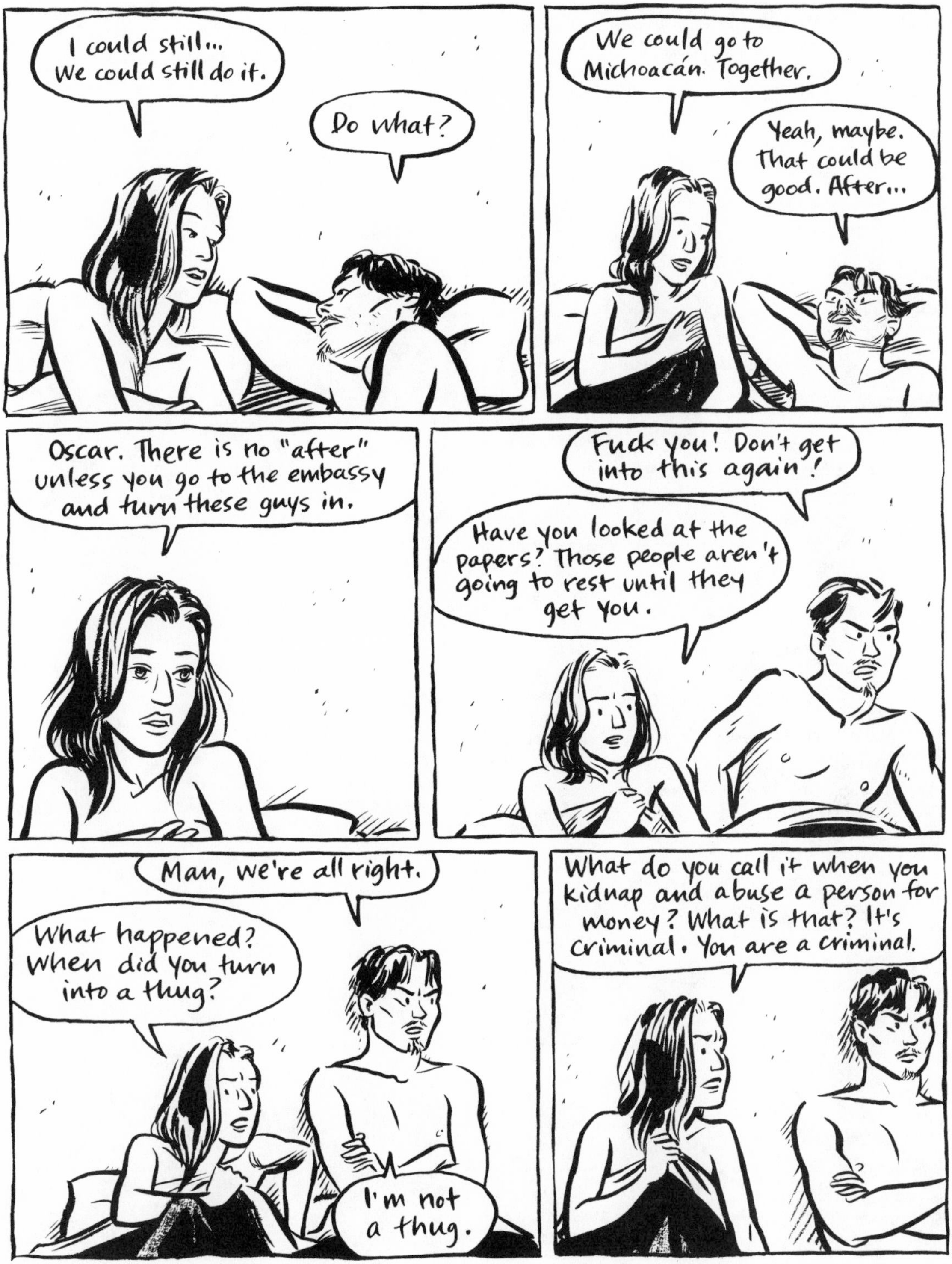

I could still... We could still do it.
Do what?
We could go to Michoacán. Together.
Yeah, maybe. That could be good. After...
Oscar. There is no "after" unless you go to the embassy and turn these guys in.
Fuck you! Don't get into this again!
Have you looked at the papers? Those people aren't going to rest until they get you.
Man, we're all right.
What happened? When did you turn into a thug?
I'm not a thug.
What do you call it when you kidnap and abuse a person for money? What is that? It's criminal. You are a criminal.

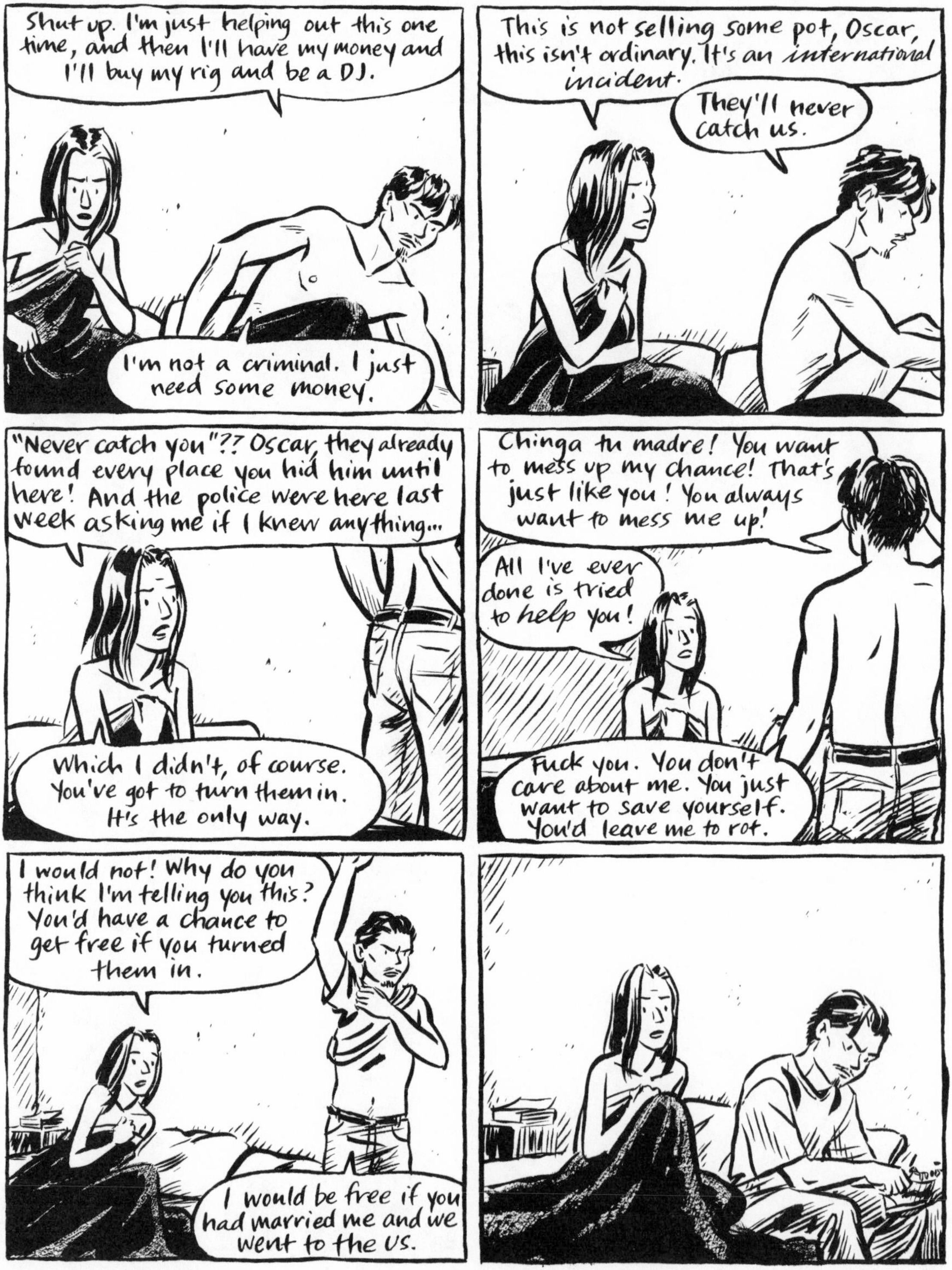
Shut up. I'm just helping out this one time, and then I'll have my money and I'll buy my rig and be a DJ.
I'm not a criminal. I just need some money.
This is not selling some pot, Oscar, this isn't ordinary. It's an international incident.
They'll never catch us.
"Never catch you"?? Oscar, they already found every place you hid him until here! And the police were here last week asking me if I knew anything...
Which I didn't, of course. You've got to turn them in. It's the only way.
Chinga tu madre! You want to mess up my chance! That's just like you! You always want to mess me up!
All I've ever done is tried to help you!
Fuck you. You don't care about me. You just want to save yourself. You'd leave me to rot.
I would not! Why do you think I'm telling you this? You'd have a chance to get free if you turned them in.
I would be free if you had married me and we went to the US.

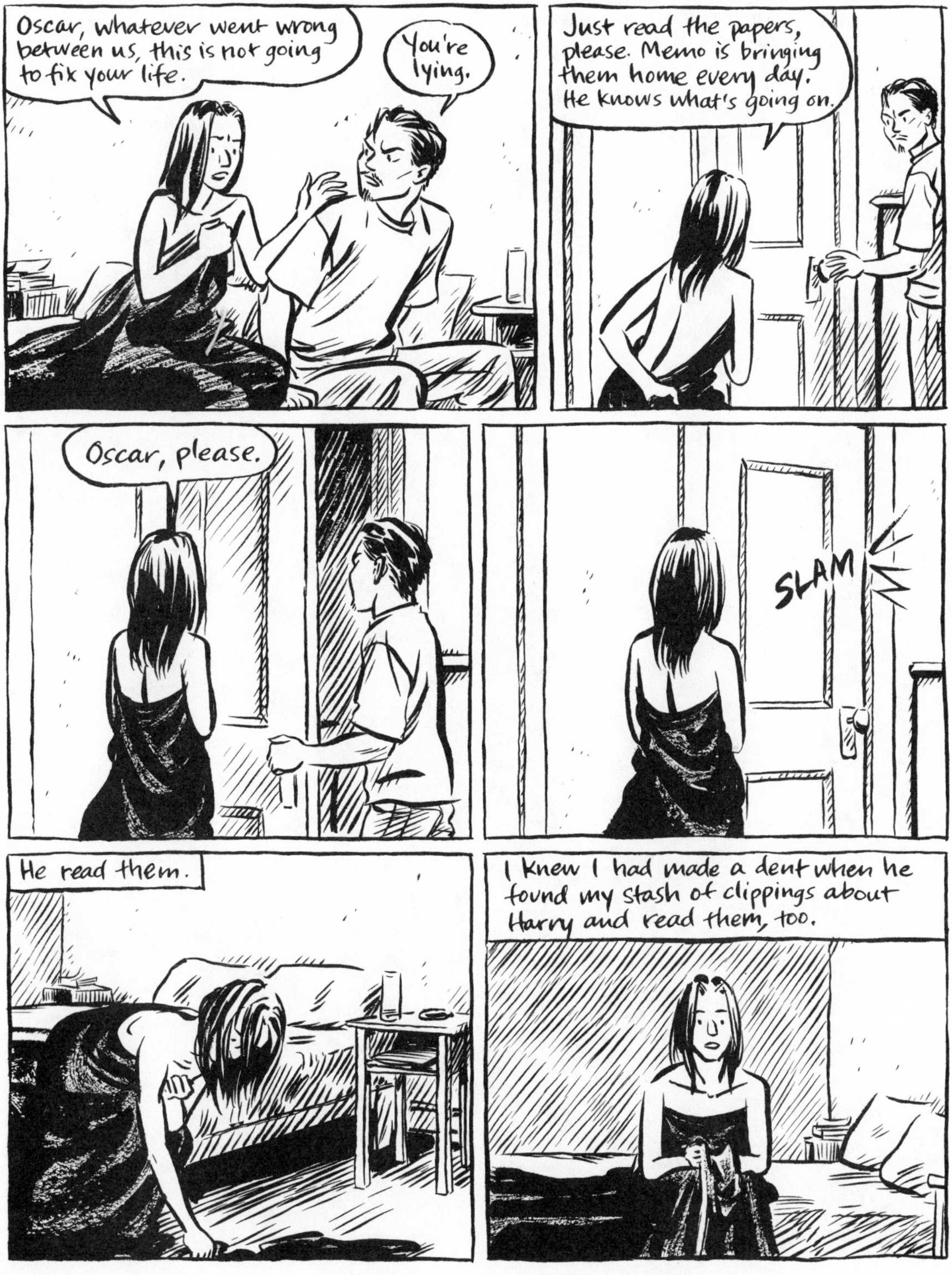
Oscar, whatever went wrong between us, this is not going to fix your life.
You're lying.
Just read the papers, please. Memo is bringing them home every day. He knows what's going on.
Oscar, please.
SLAM
He read them.
I knew I had made a dent when he found my stash of clippings about Harry and read them, too.

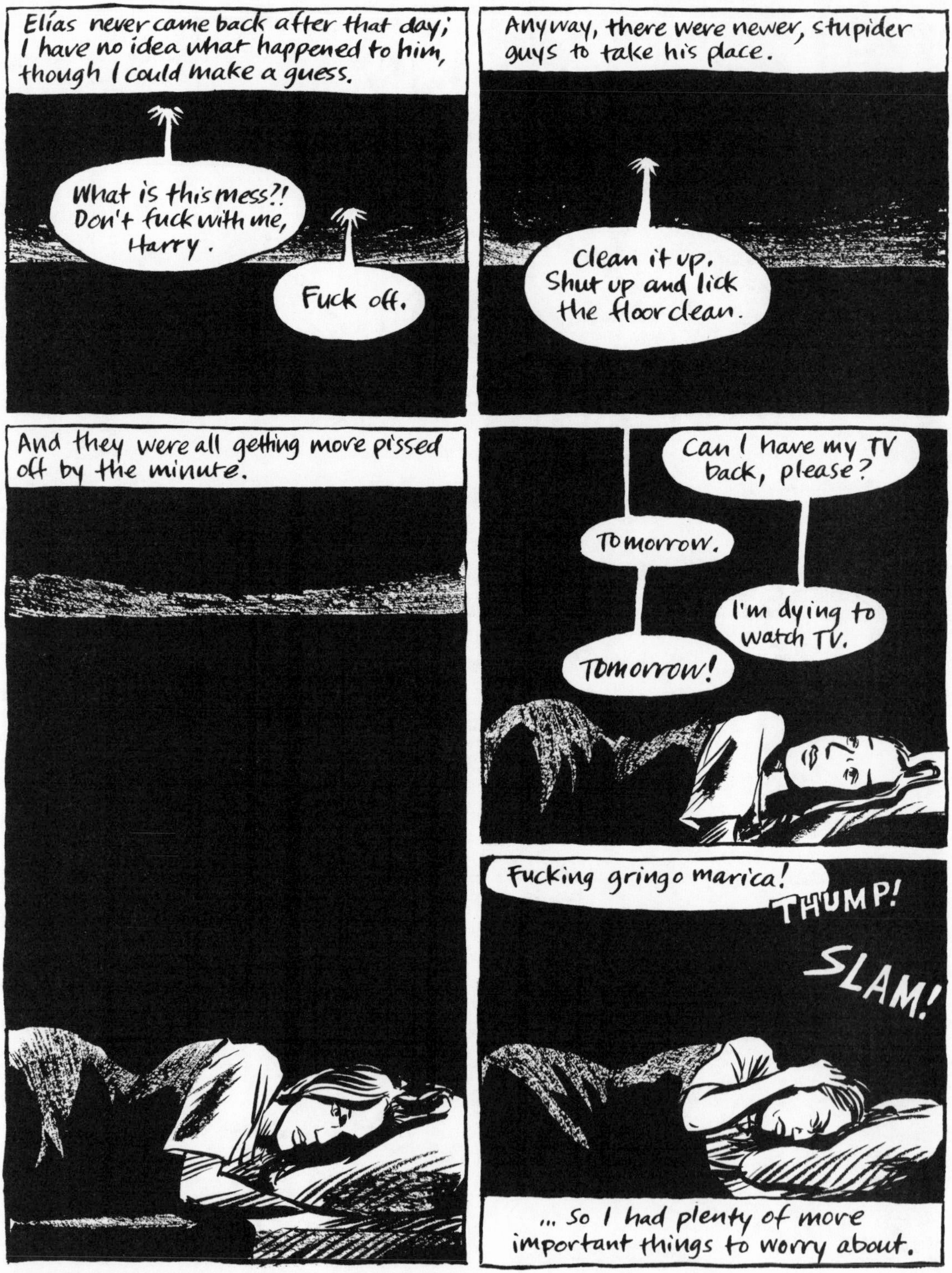

Elías never came back after that day; I have no idea what happened to him, though I could make a guess.
What is this mess?! Don't fuck with me, Harry.
Fuck off.
Anyway, there were newer, stupider guys to take his place.
Clean it up. Shut up and lick the floor clean.
And they were all getting more pissed off by the minute.
Can I have my TV back, please?
Tomorrow.
I'm dying to watch TV.
Tomorrow!
Fucking gringo marica!
THUMP!
SLAM!
... So I had plenty of more important things to worry about.

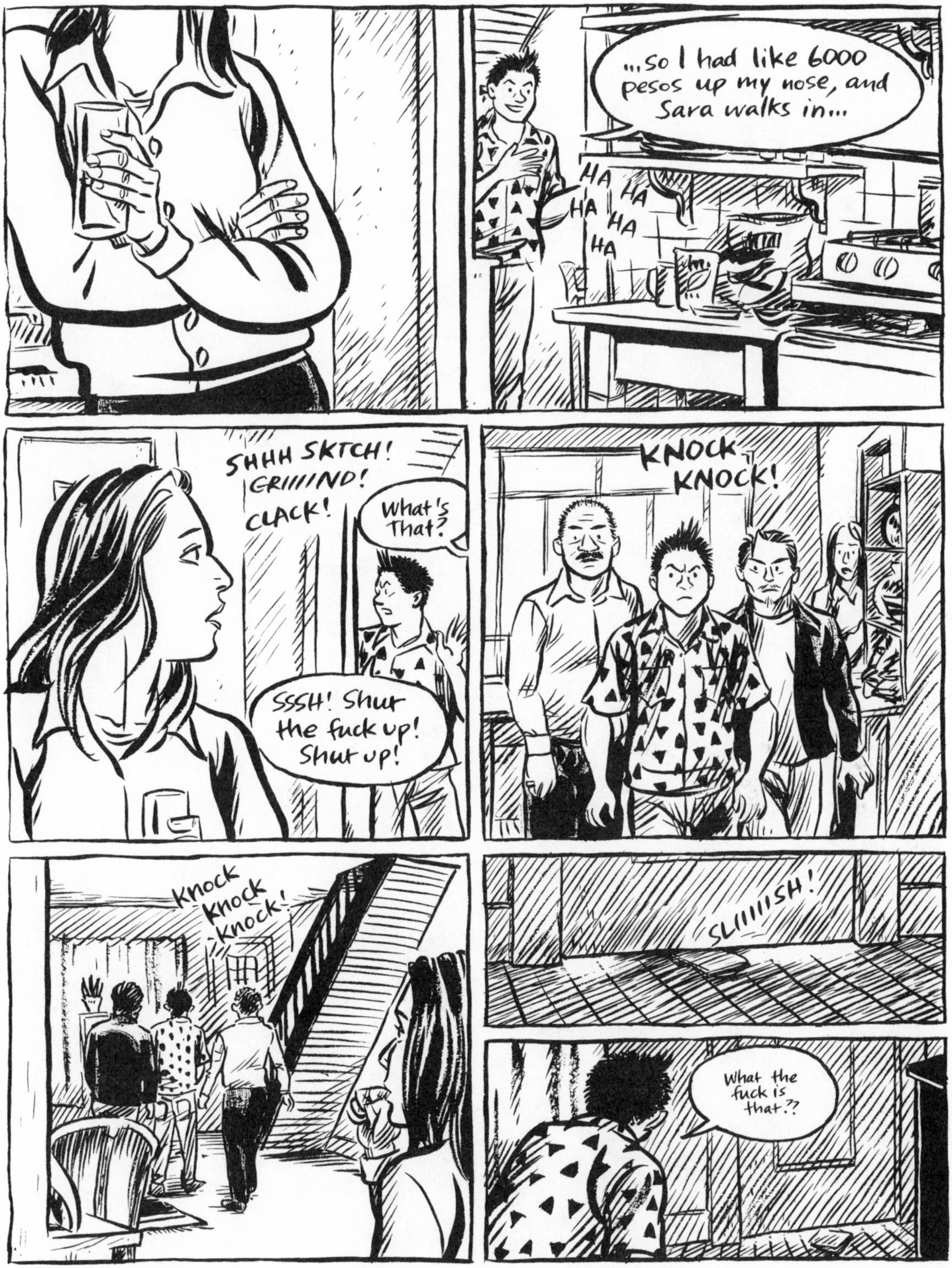
...so I had like 6000 pesos up my nose, and Sara walks in...
HA HA HA HA HA
SHHH SKTCH! GRIIIIND! CLACK!
What's That?
SSSH! Shut the fuck up! Shut up!
KNOCK KNOCK!
knock knock knock!
SLIIIISH!
What the fuck is that??

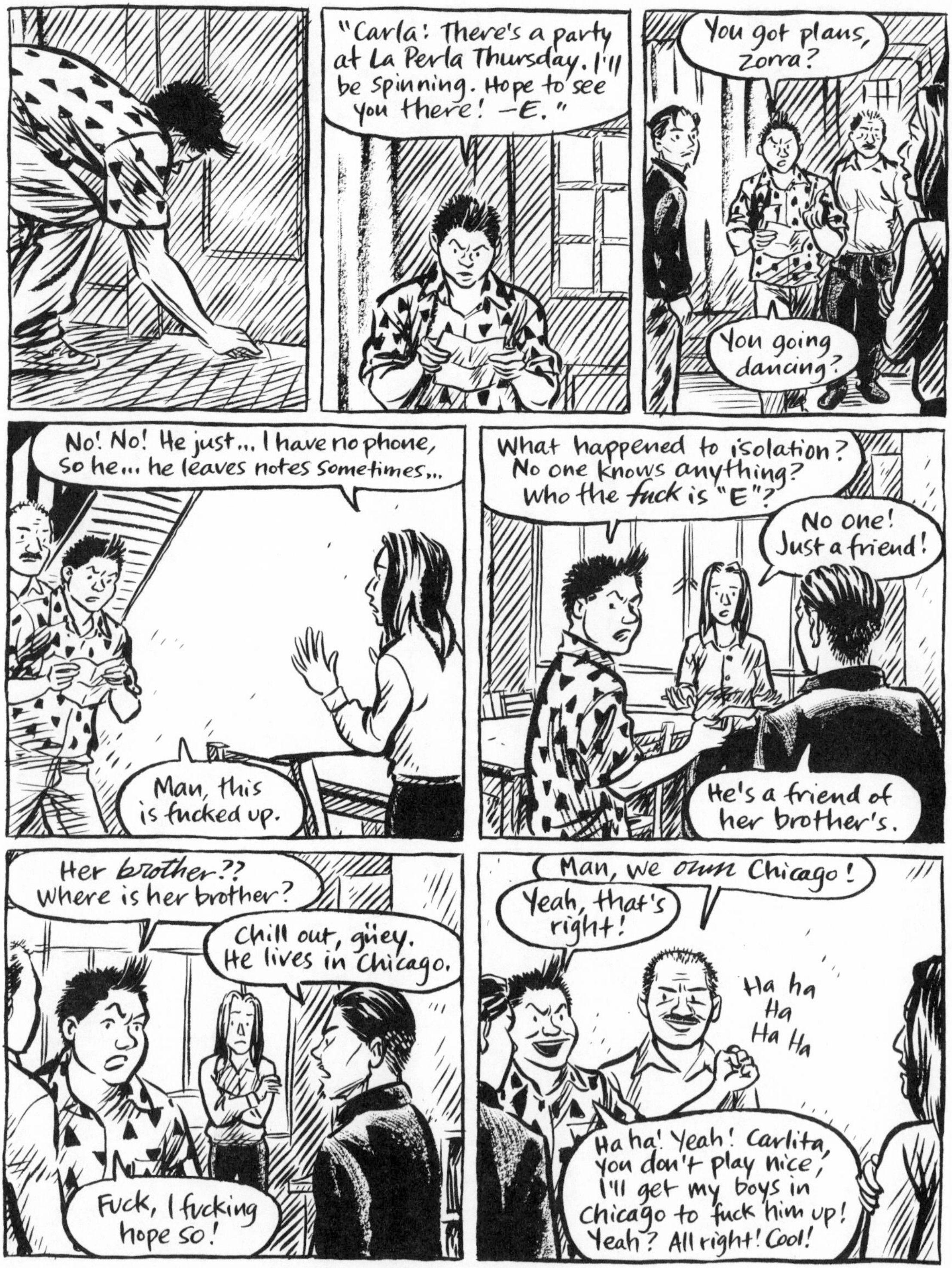
"Carla: There's a party at La Perla Thursday. I'll be spinning. Hope to see you there! —E."
You got plans, zorra?
You going dancing?
No! No! He just... I have no phone, so he... he leaves notes sometimes...
Man, this is fucked up.
What happened to isolation? No one knows anything? Who the *fuck* is "E"?
No one! Just a friend!
He's a friend of her brother's.
Her *brother*?? Where is her brother?
Chill out, güey. He lives in Chicago.
Fuck, I fucking hope so!
Man, we *own* Chicago!
Yeah, that's right!
Ha ha Ha Ha Ha
Ha ha! Yeah! Carlita, you don't play nice, I'll get my boys in Chicago to fuck him up! Yeah? All right! Cool!

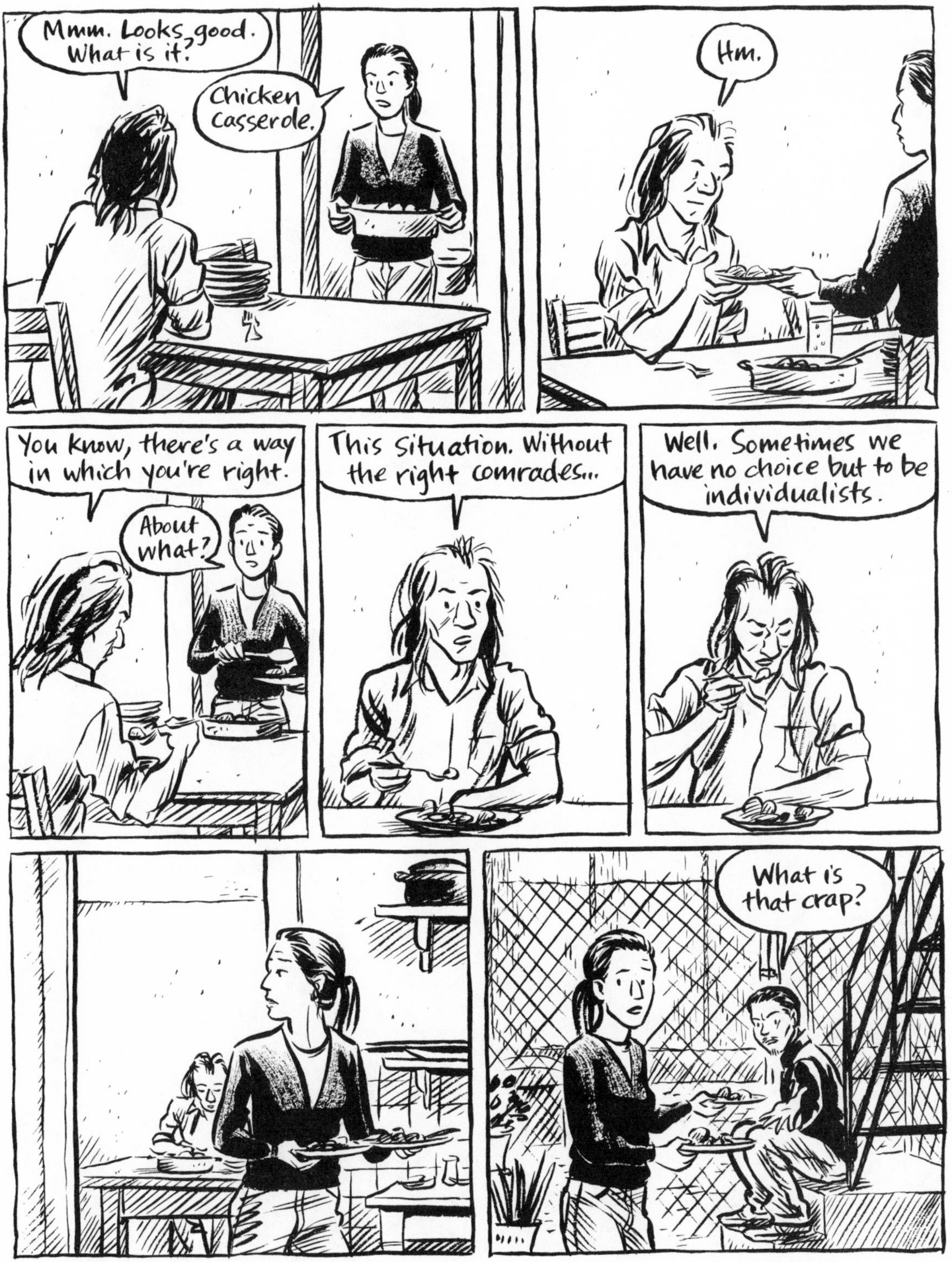
Mmm. Looks good. What is it?
Chicken casserole.
Hm.
You know, there's a way in which you're right.
About what?
This situation. Without the right comrades...
Well. Sometimes we have no choice but to be individualists.
What is that crap?

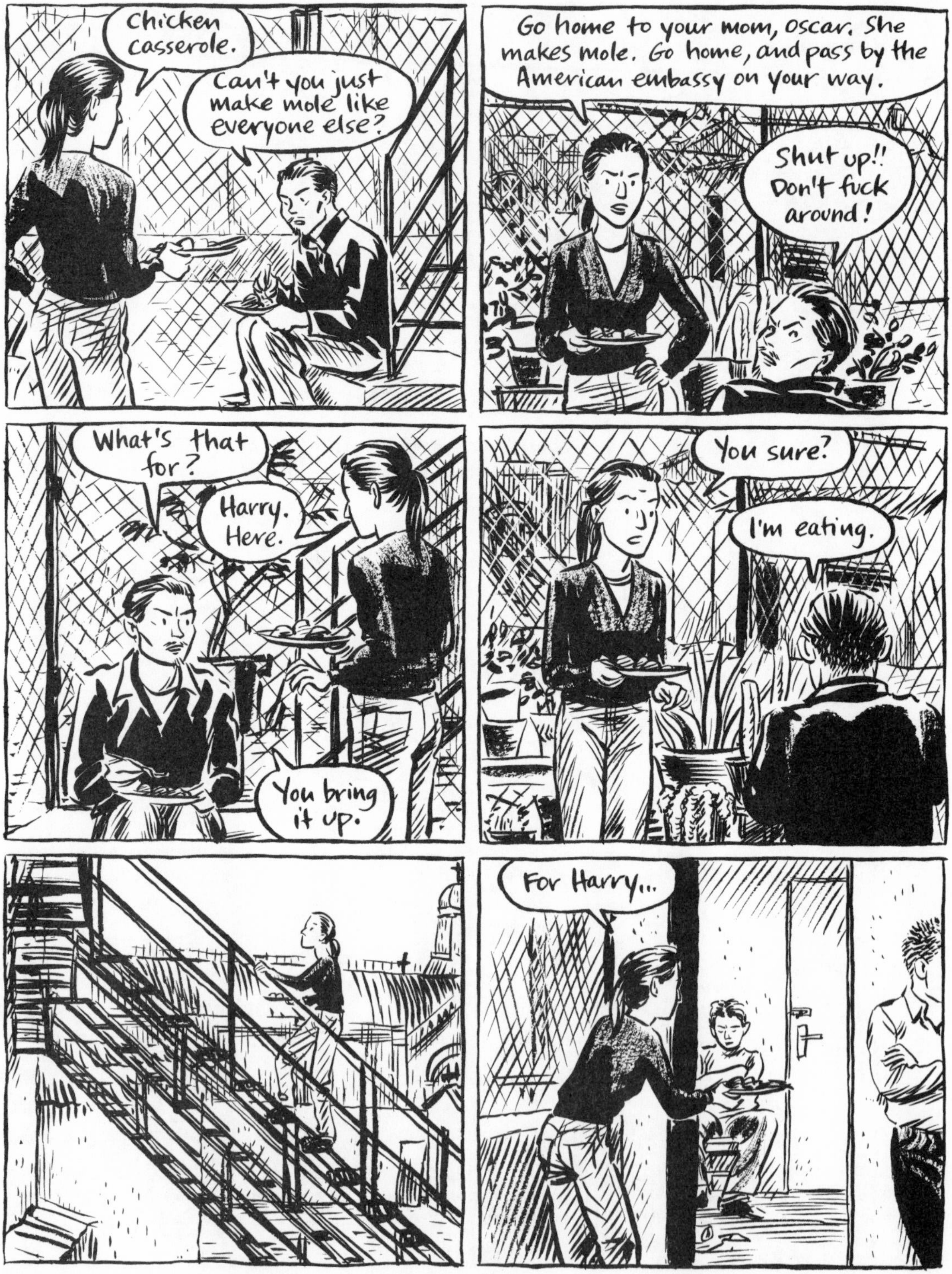
Chicken casserole.
Can't you just make mole like everyone else?
Go home to your mom, Oscar. She makes mole. Go home, and pass by the American embassy on your way.
Shut up!! Don't fuck around!
What's that for?
Harry. Here.
You bring it up.
You sure?
I'm eating.
For Harry...

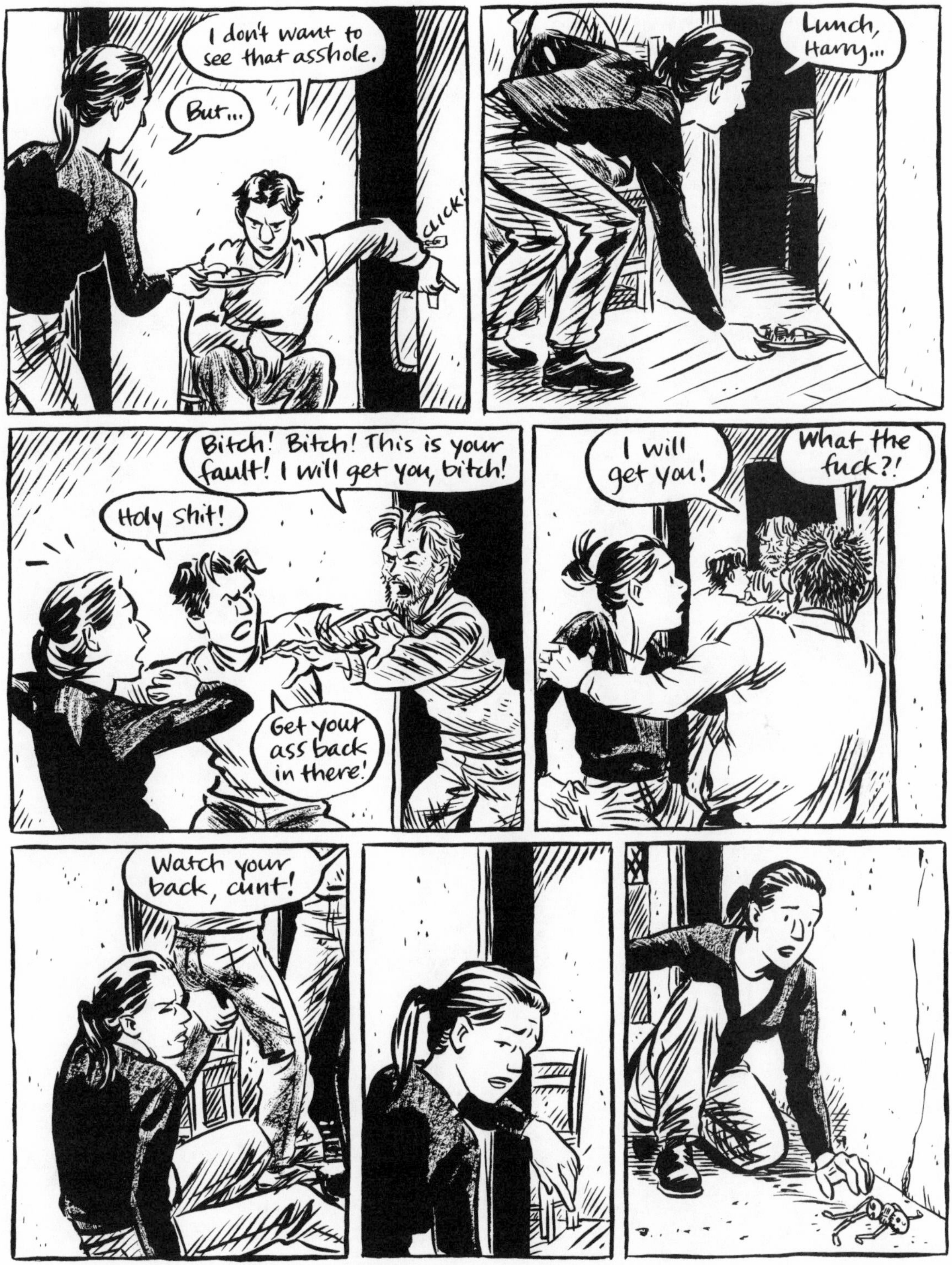

I don't want to see that asshole.
But...
CLICK!
Lunch, Harry...
Bitch! Bitch! This is your fault! I will get you, bitch!
Holy shit!
Get your ass back in there!
I will get you!
What the fuck?!
Watch your back, cunt!

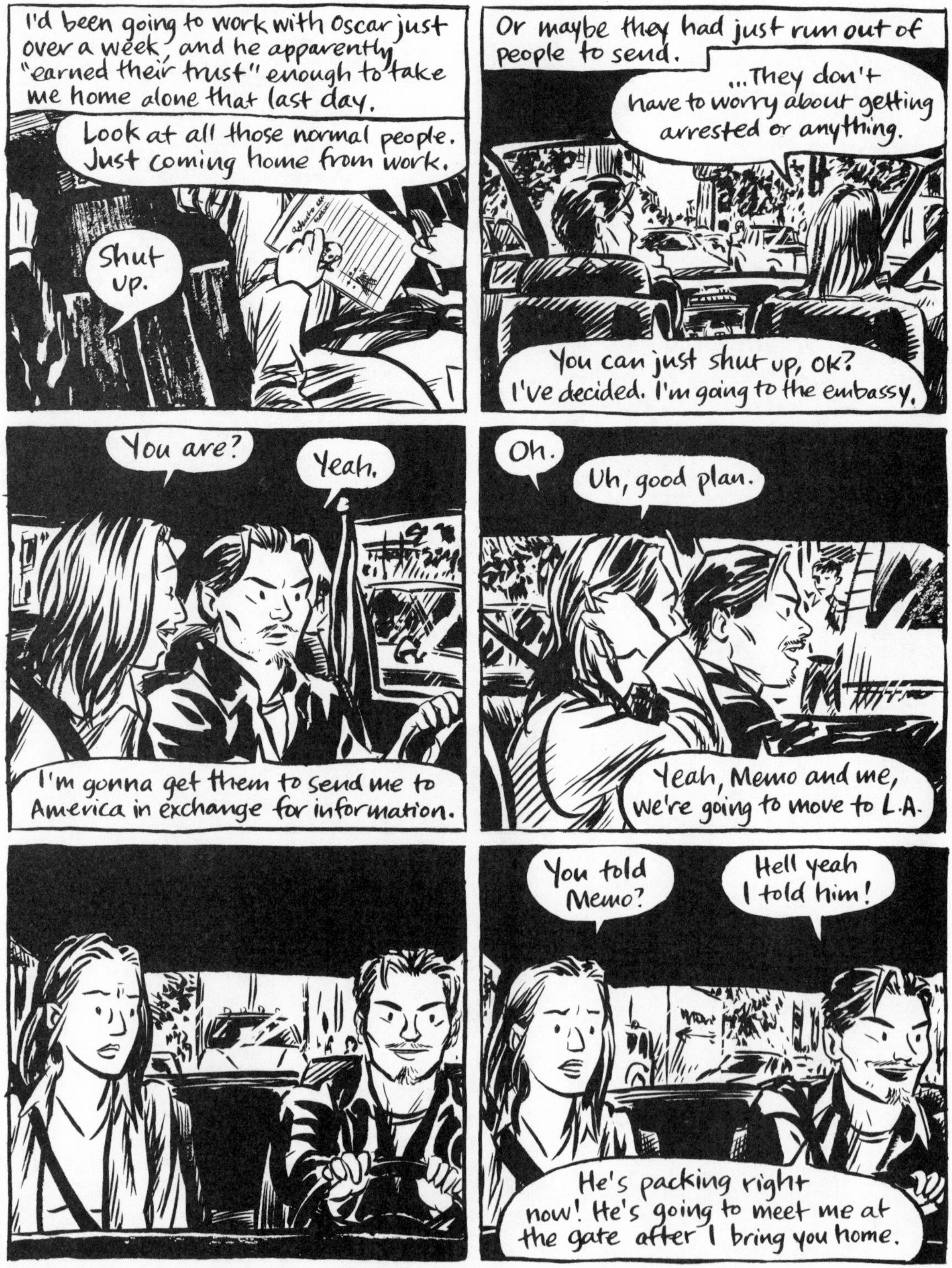
I'd been going to work with Oscar just over a week, and he apparently "earned their trust" enough to take me home alone that last day.
Look at all those normal people. Just coming home from work.
Shut up.
Or maybe they had just run out of people to send.
...They don't have to worry about getting arrested or anything.
You can just shut up, OK? I've decided. I'm going to the embassy.
You are?
Yeah.
I'm gonna get them to send me to America in exchange for information.
Oh.
Uh, good plan.
Yeah, Memo and me, we're going to move to L.A.
You told Memo?
Hell yeah I told him!
He's packing right now! He's going to meet me at the gate after I bring you home.

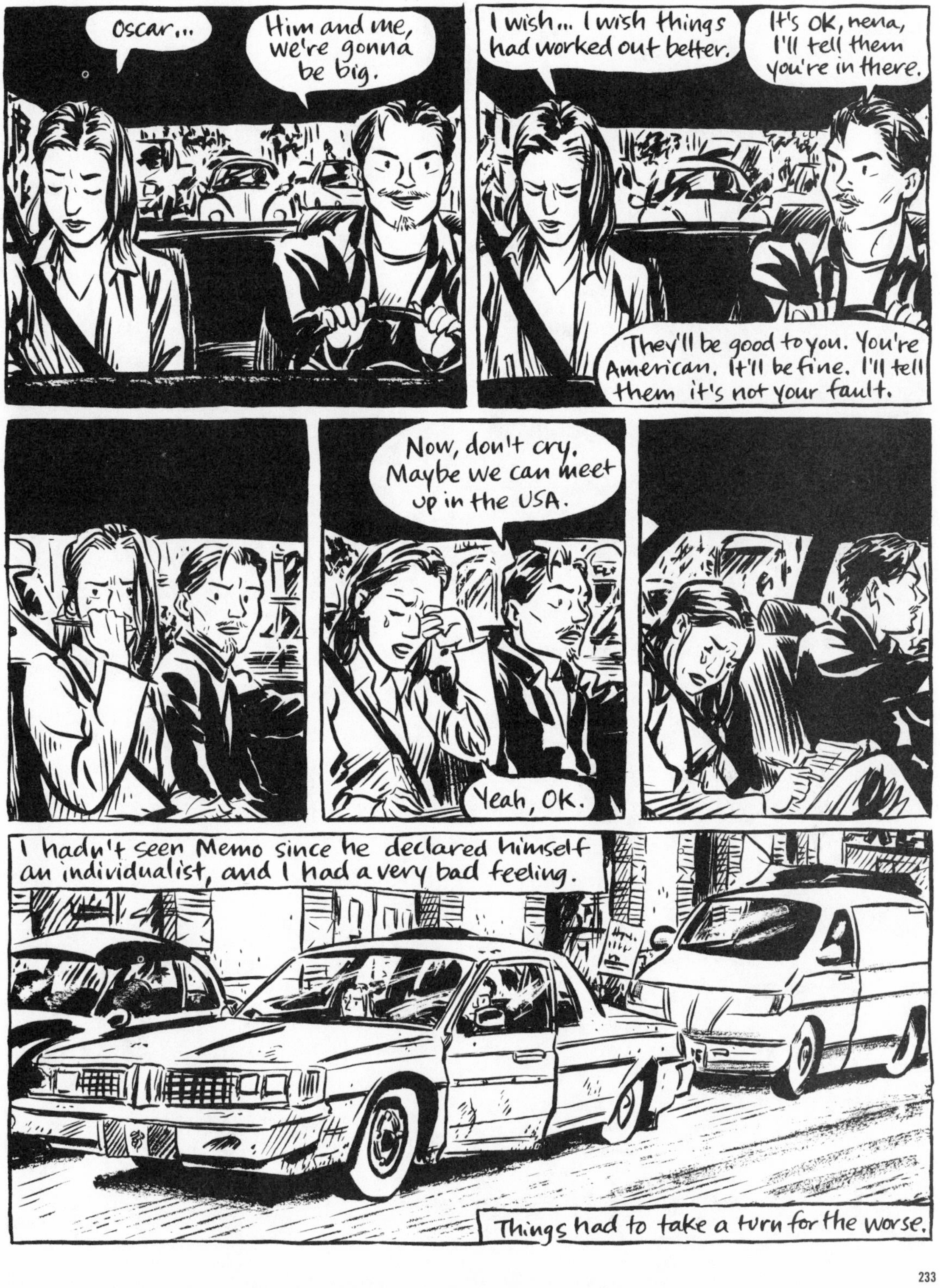
Oscar...
Him and me, we're gonna be big.
I wish... I wish things had worked out better.
It's OK, nena, I'll tell them you're in there.
They'll be good to you. You're American. It'll be fine. I'll tell them it's not your fault.
Now, don't cry. Maybe we can meet up in the USA.
Yeah, OK.
I hadn't seen Memo since he declared himself an individualist, and I had a very bad feeling.
Things had to take a turn for the worse.

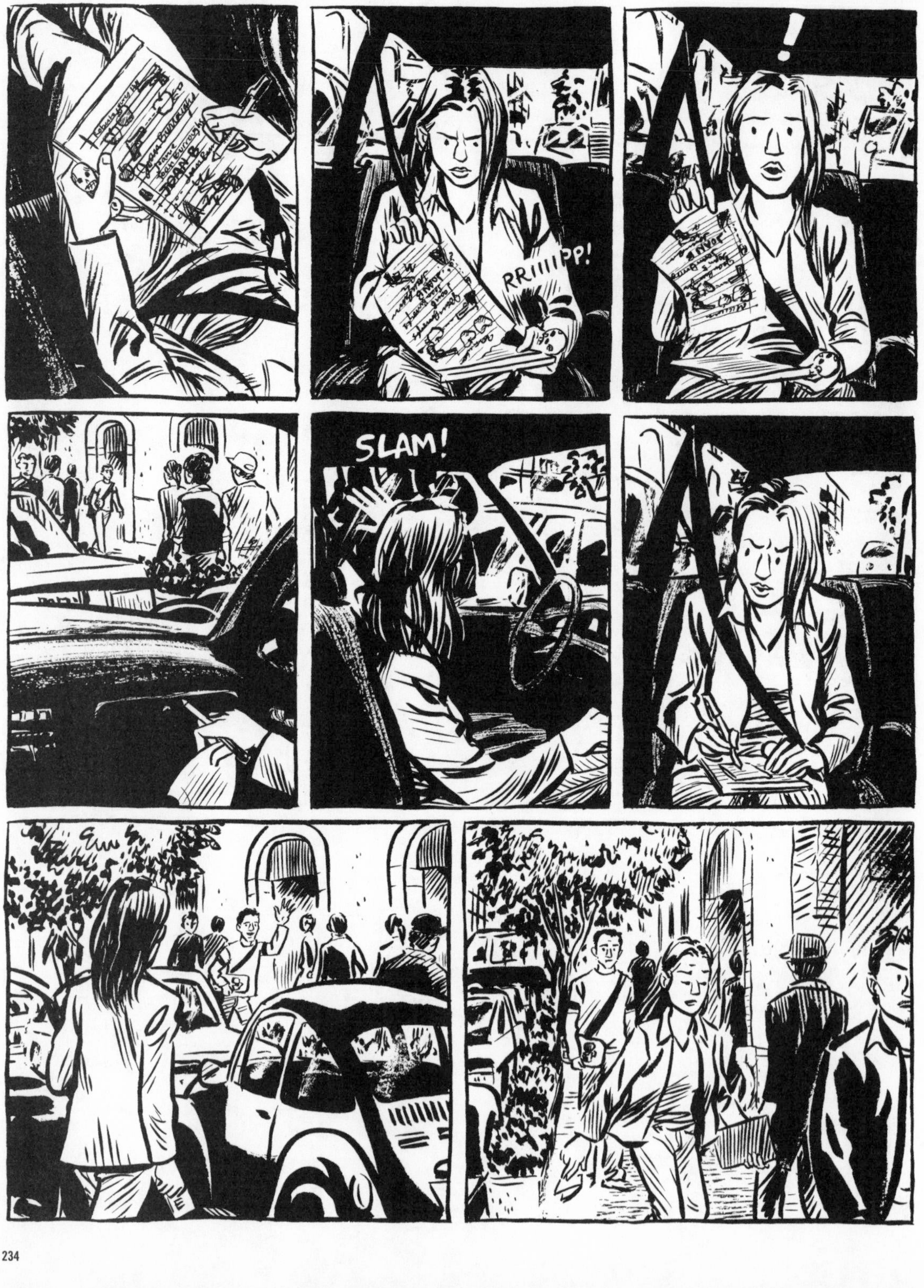
RRIIIIPP!
!
SLAM!

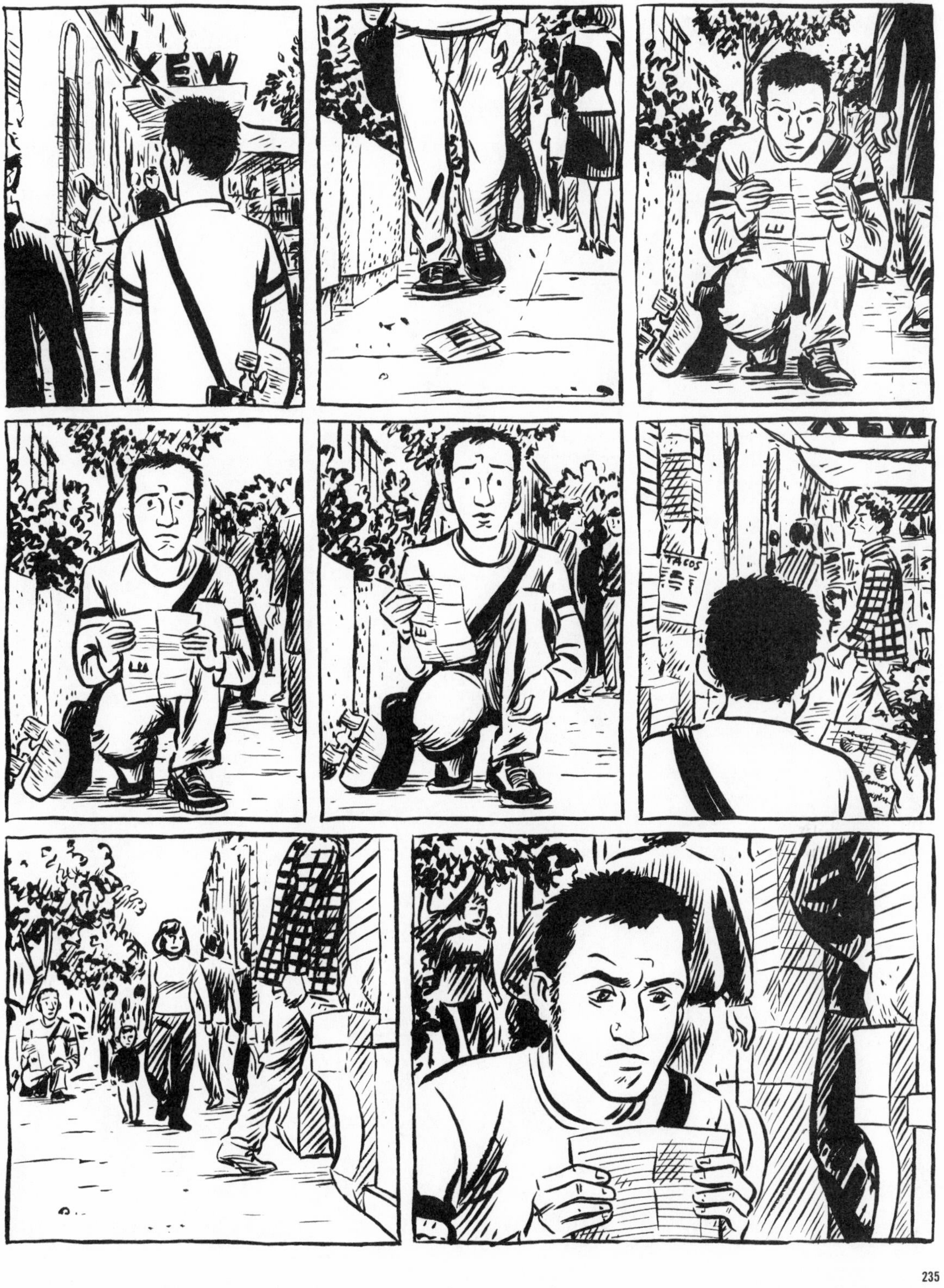
XEW
TACOS

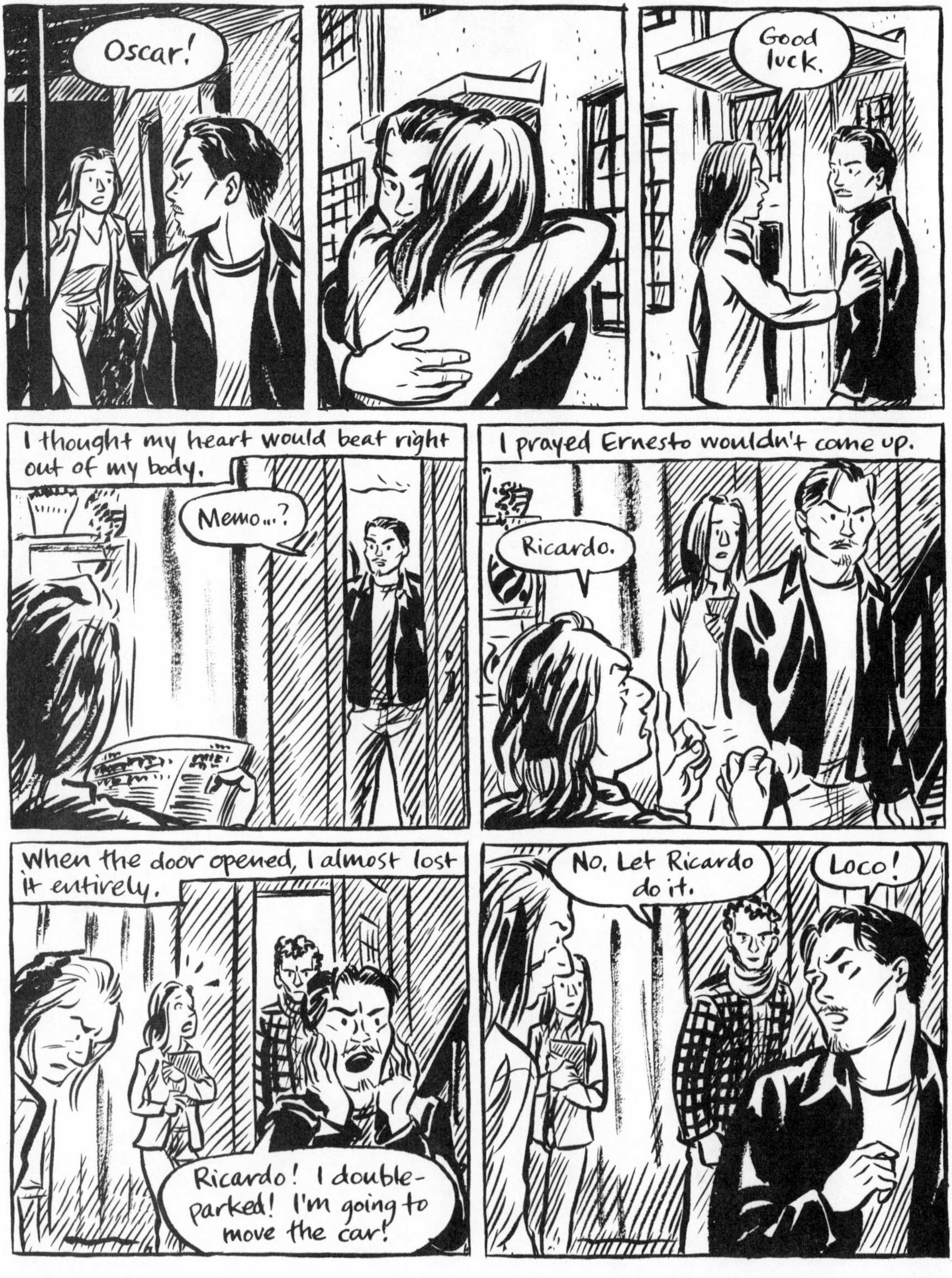
Oscar!
Good luck.
I thought my heart would beat right out of my body.
Memo...?
I prayed Ernesto wouldn't come up.
Ricardo.
When the door opened, I almost lost it entirely.
Ricardo! I double-parked! I'm going to move the car!
No. Let Ricardo do it.
Loco!

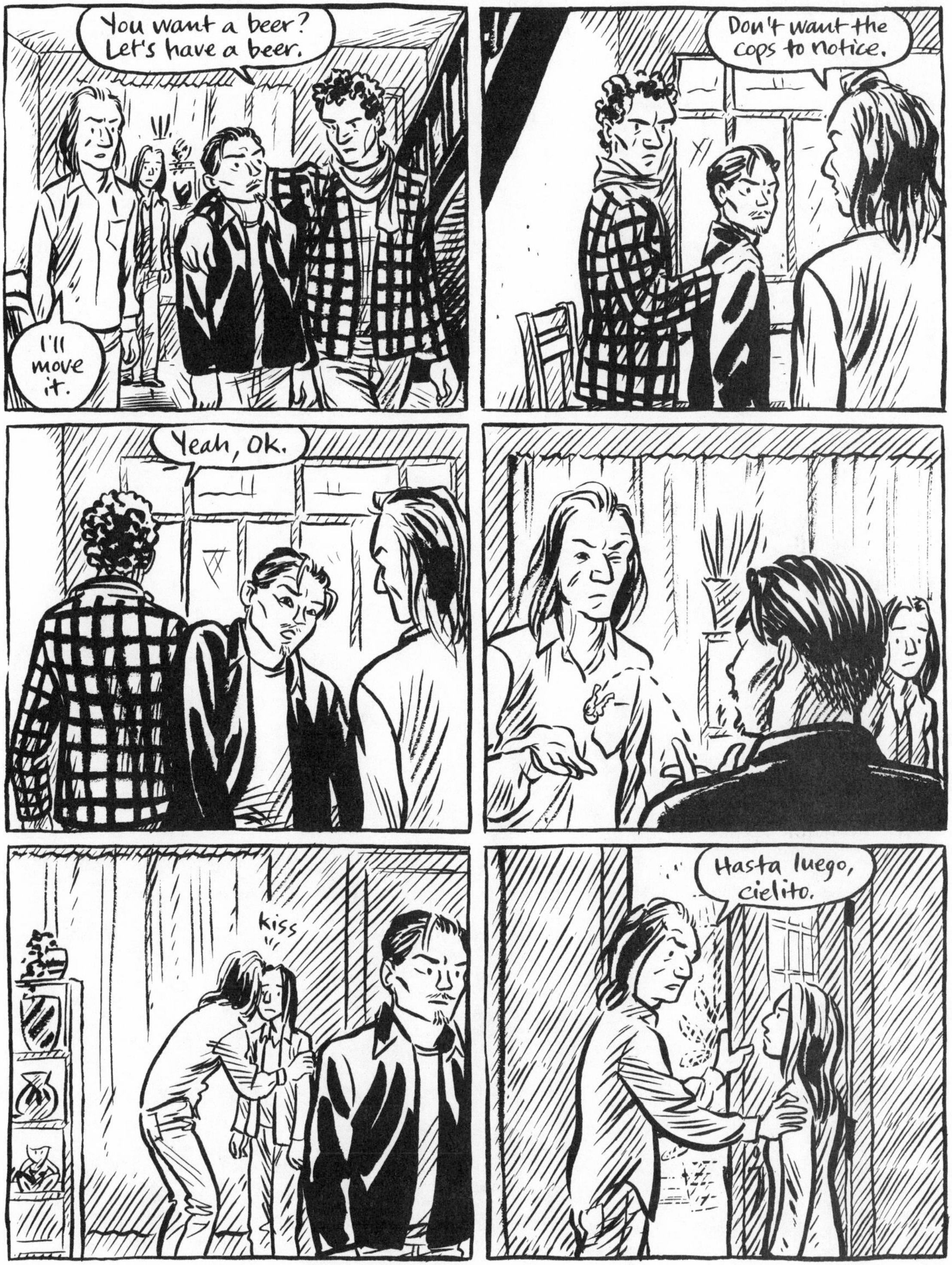
You want a beer? Let's have a beer.
I'll move it.
Don't want the cops to notice.
Yeah, Ok.
kiss
Hasta luego, cielito.

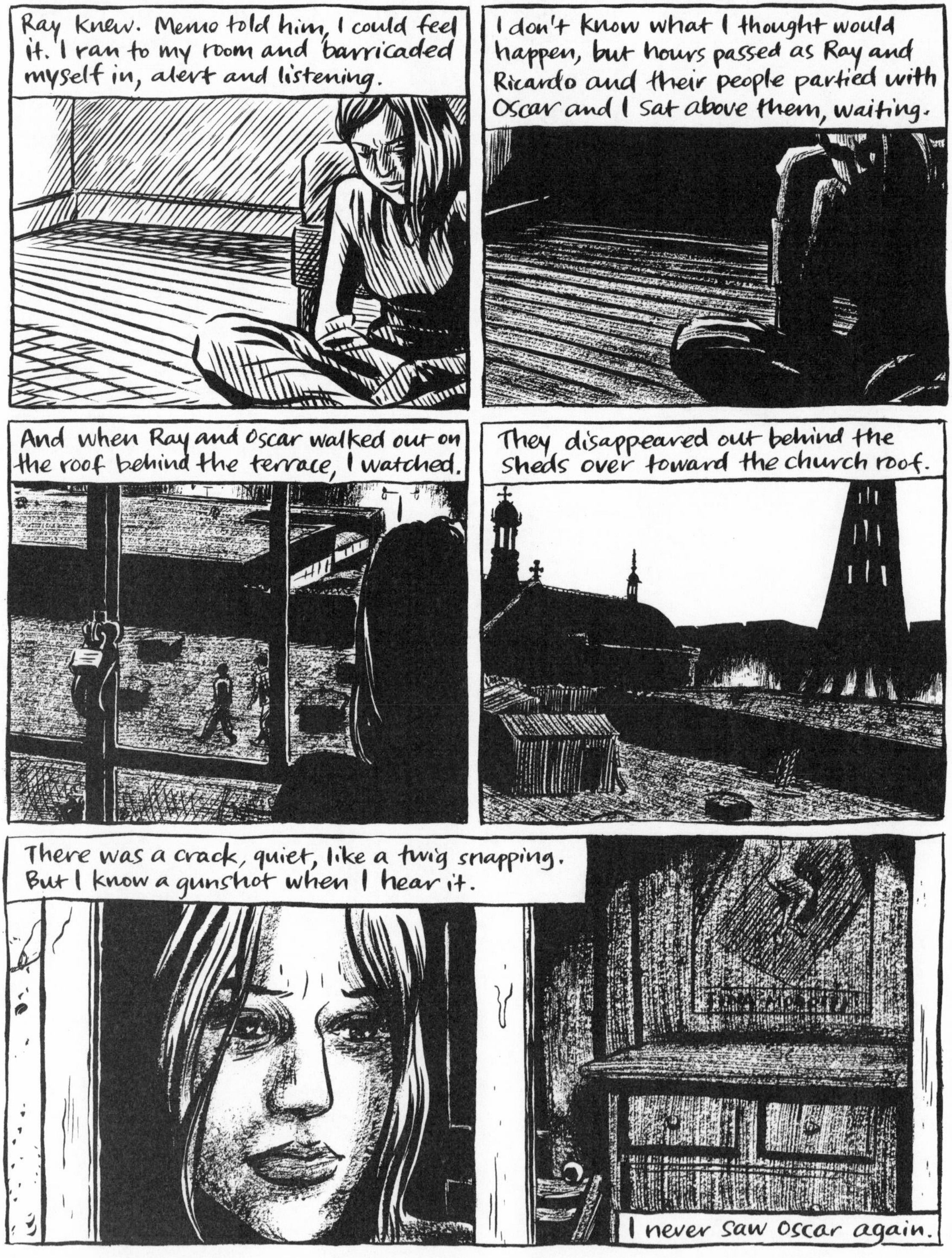
Ray knew. Memo told him, I could feel it. I ran to my room and barricaded myself in, alert and listening.
I don't know what I thought would happen, but hours passed as Ray and Ricardo and their people partied with Oscar and I sat above them, waiting.
And when Ray and Oscar walked out on the roof behind the terrace, I watched.
They disappeared out behind the sheds over toward the church roof.
There was a crack, quiet, like a twig snapping. But I know a gunshot when I hear it.
I never saw Oscar again.

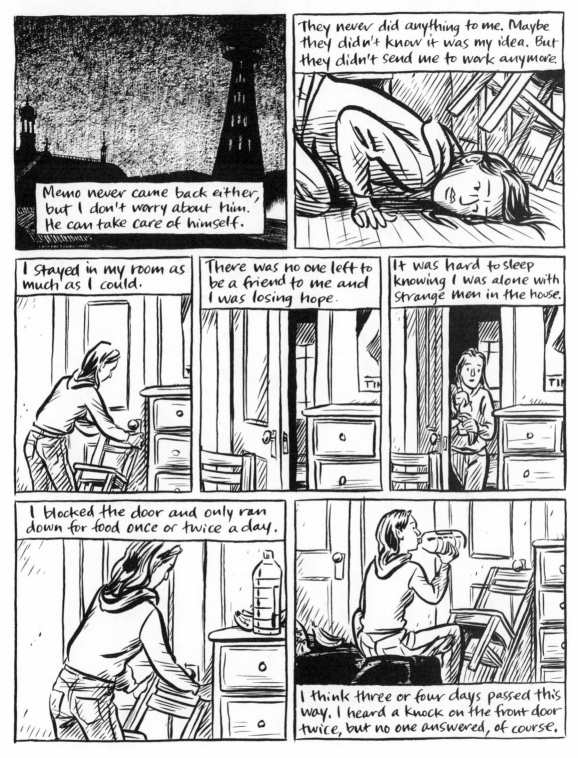

Memo never came back either, but I don't worry about him. He can take care of himself.

They never did anything to me. Maybe they didn't know it was my idea. But they didn't send me to work anymore.

I stayed in my room as much as I could.

There was no one left to be a friend to me and I was losing hope.

It was hard to sleep knowing I was alone with strange men in the house.

I blocked the door and only ran down for food once or twice a day.

I think three or four days passed this way. I heard a knock on the front door twice, but no one answered, of course.

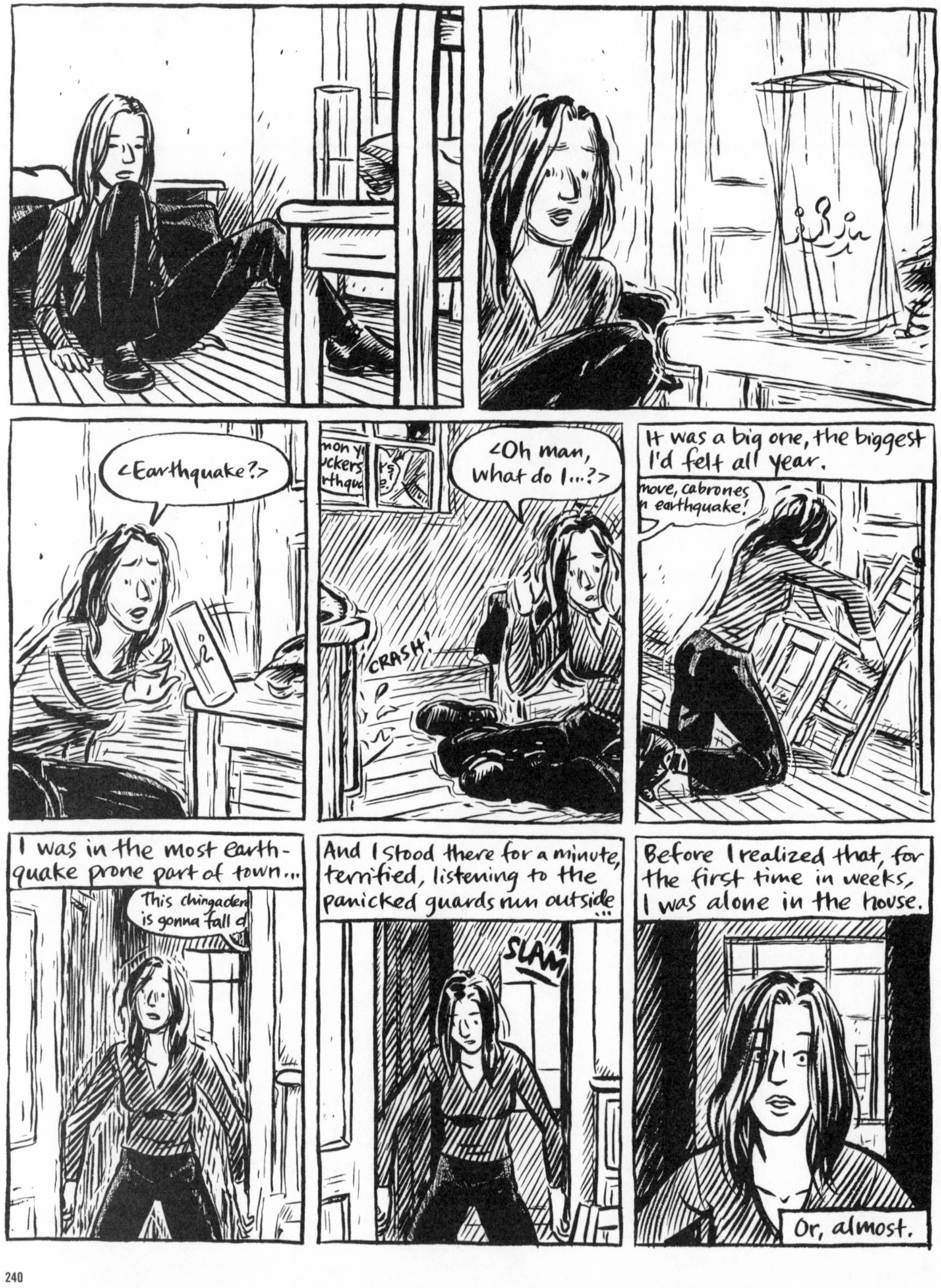

<Earthquake?>
<Oh man, what do I...?>
CRASH!
It was a big one, the biggest I'd felt all year.
move, cabrones
n earthquake!
I was in the most earth-quake prone part of town...
This chingadera
is gonna fall
And I stood there for a minute, terrified, listening to the panicked guards run outside...
SLAM
Before I realized that, for the first time in weeks, I was alone in the house.
Or, almost.

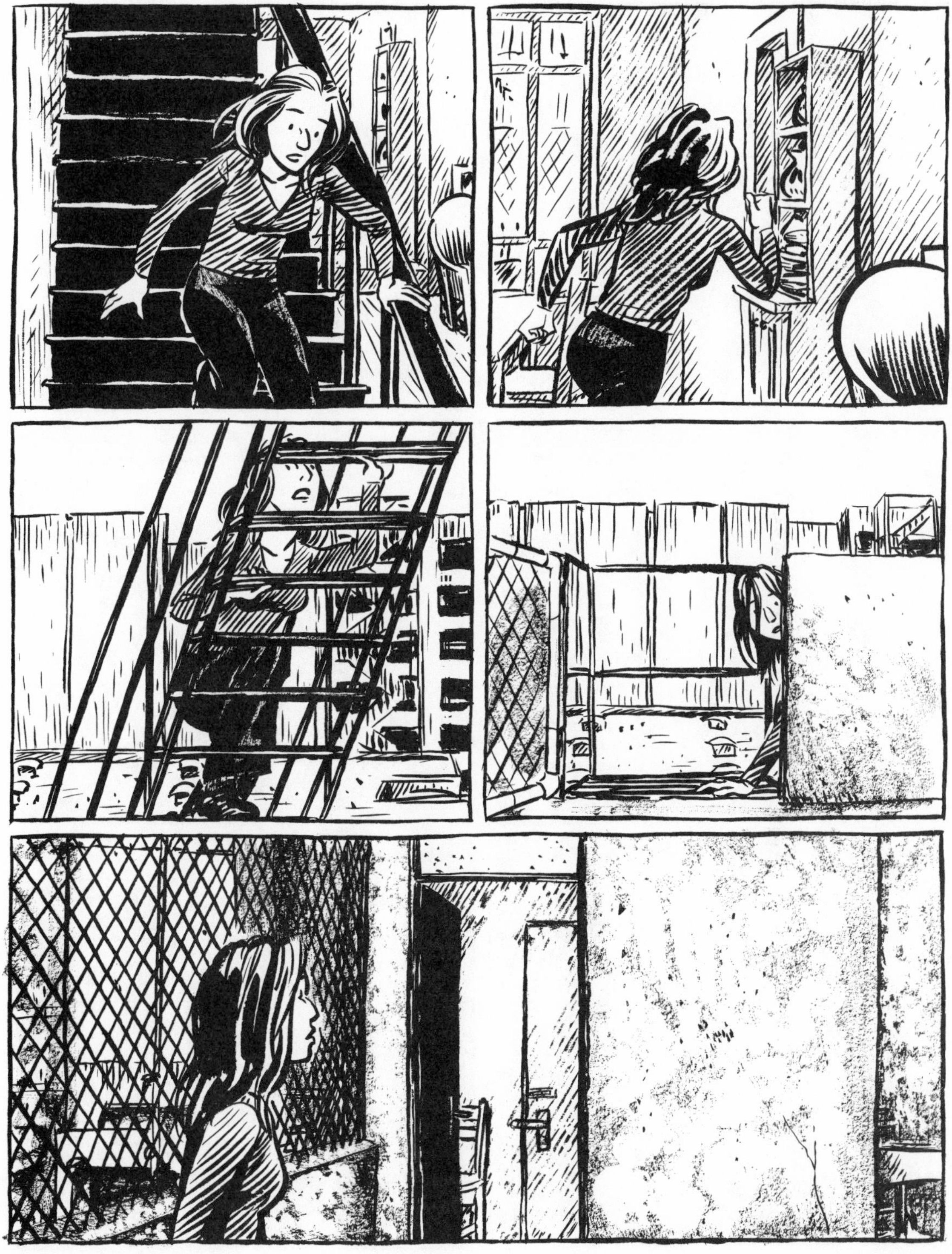

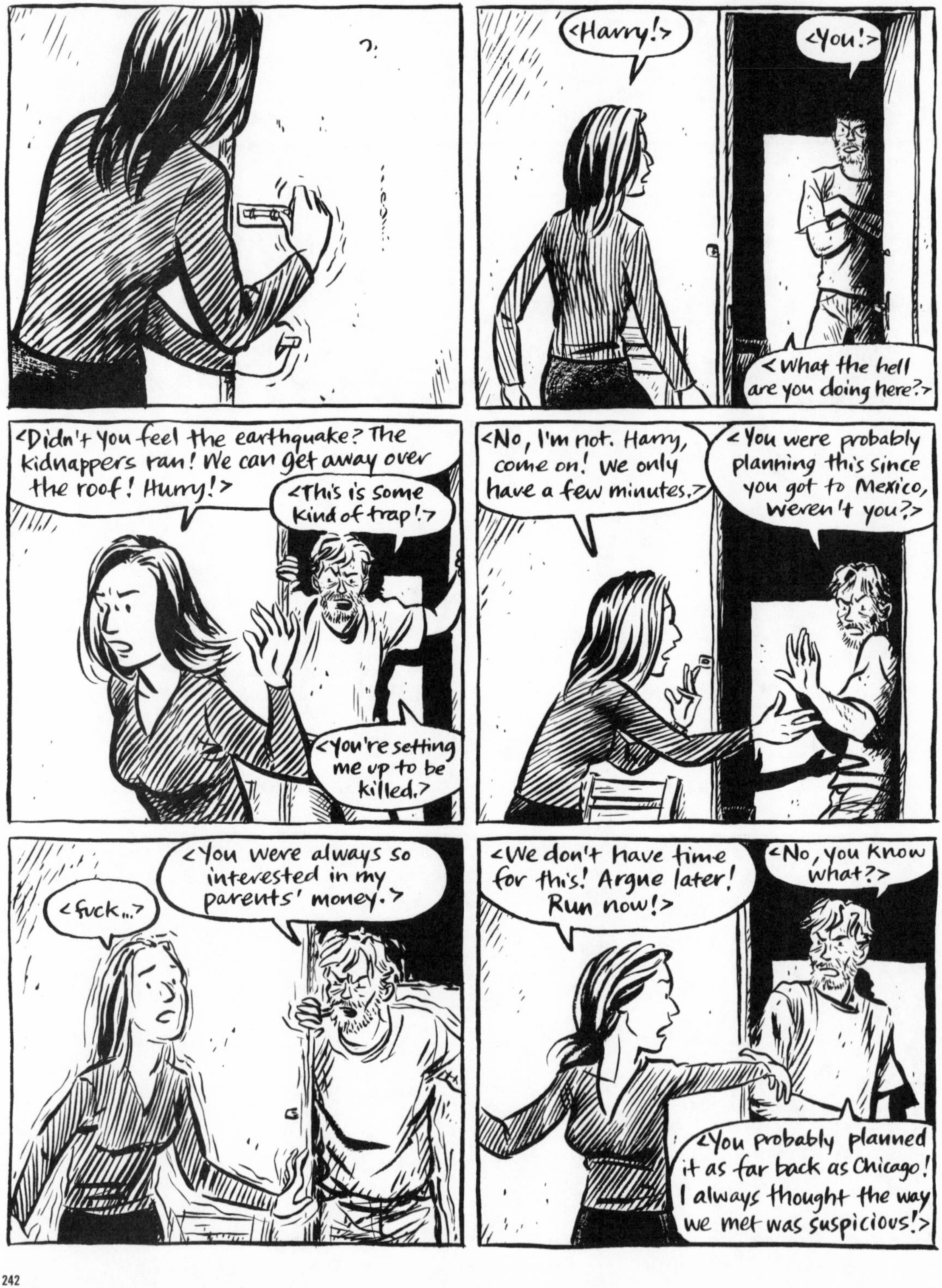
<Harry!>
<You!>
<What the hell are you doing here?>
<Didn't you feel the earthquake? The kidnappers ran! We can get away over the roof! Hurry!>
<This is some kind of trap!>
<You're setting me up to be killed.>
<No, I'm not. Harry, come on! We only have a few minutes.>
<You were probably planning this since you got to Mexico, weren't you?>
<fuck...>
<You were always so interested in my parents' money.>
<We don't have time for this! Argue later! Run now!>
<No, you know what?>
<You probably planned it as far back as Chicago! I always thought the way we met was suspicious!>

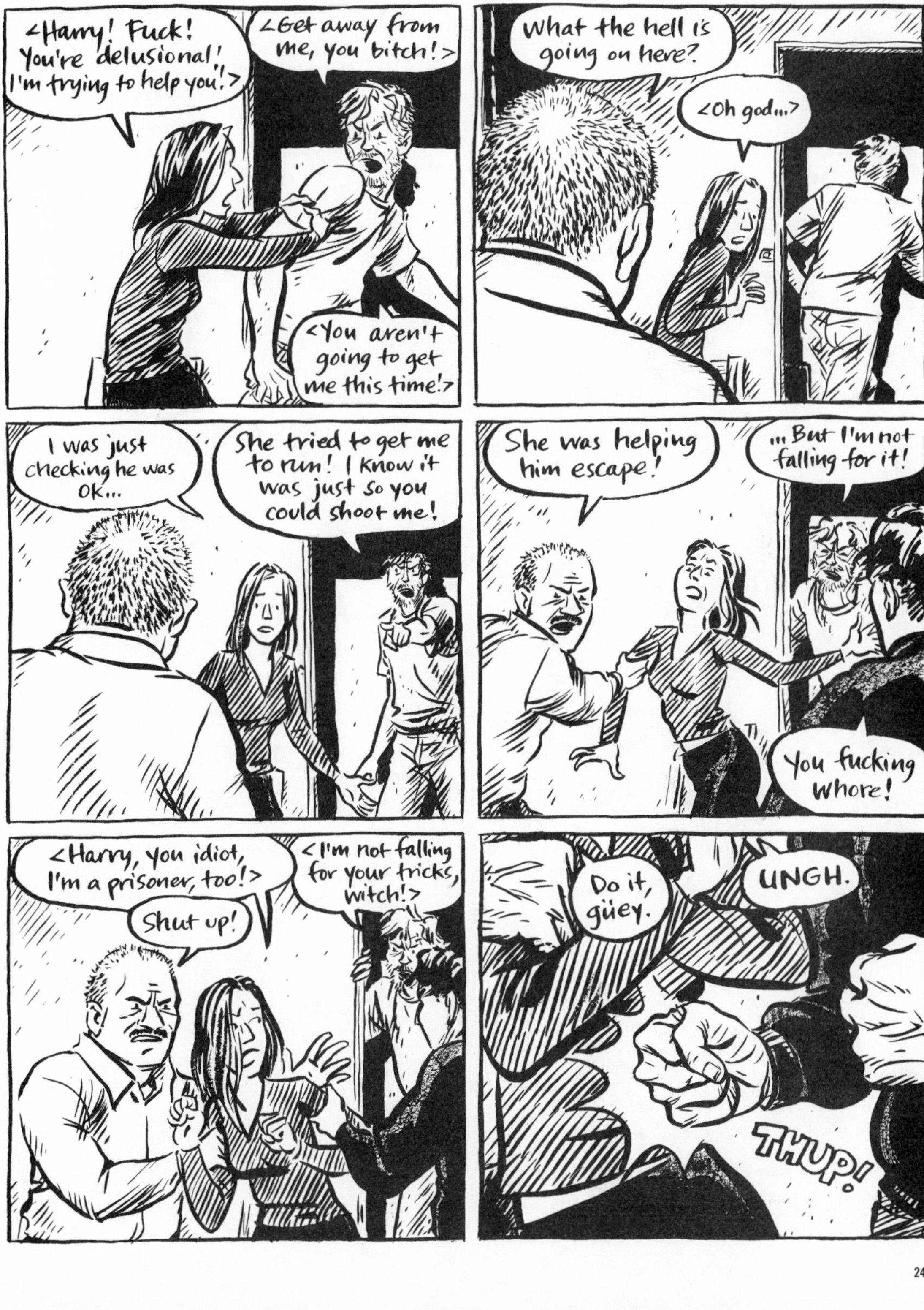
<Harry! Fuck! You're delusional! I'm trying to help you!>
<Get away from me, you bitch!>
<You aren't going to get me this time!>
What the hell is going on here?
<Oh god...>
I was just checking he was OK...
She tried to get me to run! I know it was just so you could shoot me!
She was helping him escape!
...But I'm not falling for it!
You fucking whore!
<Harry, you idiot, I'm a prisoner, too!>
Shut up!
<I'm not falling for your tricks, witch!>
Do it, güey.
UNGH.
THUP!

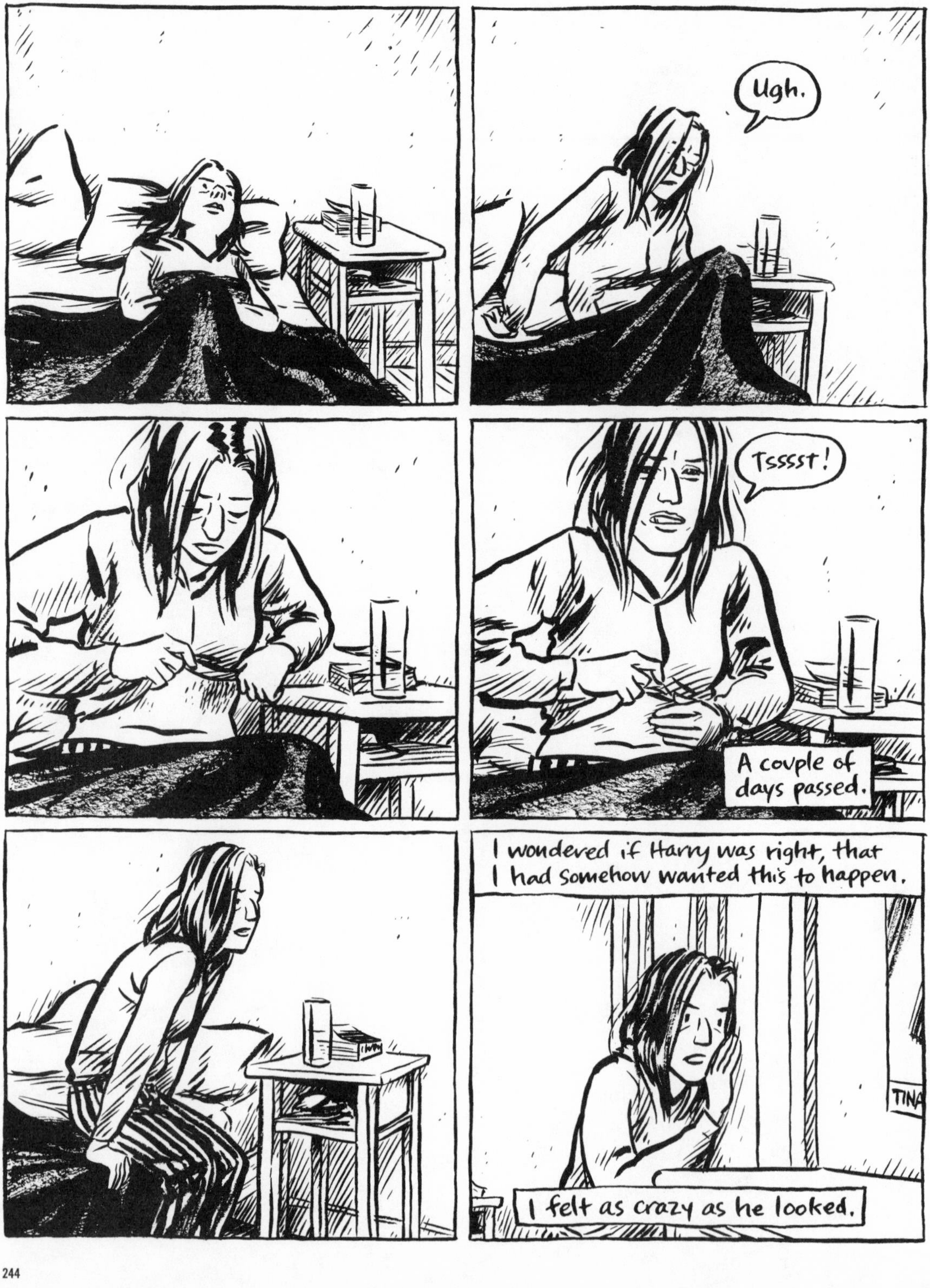
Ugh.
Tssssst!
A couple of days passed.
I wondered if Harry was right, that I had somehow wanted this to happen.
TINA
I felt as crazy as he looked.

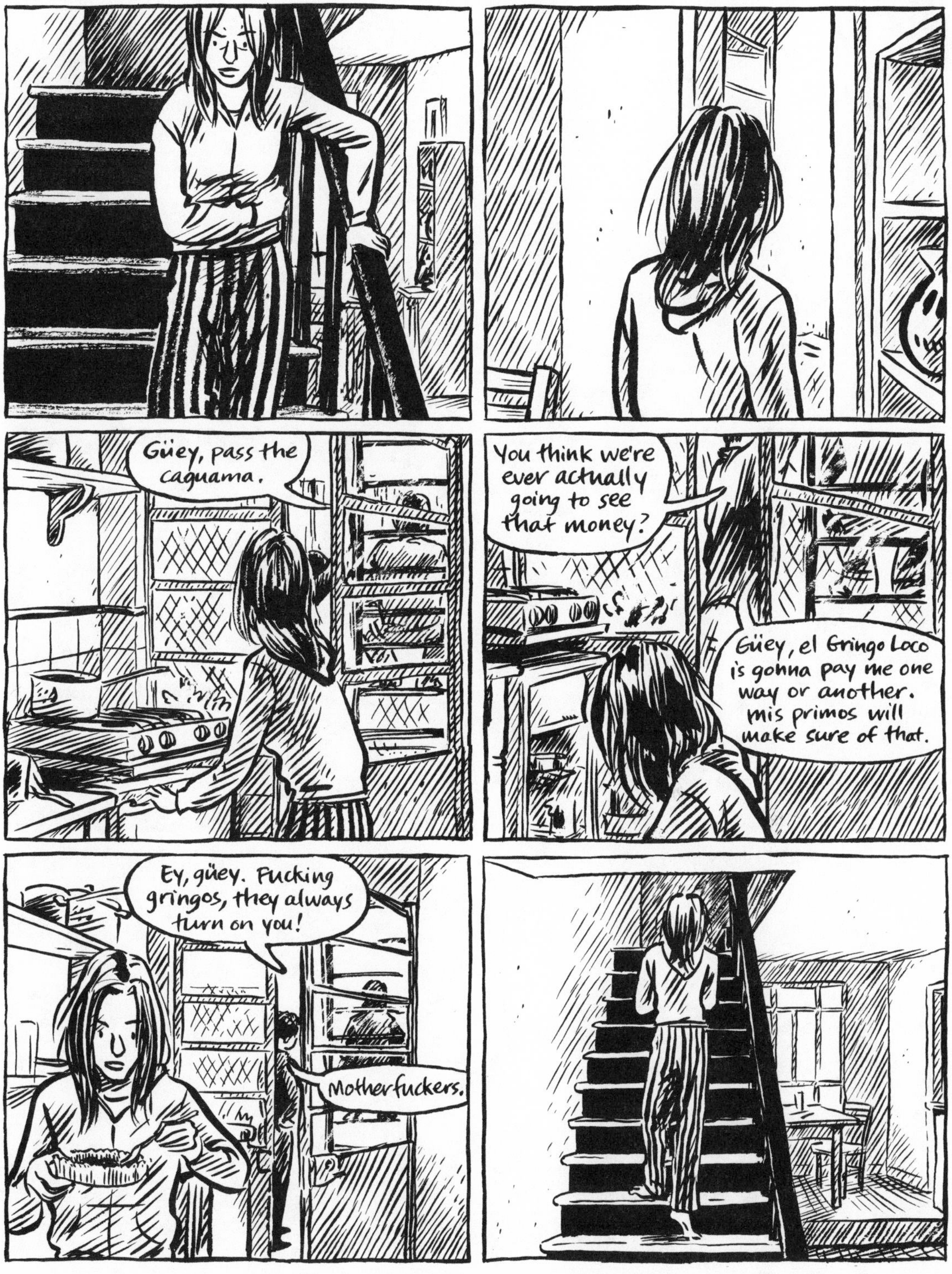
Güey, pass the caguama.
You think we're ever actually going to see that money?
Güey, el Gringo Loco is gonna pay me one way or another. mis primos will make sure of that.
Ey, güey. Fucking gringos, they always turn on you!
Motherfuckers.

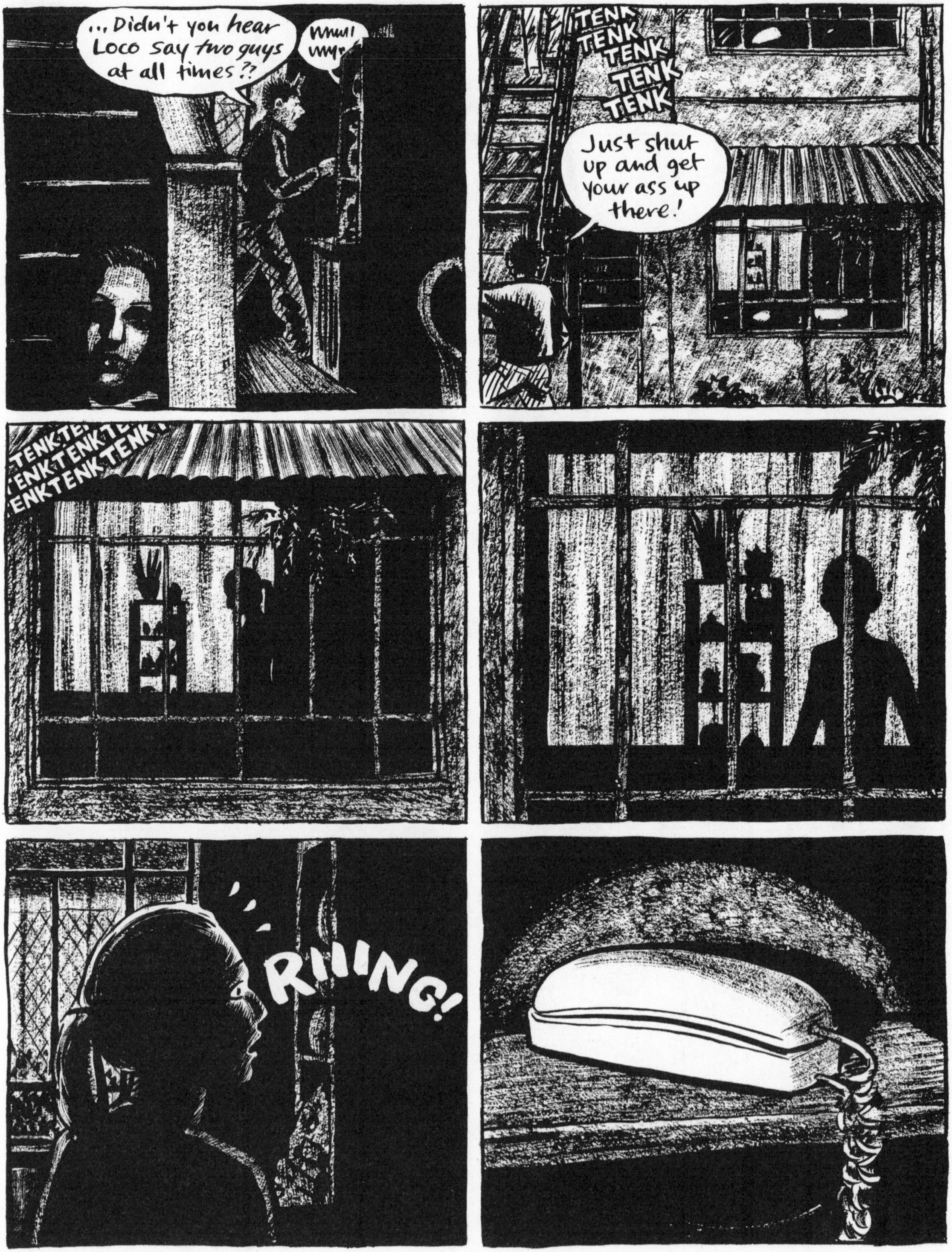
..., Didn't you hear Loco say two guys at all times??
TENK TENK TENK TENK TENK TENK
Just shut up and get your ass up there!
TENK TENK TENK TENK TENK TENK
RIIING!

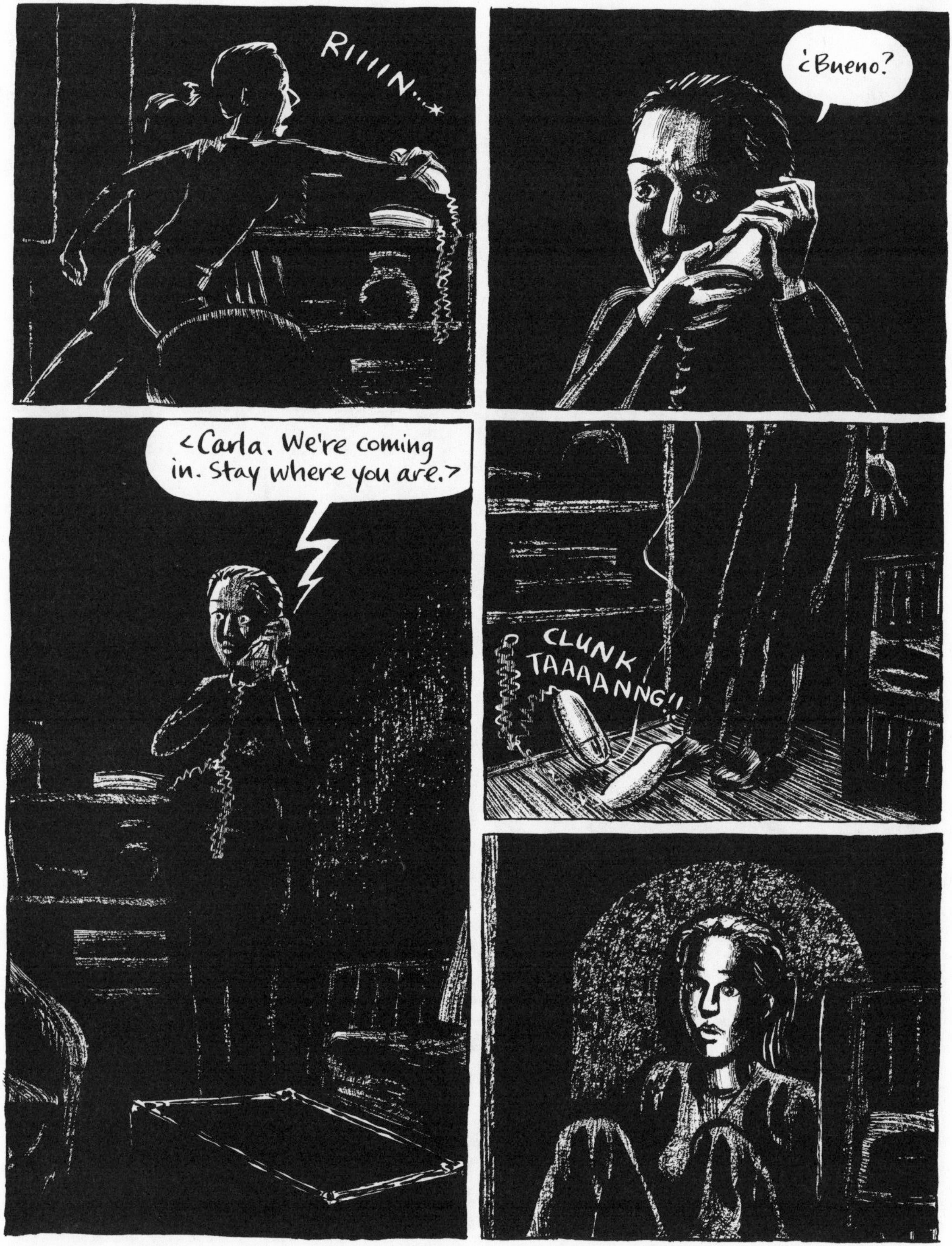
RIIIIN...
¿Bueno?
<Carla. We're coming in. Stay where you are.>
CLUNK
TAAAANNG!!

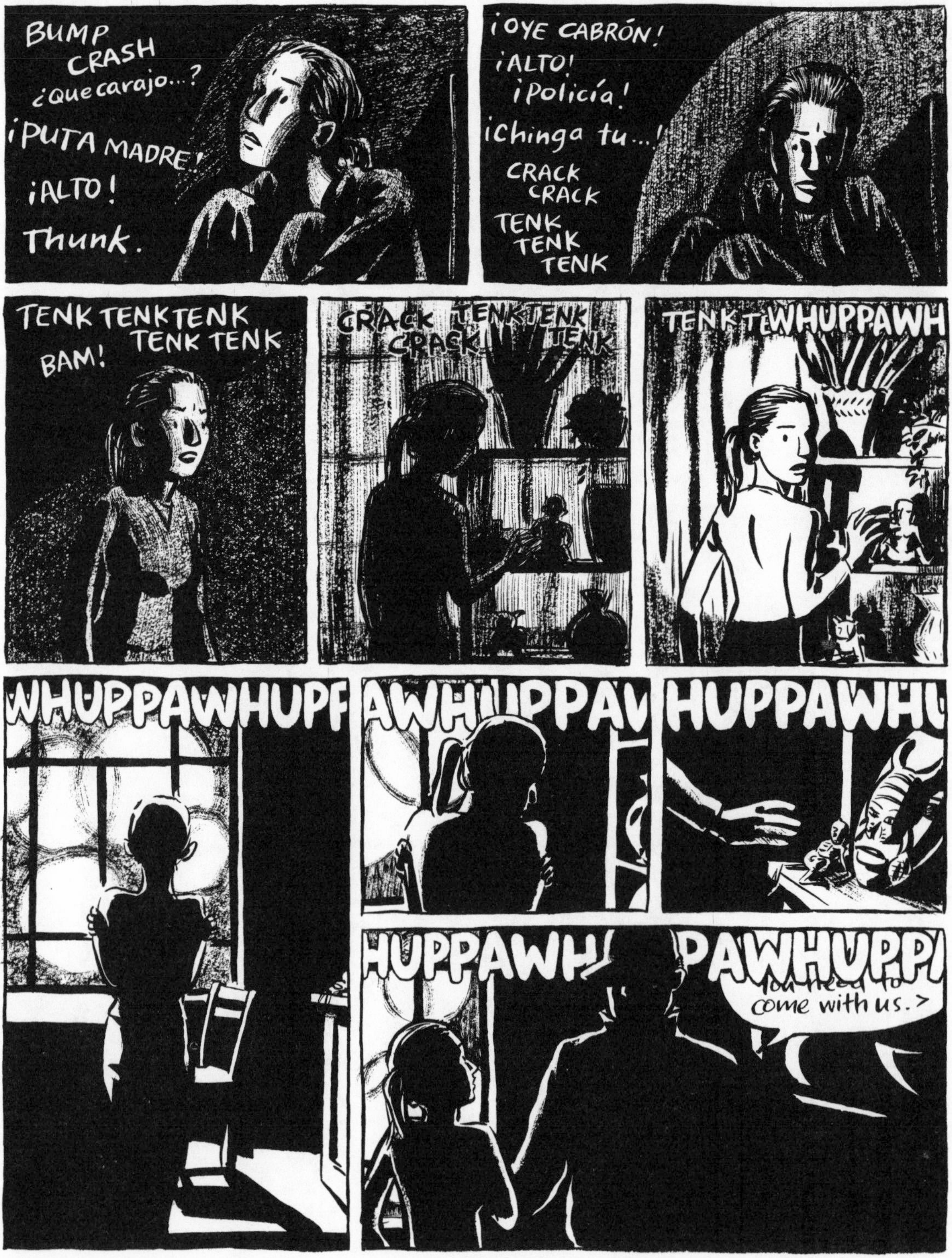
BUMP
CRASH
¿Que carajo...?
¡PUTA MADRE!
¡ALTO!
Thunk.
¡OYE CABRÓN!
¡ALTO!
¡Policía!
¡Chinga tu...!
CRACK
CRACK
TENK
TENK
TENK
TENK TENK TENK
TENK TENK
BAM!
CRACK TENK TENK
CRACK TENK
TENK TEWHUPPAWH
WHUPPAWHUPP
AWHUPPAW
HUPPAWHU
HUPPAWH
PAWHUPP
You need to come with us.>

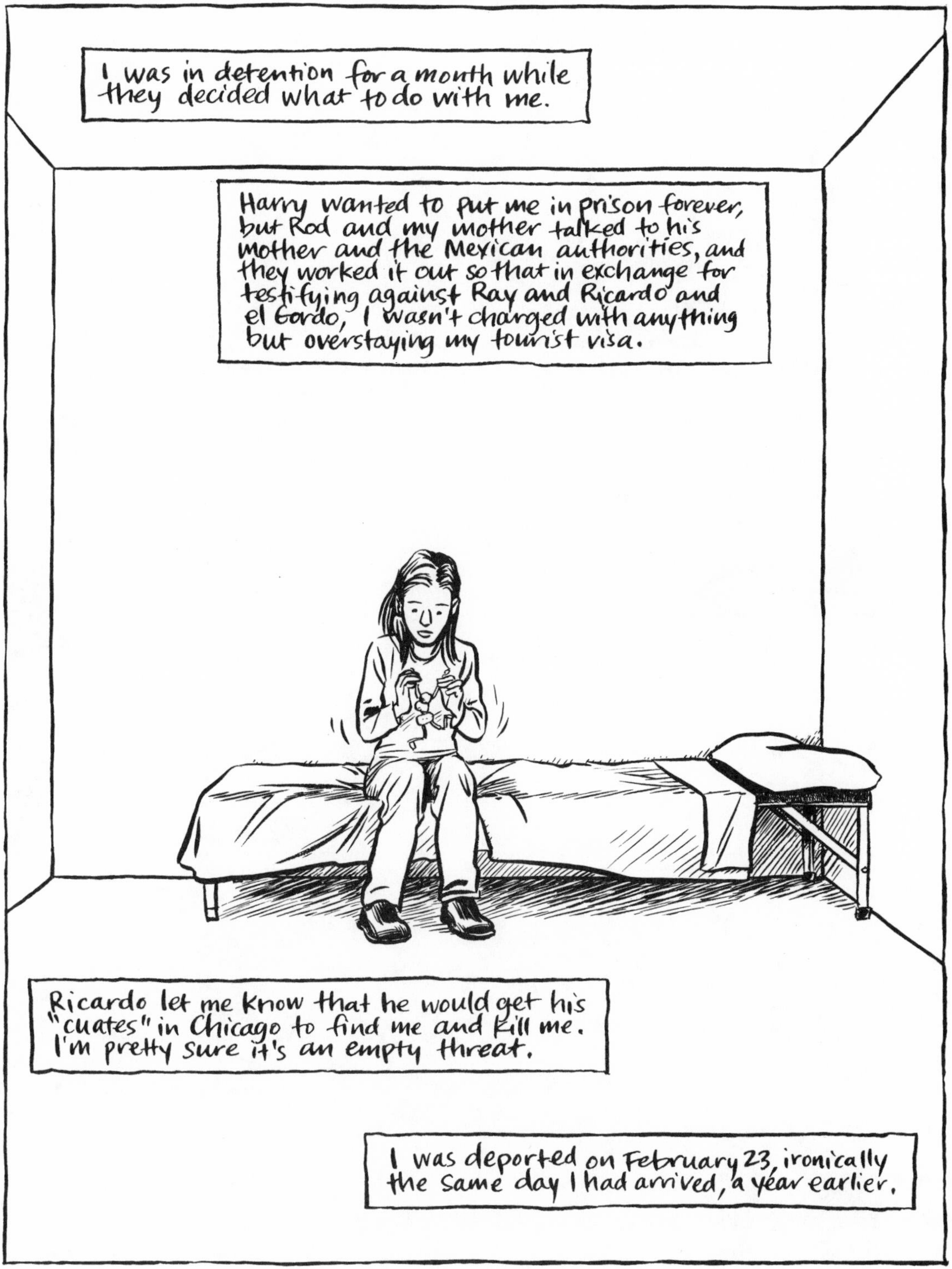
I was in detention for a month while they decided what to do with me.
Harry wanted to put me in prison forever, but Rod and my mother talked to his mother and the Mexican authorities, and they worked it out so that in exchange for testifying against Ray and Ricardo and el Gordo, I wasn't charged with anything but overstaying my tourist visa.
Ricardo let me know that he would get his "cuates" in Chicago to find me and kill me. I'm pretty sure it's an empty threat.
I was deported on February 23, ironically the same day I had arrived, a year earlier.

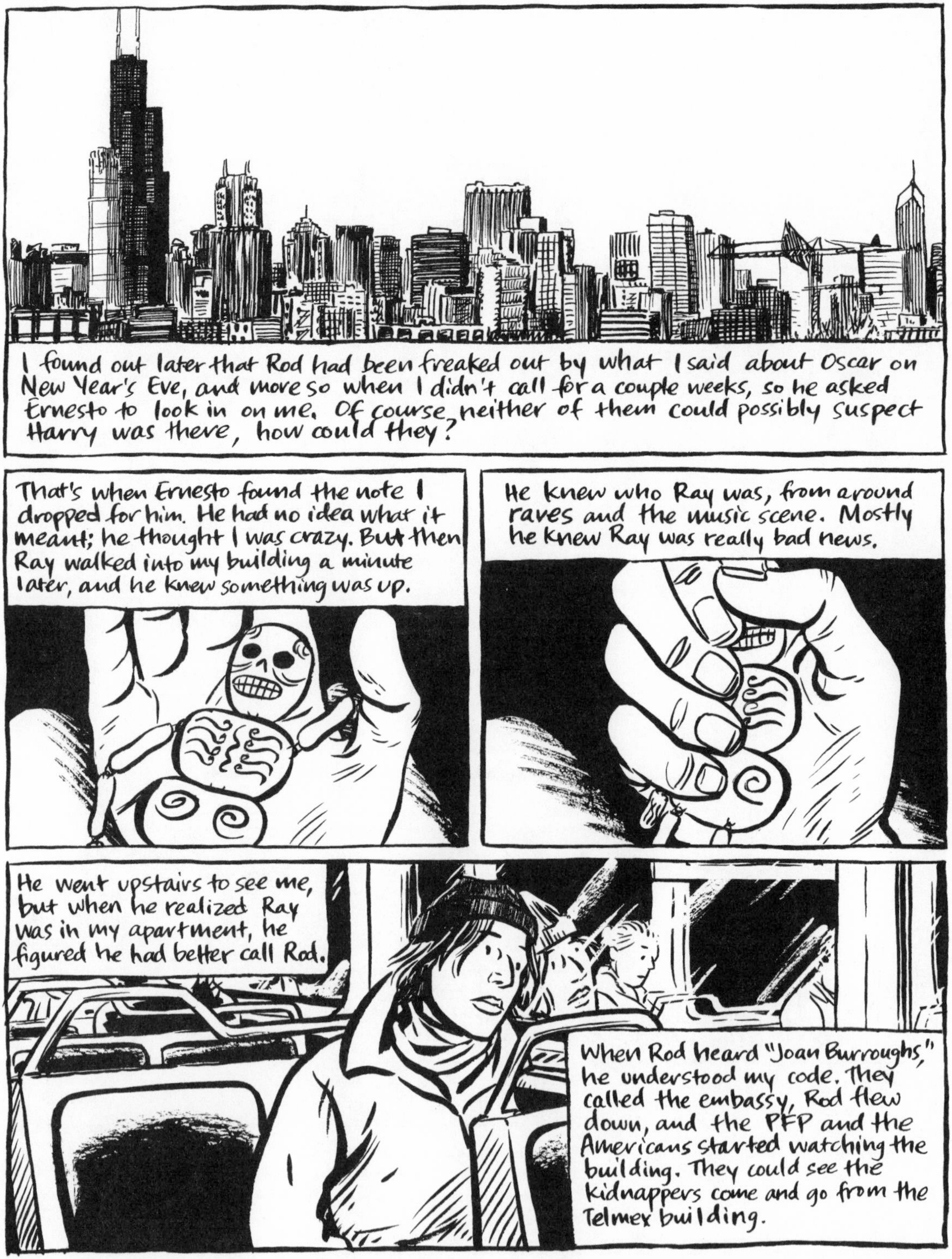
I found out later that Rod had been freaked out by what I said about Oscar on New Year's Eve, and more so when I didn't call for a couple weeks, so he asked Ernesto to look in on me. Of course, neither of them could possibly suspect Harry was there, how could they?
That's when Ernesto found the note I dropped for him. He had no idea what it meant; he thought I was crazy. But then Ray walked into my building a minute later, and he knew something was up.
He knew who Ray was, from around raves and the music scene. Mostly he knew Ray was really bad news.
He went upstairs to see me, but when he realized Ray was in my apartment, he figured he had better call Rod.
When Rod heard "Joan Burroughs," he understood my code. They called the embassy, Rod flew down, and the PFP and the Americans started watching the building. They could see the kidnappers come and go from the Telmex building.

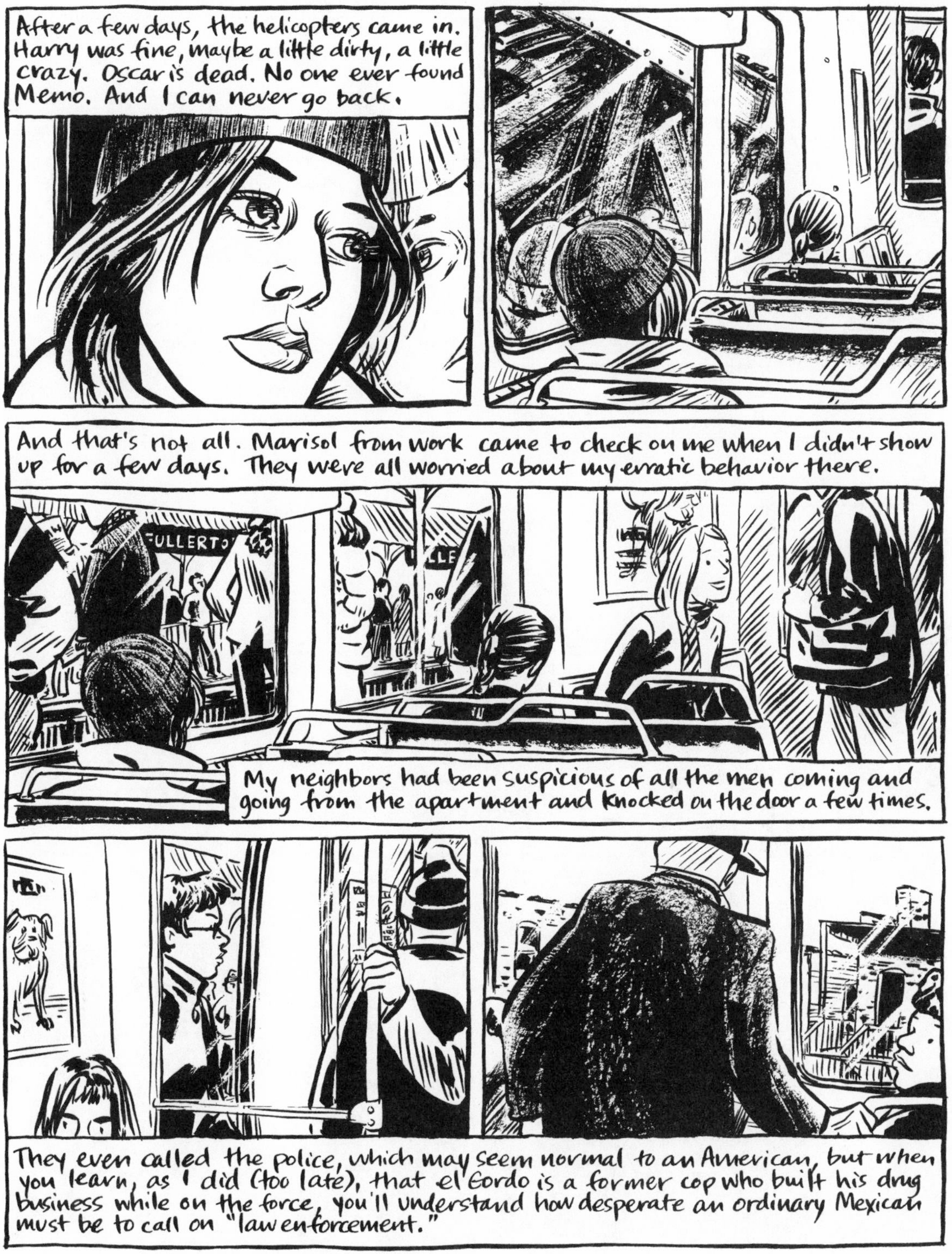
After a few days, the helicopters came in. Harry was fine, maybe a little dirty, a little crazy. Oscar is dead. No one ever found Memo. And I can never go back.
And that's not all. Marisol from work came to check on me when I didn't show up for a few days. They were all worried about my erratic behavior there.
FULLERTO
My neighbors had been suspicious of all the men coming and going from the apartment and knocked on the door a few times.
They even called the police, which may seem normal to an American, but when you learn, as I did (too late), that el Gordo is a former cop who built his drug business while on the force, you'll understand how desperate an ordinary Mexican must be to call on "law enforcement."

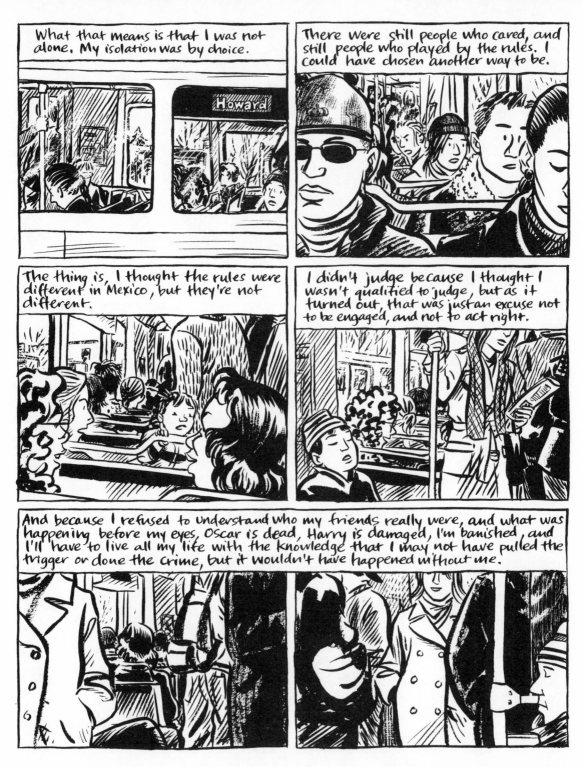

What that means is that I was not alone. My isolation was by choice.

There were still people who cared, and still people who played by the rules. I could have chosen another way to be.

The thing is, I thought the rules were different in Mexico, but they're not different.

I didn't judge because I thought I wasn't qualified to judge, but as it turned out, that was just an excuse not to be engaged, and not to act right.

And because I refused to understand who my friends really were, and what was happening before my eyes, Oscar is dead, Harry is damaged, I'm banished, and I'll have to live all my life with the knowledge that I may not have pulled the trigger or done the crime, but it wouldn't have happened without me.

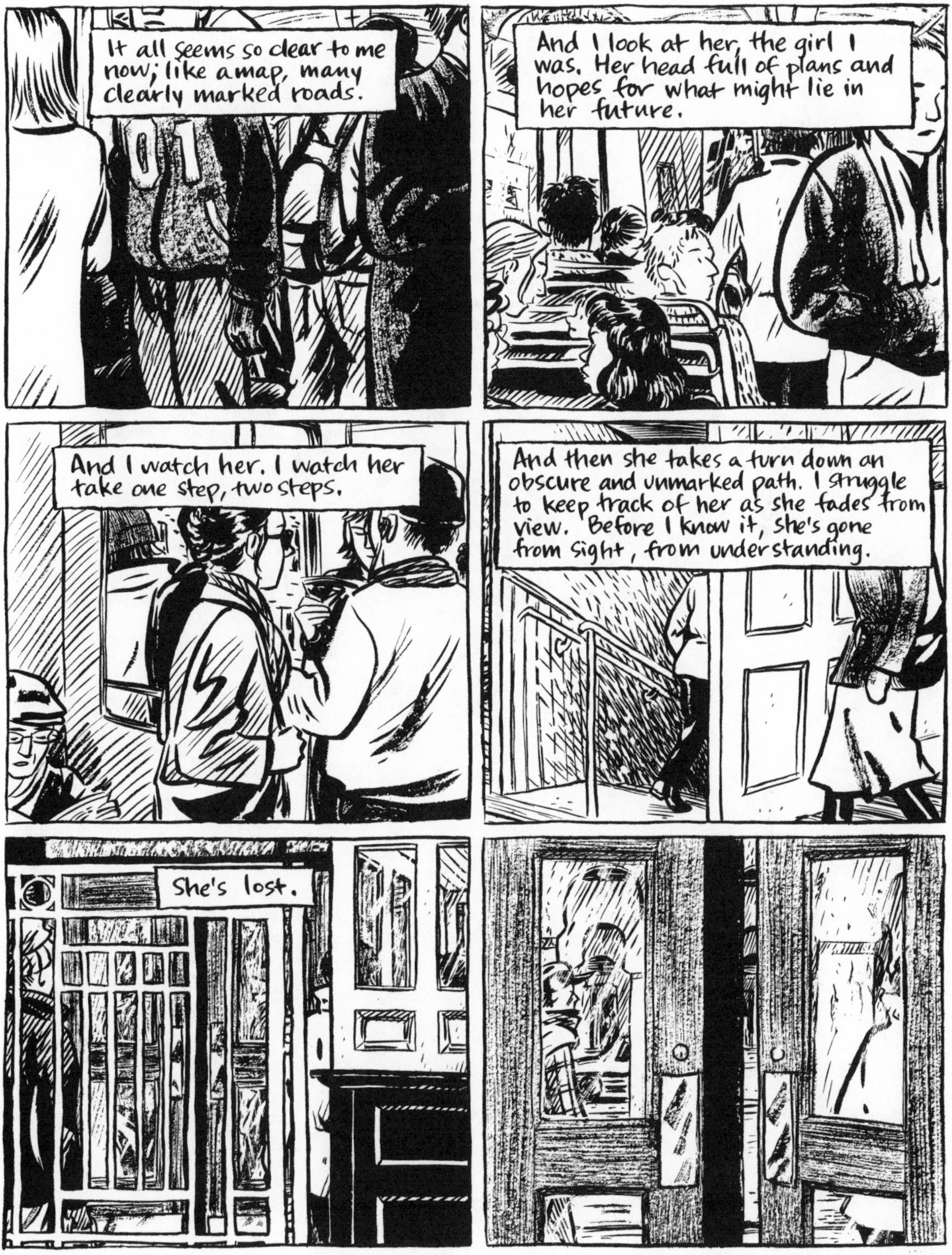
It all seems so clear to me now; like a map, many clearly marked roads.
And I look at her, the girl I was. Her head full of plans and hopes for what might lie in her future.
And I watch her. I watch her take one step, two steps.
And then she takes a turn down an obscure and unmarked path. I struggle to keep track of her as she fades from view. Before I know it, she's gone from sight, from understanding.
She's lost.

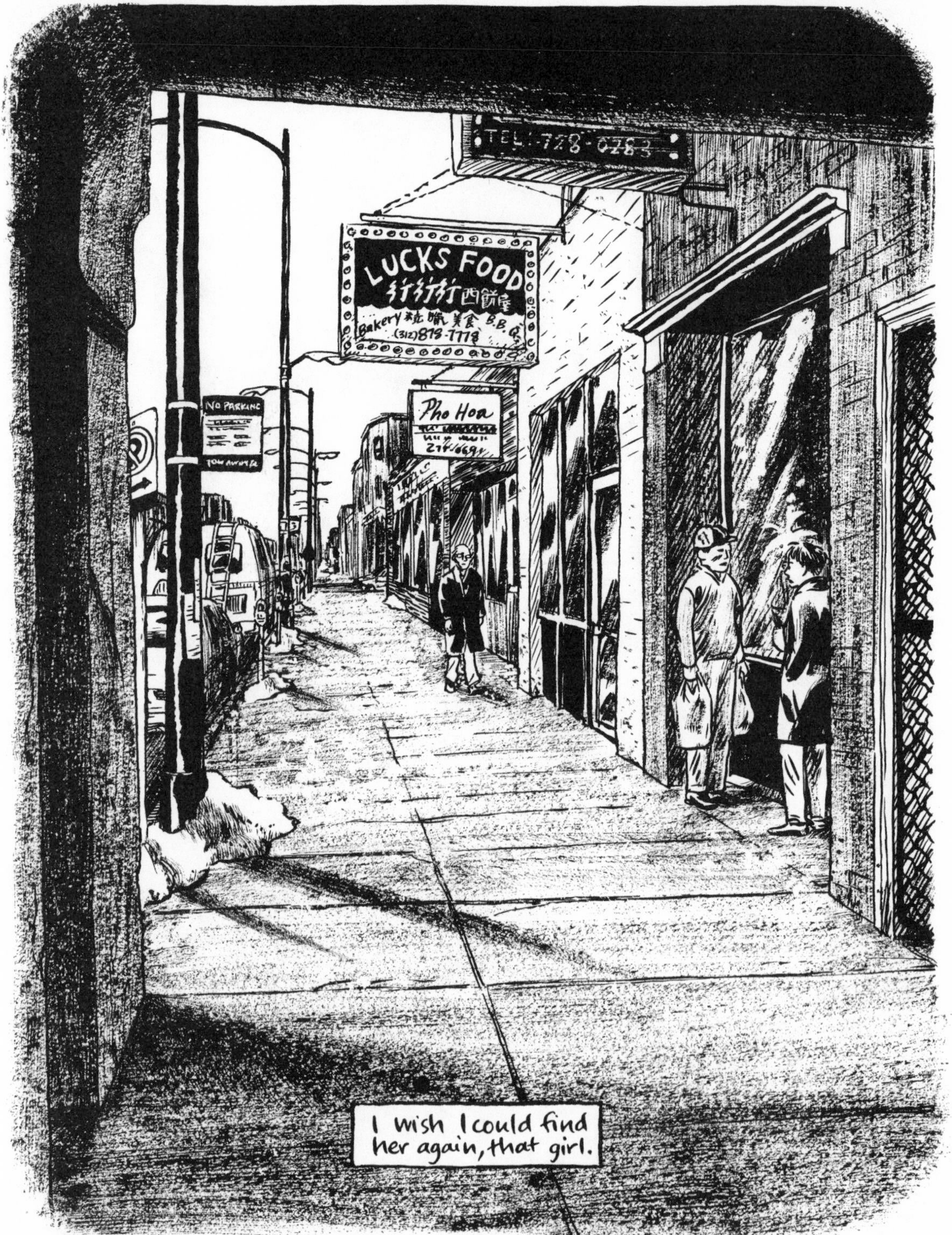
LUCKS FOOD
Bakery
B.B.Q.
(312) 878-7778
Pho Hoa
NO PARKING
I wish I could find her again, that girl.

Glossary

NB: When it's called for, I've noted differ-ent forms of words and/or different end-ings, such as masculine/feminine or singular/plural, with a slash between them.

abuela – Grandmother.

el Ajusco – A national park in the moun-tains to the south of Mexico City.

alto – Stop, as in a stop sign or a command: "Stop!"

amor – Love; also used as a term of endear-ment.

AP – The Associated Press, an international news-gathering organization.

Avenida Amsterdam – Amsterdam Avenue, a lovely, tree-lined circular avenue that used to run around a horse track, and now defines a small neighborhood between *colonia* Roma and *colonia* Condesa, known as *colonia* Hipódromo Condesa, or the Condesa Horse Track neighborhood.

bienvenido/a – Masculine/feminine forms of "welcome."

Blue Demon – My favorite *luchador,* or wrestler. I haven't translated his name here because it was always in English, Blue Demon, and never *el Demonio Azul.* He was affectionately called Blue, Blucito ("Little Bluie"), and Manotas ("Paws," or, strictly speaking, "Giant Hands"). Blue Demon came on the scene in 1948, shortly after el Santo (see below). Initially a *rudo* (a wrestler who plays dirty), he became a *técnico* (who plays by the rules) a few years later. He won the welterweight championship from el Santo in 1953, the beginning of a long and bitter rivalry. A technically excellent wrestler, Blue was a great per-former (which is, or course, more impor-tant in pro wrestling), and had a very honest and forthright public persona. He starred in a number of psychotronic movies, both alone and with el Santo, and he had his own *fotonovela* (photo comic), as well. After his retirement in 1988 (at the age of sixty-six!), and during his long post-ring life, Blue never revealed his secret identity, and in fact ran a boxing and wrestling gym in his Blue Demon mask until his death in

2000. His son, Blue Demon Jr., is currently active as a wrestler. Blue dictated a truly charming autobiography, available in Spanish (if you can find it): *Blue Demon: Memorias de una máscara* (Clío, 1999).

botana – A small tasty snack, such as those offered free with drinks at cantinas. Could be anything from peanuts or potato chips with salsa to a complete three-course meal (in some old-school cantinas)

"Buenas," "Buenas tardes" – There are several forms of everyday greetings, depending on the time of day: *Buenos días*, "Good morning," is used until noon; *Buenas tardes*, "Good afternoon," is used until dark, or sometimes a bit later; and *Buenas noches*, "Good evening," is used at night. In some parts of the Spanish-speaking world, the shortened version, *Buenas,* is used at all times of the day or night. This is not common in Mexico, however.

Bueno – This means "good," but can also mean "well," as in "Well, what now?" In Mexico, *bueno* is used when answering the telephone.

Burroughs, William, and Joan – William S. Burroughs (1914–1997) was an American novelist and essayist, whose work is associated with the Beats. Though he knew himself to be gay from very early on, he formed a relationship with Joan Vollmer in 1944. They never married, but she became Burroughs's common-law wife, and they had a son together. The couple, their son, and Joan's daughter fled a drug charge in New Orleans in 1948, moving to Mexico City. Burroughs shot Joan in a game of William Tell at a party in Mexico City in 1951. The death was ruled accidental, and Burroughs spent only thirteen days in jail, but he felt the repercussions of his act all his life. He often attributed the fact that he became a writer to Joan's death. One of his most well-known books is *Naked Lunch* (1959), which was made into a film by David Cronenberg (see below). The Burroughses lived in *colonia* Roma, on Orizaba Street.

cabrón/cabrones – Literally "billy goat," this word has overtones of "cuckold," but in common usage basically means "asshole." When applied to an object or event, it means "really difficult." Between friends, it's more along the lines of "guy" or "dude" (see *güey*, below, for a similar case).

caguama – Literally, this is a female sea turtle. In common usage (in Mexico), it's a one-liter glass bottle of beer.

calle – Street.

"Cálmate ya" – "Chill out." "Calm down already."

cámara de comercio – Commerce Department, chamber of commerce.

cantina – A kind of bar particular to Mexico, a cantina will serve lunch, then remain open all afternoon. They usually have another rush in late afternoon, when office workers and neighborhood people come in for a few beers and *botanas,* and to play dominoes and chat. Cantinas usually close around 11:30 p.m., with some exceptions, where they may close earlier or later.

carajo/al carajo – Literally "penis," used alone, *¡carajo!* means something like "Damn it!" *Al carajo* means something more like "to hell," as in *¡Al carajo con eso!,* or "To hell with that!" It can be used with people or things.

cariño – As a description: "tenderness," "sweetness," "love." As a name: "my dear," "my sweet."

Catedral Metropolitana – The giant main cathedral of Mexico City, located on the north side of the Zócalo. The building was constructed essentially on top of the Great Pyramid (el Templo Mayor) of Tenochtitlán, the capital city of the Aztecs. Well, all of Mexico City was built on top of Tenochtitlán. But anyway, the funny part is that the gigantic pyramid was *lost* for hundreds of years. No one knew where it was until some construction was being done during the first part of the 1900s, right next door to the cathedral, and lo and behold, there it was. The Spaniards had simply taken a lot of the stone from the pyramid to build the rest of the colonial city, so the pyramid got smaller and was covered up. Originally, it had been as tall as or taller than the cathedral. Excavations on el Templo Mayor found lots of artifacts still in place, however, and it's a fascinating site (see el Museo del Templo Mayor, below). Ironically, excavating the area has made it lighter, so the pyramid is rising from the soft subsoil, which is causing the cathedral to sink sideways into the ground.

el Centro – Short for el Centro Histórico. This is the old colonial center of Mexico City, where the main government buildings and the cathedral are located, along with a great number of beautiful residential and commercial buildings that date from the Spanish era of Mexico's history. Despite these magnificent buildings, the Centro has traditionally been a very crowded, poor and working-class area, filled with street vendors and, in general, *el pueblo* (see below). At the moment, the Centro is in the midst of a gentrifcation wave, and a lot of the apartments are going for sky-high rents. However, you'd never know it to look at it from the outside. It still appears to be as crowded and crazed as ever. The Centro has always been a major nightlife area, home to lots of restaurants and bars, such as la Faena and el Salón Corona (see below). Also, the boundaries of the neighborhood extend beyond the purely colonial zone right at the epicenter of the the city to several busy business districts nearby, including the plumbing-store area where Carla lives.

el Cerro de la Estrella – "The Hill of the Stars" is a bad neighborhood, part of

Iztapalapa, a giant, poverty-stricken borough of Mexico City.

Che – Ernesto "Che" Guevara, an Argentinian communist hero. *Che* is a common slang word for "guy" or used as something like "hey" in Argentina.

chela – Mexican slang term for a beer.

chicano – A Mexican-American.

chico/a – Literally: as noun, "boy" or "girl"; and as an adjective, "small." The plural *chicos* is used in a genderless sense, like "guys," as in, "Hey you guys!"

chido/-ísimo – *Chido* means "wicked cool" in Mexico, and *chidísimo* means "really really wicked cool."

chingar, chinga, chingado/a, chingadera, chinga tu madre, no chingues – *Chinga* is a particularly Mexican all-purpose word that they use like we use "fuck." *Chingar* = to fuck or to fuck up. *Chinga* = the imperative form of chingar. *¡Chinga!* = used as an interjection, i.e., "Fuck!" *Chingado/a* = people that are truly fucked, description of a thing that's fucked up. *Chingadera* = something that's a piece of shit. *Chinga tu madre* = fuck your mother. Used more generally like we use "Fuck you." *No chingues* = a vulgar way of saying "No way!" There is a multitude of variations on the above as well as other usages I haven't listed (including many I don't know, I'm sure). This expressive, multipurpose *mexicanismo* has been paid literary tribute in famous works by Octavio Paz and Carlos Fuentes.

chiquita – This is a diminutive form of *chica*, or girl, so is something like "girlie."

cielo/cielito – Literally "sky" or "heaven," as a term of endearment, it's more like "dear" or "sweetheart."

colonia – neighborhood

Comercializadora Deportiva de Méx. – Sportswear of Mexico, or something along those lines: *comercializadora* means "distributor" or "seller of," and *deportiva* means "sports."

"¿Cómo estás?" – "How are you?," a common greeting. *Estás* is the *tú* form, thus informal.

"¿Cómo se dice?" – "How do you say it?" This is the most common phrase used to ask for help with an unknown word.

la Condesa – Literally "the countess," the more correct name would be *colonia* Condesa, or Condesa neighborhood. Condesa is a somewhat ritzy and very fashionable and arty neighborhood in Mexico City. It's characterized by loads of beautiful Art Deco apartment buildings and small, quiet, tree-lined streets, as well as expensive, pretentious restaurants filled with yuppies (i.e., *fresas;* see below). In the late 1990s, the vast majority of expats (see below) in journalism and the arts chose to live in Condesa and in *colonia* Roma next door (they probably still do).

contra – Against or versus, as in, *el Santo contra los Zombies*, "the Saint vs. the Zombies."

conquistador/a – Conqueror. This is the name given to the Spanish explorers and invaders of the fifteenth through seventeenth centuries.

Coyoacán – Formerly a separate town to the south of the capital, Coyoacán is now a neighborhood of Mexico City. The painter Frida Kahlo was born and raised there, and her family home, known as *la Casa Azul*, or the Blue House, is now a museum devoted to her life and work. Her husband, painter Diego Rivera, also lived in Coyoacán, and there are several other sites devoted to him and Kahlo around the south of Mexico City.

Cronenberg, David – David Cronenberg is a Canadian film director who made the film version of *Naked Lunch*, one of William Burroughs's best-known books, in 1991.

cuadrilátero – A boxing or wrestling ring (also simply a four-sided thing).

cuate – (Mexico) Literally "twin" or "similar," in common usage *cuate* more often is used to mean "buddy," or "pal." It's a kind of cheesy, old-fashioned way of saying it.

Día de la Independencia – Independence Day. Mexico declared its independence from Spain on September 16, 1810.

Edificio Elegancia – The Elegance Building. A made-up name, but there are tons of buildings in Condesa with fancy names like that.

el DF, el Distrito Federal – The Federal District, or Mexico City. Like the United States, Mexico has a capital that is not part of any state but has its own little piece of land. The name "Mexico City"—*la Ciudad de México*—is not used in Mexico, although you'll be understood if you call it that. The most common name for the city is in fact *el DF* (pronounced *el day-EF-ay*) or simply *México*.

escuincle – A common working-class way of referring to little kids, it comes from the word *xoloitzcuintle*, for little native Mexican hairless dogs.

ese/ése – That/that one. In addition to its more general meaning, it's a common way to refer to a person.

"¡Éso sí!" – "That's it!" or "That's the way!"; basically means "I approve!"

expatriate/expat – A person who lives outside his or her native country but identifies this situation as temporary. Often the reason for the move is work-related. This is different from an immigrant, who has moved permanently to another country, or an exile, who is outlawed from living in his or her native land.

la Faena – A bullfighting-themed bar in the historic center of Mexico City. *La faena* is the word used to describe a bullfighter's actions in the ring.

Feliz Año Nuevo – Happy New Year.

flaco/a – Skinny.

folclor/folclórico – Also sometimes spelled in the English manner, *folklor/órico,* this is just what it appears to be: folklore or folkloric. From the English word.

fresa – Literally, "strawberry." However, in Mexico City slang it means a yuppie.

gallo – A rooster or fighting cock.

los Girasoles – This is the fictional name I gave to the restaurant below the apartment where Joan Burroughs was shot. It means "The Sunflowers." There is a restaurant in that building, at 122 Monterrey, but the restaurant I drew is fictional. The site of the shooting is, ironically, about half a block from the school that I used as the basis of Carla's school. She actually walks right past the school on her way to Insurgentes Avenue and across to Condesa.

gringo/a – The word *gringo* is known to most or all Americans, but what most don't realize is that it's not always used generically, as description; it can also carry a negative connotation, sort of a "you're just an American, what would you know?" attitude. It's not as bad as our "wetback" or something, but it can be dismissive (though it can also be friendly). Some people theorize that the word *gringo* derives from the color of American army uniforms and the resultant phrase "green go home." *Gringuita* can be used to describe a good-looking American woman who is naive about Mexican customs. A *gringa* is also a

roasted pork taco, in a flour tortilla (tacos are always otherwise in corn tortillas) with melted cheese on top. Urban legend attributes this innovation to an American tourist.

el Gringo Loco – The Crazy Gringo. In this case, as is true of many badass nicknames, the negative has a positive connotation.

el Gordo – This is a common nickname, meaning "Fatty." I know, it's incredible anyone would willingly accept being called fat in this day and age, but there you have a perfect example of cultural differences. Both this nickname and el Gringo Loco, above, demonstrate the tendency to put the article *el* or *la* in front of pet names. When speaking directly to the person in question, you'd call him *Gordo,* but when you're speaking about him, the word shifts from a name, "Fatty," to an adjectival description, "the Fatty." It's a weird distancing phenomenon that relates to the use of *ese/ése,* "that" and "that one," as a way to talk about people.

guapo/a – Handsome, good-looking.

güey – This word derives from the way Mexicans pronounce *buey,* which means "ox" (it sounds a bit like "waay"). Calling someone *güey* is like calling them an idiot. It can be used in a positive or negative sense, and also as an adjective, as in *"¡Estás güey!,"* or "You're such an idiot!" In common usage, it has essentially become "dude." It is particularly common in Mexico City, but not exclusive to that area. And if you think I'm exaggerating how often people use it, believe me, I'm not!

hamburguesa – Hamburger.

"Hasta luego" – "See you later." The most common phrase used to take leave.

hijo de puta – Son of a bitch. Literally, however, it means "son of a whore."

hola – Hello.

"No, hombre" – This literally means "No, man," but is used as an intensifier (pronounced kind of as one word: "¡N'ombre!"), as in "*¡No, hombre, pero es fantastico!*," or, "No, but that's so great!"

indio – Literally, "Indian." Mexicans have a bit of a problem in that they call Asian Indians *hindues*, regardless of their religion, in order to distinguish them from *indios*, or Native Americans (in more official forums, Native Americans are called *indígenas* or *poblaciones autóctonas*). Just as in the U.S., the word "Indian" used imprecisely in this manner sounds rough and tends to be depreciative. In common use it can be an insult, meaning something like "peasant" or "stupid and uneducated," but of course, the person who uses this insult shows his own lack of education by using it.

la Isla de las Muñecas – The Island of the Dolls is a real place in the "ecological reserve" portion of Xochimilco (see below). The normal boat tour of the canals takes about two hours. If you arrange for it, you can take a longer tour that passes through the much larger area on the other side of a set of water locks. It's a lovely, quiet, isolated stretch, and out there in the middle of nothing is an old man who lives on an islet entirely decorated with old, broken, dirty dolls. He claims he found the island that way. He grows his own food there (again, so he claims), and accepts change as a donation for visiting. He doesn't seem to use much of it, though, since he had a basket full of pesos when we visited.

-ito/-ita – You'll see it all through this glossary, but this diminutive ending is worth highlighting. Other Spanish-speaking peoples find the Mexican tendency to add "*–ito*" or "*-ita*" to the end of just about anything frankly hilarious. When an Argentinian says *la cervecita*, she surely means "the little tiny beer." And she'd be unlikely to say it. When a Mexican says *la cervecita*, he is more likely to mean a beer particularly for you, an unthreatening beer, just a beer, a special beer, just plain beer, or "How about a little beer?" Here's one for you: the Mexican expression *ahorita* is basically nonsensical: it comes from *ahora* ("now") + *-ita*. Now-ey? Now-ish? It usually means "real soon." Useful as the dickens, too.

jefe/a – Boss.

joder – As an exclamation, it means "Fuck!" This word is much more common in

Spain than Mexico, but you do hear it. The actual meaning can have to do with sex, as "fuck" does, but also has the sense of playing a nasty trick or messing something up.

Kerouac, Jack – Jack Kerouac (1922–1969) was an American novelist and poet and one of the central figures of Beat literature. His *Mexico City Blues,* published in 1959, is a series of 242 "choruses," or improvised poems, that he wrote in 1955. Kerouac also lived in *colonia* Roma, and also on Orizaba Street, as well as, at another time, on Medellín.

una lana – Literally, *lana* means wool. *Una lana* can be "some money" or "an unspecified, yet large amount of money" (that means "large amount" for the speaker; it could be a very small amount). *Tiene lana* means "He or she is wealthy."

Lecumberri – A famous, or infamous, Mexico City prison from 1900 to 1980.

luchador – A pro wrestler. Literally, it means "fighter."

de poca madre – One of a zillion *madre,* or "mother," phrases in Mexico. This one means "extremely excellent," "awesome." OK, literally it means, "a bit of mom."

"No mames" – This is Mexican slang for "Don't lie" or "You're full of shit" or "Stop acting like a prick" or "No way!" But, disgustingly, it literally means

"Don't nurse!," as in, don't suck milk from my tit. *Mamón* is a related word for a person who is full of shit or of himself.

maquiladora – A factory, usually of textiles, usually near the U.S.-Mexico border.

marica – This—and variations on it, such as *maricón*—is a depreciative word for gay men. In a word, "fag."

marro – Mexican slang: "cheap."

Mazunte – A small resort town on the Pacific coast in Oaxaca state. It's still not all that well known, thus Harry's desire to go there.

Memo – Not related to "memorandum," Memo is instead the commonest nickname given in Mexico to boys named Guillermo (William). Essentially, it's the Mexican "Bill."

mercado – A market. In particular, a large indoor public market filled with small vendor stands.

metro – The subway in Mexico City.

México – The name of the country to the south of the USA should have an accent over the "e," and is pronounced "MEH-hee-ko." I have used the accent when the character is pronouncing the word in Spanish, and left it off when he or she is pronouncing it in English.

Mexico City Blues – See Jack Kerouac, above.

mi – My, as in "my life" or "my desk."

la migra – The nickname Mexicans give to the Immigration and Naturalization Service, now known as U.S. Citizenship and

Vámonos ya: "C'mon, let's get going," or, literally, "Let's go already." By the same token, *¡Basta ya!,* commonly seen on political posters, literally translates as the kvetchy "Enough already!"

"Vete al carajo" – "Go to hell." See *carajo,* above.

mi vida – A term of endearment: "my life."

Xochimilco – Xochimilco (pronounced so-chee-MEAL-ko) is an agricultural area in the south of Mexico City where many of the city's flowers are grown. (The name means something like "flower plantation." If you ever meet a Mexican woman with the lovely name Xochitl, it means "flowers.") It is crisscrossed with canals that date back to Aztec times. Tenochtitlán was on a small island in the midst of several large, very shallow lakes. The Aztecs would build large rafts *(chinampas)* in the lakes and farm on them. Eventually, the rafts rooted to the bottom, and thus the city was made up of a series of extremely fertile islets separated by canals. Xochimilco is the only part of the Valley of Mexico that still has these canals. Traditional flat boats, called *trajineras,* have forever plied the canals for both work and pleasure. Many Mexican families head down to Xochimilco for boating picnics with regularity, and it's a common tourist destination. Smaller *trajineras* come up alongside and offer drinks, food, and handicrafts. See more under la Isla de las Muñecas, above.

ya – Already, or enough (in which case it's short for "*¡Basta ya!*").

"Yo soy . . ." – "I am . . ."

Zapatistas – See above, Subcomandante Marcos.

el Zócalo – The central plaza of Mexican towns is usually called the *zócalo.* This usage is unique to Mexico, as far as I know. A *zócalo* is the pedestal on which a statue is placed. Apparently there was a pedestal for a statue in the middle of the main plaza of Mexico City for a long time, but it always lacked a statue. Thus people started referring to the place as "the pedestal," and afterward the word was generalized to mean all central plazas in all towns.

zorra – Literally a female fox, it's used something like "bitch," but seems to have some sense of sneaky backstabbing in there with the usual sense. Apparently it more specifically means "whore." Yes, that means el Zorro is "the Fox."

Acknowledgments

Bringing a fat comic book like this one into existence is a tough job at best, and I certainly couldn't have done it on my own. My special thanks go to the raft of clear-eyed editors who helped me along: Matt Madden, Tanya McKinnon, Nick Bertozzi, Jason Little, Anjali Singh, and especially Ernesto Priego. My thanks go also to my publishers and longtime supporters Gary Groth, Kim Thompson, and Eric Reynolds, as well as Bill Smith and the *LA Weekly*, who first published "Xochimilco," and to my studio assistants Marina Corral and Nic Breutzman.

Numerous friends, both *chilangos* and expats of various stripes, helped me understand the story I wanted to tell. In particular, my first friends in Mexico, Rogelio Villarreal, Chris Burden, Rachel Salaman, and Brian Jones, who opened so many doors, and Agnes Crane and John Watling (and by extension Heather Biery), who "lent" Carla their apartment.